THE UNITED STATES
AS A WORLD POWER

The Big Three at Yalta, 1945

(Left to right: Churchill, Roosevelt, Stalin. Admiral Leahy is standing behind the President.)

THE
UNITED STATES
AS A WORLD POWER

A Diplomatic History 1900-1950

SAMUEL FLAGG BEMIS

Sterling Professor of Diplomatic History
and Inter-American Relations—Yale University

HENRY HOLT AND COMPANY

New York

PREFACE

The present volume is essentially a reprint, adapted and slightly revised, of Part III, "The Twentieth Century," of my *Diplomatic History of the United States,* Third Edition, 1950. It is intended not only for the inquiring mind of the general reader who lacks the time to cover the earlier history of American foreign policy and diplomacy, but also for teachers and students of international relations who wish a shorter text to give them a more immediate background for contemporary international relations of the United States. It begins with the new picture of power and politics reflected at the turn of the century by the triple birth of new world powers: the United States, Germany, and Japan. It ends with the Diplomatic Revolution of the United States in mid-century: from isolation to collective security in the United Nations and the North Atlantic Alliance. An introductory chapter recalls the foundations of American foreign policy as they were laid in classic form during the first fifty years of independence of the United States and practiced successfully throughout the nineteenth century; these historic fundamentals may be compared with the "guiding principles" listed by President Truman after the Second World War, and printed at the end of the book on pages 466-468. A final chapter focuses a half-century of American diplomatic history on the continuing crisis of thought and action between the United States and Russia, commonly called the Cold War, essentially a conflict between a World Family of Democratic Nations and a World Union of Soviet Socialist Republics.

In the preparation of the original *Diplomatic History of the United States* I was indebted to a long list of institutions and individuals, mentioned in the Prefaces of that publication and its successive editions, and to a large body of historical scholarship, partly set forth bibliographically (that is, down to 1935) in the *Guide to the Diplomatic History of the United States, 1775-1921,* prepared by me with the collaboration of Grace Gardner Griffin, and published by the Library of Congress in 1935. My obligations to these authors, and to others, appear in footnotes throughout the present pages. I am further grateful to many people, including teachers and students, for suggestions and corrections throughout the years.

I wish to thank Alfred A. Knopf, Inc., for permission to reproduce in Chapter 1 the sense of the historical summary of the fundamentals of

United States foreign policy as expressed in my *John Quincy Adams and the Foundations of American Foreign Policy,* which they published in 1949, and Thomas Y. Crowell Company for use of some of my passages in a contribution to their publication, *World Political Geography,* published in 1948.

S. F. B.

New Haven, Connecticut
August 1, 1950

CONTENTS

LIST OF MAPS

(designed by S. Whittemore Boggs)

LIST OF TABLES AND DIAGRAMS

THE UNITED STATES
AS A WORLD POWER

1

Historical Foundations of American Foreign Policy

THE diplomatic history of the United States may be divided readily into three periods: the Foundations, 1776-1826; Continental Expansion, 1826-1898, so tragically annealed by the Civil War; and, from 1898 to 1950, World Power and World Wars.

The first of these epochs measured also the Age of Emancipation, during which three great revolutions enshrined the Rights of Man in written constitutions throughout the Atlantic world and galvanized Western civilization with the spirit of nationalism, strongest force in modern history. These were the Anglo-American Revolution, the French Revolution, and the Latin-American Revolution.

The revolt of the English colonies in North America to preserve the rights of English freemen was successful only because of the intervention of absolutist France in the War of American Independence in order to restore the balance of power in Europe. The resulting strain on the French royal treasury led in turn to the meeting of the Estates General and precipitation in 1789 of the long-smoldering French Revolution. The victorious French Republic, after resisting the armies of monarchical Europe, turned into an instrument of propaganda and intervention, then of dictatorship, empire, and conquest under Napoleon Bonaparte. The peoples of conquered Europe, stirred by the infectious spirit of nationalism, finally rose and threw off the Napoleonic yoke only to slip back, as if exhausted, into the clasp of their "legitimate" kings. But the spirit of emancipation remained kindled and soon flared into new constitutions for self-government. In South America the Spanish Colonies seized upon the intrusion of Joseph Bonaparte, the brother whom Napoleon had set upon the throne of Spain, as a pretext to revolt against their mother country, not to preserve ancient liberties as in the case of the Anglo-American Revolution of North America but rather to secure them for the first time.

Thus it was that wars and rivalries of the Old World made possible in their turbulence the independence of both the United States of North

America and the new states of Latin America. The fatigue of imperialist Europe following that cycle of wars, and the detached and distant position of the fledgling nations of the West, secured for these nations their place in the world and gave them time to grow up to the responsibilities of sovereign independence and self-government. Europe's distresses were America's advantage. Asia was not yet a factor.

The first great steps of Continental Expansion had already been taken during the Age of Emancipation: Thomas Jefferson's fortuitous Louisiana Purchase of 1803 and John Quincy Adams's studiously successful Transcontinental Treaty with Spain of 1819-1821. Both are striking examples of America's advantage from Europe's distresses: the Louisiana Purchase was a by-product of the Napoleonic Wars, and the Transcontinental Treaty was a North American harvest from the Peninsular Wars and the revolution of Latin America. These two achievements bridged the periods of Foundations and Continental Expansion.

Singularly felicitous for the United States was the posture of world politics throughout the ensuing Continental period. There was no power, unless it were Great Britain, to cudgel the protean Republic of the West out of its favored position or to gainsay its Manifest Destiny of continental expansion. The populous seacoasts of the United States lay at the mercy of the British fleet, but Great Britain was exhausted from her titanic struggles of a quarter century of warfare, and before she could stir from the long period of appeasement and repose that followed Waterloo, a hostage had grown up in British North America to insure the benevolent conduct of the royal navy toward the United States: the rapidly increasing military potential of the Continental Republic *vis-à-vis* Canada across the latter's indefensible frontier forbade another war between the two English-speaking peoples.

At no time after 1815 did the Mistress of the Seas choose definitively to challenge the growth of the United States, whether over the northeast boundary, over Texas, over Mexico, over Oregon, over the Isthmian Question, or over the revolted Southern Confederacy. The United States enjoyed a unique security. Is not the fact that it was able to indulge without molestation in a great Civil War a complete demonstration of its foolproof position? It emerged from that conflict with no permanent lesion in its foreign policy. For a generation more, while Europe was balanced evenly in power, while the British Navy dominated the oceans, and Canada the Hostage stood in freedom north of the line of forty-nine, this favorable dispensation prevailed.

There were, of course, other more satisfying reasons that made war between the United States and Great Britain "unthinkable." If Canada had been under the dominion of any other power than Great Britain during the relatively peaceful British Century—most blessed for liberty and self-government in the annals of mankind—she would not have been a Hostage or a Linchpin for peace: she would have been a vestibule for invasion of the United States. If the United States had been an aggressive imperialist nation, Canada would have fallen easy prey to American annexation. Back of the Long Peace north and south of the line there was a compelling kinship for freedom.

What were the principles of American foreign policy as they crystallized in classic shape during the Age of Emancipation? What were the fundamentals invoked and practiced during the remainder of the nineteenth century as the United States spread out on its continental pedestal for later world power? In this chapter we can only list them. They were:

1. Freedom of the Seas, and freedom of international straits and rivers.

2. Freedom of commerce and navigation—that is, reciprocal equality of treatment without discrimination against the subjects or ships of any nation, whether in homeland or colonies or spheres of protection of influence. Later, this developed into the Open Door Doctrine and the New Reciprocity.

3. Abstention from the *ordinary* vicissitudes and the *ordinary* combinations and collisions of European politics and wars. This maxim of Washington's Farewell Address later was included in the Monroe Doctrine of 1823.

4. The Non-Transfer principle of 1811—opposition to the transfer of adjacent, later of any, European colonial dominions in the New World from one European sovereign to another. President Grant attached this principle to the Monroe Doctrine in 1869.

5. Continental expansion—the Manifest Destiny of the United States to become a Continental Republic in dimension and significance, the territorial basis of later world power—this was a compulsive national feeling of deep inner reality.

6. Self-determination of peoples, exemplified by early recognition of independence of the revolted peoples of Latin America and championship of their independence ever since.

7. No further European colonization in the New World—also pronounced in the Monroe Doctrine of 1823.

8. Nonintervention—also proclaimed in the pristine Monroe Doctrine —to Europe, Hands Off the New World; to the United States itself (as

illustrated in the instructions of Henry Clay to the intended plenipotentiaries to the Congress of Panama), nonintervention in the internal
affairs of other nations of the Western Hemisphere.

9. The right of expatriation and the wrong of impressment.

10. Suppression of the African slave trade—belatedly.

11. Pan-Americanism, or "Good Neighborhood," to use the phrase
of Henry Clay's instructions to the plenipotentiaries appointed in 1826
to attend the Congress of Panama.

12. International arbitration by voluntary agreement. This grew into a
pledge—the right of self-defense—to settle all controversies by peaceful
means (1928) and the obligation toward many countries (1945) to submit all "legal" disputes not involving matters of domestic jurisdiction to
the International Court of Justice.

Implicit in all these fundamentals was anti-imperialism, stemming
from the Anglo-American Revolution itself and also from the Latin-
American Revolution.[1]

Thanks to its singularly fortunate place in the world, the United States
was on the whole successful in its support of these principles during
the eighteenth and nineteenth centuries. But at the turn of the twentieth
century a new picture of power and politics began to take shape which
threatened the traditionally happy situation of the Continental Republic.
The altered outlook resulted from a tremendous phenomenon in modern
history: *the simultaneous appearance of three new world powers*.[2] They
were Germany, the United States, and Japan.

The sudden appearance of one new world power in itself would have
been a rare phenomenon. Three new constellations of major significance
in the international firmament upset the older calculations of diplomatic
astrologers and gave forth new signs and portents of great omination for
the daily welfare, indeed for life and death, of hundreds of millions of
people on this earth. They boded a new century of perturbations and
wars, of vast territorial changes, of epoch-making economic, ideological
and social upheavals, of tremendous alterations of national power and
identity. In these cycles of change the Atlantic nations, the Pacific countries, soon the whole world, would feel the shake of heavy transformations
following this triple birth of world power.

[1] See the author's *John Quincy Adams and the Foundations of American Foreign
Policy* (Alfred A. Knopf, Inc., New York, 1949), Ch. XXVII. There fourteen fundamentals (including sovereign independence and anti-imperialism) are listed. Here I
stress sovereign independence and anti-imperialism, but explicitly enumerate only the
other twelve as guiding principles.

[2] By world powers I mean powers which have to be taken into consideration in the
determination of most major international issues.

In the new frame of international politics the United States confronted the other two new world powers, Germany and Japan, one across each ocean. Both had formidable armies. Both were building up first-class navies. Either could threaten one of the populous seacoasts of the United States. Neither had a hostage such as Canada to guarantee the benevolence of its fleet toward the United States. Nor did they manifest any kinship for freedom with the English-speaking peoples. In the new picture of power and politics the British Empire became a world archipelago threatened by the hostile continents of Europe and Asia. North America gradually became an island-continent menaced by inimical potentials of power. The United States and Great Britain looked more and more to each other for their own security and freedom. Great Britain was first to feel the significance of the new order. The United States did not realize it fully until the First World War.

Historians generally accept the year 1898—that is to say, the events of the Cuban-Spanish-American War—as marking emergence of the United States as a world power. The cause of that war was the Cuban Question, but behind the Cuban Question lay the Isthmian Question. Ever since completion of the Continental Republic, American opinion had focused increasingly upon the project of an Isthmian canal to connect the commerce and defenses of the two seacoasts. Such was the "Large Policy" of Colonel Theodore Roosevelt and young Senator Henry Cabot Lodge, the leading Expansionists of 1898,[1] and of their historical mentor, Captain Alfred T. Mahan. The new frame of sea power made an inter-ocean naval life line indispensable for national security. Without a canal two navies would be required. With a canal one powerful navy might be enough. A single fleet could be passed back and forth through the Isthmus to protect either coast as circumstances might require. No one seems to have feared, in the early decades of the twentieth century, that the United States might have to fight a double conflict, a two-ocean war with a one-ocean navy.

The Cuban Question lay conveniently at hand for the statesmen of the period—the Mahans, the Roosevelts, the Lodges—who wished to secure control of the Isthmus and its maritime approaches from both oceans. The United States emerged from the Cuban-Spanish-American War sovereign of Puerto Rico, protector of Cuba, mistress of the Caribbean, ready and eager to build, control, and fortify a canal across the narrow part of Central America.

[1] Julius W. Pratt has portrayed the *Expansionists of 1898* (Baltimore, 1936).

In the Pacific, as a consequence of the war, the United States annexed the Hawaiian Islands (1898) and forced Spain to sell, for $20,000,000, the Philippine Islands and to cede Guam (1898). The United States had already become a Pacific power in a small way during the nineteenth century when it acquired a number of guano islets in the 1850's—that is, Howland, Baker, and Jarvis. Midway was annexed in 1867, Wake Island not until 1899. From 1889 the United States had been engaged in a quarrelsome operation with Great Britain and Germany, particularly Germany, for the administration of the Samoan Islands. Great Britain got out of Samoa in 1899 in return for compensation from Germany in other parts of the South Seas and in Africa. By a tripartite treaty the United States in the same year took over Tutuila with the harbor of Pago Pago and the islets east of longitude 171° W, while Germany remained sovereign (until 1919) over the rest of the islands of the group.[1]

There was certainly common sense in the American acquisition of these small islands, including the Hawaiian group, as defensive outposts for the Continental Republic. Even so, there had been much opposition to this exercise of dominion over alien peoples, this budding imperialism, so foreign to American concepts of self-government. And before the war no one in the United States—not even Theodore Roosevelt—thought of acquiring territory on the littoral of Eastern Asia. Public opinion did not demand the Philippines. It has been characterized as the Great Aberration of 1898.[2]

These epoch-making events are already behind us as this history begins at the end of the nineteenth century. It will show how in the terrible twentieth century the American people became involved against their desire, but not beyond their stretch of will, in the global whirlpool of harrowing tensions and tendencies arising outside their own continent. It will show further how the development of modern science and the accelerating release and application of physical energy conspired with the new picture of power and politics to effect a veritable revolution in the foreign policy of the United States—from isolation to alliance as the basis for the security of the nation and what the nation stands for in the world.

It is most convenient to begin with the development of Far Eastern affairs that followed the sudden acquisition of the Philippine Islands, then

---

[1] Some of these passages are taken, with permission of Thomas Y. Crowell and Co., from the author's chapter on "The United States as a World Power," in *World Political Geography* (New York, 1948), pp. 54, 55, 56.

[2] My *A Diplomatic History of the United States,* 3d ed. (New York, 1950), p. 475.

to return to the activities of American policy in the Caribbean and the Isthmus and their borderlands, following that fateful war with Spain, next to take up the diplomacy of the United States preceding and during the First World War, and between the two World Wars, again during a Second World War, with final focus on the great contest between the ideals and power of a World Family of Democratic Nations and a World Union of Soviet Socialist Republics—for such in essence was the continuing crisis which the nations and peoples of the world found themselves facing at mid-century.

2

The Open Door and the Far East

DURING the nineteenth century the United States had remained comparatively a passive spectator of the Far Eastern scene. Unlike the European powers it had no imperialistic designs. Its principal concern was the advancement of commercial relations with China and Japan and protection of the persons and property of American citizens, including missionaries residing in those countries.

The Treaty of Wanghia with China of 1844, and the treaties of 1854 and 1856 with Japan, had placed American relations with these Oriental empires on the basis of the most-favored-nation principle, to obtain equal opportunity of commerce, and of the right of extraterritoriality, to secure the protection of nationals. By the most-favored-nation principle the American Republic picked up in the wake of French, British, and Russian imperialism privileges of trade and residence equal to those extracted by the European powers after victorious wars with China. But the United States never sought for *territorial* compensation to match the conquests of the European nations.

The aim of American diplomacy was to use all peaceful means to preserve the integrity of the nations of the East, notably China, Japan, Korea, if only to maintain an equality of trading opportunity with the rival powers. This was also the principal object of British diplomacy as the nineteenth century came to a close, but with one difference: Great Britain had ensconced herself in a fortified position (Hong Kong) in Eastern Asia and was willing if necessary to do battle for her commercial interests, actually had done so. And Great Britain was ready if there were no other choice to join in a further scramble of the powers for Chinese territory in order to prevent any one of them or combination of them from encroaching on China to Britain's disadvantage. In the competitive imperialism of national capitalism China had become "the back yard of European politics." [1]

[1] Tyler Dennett, *Americans in Eastern Asia* (New York, 1922), p. 472.

8

Before 1898 the United States kept out of that wretched back yard terri-
torially but desired that no special gates should be cut through the Chinese
fence which would not be equally open to its missionaries and traders.
The European powers and Japan meanwhile sought to make their
own exclusive gates and widen them by interpretation and manipulation
of their treaty privileges. In China a hostility to all things foreign continued and smoldered among the people who sensed that treaties and
foreigners encroached inevitably upon their territory and their independence. During this continuance of feeble interest by the United States
in Asiatic affairs, two diplomatic questions stand out: the issue of
Oriental immigration (which is best considered in a later chapter)
and Korea.

Rather casually an American expedition under Admiral John Rodgers
was sent in 1870 to escort an American Minister to China, F. F. Low,
to Korea to open up treaty relations with the Hermit Kingdom, under a
show of force, as Perry had done with Japan in 1854. The Koreans, who
still kept their strategic peninsular kingdom closed to the Western world,
fired on Rodgers' ships in the Salee River below Seoul, the Korean capital.
Rodgers fired back and destroyed five forts (May, 1871), but he had
not authority to involve the United States in further hostilities. He retired
without a treaty, and the Koreans jubilantly felt they had successfully
repulsed a Western power. In 1880 Commodore Robert W. Shufeldt [1]
attempted to approach Korea through Japan, but the Japanese endeavored to manipulate the negotiations so as to make Korea appear to
be a Japanese protectorate. Exasperated, Shufeldt then sought the good
offices of China to obtain a treaty with Korea, only to find the Chinese,
on their part, seeking to show Korea as a Chinese protectorate. Shufeldt this time signed a treaty (May 22, 1882, ratified February 13, 1883)
generally similar to the sum of the two previous American treaties
with Japan, which avoided any reference to Korea as a dependent
state of China.[2]

Straightway the other principal powers (except Russia) made treaties
with Korea, treaties which would have been much more one-sided had
it not been for the American model. Japan already (1876) had made a
commercial treaty with Korea which had described that kingdom as
an independent state, and the presence of Japanese forces at the Korean

[1] Shufeldt had already commanded an unsuccessful expedition in 1867 to investigate
the destruction, with her crew, by Koreans of an American schooner, the *General
Sherman*.

[2] C. O. Paullin has described these naval diplomatic missions to Korea in his *Diplomatic Negotiations of American Naval Officers* (Johns Hopkins Press, 1912), pp. 282-328.

capital in 1882 was responsible for Shufeldt's successful avoidance of an article acknowledging Korea's dependence on China. In the background was Russia with far-reaching designs of her own to make Korea an outlet for Russian expansion southward from Siberia across Chinese Manchuria.

In opening Korea to Western commerce and Western political rivalry, the United States had unwittingly stepped on the very touchstone of Far Eastern diplomacy. For three hundred years China and Japan had contested for a protectorate over that isolated nation, a buffer among three powers, Russia, Japan, and China. Japan was now resorting to a policy of recognition of the nominal independence of Korea as a means of cutting it loose from any traces of Chinese sovereignty. Once independent, Korea would be weak enough, and close enough to Japan, to pass eventually under the latter's control, if Russia should not intervene. By making a treaty with Korea as an independent state, the United States, followed by the other powers, really played into the first designs of Japanese expansionists. China, resenting this turn of affairs, began to contest Korea's independent status. The result was the disastrous war with Japan of 1894-1895, in which the victor took (Treaty of Shimonoseki, 1895) Formosa, the Pescadores Islands, and the Liaotung Peninsula, and occupied Weihaiwei as security for the payment of an indemnity of 200,000,000 *taels* ($145,800,000 at par).

It was at this point that Russia (by previous understanding with China), France, and Germany stepped in to make Japan give up the Liaotung Peninsula—outlet of Manchuria to warm water—and then took over for themselves a portion of Japan's spoils. France unwisely supported Russia's advance in Manchuria in return for Russia's alliance with France in Europe. Germany encouraged it as a lightning rod to draw Russian energies away from the tension of Western Europe (as similarly she had encouraged French colonial adventures in Indo-China and North Africa). Great Britain had not joined the three powers to take from Japan her plunder, but anxiously she joined the scramble for concessions in 1898, lest the door be closed against her growing trade in China.

Never was a more fateful mistake made than by this application of Europe's international rivalries to the "back yard" of Asia. It nerved the Japanese to prepare for the expulsion first of Russian, then of German, finally of all European or Occidental influence from Eastern Asia. Little could the desperate Japanese then realize how events in Europe and America within the next generation would conspire for their success, as the convulsions of Europe a century before had conspired for the success of an independent, continental United States of America.

The acquisition of the Philippines in 1898 led rapidly to involvement in the United States in the politics of Asia and through them of Europe, and to a long row of further diplomatic problems. First of these was the menace to the American principle of equal trading opportunity cast up by the threatened partition of China at the close of the nineteenth century.

China in 1898 on the brink of dissolution presented to Great Britain a vital problem of world power and world commerce: if the vast area of independence and free trade should be partitioned British trade would be shut out or discriminated against in favor of the partitioners. Great Britain was eager to sustain the principle of equal opportunity of trade for all nations because, on the basis of even competition at that period, she could dominate the market with her goods and her ships; moreover, she then controlled the sea from Gibraltar to Hong Kong, and in a war she could close to her enemy all the ocean trade routes from Europe to the East, and keep them open to herself. Thus the Open Door in China was a British even more emphatically than an American policy, for Great Britain was willing to take positive action to keep it open. The events of 1898 and 1899, with partition every day more imminent, meant that Great Britain must either: (1) stand by and see China partitioned; (2) join the partitioners; (3) take action alone to stop it, which meant war with one or more powers; or (4) secure some international sanction for the integrity of China. The British Government naturally inclined to the last; and it was during this period 1898-1902 that it was shopping for allies. We must remember constantly that Great Britain was at this time involved in intense rivalry with France in Africa (until 1904), with Russia in the Near East (until 1907), and with Germany in commercial and naval problems, and that she was engaged with the Boers in open warfare in South Africa (1899-1902). With the United States now present in force in the Far East, and Great Britain withdrawn in force and in policy from the Caribbean, the kindred American Republic of the West seemed the most redoubtable as well as the most compatible of possible allies; but there were also Germany and Japan as offsets against Russia and France, then the potential enemies of Great Britain. In March, 1898, the British Government, aware of the trend of rapidly developing events in China, confidentially invited the United States to co-operate in opposing any action by foreign powers that might violate the Open Door in China.[1] At this time the British-proposed Open Door meant more than equality of trade rights throughout China; it meant equality of rights for economic concessions and privileges and the integrity of China against further territorial cessions.

President McKinley, engrossed with the Cuban Question and the impending war with Spain, instructed Secretary of State John Sherman to decline the invitation. He minimized the danger to the Open Door and saw no reason for departing from the traditional policy respecting foreign alliances. The Open Door to Chinese trade was of no such vital interest to the United States as, say, the Monroe Doctrine—there were strategic and defensive interests in America that were not at stake in China.

The acquisition of the Philippines changed the shadings of the Eastern picture, and more complete information showed the danger of partition to be very real. The paramount motive for acquiring the distant archipelago had been the trade of the East. Should China be partitioned, so it was feared, that prospect of commerce would soon vanish behind the restrictions of the partitioners.

John Hay, recently Ambassador in London, who had now become Secretary of State, knew well the attitude of the British Government. He realized that Great Britain might leave the United States a free hand in the New World and desired in return a joint hand in Eastern Asia. He was taking advantage of this change in British policy in his efforts to revise the Clayton-Bulwer Treaty of 1850 and to secure control of the future isthmian canal. He felt that the Open Door in China fitted into American policy as well as into British, if not so vitally. John Hay knew that American public opinion was set against anything resembling a foreign alliance, and that the "unspeakable Senate" would not ratify any formal treaty. Hay had as an adviser on Far Eastern affairs W. W. Rockhill, who had served briefly in the American diplomatic service in China and who was a close student of Oriental affairs. Rockhill represented to Hay that the policy best suited to American interests was not a British one, for England had been as great an offender in China as Russia herself. Hay accepted the advice [2] of Rockhill to take an independent step (not unlike the pronouncement of the Monroe Doctrine in 1823) for the preservation of China—and with it of American trade through an open door there—by an appeal to the jealous powers to guarantee

---

[1] Alfred L. P. Dennis, *Adventures in American Diplomacy, 1896-1906* (New York, 1928), Ch. VII.

[2] Rockhill's memorandum was called forth by the lectures, conferences, and publications of Lord Charles Beresford, a quasi-official British propagandist who circled the globe in 1899 urging a joint Anglo-American policy in the Orient.

to all nations equality of opportunity within their special spheres. Since 1928 it has been known[1] that Alfred E. Hippisley, a British subject formerly in the Chinese customs service, who arrived in the United States in 1899, had a strong hand in formulating the basis of the Open Door notes—previously attributed to Rockhill—and persuading Hay to issue them.[2] More recently it has been established that a small pressure group of American exporters to North China (Manchuria) organized a powerful propaganda which seems to have had its effect on the Department of State.[3]

The Hay notes, to Great Britain, Russia, Germany, France, and Japan, dated September 6-November 17, 1899, stated:

The principles which this Government is particularly desirous of seeing formally declared . . . by all the great powers interested in China, and which will be eminently beneficial to the commercial interests of the whole world, are:

First. The recognition that no power will in any way interfere with any treaty port or any vested interest within any leased territory or within any so-called "sphere of interest" it may have in China.

Second. That the Chinese treaty tariff of the time being shall apply to all merchandise landed or shipped to all such ports as are within said "sphere of interest" (unless they be "free ports"), no matter to what nationality it may belong, and that duties so leviable shall be collected by the Chinese Government.

Third. That it [each power] will levy no higher harbor dues on vessels of another nationality frequenting any port in such "sphere" than shall be levied on vessels of its own nationality, and no higher railroad charges over lines built, controlled, or operated within its "sphere" on merchandise belonging to citizens or subjects of other nationalities transported through such "sphere" than shall be levied on similar merchandise belonging to its own nationals transported over equal distances.

That the United States was now a power established with military and naval forces in the Philippines, that its policy, if independent, accorded with that of Great Britain—as also with that of Japan in 1899—made Germany, France, and Russia more attentive to Hay's proposals. Great

---

[1] Dennis, *Adventures, op. cit.,* p. 186, and Tyler Dennett, *John Hay: From Poetry to Politics* (New York, 1933), Ch. XXIV.

[2] It would be interesting to know if Mr. Hippisley had any connection, direct or indirect, with the British Embassy, in Washington, or with the Foreign Office. The *British Documents on the Origin of the War, 1898-1914* omit the documents relating to the Open Door notes, though copious selections of documents relating to other Far Eastern affairs of that time are printed.

[3] Charles S. Campbell, Jr., "American Business Interests and the Open Door in China," *Far Eastern Quarterly,* I (November, 1941), 43-58.

Britain adopted them conditionally, in language which reserved Hong Kong and Kowloon. Germany accepted on condition that the other powers would; so did France, Japan, and Italy (which had failed to establish a sphere), but Russia evaded. By what then passed for a skillful coup, Hay replied in identical language to all the powers, severally, that all having complied with the proposals of the United States, the latter (in each case) would consider the assent given to the principles as "final and definitive." Russia still kept silent.

The notes were extremely gratifying to England,[1] and undoubtedly helped Hay in adjusting the Isthmian Question and the Alaska boundary dispute, although there is no evidence of a specific diplomatic bargain. As the leading authority on this phase of American diplomatic history has put it, the net result was that Great Britain got out of the Caribbean and the United States got into Asia.[2] It should be noted that the Open Door, an international understanding of doubtful[3] binding power, was then limited in its application to tariff, railroad charges, and port dues. It did not open the door to equal opportunity of investment or of industry. It did not, in 1899, attempt to preserve the territorial integrity, the administrative entity, or the independence of China, as the British Government had suggested in March, 1898.

Was Hay's policy a wise one? As a temporary expedient, perhaps yes, it was good as long as the diplomatic equipoise should last in the Far East. As a farsighted permanent policy to stick to and defend like the Monroe Doctrine, no. The Open Door would not stay open should the territory of China or its administration pass under the full control of any other power—that is, should China's independence be threatened. The fate of Korea was soon to be a complete example of this truth. In the ensuing years, to keep the Open Door in China the Government of the United States was drawn further and further into the diplomatic entanglements of the Far East by expanding the doctrine so as to include the territorial and administrative integrity and the independence of China. This was assuming responsibilities of policy compensated by no corresponding advantages to the United States. The structure of the Open Door would be threatened as soon as any one power in the Far East

---

[1] Allan Nevins, *Henry White, Thirty Years of American Diplomacy* (New York, 1930), p. 167.

[2] Tyler Dennett, "The Open Door," in *Empire in the East,* ed. by Joseph Barnes (Garden City, New York, 1934), p. 280.

[3] Each power made its acceptance conditional upon the full acceptance by all the other powers. Since Russia did not accept, and Great Britain excluded the leasehold of Kowloon, this left everything much qualified indeed.

should become paramount. Then the United States would have to fight for the Open Door or retreat in the face of the world from its declared principles. At no time have the American people been willing to fight merely for the Open Door in any part of Asia, or indeed in any other land. Again, it cannot be shown that, even if China had been partitioned and its territory placed under other sovereignties, the opportunity of American trade would have been smaller instead of greater. It is noticeable how American trade with the sovereign Japanese Empire, one of the putative partitioners, increased while that with China unpartitioned further (until 1931) relatively languished.

The Open Door notes did not prevent an explosion in China on the part of patriotic groups resentful of foreign exploitation and of the imperial Manchu Government which had succumbed to it. The Boxers, a patriotic society in North China, stirred up the people to end the encroachments by wiping out the hated barbarians and their Christian converts. The Dowager Empress encouraged the movement, which pillaged and murdered foreign missionaries and other residents in the provinces, and finally attacked and besieged the legations in Peking, after killing the secretary to the Japanese legation and the German Minister. A total of 231 [1] (mostly missionaries and their families) were massacred between June 24 and July 24, 1900, including 53 children. The Manchu authorities, caught between native resentment and foreign punitive measures, managed to prevent a general slaughter. For a month Peking was totally cut off from the outside world, which assumed that the 920 foreigners penned in the legations had perished. Intervention seemed imperative, but would it stop short of war and partition? The Western powers and Japan hastily brought up from their naval bases and ships an aggregate of approximately 19,000 troops, and, after some sharp engagements, relieved the legations (August 14, 1900) after a seven weeks' siege, opened up communications with Tientsin and the sea, and occupied Peking and Chili province. Other contingents of troops reinforced the occupation after the taking of Peking. The United States had finally a total of 5,000 troops in China. The international settlement at Shanghai was also reinforced. After prolonged negotiations the powers imposed punishment and reparations on China.

During the Boxer crisis Secretary Hay successfully strove to prevent an actual war (although China had declared one when the foreign troops came), to limit intervention to the protection of foreign nationals, to

---

[1] Exclusive of the Marine guards (76 killed, 179 wounded) defending the legations during the siege, and, of course, of military casualties during the ensuing intervention.

withdraw troops promptly, to stop the jealous, avaricious powers from vengeful extensions of their existing leaseholds and spheres, and to keep down the total of reparations to be demanded from China. This was also the policy of Great Britain, then engaged in the Boer War in South Africa. The Secretary of State issued a circular (July 3, 1900): "The policy of the Government of the United States is to seek a solution which may bring about permanent safety and peace to China, *preserve Chinese territorial and administrative entity*,[1] protect all rights guaranteed to friendly powers by treaty and international law, and safeguard for the world the principle of equal and impartial trade with all parts of the Chinese Empire." It was the capstone of American policy in the Far East.

Only Great Britain, France, and Germany responded favorably to this principle; nevertheless its application softened the terms imposed on China. Unfortunately Hay contradicted himself by asking the Japanese Government if it would have any objection to the United States establishing a naval coaling station at Samsah Bay, Fukien Province (within the recently established Japanese sphere of influence). Japan replied that she would indeed have objection: "The Imperial Government harbor no territorial designs on China; their policy, on the contrary, is directed to the maintenance of her territorial integrity; and they have noted with entire satisfaction the declaration made on several occasions by the Secretary of State that the United States were also anxious to preserve the territorial entity of that empire."[2]

The protocol[3] of September 7, 1901, imposed on China by the intervening powers including the United States, stipulated for the punishment by death or exile enumerated Chinese officials implicated in the outbreak, the erection of expiatory monuments where foreigners had been killed or outraged, or tombs defiled, protection of foreign communications between Peking and the sea, and the payment of 450,000,000 *taels* ($333,000,000) reparations. Of this the United States had claimed only $25,000,000. This proved more than adequate to indemnify the claims of nationals, and in 1907 $10,785,286 was returned to the Chinese Government. This generous act ingratiated the United States further in Chinese estimation. The Chinese Government placed the money in a trust fund

[1] Italics inserted.

[2] *Foreign Relations of the United States, 1915* (Washington, G.P.O., 1916), p. 115, note.

[3] Not a treaty ratified by the Senate.

for the education of Chinese youths in China and in the United States. $6,137,552.90 more was remitted by the United States in 1924.[1]

Following the July circular of 1900, the American policy of the Open Door rapidly proliferated into preservation of all China in full sovereignty against foreign encroachments. During the occupation of Peking, Russia had occupied Manchuria and, despite subsequent promises, refused to get out unless the Chinese consented to place Manchuria under Russian protection. Secretary Hay made successive protests against Russian advances on Chinese sovereignty. He protested (February 1, 1902) against the granting to Russia of any exclusive mining or railroad privileges as wrecking the policy of "absolute equality of treatment of all nations in regard to trade, navigation, and commerce within the confines of the Empire," and against any commercial monopoly as a violation of the Open Door "accepted by all the treaty powers having commercial interests in that Empire." He protested (April 25, 1903) against a proposed Russo-Chinese convention then being pressed on China which would have prohibited treaty ports and foreign consuls in Manchuria, and would have excluded all foreigners except Russians from Chinese public service in North China; and in the Chinese-American treaty of commerce (October 8, 1903) the Open Door Doctrine was asserted in treaty form, accompanied by the opening of Mukden and Antung in Manchuria to foreign trade, thus thwarting Russian attempts to close it. At the outset of the Russo-Japanese War the United States appealed (February 10, 1904) to both belligerents to limit as much as possible their military operations in order to preserve the neutrality and "administrative entity" of China (with no mention of Korea), and joined the neutral powers in a disclaimer of compensation for themselves with Chinese territory. At this time the war was being fought in Chinese territory. Hay then stated (January 13, 1905) the broad policy of the United States to maintain "the integrity of China and the 'Open Door' in the Orient."[2]

Secretary Hay had advanced from a policy of a limited Open Door to a policy of preserving the sovereignty and territorial and administrative entity of all of China's vast empire. At the very time he was writing these fine words, Russia and Japan were engaging in a duel, at first in peace and then in war, ultimately to possess themselves

---

[1] During the war of 1917-1918, payment was by agreement of the Entente allies suspended for five years. Germany had renounced hers by the peace of 1919 (also returning artistic and scientific treasures plundered from Peking in 1900), and the Soviet Government renounced its remaining share in 1920.

[2] M. J. Bau, *The Open Door Doctrine in Relation to China* (New York, 1923).

of large portions of Chinese territory. Under the guidance of Hay, American policy in Eastern Asia was rapidly assuming responsibilities far greater than any advantage promised or interests involved.

We have said that the success of the Open Door policy—not to mention now its proliferations—depended on a complete equipoise in the Far East, that it could not be maintained if one power should upset the balance. That power began to emerge to a position of challenge very soon. It was Japan.

In the situation heading up in Asia, Japan, like Great Britain, needed an ally. Great Britain, engaged in the Boer War, at odds with France in Europe and Africa, and with Russia in the Near East and Asia, and desiring to preserve the territorial integrity of the remainder of China and the Open Door there, unable to make friends with Russia, had deserted her traditional policy of "magnificent isolation." She had looked first hopefully to the United States, glanced distrustfully at Germany, and then turned again to her traditional adversary Russia [1] as possible allies. None would commit itself. Japan was now confronted with Russia, established in the Liaotung Peninsula and building with French loans a railroad south across Manchuria to a naval base at Port Arthur. This was the concession which China had secretly promised to Russia in return for getting the three powers to thrust Japan out of her conquests in 1895. After the Sino-Japanese War Japan considered nominally independent Korea as her preserve and looked beyond it toward Manchuria. Russia considered Manchuria as her preserve and looked beyond it toward Korea.

In back of the immediate ambitions of both rival powers in Korea and Manchuria lay their larger ambitions and rivalry for the ultimate domination of all China. Japan prepared for another war but wished to make sure that Russia would have to stand alone, without allies. The result was the Anglo-Japanese alliance of January 30, 1902. The contracting powers declared themselves to be actuated solely by a desire to maintain the *status quo* and general peace in the Far East, being moreover specially interested in maintaining the independence and territorial integrity of the Empire of China and the Empire of Korea, and in securing equal opportunities in these countries for the commerce and industry of all nations. Disavowing aggressive tendencies in China and Korea, they recognized the right of either ally to take such measures as might be necessary to safeguard its existing interests; and in case either should

---

[1] W. L. Langer, *The Diplomacy of Imperialism* (2 vols., New York, 1935), II, pp. 711-786, describes in detail these negotiations with Germany, Russia, and Japan.

become involved in war with a third power in defense of those interests, the other party would remain neutral but would come to the defense of its ally in case the enemy were joined by another power. The treaty was to remain in force for at least five years.

Before the first five years had elapsed Great Britain had pacified South Africa and, in the face of the German advance, had liquidated her historic issues with France in Morocco, Egypt, and other parts of the world by the Entente of 1904, and Japan was engaged in the war with Russia. The early Japanese victories at Port Arthur and on the plains of Manchuria, Britain's concern to protect the northwestern frontiers of India against future Russian expansion, and the continuing menace to England of the rising German navy made it possible for Japan to reframe the alliance in 1905 during her peace negotiations with Russia. The object of the alliance, renewed for ten years, was now (August 12, 1905) stated to be: "(a) The consolidation and maintenance of the general peace in the regions of Eastern Asia and of India. (b) The preservation of the common interests of all powers in China, by insuring the independence and integrity of the Chinese Empire and the principle of equal opportunities for the commerce and industry of all nations in China. (c) The maintenance of the territorial rights of the high contracting parties in the regions of Eastern Asia and of India, and the defense of their special interests in the said regions." Great Britain agreed to go to Japan's assistance in case, during the existing war, Russia should be joined by a third power. Further, if by reason of unprovoked or aggressive action *wherever arising,*[1] on the part of any other power or powers, either party should be involved in war in defense of its territorial rights in "the regions of Eastern Asia and of India," the other party would at once come to the assistance of its ally. As for the future, Great Britain explicitly recognized a free hand for Japan in Korea, subject to the maintenance of the Open Door there, and Japan implicitly and tacitly gave to Great Britain a free hand to sap Chinese suzerainty in Tibet, which had been penetrated by British forces in 1904.

[1] Under this phrase the aggressive action might arise in Europe or in America. In 1911 the alliance was renewed for ten years from date, to continue thereafter until abrogated by either party at one year's notice. It contained a modification intended to remove the United States from its scope: "Should either high contracting party conclude a treaty of general arbitration with a third power, it is agreed that nothing in this agreement shall entail upon such contracting party an obligation to go to war with the power with whom such treaty of arbitration is in force." Great Britain was then negotiating a general treaty of arbitration of justiciable questions with the United States, but it was never ratified.

The new alliance enabled Japan to clinch its hold on Korea in the coming treaty of peace with Russia, and it made it possible for Great Britain to concentrate her sea power in European waters. At the same time Japan pledged herself to observe the Open Door in Korea, and in China the Open Door and "the independence and integrity" of that Empire.

The peace negotiations had opened meanwhile at Portsmouth, New Hampshire. To understand the background of President Roosevelt's proffer of good offices to the belligerents in 1905, we must bear constantly in mind the relationship of the "back yard" of European diplomacy in Asia to its front yard in Europe. With Russia "mired" in Manchuria after the Japanese victory at Mukden (March 10, 1905), the German Kaiser and his advisers determined to reap the diplomatic profits arising in Europe from their inveiglement of Russia into Asiatic adventure by: (1) breaking the new Anglo-French entente on the anvil of Morocco, and, (2) nullifying the Franco-Russian alliance through attaching a salvaged Russia to Germany in a defensive alliance against France. As the first move the Kaiser disembarked at Tangier (March 31, 1905) to greet the Sultan of Morocco in his position as an independent sovereign. This German challenge to the dual entente for an open door in Morocco precipitated a major European diplomatic crisis. We shall see in a later chapter,[1] how the exuberant Roosevelt went out of his way unnecessarily to participate in the first Moroccan crisis— the first of a series that led to the outbreak of the First World War in 1914. He also went out of his way to play unnecessarily a part in the Asiatic sphere of world policy.

During the first Moroccan crisis, France's embarrassment at the paralysis of her Russian ally inspired her to suggest to Japan her willingness to be a peacemaker. The Japanese Government suspected French disinterestedness. It was nevertheless eager for a peace which would preserve its victories against the danger of exhaustion by a long war of attrition in northern Manchuria. It ceased major military movements and intimated to President Roosevelt a preference and readiness for his good offices. Germany, whose policy had been to push Russia along diplomatically into the Manchurian quagmire in order to paralyze France's ally in Europe, was now content with the predicament of Russia and somewhat alarmed at the possibility of revolutionary disorder in European Russia, which might infect Germany and endanger the mon-

[1] For the first Moroccan crisis, see below, pp. 113-116.

archical principle there. The Kaiser therefore supported the move for peace, through Roosevelt. He also was planning a secret treaty with weakened Russia (Björkö, July 25, 1905) which would detach her from the Franco-Russian alliance, and he desired to win Roosevelt's support for that.

Roosevelt [1] had let the Japanese know that he thought that they deserved to have Korea, and Secretary Hay's [2] note on the Open Door had ignored that expiring kingdom. The President now attached one condition for his services to bring about a peace: that Japan pledge herself to the doctrine of the Open Door in Manchuria. Having secured from the Czar—after the destruction of the Russian fleet at Tsushima Straits— an agreement to meet the Japanese, Roosevelt made to both parties a formal offer of good offices (June 8, 1905). The belligerents accepted and successfully worked out indirect negotiations without the presence of a formal mediator, the peace of Portsmouth, New Hampshire (signed, September 5, 1905).

While the Japanese envoys were *en route* to the peace conference, President Roosevelt confirmed the bargain with Japan concerning Korea and the Philippines: the secret [3] Taft-Katsura memorandum (July 29, 1905). This avowedly had no constitutional force binding upon the United

[1] Tyler Dennett in his distinguished study, *Roosevelt and the Russo-Japanese War* (New York, 1922), p. 2, quotes an authentic letter of Theodore Roosevelt to the British diplomatist, Sir Cecil Spring-Rice, dated July 24, 1905, in which he said: "As soon as the war broke out, I notified Germany and France in the most polite and discreet fashion that in the event of a combination against Japan to do what Russia, Germany and France did to her in 1894 [*sic*], I should promptly side with Japan and proceed to whatever length was necessary on her behalf. I, of course, knew that your government would act in the same way, and I thought it best that I should have no consultation with your people before announcing my own purpose."
The Anglo-Japanese alliance itself had never promised more than this, and (so far as we know) Great Britain had never served such notice. That Roosevelt really did do precisely this is doubtful, like his now disproven "ultimatum" to Venezuela of 1902-1903. Alfred Vagts, *Deutschland und die Vereinigten Staaten in der Weltpolitik* (2 vols., London, 1935), II, p. 1178, could find no trace of it in the archives of the Department of State, the German Foreign Office, or in the personal papers left by Roosevelt or John Hay.
[2] Secretary Hay was now ill and on leave. He died July 1, 1905. Roosevelt meanwhile had taken over the administration of foreign affairs, leaving Secretary of War Taft in nominal control of the Department of State. Taft presently was sent on a mission to the Philippines via Japan.
[3] The text, without mention of Taft's name, is printed in Dennett, *op. cit.* P. C. Jessup, *Elihu Root* (2 vols., New York, 1938), II, p. 5, makes out that Taft did this on his own initiative. "Your conversation with Count Katsura absolutely correct in every respect," Roosevelt cabled to Taft, July 29, 1905. "Wish you would state to Katsura that I confirm every word you have said." See also Henry F. Pringle, *Theodore Roosevelt, a Biography* (New York, 1931), p. 384. Great Britain informed Roosevelt of the substance of the alliance during its negotiation. He did not object. L. M. Gelber, *Rise of Anglo-American Friendship* (New York, 1938), pp. 216-250.

States; but President Roosevelt, speaking in the most noncommittal way through Secretary of War William H. Taft, then in Tokyo on a mission to Manila, approved a free hand for Japan in Korea, and Count Katsura, the Premier of Japan, disavowed "any aggressive designs whatever on the Philippines."

The Treaty of Portsmouth, a landmark in the diplomatic history of the modern world, contained these terms: (1) Russia recognized that Japan had "predominant political, military, and economic interests in Korea," and agreed not to interfere with them in any way. (2) Both countries agreed "to completely and simultaneously evacuate Manchuria" and to restore it to "the exclusive administration of China," excepting always the Russian leasehold with all concessions in Liaotung, which was transferred completely to Japan. Russia declared she had no "territorial advantages or preferential or exclusive concessions in Manchuria of such a nature as to impair the sovereignty of China or which are incompatible with the principle of equal opportunity." [1] Both parties mutually pledged themselves not to place obstacles in the way of general measures, applying equally to all nations, which China might adopt for the development of commerce and industry in Manchuria. Russia transferred to Japan her mining and railroad concessions in southern Manchuria, south of Changchun. Both countries reserved the (arbitrary) right to maintain railway guards to a maximum of fifteen per kilometer. (3) Russia ceded to Japan the southern half of Sakhalin Island. This treaty was a striking triumph for Japan, definitely establishing her position as a world power, an epoch-making step for that nation on the continent of Asia.

President Roosevelt thought the peace just to Russia and Japan and also good for England and the United States. It is difficult to see how the President's diplomacy in this instance benefited the United States. The Open Door was not really strengthened by the substitution of Japan for Russia in southern Manchuria, as Mr. Roosevelt came presently to realize. In Japan a disappointed populace raged at the failure to secure an indemnity and the whole of Sakhalin Island, and attached, unreasonably, the odium for this to the United States where the treaty had been signed. From this time begins a steadily mounting feeling of enmity in Japan against the United States, hitherto her best and most disinterested friend. The feeling was sharpened by

---

[1] Note that this was not a disavowal of territorial advantages or exclusive concessions. In fact, the Russian reply of itself was sufficiently equivocal to nullify any general binding agreement.

the immigration policy of the United States, and, more and more, by the Open Door policy, which stood in the way of Japanese expansion on the continent of Asia, for which the way had been prepared by the winning of the war against Russia.

President Roosevelt received the Nobel peace prize and the plaudits of the world for his conspicuous diplomacy, but the peace treaty of Portsmouth did some harm and no good to the United States. It left Japan in a position of power to threaten the whole American policy in the Far East, part and parcel of the growing Open Door policy which had been the immediate sequel to the fateful aberration of 1898. It is to be noted that Great Britain, whose interests in China surpassed those of all other powers, kept clear of all these peace negotiations, except to confirm and reshape her alliance with Japan, as above noted, recognizing the new Japanese position in Korea.

During the decade after Portsmouth, American diplomacy in the Far East is featured on the one hand by continuing efforts to hold the door open in China, including, after Roosevelt's departure from office, Manchuria, and to preserve its territorial and administrative integrity and independence, and on the other hand by the appearance of new issues between the United States and Japan arising out of domestic legislation within the United States on matters of immigration and alien landholding. We must reserve the last of these questions for special consideration later.[1]

Japan had stepped into a continental foothold and a policy of expansion which must necessarily envisage Korea, China, or Russian Siberia— in the long run all of them. Over Korea she established a protectorate during the war (1904), which rapidly, and despite disclaimers of any intention to annex, developed into outright possession (1910). In China, Japan confronted the concessionaire powers and the doctrine of the Open Door blossoming into the preservation of that country. Siberia was not of immediate importance, and the account was already squared with Russia for that generation. As to China, until the First World War and the preoccupation of the Western powers with other problems it was necessary to speak softly and go slow. Japan therefore did lip service to the Open Door and its expanding principles, which really stood in the way of her "manifest destiny," and concentrated her diplomacy on establishing a special position in that part of China known as Manchuria. She quickly secured from China (treaty of Peking, 1905) an acquiescence in the transfer of the Russian leasehold and

[1] See Chapters 10 and 11.

attendant railway concessions and a secret statement [1] that China would not allow any parallel or branch railways prejudicial to the interests of the South Manchuria Railway. She then started a development of the railway and ancillary concessions directed toward the economic and, eventually, the political control of Manchuria. The first step was to work quietly for treaties with individual powers, which, while recognizing in a general way the principle of the Open Door and the integrity of China, would nevertheless confirm—in return for equivalent recognitions by Japan in other spheres—Japanese special interests and the network of particular treaty rights regarding Manchuria.

Japan signed such treaties [2] with both France and Russia in the summer of 1907 and considered the negotiation of one with the United States, but the time was then unpropitious for this last because of the serious tension between the two nations arising from the California immigration question. After the temporary adjustment of that issue, and the acceptance by the United States of Japan's invitation for the American fleet to visit her ports on the famous cruise around the world, there was worked out the Root-Takahira executive agreement, November 30, 1908; not a treaty to be sure, but an understanding of the first importance, binding at least on the Roosevelt Administration.

In this exchange of notes—which followed the spectacular American naval demonstration in the Pacific—the United States and Japan declared themselves to be: (1) uninfluenced by any aggressive tendencies in their policy to maintain the "existing *status quo*" in the "region of the Pacific Ocean," (2) resolved to respect the territorial possessions belonging to each other in that region, and (3) "determined to preserve the common interests of all powers in China by supporting by all pacific means at their disposal the independence and integrity of China and the principle of equal opportunity for commerce and industry of all nations in that Empire." "Should any event occur threatening the *status quo* as above described or the principle of equal opportunity as above defined, it remains for the two Governments to communicate

---

[1] The Lytton Report of 1932 (below, pp. 343-345) showed that this was not an agreement, but merely a statement in the minutes of the discussion between the representatives of the two governments.

[2] For English text of the treaties, and of all other treaties revealed before 1919, see the standard compilation by J. V. A. MacMurray, *Treaties and Agreements with and Concerning China, 1894-1919* (2 vols., New York, 1921), I, pp. 640, 657.

The French treaty (June 10, 1907) recognized the "independence and integrity of China." The Russian treaty (July 30, 1907) recognized "the independence and territorial integrity of the Empire of China."

with each other in order to arrive at an understanding as to what measures they may consider it useful to take."

The Root-Takahira understanding, so studiously phrased, was another executive adventure of Roosevelt—unsustained by the Senate. It supplemented the earlier Taft-Katsura "agreed memorandum." It appears to have been calculated to recognize indirectly Japan's increasing interests in Manchuria. One should note: (1) that there is a distinction between the region of the Pacific Ocean (where lie the Philippines and Formosa) and China; (2) that only "peaceful means" are mentioned; (3) that the phrase "integrity of China" is not preceded by the qualifying word "territorial." It suggests that Roosevelt was preparing to give to Japan a free hand in Manchuria as he had done already in Korea.

He had already come to feel that the Philippines—for the conquest of which he had been so ardent in 1898—were the "Achilles heel" of the United States, and that the United States could not fight Japan over Manchuria. His executive agreements reflect this conviction, the greatest anxiety of his Eastern policy.

If the Root-Takahira agreement might be construed to make, tacitly but realistically, some concessions to Japan's ambitions in Manchuria, at the expense of China's complete territorial integrity, the policy of President Taft ignored such an interpretation. He endeavored to push the door still wider open by a highly legalistic reliance on the construction of the Open Door and the territorial integrity of all China, including Manchuria. Taft was a constitutional lawyer; so was his Secretary of State, Philander C. Knox.

Taft and Knox saw that the territorial integrity and political independence of China in Manchuria were being menaced by the railway concessions to Japan and Russia, and were convinced that this was contrary to the spirit and letter of the Open Door and ought to be stopped. Secretary Knox believed that if these special railway concessions—to gain which it is remembered the two nations had gone to the point of war, and to war itself—could be done away with, the Open Door and China's sovereign rights would be protected. To achieve this he relied on paper and ink: a memorandum (December 14, 1909), the principle of which the British Government had agreed to support diplomatically, which he presented to the Governments of China, Japan, France, Russia, and Germany, proposing a joint loan to enable China to buy up all the railways, including those in Manchuria, in her territory which were then under foreign lease or hypothecation; or, alternately, to construct south to north through Manchuria from

Chinchow to Aigun another railway under neutral administration—a scheme of "commercial neutralization."

Thus would the Open Door be guaranteed by neutral administration throughout Manchuria and all other parts of China, and thus would China eventually throw off the trammels which the railway concessions had established upon her sovereignty. This, said Secretary Knox, was "perhaps the most effective way to preserve the undisturbed enjoyment by China of all political rights in Manchuria and to promote the development of those Provinces under a practical application of the policy of the open door and equal commercial opportunity." Neither Russia, who had never agreed with the United States to the Open Door, nor Japan, who found it irksome, desired any practical application of that doctrine in Manchuria, particularly after they had reached understandings with some of the powers (including the Root-Takahira agreement) which appeared to confirm their special interests there.

The Knox neutralization proposal was an unsuccessful *démarche* of American diplomacy. Despite the willingness, in principle, of China, Great Britain, and Germany to accede to it, the ill-considered proposal had no chance of success [1] with the three other powers opposed. Its only result was to impel Japan and Russia to delimit and agree to defend their respective special interests in Manchuria and also the adjacent area of Eastern Inner Mongolia (treaties of July 4, 1910,[2] and June 25, 1912). It undid Roosevelt's dubious policy of give-and-take with Japan. It did not help keep the door open in Manchuria, and it brought resentment from both powers, particularly Japan, against the government which had initiated the proposal. Japan proceeded to construct feeder lines to the South Manchuria Railway, particularly for the exploitation of the rich coal fields, and to connect with a trunk line through Korea to its southern tip. Along the new railroad trackage Japan extended her military guards and developing political jurisdiction over the loosely defined railway zones.[3] In northern Manchuria, Russia likewise expanded her political influence.

[1] France, true to the spirit of her Japanese treaty of 1907, declined the proposal unless it was acceptable to Russia and Japan.

[2] Ironically, this treaty reaffirmed attachment to the principles of the previous convention of July 30, 1907, in which the two powers had recognized the "independence and territorial integrity of China and the principle of equal opportunity" and agreed to defend the *status quo* and respect for this principle by all pacific means within their reach. The *status quo* and the principle were of course incompatible.

[3] The original contract of September 8, 1896, granting to the Russo-Chinese Bank the right to construct a railroad, under the organization of the Chinese Eastern Railway Company, stated that the company might hold "the lands actually necessary for the construction, operation and protection of the line"; and that "the company will have

After the failure of the neutralization proposal, Taft and Knox desired a share for American corporations henceforth in China's foreign loans and big construction contracts. The service of these loans had demanded the pledging of various classes of internal revenues, and even Chinese employment of designated foreign subjects for the collection and administration of the hypothecated revenues. Hence there was grave danger of eventual political control by the powers so eagerly competing to be China's creditors. As in 1898 the powers strove for geographical spheres of political influence, so now the rivalry was for political control, or to prevent unique political control through the supervised service of the loans. In 1910 French, German, British, and American banking groups, with the support of their respective governments, signed an agreement for joint action and participation in foreign loans to China. Into this consortium, further perfected in 1913, were admitted Russia and Japan in 1912.[1]

The consortium loaned to the Chinese Government a total of only £27,000,000. American bankers furnished but $7,299,000 [2] of this. It has not yet been made clear how the favored corporations secured government support for their entrée. The American share of the consortium loans were only a tiny fraction of the immense Chinese foreign debt of $835,000,000 [3] at the end of 1913. In addition to this $7,299,000 share of the public debt of China by favored American banking cor-

the absolute and exclusive right of administration of its lands." Russia and Japan used this clause to justify political control of the railway zones including administration of cities, within their respective spheres, and to guard the road with troops. It has been noticed already that both powers incorporated this into the treaty of Portsmouth. Japan's right to do so was confirmed by an interpretative additional agreement to the treaty of Peking of 1905. See the three volumes by C. Walter Young: *Japan's Special Position in Manchuria; The International Legal Status of the Kwang-Tung Leased Area;* and *Japanese Jurisdiction in the South Manchuria Railway* (Johns Hopkins University Press, 1931).

[1] Space forbids any more detailed analysis of the political and economic aspects of these loans. We refer the reader to Stanley K. Hornbeck, *Contemporary Politics in the Far East* (New York, 1916); W. W. Willoughby, *Foreign Rights and Interests in China* (Johns Hopkins Press, 1927); H. B. Morse and H. F. MacNair, *Far Eastern International Relations* (N. Y., 1931); and more particularly to C. F. Remer, *Foreign Investments in China* (New York, 1933); Frederick V. Field, ed., *Economic Handbook of the Pacific Area* (New York, 1934), for the Institute of Pacific Relations; Edward H. Zabriskie, *American-Russian Rivalry in the Far East* (University of Pennsylvania Press, 1946), and Pauline Thomkins, *American-Russian Relations in the Far East* (New York, 1949).

[2] This was their share in the so-called Hukuang railway loan of £6,000,000. Charles F. Remer, *Foreign Investments in China* (New York, 1933), pp. 268-272.

[3] Of this $174,600,000 was on account of a loan to pay off indemnity to Japan after the Sino-Japanese War; and $309,200,000 was outstanding on account of the Boxer indemnity—that is, obligations on account of these two indemnities then constituted 57.9 per cent of China's total foreign indebtedness.

porations, American private business of one kind or another—merchants, shippers, navigation—had $42,000,000 invested in China in 1914, plus mission property of $10,000,000.

The whole stake was very small indeed,[1] but President Taft felt that uncontrolled rivalry by the powers for loans to China and their supervision would lead to bankruptcy and political intervention, that American participation and co-operation were necessary to prevent such a catastrophe and to preserve the integrity of the nation.[2] President Wilson promptly reversed this policy (March 18, 1913) when he took office, on the ground that the conditions of such loans very nearly touched the administrative independence of China. He would not accept the responsibility which would be implied in requesting bankers to undertake loans "which might conceivably go the length in some unhappy contingency of forcible interference in the financial and even the political affairs of that great oriental state." The Wilson policy (abandoned in 1917) put an end to American banking loans to China.

Following the exit of the United States from the consortium, the powers resumed their rivalry for supervision of Chinese loans and finances, a rivalry in which the European governments gave way to Japan after the outbreak of the First World War in 1914. During these years of international contest for loans and public works the Chinese revolted against the Manchu Imperial Government, which had led them into the increasing entanglement of foreign concessions and control, and set up (1911) a republic, out of which it was hoped would develop a strong national government able to cope successfully, like the Japanese, with foreign nations. The United States, with overoptimistic expectations, eagerly welcomed the new government into the family of nations.

Throughout this period of 1898-1914 American policy had endeavored by diplomacy to support the independence and integrity of China in order to share with the world an open door to the foreign trade and investments of that crumbling Empire. The diagram on page 29 shows the actual American (all *privately owned*) stake in China as compared with other foreign nations. It shows that Great Britain and

---

[1] Remer, *op. cit.*, pp. 125-130, 272-274.

[2] "I have an intense personal interest in making the use of American capital in the development of China an instrument for the promotion of the welfare of China, and an increase in her material prosperity without entanglements or creating embarrassments affecting the growth of her independent political power and the preservation of her territorial integrity." President Taft to the Prince Regent of China, July 15, 1909. *Foreign Relations of the United States*, 1909, p. 178. There is no reason to believe that Taft had other than the interest of China at heart.

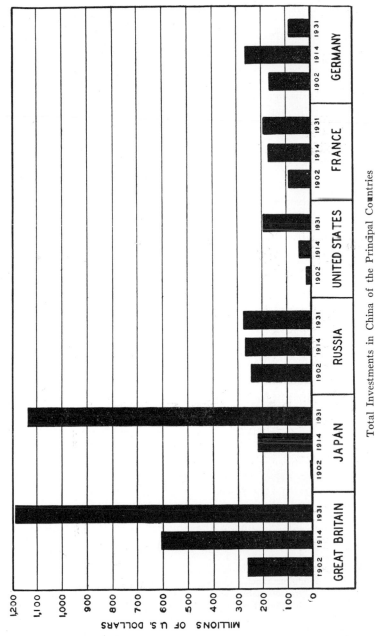

Total Investments in China of the Principal Countries

From C. F. Remer, *Foreign Investments in China*, p. 75. (Acknowledgments to the Macmillan Company.)

Japan by 1914 were, as they still were in 1939, the principal capitalistic [1] and indeed political rivals in China—next came Russia, Germany, and France.

The United States had committed itself before the world to a policy of obligingly helping to hold open a door used far more by Great Britain, Japan, Russia, France, and Germany than by itself, to defending at least by peaceful means the independence and integrity of a distant, vast, and uncertain country where its interests were less than those of any other great power and not in any sense vital.[2] Until 1914 this had been possible because of the diplomatic equipoise in the Far East which sustained the Open Door and its proliferation. The First World War was to upset that balance in favor of Japan. After that the Open Door remained only a verbal and paper challenge to Japanese ambitions of expansion and hegemony in Eastern Asia, spiritedly backed by bayonets and battleships strategically placed.

If the expansionists of 1898 could have read the future as we can read the past, or if they had even taken the pains to study a few statistics of trade and investment demonstrative of the small stake which the United States had in the Far East compared with other parts of the world, or the problems of strategy involved, we are constrained to believe that they would not have embarked so precipitately upon the conspicuous but unprofitable and foolhardy venture into the world politics of Asia, so alien to American continental traditions and interests, so dangerous to the welfare of the United States. Perhaps they would have applied logically to Asia that dictum of the Monroe Doctrine which opposed American participation in the entanglements of Europe. It is significant that, except for the Treaty of Paris of 1898, which terminated the Spanish-American War, the whole structure of American foreign policy in the Far East from 1898 to 1914 rested on executive act and executive agreements and not on the expressed sanction of the Senate or of the Congress.

The Philippine Islands under the sovereignty of the United States became a monument to American good works and good will, a model for

---

[1] As regards exports and imports, the United States stood third, after Great Britain (including British dominions and colonies); in 1932 and 1933 American trade with China surpassed Japan's, presumably because of Chinese boycotts. Commercial tabulations of China's trade with the principal countries may be found in Field, *op. cit.*, pp. 424-425.

[2] The exports of the United States to China in 1914 were less than 1 per cent of the total exports; the imports from China to the United States only 2 per cent of the total imports into the United States. The investments of the United States in China in 1914, $42,000,000 (exclusive of $10,000,000 mission property) were 2.8 per cent of the total American investments abroad.

colonial dominion and administration in the world. They also became a military and a diplomatic liability. They were a hostage to Japan for American foreign policy in the Far East. Time and again Theodore Roosevelt and other American diplomatists had to make concessions to Japanese aggression on the continent of Asia in return for Japanese disavowal, either explicit or implicit, of aggressive intentions toward the Philippines. The principal concern of the United States in the Islands became that of liquidating decently and honorably an uncomfortable imperialism there, leaving them able to sustain their independence in a sea of sharks. In the Second World War they served as a battleground for a magnificent rear-guard action that may have held up the Japanese juggernaut just long enough to make all the difference between final defeat or victory for the United Nations in that conflict. But it wasn't planned that way in 1898.

The Platt Amendment; The Isthmian
Life Line

THE Cuban-Spanish-American War signalized the predominance of the United States over the future isthmian canal. The primary concern of American foreign policy in the years between the Peace of Paris of 1898 and the First World War was to consolidate the newly established position in the Caribbean and Central America, to make the necessary diplomatic arrangements for the construction and control of the canal, and to assure the protection of the approaches from both coasts of the United States. After the War the exhaustion of Europe, comparable only to its exhaustion a century before following the Napoleonic wars, and the consequent strengthening of the position of the United States on this side of the Atlantic diminished the danger of intervention and diluted the established measures of control. This and the following chapter will bridge the period of the First World War and will witness the rise of American[1] imperialism in the Caribbean and Central America, and in turn some indications of its decline. A third sequent chapter will deal with Mexico; further on, after we have covered the

[1] The name United States of America first appears in the Declaration of Independence. The Franco-American treaties of 1778 used the phrase United States of North America, occasionally employed thereafter in official pronouncements; but Congress resolved, July 11, 1778, in favor of the name United States of America, to be used on its bills of exchange, and it has been used since as the official name. See E. C. Burnett, "The Name 'United States of America'" in *American Historical Review*, XXXI, (October, 1925), 79-81.

The proper noun *America* is entirely proper to describe the nation comprised by the United States, and *American* to designate a citizen of the United States of America. Our South American friends have sometimes thought this presumptuous, but the fact is that the word was first used in Europe, particularly in the early diplomatic correspondence of Spain and France. Before the Revolution they spoke of *Anglo-Americans* to distinguish from the Spanish-Mexicans, i.e., Chileans, Peruvians, etc. Afterward they logically dropped the word *Anglo*. It was only natural for the people of the United States to adopt this European usage, which is now confirmed. Historical pedants who nowadays are reviving usage of the awkward phrase *Anglo-Americans,* to distinguish between Americans and other nationals inhabiting North America, such as Mexicans, are guilty of committing a gratuitous solecism. If this anomalous designation could be justly applied to any people, I would suggest the Canadians as more appropriate; but certainly they would not approve.

diplomacy of the First World War, the peace settlement, and its aftermath, we shall touch on general Pan-American relationships and problems.

The Teller Amendment at the beginning of the Spanish-American
War had pledged the restoration of Cuba to the Cubans—Cuba, that
island so close to the United States, so important to the strategy of the
Caribbean which was in turn to be the strategy of Panama, the strategy
of American naval defense. At the close of the war the Senate had
refused by the casting vote of the Vice President to pledge the country
to restore the Philippines to the Filipinos, those Philippines and those
Filipinos on the other side of the globe, those islands and people where the
United States had no vital interests. Who can penetrate the mysterious
inconsistencies of such expressions of policy?

The reconstruction of Cuba by the American army authorities during
the military occupation of 1898-1902, the sanitation of the island, the
start of the Cubans on the road to self-government at first so promising,[1]
all these Samaritan achievements in Cuba, as in the Philippines, are
outside the scope of this history, which must stick closely to American
diplomacy. The United States kept the pledge of the Teller Amendment, though the expansionists of 1898 regretted this hasty expression.
An amendment to the army appropriation act of March 3, 1899 (the
Foraker Amendment) provided:

> That no property, franchises, or concessions of any kind whatever shall be
> granted by the United States, or by any military or other authority what-
> ever, in the island of Cuba during the occupation thereof by the United
> States.

It was Elihu Root, Secretary of War, who formulated the future relationship of Cuba to the United States, the same notable jurist who
was responsible for the structure of government in the Philippines, the
island of Puerto Rico, and the other overseas possessions. Root was
determined that the United States should not be placed after the war
with Spain in a worse position in regard to its vital interests in Cuba
than it had been while the island was in Spanish possession. He wished
to make it certain that no foreign power other than the United States
should interfere with the destiny of Cuba—and this meant a protectorate. Root submitted to the Cuban constitutional convention the pro-

---

[1] Charles E. Chapman has told with penetrating understanding the history of the
formation of the Cuban Government and its subsequent shortcomings in his *History of
the Cuban Republic, a Study in Hispanic American Politics* (New York, 1927). A
very serviceable review of Cuban-American relations, is Russell H. Fitzgibbon, *Cuba and
the United States, 1900-1935* (Menasha, Wis., 1935).

posals which soon afterward were embodied in the Platt Amendment
(to the army appropriation bill passed by the Congress of the United
States, March 2, 1901), but the Cubans rejected the provisions, which
gave the United States a right to intervene in order to maintain a
stable government in Cuba and to have naval bases there. The Platt
Amendment provided that the United States would leave the government and control of the island of Cuba to its people as soon as they
would imbed in their constitution the following terms:

1. Cuba not to enter into any treaty or other compact with a foreign
power which would impair its independence, or permit colonization
for military or naval lodgment of control.

2. Cuba not to contract any public debt beyond its resources reasonably considered.

3. The United States to have a right to intervene "for the preservation of Cuban independence, the maintenance of a government adequate
for the protection of life, property, and individual liberty," and for discharging the obligations assumed by the Treaty of Paris.

4. Ratification of all the acts of the United States during the military
occupancy.

5. Execution by Cuba of the sanitary arrangements already undertaken by the United States, thereby assuring protection against infectious diseases "to the people and commerce of Cuba, as well as to
the commerce of the southern ports of the United States and the people
residing therein."

6. The title to the Isle of Pines to be left for future adjustment.[1]

7. The United States, for its defense as well as that of Cuba, to have
the right of purchase or lease of two naval stations.

8. These provisions to be embodied in a permanent treaty with the
United States.

The fact that the Platt Amendment was the indispensable condition precedent of American evacuation overcame the Cuban objections
to the right of intervention and the naval stations. Secretary Root
took pains to explain, for the President, that the Amendment was
"not synonymous with intermeddling or interference with the affairs of
the Cuban Government, but the formal action of the Government of
the United States, based upon just and substantial grounds, for the

---

[1] This island contains 1180 square miles and is located 35 miles off the southwest coast
of Cuba. A Cuban-American treaty signed March 4, 1904, recognized Cuba's sovereignty
over the island, but was not ratified by the United States until 1925. The delay was
due to the influence of the American colonists who had gone there in the belief that
they were settling under the American flag.

preservation of Cuban independence and the maintenance of a government adequate for the protection of life, property, and individual liberty, and adequate for discharging the obligations with respect to Cuba
imposed by the Treaty of Paris on the United States." [1]   The terms
were embodied both in a treaty (May 22, 1903) and in the Cuban constitution itself.   General Leonard Wood, the military governor—intimate
of President Roosevelt, the leading expansionist of 1898—privately
thought that the Platt Amendment would practically annex Cuba,[2]
and many Cubans feared so; but American public opinion steadily
moved in a different direction particularly after the First World War.
Trusteeship of Cuban independence thus assumed and maintained by
the United States compatibly with its own vital strategical interests
in the Caribbean has stood as a notable example to the powers.

The Cuban protectorate brought its problems for the United States.
One problem since 1902 has been to resist the importunities of Cuban
political parties to place or maintain them in power during inveterately
recurring political disorder.   Another has been to arrange beneficent
commercial treaties with Cuba which should not be too painful for
sugar growers in the United States.   Finally, in a safer age, there has
been the problem of modifying or dissolving the Platt Amendment.
During the lifetime of the Platt Amendment, however, the principal
problem was the maintenance, with a minimum of intervention, of peace
and stable government in the island.   With great reluctance the United
States intervened and set up a provisional régime, 1906-1909, after the
second Cuban national election had paralyzed the island's government.
The people, who had not submitted to 200,000 Spanish troops in 1898,
made no resistance to a handful of soldiers in the second American intervention because they had confidence in its righteousness.   The action
conferred a benefit by stiffening for a time the stability of the government.   Since then the United States has followed a preventive policy
of seeking by diplomatic methods to avoid intervention.   In 1911, on the
occasion of a Negro revolt, and again during the war with Germany, a few
companies of marines were stationed in Cuba, mostly at the United
States naval base at Guantánamo, to lend aid in case the established

[1] Article XVI, Treaty of Paris of December 10, 1898: "It is understood that the
obligations assumed in this treaty by the United States with respect to Cuba are limited
to the time of its occupancy thereof; but it will, upon the termination of such occupancy,
advise any Government established in the island to assume the same obligations."
[2] Professor Herminio Portell-Vilá, of the University of Havana, brought this out in a
paper read before the American Historical Association at Urbana, Ill., in 1933, citing
a letter of General Wood to President Roosevelt, October 29, 1901.

government should not be able to ward off anarchy; and from time to time various American missions have been sent to the island to untangle electoral difficulties or straighten out financial troubles.[1] A reciprocity treaty, ratified early in 1903, was the basis of Cuban-American commercial relations until it was superseded by the agreement of 1934. It gave special reductions, of 20 per cent under the general tariff line of the United States, to Cuban products, and of 20 to 40 per cent upon importations into Cuba from the United States. Under it Cuba enjoyed a rousing economic prosperity based on sugar, until after the First World War.

Despite persistent Cuban dissatisfaction with the protective status imposed by the Platt Amendment, the entrance of the United States into the First World War furnished a test of that relationship. Cuba declared war on Germany the day following the resolution of Congress that a state of war existed between the United States and Germany. The island republic, instead of finding an opportunity to press for readjustment of the protectorate, manifested a sentiment of complete solidarity and loyal co-operation with the United States.[2] Cuba's principal contribution to the war proved to be her economic undoing, immensely profitable as it was at first: the stimulation of sugar production under high price control. In the months of unexampled prosperity that followed, both the Cuban Government and Cuban business, in many instances representing American capital, were able to borrow huge sums within the Platt Amendment. Cuba's principal export crop of sugar expanded far beyond its normal base of the preferential market of the United States. Its collapse at the end of 1921 brought widespread bankruptcy in its wake, though a mission from the United States under General E. H. Crowder succeeded in restoring order to the finances of the Government.

Economic conditions ameliorated, but collapsed again with the Great Depression that plunged the world into misery in 1929. Cuban politics went from bad to worse. A revolution began to smolder in 1932 against the repressive administration of President Gerardo Machado. Determined to smother it, he resorted to a veritable reign of terror, with excesses which, in the case of individuals, rivaled those of the Spanish régime. The Cuban revolutionists importuned the United States to in-

[1] Dana G. Munro has summarized Cuban-American relations after digesting the voluminous literature, both Spanish and English, in *The United States and the Caribbean Area* (World Peace Foundation, Boston, 1934). See also Fitzgibbon, *op. cit.*

[2] Percy Alvin Martin, *Latin America and the War* (Johns Hopkins Press, 1925), pp. 107-172.

tervene. Intellectuals in the United States meanwhile urged a revision
of the Platt Amendment, echoing the propaganda of Cuban liberals. The
economic collapse added to the distresses of the island. The result was,
in the second year of the Administration of President Franklin D. Roosevelt, a radical revision of Cuban-American relationship. Machado was
eased out of office, what with the pressure of the revolutionists, without military intervention of the United States; and after a period of
diplomatic uncertainty, because of succeeding provisional governments,
the United States recognized a new but none-too-stable régime and ratified a treaty "of general relations" (1934), and signed an executive
agreement (under authority of the act of Congress of June 12, 1934),
putting into effect reciprocal preferential tariffs, suspending, during the
existence of the new agreement, the old reciprocity treaty of 1903. The
new treaty abolished the Platt Amendment and the protectorate, retaining the naval station at Guantánamo.

Cuban politics continued to be highly volatile, with the "outs" continually importuning the United States to put them in power, and the
"ins" persistently asking for intervention to repress the insubordination
of the "outs." The abandonment of the protectorate and the right of
intervention, coupled with ratification by the United States of the Pan-
American treaty of the rights and duties of states, which renounced the
right of intervention, meant that henceforth the United States would
not intervene in Cuban politics no matter how unsavory they might
become. To use a vulgar phrase, Cuba, like all other Caribbean and
Central American states, must now stew in its own juice, except should
a non-American power attempt to season the dish; then the United States
might be expected to say hands off, under the Monroe Doctrine. It is
still too early, and the domestic situation in the United States is too
uncertain economically and politically, for us to know how the new
tariff relationships will work out for both countries after the commercial
disturbances of the Second World War, but it can be said that great
and sympathetic effort was exerted in its negotiation really to benefit
Cuba as well as the United States. The United States in its present
system of unconditional most-favored-nation treatment [1] for nations
enjoying treaties of commerce, has uniformly reserved a privilege of
special preferential tariffs with Cuba.

Puerto Rico never presented any diplomatic problem after its outright
annexation in 1899. Since 1917 Puerto Ricans have become American

[1] See below, p. 284.

citizens, and the island enjoys a territorial form of government in all but name.

Contemporaneously with this installation of the Cuban protectorate, the State Department, under Secretary John Hay, had been negotiating with Great Britain for a modification of the Clayton-Bulwer Treaty of 1850, which had internationalized and neutralized the status of any isthmian canal under the joint control of Great Britain and the United States and any other nations which might adhere to the instrument. Repeated attempts by corporations, both American and French, to build a canal had demonstrated that it was beyond the resources of private capital. If any government should construct the waterway it was incompatible with American interests that this should be any other than the United States. If the United States should build a canal under the Clayton-Bulwer Treaty it would assume all the risks and expenses, with Great Britain equally in control of the canal and all the world sharing its facilities equally. The United States could not even fortify it. For half a century this treaty had barred the way to any "American canal on American soil for the American people."

After the West had filled up, the people of the United States had turned their attention back to the canal. The naval operations of the war with Spain—including the long and dramatic voyage of the U.S.S. *Oregon* from the Pacific Coast to the Caribbean around South America— had vividly emphasized the necessity of full national control over the future waterway; in fact the underlying motive of the expansionists of 1898 was to clear the way for the control of the canal, the future nodal point of American naval defense from ocean to ocean. Political parties and successive governments were increasingly annoyed at the persistence of the Clayton-Bulwer Treaty estoppel. Immediately after the war an act of Congress (approved March 3, 1899) authorized an investigation into all possible isthmian routes, with a view of digging the canal as a government enterprise.

Hay's task of modifying the Clayton-Bulwer Treaty was eased by Great Britain's new decision to strengthen her position by withdrawing from any contest for predominance in America and by cultivating the United States as a possible ally in Asia. From the Venezuela boundary arbitration in 1896 to the signature of the Anglo-Japanese alliance of 1902 it was the effort of Great Britain to seal an Anglo-American alliance in preference to some other. Hay was personally not averse to an alliance, but he knew that the Senate was dead set against it; he therefore made, as he thought, the best of the situation by arranging a new canal treaty, and, subsequently, a settlement of the Alaska boundary dispute. British diplomacy tried to couple the two questions, but the outbreak of the Boer War weakened this attempt to secure compensations in Alaska for concessions in the Isthmus.

The terms of the first Hay-Pauncefote treaty, signed on February 5, 1900, but never ratified, modified the continuing Clayton-Bulwer Treaty to permit the construction of a canal anywhere across the Isthmus under the auspices of the United States, to be maintained by the United States; but the United States could not fortify it, or blockade it; it was to be open in time of peace and in time of war to the vessels of peace and of war of all nations, on terms of entire equality, under rules of neutralization substantially similar to the international convention for the regulation of the Suez Canal. That is, the United States could go to the expense of constructing the canal and maintaining it, but could have no special advantage of any kind, even in case it were engaged in war; in time of war an enemy might sail its fleet right through the canal to attack San Francisco or Savannah. As Governor Theodore Roosevelt objected to his friend, Hay, the proposed canal under such conditions would fetter the navy rather than assist it: "Our fleet would have to watch it, and therefore do the work which a fort should do; and which it could do much better."

The first Hay-Pauncefote treaty would have thrown away the real victory of the Spanish-American War. The refusal of the Senate to ratify it as it stood is at least one striking example of the advantages of the Constitution in requiring the advice and consent of the Senate for the ratification of treaties. The three amendments attached to the treaty by that body, as a condition of its consent, were: (1) The Clayton-Bulwer Treaty is superseded; (2) the United States might take measures "for securing by its own forces the defenses of the United States and the maintenance of public order"; (3) other nations might not adhere to the treaty.[1] Great Britain refused to accept these changes. Hay resigned in disgust, but President McKinley, who had not lifted a finger to help his Secretary's treaty through the Senate, persuaded him to stay and try again with Great Britain. The multifarious exigencies of Great

---

[1] The Senate adopted unanimously the first and third of these amendments, the second by a vote of 65-17; it then advised and consented to ratification by a vote of 55-18. This time party politics had little to do with the vote, except in the sense that an endorsement of Hay's treaty as it stood would have jeopardized any party in power in the coming national elections. William S. Holt in *Treaties Defeated by the Senate* (Johns Hopkins Press, 1933) has a sharp eye for all possible political implications of the treaty.

Britain in other parts of the world made her amenable to further negotiation.

The second Hay-Pauncefote Treaty (signed November 18, 1901, ratified February 21, 1902, after a Senate vote of 72-6) was a compromise between the first treaty and the Senate amendments. The text stated that it "superseded" the Clayton-Bulwer Treaty.[1] In the preamble it declared its purpose to remove any objection that might arise under that treaty to the construction of the canal under the auspices of the Government of the United States, without impairing the "general principle" of neutralization established in Article VIII of that convention. It incorporated "substantially" the rules of neutralization for the regulation of the Suez Canal as in the convention of Constantinople of 1888, but rewritten here with certain small changes from the text of the first Hay-Pauncefote treaty and with this vitally important difference: the omission of any article prohibiting fortification of the canal by the United States. It was further agreed that no change in the territorial sovereignty of the canal would alter the obligation of the parties to the treaty. There was no provision for other nations to adhere.

In the interim between the two negotiations Theodore Roosevelt had become President. He vigorously supported the new treaty. By the implication of silence, as compared with the first rejected treaty, it would appear that the second Hay-Pauncefote Treaty gave the United States the right to fortify the canal and defend it against enemies in time of war. Academicians argued that omission of prohibition did not give consent to fortification, particularly in view of the rules for neutralization which expressly prohibit the exercise of any act of war

---

[1] President Roosevelt carefully stated in his annual message of December 3, 1901, that the Clayton-Bulwer treaty "is abrogated"; and the British Government in its note of November 14, 1912, declared it was "superseded." It was the rules incorporated in the Hay-Pauncefote Treaty rather than the Clayton-Bulwer Treaty on which Great Britain chose to rest her successful protest against the act of August 24, 1912, which exempted from tolls American coastwise vessels using the Panama Canal. Rule 1 stated: "The canal shall be free and open to the vessels of commerce and of war of all nations observing these Rules, on terms of entire equality, so that there shall be no discrimination against any such nation, or its citizens or subjects, in respect of the conditions or charges of traffic, or otherwise. Such conditions and charges of traffic shall be just and equitable."

President Wilson induced Congress to repeal the articles omitting coastwise shipping from the same burden of tolls; but Congress in the repeal declared its right to do so if it wished. Many students of the tolls question believed that the United States abandoned a perfectly good legal case for arbitration. Wilson's recommendation was the result of his personal connections, and of a tacit diplomatic bargain by which he received British support for his contemporary Mexican policy. The details reveal themselves in Charles Seymour's edition of *The Intimate Papers of Colonel House* (2 vols., Boston, 1926), I, pp. 191-206.

within the canal; but all these academic arguments have no significance because during the negotiation of the second Hay-Pauncefote Treaty, Great Britain, the only other party to the treaty, admitted the right of the United States to fortify and defend the canal against enemies.[1] These fortifications became a key to American naval defense and a fundamental factor in the foreign policy of the United States.

Within a few years after this treaty Great Britain reduced her permanent garrisons in the West Indies and withdrew her principal naval forces from that area. She rather definitely acquiesced in the predominance of the United States in that part of the world, so vital to its own interests.

The way was now clear for the diplomatic arrangements with the Central American state through which the canal must run. There had been much debate, and still is, among engineers and in public opinion which was the better route, Nicaragua or Panama. The United States had secured transit rights—but not construction rights—from both Colombia (treaty of 1846) and Nicaragua (treaty of 1867): in the former case guaranteeing "positively and efficaciously" both the neutrality of the canal route and the sovereignty of Colombia, in the latter case recognizing the sovereignty of Nicaragua over the canal route and guaranteeing only its neutrality. An official engineering commission in 1876 favored the Nicaraguan route. An American corporation, the Maritime Canal Company, working under a charter from Congress and a concession from Nicaragua, failed after three years (1890-1893) of initial construction labors there. On the Isthmus of Panama a French Company, organized by Ferdinand de Lesseps, the engineer of the Suez Canal, had gone bankrupt after spending nearly $300,000,000 (1881-1887) and digging less than a third of the way. Immediately after the Cuban-Spanish-American War, and while Hay was negotiating his canal treaties with Great Britain, another official American commission investigated the merits of the rival routes and their abandoned works. These engineers, the Walker Commission, pronounced just after the signature of the second Hay-Pauncefote Treaty, in favor of Nicaragua. The cost of a river-and-lake canal there it estimated at $189,864,062. It would cost only $144,233,358 to complete the Panama Canal—according to the estimates of this commission, which fell far short of realities—but to this must be added $109,141,500 which the bankrupt French Panama Company demanded for its concession and property rights.

[1] Memorandum of Lord Lansdowne, August 3, 1901. John Bassett Moore, *Digest of International Law*, III, pp. 212-216.

The House of Representatives quickly passed a bill for the construction of a Nicaraguan canal. If enacted, this bill meant that the stockholders of the ruined French company would get nothing. From now on the ring of men who controlled the rusting remains of this bankrupt French corporation succeeded in manipulating the destiny of the canal route and the political and international and moral factors bound up with it. The French company now quickly offered to sell for $40,000,000. Forthwith, at the suggestion of President Roosevelt, the Isthmian Canal Commission reversed its decision and pronounced for the Panama route. The United States Senate, under a powerful lobby of representatives of the Panama Company, adopted the amendment of Senator Spooner to the House canal bill, switching the site to Panama under condition that the French concession and property could be purchased for $40,-000,000 or less. If Colombia should refuse to accept this reasonable offer, the President was authorized to go ahead with the Nicaraguan route, making the necessary diplomatic arrangements with that state, and with Costa Rica, which had claims of sovereignty over the San Juan River. The law passed Congress in this form.

The act gave to the President a strategic position in dealing with the rival canal countries. After nine months of negotiations the Secretary of State signed with the Colombian Minister the famous Hay-Herrán treaty (January 22, 1903). This treaty authorized the New Panama Canal Company (the reorganized French company) to sell its properties to the United States, and granted to the United States full control over a strip across the Isthmus covering the canal site, six miles wide. For this the United States promised to pay to Colombia $10,000,000 cash, and, beginning nine years after the exchange of ratifications, an annuity of $250,000 gold. The money was the least of the great benefits to Colombia; the real value of the treaty was that it would bring suddenly to Colombia, particularly to the Colombian state of Panama, the inestimable advantage of a highly prosperous seat at the crossroads of one of the two greatest waterways of the world. Like the Hay-Pauncefote treaties, and all treaties signed by plenipotentiaries of the United States, this treaty was to come into effect when ratified according to the laws of the respective countries, which meant, in this instance, by the Senate of the United States and by the Senate of Colombia.

The Colombian Senate threw away this priceless advantage by failing to ratify the treaty. Those small-minded senators thought they might get more money both from the United States and from the Panama Company. Their conduct exasperated President Roosevelt greatly, but we must remember, we must remember most emphatically, that Colombia had a perfect sovereign right to refuse to ratify the treaty, just as the United States had a perfect right to refuse to ratify without amendments the first Hay-Pauncefote treaty, the early treaties for the purchase of the Danish West Indies, or the Treaty of Versailles, to mention only a few of those where the Senate has exercised its constitutional prerogative. That Colombia, for whatever motives, according to its constitutional forms, allowed for in the treaty itself, rejected the treaty did not give the United States a right to interfere within the internal affairs of that nation. Nor did the old treaty of 1846 give the United States any such right beyond that of guaranteeing the neutrality of the canal route; more especially, it expressly guaranteed the sovereignty of New Granada (the earlier name for Colombia) over the Isthmus.

The President was at first undecided what step to take after the Colombian Senate's rejection: whether to take up Nicaragua, or "in some shape or way to interfere when it becomes necessary so as to secure the Panama route without further dealing with the foolish and homicidal corruptionists of Bogotá." [1] A trusted adviser presented a confidential memorandum to this effect: that if Colombia should reject the Hay-Herrán treaty, then the old treaty of 1846—the one which had guaranteed so "positively and efficaciously" the sovereignty of New Granada—could be interpreted to cover intervention in Panama to prevent interruption of the transit by domestic disturbances, as well as to protect Colombian sovereignty and the neutrality of the canal route against attack by an outside power. He pointed out that the United States had repeatedly landed troops to protect the canal route against riots and insurrectionary disturbances (he did not cite instances where the United States had intervened to the advantage of insurrectionists and secessionists). "Once on the ground and duly installed," this memorandum stated, "this government would find no difficulty in meeting questions as they arose." [2] In the first draft of his proposed annual message to Congress, Roosevelt recommended that the United States should purchase all the rights of the French Panama Company, and, without any further parley with Colombia, enter upon the completion of the canal

[1] Joseph Bucklin Bishop, *Theodore Roosevelt and His Times* (2 vols., New York, 1920), I, p. 278.

[2] The memorandum, initialed "J. B. M." (presumably John Bassett Moore), is printed in the appendix to Helen Dwight Reid's *International Servitudes in Law and Practice* (University of Chicago Press, 1932). Mr. Moore was then professor of international law at Columbia University, but previously had long been an assistant secretary of state.

which the French company had begun.[1] The message was never delivered in this form.

Again the New Panama Canal Company stepped into the situation.
Philippe Bunau-Varilla, who once had been the chief engineer of
the company on the Isthmus, hurried from Paris to the United States.
He and a New York lawyer who was counsel for the French company,
organized a revolution in the state of Panama, working through the
employees of the Panama Railroad Company, a subsidiary. Bunau-
Varilla also had conferences with Professor John Bassett Moore, Secretary Hay, and President Roosevelt, who became well aware of the
imminence of a revolution for the independence of Panama. No evidence has been presented to show that these high officials of the
United States directly conspired with the plotters, but they certainly did
nothing to discourage a movement which presented itself for their convenience. The President ordered the Department of the Navy to hold
warships within striking distance of the Panama transit, on both sides.
On November 2, orders went out to the commanders of these vessels to
proceed to Panama and to "maintain free and uninterrupted transit,"
even to the extent of using armed force to occupy the route and to prevent Colombian troops being landed. Bunau-Varilla and his fellow
conspirators, including Doctor Manuel Amador Guerrero, the agent of
the Panamanians in New York and Washington, guessed that the United
States would use its naval forces to prevent Colombian troops from being
landed to put down the insurrection and prevent the secession of
Panama.[2] This is exactly what happened when the revolution occurred,
as planned, on November 3, 1903. It was the formal statement of the
United States Government to Colombia (November 11, 1903) that it

[1] H. C. Hill, *Roosevelt and the Caribbean Area* (University of Chicago Press, 1927),
p. 59.
[2] Philippe Bunau-Varilla, *Panama, the Creation, Destruction and Resurrection* (New
York, 1914).
Dr. Amador wrote to his son, Lt. Raoul Amador, a surgeon in the United States
Army at Fort Revere, Mass., October 18, 1903, that he had spoken to Bunau-Varilla
about him: "He said that if all turns out well, you shall have a good place on the
medical commission, which is the first that will begin work; that my name is in Hay's
office and that certainly nothing will be refused you. The plan seems to me good.
A portion of the Isthmus declares itself independent and that portion the United States
will not allow any Colombian forces to attack. An assembly is called and this given
authority to a minister to be appointed by the new Government in order to make a
treaty without need of ratification by that assembly." *The Story of Panama* (Hearings
on the Rainey Resolution before the Committee on Foreign Affairs of the House of
Representatives) (Washington, G.P.O., 1913), p. 371. Raoul Amador became a Panama-
nian diplomat and died, March 24, 1934, as President of the Council of the League of
Nations!

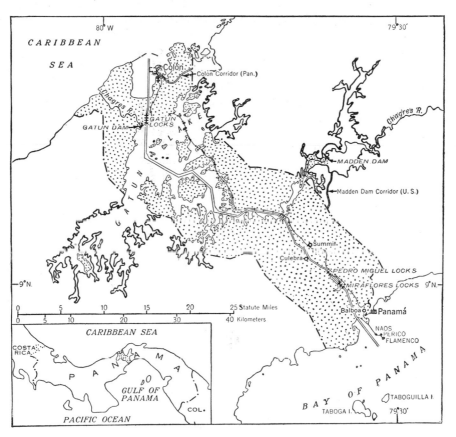

Map 1. The Panama Canal Zone

would oppose the landing of Colombian troops to suppress the insurrection, which is the touchstone of the whole affair. That guaranteed the success of the insurrection; in effect it completed it. The United States had promptly recognized the *de facto* government, November 6, and on November 18 signed a treaty with the plenipotentiary of the Republic of Panama, none other than the Frenchman Bunau-Varilla. *Ipso facto* the treaty acknowledged the independence of Panama. The European powers also quickly recognized the new state. The Latin-American republics (except Colombia) followed promptly (March, 1904) in greeting the full-fledged independence of a new sister republic.

The treaty conferred upon the United States the right to build the canal, fortify it, and to possess the Canal Zone, ten miles wide from Colon to Panama, "as if it were sovereign." For this Panama received $10,000,000 in gold coin, plus an annuity of $250,000 "in like gold

coin," [1] beginning nine years after ratification. The first article of the
treaty stated: "The United States guarantees and will maintain the
independence of the Republic of Panama." Other articles gave to the
United States the use, occupation, and control (subject to indemnification
for private owners) of any other lands and waters necessary and convenient for the construction and maintenance of the canal, the right
to intervene for its maintenance and protection, and the right of eminent
domain within the limits of the cities of Panama and Colon and adjacent
territories and waters. This, of course, made Panama a protectorate.[2]

President Roosevelt immediately set in motion the work of construction and fortification of the canal. It opened its locks to the commerce
and the warships of the world on terms of entire equality (so long as the
United States remained a neutral) in 1914. In office and out of office,
Theodore Roosevelt throughout the remainder of his life defended his
intervention in Panama. The verdict of history must be summed up in
his own frank words: "I took Panama." [3] With patience, diplomacy
could have secured control of a canal route in a more creditable way
without the use of force. The episode antagonized Latin America.
Public opinion there began to brand the sponsor-nation of the Monroe
Doctrine with the accusation of conquest in that part of the world which
it professed to have liberated from European interference. It has taken
much diplomacy and a generation of time to soften away this stigma.[4]

Despite the confidence of the President in the rectitude of his proceeding, the United States later pursued with Colombia a sort of
conscience-striken diplomacy. Even during President Roosevelt's Administration, Secretary of State Root arranged three companion treaties
intended to satisfy Colombian grievances: a treaty between Colombia

---

[1] The treaty did not specify the weight and fineness of this gold coin. After the
devaluation of the United States gold dollar in 1934 to 59.06 per cent of its former value
Panama paid coupons on her dollar bonds in the devalued currency, but insisted on
collecting her annuities from the United States in the old standard dollars. The treaty
signed on March 2, 1936 (below, p. 47), provided that Panama was to be paid in her
own currency, *balboas,* 430,000 per annum, slightly more than the equivalent of $250,000
of the old standard.

[2] The scope of this volume does not permit any history of treaty relationships and
negotiations between Panama and the United States since 1903, other than mention at
the end of this chapter of the new treaty signed in 1936, ratified in 1939, which ended
the protectorate. Munro, *op. cit.,* gives a good summary.

[3] *Autobiography.* At the University of California, March 11, 1911, he declared: "I
took the Canal Zone."

[4] Useful reviews of the diplomacy of the Panama Canal and United States intervention
are: H. C. Hill, *Roosevelt and the Caribbean Area, op. cit.;* Henry F. Pringle, *Theodore
Roosevelt, a Biography* (New York, 1931); D. C. Miner, *The Fight for the Panama
Route* (Columbia University Press, 1940), and an unpublished doctoral thesis by William
G. Fletcher, 1940, in Yale University Library.

and Panama which recognized the independence of that republic and agreed to a boundary, with certain privileges in the use of the proposed canal; a treaty between the United States and Colombia which transferred to Colombia the first ten installments of Panama's annuity; and a treaty between the United States and Panama which sanctioned these changes and started the annuity five years earlier than required by the treaty of 1903. Popular opposition in Colombia led to the rejection of this settlement. Negotiations continued. Under Woodrow Wilson's Administration Secretary of State Bryan signed a treaty with Colombia (April 6, 1914) by which the United States expressed "sincere regret that anything should have occurred to interrupt or mar the relations of cordial friendship that had so long subsisted between the two governments." It also agreed to pay $25,000,000 indemnity, and to allow to Colombia and her citizens the same treatment as the United States and its citizens in the use of the canal; Colombia in turn recognized the independence of Panama, with a specified boundary. The opposition of former President Roosevelt, who vigorously denounced it as a "blackmail treaty," was sufficient to prevent its ratification by the Senate during his lifetime. After he died, his friend Senator Henry Cabot Lodge, chairman of the Committee on Foreign Relations, supported a treaty (ratified in 1921 by a vote of 69-19) which paid the indemnity but omitted the apology. Colombian threats to refuse petroleum concessions to American capitalists seem to have been a decisive influence on Senator Lodge and his colleagues who previously had opposed paying any indemnity. This settlement closed the affair, but it took time to wipe out the rankle.

A recent, and important, adjustment in the relations between the United States and Panama is the treaty signed March 2, 1936, and finally ratified July 25, 1939. It ended the protectorate and the right of land takings by the United States in Panama by eminent domain, and substituted therefor a pledge of joint co-operation for the furtherance of common interests. Article X reads:

In case of an international conflagration or the existence of any threat of aggression which would endanger the security of the Republic of Panama or the neutrality or the security of the Panama Canal the Governments of the United States of America and the Republic of Panama will take such measures for prevention and defense as they may consider necessary for the protection of their common interests. Any measures essential to one Government to take, and which may affect the territory under the jurisdiction of the other Government, will be the subject of consultation between the two Governments.

The Senate did not advise and consent to ratification of this treaty until it was made clear by a final exchange of notes [1] that in case of great emergency the United States could act first and consult with Panama afterward; that the treaty permits expansion and new construction for the canal; and that it does not prohibit military maneuvers in Panama's territory.

The new treaty is in line with the liquidation of imperialism which began after the First World War, and the Doctrine of Nonintervention which President Franklin D. Roosevelt accepted as a part of his Good Neighbor Policy.

During the Second World War consultations between the United States and Panama resulted in the expansion of canal defenses throughout the Isthmian Republic's territory, particularly air bases. The two governments signed a new treaty (May 18, 1942) providing for the lease during the war and for one year thereafter of these new bases and areas already occupied as a result of the previous consultations.

[1] *Senate Ex. Rept.* No. 5, 1st Sess., June 21 (legislative day, June 19), 1939.

4

Development of the Panama Policy in the Caribbean and Central America

WE have said that the prospective Panama Canal had become a fundamental factor in the foreign policy of the United States. The conscious development of a policy based on this truth began contemporaneously with the negotiation of the canal treaties, and the Cuban protectorate in the first years of the twentieth century, and rapidly built up a structure of comparatively benevolent imperialism and tutelage in the Caribbean and Central America. What generally is referred to as the Caribbean Policy of the United States more appropriately might be called the Panama Policy.

Inescapably the canal is open to some danger of terrestrial accident that might close it, particularly an earthquake. With that waterway a prime factor in the naval defenses of the United States, American policy could not tolerate the risk of any political disturbance or intervention that would block it. The danger that some non-American power might welcome a pretext for effecting a lodgment within this wide strategical diameter was continually a possibility to be reckoned with alertly before the First World War. President Theodore Roosevelt was acutely conscious of this and promptly took steps to avoid it.

There were several ways to proceed. First there was the traditional Monroe Doctrine; Roosevelt resorted to this in 1902 in the Venezuelan debts controversy, and the Senate invoked it in 1912 in the Magdalena Bay episode.[1] Secondly there was the expedient of buying Caribbean islands, belonging to small powers, which otherwise might be acquired by larger naval powers contrary to the non-transfer principle historically associated with the Monroe Doctrine; such was the eventual purchase of the Danish West Indies. The third way was to assume a sort of vicarious responsibility for foreign nationals and property within those republics where law and order might collapse, intervening by force to make them behave, lest good reasons be presented for intervention by

[1] For the Lodge Resolution, see below, p. 64.

some other power less vitally interested in the strategy of the Caribbean. Theodore Roosevelt and Woodrow Wilson did this when they imposed temporary protectorates over the Dominican Republic and Haiti. Journalists unfortunately dubbed it the policy of the "big stick"; and more responsible writers have called it the "Roosevelt Corollary" of the Monroe Doctrine, an infelicitous formula lately repudiated. The fourth means, applied to Central America, was an active diplomacy aimed at stiffening the independence of those states and strengthening their economic and political stability in order to remove pretexts or justifications for foreign intervention. Taken together with the possession of Puerto Rico and the already established protectorates over Cuba and Panama, this self-interested benevolence might be said to constitute the Panama Policy of the United States from 1898 to 1934.

Publicists in both Americas, Europe, and Asia have accused the United States of intervention in the Caribbean area for motives of economic profit. Although American investments in Cuba under the Spanish régime had become quite considerable, "big business" was opposed to the Spanish-American War. That breaks down this economic interpretation of the war. In all the other states where the United States has intervened—Panama, Santo Domingo, Haiti, Nicaragua—those republics have been the regions where the least American capital,[1] or foreign capital of any kind, had been invested, and which were the least promising for economic development. Only in the Philippines—from which the United States has since withdrawn, after costs of over a billion dollars to Uncle Sam after V–J Day alone—the initial motive seems to have been economic; and even there it was the politician who led on the businessman, not the businessman who pushed the politician into the Far East.

The interventions in Central America and in the Caribbean were the result of the developing Panama Policy following the Spanish-American War. That fundamental strategical requirement of foreign policy becomes all the stronger when international agreements impose a limitation of naval armament, as they did between 1922 and 1936. The naval limitations of those years were, of course, adjusted to the strategic advantages and possibilities of the finished canal. Having described in the previous chapter the intervention in Cuba and the episode of the creation of the Republic of Panama and its sequent problems, we may

---

[1] Max Winkler, *Investments of United States Capital in Latin America* (World Peace Foundation, Boston, 1928) tabulates comparative statistics.

now review [1] the rapidly developing diplomacy of the United States in other portions of this interesting region of the New World.

Ever since the Senate's rejection of the Danish treaty in Grant's Administration the executive branch of the Government had been apprehensive of recurring rumors that Denmark was preparing to sell or exchange her West Indian islands to Germany or France, particularly Germany. Denmark had been eager to dispose of them to the United States, but successive Presidents had hesitated to sign another treaty for fear that the Senate might again reject it. Sentiment for acquisition increased as an American canal became more likely. The expansionists of 1898 favored the purchase and committed the Republican Party to it. The movement gained headway after the turn of the century from rumors that Germany was seeking to acquire the islands for a naval base in the Caribbean. Researches [2] in the German archives have revealed that Admiral Alfred von Tirpitz wanted such a base in the Danish West Indies. He was also actively interested in the Galápagos Islands, belonging to Ecuador, on the Pacific side of the Isthmus, 640 miles at sea from Panama, and in the possibilities of naval *fulcra* along the coast of Costa Rica, Colombia, and Venezuela, within touch of the Canal; but the Foreign Office hesitated to challenge the Monroe Doctrine for these demands of the Admiralty.

Much discussion, formal and informal, finally resulted in the signature of a Danish-American treaty (January 24, 1902) for the purchase of the islands for $5,000,000. This time the Senate readily ratified the treaty, but the upper house of the Danish Parliament rejected it by one vote. It was not until 1917 that both governments were able to exchange ratifications of a treaty of purchase; by then, in the atmosphere of war, the price had gone up to the exorbitant figure of $25,000,000. Though Denmark had held the islands at a budgetary loss for decades, it was all made up, with a handsome profit, by this lucrative sale.[3] The poverty-stricken Virgin Islands, as they are now called in the possession of the

---

[1] There is, of course, a voluminous literature on this subject, little of which can be cited here. For some detailed classified bibliography, with a modicum of critical comment, see Bemis and Griffin, *Guide to the Diplomatic History of the United States, 1775-1921* (Library of Congress, G.P.O., 1935). The best summary by an American authority is Dana G. Munro, *The United States and the Caribbean Area, op. cit.*. Raúl de Cárdenas y Echarte, *La Política de los Estados Unidos en el continente Americano* (Havana, 1921), is one of the most temperate Latin-American reviews, and Manuel Ugarte, *The Destiny of a Continent* (New York, 1925, translated from Madrid edition of 1923), is the most passionate Latin-American polemic against the policy of the United States.

[2] Alfred Vagts, *Weltpolitik, op. cit.*, II, pp. 1410-1524.

[3] The Danish Parliament did not ratify until after a national plebiscite had voted overwhelmingly in favor of the change in sovereignty.

United States, have proved to be a worth-while insurance policy against the violation of the non-transfer principle of the Monroe Doctrine.[1]

An international incident in Venezuela made American opinion fear, in 1902, that the new isthmian diplomacy of the United States might be frustrated by the lodgment of Germany within striking distance of the future canal. The Venezuelan dictator Cipriano Castro had played fast and loose with foreign creditors and bondholders, who had also played fast and loose with the risky credit of his country. Citizens and corporations of Great Britain, Germany, Italy, France, Belgium, Mexico, the Netherlands, Spain, Sweden, and Norway, and also of the United States, had claims against the Venezuelan Government for default on contracts. Castro treated these claims quite frivolously. Diplomatic soundings at Washington had given the German Government the impression that a chastisement of Venezuela would meet with no objection on the ground of the Monroe Doctrine provided action led to no "lasting" occupation of Venezuelan territory. So reported the German Ambassador von Holleben after conversations with President Roosevelt and Secretary John Hay.[2] Under this impression Germany resolved to use force and to occupy one or more Venezuelan harbors, and perhaps the customs, as security for the flouted credits of German nationals. When this intention became known, Great Britain proposed a joint intervention. The precise reasons[3] for this will remain unknown until British confidential archives are unlocked. A good guess is that the British Government, feeling that the United States was not going to object to, and would not join a non-American intervention, was loath to see Germany take steps alone and perhaps set up a régime similar to that of Egypt. As the intervention ripened, Germany's nominal ally Italy[4] was allowed to join. The three powers blockaded[5] the Venezuelan ports, in December, 1902, bombarded two forts, and seized several Venezuelan gunboats.

[1] Charles C. Tansill in his detailed study of *The Purchase of the Danish West Indies* (Johns Hopkins University Press, 1932) was unable to find, in searches made for him in the Danish and German archives, any evidence of German pressure being responsible for Denmark's rejection of the treaty of 1902. Vagts, *Weltpolitik, op. cit.*, in a more detailed personal search does not seem to have found any.

[2] Vagts, *Weltpolitik, op. cit.*, II, p. 1540.

[3] Vagts guesses it may have been a feeler of England toward a more permanent German alliance. These were the months when England was seeking everywhere a serviceable ally, presently first found in Japan.

[4] Italy participated only in the blockade.

[5] The German Government maintained that this was a "pacific blockade." The British Prime Minister, Arthur Balfour, declared in the House of Lords that "there can be no such thing as a pacific blockade," but that "evidently a blockade does not involve a state of war." When Lincoln in 1861 declared the Southern ports blockaded, Great Britain considered that tantamount to a declaration of war which justified the British proclamation of neutrality, without consultation with the United States Government.

Despite the aggressiveness of Great Britain in handling the Venezuelan question and the joint responsibility which she had assumed, the Department of State was much more apprehensive about the real intentions and designs of Germany; British intention to relax in the Caribbean became plain with the Hay-Pauncefote Treaty. German policy on the other hand, though never venturing to challenge the Monroe Doctrine outright, in the existing naval strength of the Empire, had consistently resented it, the more strongly after the United States in 1898 had seemed to wander into the Far East contrary to the original isolationist dogma of that Doctrine. German leaders felt that if the United States had deserted the Doctrine to this extent, for its own advantage, it was unfair to cling to the rest of it in the Caribbean and in South America. They secretly nursed the ambition some day to break it down, particularly in southern Brazil, where German immigrants were strongly concentrated (though exasperatingly lukewarm toward *Deutschtum*), and also in the Caribbean near the approaches to the future canal.[1]

During the development of the Venezuelan crisis the powers had notified the United States of their intention to use force against Venezuela if their claims were not requited. Germany stated that in no circumstances did she in her proceedings intend the acquisition or the "permanent occupation" of Venezuelan territory, but did not exclude a "temporary occupation" and collection of customs duties to pay the debts. In answer Secretary Hay invoked the Monroe Doctrine, but was careful to quote President Roosevelt's recent exposition of it: "We do not guarantee any state against punishment if it misconducts itself, provided that punishment does not take the form of the acquisition of territory by any non-American power."[2] He professed to believe that Germany would not undertake any "occupation."[3] The British Secretary for Foreign Affairs, Lord Lansdowne, declared in the House of Lords three days after the bombardment that there was no intention to land a

---

[1] Alfred Vagts, *Weltpolitik, op. cit.*, has dissected German policy, and German-American naval and imperialistic rivalry after a close examination of German and American archives. For the Monroe Doctrine, see particularly pp. 1452-1814.

[2] Annual message, December 3, 1901. Note that this is not qualified by the adjective *permanent*, or "lasting," as von Holleben had reported in his earlier despatches.

[3] The insincerity of the German professions is demonstrated by the instructions to Prince Henry during his visit to the United States, as quoted by Dennis out of the *Grosse Politik:* ". . . should the Americans manifest concern about German ideas of acquisition or of influence as regards Central and South America, that should be disclaimed as an absurd fantasy by pointing to the pacific character of His Majesty's policy and to the many problems we have to solve elsewhere in the world, without, however, imparting the character of a solemn declaration to such a rather ironical denial."

British force "and still less to occupy Venezuelan territory." Germany made similar professions.

Roosevelt had informed both Great Britain and Germany, as the crisis approached, that he hoped a peaceful solution could be worked out, such as the American claimants were trying to do in Venezuela. Castro paid no attention to the threatening powers until they presented their ultimata; then he ran under cover of the Monroe Doctrine by requesting the United States to transmit to Great Britain and Germany his proposal that their claims be arbitrated by the United States Minister to Venezuela. Great Britain promptly agreed to arbitrate certain classes of the claims, and urged Germany to do so. Germany hesitated but soon acquiesced, as American public opinion presaged a collision with the Monroe Doctrine. Admiral George Dewey's fleet had been mobilized in the Caribbean off Puerto Rico,[1] a natural wintering place, but there seems to have been no formal or informal demands by President Roosevelt on the intervening powers. Italy, of course, followed along with the other two blockading powers. We may regard the Venezuelan incident of 1902 as a feeler by Germany to see to what extent the United States would really defend the Monroe Doctrine.

The claims of all the creditor powers were adjudicated by a group of mixed commissions sitting at Caracas, all except certain reserved claims of Great Britain and Germany which were settled by diplomatic conversations through the good offices of the United States at Washington. The question then arose whether the blockading powers should receive preferential treatment in payment of their claims. This went to the Hague Permanent Court of Arbitration. The tribunal in its decision put a premium on the use of force for the collection of contract debts by giving the belligerent powers a prior right of payment.

Despite this discouraging decision, the Venezuelan debts question led to the outlawry of force for the collection of contract debts if debtor powers agreed to arbitrate. During the dispute Luis M. Drago, the Minister of Foreign Relations of the Argentine Republic, submitted

[1] Theodore Roosevelt some years later (during the World War) in a celebrated letter of August 21, 1916, to one of his biographers, W. R. Thayer, described how he notified the German Ambassador that he would send the fleet to Venezuela if the Kaiser would not arbitrate. Historians have not been able to discover any evidence of this in the German correspondence printed in the *Grosse Politik*. Hill, *Roosevelt and the Caribbean, op. cit.*, dismisses this as a vainglorious boast *ex post facto*, but Dennis, *Adventures, op. cit.*, and Pringle, *Theodore Roosevelt, op. cit.*, introduce bits of contemporary evidence to confirm the impression of a suggested and informal warning. Vagts's and Perkins's subsequent thorough researches in German and American archives revealed no additional support for Roosevelt's later dramatic statement. But see S. W. Livermore's recent naval study in *American Historical Review.*, LI (April, 1946), 452-471.

to the United States a note embodying a proposition that has since been associated with his name. He proposed "that the public debt cannot occasion armed intervention nor even the actual occupation of the territory of American nations by a European power." [1]   In reply Hay referred to "the general position" of his Government, as expressed in President Roosevelt's recent message (December 3, 1901). Convention II adopted at the Hague Conference of 1907 finally made international law of a modified form of the Drago Doctrine: [2]

> The Contracting Powers agree not to have recourse to armed force for the recovery of contract debts claimed from the government of one country by the government of another country as being due to its nationals.
>
> This undertaking is, however, not applicable when the debtor State refuses or neglects to reply to an offer of arbitration, or, after accepting the offer, prevents any "Compromis" from being agreed on, or, after the arbitration, fails to submit to the award.

The Drago Doctrine supplemented the Monroe Doctrine by an international convention; and in turn it foreshadowed the Pact of Paris of 1928 by which all the nations agreed not to have recourse to war as "an instrument of national policy." American diplomacy played a decisive part in the adoption of both these great formulas of peace.

Between Cuba and Puerto Rico the island of Hispaniola bridges the approaches to the Caribbean and the canal from the North Atlantic. It had long been a matter of strategic interest to American diplomacy. That interest received additional emphasis as the United States turned to the construction of the canal. The two native republics, the Dominican Republic in the eastern half of the island, and Haiti in the western half, had been the scene of perennial revolution, war, confusion, and intermittent dictatorial tyranny even since their independence. Injuries to the citizens and property of European powers had frequently threatened intervention. The default on bonds and other obligations of the Dominican Republic threatened in 1904 to bring about another situation similar to that of Venezuela a few months before. The public debt was about $32,000,000, of which European creditors claimed title to $22,000,000. The distressed government had hypothecated various port revenues to

[1] Moore, *Digest, op. cit.*, VI, p. 593.
[2] Not to be confused with the "Calvo clause" which denies the right of a foreigner to appeal to his own government for enforcement of contracts. It is the custom of Latin-American governments to introduce into the contract of a concession to a foreign national a so-called Calvo clause by which the concessionaire formally renounces his right of appeal to the protection of his own government for the execution of the contract. Whether the foreigner can of his own act sign away his right is a question.

Belgian, French, German, Italian, and Spanish bondholders. In October, 1904, after an arbitration, the Dominican President turned over to an American agent the collection of customs at Puerto Plata, to satisfy the debts to a New York corporation, the Santo Domingo Improvement Company, which had transferred its property to the government. This was over the protests of the other foreign creditors.

The Dominican President looked to the United States as an alternative to imminent European intervention. Reluctantly, Roosevelt, as a means of preventing a repetition of the Venezuela incident, decided to accept the protecting responsibility of a collection of the Dominican customs and an arrangement with all creditors. With the assistance of a naval officer, who served as special commissioner, the American Minister to the Dominican Republic drafted the protocol of an agreement (February 7, 1905) which provided for the installation, and protection by the United States, of a collector of customs who would apply 45 per cent of the revenue to the current needs of the Dominican Government and turn the rest over pro rata to the creditors on an equal basis. The original rejected protocol contained a guaranty of the territorial integrity of Santo Domingo. The way in which the negotiations were carried on suggests that the President had not planned to submit this to the Senate for advice and consent, but to let it stand as an executive agreement; at the last moment, however, it was deemed the better part of wisdom to insert an article requiring the consent of the Senate, lest that body accept a challenge of its constitutional powers, and to substitute for the territorial guaranty a pledge to respect the sovereignty of the Dominican Republic.[1]

The Senate adjourned its session without a vote on the treaty, and for two years it refused its advice and consent. Meanwhile American agents collected and administered the customs of the republic according to an executive *modus vivendi* under the protecting presence of warships, which refrained from intervening in local political strife. The consequent increase in revenue was quite astonishing. Arrangements with the foreign creditors scaled down the outside debt to $12,407,000, mutually acknowledged, so that the total national debt, with arrears of interest, stood at $17,000,000, which the republic could handle quite solvently so long as the existing collectorship continued. A new issue of $20,-000,000, fifty-year bonds at 5 per cent, depended on the ratification of a treaty formalizing the new relationship.

[1] Holt, *Treaties Rejected, op. cit.,* pp. 212-229.

In presenting the agreement of 1905 to the Senate, President Roosevelt said:

It has for some time been obvious that those who profit by the Monroe Doctrine must accept certain responsibilities along with the rights which it confers; and that the same statement applies to those who uphold the doctrine. It cannot be too often and too emphatically asserted that the United States has not the slightest desire for territorial aggrandizement at the expense of any of its southern neighbors, and will not treat the Monroe Doctrine as an excuse for such aggrandizement on its part. . . . The justification for the United States taking this burden and incurring this responsibility is to be found in the fact that it is incompatible with international equity for the United States to refuse to allow other powers to take the only means at their disposal of satisfying the claims of their creditors and yet to refuse, itself, to take any such steps.

This is the "Roosevelt Corollary," recently repudiated, to the Monroe Doctrine. Not without a good deal of bitter debate over constitutional residues of treaty-making power did the Senate ratify, in 1907, a Dominican treaty. The new treaty put into effect an arrangement which continued, with certain modifications, until 1941. The President of the United States appointed a receiver general of customs, who collected the Dominican customs and applied their proceeds: (1) to the expenses of the receivership, not to exceed 5 per cent of the collected revenue; (2) to interest and amortization on the consolidated new issue of bonds; (3) to the Dominican Government. The United States had the right to protect the receiver general and his assistants in the performance of his duties, and the total of the Dominican debt was not to be increased or customs duties changed except on agreement with the Government of the United States.

Ratification of this treaty salvaged financial and political law and order in this Caribbean republic, at least for the next four years, and led to an expansion of trade and public works. Revolutions were nonexistent for several years, thus damming up an accumulation of resentment and hatred among the Dominican politicians at interference with this traditional right. But there was no economic exploitation of the island at the expense of natives or foreigners and no interference with constitutional liberties until 1916, when, after three years of efforts to quiet by diplomatic means revolutionary disturbances chronic since 1911, President Wilson finally resorted to an armed intervention which lasted until 1924. A new constitution was adopted under American tutelage, elections under it took place under American policing, and a program of public works, sanitation, and education marched rapidly ahead. The United States permitted new Dominican bond issues to care for this. The terms of evacuation, written into a second treaty in 1924 by which the military government ended, validated all the acts of the intervention, including the new bond issues, and provided that the terms of the treaty of 1907 should continue during the lifetime of the bonds (they were all paid off before 1950), with a new provision for arbitration of any disputes arising under it.[1] The "financial protectorate" over the Dominican Republic looked very positively toward a termination. A third treaty in 1941 ended the protectorate and receivership.

Events in Haiti paralleled those in Santo Domingo a few years later in time. Germany was just about to land marines there when the First World War began. A state of complete anarchy appeared the following year when an enraged populace in Port-au-Prince cut into small pieces the body of President Guillaume Sam after he had arbitrarily slaughtered 167 political hostages. With promises of no designs on the political or territorial integrity of Haiti, President Wilson ordered the intervention of American naval forces in July, 1915. Haiti continued under the supervision of American marines and political, economic, and educational advisers until 1934. A twenty-year treaty imposed at the beginning of the intervention set up a régime similar to that in the Dominican Republic, but more extended: it added provisions for the establishment of a financial adviser as well as a receiver general, of a native constabulary under American control, and for the co-operation of the United States in the sanitation and public improvements on the islands. A degree of protection, much stronger than that of the Dominican treaties, is visible in the following provisions which resemble the Platt Amendment:

Article XI. The Government of Haiti agrees not to surrender any of the territory of the Republic of Haiti by sale, lease, or otherwise, or jurisdiction over such territory, to any foreign government or power, nor to enter into any treaty or contract with any foreign power or powers that will impair or tend to impair the independence of Haiti.

Article XIV. The high contracting parties shall have authority to take such steps as may be necessary to insure the complete attainment of any of the objects comprehended in this treaty; and, should the necessity occur, the United States will lend an efficient aid for the preservation of Haitian Independence and the maintenance of a government adequate for the protection of life, property and individual liberty.

[1] Carl Kelsey wrote for the American Academy of Political and Social Sciences an objective survey of *The American Intervention in Haiti and the Dominican Republic* (Philadelphia, 1922). There is, of course, a voluminous controversial literature.

The intervention took place not without some severe fighting, notably the "Caco Revolt" of 1918 marked by isolated atrocities which years later (after the First World War) excited justified popular indignation in the United States; but it should be emphasized that these were rare exceptions, and the constitution, approved in Washington, scrupulously avoided any particular advantages for economic exploitation by citizens of the United States as compared with other foreign nationals. The treaty provided for the arbitration of all foreign claims, and their payment by new bonds. This took place in 1919, through a new issue of $40,000,000, thirty-year bonds, of which $16,000,000 was issued in 1923, and only small amounts of the remainder in later years. A protocol supplementary to the treaty of 1915 extended American "control and allocation" of the hypothecated revenues through a twenty-five-year period (that is, to May 3, 1941). The extensive treaty service, involving a widespread control over internal affairs in the island, continued until 1934, with remarkable benefit to the people. Public opinion in the United States, however, had grown increasingly restive about this measure of intervention, until President Hoover initiated in 1931 a policy for the gradual Haitianization of the treaty service, which was written into a new "accord," in the form of an executive agreement, negotiated by the Administration of President Franklin D. Roosevelt in 1933. Under the terms of this, American military forces withdrew from Haiti in 1934. The receivership of the customs was discontinued in July, 1935, and the revenues are now collected by the Haitian government-owned national bank, in which outsiders representing the foreign bondholders' interests have a measure of control. As in the case of the Dominican Republic, the "financial protectorate" over Haiti [1] was limited in time; in fact it was not exercised after 1935.

Central America had remained since the breakup of its Confederation in 1838 a backward area, divided into five sovereign and independent states continually torn by revolutions which brought local international wars in their wake.[2] External loans to European bankers went into

[1] One may single out of the plethora of relevant literature Arthur C. Millspaugh, *Haiti under American Control, 1915-1930* (World Peace Foundation, Boston, 1931). The author was an American professor who after an experience as financial adviser to the Persian Government, was financial adviser and receiver general of Haiti, in 1927-1929.

[2] The leading American authority on the history of the diplomacy of the United States in Central America and the Caribbean is Dana G. Munro. I wish to make special acknowledgment to his two books: *The Five Republics of Central America; Their Political and Economic Development and Their Relations with the United States* (New York, 1918), and *The United States and the Caribbean Area, op. cit.*

default there, too.   Nicaragua alone attracted much attention: it was the seat of Anglo-American rivalry before the Clayton-Bulwer Treaty, and was the field of the later operations of the notorious filibuster, William Walker; the canal route and the transisthmian lake-and-railway transit gave it continuing importance.   Nicaragua abrogated, according to its provisions for so doing, Seward's transit treaty of 1867, shortly before the United States made its canal treaty with Panama in 1903.   The new Panama Policy made the United States immediately interested in promoting the tranquillity and stability of these five governments.   A rival canal route lay through Nicaragua, and the collapse of law and order in any one state might mean the danger of European intervention on the Isthmus.   It was contemporaneously with the installation of the protectorate in Santo Domingo that the United States took steps in 1906 by friendly good offices and tutelage to establish stability in Central America by promoting local treaties which would do away with the scourge of revolution and internecine warfare and thus remove the danger to foreign nationals and property.

  The Washington Government united its good offices with Mexico in 1906 to bring about a truce between Guatemala and El Salvador, which had become involved in hostilities when the Salvadorian Minister of War supported a revolution against the President of Guatemala.   Following this a general Central American peace conference met at San José, Costa Rica, and adopted a series of treaties looking toward federation.   They included one for the judicial arbitration of international disputes among them, and another by which each state pledged itself not to support revolutions against the government of another, and not to harbor revolutionists against its sister states.   When notwithstanding this a new war broke out presently between Honduras and Nicaragua, President José Santos Zelaya, dictator of Nicaragua, blocked all peace machinery and succeeded in putting into power in Honduras a new revolutionary government.   He threatened later to upset the government of El Salvador and put his man in there, too.   It was at this stage that the United States and Mexico persuaded the Central American states to participate in a conference at Washington, in 1907, from which they emerged parties to a number of treaties which set up a new international framework in Central America, a miniature league of nations. The United States was the tutelary sponsor of this political structure but not party to the treaties, nor was Mexico.   They provided for the compulsory settlement of all international disputes among the Central American nations before a Central American Court of Justice.

They neutralized the central state of Honduras, across whose territory the other states often had to go to make war on each other. They covenanted not to harbor revolutionary leaders or movements against each other. They agreed not to recognize new governments set up by revolutionary process, pending the reorganization of the government through a free election. They recommended the creation of a number of cultural institutions, such as a pedagogical institute, and technical schools allied thereto, and a Bureau of Central American Republics.

These treaties proved more than the Central American states could live up to. The United States as a consulting and advising party to the Washington treaties of 1907 was continually called upon by one or the other of the signatories to exert itself for their enforcement. Most of the complaints were directed against Zelaya, the contumacious dictator of Nicaragua. When a revolution broke out in Nicaragua against Zelaya in 1909 the United States gave its moral and physical [1] support to the revolutionists, who set up a new régime.

The collapse of Nicaraguan finances during these disturbances and the pressure of foreign creditors for adjustment resulted in the signature of the Knox-Castrillo convention (June 6, 1911) similar to the Dominican treaty of 1907, with this difference: the bankers of the new consolidated loan, for the refunding of Nicaragua's indebtedness, were to present a list of names from which the President of the United States was to nominate the receiver general of the customs, who was to be protected by the United States in the performance of his duties. The Senate, which at first had opposed the Dominican treaty, refused now to ratify this Nicaraguan protectorate and a similar one which Secretary Philander C. Knox negotiated with Honduras. President Taft gave to these proposed treaties and to his contemporary diplomacy in China the unhappy description of "dollar diplomacy," and public opinion, which did not distinguish between American policy in China and in Central America, turned against it.[2]

The New York bankers who had been willing to underwrite the proposed new bonds, contingent upon ratification of the treaty, made a series of short-time loans under arrangements of their own with Nicaragua and Honduras, thus allowing them the means of satisfying their creditors. These arrangements, which included receiver generals

[1] American cruisers prohibited the bombardment, by opposing Nicaraguans, of the revolutionary forces in the port of Bluefields, on the ground that it might injure the lives and property of American citizens.

[2] See Scott Nearing and Joseph Freeman, *Dollar Diplomacy; a Study in American Imperialism* (New York, 1925), for the classic polemic and excoriation.

of customs appointed by the local governments from nominees of the bankers, were based on consultation with the Department of State and its approval, without any guaranty of anything by the United States. Nicaragua meanwhile, like some of her sister states, agreed at the instance of American diplomacy to set up mixed commissions which adjudicated other claims of foreigners. The abortive Knox treaties and contemplated dollar diplomacy also spurred other Central American states to make satisfactory arrangements with their foreign creditors, European and American.

An agreement between factions in Nicaragua on a compromise president did not bring political peace even when extended under the good offices of the United States. At the request of a succeeding President, Adolfo Diaz, the United States in 1912 intervened to end the sanguinary political turbulence and thus strengthen the local international treaty régime. A legation guard of about 100 marines continued on in Nicaragua until 1925, during which time the intervening power labored to bring political tranquillity to that distracted country.

President Wilson repudiated dollar diplomacy only in name—except in China, where he later returned to it. Secretary Bryan signed a treaty with Platt-Amendment articles which granted to the United States an exclusive proprietary concession to build any canal through Nicaraguan territory—waiving always any proven rights of the neighboring states of El Salvador and Costa Rica over the route.[1] The treaty included a lease of Great Corn and Little Corn islands [2] off the eastern coast of the canal route; and a ninety-nine-year (renewable) lease of a naval base (never established) under American "sovereign authority" on Nicaraguan territory in the Gulf of Fonseca, into which any probable Nicaraguan canal would lead on the Pacific side; the Gulf of Fonseca is also strategically located between California and Panama. In return, by the terms of this Bryan-Chamorro Treaty (August 5, 1914), the

[1] El Salvador and Honduras claimed sovereign rights in the Gulf of Fonseca, and Costa Rica sovereign rights over the San Juan River. The Senate ratified the treaty only with the reservation that nothing in it was intended in any way to affect any existing right of Costa Rica, El Salvador, or Honduras. Notwithstanding this careful provision Costa Rica and El Salvador (but not Honduras) sued Nicaragua before the Central American Court of Justice for conveying their rights to the United States, and secured a judgment in their favor. Nicaragua refused to admit the jurisdiction of the Court. Already weakened by the political character of its judges, the Court suffered by this action a final blow, and expired in 1918, to be resurrected by the later Washington treaties of 1923. The United States has not yet been able to quiet the easements of Costa Rica and El Salvador.

[2] So far the United States has taken up only a sufficient part of Little Corn Island to establish a lighthouse.

United States agreed to pay Nicaragua $3,000,000, to be spent under American supervision for the reduction of the foreign debt and any other agreed purposes. In ratifying this treaty the Senate cut out the Platt-Amendment articles.

The Bryan-Chamorro Treaty nevertheless made Nicaragua a protectorate, though diluted in comparison with the Cuban protectorate of 1902-1934. Article II, the article leasing the naval base, states that it is in order "to enable the Government of the United States to protect the Panama Canal and the proprietary rights [to any Nicaraguan canal] granted to the United States by the foregoing article, and also to enable the United States to take any measure necessary to the ends contemplated herein." This language reflects the Panama Policy. Under it the United States has exercised a larger measure of tutelage and intervention than in Cuba. The State Department sanctioned the adoption of agreements between the bankers and foreign bondholders and Nicaragua embodying a plan for the reorganization of the country's finances by which a financial high commission was set up by Nicaragua in 1917 to supervise the expenditures of certain portions of the revenues.[1] Under this plan, modified in 1920, the debts for advances by American bankers were paid off by 1924, and the service of the foreign (British) bonds taken care of. During the Great Depression, Nicaragua, ravaged again by revolution, suspended amortization payments on its debt as did other Caribbean and Central American governments, not to mention European governments.

It was during the revolutionary disturbances in Central America and in Mexico that a circumstance occurred which brought forth a formal application of the Monroe Doctrine to any "non-American" power, as well as to any European power which the Doctrine hitherto had envisaged in all its expressions. Rumors, whether exaggerated or not, had announced that a Japanese fishing company was about to lease from the Government of Mexico an extensive tract of land on the shore of Magdalena Bay, in Lower California, an admirable location for a naval base to intercept the communications between the Pacific Coast of the United States and the Panama Canal. This promptly evoked the adoption by the Senate of the resolution presented by Senator Lodge, member of the Committee on Foreign Relations, in 1912:

[1] One member of the commission was appointed by the President of Nicaragua, one by the Secretary of State of the United States, and, when necessary, an umpire appointed also by the Secretary of State.

Roscoe R. Hill, formerly one of the commissioners, has written an authoritative history of *Fiscal Intervention in Nicaragua* (New York, 1933).

[When] any harbor or other place in the American continents is so situated that the occupation thereof for naval or military purposes might threaten the communications or the safety of the United States, the Government of the United States could not see without grave concern the possession of such harbor or other place by any corporation or association which has such a relation to another Government, not American, as to give that Government practical power of control for national purposes.

The Lodge Resolution is thus part and parcel of the Monroe Doctrine, and a logical adaptation of it to twentieth-century conditions and particularly to the Panama Policy.

The first intervention in Nicaragua had back of it the general policy of the United States, manifest since 1907, of smothering out revolutionary strife and stimulating constitutional union among the Central American states. The weakening force of the Washington treaties of 1907 and the ominous strength of chronic revolutionary symptoms and outbreaks had led, after another abortive attempt at union in 1921,[1] to the acceptance by the five states, of an invitation by the United States to a second general conference at Washington, which took place in 1922-1923. Again they adopted treaties which repeated and strengthened the provisions of the conventions of 1907. New features were: a reformation of the failing Central American Court of Justice by providing that its tribunals should be drawn from a panel of jurists instead of from political appointments; a provision for international commissions of inquiry on the model of the Bryan "cooling-off" conciliation treaties then in effect between the United States and most countries; and an agreement not to recognize the legal existence of governments installed by revolution. The United States was a party to only the conciliation treaty, but during the lifetime of the quintuple treaty of peace and amity, namely, until January, 1934, it considered itself morally bound not to recognize revolutionary governments in Central America. To implement this policy—not only in Central America but elsewhere—Congress empowered the President to embargo the shipments from the United States to revolutionists, of arms, ammunition, and implements of war. The resolution of January 21, 1922 (extending one of March 14, 1912) declared:

That whenever the President finds that in any American country, or in any country in which the United States exercises extraterritorial jurisdiction, conditions of domestic violence exist, which are or may be promoted by the

[1] The history of the movement for federation in Central America is presented, in a careful factual manner, by Laudelino Moreno, *História de las relaciones interestatuales de Centro-América* (Madrid, 1928).

use of arms or munitions of war procured from the United States, and makes proclamation thereof, it shall be unlawful to export, except under such limitations and exceptions as the President prescribes, any arms or munitions of war from any place in the United States to such country until otherwise ordered by the President or by Congress.

President Coolidge put this into effect in respect of Honduras (March 22, 1924), and in respect of Nicaragua (September 15, 1926), and President Roosevelt in respect of Cuba (June 29, 1934). On October 10, 1935, the Secretary of State, acting under authority delegated by the President, announced that the exportation of arms, ammunition, and implements of war [1] to Cuba, Honduras, and Nicaragua would be licensed only when the Department of State had been informed by the respective legations of those countries in Washington that it was the desire of the government concerned to have the exportation authorized.[2]

The Panama Policy of the United States has built up, through the Washington Conferences of the Central American nations, in 1907 and 1923, a special treatment of these nations in the effort to bring about union and political stability and tranquillity. The great project of federation has so far failed, but there is no question that the preventive features of the Panama Policy as applied to Central America, as well as the Caribbean, brought comparative prosperity and peace to that portion of the Western world. The assistance by American commissions, under the general supervision of the State Department, in the regeneration of broken-down finances,[3] in the settlement of boundary disputes,[4] and in the reference of international controversies to peaceful means of settlement has also lessened the ravages of war, international and civil. The motive of it has been the security of the Panama Canal.

Nicaragua continued to be a source of disturbance and of danger to the peace of Central America.

The presence of the legation guard of 100 marines from 1912-1924 gave passive assistance to the efforts of American diplomacy to steady Nicaraguan politics by supervising elections. The persistent voicing of

[1] As defined by the proclamation of that date putting into effect the neutrality legislation of August 31, 1935 (see below, pp. 196-197).

[2] This regulation also applied to China. *International Traffic in Arms; Laws and Regulations Administered by the Secretary of State Governing the International traffic in Arms, Ammunition, and Implements of War* (Washington, Department of State, 1935).

[3] In Honduras, El Salvador, and Guatemala, without treaty contracts. The State Department was not involved in Costa Rica's successful refunding of her foreign bonds in 1911.

[4] The United States has mediated to secure the arbitration of boundary disputes between Honduras and Guatemala and between Costa Rica and Panama.

popular opposition in the United States to "imperialism" in Nicaragua and Hispaniola led to a withdrawal of the handful of marines remaining there in 1925. Nicaragua immediately reverted to its traditional revolutionary anarchy, and in a few months revolutions undid much of the healthful salvage work that had been accomplished since 1912. The marines returned almost immediately, and during a second intervention American diplomacy laboriously repeated its prophylactic labors to clean up new revolutions and prevent further ones. This time the forces stayed in Nicaragua until January 1, 1933. President Coolidge explained to a Congress and to a puzzled public at home that the intervention was due to the necessary implications of Nicaraguan disturbances as they affected the Panama Canal and to the confirmed policy of the United States to protect the lives, property, and interests of its citizens and of the government itself. President Coolidge expressed the Panama Policy of the United States in its most brusque form, a form from which his successors retreated. He next sent Colonel Henry L. Stimson, formerly Secretary of War, to Nicaragua in 1927 to assist the existing government in the reform of electoral machinery and to supervise a fair election under the policing of American forces, which in 1928 amounted to over 5,000 men. Elections were supervised again in 1930 and 1932. The Administration of President Hoover followed a policy of tapering off the military forces and turning over responsibility as fast as possible to the existing local government. Despite the persistence of guerrilla insurrectionary warfare under a native leader, Sandino (killed by Nicaraguan forces in 1934), the American marines were withdrawn altogether at the beginning of 1933.

It was Colonel Stimson himself, Secretary of State under President Hoover, who reversed the Coolidge policy, when in 1931 he said that the Government would refuse to send more marines to Nicaragua, following the cold-blooded murder by Sandino forces of eight American citizens.[1] The United States would not assume general protection of American nationals throughout the territory of Nicaragua: "To do so would lead to difficulties and commitments which this Government does not propose to undertake." He warned all American citizens who did not feel secure to withdraw from the country or at least to the coast towns from which they could be easily evacuated.

This warning—similar to warnings by the Wilson Administration to

---

[1] This occurred after a fearful earthquake which destroyed the city of Managua, when the marines already at that capital were engaged in relief activities and the normal forces of the local government were completely paralyzed.

citizens sojourning in revolutionary Mexico—foreshadowed the later policy by which the "Roosevelt Corollary" of the Monroe Doctrine has been completely repudiated, and the preventive features of the Panama Policy largely discarded.   The time had come when Europe did not appear to challenge the United States by intervening in the strategic area of the isthmian canal.   The Department of State published officially in 1930 an exegesis of the Monroe Doctrine, the so-called Clark Memorandum, which had the effect of pruning the "Roosevelt Corollary" from the historical structure of the Doctrine and suggesting that the United States would no longer guarantee that the American republics must behave responsibly toward foreigners or suffer the "big stick."   The prohibitions against non-American intervention still exist, but not the "corollary."

The Panama Policy of the United States was thus brought back to the pristine Monroe Doctrine, plus the possession and protection of the Canal Zone, plus an optional canal route in Nicaragua.   The Panama protectorate, the Cuban protectorate, and the two protectorates in Hispaniola were liquidated.   More than that, the United States ratified (1935, 1937) a treaty abjuring the right of intervention, directly or indirectly or for whatever reason, within the internal or external affairs of any other American state.[1]

It remains to be seen whether this benevolence will stand the tests of time and tropics.

---

[1] "The High Contracting Parties declare inadmissible the intervention of *any one* of them directly or indirectly, and for whatever reason, in the internal or external affairs of any other of the Parties." (Italics inserted.)   Article 1 of Additional Protocol Relating to Nonintervention, of Buenos Aires, 1936, supplementing the Montevideo Treaty on the Rights and Duties of States of 1933.   See below, p. 306.

5

The United States and Mexico

It has been the habit of a certain school of publicists to cite the relations between the United States and Mexico as exhibiting a shameful aggression which serves historically as a sorry model for other nations to vex the peace of the world today. Nothing could be more false, even if we go back a hundred years in history. Texas, recognized as an independent state by the world for nearly a decade, and later annexed by its own choice to the United States by what was tantamount to a national plebiscite, was certainly no Manchuria. Those who have studied carefully the diplomatic history preceding the outbreak of the war of 1846-1848 must be convinced that the war, which resulted in the purchase of those vast but almost vacant domains of northern Mexico, was as much the fault of Mexico as of the United States. When the student turns to the history of Mexico in the last century he must see in the United States the great example of the peaceful disposition, patience, complaisance, and self-sacrifice of a powerful people, and their friendliness, largely unrequited, for an unfortunate and helpless neighbor burdened with tragic domestic problems. It is true that there have been individuals and groups within the United States who have advocated intervention during the revolutionary disturbances of 1910-1925, and there have been a few persons who would have willingly annexed more Mexican territory; they can scarcely be said, however, to be leaders of American thought. Nor have the heavy investments in Mexico of American capital, the spokesmen of which advocated military intervention, had any enduring or decisive influence on the policy of the United States. With one of the richest storehouses of natural resources at its very door, where abundant provocation and justifications for intervention and control have existed, the United States has exhibited, at great cost of life and property to its citizens, almost a Galilean forbearance. The ideals of Woodrow Wilson largely explain this. Where else in the world is there such another example? Certainly not in Africa. Assuredly not in Asia. The history of Mexican-American

68

relations, too, is a gauge of the essentially defensive character of the Monroe Doctrine and of the Panama Policy. The United States has warned non-American nations to keep hands off Mexico, in 1867 and again in 1912, but itself has not, since 1848, laid hands on Mexico except for brief punitive actions following extreme provocations—actions which themselves exhibit rare self-restraint.

Mexican-American relations between the enforced French evacuation in 1867 and the outbreak of the Mexican Revolution in 1910 were of a routine nature,[1] but not devoid of a significant development which was to create a major problem when that Revolution occurred—the permeation of Mexico by foreign, particularly by American, capital. Mexico during this period was under the dictatorship of Porfirio Diaz, who smothered the hitherto chronic revolutionary strife at the price of stifling individual liberty and the continuation of a benighted peonage, akin to serfdom, for the masses of the people. The United States during these same years was occupied by the settlement and exploitation of the new West, by the rising crescendo of the Industrial Revolution, and by the new foreign problems ushered in by the Spanish-American War. As the republic approached its climax of expansion without ambitions for further continental territory to the south, those who governed Mexico, heartened by the events of 1867, became less and less fearsome of their northern neighbor. Diaz, wishing to advance the material progress of his impoverished country, without equal regard for the elevation of human values, invited foreign capital, under broad and frequently lavish concessions, to exploit its natural resources and to organize its economic life. Two billion dollars poured in from abroad—one half of it from the United States—by the year 1912, for the development of Mexican mines, petroleum, power, railroads, agriculture.[2]

These funds flowed into Mexico in good faith, as similarly foreign capital went into Canada during the same years, and as it had been

---

[1] A general claims commission was provided in the treaty of 1868. It adjudicated all claims accumulated on either side since 1848. It awarded a total of $4,125,622.20 on a total of claims of citizens of the United States originally entered at an aggregate sum of $470,126,613.40, and a total of $150,498.41 of a total of 998 claims of citizens of Mexico originally filed at an aggregate of $86,661,891.15. J. B. Moore, *International Adjudications* (5 vols., New York, 1929-1933), II, pp. 1314-1320.

Numerous conventions and agreements took place during this period for the settlement or arbitration of minor boundary disputes (including the unsuccessful and still unsettled controversy over the Chamizal tract, near El Paso, Texas, and Ciudad Rodriguez, Chihuahua); for regulation of frontier water courses, notably on the Rio Grande and Colorado rivers; and for mutual trans-frontier pursuit of hostile Indians.

[2] J. Fred Rippy, *United States and Mexico*, rev. ed. (New York, 1931), discusses this inflow of capital and its results.

invested in the United States itself during a previous generation. The foreign investors took the constitution and laws of Mexico at their face value, which was valid so long as Diaz held power, and they did not inquire into, nor were they interested in, the deeper implications of Porfirianism for the history of the Mexican nation or the appropriateness of those policies for the people of that land. The concessions to foreigners aroused a smoldering popular hostility not altogether dissimilar to that which animated the Boxer movement in China. This directed itself most strongly against the United States, nearest of the foreign exploiting nations. Diaz kept it down, but under unsettled conditions it could flame into great intensity and express itself in horrible atrocities.

The economic invasion of Mexico was not so formidable as the contemporary flow of foreign including American capital into Canada in the north; but Mexico had a different historical heritage from that of Canada, a heritage which combined with these new economic forces in the most explosive way.

The English colonies, from which the United States and the Dominion of Canada have risen to nationhood and expanded across a practically empty continent to interoceanic domains, had a fundamental difference from the Spanish colonies out of which came Mexico: they were settled by homemakers and state-builders alive with English ideas of self-government; Mexico was conquered by Spanish adventurers who wanted to go home with their plunder. Their women did not come in large numbers to Mexico. The conquerors imposed in feudal forms the forces of Spanish absolutism, in state and church, on the masses of Mexican aborigines. The Spaniards who stayed there mixed frequently with the aboriginal stock. Throughout the Spanish colonial period, throughout the history of independent and nominally republican Mexico during the nineteenth century, the Creole element kept in power. The native Indians and the mestizos, constituting nine tenths of the population, dwelt in poverty, ignorance, superstition, and disease. No significant middle class developed, capable of advancing self-government.[1]

The policies of Porfirianism organized many of the economic resources of Mexico, but the mass of the benighted people remained as badly off as before. The profits of the foreign concessions paid the fees of a small group of Mexican lawyers, bureaucrats, and politicians who lived in Mexico City, provided the salaries of young foreign engineers, swelled the estates of foreign residents, or flowed abroad as dividends to stockholders,

[1] Ernest Gruening has made this abundantly clear, with philosophical insight supported by a plethora of reality, in his *Mexico and Its Heritage* (New York, 1928).

There was practically no progress in education, in sanitation, in public welfare, in social improvement. In Canada during this period and in the United States earlier, the forces of human freedom, enlightenment, and self-government—the heritage from England as compared with the heritage from Spain—prospered under a similar flow of foreign capital and were able to make it useful to themselves while generally protecting it for the investors. This could not be so in Mexico.

The Revolution which broke out in 1910 continued in movements of action and reaction throughout the next ten years—a decade which witnessed also the First World War. Like all violent revolutions it went through successive phases. It began as a revolt, under Francisco I. Madero, for the restoration of constitutional liberties ruthlessly suppressed by the dictator Diaz. It ended with the completion of a revolution under the leadership of General Alvaro Obregón and finally Plutarco Calles for the social regeneration of the destitute masses of the Mexican people, a revolution which included the bridling of foreign concessions to Mexican sovereign control. During these gruesome years of civil warfare there were chaos and anarchy, banditry and plunder, robbery and cold-blooded butchery, with short intervals of promised order as successive revolutionary leaders came for brief times on the scene.

A comparatively orderly type of warfare such as prevailed in the United States during the Civil War was impossible in a country with Mexico's historical heritage, which included an accumulated hostility to foreigners. The history of the Revolution has not yet been fully written, nor has any complete census been compiled of the casualties and deprivations of foreign nationals, to say nothing of the loss of native life. The best estimate [1] for American citizens, from 1910 to 1920, is:

American citizens (civilians) killed in Mexico............ 397
United States soldiers killed in Mexico.................. 64
American citizens killed along the border, in the United States 58
United States soldiers killed along the border, in the United States 68
American citizens (civilians) outraged or wounded in Mexico 32
American soldiers outraged or wounded in Mexico.......... 29
American citizens (civilians) wounded on the border, in the United States 90
United States soldiers wounded on the border, in the United States 47

[1] The names are given in the "Partial Report" of the Fall subcommittee of the Senate Committee on Foreign Relations, Sen. Rept. No. 645, 66th Cong., 2d Sess., pp. 77-90.

In many instances the slaughter and outrages were not inescapable results of a revolutionary disorder; they were perpetrated on the victims simply because they were citizens of the United States. A rough estimate of actual property damages is $170,400,000 (Mex.),[1] much of which, of course, shared the companion fate of similar Mexican property, without recourse; but other portions suffered by violence to American citizens alone. Forty to fifty thousand American citizens abandoned their property and left the country, either on their own impulse or under the reiterated advice of the Department of State to do so. Only judicial inquiry—which has proved impossible—could determine how many of these violent deaths were casualties of the Revolution, shared by native and foreigner alike, and beyond the control, and thus beyond the responsibility of the existing Mexican governments. It should also be remembered, as Secretary of State Lansing did justly note in 1915, that 92 Mexicans were reported killed in American territory during the years 1913, 1914, and 1915, victims of the incomparably high ordinary homicide rate which the people of the United States permit themselves in so-called times of peace and for which the Government of the United States assumes no responsibility toward foreign governments unless the foreign nationals are murdered because of their nationality. This compares with 47 Americans who lost their lives in Mexico during the first three years, 1910-1912 inclusive, of the Revolution, and 76 during the three years 1913, 1914, 1915. Incomplete estimates of the number of other foreign nationals killed in Mexico during the Revolution are 927,[2] their property destroyed $134,900,000 (Mex.).[3]

The greater part of this violence took place after the outbreak of the First World War in Europe in 1914, when the European powers were in no position to take steps to protect their nationals. Even before the World War, Great Britain, after some hesitation, decided to co-operate with President Wilson's Mexican policy of "watchful waiting" and the other powers followed suit. They did not again challenge the Monroe

[1] Based not on the Fall Committee's estimate of $505,002,434, but on Turlington's calculation of one tenth the amount of claims later presented.

[2] Chinese, 471 (303 of whom perished in the Torreón massacre).

Spanish,	209	Italian,	16	Japanese,	10
Arabs,	111	French,	14	Miscellaneous,	58
British,	38				

See Report of Secretary of State Robert Lansing to President Wilson of December 3, 1919, transmitted to the Senate by the President December 5, 1919. Sen. Doc. 165, 66th Cong., 2d Sess.

[3] E. W. Turlington, *Mexico and Her Foreign Creditors* (Columbia University Press, 1930), presents the following estimates of property damages to foreign nationals, based in large part on one tenth of the amount of claims subsequently presented to mixed

Doctrine in Mexico; but had it not been for the protecting circumstances of the European War during the later and more bitter phases of the Mexican Revolution, the United States might have been forced by the pressure of foreign powers to an intervention in Mexico.

In order to understand the diplomatic issues which emerged during and after this confused decade of Mexican history, we must carry in mind the several movements through which the Revolution passed.

1. The revolt of Francisco I. Madero, 1910-1913. Madero's democratic revolt rested on an appeal for the restoration of constitutional liberties which had been suppressed by the dictator Diaz. It was purely political. Installed in power, he allowed to his political foes complete use of the new liberties. They soon overwhelmed him, by a treacherous *golpe de cuartel*, and murdered him and the Vice President, Suárez (February 23, 1913).

2. The reactionary régime of Victoriano Huerta, February, 1913–July, 1914. Huerta represented a counterrevolution back toward Porfirianism. His success would have restored a dictatorship and, presumably, law and order until the pent-up forces of Mexican misery found a chance to explode. The refusal of President Wilson to recognize him brought about his downfall (July 15, 1914) and released the radical forces.

3. A period of confusion, April, 1914–October, 1915, and of strife between various Mexican military leaders for control of the nation, in which they introduced promises of radical social reform [1] now in line with half-articulate public opinion. This lasted from the downfall of Huerta to the recognition by the United States of the *de facto* government of Carranza, October 19, 1915.

4. The régime of Carranza, October, 1915, to April, 1920.

commissions, and justifying this calculation by the general history of international awards:

United States	$170,400,000	(Mex.)
Spain	68,800,000	"
Great Britain	35,100,000	"
France	19,200,000	"
Germany	6,800,000	"
Netherlands	1,600,000	"
Belgium	1,800,000	"
Switzerland	1,600,000	"
Total	$305,300,000	"

Adjudication by the mixed claims commissions suggested that an estimate of 3 per cent is closer than 10 per cent.

[1] Frank Tannenbaum has made much simpler the intricate question of Mexican national and regional sociology in *The Mexican Agrarian Revolution* (Washington, Brookings Institution, 1930).

Carranza, after his election, was recognized *de jure* by the United States, April 17, 1917. The new Mexican Constitution of 1917 was adopted, embodying the political, agrarian, and other economic and social reforms of the Revolution. Carranza proved more ready to proclaim the revolutionary reforms than to execute them with integrity, and was highhanded, ruthless, and not incorrupt. He in turn was overthrown and murdered, in 1920, by a new uprising led by General Alvaro Obregón.

5. The régime of orderly government, from 1920, which ended the Revolution and began to consolidate its reforms in detailed legislation.

The principal diplomatic problems brought forth by the revolutionary disturbances were: recognition of new Mexican governments, protection of American citizens and property and of foreign nationals, and the honorable chastisement of provocative insults and attacks. These in turn involved the grave decision of policy, whether it would be necessary to intervene by force in Mexican affairs to achieve this protection.

President Taft was inclined to look on the Madero revolution through conventional legal eyes. He immediately recognized the new government, and, fortified by the resolution of Congress of March 14, 1912,[1] he embargoed shipments of arms destined for Madero's subversive opponents. As Madero's authority weakened, Taft and Secretary of State Knox became alarmed lest he be unable sufficiently to protect American citizens and their property according to their existing legal rights. On the advice of the American Ambassador to Mexico, Henry Lane Wilson, Secretary Knox sent a stiff note to the Madero Government, enumerating a number of grievances of American citizens (they were so few at that time that they could be enumerated) and demanding that the administration of Mexico actively and competently bestir itself "to fulfill its international duties toward American citizens and their interests," or else the United States might have to abandon its policy of friendliness.[2] The answer to this was an able refutation of the specified charges, an allusion to contemporary attacks on Mexican citizens in the United States, a willingness to do complete justice, with an expression of the difficulties involved by domestic turbulence. Ambassador Wilson recom-

---

[1] "That whenever the President shall find that in any American country conditions of domestic violence exist which are promoted by the use of arms or munitions of war purchased from the United States, and shall make proclamation thereof, it shall be unlawful to export except under such limitations and exceptions as the President shall prescribe any arms or munitions of war from any place in the United States to such country until otherwise ordered by the President or by Congress."

[2] The correspondence is printed in *Foreign Relations of the United States, 1912, 1913.*

mended to Washington vigorous and drastic action. "These Latin-American countries," he wrote, "should be dealt with justly and calmly but severely and undeviatingly." To act otherwise would "bring disaster and forfeit to us, in the estimation of these peoples, the respect and awe with which they have been taught to regard us." On his part, in Mexico City, he used his influence to weaken Madero, and even to organize a demand on the part of the diplomatic corps that Madero resign.

President Taft had ordered the mobilization of 100,000 troops in Texas to enforce neutrality, and the Secretary of State intimated that, if Mexico did not succeed in protecting "American interests," the President might open the sluiceways of munitions across the frontier to Madero's insurrectionary foes; but he shrank from any policy of intervention. Such was the situation when Huerta came into power following the *coup d'état* of February 9, 1913, less than a month before the end of the Taft Administration.

Henry Lane Wilson at once congratulated Huerta upon his seizure of the presidency. He urged President Taft to recognize the new government *de facto*. Had his advice been followed by Taft or by Woodrow Wilson it is possible that another epoch of Porfirianism, safe for foreigners, might have followed for years. But Taft was too shocked at Madero's brutal death to recognize in any way the régime of his murderers. He left the Mexican question to President Wilson.

Woodrow Wilson viewed the Mexican problem in a new light. A reformer himself, he was sympathetic to the reform movement in Mexico, particularly to the Madero program, and to the revealing necessity of agrarian reforms. Henry Lane Wilson, the ambassador of the Taft Administration, pressed the Department of State to recognize Huerta *de facto* and to hasten arrangements with him, as the other governments were doing, for the satisfaction of all claims. The President ignored this advice and gave expression to a new policy of recognition of Latin-American governments: the United States would not recognize those which were not constitutionally right. Judging by the past, during which so many Latin-American governments had established themselves as durably by revolution as by constitutional procedure, and in a congeries of states where so many different constitutions existed, this novel policy would require a wide and penetrating scrutiny into the internal affairs of the governments involved. It nevertheless rested on lofty motives. Said the President a week after his inauguration:

We hold . . . that just government rests always upon the consent of the governed, and that there can be no freedom without order based upon law and upon the public conscience and approval. . . . We shall lend our influence of every kind to the realization of these principles . . . knowing that disorder, personal intrigue and defiance of constitutional rights weaken and discredit government and injure none so much as the people who are unfortunate enough to have their common life and their common affairs so tainted and disturbed. We can have no sympathy with those who seek to seize the power of government to advance their own personal interests or ambitions.

Later, in a public address at Mobile, Alabama (October 27, 1913), Woodrow Wilson, after first declaring that the United States would never again seek to add additional territory by conquest, opposed by implication the policy of the European powers which had recognized Huerta *de facto* with the hope of securing the vested interests of their citizens by choking off further revolutionary disturbances with another dictatorship: "We have seen material interests threaten constitutional freedom in the United States. Therefore we will know how to sympathize with those in the rest of America who have to contend with such powers, not only within their borders but from outside their borders also."

President Wilson, determined not to recognize "the unspeakable Huerta" in any way, endeavored by his counsel peaceably to direct the Mexican situation into some constitutional channel. He accepted the resignation of Ambassador Henry Lane Wilson—who thenceforth became a confirmed but powerless advocate of forcible intervention in Mexico and an American protectorate there—and dispatched a personal representative, former Governor John Lind (of Minnesota), in a vain attempt to bring the leaders of the Revolution to an agreement which would eliminate Huerta, set up a provisional president, and proceed to fair elections of a clean government and president by constitutional methods. Lind was authorized to say that if the Huerta government acted favorably, and at once, on these suggestions, the President would inform American bankers that the United States approved the extension of an immediate loan sufficient to cover the temporary demands of those holding possession of the government in Mexico.[1] This was a curious overture from an opponent of "dollar diplomacy." Huerta would not step down. Lind reported that the Mexicans respected only force, and he too urged a military occupation of the capital. Wilson persisted in his peaceful endeavors to get Huerta out. He made the tacit diplomatic bargain by which Great Britain ceased to oppose American policy in Mexico and the President secured from Congress a repeal of the exemp-

[1] George M. Stephenson, *John Lind of Minnesota* (University of Minnesota Press, 1935).

tion from tolls of coastwise vessels of the United States using the Panama Canal.[1] Armed with this the Secretary of State explained to the diplomatic corps at Washington (November 24, 1913) that such usurpers as Huerta

. . . put the lives and fortunes of citizens and foreigners alike in constant jeopardy. . . . It is the purpose of the United States therefore to discredit and defeat such usurpations whenever they occur. The present policy . . . is to isolate General Huerta entirely; to cut him off from foreign sympathy and aid and from domestic credit, whether moral or material, and to force him out. It hopes and believes that isolation will accomplish this end and shall await the results without irritation or impatience. If General Huerta does not retire by force of circumstances it will become the duty of the United States to use less peaceful means to put him out. . . . Beyond this fixed purpose the Government of the United States will not go. It will not permit itself to seek any special or exclusive advantages in Mexico or elsewhere for its own citizens but will seek, here as elsewhere, to show itself the consistent champion of the open door.

To Congress in his annual message (December, 1913) the President disclaimed any intention of intervention. The foreign powers accepted this policy. Under British leadership their diplomatists in Mexico City formally advised Huerta to accept the demands of the United States. This the usurper refused to do. The United States now offered to act as an intermediary for foreign powers in cases needing the protection of their citizens. Wilson removed the embargo on shipments of arms and munitions to Mexico, thus replenishing Huerta's armed opponents, and stationed naval vessels off Vera Cruz to make sure that the dictator did not get shipments from Europe, where he was making a desperate loan for such purchases.

The presence of American warships in Mexican waters, and the anti-American feeling rapidly mounting among Huerta's followers, produced a provocative incident, which at the disposition of a less patient and humanitarian President of the United States might have led to prolonged intervention. A party of uniformed American sailors went on shore with a launch at the port of Tampico to buy gasoline. Local military officials summarily arrested them and took them from the boat flying the American flag to headquarters, where they were quickly released. Admiral H. T. Mayo, commander of the naval forces, demanded a salute of the American flag by way of reparation.

Huerta saw a possible chance, by provoking the United States into

[1] See above, p. 40, n. 1.

forceful action, to strengthen his position by rallying opposing Mexican factions behind him. He refused the salute. President Wilson backed up the Admiral. He informed Huerta that if the salute were not given he would turn the question over to Congress. When a President of the United States resorts to such a statement he usually is sure that Congress will support forcible action. Huerta still adamant, Wilson informed Congress that Tampico was only one spectacular incident in a series of events which showed contempt for American rights. Disclaiming aggression or purpose of intervention, he asked for authority to use force if necessary to bring about a proper respect for the flag of the United States. Congress supported this request overwhelmingly and immediately; [1] but the President had to act before the resolution passed the Senate. Just as the German merchant ship *Ypiranga* was about to land a cargo of arms at Vera Cruz, Admiral Mayo's forces shelled the defenses there (April 21, 1914) and, after some sharp fighting, took the customhouse and the entire city, and seized the ship. There followed a proclamation prohibiting the importation of arms into Mexico. This incident caused a complete cessation of all relations between the two governments. The American *chargé d'affaires,* who had remained in Mexico in informal and personally friendly contact with Huerta, now left the country. The President strengthened garrisons on the frontier and restored the embargo on shipments of munitions to Mexico; and the Department of State advised American citizens to leave Mexico at once. Huerta sought in vain to rally all armed Mexicans to a united resistance of the "invader." The "constitutional" opposition, under Carranza and other leaders, looked with increasing disfavor upon the American occupation of Vera Cruz, "a violation of the national sovereignty," as Carranza notified the Department of State, but, with success so imminent, they would not rally to Huerta.

President Wilson's position at Vera Cruz was as unwelcome to himself as it was to his opponent. He accepted with alacrity an invitation of the diplomatic representatives of the Argentine, Brazil, and Chile in Washington to mediate.[2] This cleared him from the imputation of any contradiction of his declared policy of nonintervention, and molded good will for the United States over all South America. It was the point of departure also for a new Latin-American policy, sug-

---

[1] The vote in the House of Representatives was 323-19 (April 20); in the Senate, 72-13 (April 22, 1914).

[2] Rippy, *op. cit.,* has some interpretative chapters summarizing the noninterventionist Mexican policies of Presidents Taft, Wilson, Harding, and Coolidge.

gested to the President by his intimate adviser, Colonel E. M. House —that of Pan-Americanizing the Monroe Doctrine by an inter-American pact mutually to guarantee the territorial integrity and political independence of each contracting state.[1] From then on, the President, favoring this policy, was scrupulous not to stultify it by the exhibition of any aggression by the United States toward Mexico. His Mexican policy added to the moral force of his diplomacy of war and peace in Europe in 1917-1919.

Huerta, isolated at home and abroad, was obliged to accept the advice of the ABC powers. The *Carranzistas* also accepted an invitation to send a delegate. In Mexico, the "constitutional" forces under Carranza were rapidly gaining in the field when the ABC mediation conference met at Niagara Falls, Ontario. The mediators proposed the following settlement: elimination of Huerta; the installation of a provisional government "actually, avowedly and sincerely in favor of the agrarian and political reforms" advanced by the revolutionists; a commission to arrange settlement with the new provisional government of foreign claims for indemnity; agreement of the mediating powers to recognize the provisional Mexican government on this basis; no indemnity for the United States for the expenses of occupation. This the delegates of the United States accepted, under reservation of not recognizing in any way the government of Huerta.[2] The *Carranzistas* would not sign. When the terms of the protocol were read at Mexico City the Huerta Government collapsed, and the General left for Europe. The government of Mexico fell among rival armed factions, temporarily to the *Carranzistas* who at all times denied the right of foreign powers to mediate in any settlement of Mexican affairs. Huerta eliminated, but Mexico still in ferment, American forces evacuated Vera Cruz (November 23, 1914).[3]

The elimination of Huerta did not bring peace to Mexico. Rival revolutionary armies, under Zapata in the southwest and the bandit Villa in the north among others, ravaged the country. Wilson's task now was to get placed in authority a group which could command

[1] Seymour, *Intimate Papers of Colonel House, op. cit.,* I, pp. 207-234. See below, Chapter 14.

[2] Chapter XII in J. M. Callahan's *American Foreign Policy in Mexican Relations* (New York, 1932) gives us a timetable of these happenings, a *précis* in effect, of the correspondence published in the official series *Foreign Relations.*

[3] Ray Stannard Baker's review of the Mexican crisis, to the evacuation of Vera Cruz, in the fourth volume of his *Woodrow Wilson, Life and Letters* (8 vols., New York, 1927-1939), is most sympathetic to Wilson's idealistic policy.

the support of the people of Mexico as a provisional government that could receive the sanction of later free elections, a government from which satisfactory guaranties could then be had for the protection of American and other foreign life and property in Mexico. The *Carranzistas,* despite their unsympathetic response to Wilson's attitude, seemed to offer the best chance of such a government.

Confusion worse confounded, murder, and pillage swept Mexico. Anxious to hasten the establishment of order, President Wilson summoned a conference of diplomatic representatives of six Latin-American powers—the Argentine Republic, Brazil, Chile, Guatemala, Bolivia, and Uruguay—at Washington (August, 1915) to advise on which warring faction to recognize and support as the government *de facto* of Mexico.

The conference invited representatives of the Mexican groups to participate. Despite the fact that Carranza refused the invitation and consistently denied the right of outside parties to give advice to Mexico, the conferees announced their decision that the *Carranzista* party was "the only party possessing the essentials of recognition as the *de facto* government of Mexico." This was an anxious response to the desire to see somebody in authority in Mexico whom foreign powers could support and with whom they might expect to make conventions for the settlement of claims and the protection of lives and property of their nationals. The United States then promptly (October 19, 1915) recognized *de facto* Carranza's authority, followed by similar action by the six Latin-American conferee powers. "We will aid and befriend Mexico," President Wilson explained to Congress,[1] "but we will not coerce her."

The *de facto* recognition of Carranza proved premature. He was unable to control the ravaging chieftains who refused to accept his leadership. The most notorious and bloodthirsty of these, Pancho Villa, operating in the northern states, deliberately attempted, by a series of sanguinary incidents, to provoke an armed intervention of the United States which might enable him to supplant Carranza in public estimation as a leader of a patriotic revolutionary Mexico to repel the hoped-for invasion. Carranza had invited American mine owners, who had abandoned their properties on advice of their Government, to return and operate the mines. A group of fifteen graduate engineers promptly entered the State of Chihuahua for this purpose. Villa's forces took the young men from a railroad train and murdered them in cold blood

[1] Annual message of December, 1915.

at Santa Ysabel (January 10, 1916). In the Congress of the United States resolutions for armed intervention were introduced, but Wilson accepted, this time, the promise of Carranza to punish the perpetrators of the massacre. To this day they have gone unpunished. Next Villa led a hostile raid on American soil, "shooting up" the town of Columbus, New Mexico, with the loss of seventeen American lives—innocent citizens killed within their own country, in their own home town (March 9, 1916).

President Wilson with the quick approval of Congress immediately sent a punitive expedition of 15,000 men under General John J. Pershing in hot but ineffective pursuit of Villa's band across the Chihuahua desert. The President mobilized 150,000 militia on the southern frontier against further contingencies, to supplement the regular army, a military episode which exhibited to the world such a lamentable unpreparedness for war that it encouraged Mexicans of all groups, including Carranza, to resist American demands, however reasonable. The untamed Villa perpetrated new raids into Texas (affairs of Glen Springs and Boquilla, May 5, 1916), which happened at the time of the *Sussex* crisis with Germany.[1]

From now on the increasing uncertainty of American neutrality *vis-à-vis* the war in Europe exerted its influence on the benevolent "watchful waiting" of the exasperated President Wilson. Carranza refused to accept American requests for co-operative action for the suppression of Villa with American troops on Mexican soil. Another column of 8,000 crossed the frontier over the rising protests of Carranza. The Department of State again publicly advised all American citizens remaining in Mexico to leave. The American President was sincere in his explanations that these punitive expeditions were necessary to prevent further and general intervention, for which public opinion within the United States began to clamor, led by Theodore Roosevelt, and backed of course by those people whose legitimate investments in Mexico were being wiped out. The second pursuit of *Villistas* led to a collision with Carranza's forces at Carrizal. Other smaller attacks on American naval or land forces on the ports and frontiers of Mexico showed the eager enmity of Carranza's Government. General hostilities seemed to have been averted only by a hair's breadth by Carranza's prudence in accepting Wilson's demand (June 25, 1916) for the immediate release of seventeen American troopers who had been cut off and made prisoners at Carrizal.

[1] See below, p. 131.

A series of futile conferences (at New London, Atlantic City, Philadelphia, and New York) between commissioners of the United States and of the *de facto* Mexican Government, endeavored in vain to agree on bases for evacuation of Pershing's regiments, based on a right to intervene again when necessary and sufficient promises of protection by the Carranza forces. Only when the crisis of approaching war with Germany developed, in January, 1917, did Wilson order the withdrawal of the troops, without adequate guaranties. The Mexican Congress, acting as an electoral college, elected Carranza as President, March 11, 1917, and adopted a new constitution, embodying the reforms of the Revolution. Wilson now hastily recognized the new government *de jure*. When Henry P. Fletcher, the new Ambassador of the United States, entered the Chamber of Deputies, the members received him with hisses, in shameful contrast to the applause which greeted the German Ambassador, whose proposal to Mexico the British secret service and Washington Government had just ventilated to the world: a war alliance, to include Japan, for the purpose of conquering back from the United States "the lost territory" in the states of Texas, New Mexico, and Arizona.

It was a spectacular victory for Carranza, who maintained his authority successfully—though not faithfully to the principles of the Revolution—in Mexico during the remainder of the First World War, in which the United States was now involved.

Despite his loss of respect in Mexico for the time being, Wilson had gained the good will of Latin America in general and had prevented the United States from becoming involved in a war with Mexico on the eve of its entrance into the war in Europe. The settlement of Mexican-American affairs and liquidation of claims of foreign nationals now had to await the settlement of the far greater issues of the conflict.

After the American Civil War, the United States with a million men under arms did not take advantage of its power to march into Canada, despite provocations. It was the same after the First World War in regard to Mexico although the provocation was unspeakably greater. The demand for it, too, particularly on the part of the despoiled investors, was great. In Washington in the upper house Senator Albert B. Fall of New Mexico, spokesman for the Doheny oil interests,[1] presided over

---

[1] Senator Fall was later convicted of betraying public trust, in connection with the award to Doheny interests of the Elk Hill oil leases on United States public lands while he was Secretary of the Interior during the Harding Administration. Doheny "loaned" Fall $100,000 and destroyed the latter's note, at the time of passing the leases. Fall spent a year in a federal prison. The public utterances of this person in regard to

a subcommittee of the Committee on Foreign Relations, which diligently collected evidence concerning the multitude of outrages. These were embodied in a *Preliminary Report and Hearings* of 3,000 printed pages, parts of which were widely distributed in 1919 as fuel for warming public opinion to demand a more positive Mexican policy. This protest was gathering volume when suddenly the end of the Revolution in the spring of 1920 vindicated Wilson's policy. The radical party, under the leadership of General Alvaro Obregón, overthrew the corrupting Carranza Government. Obregón was then elected President by national suffrage (September, 1920). The Fall Committee limited its recommendations to: diplomatic pressure for the security of American property and citizens in Mexico; no recognition of Obregón without a specific agreement to that effect and a settlement of all claims for damages; only in case of failure ought intervention to be considered.

Both political parties in their platforms of 1920 expressed unwillingness to recognize the new Obregón Government without a specific understanding for the adjudication and payment of American claims and the protection of American nationals and property. This was the policy of the Wilson Administration in its closing days and of the new Republican Administrations of Presidents Harding and Coolidge. Did it mean that such an agreement must be written into a formal treaty as the price of recognition, a treaty which would be binding on the Mexican nation, or merely a diplomatic agreement which would not bind any other than the Mexican Government at that time in power? Bainbridge Colby, Wilson's last Secretary of State, seemed to mean a treaty.

The legacy of issues [1] between the United States and Mexico which had come down from the decade of revolution was intricate and confusing. We are straining for simplicity when we summarize them as follows: claims for damages to American citizens suffered since the last mixed commission of 1868; claims for damages of American citizens and their property by violence or arbitrary decrees during the Revolution; claims for damages for the appropriation of lands, owned in good legal title by American citizens, for the restoration by the new reforms

---

Mexico must be always suspect. President Wilson must have realized this when he remarked to his private secretary [as quoted by Joseph Tumulty, *Woodrow Wilson as I Knew Him* (New York, 1922), p. 146]: "I have to pause and remind myself that I am President of the United States and not of a small group of Americans with vested interests in Mexico."

[1] F. S. Dunn, *The Diplomatic Protection of Americans in Mexico*, prepared for the Columbia University Council for Research in the Social Sciences (Columbia University Press, 1933), has a succinct account of the technical points involved in these issues.

of communal holdings or *ejidos* for the agrarian population of Mexico; damages to American citizens by virtue of the nationalization of sub- soil deposits according to the provisions of Article 27 of the new Mexi- can Constitution of 1917; claims based on the nonpayment of interest or principal of Mexican Government bonds. A brief description of each category is in order.

The so-called general claims since 1868 were routine claims under in- ternational law and treaty provisions; the tranquillity of the Porfirian régime had kept these within normal limits. The special claims for damages arising from the events of the Revolution were various and multitudinous: they included deaths, mutilations, and other injuries to persons, damage or confiscation of property, inadequate police protec- tion, denial of justice, to mention only the more prominent.

The claims for *ejido* land takings arose out of the most fundamental reform of the Revolution, the effort to restore to the agrarian population the communal land holdings, the custom of which dates back to abo- riginal history, of lands of which they had been despoiled during the cen- tury of Mexican independence. In the great agrarian states of Mexico over 90 per cent of the population was landless and in a system of peon- age no better than slavery; their misery was profoundly pitiful, worse than the Negro slave in the United States before the Civil War, and it had been growing steadily worse decade by decade; because of this Mexico herself, once a country self-sufficient for foodstuffs, had de- creased in production and depended, in the last years of the Diaz ré- gime, on imports of foodstuffs.[1] The redistribution of the colossal private landholdings accumulated largely by fraud and graft under legal forms, some of them held by foreign citizens, innocent investors, was the great- est problem of the Revolution. One factor in it was the historic custom among these native peoples of holding and working their land in common, in the environs of their village communities. The redistribution of land under Article 27 of the new Constitution, and earlier decrees and subse- quent legislation, was adapted to this custom. Article 27 of the Con- stitution of 1917 declared the ownership of all lands and waters, and of the mineral deposits under them, to be vested in the nation, which might then prescribe the conditions under which private property might be held in the public interest. At the same time it stated that private property so defined should not be expropriated except for reasons of

---

[1] For a sympathetic and luminous description of the agrarian population, and its fundamental relation to the Mexican Revolution, see Gruening, *op. cit.*

public utility and by means of indemnification. Under this principle the land which was redistributed in the agrarian reforms for the re-establishment or creation of *ejidos* was not confiscated from the *hacendados,* or proprietors; the Government took it by eminent domain at appraised valuation, with payment in national bonds which had no live value, and gave it over to native agrarian communal holdings. Protests arose over the appraisals and the method of payment. The Mexican Government contended that foreigners received no worse treatment than Mexican proprietors in this respect, and that, as to payment in bonds, it was a recognition and a promise, and the only way during a great and vital emergency to execute a reform indispensably necessary for the restoration of peace and public tranquillity.

Another fundamental principle of the Mexican Revolution was "Mexico for the Mexicans": the liquidation of foreign economic dominion, particularly of natural resources which constituted the material patrimony of the nation. Before the Revolution the mineral subsoil products, *excepting carboniferous minerals including petroleum,* had been separated by law from the surface ownership and vested in the state, which licensed their exploitation under regulatory laws and decrees. On the basis of this exception the extensive petroleum industry had rested upon private ownership, almost altogether foreign, predominantly American owners who had bought vast tracts of land (including subsoil petroleum) for this purpose under good title according to the existing legal system. Some of this land was held in reserve for future exploitation.

The new Constitution of 1917 in Article 27 now brought subsoil petroleum deposits also under the ownership of the state. A series of provisional decrees, pending the enactment in 1925 of an organic national petroleum law, laid down the new conditions under which petroleum operators, hitherto owners outright, now might continue to exploit their holdings, for terms of not more than fifty years, under license and confirmatory concessions, which must be registered within two years under pain of total lapse of all title. The new registration required: new taxation, Mexicanization of corporations, and of a controlling fraction of their stock; limitation of existing titles of foreign individuals to one life after which the holdings must be liquidated to Mexican citizens or corporations; exploitation by some "positive act" of all land held; agreement by foreign concessionaires not to call upon their governments for support of their titles against the Mexican Government (the so-called "Calvo clause" increasingly in usage in contracts of

Latin-American states with foreign nationals), and prohibition of concessions to foreign citizens or corporations in coastal or frontier zones.

The foreign holders of petroleum lands saw their titles suddenly converted into fifty-year leaseholds under increasingly complex conditions
and growing tax burdens. It looked to them as though the Mexican
Government was deliberately trapping the funds and ability which they
had been invited to invest under constitutional guarantees. The United
States Government took the position, in the diplomatic disputes which
followed, that, while not denying the right of the nation to reform its
constitution and legislation in its own way, such reforms could not (as
the new Mexican Constitution itself said they could not) be applied
ex post facto to property rights already secured by foreign nationals in
contracts in good faith under earlier constitutions and laws. This legalistic position, at least debatable, paid no attention to the circumstances,
propriety, or morality under which such a former legal system had
existed. The United States also contended that a foreign national
could not, without the consent of his government and solely by his own
will, sign away any right to protection by his government.

The issue of defaulted interest on loans abroad, either by the Mexican
Government or by railroads or states guaranteed by Mexico, was, due to
the impoverished condition and political insufficiency of the country,
a large but simple question of adjustment between debtor and creditor, although complex in its details. The Revolution bankrupted the
country and brought about a suspension of interest and amortization
on its bonded public debt, nearly all of which was held by foreign nationals, mostly in the form of Mexican external bonds contracted in
foreign currencies. As suspension continued for two decades, arrears
of interest rapidly added to the total indebtedness. French citizens
held the largest share of this direct foreign debt, next British, next
Americans, with smaller shares for German, Dutch, Belgian, Swiss, and
Spanish nationals. Foreign governments by international law had the
right to interpose their authority for the settlement of the portion of
the external debt contracted with their nationals; but, since the Second
Hague Convention [1] of 1907, they had no right to the use of force for
the recovery of such contract debts unless Mexico should refuse to
arbitrate or, having arbitrated, refuse to pay the adjudicated awards.
We shall see that the warring foreign governments did not officially
interpose for the settlement of these debts. They left the negotiations

[1] See above, p. 55.

to representatives of the bondholders under the leadership of American bankers.

President Obregón, seeking full recognition of his government, offered his personal assurances for the security of American property and citizens in Mexico and the ownership of lands acquired by American citizens before the adoption of the new Constitution on May 1, 1917. He would shape his policy, he said, "according to the dictates of law and morality." These ambiguous promises bound only Obregón and his actual government; similar promises from one man and one administration previously in the case of Carranza had been worth nothing. Apparently, too, there was a loophole left for the alienation of title to the subsoil products of such lands on which no "positive act" of exploitation had taken place before 1917. Secretary of State Charles E. Hughes, in the new Republican Administration of President Harding, insisted that recognition must be contingent upon a treaty which would explicitly bind the Mexican nation itself to adequate guaranties. Obregón refused this. Eventually Hughes gave way and accepted, instead of a treaty, a statement of agreement written into a protocol of informal conferences in Mexico City—the so-called Bucareli Conferences—of a commission composed of delegates from the two countries.

In these Bucareli Conferences the American spokesmen were willing to accept in general the position of the Mexican Government that it had an unquestioned right to regulate the oil industry according to the new reforms providing they did not apply to property acquired under other conditions before the new Constitution went into effect; and they denied the necessity of having performed *before May 1, 1917,* "a positive act" of exploitation in order to validate continuing title to petroleum lands acquired before that date. Such a necessity, laid down in principle in a then recent case of the Supreme Court of Mexico involving the Texas Corporation, they held to be *ex post facto.* The Mexican representatives set forth a definition of a "positive act" which they said "has constituted and will constitute in the future the policy of the Mexican Government." This definition, while clinging steadfastly to the theory of the necessity of such an act before 1917, nevertheless was so phrased that the merest trace or wisp of action, such as payment for the lands of a higher price than their surface value alone would justify, or even manifestation of intent to exploit, would suffice for the indispensable "positive act."[1] This new statement seemed to mean that such lands

[1] Such as "drilling, leasing, entering into any contract relative to the subsoil, making investments of capital in lands for the purpose of obtaining the oil in the subsoil, carry-

and their subsoil products were excluded from the nationalization program of Article 27. In the cases of owners who had not, indeed, performed such a positive act, they would have preferential rights, to the exclusion of third parties, for the exploitation of the subsoil. In answer the American delegates on behalf of their government said that they reserved all the rights of citizens of the United States in respect to the subsoil of lands in Mexico owned by citizens of the United States, or in which they had an interest in whatever form owned or held, under the laws and constitution of Mexico in force prior to the promulgation of the new constitution, May 1, 1917, and under the principles of international law and equity.

At the same conference the representatives of the United States accepted a statement of the Mexican representatives of the principles that takings of land for *ejidos, for existing villages,* could be paid for in bonds, up to 1,755 *hectares;* all taking of acreage above that figure was to be compensated in cash; and the former owner might appeal to a general mixed claims commission (to be mentioned directly) the appraised valuations. The payment in bonds of this limited class of agrarian claims was not to constitute a precedent for any future expropriations; and other types of existing, disputed agrarian claims were to be settled by the general claims commission. This settlement in principle was an acceptance of the Mexican argument that the emergency nature of the appropriations justified in some cases the particular form of payment, the only form immediately possible.

Finally, in the Bucareli Conferences, the Mexican spokesmen agreed that their government, when recognized, would negotiate two claims conventions for the settlement of all outstanding claims between the two governments: one, a general claims commission for claims accumulating since the last liquidation by the mixed commission of 1868; the other, a special claims convention for claims arising out of the Revolution, 1910-1920. The separation of the claims into two classes implied that they were susceptible of separate treatment.

On the basis of this understanding the United States formally recog-

ing out works of exploitation or exploration of the subsoil, and in cases where from the contract relative to the subsoil it appears that the grantors fixed and received a price higher than would have been paid for the surface of the land because it was purchased for the purpose of looking for oil and exploiting same if found; and, in general, performing or doing any other positive act, or manifesting an intention of a character similar to those heretofore described." The exchanges are printed in *Proceedings of the United States-Mexican Commission Convened at Mexico City, May 14, 1923* (Washington, G.P.O., 1925), p. 47.

nized (August 31, 1923) the Government of Mexico, *de jure,* under the presidency of General Obregón.

The claims conventions were quickly negotiated and ratified. British, French, and other foreign recognition followed. The other powers made similar claims conventions with Mexico. When a revolution broke out in the north against the established Mexican Government, the United States saved it by selling, on deferred payment, munitions to the constituted authorities.

The long years of controversy between the United States and Mexico appeared, thanks to the inveterate forbearance and persistent patience of the stronger nation, at last well on the way to a satisfactory settlement. But when in 1925 the Mexican Congress enacted permanent legislation for the application of the petroleum and agrarian reforms of the Constitution of 1917, hitherto embodied only in temporary decrees, further controversy immediately ensued. Secretary of State Frank B. Kellogg, in the Administration of President Coolidge, saw in these laws a violation of the Bucareli understandings. The Secretary made it clear in a public manner, as this legislation impended, that the United States would continue to support the Mexican Government against revolutionary movements only so long as it protected American lives and American rights and complied with its international engagements and duties. When the laws were passed he made public an *aide-memoire* to the Mexican Ambassador (November 17, 1925) in which he referred to clouds gathering on the horizon of friendship. It was a few months after this that Mexico interfered in American policy in Nicaragua by shipping munitions to the insurrectionists there.[1]

The new Mexican laws [2] violated the Bucareli understandings and emphasized the wisdom of Secretary Hughes's original preference for treaty guaranties. They required, under pain of forfeiture, all foreign owners of petroleum lands on which positive acts of exploitation had taken place before 1917, to confirm their holdings by fifty-year licenses to exploit, renewable upon expiration provided the licensee had observed the terms of the concession. They defined the "positive act" much more narrowly than the Bucareli definition. They omitted reference to previous owners who had not performed a positive act. They seemed to

[1] See above, p. 66.

[2] C. W. Hackett prints an English translation of these laws in the appendix to his pamphlet on *The Mexican Revolution and the United States, 1910-1926* (World Peace Foundation Pamphlets, IX, No. 5, Boston, 1926).

apply only to individual foreign nationals, and not to corporations at all. They required a "Calvo clause" for all licenses.

To the protests which followed, the newly elected (1924) Calles Government, which had succeeded Obregón by orderly constitutional process, replied that the promises made in the Bucareli Conferences were not binding on the Mexican Congress—exactly what Secretary Hughes had feared. The diplomatic discussions came to a deadlock. Most of the American oil corporations meanwhile had refrained from applying for concessions under these conditions, and were, consequently, in danger of having their properties utterly lost by the contingencies of the protested laws. The Mexican Government made no step, however, to execute the annulments, which would have taken effect January 1, 1927; and in November of that year the Supreme Court of Mexico declared unconstitutional the provisions of the act which limited to a period of years the confirmed titles of subsoil rights in lands acquired before 1917 on which a positive act of exploitation had taken place before that date. President Calles thereupon recommended to Congress amendments to the oil legislation, in conformity to this decision, which were duly enacted in January, 1928. The new amendments removed one issue. New regulations for the administration of the oil laws defined a "positive act," now in language identical with that of the Bucareli protocols, dropped the requirement for the Calvo clause, and recognized the position of foreign corporations as well as individuals.[1] These new interpretations and changes satisfied the Government of the United States, and the Department of State issued (March 28, 1928) a statement that, with this basis, future questions could be adjusted through the Mexican administrative departments and the Mexican courts.

In the compromise which thus set at rest the tangled issue both governments had achieved in substantial degree their practical aims: the United States had secured the substance for which it contended, but the Government of Mexico had succeeded in protecting the full integrity of its constitutional and legislative independence; it did so only by refraining from exercising them in an unreasonable way.

Instrumental in achieving the administrative features of this compromise was Ambassador Dwight W. Morrow, a personal friend whom President Coolidge sent to Mexico in October, 1927, after the Senate unanimously had passed (January 25, 1927) a resolution for the arbitra-

---

[1] In one respect these new laws and regulations left unfilled one of the Bucareli promises: they reserved no preferential rights for owners of petroleum lands who had made no positive act of exploitation before May 1, 1917.

tion, if necessary, of the outstanding issues with Mexico. Ambassador Morrow succeeded in restoring an abundant measure of good will between the estranged peoples and governments. He showed a sympathetic understanding of Mexico's heavy problems, which President Coolidge shared, and he was resourceful in his manner of turning public opinion to friendly appreciation. One of the spectacular devices thus promoted was the exchange of nonstop aerial flights between the two capitals by American and by Mexican aviators. The American hero of the air, Charles A. Lindbergh, led off in this pleasing gesture, and, as every schoolgirl in both countries then knew, ended up by marrying one of Mr. Morrow's talented daughters.

The portion of controversy which had been shelved for settlement by the mixed claims commission had an even more labored history. The general mixed claims commission met in 1924, composed of one Mexican commissioner, one United States commissioner, and a neutral umpire. After repeated extensions of its conventional lifetime it lapsed in 1931, after having adjudicated only 148 claims out of a total of 3,617 filed by both governments,[1] to be renewed again in 1932, subject to the exclusion from it of all agrarian claims.

The administration of President Franklin D. Roosevelt made an executive agreement (April 24, 1934), which created new machinery for expediting the adjudication of the remaining claims within two years, by commissioners, respectively, of the two governments; in case of disagreement of the two commissioners meeting together later to compare their decisions, the disagreed cases were to be finally settled by a special convention still later to be negotiated by both governments. This could dispose of the disputed claims (together with the agreed awards) *en bloc*, or refer them to an umpire under terms to be fixed in the future convention. Certain agrarian claims which it had been agreed previously to submit to this commission were reserved for further discussion. Thus the two governments speeded up the grinding of the general claims mill without definitely agreeing upon a means of payment of the final awards.

The special (revolutionary) claims commission met first in Mexico City in 1924. At the proposal of the United States as a gesture of good will the two governments chose a Latin-American umpire for the third com-

---

[1] The claims filed before 1931 were:

	Number	Amount
United States against Mexico	2,781	$513,649,267.17
Mexico against the United States	836	245,158,395.32

Dunn, *op. cit.*, p. 404.

missioner. The commission's labors were contentious and consequently slow, and its lifetime was repeatedly extended by mutual agreement until it expired in 1931. Only two groups of claims went before this commission in its seven years' history: the Santa Ysabel massacre claims, and one other individual death claim, selected because of their flagrant nature. In both instances the umpire threw out the claims on the ground that the United States could not show that the Mexican Government had not taken reasonable steps to suppress Villa (who was later granted amnesty and pardon by the Carranza Government). It seems to have been a mistake to suggest a Latin-American national for such an umpire, in view of implications of such claims for countries in which revolutions are frequent: if the cases had been presented to a tribunal of the Hague Court presumably they would have been acted on with more celerity and different interpretations of justice.

After the failure of the commissions to pass on the mass of claims, a settlement in this manner was no longer expedient.

It had been only an executive agreement which had expedited the final settlement of the general claims, a part of which were of Mexican citizens against the United States. A formal treaty, signed the same day (ratified, 1935), arranged a settlement *en bloc* of the special (revolutionary) claims, all of which were of the citizens of the United States against Mexico. That government now agreed to pay to the United States, in total quittance of all this class of unsettled claims, a sum of money equal to the proportion of the total in money of final awards to the total in money of original claims as decided by all the other mixed claims commissions then at work with Mexico adjudicating the claims of European governments (Belgium, Great Britain, Italy, and Spain). Mexico agreed to pay for the American claims in installments of $500,000 per annum, beginning January 1, 1935, until paid.[1] The expenses to the United States for its share of the maintenance of the two mixed claims commissions were $350,000 a year from 1927 to 1932: total, 1925-1932, $2,574,730.[2] In this very general way, after much negotiation and much patience, the United States secured for its nationals a treatment approximately equal to that of the nationals of European claimant governments; and payment began in small and insufficient annual

[1] The first and second installments of $500,000 were paid promptly in January, 1935, and January, 1936.

[2] A. H. Feller has presented a thorough analysis of the history and procedure of all these mixed claims commissions, including the two Mexican-American ones, in *The Mexican Claims Commissions, 1923-1934, a Study in the Law and Procedure of International Commissions* (New York, 1935).

driblets.[1] Considering the obligations of Mexico also to other governments and its foreign bonded debt, this was perhaps all that could
be expected. It was generous and fair to Mexico, and exemplary.

The United States Government kept its hands off the question of
Mexico's bonded indebtedness to foreign nationals, including American
citizens. Representatives of the foreign bondholders, organized through
an international committee of bankers, treated directly with the Mexican
treasury. The total foreign debt of Mexico (including certain internal
bonds mostly held by foreigners, and railroad bonds guaranteed by the
Mexican Government, but exclusive of obligations for claims) was in
1922 about 1,000,000,000 *pesos*[2] bonded in various foreign currencies.
Arrears of interest added 40 per cent. Repeated attempts to reach agreements to refund proved abortive. Between 1922 and 1928, however, the
Mexican Government remitted $43,000,000, then stopped. In 1943 it
began to make current interest payments on the direct debt, after an
offer to discharge back interest with a token payment and pay off the
principal in *pesos* for dollars by 1968, including future interest in *pesos*
at 4.35 per cent. A somewhat similar offer was made in 1946 to holders
of Mexican railroad bonds under a schedule to extend to 1974, and eventually accepted by a majority of the bondholders. The hands-off policy
enabled the Mexican Government to re-establish itself financially at
the expense of American bondholders.

Because the policy of the United States has been not to support diplomatically the collection of contract debts due to its nationals by defaulted
foreign states, Mexico's vast defaults thus have been excluded from the
area of diplomatic controversy. Therefore we can say that by December,
1936, Mexican-American relations had been adjusted, except for the
claims arising from expropriations of agrarian lands owned by citizens
of the United States. Even on this score the Mexican Government had
slowed down its program of landtakings. It was in December, 1936,
that the United States signed at Buenos Aires, at the special inter-
American Conference for the Maintenance of Peace, the Additional
Protocol Relative to Nonintervention (additional to the Montevideo
multilateral Treaty on the Rights and Duties of States, of 1933): "The

[1] If the lump sum proves to be one tenth of the total claimed, or $42,130,000, it
would take over eighty-one years to pay off at $500,000 per year, exclusive of interest.
The awards of the mixed commissions of Mexico with other foreign nations indicate,
however, an average of about 3 per cent of the amount claimed.

[2] Throughout 1941 a *peso* equaled about 20 cents United States currency. When
the bonds were issued it was near par, approximately 50 cents. In 1950 the *peso* was
worth approximately 11.50 cents.

High Contracting Parties declare inadmissible the intervention of any one of them, directly or indirectly, and for whatever reason, in the internal or external affairs of any other of the Parties."

Just as soon as this Protocol had been ratified by the two nations, the newly elected (1934) radical government of President Lázaro Cárdenas launched a thoroughgoing expropriation of agricultural and grazing properties remaining in the possession of United States nationals. There was no longer even a pretense of paying for these new takings for communal agrarian reform—the *ejido* system [1]—and the older expropriations, since 1927, remained uncompensated.

Resting for political support on the aggressively organized labor organizations of Mexico, the Cárdenas Government next passed labor laws that bore down destructively on the operations of foreign corporations. Tacitly it encouraged the labor unions to strike against the foreign-owned concerns for heavy increases in pay, shorter hours, double pay for overtime, automobiles and chauffeurs for labor leaders, labor halls for union meetings, holidays, vacations and vacation travel for employees and families (numerously construed), and an increasing control over books and management. These demands abruptly drove up the costs of the foreign corporations, particularly the petroleum companies (American, British, and Dutch) which had been operating under the guaranties of 1928, which said nothing about labor.

One suspects that the purpose of the labor demands was not only a rapid rise in the standard of living for the Mexican workers (such of them as were lucky enough to be employed by the foreigners, who notoriously afforded higher pay and better working conditions than most Mexican employers), but also to make it financially impossible for the foreign oil companies—and after them foreign mining and other properties—to operate, so that the Mexican Government might then take them over by default.

New legislation had opened the way for this program. A federal expropriation law of November 13, 1936, had provided for the expropriation of private property of public utility "to satisfy collective necessities in case of war or interior upheaval." To make sure that the courts would interpret the new laws to suit his purpose, President Cárdenas put through Congress a law reducing the life tenure of the judges of the Supreme Court to the tenure of the President who appointed them.

[1] Eyler N. Simpson published a highly sympathetic, and not unbiased, study of *The Ejido, Mexico's Way Out* (University of North Carolina Press, 1937), with a commendatory introduction by Mexico's principal diplomatic dialectician, Ramón Beteta.

The judges now became creatures of the executive, and the executive, if only because of the Buenos Aires Protocol, no longer had any reason to fear intervention by the United States, direct or indirect, or for whatever reason, to protect its nationals against denials of justice in American republics. All that the United States could resort to was diplomatic expostulation. There were some Latin Americans who claimed that even this was "indirect intervention"! There were, of course, various domestic resources of economic retaliation against Mexico, but this was not much to be feared because economically the United States depended on Mexico more than Mexico depended on the United States. It would also have been politically dangerous to hold Mexico too categorically to account, because organized labor in the United States—on which the New Deal depended heavily for its political existence—sympathized with the demands of organized labor in Mexico as championed by the Cárdenas Government. Mexican and American labor organizations and leaders fraternized conspicuously in the capitals of both countries. Labor had now become a factor to be reckoned with in American diplomacy.

The expropriation issue came to a head when President Cárdenas ordered (March 18, 1938) properties of the foreign-owned petroleum corporations to be taken over by the state after they had failed to accept the award of a Mexican labor board, confirmed by the Supreme Court of Mexico following a strike of the petroleum workers. The award called not only for drastic increases in pay retroactive to the beginning of the strike (26,000,000 *pesos*) and the radical easement of work—terms which the Mexican Government itself proved unable to meet when it took over operation of the properties. It also enjoined a degree of control by the union over books and management. The companies proved not unwilling to accept the other terms, but stuck at the intrusion of labor unions into management. The properties thus expropriated were valued by the owners at approximately $450,000,000 of which $200,000,000 was American-owned. Mexico contended they were worth a total of $262,000,000, and advanced various ingenious devaluations and set-offs to bring American properties down to less than $50,000,000.[1]

[1] There is an enormous literature, documentary and secondary, on this controversy. The American companies have published the memoranda stating their grievances with appendixes of official documents, in the following publications: *Mexico Labor Controversy, 1936-1938* (no place or date of publication); *Mexico, Expropriation of Foreign-owned Oil Properties,* 1938, Huasteca Petroleum Co., "printed in the U. S. A.," preface dated, 1938; *The Reply to Mexico* (Standard Oil Co. [N. J.], New York, 1940); *Present Status of the Mexican Oil "Expropriations," 1940* (Standard Oil Co. [N. J.], New York, 1940). *Donald R. Richberg's Story, The Mexican Oil Seizures (circa 1939)* digests these data of the oil companies into an appeal to public opinion for justice to the expropriated

The United States never contended that the Mexican or any other government had no right to expropriate property, including foreign property, for purposes of internal reform. What it objected to was expropriation without compensation. That meant confiscation. In a series of protests,[1] Secretary Hull insisted that "recognized rules of law and equity require the prompt payment of just compensation for property that may be expropriated." But the Department of State was quicker to insist on settlement for the agrarian takings, "farms," from individual United States citizens than for the expropriation of petroleum property from United States nationals in the form of corporations. The word "farm" was politically popular among the electorate in the United States at this time; the word "corporation" was politically hateful.

Mexico agreed in 1938 to pay for the expropriated agrarian properties, estimated by the owners as worth a total of approximately $10,000,000, after their value had been fixed before June 1, 1939, by a mixed commission composed of one representative of each government. In cases where the commission disagreed, an umpire, to be designated by the permanent commission established by the Gondra Conciliation Convention,[2] was to decide within two months after his intervention had been requested. Meanwhile the Mexican Government agreed to pay $1,000,000 (U. S.) in May, 1939; after that at least $1,000,000 (U. S.) on each June 30 until the awards had been paid off. In agreeing to this settlement, the Mexican Government asserted that it should not constitute a precedent "in any case, nor for any reason"—that is, it agreed to adjudicate and pay the agrarian claims, nothing else.

The United States Government did not abandon the petroleum claims, but it did not press them decisively until after the Presidential elections of 1940 in the United States and in Mexico. In the United States President Roosevelt was re-elected for a third consecutive term; in Mexico a middle-of-the-road government under President Avila Camacho came into power. Meanwhile the Second World War had broken out and the neu-

owners. Richberg was formerly NRA Administrator and Co-ordinator in the Roosevelt Administration whom the companies employed as counsel. Roscoe B. Gaither, not a representative in any way of the companies, has published a revealing account of the legal injustice of *Expropriation in Mexico: The Facts and the Law* (New York, 1940). Josef L. Kunz has an objective analysis, in international law of *The Mexican Expropriations* (New York University School of Law, Contemporary Pamphlets, 1940, Series 5, No. 1).

[1] *Compensation for American-owned Lands Expropriated in Mexico: Full Text of Official Notes, July 21, 1938, to November 12, 1938.* In English with Spanish translation, Department of State Publication 288, Inter-American Series 16.

[2] See below, p. 290.

trality of the United States had collapsed. A treaty between the United States and Mexico, signed April 1, 1941 (ratifications exchanged April 25, 1941), provided for the reciprocal passage, refueling, and supplying "for the duration of the present state of possible threats of armed aggression against either of them" of military airplanes and seaplanes in the territory of each party, a great advantage for the United States in communications with Panama. This testified to the cordiality existing between the two governments in the face of dangers from the Old World. On November 19, 1941, less than a month before the Japanese attack on Pearl Harbor, the Department of State announced "with deep satisfaction" that a comprehensive agreement had been reached with the Mexican Government on various matters,[1] including the expropriated petroleum properties.

As to the expropriated petroleum properties, an exchange of notes of that date provided for a mixed commission of experts, one from each government, to determine the just compensation to be paid the American owners for their properties and rights and interests. Simultaneously with the exchange of notes the Mexican Government made a cash deposit of $9,000,000 on account of the compensation to be paid to the affected American companies. If the American and Mexican experts agreed on the amount to be paid, they were to render a joint report to their two governments within five months. They promptly agreed. Their joint report, April 17, 1942, stated:

Expropriation, and the exercise of the right of eminent domain, under the respective constitutions and laws of Mexico and the United States, are a recognized feature of the sovereignty of all states.

Accordingly they awarded the sum of $23,995,991 (U. S.) covering all elements of tangible and intangible value.[2] They "recommended" that the balance due by the Mexican Government for the payment of the sum awarded be paid as follows: one third on July 1, 1942, and the balance in five equal annual installments, the debt to carry 3-per-cent interest.

By a claims convention of the same date, November 19, 1941 (ratifications exchanged April 2, 1942), the Mexican Government agreed to pay to the United States the sum of $40,000,000 (U. S.) in full settlement

[1] Multigraphed *Press Release* No. 555 (November 19, 1941) of the Department of State, with the text of exchange of notes of November 19, 1941, for settlement of expropriated petroleum properties.
[2] Department of State *Press Release,* No. 165 (April 18, 1942).

of other outstanding property claims, including the hitherto unsettled general claims, and the agrarian claims on which $3,000,000 had been paid to date on claims arising between August 30, 1927, and October 7, 1940. Payments were to be made as follows: $3,000,000 on account at the exchange of ratifications of the convention (paid on April 2, 1942), the balance of $34,000,000 to be liquidated in annual payments of $2,500,000 beginning in 1942.[1]

The dangerous status of American negotiations with Japan impelled Secretary of State Cordell Hull to hasten this general settlement with Mexico.[2] Any sacrifice of just interests of the property owners was therefore for the benefit of the United States and its people at large.

Coincidentally the two Governments announced their decision to negotiate a reciprocal trade agreement; the United States Treasury Department agreed to co-operate with the Mexican Government and Bank of Mexico to help stabilize the *peso* by purchases with dollars, and announced its "willingness" to purchase newly mined Mexican silver on a basis similar to that under which purchases were made prior to 1938. Finally, the official Export-Import Bank of the United States opened a credit to the Mexican Government by purchase of "certain" highway bonds of the Mexican Government as a means of expediting construction work in Mexico which incidentally would advance toward ultimate completion the projected Inter-American Highway. The official bank took up these bonds which no privately owned bank would think of buying, after Mexico's wholesale repudiation of her obligations. The Export-Import Bank even announced its readiness to consider sympathetically other requests for credits, to be guaranteed by the Mexican Government, for development in Mexico.

Such was the design for Mexican-American harmony at the end of 1941. After Pearl Harbor, Mexico established a joint defense commission with the United States, and declared war on Germany, Japan, and Italy in the darkest days of the Second World War, June 1, 1942. Mexico welcomed the declaration known as the Act of Chapultepec for reciprocal assistance and American solidarity during the war, signed in her capital (March 6, 1945), and was one of the first to ratify the inter-American treaty, the Pact of Rio de Janeiro (September 2, 1947), for the future defense of the Western Hemisphere.[3]

[1] The eighth installment was regularly paid in November, 1949.
[2] *Memoirs of Cordell Hull* (2 vols., New York, 1948), p. 1141.
[3] See below, Chapter 14.

During the Second World War Mexico experienced the golden flood of lend-lease ($38,639,450.63 to Mexico out of $491,456,432.64 to all Latin America during hostilities) [1] and the rising tide of inflation that bathed all Latin America, and greatly profited from the prodigious purchases of belligerent requirements. The United States Government extended loans on easy terms to Mexico, through the Export-Import Bank totaling $18,900,000 for the development of Mexican resources and to ease adjustments to war economy; and since the war a total of $73,000,000 [2] plus post-V–J Day lend-lease of $600,000 and outright gifts: $7,500,000 "grants-in-aid" from the United States Office of Inter-American Affairs during the war, and $4,800,000 since—for food supply, health and sanitation, and education; and $45,000,000 (to April 1, 1949) to help stamp out the hoof-and-mouth disease (Mexico contributed about $2,000,000) before it spread to American herds north of the border. These government loans and gifts poured forth lavishly to the neighbor south of the Rio Grande whose defaults on her foreign debt to private American citizens and corporations and wholesale expropriations (with meager compensation) of their private property trapped in Mexico, had made it difficult for that Republic any more to borrow in the money markets of the world. Such is the new "dollar diplomacy"!

Mexico successfully negotiated a water treaty (signed February 3, 1944, ratifications exchanged November 18, 1945) securing an equitable share, to say the least, of water flowing down from the United States in international rivers (Rio Grande, Colorado, Tiajuana) to water the arid regions of her northern states. This important treaty, supplementing earlier conventions of 1889 and 1905, placed the common waterways and waterworks under the regulation and administration of an International Boundary Commission, United States and Mexico, but without any independent arbitral function.

At the mid-century mark no serious issue existed between the United States and Mexico. The only dispute remaining unsettled was the long-standing legal question of sovereignty over the Chamizal area left uncertain by the meandering of the Rio Grande River.[3] By ratifying the

[1] *Twenty-fifth Report to Congress on Lend-Lease Operations* (State Department Publication 3064, Washington, 1948).

[2] To end of fiscal year, June 1, 1948. See *Fuel Investigation, Mexican Petroleum,* 80th Cong. H. Rept. 2470 (Washington, G.P.O., 1949), p. 86.

[3] Involved is a tract of 600 acres of land near El Paso, Texas, left in dispute by the sudden shift of the Rio Grande boundary river. The United States refused to accept an arbitral award of 1910 which "split the difference" instead of awarding the whole tract to Mexico or to the United States, as required by the Arbitration Treaty.

United Nations Charter and the International Court of Justice both nations have bound themselves, along with the obligations of the inter-American peace pacts, to the peaceful settlement of their disputes, including international adjudication of all legal questions.[1]

[1] Both the United States and Mexico have accepted as compulsory *ipso facto* the obligation to submit any legal question to the decision of the International Court of Justice, but both have reserved therefrom any dispute which in their opinion involve questions of domestic jurisdiction.

6

Africa and Europe

In the period of the twentieth century, before 1914, American foreign policy tended to follow the geographical distinctions emphasized by Captain Mahan: predominance in the Caribbean and its periphery; "co-operation"—that is, participation in the politics of the Far East; abstention from European political questions. Excluding non-American and non-Asiatic questions, one is impressed by the routine character of American diplomatic contacts with the European countries. As long as the question of neutral rights remained asleep the United States could keep profitably aloof from all European politics and generally did so. Aside from those affairs of the Pacific and the Far East, and of Latin America, described in the previous four chapters—and with the one exception of Morocco and the Algeciras Conference, 1905-1906—the diplomacy of the United States in Europe was limited to the maintenance of friendly commercial and cultural contact, the technical problems of citizenship and immigration, and participation in multilateral international conferences of a humanitarian rather than a political nature.

This type of international conference came into existence during the last half of the nineteenth century. The growing complexity of civilization rapidly increased their number until now there are several international gatherings at work every day of the year. The United States began the practice of attending such conferences in 1875, when it signed and ratified an international convention for regulation of weights and measures. In 1882 it formally adhered to the Geneva Convention of 1864 for bettering the condition of the wounded in time of war. The Senate between 1883 and 1898 ratified five multilateral treaties signed in European international conferences by representatives of the United States: they dealt with protection of industrial property, submarine cables, exchange of official publications, repression of the African slave trade, and the publication of customs tariffs. After the Cuban-

101

Spanish-American War these contacts and engagements multiplied: The two Hague Peace Conferences of 1899 and 1907, and the London Naval Conference of 1909; and a long series of Pan-American conferences which will receive attention in another chapter. There was a great increase in nonpolitical conferences in the period 1898-1914, sixteen in all, producing treaties signed and ratified by the United States, a multifarious nexus: sanitation, traffic in white women, hospitals, institute of agriculture, amelioration of wounded in the field in time of war, public health, importation of spirituous liquor into Africa, pharmacopoeial formulas, etc. The First World War interrupted the good work; since then, of course, these gatherings have taken place very largely under the auspices of the League of Nations, with the United States sitting in *ad hoc,* and the United Nations, with the United States an active and leading member.

These conferences were nonpolitical. The unnecessary contact of the United States with the opposing systems of European political alliances came through its Far Eastern diplomacy and its touch with the Moroccan Question.

Mention of Morocco brings up the subject of Africa. The American people had manifested a passive interest, mostly of a humanitarian and scientific nature, in the opening of that continent to civilization and commerce, but had assumed no political responsibility in the European partitions of its vast domains and had engaged in no participation in the imperialistic rivalries of the powers for dominion there.

The origin of American interest in Africa was the establishment by the American Colonization Society, with the assistance of the United States navy, of a colony of freed Negroes in Liberia, on the coast of Guinea in 1821. All told about 15,000 Negroes were transported thither by 1870. This is the only overseas colony which the United States ever has begotten. It continued to be a receiving station for free American Negro immigrants sent out by the Society and of captured Africans who had been liberated from condemned slavers by the United States courts. Theoretically the Colonization Society and the United States Government had distinct functions, the one tutelary, the other mildly protective, but actually agents of each worked together and frequently were one and the same person. The colonial government occupied an anomalous position in Africa; it was not itself a sovereign state nor would the United States assume a formal protectorate over it. It continued to be a convenient distant dumping place for American free Negroes and liberated Africans. European authorities in adjacent areas, such as the British in Sierra Leone, would not respect the colonial officials; to secure a more regular place in the society of nations a republic declared itself in Liberia in 1847, and was recognized as such soon afterward by the principal European states but not by the United States, its parent. Though the United States expressed "sympathy and solicitude" for Liberia, the slavery question in American politics prevented any recognition of Negro republics until 1862 after the Southern states had seceded from the Union; then diplomatic relations were established with Liberia, as with Haiti (1864), and the Dominican Republic (1866).

American Negro emigration to that African shore slackened with the passing of the sailing ship. The "scramble for Africa" in 1884 made the rival powers cast covetous eyes on Liberia. Though they at least respected its independence, Great Britain from the west and France from the east and north picked boundary disputes, and by settling them through aggressive diplomacy successively cut down the area of the black republic into a small coastal enclave. If the United States had unwisely desired to plunge into the scramble for Africa, a Liberian protectorate—eagerly solicited—would have offered a jumping-off place.

Though no protectorate was ever admitted to exist, the United States repeatedly has manifested a benevolent and active interest in the perpetuation of Liberian independence. In 1880 the Department of State was disposed to maintain that "peculiar relations" existed between Liberia and the United States, which was "prepared to take every proper step to maintain them"; and Secretary Hay declared in 1899, that "our position in reference to the citizens of Liberia is such that we could not be justified in regarding with indifference any attempt to oppress them or deprive them of their independence."[1] When Germany threatened to interfere in Liberia, Hay stated the "grave concern" which the United States would have at any threat to the liberty or the independence of the African republic. He was also prepared, in the same year, 1899, to say the same to France, if possible to say it in co-operation with Great Britain; and he endeavored to prevent the granting by Liberia of any monopolistic concessions to foreign powers.[2] But at no time would the United States acknowledge legitimate paternity of this foundling which it had left on Africa's doorstep.

The Liberian Government, fearful of its remaining territory being absorbed by Great Britain and France, in 1908 sent a commission to

[1] Moore, *Digest, op. cit.,* V, pp. 762-768.
[2] Dennis, *Adventures, op. cit.,* pp. 437-441.

the United States to seek a treaty which would guarantee the independence and territorial integrity of the republic. Incompetent policing and management of finances were inviting foreign intervention. President Roosevelt dispatched a commission of investigation. It recommended [1] a protectorate similar to that previously established over the Dominican Republic, and later over Haiti. With proper prudence, the United States declined a protectorate; with the rueful exception of the Philippine Islands, American imperialism had not yet ventured, even for philanthropic purposes, into regions in which the Republic has no vital interests and which it could not defend, whether in Liberia or in Turkish Armenia. [2] Instead the United States co-operated with an international commission which helped to straighten out the financial affairs of Liberia and to strengthen her internal condition, with an American citizen as financial adviser. The fact that Liberia has been able to claim the United States as a godparent, and that the United States has appealed to the world to lend a friendly sympathy to that infirm and dubious little state, undoubtedly helped to sustain its shaky independence.

Serious charges of slave traffic in native Negroes within Liberia (founded by liberated slaves!) within recent years have supported impressive arguments for European intervention. [3]

Southeastwardly from Liberia, around the bight of Guinea, lie the vast regions of equatorial Africa, drained to the westward by the mighty river Congo. An Anglo-American journalist-explorer, H. M. Stanley, who

[1] Roland P. Falkner, chairman of the commission, wrote an informative summary of the relations of "The United States and Liberia," *Am. Jour. International Law,* IV (1910), 529-545. The commission's report is in Senate Doc. 457, 61st Cong., 2d Session, March 25, 1910.

[2] The shocking and widespread massacre of thousands of Armenian men, women, and children by the Turks, in 1894 and 1895, elicited expansive sympathy in the United States and Great Britain, coupled with demands from humanitarian groups and leaders to intervene. Secretary Olney, speaking for the Cleveland Administration in answer to a British request whether it would join in any action with regard to Turkey, said that "if England should now seriously set about putting the Armenian charnel-house in order, there can be little doubt that the United States would consider the moment opportune for vigorous exertion on behalf of American citizens and interests in Turkey . . . its attitude would morally and materially strengthen the hands of England." (Dennis, *Adventures, op. cit.,* p. 450). This was too vague an assurance to engage Great Britain in intervention. The Cuban crisis soon crowded Armenia out of American attention, and the Boer War and succeeding international complications monopolized British concern. As the prospect of intervention disappeared the revolutionary plottings of the Armenians subsided and the bloody Turkish reprisals abated.

American diplomacy was active from 1900 to 1914 in securing equal rights and treatment among foreigners, for missionaries, schools, traveling nationals in the Ottoman Empire, the collection of small claims, and the protection of neutral interests during the Balkan Wars, but wisely steered clear of any political commitments in the Near East.

[3] See "Note on the Problems of Liberia," pp. 118-120.

in 1870 set out under the auspices of the New York *Herald* to the relief of the celebrated English missionary-explorer, David Livingstone, had been the first person to make known to the world (1874-1878) the true nature of the Congo Basin. At that time most of the "dark continent" was still unpartitioned—only four European powers claimed any dominion: Great Britain in the Cape Colony region, and on the west coast at Gambia, Sierra Leone, the Gold Coast, and Lagos—old coastal stations for the abolished maritime slave trade; France in Algeria, and on the west coast at the Senegal and Gabon rivers, also old slaving coasts; Spain opposite Gibraltar, with bits of shore along the west coast of Morocco, and trading stations along the Gold Coast; and Portugal, at Angola and Mozambique as well as her ineffective claims from the Congo River south along the Atlantic shoreline shadowing away from old trading posts on that coast. The remainder of Africa had remained unclaimed by any power. Not until 1881 did France take Tunis, and, 1882, did Great Britain occupy Egypt.

King Leopold II of Belgium saw in the newly discovered regions of the Congo an opportunity for building up a great personal fortune and ultimately a colonial empire for Belgium. Capitalizing the world-wide interest aroused by the exploits of Livingstone and Stanley, he organized the International African Association in 1876, with branches in all the principal countries of Europe and America, to discuss ways and means of opening equatorial Africa to civilization. Out of this quickly developed the International Association of the Congo. The Association engaged explorers, among them Stanley, to establish a line of stations to help open the country, to assist in abolishing the slave trade, and to make treaties with the native chieftains. The treaties placed the natives under the patronage and protection of the Association, but jurists debated its power to assume sovereignty without some sort of international mandate or agreement. Stimulated by these activities Portugal, Great Britain, and France [1] began advancing claims from the borders of the Congo Basin toward the river.

The territorial claims of the organization were facing extinction when (April 22, 1884), the United States Government recognized the flag of the Association as "that of a friendly Government," and negotiated a treaty of friendship and commerce. The preservation of the Association

---

[1] The French Committee of the International African Association sent out an explorer, de Brazza, who in 1880 made treaties with chieftains not in the name of the Association, but of France. Thus France established claims to the north bank of the Congo far into the interior.

offered the least possibility of discrimination against American trade.[1] France and Germany followed suit. We are now in a feverish and decisive year in the history of Africa. Germany, viewing the vacant places of the earth as about to pass under sovereignty of one or another power, had suddenly become a competitor for colonial empire, and thus precipitated the European scramble for Africa in which the powers quickly appropriated the remaining empty portions. Bismarck, fearing some one or more powers might lay hold of the Congo country to the exclusion of German trade, invited them (October, 1884) to a conference at Berlin to agree on the following principles: 1. freedom of commerce in the basin and mouths of the Congo; 2. freedom of navigation of the Congo and Niger rivers; 3. definition of formalities to be observed so that new occupations on the coast of Africa might be considered effective.

By this announcement and by occupation of coastal districts in Togoland, Kamerun, and also in East Africa and Southwest Africa, did Germany proclaim to the world her determination to be considered in any partition of the remaining unappropriated parts of the continent. The powers, including the United States, accepted the invitation to the conference at Berlin. Secretary of State Frederick T. Frelinghuysen directed the United States Minister to Germany, John A. Kasson, to accept the invitation with the understanding that the discussion be strictly limited to the three heads mentioned, without assuming to decide any territorial claims, and that all arrangements reached be *ad referendum* so far as the United States was concerned. This caution was due to an unwillingness to depart from the traditional policy of noninterference in European questions; yet in the same instructions the Secretary indicated his preference for a neutralization of the Congo Basin, to be held in trust for the benefit of all peoples. Is this not the germ of the idea of international mandate for backward areas? Ironically enough, this great basin of equatorial Africa, Belgian after 1908, escaped any proposal of international mandate in 1919.

The Berlin Conference adopted a General Act which established freedom of commerce and navigation for all nations in the Congo Basin, both in time of war and of peace, outlawed the overland slave trade,[2] established freedom of religion and of proselyting for all faiths, defined freedom of navigation of the Niger River, drew up rules for *future* new

---

[1] Otto Graf zu Stolberg-Wernigerode, *Deutschland und die Vereinigten Staaten von Amerika im Zeitalter Bismarcks* (Berlin and Leipzig, 1933), pp. 223-231.

[2] The maritime slave trade had long since been declared piracy.

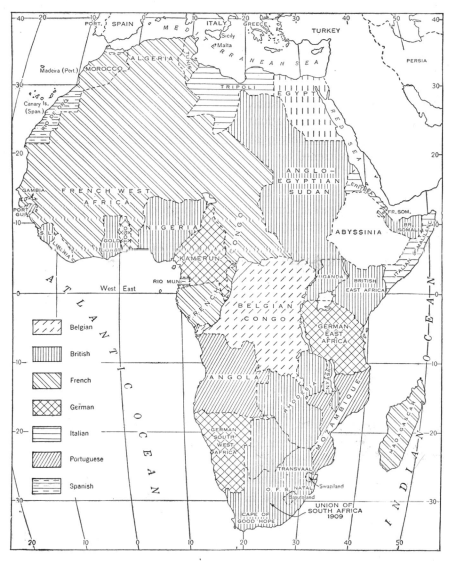

Map 2. Africa, 1914

coastal occupation of African territory (the coast had by now been nearly all occupied), and established an international commission (one delegate from each signatory) to execute the provisions of the Act. The commission had power to call upon warships of the signatory powers to enforce its execution, unless the commanders were instructed to the contrary, and to negotiate a loan for improvement of navigation. It is desirable to mention this commission, even though it never came into existence because of the refusal of any of the powers to assume any responsibility for guaranteeing its acts, because it displays the degree of international involvement contemplated by the Act.

The Conference ended by recognizing the International Association of the Congo as a sovereign state, thus giving it powers to exercise the rights as well as the obligations conferred on it by the Act, including that of a rather elaborately qualified neutrality.[1] Thus did an artificial new state, just welcomed by the United States, emerge full-fledged in the heart of Africa,[2] filling up a vacuum there which might have brought the powers of Europe into conflict. A series of bilateral treaties, including treaties between European powers with conflicting African territorial limits, fixed its frontiers. King Leopold, organizer of the Association which was now a state, proclaimed (May 29, 1885) the existence of the Congo Free State, and he became its separate sovereign, thus constituting an absolute monarchy under a personal union with Belgium, a vast appanage which the self-created monarch began to exploit, eventually to the horror of Christendom, for his own profit. Leopold devised the Congo Free State to go to Belgium after his death. As sovereign of the Congo he had become debtor for loans advanced from the Belgian treasury. The maladministration of the Congo, stimulating demands from the old treaty powers for another general conference, hastened reforms and also hastened annexation in 1908 after long negotiations between the two states. Europe eventually acquiesced in the transformation of Leopold's wretched political monstrosity, the Congo Free State,[3] into a Belgian colony.

The United States had never ratified the Berlin Act, as did the other powers, although it continued in treaty relations with the Congo Free State until its absorption by Belgium. President Cleveland had come into office immediately after the conclusion (February 26, 1885) of the Conference, and he refused to submit the Act to the Senate for advice. He reminded the country in his first annual message that the delegates

---

[1] The signatory powers engaged themselves to respect the neutrality of the territories, and parts of territories, belonging to the various powers *in the conventional area* as long as the duties of neutrality were observed. The conventional area, in which free trade applied no matter under what sovereignty, was much larger than the Congo Basin— a belt from coast to coast approximately the width of the most extreme latitudes of the Basin.

[2] Jesse S. Reeves has carefully described the establishment of the new state in *The International Beginnings of the Congo Free State* (Johns Hopkins University Studies, 12th Series, Nos. XI-XII, Baltimore, 1894).

[3] A. B. Keith, *The Belgian Congo and the Berlin Act* (Oxford, 1919).

of the United States had attended the Berlin Conference under the understanding that their part should be merely deliberative. Notwithstanding this specific reservation they had signed the Act, "thus making the United States appear, without reserve or qualification, as signatories to a joint international engagement imposing on the signers the conservation of the territorial integrity of distant regions where we have no established interests or control." [1] Cleveland's abstention from an "alliance" to enforce the European balance of power in Africa was a well-justified caution in line with the clear-cut definitions of American foreign policy. The President refused to sanction such a departure as twenty years later was to be made by executive action in Asia after the Expansionists of 1898 had entangled the United States in the European balance of power in that distant continent. When Belgium annexed the Congo in 1908 the United States was free to recognize the new régime, as it was in the case of Korea in 1910. It had assumed no such policy of preservation of the Open Door and territorial integrity as later were to become so embarrassing in China and Manchuria.

Another danger spot in Africa was Morocco. A "white man's land" nearest to Europe of any part of Africa, it was a region of small immediate but great future importance for European expansion. Only the fact that three powers had been rivals for its control had preserved the independence of that backward country under the corrupt, weak, and semibarbarous rule of the native Sultan, "his Sherifian Majesty." Great Britain was determined not to allow any power to ensconce itself in Morocco, lest a naval base might offset Gibraltar, and for fear that foreign political control might erect discriminations against the preponderant British trading interests (two thirds of the small Moroccan trade by 1880). The hostile incursion of turbulent Moroccan tribesmen across the unnatural Algerian frontier continually invited French intervention, and the fact that France had marked out Morocco for colonial expansion made her insistent that no other power should block her ambition in that direction. Spain also desired to keep foreign hands off Morocco: she did not care to be hemmed in by two French frontiers, north and south; she did not want Gibraltar supported by a British hinterland across the straits; she esteemed herself to have a "mission" in Morocco, by history, culture, tradition, and geography destined with Portugal and Gibraltar to pass eventually under Spanish sovereignty. So the Sultan of Morocco sat on his trembling throne and still commanded

[1] J. B. Moore, *Digest, op. cit.*, I, pp. 117-119.

with diminishing authority an independent but wretchedly misruled nation.

The sharpening of European imperialism in the late 1870's made the *status quo* more difficult to maintain in all North Africa, from the Red Sea to the Atlantic. The rivalry of the three powers and a drift of internal affairs toward anarchy brought Morocco to the threshold of foreign intervention in 1880.

We must remember constantly that the atrocious government of the country abundantly justified extraterritorial protection for foreigners sojourning there. But Morocco is an impressive example of how abuse of the rights of extraterritoriality can undermine the sovereignty and independence of a weak state on which powerful neighbors cast covetous eyes. Foreign nationals were able to take increasing numbers of natives under their extraterritorial protection. The American consul at Tangier was no exception to this, although no one accused his country of political ambitions in Northwest Africa. To end the threat of this practice to Moroccan independence, British diplomacy, which favored for reasons of policy the integrity of the Sherifian Empire, and Spanish diplomacy, which supported it also during the period of Spain's recovery from the prostration of her civil wars, called the Conference of Madrid in 1880. It was proposed to reach some agreement even by the adjustment of previous treaties which would end the abuse of extraterritorial protection to native Moroccans attached in loose ways or pretenses to foreign officials or merchants. France refused to make any concessions of treaty rights sufficient to permit this. Germany, anxious to draw French national energies away from Alsace-Lorraine toward colonial adventure, supported France. Though the powers agreed to a treaty at Madrid, it was inadequate to the purpose. The abuse of protection continued. Presently France took under her protection one of the potential pretenders to the throne of Morocco. Each of the powers with interests in the country now strove not to be outdone by rivals in the number and importance of protégés. The Sultan ceased to have control over thousands of his subjects, much to their comfort and satisfaction. The Madrid Conference nevertheless had served to bring the Moroccan Question within the purview of the European concert of powers; any attempt in the future by one or two powers to upset the *status quo* in Morocco could be a cause of legitimate grievance to the other conference powers, should any of them desire to make an issue of it.[1]

[1] Earl Fee Cruickshank has examined with great detail and multiarchival research the early phases of the Moroccan Question in his *Morocco at the Parting of the Ways; the Story of Native Protection to 1885* (University of Pennsylvania Press, 1935).

The United States, which was the only non-European government (aside from that of Morocco) to participate in the conference, ratified the Convention of Madrid without reservation.[1] Since it contained merely a definition of extraterritorial protection, and no provisions for international sanction, there was a minimum of political involvement therein, as contrasted with, say, the later Berlin Act of 1885 for the regulation of the Congo Basin. American political interests in Morocco were nil; commercial interests were as small as they could be. There was little likelihood of entanglement, so it would seem, in this treaty. But the fact that the United States had sat in with the European concert gave it a voice in Moroccan affairs; in a later day of world power an American President was persuaded to use this voice to speak in major European affairs.

In Theodore Roosevelt's Administration the Moroccan Question came up again, as an aftermath of the Anglo-French *entente* of 1904. In the general liquidation of colonial rivalry by which France and Great Britain drew together in the face of rising German power, Great Britain gave France a free hand to do whatever she wished in Morocco in return for a free hand similarly for Great Britain in Egypt. By secret articles Great Britain agreed to a partition of Morocco between France and Spain—this was in turn specified in a secret Franco-Spanish treaty which left to Spain, in any future partition, the narrow Rif strip opposite Gibraltar, most of the rest to France. By agreeing (1902) to future Italian control of Tripoli, France already had pledged Italy to the new trend of affairs in Morocco. The other treaty powers were not consulted about these arrangements. Germany had meanwhile built up an appreciable commercial interest in Morocco, and certainly had a right, as had the United States or Denmark, to be consulted in any modification of the treaty regulation of the Sherifian Empire. To the United States or Denmark it made little difference who controlled Morocco—the country in fact would be a better place to live in under the domination of almost any European power. To Germany Morocco came to be a *Machtfrage,* a question of power. To stand aside while that country was being arranged for partition would mean for Germany a loss of power and prestige in Europe. One of the putative advantages of the imperial system of government in Germany was its supposedly more effective control and conduct of foreign affairs. The Liberals in that Empire were now pointing out derisively that the diplomatists of the democratic countries, France

[1] The United States also ratified in 1865 a multilateral convention for the maintenance, under Moorish sovereignty, of a lighthouse on Cape Spartel.

and Great Britain, were outwitting the Wilhelmstrasse.[1] Prince von Bülow, the Chancellor, and his inherited adviser, Baron von Holstein, men who at first had reacted rather complacently to the new dispensation in Morocco, now resolved to make it a test of German power in Europe.

In her efforts to scotch the newly formed Anglo-French *entente cordiale* Germany succeeded in enticing the United States unprofitably into European affairs for Germany's purpose, but not, as calculated, to her ultimate advantage. Morocco afforded the opportunity. The United States was a signatory to the Madrid Convention and quite recently had intervened at Tangier in a spectacular way to release one Jon Perdicaris, an alleged American citizen, from bandits. On the eve of the Republican nominating convention in the summer of 1904, the notorious Riffian bandit Raisuli had kidnaped Perdicaris and his stepson, a British subject, from their villa three miles from Tangier. The Department of State made most vigorous representations to the Sherifian Government. American and British warships were rushed to Tangier. Three or four American marines were actually landed to protect the consulate and to guard Perdicaris's home. He was released on ransom (eventually repaid by the Moorish Government, with $4,000 additional for American expenses) just as Secretary Hay was dispatching a celebrated telegram, indited after conference with the President: "We want Perdicaris alive or Raisuli dead" (but also instructing not to land marines, though this was not published). The Chicago convention roared its patriotic applause, and the press echoed. It remained for historians later to discover that Roosevelt knew when he authorized the message that the American citizenship of Perdicaris was questionable.

Doubtless the abduction for ransom of Perdicaris had been encouraged by the successful kidnaping in Turkish European territory by Macedonian political bandits in 1901 of Miss Stone, an American missionary. With wide publicity in the following months a ransom of $65,000 was collected by public subscription in the United States from pious folk. Quite shockingly, the Department of State had allowed this to be paid to the kidnapers, and the lady was released. No government or person was held to account for the outrage.

The Perdicaris affair seemed to indicate a possible active American interest in Morocco. Furthermore, the exuberant temperament of the robust Roosevelt, who personified the appearance of the United States as a world power, and who was already busying himself in Far Eastern

---

[1] Alfred Vagts, *Weltpolitik, op. cit.,* II, pp. 1841-1913, has presented the most detailed account of American-German relations during the first Moroccan crisis.

affairs, invited contacts. Early in 1905 the German Foreign Office, feeling irked by Liberal derision, determined to do something in Morocco. It sounded President Roosevelt whether it would not be worth while for Germany and the United States separately to take a stand against any one-sided disposition of Moroccan sovereignty, which was now being threatened by new French demands shaping toward a protectorate, demands which the Sultan was resisting by referring them to an assembly of notables. Despite the President's noncommittal language, it was believed that he had given some encouragement. As we have already observed, the paralysis of Russia in Manchuria presented a favorable juncture for Germany to make an issue of the Open Door in Morocco in the spring of 1905. Somewhat against the Emperor's will, Prince von Bulow, the Chancellor, and Holstein, *die graue Eminenz* of the German Foreign Office, persuaded the Kaiser to disembark from his yacht at Tangier (March 31, 1905), and make an ostentatious official call on the Sultan. The Kaiser declared:

I hope that under the sovereignty of the Sultan a free Morocco will remain, open to the peaceful rivalry of all nations without monopoly or annexation, on the basis of absolute equality. The object of my visit to Tangier is to make known that I am determined to do all in my power to safeguard efficaciously the interests of Germany in Morocco, for I look upon the Sultan as an absolutely independent sovereign.

Germany thus proclaimed to the world her determination to be consulted in any settlement of the Moroccan Question. On the face of it, this was to support the Open Door, like the United States in China. Under German suggestion the Sultan called for a conference of the powers to propose reforms instead of adopting the French demands for a reorganization of his army and police by French instructors, control by France of his finances, and a treaty excluding the political influence of all other nations except France in Morocco. The French Foreign Minister, Théophile Delcassé, who had built up the *entente* with England, opposed a conference. The British Government backed him, but Delcassé could not command his own Cabinet, which feared war with Germany and knew that even if Great Britain should support France with force it would be difficult to withstand Germany on the land frontier. Accordingly, with the connivance of Germany, the French Government dropped its own Foreign Minister (June 6, 1905) to make way for compromise. This was a humiliation for France, a triumph for Germany. It was even then difficult to find a formula for a conference which if agreed upon would relieve the tension. Germany ardently desired a diplomatic victory, and was not wholly unwilling to go to war. The Kaiser appealed to Roosevelt to urge France to accept a conference and to advise Great Britain against lending military support to France. His most effective argument was that the destruction of the German navy in any war would leave Great Britain and France free to partition China, and would endanger the President's peace maneuvers between Russia and Japan. Whatever decision the President would consider the most fair and practical, the Kaiser said he would accept and support. Roosevelt told France he would not urge a Moroccan conference unless France wanted it, but strongly advised her to accept, intimating that he would support the French position in a conference. The French Government agreed, and a conference was called to meet at Algeciras, in southern Spain, January 16, 1906.

As the powers prepared for the conference, the Kaiser persisted with his efforts to wean a weakened Russia away from the French alliance and to attach her to Germany. In a meeting on their yachts at Björkö (July 24, 1905) in the northern Baltic, the two Emperors signed with solemn vows under heaven a secret treaty unknown to the Czar's most intimate advisers, by which they agreed to lend each other mutual help in case either were attacked in Europe by a third power, and to ask France to be a co-signatory. This "reinsurance" treaty was to come into effect immediately upon the conclusion of peace between Russia and Japan. Though nominally defensive, it was incompatible with Russia's obligations to France. The jubilant Kaiser was bitterly disappointed when Nicholas II, upon advice of his Foreign Minister, backed out of the agreement (October, 1905).[1] Had this secret treaty held, Germany would have been in a position to make radical demands at the Algeciras Conference.

The powers at Algeciras [2] presented a cleavage foreshadowing the opposing belligerents in 1914. France would have preferred a mandate for Morocco south of the Rif, but failing that wished to staff the Sultan's army and police with French, or, at least, French and Spanish officers,

[1] The voluminous literature on the personal negotiations between Kaiser and Czar in 1904-1905, including Herman Bernstein's publication of *The Willy-Nicky Correspondence, Being the Secret and Intimate Telegrams Exchanged between the Kaiser and the Tsar* (New York, 1918), is thoroughly digested by Sidney B. Fay in the chapter on the Moroccan crisis of 1905 in his *The Origins of the World War* (2 vols., New York, 1928).

[2] Eugene N. Anderson has published a detailed study of the intricate diplomacy of Morocco, *The First Moroccan Crisis, 1904-1906* (University of Chicago Press, 1930), in which he was able to utilize the correspondence published in the German and British series of diplomatic correspondence preceding the First World War, but not the French, which series is not then printed for those years.

and to have charge of an international bank to salvage Moroccan finances; this would have turned Morocco into a French sphere of influence. Germany preferred to see several powers, including herself, put in charge of police in particular ports, thus implying a future partition; failing this, that the Sultan be free to select such foreign officers as he chose, with an evenly balanced international control of the finances. As the greatest concession Germany would accept the officering of the Sultan's police and army with soldiers from some small minor power without political interests in Morocco, like Switzerland or Denmark. England supported the French position, but hesitated about pledging certain military support in case of war, although Sir Edward Grey, the new British Secretary for Foreign Affairs, told the German Ambassador in London (January, 1906) that "In the event of an attack upon France by Germany arising out of our Moroccan agreement, public feeling in England would be so strong that no British Government could remain neutral." Italy favored France, following her secret treaty of 1902, exchanging a free hand in Morocco for one in Tripoli. Spain in her feeble way clung to the bargain she had made with France. Austria-Hungary supported Germany. Russia could support France in word only.

At Algeciras the United States was represented by the experienced diplomatist Henry White, then Ambassador to Italy, and Samuel Gummeré, Consul General to Morocco. White followed Roosevelt's instructions to "keep friendly with all" but "to help France get what she ought to have." In the end Roosevelt suggested a compromise which in effect the powers adopted. The Act of Algeciras, signed April 7, 1906, by the plenipotentiaries of the United States and the other powers assembled there provided: (1) recognition of the "triple principle of the sovereignty and independence of His Majesty the Sultan, the integrity of his domains, and economic liberty without any inequality"; (2) organization of the police under Spanish and French officers; (3) a state bank divided into fourteen equal shares of which one share was allotted to each of the twelve signatory powers and the other two to French banks. Though France and Spain in this way became the mandatories of the conference powers, they also received a privileged position, and France more so than Spain. Germany triumphed in her insistence on a conference; France won the conference. If one could justify President Roosevelt's diplomatic interference at all, one would recognize the skill and adroitness with which he had brought the powers to a peaceful compromise. What is more, both sides were pleased with the result, in contradistinction to Portsmouth the year before. It was risky business, and the United States had nothing to gain by it. That Roosevelt prevented a European war is to be doubted; the crisis had passed when Delcassé resigned in June, 1905. The collapse of the Björkö treaty insured against a second crisis in 1906. The President derived enormous satisfaction from his perilous but successful rôle as world statesman, for which the Kaiser had really given him the cue.[1]

The Senate considered the Algeciras Convention more soberly and objectively. It prudently embodied in its resolution of advice and consent to ratification a statement and reservation that

[The participation of the United States in the Conference and the General Act] was with the sole purpose of preserving and increasing its commerce in Morocco, the protection as to life, liberty, and property of its citizens residing or traveling therein, and of aiding by its friendly offices and efforts, in removing friction and controversy which seemed to menace the peace between powers signatory with the United States to the treaty of 1880, all of which are on terms of amity with this Government; and without purpose to depart from the traditional American foreign policy which forbids participation by the United States in the settlement of political questions which are entirely European in their scope.

Had the Senate realized the extent to which President Roosevelt had concerned himself with a critical and purely European question, in which the United States had no vital or even substantial interest, we may well doubt whether it would have ratified the Act at all. This wise reservation relieved the United States from any responsibility in Morocco when in 1911 another crisis between France and Germany, between the Triple Alliance and the Triple Entente, again strained the peace of Europe. In great contrast to Roosevelt, President Taft kept out of the Agadir affair, which signalized the second Moroccan crisis.[2] From 1899 on the Senate cautiously has attached such a reservation to all multilateral treaties which had the slightest political implication, even Hague Conventions for international arbitration, and the unratified Declaration of London with its code for naval warfare.

[1] Joseph Bucklin Bishop published in his *Theodore Roosevelt and His Time, op. cit.*, selected letters from Roosevelt's papers illustrating his participation in the Moroccan crisis. Dennis, *Adventures, op. cit.*, Nevins, *Henry White, op. cit.*, and Pringle, *Theodore Roosevelt, op. cit.*, have reviewed the subject more critically with fuller information.

[2] By a convention between France and Germany, November 4, 1911, Germany yielded to France an implied protectorate *de facto* in Morocco, in return for the cession to Germany in the French Congo of two prongs of territory to bring the German Kamerun into contact with the Ubangi and Congo rivers, respectively.

Morocco was made a French protectorate by the Franco-Spanish convention of November 27, 1912. The United States recognized it in 1914.

The repeated European crises—first Moroccan crisis of 1905-1906, the first Balkan crisis of 1908, the second Moroccan crisis of 1911, the second Balkan crisis of 1913—betokened to informed observers that European diplomatists were lighting their cigarettes over an enormous powder bin. Of the precarious nature of European peace the American public knew little and cared less. Only a few individuals, and these outside the general diplomatic personnel, had any imaginative penetration into the critical balance of power between the opposing European alliances, the Triple Alliance and the Triple Entente, and into the bases of this international imperialistic rivalry and fear which pointed toward war: the contest for control of the backward regions of the world and their enormous potentials for trade and the supply of raw materials for modern industry, a contest which approached a climax as the German navy pushed toward parity with Great Britain; the latent French desire for the return of Alsace-Lorraine; and the complications of nationalism in the Balkans and within the Austro-Hungarian Empire.

The mind of President Wilson, when the new Democratic Administration came into power in 1913, was occupied almost exclusively with domestic questions. His chief adviser in domestic policy and in political strategy was Colonel E. M. House, of Texas, with whom the President formed one of the strangest friendships in history.[1] Without consultation of the Department of State, over which William Jennings Bryan now presided, House envisaged the unsteady European situation, and directly after the triumph of the Democrats in the election of 1912 he set his mind to play on it. To President Wilson he proposed a roving mission for himself to the capitals of Europe to suggest by tête-à-tête conversations with the ruling personalities some new arrangement which would tranquilize European diplomacy and stabilize peace. He had in mind, rather vaguely as to precise details, an understanding among the United States, Great Britain, Germany, and France, by which Germany might be promised a greater activity in overseas regions (including South America), and in return for which she might be willing to check her naval building. He felt that this might lead to some general agreement for the peaceful development by the capitalistic powers of the economically and politically backward regions of the world, notably the tropics, and to progressive limitation of armaments and the dissipa-

[1] George Sylvester Viereck, *The Strangest Friendship in History: Woodrow Wilson and Colonel House* (New York, 1932).

tion of fear.[1] Wilson permitted the inexperienced House to undertake
this unprecedented personal mission without precise instructions, and
gave to it his affectionate personal blessing.[2]

These were as bold ideas as even Theodore Roosevelt ever played
with: bringing in discussion of South America [3] suggested sacrifices by
the United States for the peace of Europe; but House felt that the
peace of Europe might mean the peace of the world, and he romanti-
cally thought of his peripatetic mission as the Great Adventure.   In
the spring of 1914 he had conversations with the German Kaiser and
then with the leaders of the British Government.   They listened politely
to the softly challenging Texan, because they knew he represented the
President in an intimate way, and they made noncommittal statements
of amenity and willingness to talk about his points.   In bitter postwar
days these men thought back to House and his idealistic proposals and
attached more significance to his ideas than they did in 1914.   Whether
House could have brought Germany and Great Britain to a friendly
arrangement, basking in French and Russian countenance, is highly
problematical, but before his suggestions had made any real headway
war suddenly engulfed Europe.

NOTE ON THE PROBLEMS OF LIBERIA

An international inquiry into the slave traffic in 1930, initiated by the
United States in response to discussions in the antislavery commission of the
League of Nations, reported in essence that the attempt to establish an in-
dependent civilized Negro state in West Africa had nearly failed. Technically
the inquiry was set up by the Liberian Government, with one representative
of the United States, one of the League of Nations, and one of Liberia.
The report is printed in Department of State, Publication 147 (Washington,
G.P.O., 1931), or League of Nations official publication Nos.: C. 658.
M. 272. 1930. vi.

[1] The mission is described and essential documents are printed in Seymour's publication
of *The Intimate Papers of Colonel House, op. cit.,* I, pp. 235-275.

[2] "In short," says Wilson's biographer, "this is the first demonstration of the working
of that strange and unclear relationship which was to becloud American foreign policy
and exasperate European diplomats until, in the end, a revelation of the real disparities
led to serious difficulties. On Wilson's part it seemed always to have been a relationship
of faith without complete understanding, of trust without actual commitment—wholly
creditable to neither, and deplorable in some of its results. But it was one of those
'necessary friendships' which throughout his life so often influenced, and sometimes
warped, Wilson's clear-running judgment." Ray Stannard Baker, *Life and Letters of
Woodrow Wilson, op. cit.,* V, p. 50.

[3] Roosevelt had suggested to a German agent in 1903 the establishment of an independent state by Germans in Brazil, *Die Grosse, Politik der Europäischen Kabinette,
1871-1914* (Berlin, 1924), XVII, No. 5151, cited by Dennis, *Adventures, op. cit.,* p. 296.

In 1926 an American corporation, the Firestone Tire and Rubber Company, entered into a contract with the Government of Liberia for the rental of 1,000,000 acres for a rubber plantation, and (through subsidiaries) for a 7-per-cent loan, to be floated at 90, to refund Liberia's outstanding foreign indebtedness and commence a program of public works, including dock facilities, under supervision of the American financial adviser to the Liberian Government and an increased staff of expert assistants. The Great Depression and eventual default by Liberia on the new loan cut short this program. The United States suspended formal diplomatic relations with Liberia, 1930-1935, and co-operated with the Council of the League of Nations in long and complicated negotiations to place the Government of Liberia under a chief adviser responsible ultimately to the Council, with a salvage of the outstanding Firestone investments (most of which up to that time had gone to pay off the older European loans) in co-operation with that capitalist. This seemed to be working toward a species of mandate for the Council over Liberia, when the plan was rejected by Liberia in 1934.

In 1935 Premier Hertzog of the South African Union made the unpopular suggestion that Liberia—as well as former German Southwest Africa—be placed under mandate to Germany in case that power should re-enter the League of Nations. It was very soon after this that the Department of State announced formal recognition of a new Liberian Government, of President Edwin Barclay, who agreed to a program of adjustment of the Firestone contract debts which allowed a reduction in interest charges from 7 per cent to 5 per cent. The devaluation of the American dollar meanwhile had already cut the principal and the interest burden 40 per cent. Contemporary announcements foreshadowed the withdrawal of the American financial adviser.

Two eminent scholars have sharply criticized the Firestone contracts and the policy of the United States: R. L. Buell, in *New Republic*, LXXVI, 17-19 (August 16, 1933), and W. E. B. DuBois, "Liberia, The League and the United States," *Foreign Affairs*, XI (July, 1933), 682-695. For a Liberian scholar's analysis, see N. Asikiwe, *Liberia in World Politics* (London, 1934). More justificatory is Charles Morrow Wilson's study of the sociology and economy of *Liberia* (New York, 1947).

Located 750 miles south of Dakar, so close to the "Atlantic Narrows," opposite the easternmost bulge of Brazil, Liberia occupied an important strategic position during the Second World War. The historically friendly nonimperialistic affinity between the United States and the little African republic bore good fruit. Liberia placed herself under the protection of the United States for the duration of the war (executive agreement of March 31, 1942); became a member of the United Nations by adhering to the Declaration of January 1, 1942, and also the Atlantic Charter; enjoyed lend-lease and other assistance from the United States; declared war on Germany and Japan (January 27, 1944); and served as a valuable military base for the transport of American personnel and supplies by air and by sea to the North African, European, and Asiatic fronts (executive agreements of June 8 and December 31, 1943). President Roosevelt visited President

Barclay at Monrovia on his way back from Casablanca in January, 1943, and President Barclay returned the visit as a guest at the White House in Washington in May of the same year. See Documents on *American Foreign Relations* (World Peace Foundation, 1944-1945), V, 600-604, VI, 213-214, 222; and *Dept. State Bulletin* VIII (No. 207, June 12, 1943), 515-517.

7

Woodrow Wilson and American Neutrality

THE world war that broke out in August, 1914, was caused by the dislocation in the European international system accompanying the development of the German Empire. Amid all the conflicting opinion about the immediate circumstances that precipitated that conflict, one thing is historically certain: the United States was the only great power completely disassociated from the controversies which led to the outbreak of the war. Neither the people of the United States nor the persons whom they had placed in governance knew very well what it was all about. This included the diplomatists, several of them literary personages, most of the others political appointees, newly installed in the principal capitals of Europe by the incoming Wilson Administration. At home, all leaders of American life were in favor of neutrality, when the President promptly proclaimed it.

President Wilson at the outset offered the good offices of his government for peace. Both groups of belligerents politely declined them. The President enjoined his countrymen to be neutral in thought and feeling as well as in outward act. To be neutral in thought and feeling proved eventually impossible even for the President himself, to say nothing of his ambassadors [1] and ministers abroad. Even before the engines of belligerent propaganda had begun to function in the United States the great majority of the people were immediately sympathetic to the "Allied"—that is, to the Entente—side, which contained the two great democracies of Great Britain and France. This feeling was confirmed by the tone of the American foreign press service which filtered through British channels, at least at the beginning of the war. [2] The

[1] Walter Hines Page, Ambassador in London, quickly developed into an avowed Anglophil and interventionist. His remarkable letters to President Wilson, supplementing his official despatches (printed in *Foreign Relations*), are interesting principally for his urging of England's cause. Burton J. Hendrick printed them in *The Life and Letters of Walter Hines Page* (3 vols., New York, 1922-1926).

[2] Walter Millis has emphasized this in his *Road to War; America, 1914-1917* (New York, 1935), a historical study of national psychology which must be used with greatest caution by the experienced reader, and which because of its captivating style is as

violation of Belgian neutrality gave to the Allied cause at the outset a potent moral instrument of propaganda, powerful because of its awful validity. As the weeks wore on, British and Allied propaganda [1]—some of it most unscrupulous—steadily reinforced American sympathies. It was difficult for Germany to reply in kind to this sort of stuff: first, because of her own conduct, but also because of limited understanding of American history, character, thought, and institutions, which were historically more associated with Great Britain and France; and, later, because of American public indignation at the sabotage covertly practiced by German and Austrian authority in American munitions factories filling orders for the Allies,[2] as they had a right to do by existing international law.

Behind the neutrality of the Government there was more than a cultural attachment to the Allied cause. Loans to the Allied governments by American banks, which set in motion during the second year of the war, created an economic tie-up.

Under the leadership of J. P. Morgan and Company, purchasing

effective a persuasion for the average reader as was the Allied propaganda which the author excoriates. Millis does not discuss, for example, the moral and political implications of Belgian neutrality, nor does he seek for the least validity in any of the Allied propaganda, although he suggests much validity in German counterpropaganda. This book, undocumented, reflects conspicuously the labors of research embodied in the earlier, carefully documented work, of similar tendency, by C. Hartley Grattan, *Why We Fought* (New York, 1929).

    Charles Seymour, *American Diplomacy during the World War* (Johns Hopkins Press, 1934), was the first and most objective analysis of American problems of neutrality. He has further discussed disputed problems in his *American Neutrality 1914-1917* (Yale University Press, 1935). By far the best of the controversial works is Charles C. Tansill, *America Goes to War* (Boston, 1938).

    [1] J. Duane Squires has described the machinery of *British Propaganda at Home and in the United States from 1914 to 1917* (Harvard University Press, 1935).

    [2] It was because of their connection with this sabotage, revealed by the British secret service, that the United States requested the recall of the German military and naval *attachés,* Captains von Papen and Boy-Ed, and the Austrian Ambassador, Konstantin Dumba.

    In previous wars Germany and Austria-Hungary as neutrals had allowed their subjects to export munitions and other contraband to belligerents without regard to the special circumstances of the belligerents. There is nothing in international law to prohibit this, although the belligerent may capture neutral ships taking contraband to the enemy. During the World War of 1914-1918 British sea power, as in some previous wars, prevented the Central Powers from access to American markets. They therefore requested that the United States in its neutrality maintain an attitude of "strict parity with respect to both belligerent parties." In a notable state paper directed to the Austro-Hungarian Government (August 12, 1915) Secretary of State Lansing said, in effect, that it would not be consonant with strict neutrality to change the rules while the game was in progress.

    International law does not forbid a neutral to prohibit the export of munitions or other contraband; this would be a matter of policy. See below, pp. 196-197.

agent [1] for Great Britain and France, prominent banking firms underwrote loans for popular subscription, in the autumn of 1915, after Secretary of the Treasury William G. McAdoo and Secretary of State Robert Lansing persuaded the President to alter former Secretary Bryan's policy of officially frowning on private loans to belligerent governments as inconsistent with the spirit of neutrality.[2] During the remaining period of neutrality a total of $1,900,000,000 in loans was extended privately in the United States to Allied governments, compared with only $27,000,-000 to Germany.[3] American trade, because of British control of the seas, became increasingly identified with Great Britain and France, and with it the national prosperity which early in 1914 had been declining in a serious way. This new business included the lucrative manufacture and sale of munitions of war. It is now known that, following technical defaults on rifle contracts, the British Government, anxious to keep up deliveries of desired weapons, felt obliged to take over control, but not ownership, of some leading American arms factories.[4]

These emotional, cultural, and economic factors predisposed the people of the United States in favor of Great Britain, Canada and the other Dominions, and France and Belgium, *but not to fight for them.* As the able German Ambassador, Count von Bernstorff, recognized, the United States, though predisposed in favor of the Allied cause, was a profoundly pacifistic nation and people, under a peace-loving President, anxious to keep out of war.[5] The obvious fact is that until April 6, 1917, the United States did not join the war, notwithstanding the exhortations of former President Roosevelt and other minority leaders. It went to war in 1917 because Germany had announced a renewal of her un-

---

[1] J. P. Morgan testified that during the period of American neutrality his firm ordered in the United States about $3,000,000,000 of materials of different sorts, receiving therefor a commission of roughly 1 per cent, or $30,000,000. New York *Times,* January 8, 1936.

[2] For this policy of disapproval of such loans and its reversal, see *Foreign Relations, 1914, Supplement,* xii, 580; *1915, Supplement,* 820; and Baker, *Life and Letters, op. cit.,* V, pp. 175-177, 381-383; and particularly the testimony before the Senate Munitions Investigation Committee, January 7-11, 1936, as published contemporaneously in the New York *Times.*

In previous wars, notably the Russo-Japanese, neutral bankers, including German, French, English, and American, loaned to either or both belligerent governments.

[3] The figures for the Allies are computed from the estimates of foreign loans, 1914-1919, in a letter of the Secretary of the Treasury to the President of the Senate, January 27, 1920. 66th Cong., 2d Sess. Sen. Doc. 191. The estimate of loans to Germany is from Grattan, *op. cit.,* p. 159. R. W. Van Alstyne digests press comment in "Private American Loans to the Allies, 1914-1916," *Pacific Historical Review,* II (1933), 180-193.

[4] *Report* of the Senate Munitions Investigation Committee, Sen. Rept. No. 944, Part V 74th Cong. 2d Sess., pp. 88-97, *et passim.*

[5] J. C. von Bernstorff, *My Three Years in America* (New York, 1920).

restricted submarine warfare. If it had not been for that great mistake in German policy the United States would not have intervened, despite the overwhelming sympathy for the Allies in all but German-American and Irish-American constituencies. In that case the war would have ended much differently. In any diplomatic history of the United States, therefore, the obvious fundamental for the years 1914-1917 is the intricate and unwelcome question of neutral rights.

The erection of opposing belligerent maritime systems and their effect on the rights of neutrals, in so far as those rights were securely defined in international law, was a repetition of the great struggle between England and Napoleon: the off-shore blockade versus the continental system. To adapt himself to the twentieth-century struggle the historian need but substitute Imperial Germany and her allies for Napoleonic France and her allies, submarine warfare for the continental system. During the Napoleonic period the opposing belligerents professed to be resorting to admittedly illegal conduct against neutral shipping only because driven in desperation to retaliation and reprisal by the enemy's disregard for international law. So it was in the world wars of the twentieth century. Each mighty belligerent was eager to draw forth and to use mercilessly his most deadly weapon of war: economic strangulation and starvation. With Great Britain that weapon was the blockade, which raised at least moot points of international law. With Germany it was the unrestricted use of the submarine for the destruction on the high seas of merchant ships, enemy or neutral, coming to the British Islands, destroying them without examination or warning; this was clearly contrary to established law.

There was some delay by both Great Britain and Germany in forging and using these deadly weapons.

Great Britain had to feel her way carefully because too confirmed an opposition by the United States to interference with neutral rights might produce a general embargo and deprive the Allies of an indispensable source of raw materials and munitions, without which they could not equip armies to survive the onslaughts of Germany on the continent.[1]

---

[1] Sir Edward Grey, the British Secretary for Foreign Affairs, later stated this very clearly in his memoirs after the war.

"After Paris had been saved by the battle of the Marne, the Allies could do no more than hold their own against Germany; sometimes they did not even do that. Germany and Austria were self-supporting in the huge supply of munitions. The Allies soon became dependent for an adequate supply on the United States. If we quarreled with the United States we could not get that supply. It was better therefore to carry on the war without blockade, if need be, than to incur a break with the United States about contraband and thereby deprive the Allies of the resources necessary to carry on the war

It is clear that in an embargo, at least on munitions of war, if necessary on other commodities, applied equally to all belligerents, the United States had available an unexceptionable weapon by which peaceably to force Great Britain to an observance of American definitions of international law. It is also certain that an embargo would have brought an abrupt and calamitous decline of trade, as in Jeffersonian times; it would have precipitated the United States, which was sliding at the outset of the war toward an industrial depression, into a real economic tailspin which might have thrown the Democratic Party out of its seat. Such an economic catastrophe would have been calamitous, but by no means as disastrous as war. Great Britain astutely deferred her blockade measures until the developing war trade of the Allies had stayed the United States from the brink of an imminent depression and made its swelling prosperity contingent upon acquiescence, under protest, in the British maritime measures, which after all were in large degree moot.

Germany delayed her maritime system: first, because she hoped to end the war by a quick campaign on land before her great pile of military stores, man power, and foodstuffs could run low; this expectation was ruined by the Battle of the Marne and the ensuing stalemate in the trenches. Secondly, her fleet of twenty-eight sea-going submarines at the beginning of the war did not seem certainly adequate to the task of starving out England by unrestricted operations against merchant ships. Thirdly, Germany feared to some extent the effect of such measures, in the face of international law, on the United States. German counsels were divided, however, on this last point. The naval advisers believed that, given the submission to British sea power, the United States could not be in a much more unfriendly position as to Germany, even in case of war. No one then dreamed that two million American troops would or could be sent to France.

The existence of this compelling weapon of the embargo has led one school of historical writers to argue that the United States could have avoided the First World War if only it had used this legitimate weapon of policy to make Great Britain conform to American interpretations of international law, that the unwillingness to use it was due to the effect which it would have had on economic conditions in the United States and consequently upon the fate of the Democratic Party.[1] This thesis

at all or with any chance of success. The object of diplomacy, therefore, was to secure the maximum of blockade that could be enforced without a rupture with the United States." *Twenty-five Years, 1892-1916* (2 vols., New York, 1925), II, p. 107.

[1] The leader of this school was the late Joseph V. Fuller. This serious scholar died before his thesis could be developed fully, but see his (anonymous) sketch of W. J.

assumes that if Great Britain had conformed, Germany, deprived of pretexts for retaliation, would have conformed too, there would have been no unrestricted submarine warfare on merchant ships, and American neutral rights would have been safe. The argument is very plausible; for one thing it is based on the correct assumption that it was the issue of submarine warfare that finally brought the United States into the war. But it assumes further that Germany would not have found some other pretext for unrestricted submarine warfare, or that she would not have resorted to it anyway without pretext, as she violated Belgian neutrality, on the principle that self-preservation knows no law. Nevertheless there is no question but that the Wilson Administration willfully refused to raise up this effective weapon of an embargo on all shipments of munitions to belligerents, a weapon so feared by British diplomacy.[1] The historian must be very suspicious of political motives for not using an embargo at the outset of the controversy over neutral rights.

With these fundamental factors in mind we may now turn to the development of the opposing maritime systems of the belligerents and the relation of the neutral United States thereto.

International maritime law was to a large degree in an uncertain state when war broke out in 1914, even as it is now. There had been no great maritime war for a hundred years. The important developments in law had been the Declaration of Paris of 1856 (following the Crimean War) and the accepted Civil War practice of the United States. The Declaration of Paris had stated in 1856 that: "Blockades, in order to be binding, must be effective; that is to say, maintained by a force sufficient really to prevent access to the coast of the enemy." It did not say precisely where the ships must be stationed. Since 1856 the powers had not been able to agree to any further definitions of blockade. The United States, however, in the Civil War invoked the doctrine of continuous voyage to extend a blockade to the interception of neutral

Bryan's diplomacy, in *American Secretaries of State and Their Diplomacy*, X, pp. 22-44; and his article, "The Genesis of the Munitions Traffic," *Journal of Modern History*, VI (September, 1934), 280-293.

[1] An important group of Democratic members of Congress, headed by no less a person than the majority leader of the House, Claude Kitchin, and the Speaker, Champ Clark, urged the President to threaten such an embargo, and in February, 1916, Kitchin advocated an actual embargo, and believed that Congress would pass one, except for the opposition of the President. It was this same group that believed, as Secretary Bryan had urged, that the United States should warn its citizens against traveling on the armed vessels of the belligerent powers and disclaim responsibility for those who insisted on so doing.

Professor A. M. Arnett read at the Chattanooga meeting of the American Historical Association, December 27, 1935, an enlightening paper, based on Kitchin's personal papers, on *Claude Kitchin and the Wilson War Policies* (Boston, 1937).

cargoes bound to a neutral port on the first leg of a voyage *en route* to the enemy by a sequent short *maritime* leg. Great Britain had been careful to make no objection to that step; because later she might want to do the same,[1] and take another step in addition—that is, to stop neutral cargoes continuously *en route* to a blockaded belligerent where the second leg of the voyage lay *overland* via contiguous neutral countries.

In addition to the definition of blockade, the Declaration of Paris, protected neutral property on enemy ships as well as enemy property on neutral ships (free ships free goods) except contraband of war. But what was contraband? There was no universal agreement on that. The spreading relationship to the conduct of war of previously innocent articles made contraband much more difficult to define in the twentieth century than a hundred years before.

Attempts at the Hague Peace Conferences of 1899 and 1907 and at the London Naval Conference of 1909 to codify rules for maritime and for land warfare had met with meager success because of failure of complete ratification.

The Senate of the United States advised and consented to ratification of the Declaration of London which among other things validated, in effect, the American Civil War practice as to continuous voyage; but protected neutral commerce in conditional contraband when bound to neutral countries. The German Government embodied it intact in its prize law. It was favorable to German strategy because it protected such a large degree of neutral trade; and in a future maritime war Germany could draw on adjacent neutrals for supplies. In Great Britain the House of Lords blocked ratification for the same reason which impelled the German Admiralty to accept it: it was too favorable to neutral commerce. When Great Britain rejected the Declaration, the President of the United States withheld final ratification. So did the other governments. So the Declaration of London, *qua* Declaration, never became international law, although most of its articles represented an international juridical consensus on the existing law of the sea, together with some innovations as to precise classification of contraband and a revised definition of blockade.

What was "existing law"? In view of the lack of explicit agreements by the nations, this was difficult to state with all security. According to a careful study of this question, an international lawyer might advise a neutral client in regard to maritime law in war in 1914, as follows:

---

[1] See my *Diplomatic History, op. cit.,* p. 376.

1. "Paper" blockades are illegal. A blockade to be binding must be effectively maintained by an "adequate" naval force.

2. Even enemy goods are safe on a neutral ship, *if* they are not contraband and *if* they are not destined for a blockaded port: "Free ships make free goods."

3. Neutral goods are safe even on an enemy ship, *if* they are not contraband and *if* they are not destined for a blockaded port.

4. *A fortiori*, neutral goods are safe on a neutral ship *but* only if they are not contraband and if they are not destined for a blockaded port.

5. Contraband goods are divided into two categories: absolute and conditional.

6. Absolute contraband consists of goods exclusively used for war and destined for an enemy country, even if passing through a neutral country en route; the rule of "continuous voyage" applies.

7. Conditional contraband consists of goods which may have a peaceful use but which are also susceptible of use in war and which are destined for the armed forces or a government department of a belligerent state; the rule of "continuous voyage" does not apply.[1]

As soon as the war began Great Britain declared that Germany was violating international law by planting mines "of the prohibited class" in the open waters of the North Sea, and doing it with cruisers disguised with neutral flags. Having stated this, the British Government reserved full freedom to take retaliatory measures. Germany denied that she had been laying mines illegally, and pointed out that the Hague Convention on mines was not binding because not ratified by all belligerents.

Here is the starting point for retaliation from which the opposing belligerents so eagerly reached for their deadliest weapons. Belligerent use of the neutral flag had always been a legitimate *ruse de guerre*—as the British Government was soon to argue to the United States on another issue—but who can now tell or could then tell whether the mines were "legitimate" or not? In acknowledging this notice the United States tolerantly stated that hostile measures on the high seas should not increase the hazards of neutral shipping, "so far as the exigencies of the war permit." Encouraged by this noncommittal response, the British Government notified (October 2, 1914) the neutral world of retaliatory measures: in consequence of the German policy of mine laying, combined with their submarine activities, the British navy would now itself take countermeasures and lay mines in "designated areas" or "zones," through which it would be dangerous for neutrals to pass. Sub-

[1] Philip C. Jessup, in Preface to Volume III, *The World War Period*, by Edgar Turlington, of *Neutrality, Its History, Economics and Law* (4 vols., Columbia University Press, 1936).

sequently (November 3, 1914) Great Britain declared the whole of the North Sea to be a "military area" into which neutrals would go at their own risk except in accordance with Admiralty instructions. The risk, of course, was from mine fields.

There was no settled international law of "military areas" on the high seas. The United States did not protest:[1] but in 1917—after its rupture with Germany over unrestricted submarine warfare—it made a statement reserving "all its rights in the premises."[2]

Uncommitted to the Declaration of London, Great Britain and her allies proceeded in 1914 and after to define contraband to suit themselves, being cautious at first not to include even as conditional[3] contraband commodities such as cotton and tobacco, resin and turpentine which might antagonize too large a section of American opinion and thereby possibly raise in the Congress of the United States the menace of an embargo. Foodstuffs were treated from the beginning as conditional contraband, and after the German Government extended its control over all foodstuffs (January 26, 1915) for the purpose of rationing, the British navy seized such cargoes bound to Germany directly or in-

[1] "You may inform the Minister for Foreign Affairs that this Government does not see its way at the present time to joining other governments in protesting to the British Government against their announcement that ships entering the North Sea after November 5 do so at their own peril." Secretary of State W. J. Bryan to United States Minister in Norway, November 10, 1914. *Foreign Relations, Supplement, 1914,* 466.

"As the question of appropriating certain portions of the high seas for military operations, to the exclusion of the use of the hostile area as a common highway of commerce, has not become a settled principle of international law assented to by the family of nations, it will be recognized that the Government of the United States must, and hereby does, for the protection of American interest, reserve generally all of its rights in the premises, including the right not only to question the validity of these measures, but to present demands and claims in relation to any American interests which may be unlawfully affected, directly or indirectly, by virtue of the enforcement of these measures." Secretary Lansing to the British Ambassador, February 19, 1917. *Ibid., 1917, Supplement* I, 519.

The voluminous correspondence with foreign governments, belligerent and neutral, in regard to neutral rights, is fully printed in the Supplements to this official series, for 1914, 1915, 1916, 1917.

[2] American participation later as a belligerent in laying the antisubmarine mine barrage across the northern entrance to the North Sea stultified the earlier caveat to Great Britain on this score. On some other questions of neutral rights—blockade measures, diversion for search, mails, etc., the United States carefully refrained from any belligerent conduct which would be irreconcilable with its earlier neutral protests to Great Britain. American belligerent definitions of contraband were very sweeping. Carlton Savage, *Policy of the United States toward Maritime Commerce in War* (2 vols., Washington, G.P.O., 1934), II, p. 151.

[3] A customary definition of contraband, in the unratified Declaration of London, which comprised articles that were used generally by civilian populations as well as by armies; only where destined for army use were such to be treated as contraband.

directly.[1] The Admiralty resorted to other practices of questionable legality, such as requiring neutral ships to go into British ports for thorough and leisurely search instead of being examined at sea and censoring the mail on such ships thus forcibly diverted into British territorial jurisdiction.[2]

The United States continually protested against these practices. A classic statement was the note of December 26, 1914. This stated complacently: "The commerce between countries which are not belligerents should not be interfered with by those at war unless such interference is manifestly an imperative necessity to protect their national safety, and then only to the extent that it is a necessity." The Department of State contended that the objectionable practices were not so necessary to national safety. Henceforth Great Britain argued politely that they were indeed so necessary, and continued to extend her contraband lists, and resorted to other practices, obnoxious indeed, but difficult to outlaw: placing on the neutral carrier the burden of proof, prohibition of trade with neutral firms suspected of trading with the enemy, and denial of fuel to ships carrying goods of neutral firms enumerated on a British "black list," suspected of trading with the enemy. In these exchanges the United States, in effect, challenged the legality of British practice and reserved claims for adjudication after the war. It also informally accepted the British arrangements agreed to by neutral countries contiguous to Germany or to the Baltic Sea: the creation of private trading trusts which guaranteed not to allow the re-exportation of conditional contraband, which Great Britain thereupon permitted to be imported into the neutral countries. In return Great Britain relaxed an embargo which had been placed on the export of certain commodities indispensable to American industry, such as wool, manganese, rubber, and hides. This British embargo had been most injurious to American manufacturers and annoying to the Department of State.

In the arguments and counterarguments that followed between the two governments, over these and over later retaliatory measures of control and eventual blockade against Germany, it was a contention of the United States that such practices had not only the effect of restraining neutral commerce with the enemy but also of delivering that

[1] The seizure of foodstuffs went into effect for ships leaving home ports after January 26, 1915. These regulations were swallowed up by the more inclusive blockade measures of the "effective cordon," which went into effect March 11, 1915.

[2] Edgar Turlington has described in great detail these and other devices, and their effect on neutrals, in Volume III, *The World War Period* of *Neutrality, Its History, Economics and Law, op. cit.*

commerce over to British firms who shipped it to the enemy by neutral routings. That Great Britain was to some measure guilty of the old abuses of the Napoleonic wars, the use of war and sea power to destroy neutral commerce for commercial profit instead of employing the navy solely for purposes of war, legitimate or illegitimate, has been emphasized by British writers since the war.[1]

These earlier disputations over neutral rights with Great Britain resemble the preliminary controversies between President Jefferson and the British Government, before the announcement of the Berlin Decree by which Napoleon without a navy declared the British Islands in a state of blockade and prohibited neutral commerce with them. As in Napoleonic times, the earlier belligerent practice now soon was overshadowed by the extraordinary range of sweeping retaliatory measures on both sides.

Germany, having decided that her small [2] submarine flotilla—then twenty-seven in number—was sufficient at least greatly to harass England's importations, announced on her part (February 4, 1915) a retaliatory war zone around the British Islands into which neutral shipping would enter at its own peril because of the impossibility always of identifying it given the British practice of disguising belligerent ships with neutral flags.[3] The pretext for retaliation was the British war zones and the British practice in regard to contraband, particularly foodstuffs, both moot points in law. It was now the avowed intention of Germany to torpedo merchant ships making for ports of the British Islands, without stopping them for examination to see whether they were really belligerent or neutral. This presented not a possibly moot point, but an unquestionable violation of international law.

Age-long practice of surface navigation had confirmed the right of visit and search precisely to verify that the accosted ship, no matter what flag it had been flying, was really a belligerent and not a neutral vessel, and also to make sure that the examining cruiser provided for the safety of the crew and passengers and the ship's papers, in case destruction were justified. Only in case Germany could win the war

---

[1] For example, Montagu Consett, *The Triumph of Unarmed Forces (1914-1918)* (London, 1923).

[2] Complete statistics are given by Andreas Michelsen, *Der U-Bootskrieg, 1914-1918* (Leipzig, 1925), on which I have relied for numbers of submarines at various epochs. Only one third of the U-boats could be kept continually in the cruising waters.

[3] Great Britain ordered the use of neutral flags as a *ruse de guerre,* when necessary to protect merchant shipping (January 31, 1915). The *Lusitania* hoisted the Stars and Stripes as it neared the English coast, February 5, 1915.

could she force recognition of her new and deadly practice, deadly to neutrals on the common high seas as well as to the enemy in his own domain. She had resolved to try that chance, convinced that the unrestricted use of the submarine would help her win the war, persuaded that the United States would interpose no fatal objection.

To the German announcement the United States quickly and fatefully replied (February 10, 1915) that it would hold Germany to "strict accountability" for any American lives or property thus injured or destroyed. What did this "strict accountability" mean? Immediate coercion, or accountability later on in dollars and cents, by some adjudication? President Wilson, who edited the note, had not decided what the phrase did mean.

Germany's announcement of a submarine war zone gave Great Britain and her allies the ideal pretext for retaliation with their deadliest weapon, the long-range blockade, effective under modern naval propulsion, and, as the British Government stated, operable without risk to neutral ships or neutral life. The Allies announced that they would "hold themselves free to detain and take into port ships carrying goods of presumed enemy destination, ownership, or origin. It is not intended to confiscate such vessels or cargoes unless they would otherwise be liable to condemnation." [1] The formal announcement eschewed the word blockade; later descriptions referred to it as an "effective cordon"; but even official correspondence soon lapsed into usage of "blockade." The British made no effort to justify the new procedure by law, except through the right of retaliation, a retaliation humane to neutrals, destructive to the enemy. In Paris, Winston Churchill, First Lord of the British Admiralty, declared in an interview: "Germany is like a man throttled with a heavy gag. You know the effect of such a gag. . . . The effort wears out the heart, and Germany knows it. This pressure shall not be relaxed until she gives in unconditionally." [2] It was not.

The new practice, elaborated by successive orders-in-council, was converted into a real blockade, in effect if not in name, in February, 1917, after the United States and Germany had ruptured relations. Great Britain then frankly returned to her practice of a century before: prohibition under pain of confiscation of ship and cargo of all trade to enemy destination, or carriage of enemy property, unless with British or Allied license, or unless the neutral ship had voluntarily stopped at a British

[1] Carried into effect by the order-in-council of March 11, 1915.
[2] New York *Times*, February 3, 1915.

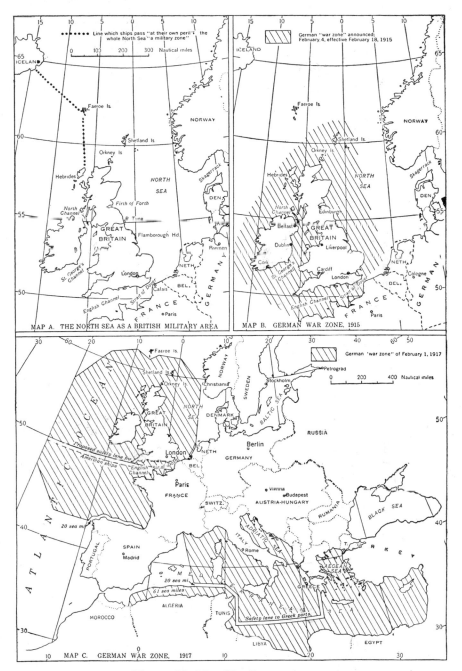

MAP A. THE NORTH SEA AS A BRITISH MILITARY AREA

MAP B. GERMAN WAR ZONE, 1915

MAP C. GERMAN WAR ZONE, 1917

Map 3. Maritime War Zones, 1914-1917

133

or allied port for examination.[1]   But the British Government no longer sold licenses for revenue, as in Napoleonic days.

To the neutral and innocent United States these rival retaliations meant the facing of grave issues, graver with Germany than with Great Britain.   The Department of State endeavored to avoid them by good offices, suggesting to the opposing belligerents a *modus vivendi* which would bring them back to general principles of international law, somewhat improved: that Germany give up mine laying and submarine attacks on merchant vessels in return for British restriction of the use of neutral flags and permission of neutral transport of foodstuffs, subject to safeguards under American supervision to guarantee *bona fide* destination to only civilian population.   The real motive of the belligerents is clear from their unsatisfactory replies, in this instance, as well as in a later instance—in May following—when the proposal was repeated informally, with the added condition of German renunciation of the use of poison gas.   Great Britain and her allies refused to consider such a proposal on the ground that Germany could not be trusted. Germany refused unless *raw materials* were added to foodstuffs—raw materials as defined in the German reply included materials that could enter into the equipment of armies in the field.   The German replies to this sane American suggestion must puncture in the mind of every careful student the later lament against the British "hunger-blockade," which had such a strong appeal to neutral opinion.

Thus the two opposing systems assumed their ominous shapes notwithstanding the anxious desire of the United States to avoid them.

Submarine warfare, so terrifying to England, so nearly the cause of her downfall, was actually a great blessing to her, finally her salvation. By taking 223 neutral American lives on the high seas [2] (28 on American ships, one on a neutral Norwegian ship, 183 on British, one on

---

[1] The American protests at these measures denied the right of a belligerent to injure a neutral by retaliating on the illegal conduct of an enemy; and they assailed the blockade measures as illegal because they did not apply equally to all nations since they did not block Scandinavian ships from entering German Baltic ports, while preventing other neutral vessels from so doing.   They also denied the application of the blockade to neutral ships bound for neutral ports (adjacent to Germany) with conditional contraband or noncontraband; in this the British were going one step ahead of the advance in continuous voyage made by the United States in its Civil War blockade.   See the United States note of October 21, 1915, to Great Britain. *Foreign Relations, 1915, Supplement,* 578-602.

[2] Prof. E. M. Borchard and W. P. Lage have adjusted for me the official figures presented in Savage, *op. cit.,* II, pp. 85, 506, by adding the Norwegian and French ships and excluding the foreigners lost on American ships.   See tables in their *Neutrality for the United States* (Yale University Press, 1937).

French, and 10 on Italian belligerent merchant ships), German practice softened by contrast the interference of the Allies with neutral commerce. "We looked forward," states Winston Churchill in his memorable
history of the war, writing of the effect on the United States of submarine
warfare, "to a sensible abatement of the pressure which the American
Government was putting upon us to relax our system of blockade, and we
received a whole armoury of practical arguments with which to reinforce
our side of the contention." [1]   By returning finally in 1917 to unrestricted
submarine warfare, after the suspension which we are about to note,
Germany caused her own downfall, and the triumph of her enemies, by
bringing the United States into the war.

The full meaning of the new German policy first fell on the United
States with dramatic horror in the torpedoing without warning of the
great British unarmed passenger liner *Lusitania*, May 7, 1915, off the
southern coast of Ireland, with a loss of 1,198 lives, including 128
Americans, of whom 37 were women and 21 children.[2]   Of 129 children
on board, of all nationalities, 94 were suffocated, including 35 babies.
The outrage raised a cry for war among a virile and vociferous minority,
which at first included the President's intimate counselor on foreign
affairs, Colonel House, then in England; but the President stayed the
clamor, and, it proved, with general popular support.   In a public address
he directed to the crisis with Germany the idealism which he had applied
so far without success to Mexico: "There is such a thing as a man being
too proud to fight.   There is such a thing as a nation being so right that
it does not need to convince others by force that it is right."   This was
the language of the Sermon on the Mount, to which neither Mexican
bandits would pay heed, nor European belligerents at their death grips.
Turning to the German Government the President resorted to a not-
impatient diplomatic debate, in which he finally had this last but not
conclusive word:

The United States understood the German Government "to accept as
established beyond question the principle that the lives of non-combatants
cannot lawfully or rightfully be put in jeopardy by the capture or destruction of an unresisting merchantman, and to recognize the obligation to
take sufficient precaution to ascertain whether a suspected merchantman is
in fact of belligerent nationality or is in fact carrying contraband of war
under a neutral flag.   The Government of the United States therefore deems
it reasonable to expect that the imperial German Government will adopt the

[1] *The World Crisis* (4 vols., New York, 1923-1929), II, p. 283.
[2] For status of *Lusitania*, see note at end of this chapter.

measures necessary to put these principles into practice in respect of the safeguarding of American lives and American ships, and asks for assurance that this will be done."

The United States elected to protect citizens traveling under a foreign belligerent flag, even on an armed merchant ship. Once this position had been assumed, of protecting American citizens against violations of international law on the high seas, even though those violations were directed against a foreign, even a foreign belligerent flag, it proved impossible to recede from when later the position was challenged by force before the world. This caused Bryan's resignation, his succession by Lansing.[1] Bryan felt that Great Britain should be held to equal accountability and that in both cases the final reckoning should be deferred. He had recommended requesting Americans to keep off belligerent ships. Lansing was an able legal technician, a subordinate by training and by temperament. Like Wilson he favored the Allied cause, but he was a political funambulator, walking the unsteady tightwire of neutrality to the end, leaving the decision to others. But he deliberately submerged in argumentative verbosity issues with Great Britain over property rights so as to leave the United States free to act if it should desire to enter the war against Germany on the side of the Allies against military autocracy.[2] From 1915 on Wilson became more and more his own Secretary of State.

Germany still hesitated. In June, 1915, she had only forty U-boats, though she was building faster now. There was still the question in the minds of the high civilian officials and the Kaiser whether the promise of submarine warfare was worth the possibility of a break with the United States. The issue was finally presented for immediate decision when the British liner *Arabic* was torpedoed without warning, August 19, 1915, with the loss of two American citizens. Without waiting for reports from the Admiralty, the German Foreign Office assured the American Ambassador that the ship must have struck a mine because instructions had been issued (secretly, it proved, on June 5 and August 27) to naval officers not to torpedo passenger ships. "What instruc-

[1] Baker, *Wilson, op. cit.,* V, pp. 323-360, narrates fully the issues which impelled Bryan to resign.

[2] In his *War Memoirs,* written shortly before his death in 1928 (published posthumously, New York and Indianapolis, 1935), Lansing pictured himself as a statesman who was consistently in favor of military intervention by the United States if necessary to prevent the defeat of the Allies. In 1939, the Department of State published the voluminous *Lansing Papers* (2 vols., Washington, G.P.O.), which show him consistently clinging to neutrality until 1917.

tions?" asked Ambassador James W. Gerard. Finally (September 1, 4, 1915) the new Secretary of State got from the German Ambassador in Washington, Count von Bernstorff, a statement that German submarines would not attack unarmed [1] "liners" which did not themselves attack German vessels or try to escape when summoned to surrender. He disavowed the act and offered reparation.

The Central Powers played two more cards before they exhausted their hand on this trick. On November 7 the Italian passenger liner *Ancona* was torpedoed, not without warning, with a loss of American lives. Demands on Germany elicited the information that this must have been an Austrian submarine (it was really a German). American protests now belabored Austria, and obtained similar equivocal assurances. On December 30, 1915, the armed British passenger liner *Persia* was torpedoed in the Mediterranean with the loss of an American consul; this time Germany and Austria-Hungary denied any part in it; Turkey was perhaps responsible, though she denied it. Protests were inconclusive, because nobody could then identify the nationality of the guilty submarine. Nevertheless the German flotilla had suspended its unrestricted operations against unarmed passenger liners, although it formally declared (February 10, 1916) that enemy merchant vessels armed with cannon could not be considered as peaceable vessels of commerce, and after March 1 would be treated as war vessels by German submarines.

It was increasingly difficult for the President to keep his country out

---

[1] *Note on armed merchant ships.* At the beginning of the war the United States treated as merchant ships British merchant ships armed solely for defensive purposes against converted German raiders, and issued a circular, September 19, 1914, setting forth criteria to test the defensive character of armaments. By an informal understanding, British armed merchant ships kept out of American waters from September 19 until after the proclamation of the "retaliatory" German submarine campaign, February 4, 1915. Then Secretary Lansing believed that the changed character of the war should cause armed merchantmen to be treated as warships. With President Wilson's approval, he tried to solve the problem by submitting to Great Britain and her allies (January 8, 1916) the following *modus vivendi:* (1) Great Britain not to arm merchantmen, (2) Germany not to attack merchantmen without visit and search and provision for the safety of the crew and passengers. At the same time, *pour encourager les Anglais,* he suggested to the Central Powers that they proclaim their intention to treat all armed merchantmen as ships of war. Germany accordingly announced (February 10, 1916) that she would treat all armed merchantmen as ships of war. Great Britain rejected the *modus* on the ground that Germany could not be trusted to observe the rules. The United States did not then insist on treating the armed merchantmen as warships, as Lansing had threatened, but went back to the old policy of September 19, 1914, in a new announcement of March 25, 1916. It would appear that President Wilson reversed Lansing's démarche because it threatened to abort the House-Grey understanding (see p. 138) *Foreign Relations, Supplements, 1914, 1915, 1916,* sections "armed merchant ships," and *Lansing Papers, op. cit.,* I, pp. 330-331.

of war if he should insist, as he had insisted, on the right of American neutrals to travel on belligerent merchant ships on the high seas. To forego such a right, voluntarily, out of policy, announced in time of peace in anticipation of war, as the United States later did in 1935, is one thing; but in the midst of a situation and at the point of a torpedo to accept orders to give up rights is another thing: dishonorable and pusillanimous. "Once accept a single abatement of right," wrote President Wilson to Senator William J. Stone (February 24, 1916) "and many other humiliations would certainly follow." The stand earlier taken in the "strict accountability" note, and in the *Lusitania* case, made it now too late to abate the right claimed so solemnly.

As one looks back upon the First World War it becomes increasingly clear that it was Woodrow Wilson's *choice* of neutral policy that brought his country into war. All within the realm of neutrality, he could have claimed protection of American citizens against violations of international law directed against a foreign flag, or he could have told them originally that they must run the risks of the flag under which they traveled.

Actually Woodrow Wilson thought that the United States would probably have to go in on the side of the Allies *if peace did not come in Europe.* "He said he had never been sure that we ought not to take part in the conflict and if it seemed evident that Germany and her militaristic ideas were to win, the obligation upon us was greater than ever." [1] Under this persuasion he authorized the eager Colonel House to initiate a correspondence with Sir Edward Grey, supplemented by another trip of House to Europe. This resulted in this proposal by House, as the President's personal representative, to the British Government: the United States, in previous agreement with Great Britain and the Allies, would invite the belligerents to a peace conference under American mediation, which would endeavor to secure peace terms not unfavorable to the Allies; if Germany refused to come, the United States would probably enter the war on the side of the Allies; if the conference met and failed because of the unreasonableness of Germany, the United States would [probably] join the war on the side of the Allies. President Wilson from the first had insisted on the contingent word *probably* before the proposal was finally sanctioned and sent back to London (February, 1916). Both contingencies must be probable because of the necessity for Congress to vote any declaration of war. At that very time the Presi-

---

[1] "One evening, in September, 1915," *"Intimate Papers of Colonel House, op. cit.,* II, p. 84.

dent was engaged in a test of control of Congress in his demand—it was
to prove successful—for the defeat of the McLemore resolution forbidding the issuance of passports to American citizens traveling on [1] armed
belligerent merchant ships.

Here was an opportunity for the Allies to get the United States into
the war and to tap its treasure chest and man power, if Germany would
not make a peace roughly conforming to the terms which the Allies had
forged among themselves by secret treaties made *after* the declaration
of war in 1914, and then not precisely known by the Government of
the United States. The British Government did not, however, accept
Wilson's offer. They were not yet ready to throw up the sponge, nor
did they wish to weaken the resolution of their allies by any mention
of an American mediation; besides, was it not possible that German submarine policy might soon drive the United States into war anyway?
The imminence of a rupture between the United States and Germany
was vividly emphasized by the torpedoing (March 24, 1916) without
warning, and with heavy loss of life, of the unarmed French cross-channel passenger packet *Sussex,* and the resulting injury of several
American citizens.[2] Nothing could be more flagrantly violative of German pledges to the United States. Again a series of notes between the
United States and Germany. This time the United States finally demanded (April 18, 1916):

Unless the Imperial Government should now immediately declare and
effect an abandonment of its present methods of submarine warfare against
passenger and freight-carrying vessels, the Government of the United States
can have no choice but to sever diplomatic relations with the German Empire
altogether.

There were in April, 1916, fifty-two U-boats, of which a relay of no
more than eighteen could keep cruising. The German Government,
still unpersuaded that unrestricted submarine warfare would be unquestionably conclusive with the inadequate flotilla then available, temporarily
capitulated, until more submarines could be launched. It promised
(May 4, 1916):

In accordance with the general principles of visit and search and destruction of merchant vessels recognized by international law, such vessels, both
within and without the area declared as a naval war zone, shall not be sunk

[1] For Colonel House's conversations and letters, and the text of the House-Grey
memorandum, see *Intimate Papers, op. cit.,* II, pp. 166-204.
[2] No American citizen was killed.

without warning and without saving human lives, unless these ships attempt to escape or to offer resistance.

But this treatment was to be conditional upon insistence by the United States that Great Britain "shall forthwith observe the rules of international law universally recognized before the war" and laid down by the United States itself in protests to England. Again President Wilson had the last word (May 8, 1916). "Responsibility in such matters," he told Germany, "is single, not joint; absolute, not relative."

The *Sussex* suggested to the Allies that it was only a matter of time before Germany would again resort to unrestricted submarine warfare; then the final test of the great war would come, but then the United States, with its man power and treasure would probably be driven into it by Germany. The United States had failed to control the problem, first by delay, then by giving away its hand in the House-Grey memorandum. Following the Allies' rebuff, the President turned back to an inveterately neutral policy. In the campaign of 1916 he permitted his supporters to appeal successfully to the electorate on the issue "He kept us out of war"; at the same time he weakened the aggressive Republican opposition by advocating rapid military preparedness, for all contingencies; particularly did he urge that the United States navy be built up to be the most powerful on the oceans.

The House-Grey memorandum was now dead. If, without German resort to unrestricted submarine warfare, the Allies should later have faced defeat and Sir Edward Grey or his successor Arthur Balfour should have turned back in desperation to the Wilson-House proposal, we may believe it could not have been resurrected.

In the autumn of 1916 the great offensive and counteroffensive (Verdun and the Somme) of the opposing armies on the western front had reached a deadlock over a million graves, with little promise of either side being able in the near future to push through the enemy's lines. Germany held Belgium and northern France, and the Central Powers had occupied Serbia and were pushing into Rumania (occupied by December). In the eastern theater they held an advantageous line for negotiations—they did not, of course, then glimpse that the coming Russian Revolution would open up that frontier completely to them. The war map was highly favorable, but German man power and materials could no longer be securely replenished against a continuing war of attrition. The only way to victory seemed to be by immediate negotiation, or by ending the war with the unrestricted submarine. The

U-boats now were 103 in number.[1] The German high staff argued by statistics that the unrestricted use of submarines then available could cut British carrying space 39 per cent in five months, and meanwhile the terror of their operations would keep neutral vessels in home ports. It was the hope for an economic paralysis of England, rather than the mere stoppage of the flow of munitions from America, that led the German Government to look again to the terror of the submarine.[2] There was of course the certainty—at least so Ambassador von Bernstorff pointed out from Washington—that this would bring the United States into the war. The German Government therefore decided first to invite direct negotiations; if this failed, then to lash out with unrestricted submarine warfare.

In the United States, President Wilson recognized the precarious situation after the *Sussex* correspondence. The possibility of war with Mexico also had to be reckoned with, as a result of the punitive expeditions of 1916. He had resolved if re-elected to invite the belligerents to a peace conference. Germany asked for American good offices. After election, questionable submarine incidents and German deportations of Belgian civilians caused him to pause.[3] Germany was impatiently asking for action. When the President hesitated, Germany anticipated him and issued, through the United States, an invitation (December 12, 1916) to the enemy to open direct negotiations. The German terms, not then divulged but indicated confidentially to Washington a few weeks later, were: "Germany to give up Belgium but retaining so-called guaranties such as railroads, forts, a garrison, ports, commercial control, etc.; a slice of France through rectification of frontier; will only give back a small part of Serbia, and Bulgaria can do as she likes with Rumania and everybody must pay indemnities to Germany, etc."; colonies for Germany "adequate to her population and economic interest"; and "the freedom of the seas."[4]

Great Britain and her allies refused negotiations when Germany would not state her terms in advance. Britain's designs for peace, as embodied

---

[1] The maximum of 140 was reached in October, 1917. At the end of the war they were reduced to 121, thanks to British, and (after April, 1917) American counteroffensive measures. During the war Germany lost a total of 178 submarines. Michelsen, *op. cit.*, p. 194.

[2] Charles Seymour has stressed this with convincing effect, from the German sources, in his *American Neutrality, op. cit.*

[3] At least so Lansing told the German Ambassador. *War Memoirs, op. cit.,* p. 178.

[4] These terms were conveyed to the United States coincidentally with the notification of resumption of unrestricted submarine warfare. See confidential letter of von Bernstorff to Colonel House, January 31, 1917, and a telegram of Gerard to the Secretary of State, February 4, 1917. *Foreign Relations, 1917, Supplement* I, pp. 35, 37, 114.

in a confidential memorandum of the new Foreign Secretary, Arthur Balfour, not made public until long afterward, were:[1] "diminishing the area from which the Central Powers can draw the men and money required for a policy of aggression" by Balkanizing Central Europe on the principle of nationality; Alsace-Lorraine for France; Constantinople for Russia; some sort of autonomy under Russian sovereignty for a Poland to include the German and Austrian provinces; and reparations for German submarine sinkings, and the damage done in Belgium, northern France, and Serbia.

The belligerents were still far apart. Discouraged, President Wilson (December 18, 1916) suggested that they state their war aims to see if approximations might be revealed which would lead to peace discussions. Germany answered, with her allies, that she would be glad to do so but only in a peace conference. The Prime Minister of Great Britain, Lloyd George, publicly summarized the Allied peace terms in the House of Commons (December 19, 1916): "complete restitution, full reparation, and effectual guarantees" for the future.[2]

It was obvious to Germany that no peace of victory by negotiation was possible at the existing stage of the war. The German Kaiser, in a conference of military, naval, and civil officials [3] (January 9, 1917), decided in favor of a prompt resumption of unrestricted submarine warfare on the first of February, and instructions were sent to Ambassador von Bernstorff to notify the United States accordingly but not until the last day of January. Unaware of this, and still more profoundly discouraged by the belligerents' refusal to talk peace, President Wilson, in a notable address to the Senate, January 22, 1917, lamented their recalcitrance and stated with prophetic insight, which the world could not then appreciate, that there could be no peace with victory. He still hoped he might bring them together for a compromise peace. The depleted finances of the Allies might have made them willing to reconsider, if Germany had held off her submarines.

[1] *War Memoirs of David Lloyd George* (4 vols., Boston, 1933-34), II, pp. 300-308. The Balfour memorandum did not discuss colonial dispositions.

[2] These were set forth more in detail in the note of the French Government, January 10, 1917. See *Foreign Relations, 1917, Supplement* I, 6.

[3] The formulation of German policy, at successive epochs of the war, is revealed in the published memoirs of Admiral von Tirpitz, Chancellor von Bethmann-Hollweg, Field Marshal von Hindenburg, Generals Ludendorff and Falkenhayn, Ambassador von Bernstorff, and in the stenographic minutes of testimony in the Reports of the First and Second Subcommittees of the Committees appointed by the National Constituent Assembly to inquire into the responsibility for the war, translated into English and published by the Carnegie Endowment for International Peace: *Official German Documents Relating to the World War* (2 vols., New York, 1923).

But a few days later the thunderbolt dropped. Count von Bernstorff delivered to the Department of State the German note:

Germany will meet the illegal measures of her enemies by forcibly preventing after February 1, 1917, in a zone around Great Britain, France, Italy, and in the eastern Mediterranean all navigation, that of neutrals included, from and to England and from and to France, etc., etc. All ships met within that zone will be sunk.

The Imperial Government is confident that this measure will result in a speedy termination of the war.

As a special concession to the United States, the note offered to permit one American passenger ship a week to go to and from Falmouth, England, without contraband, if marked with "3 vertical stripes 1 meter wide each to be painted alternately white and red," and the display at each masthead of "a large flag checkered white and red," fully illuminated by night.

The President immediately announced the rupture of diplomatic relations with Germany, according to the warning of the *Sussex* ultimatum. Did this mean war? To the press, to Congress, to the country at large, yes; to the President, no. He tried desperately but unsuccessfully to induce Austria-Hungary to desert Germany on promises of the integrity of that Empire. The United States even notified Great Britain (February 17, 1917) that it reserved the right to enter claims for any damages to American citizens resulting from British proclamation of war zones, concerning which the principles of international law were still "unsettled."[1] Wilson still hoped that Germany would not in fact resort to an "overt act." Such soon occurred, in a succession of sinkings, including American as well as enemy ships. The President then turned with despairing hope to "armed neutrality" including the arming of merchant ships by the Government under authority of an ancient statute of 1797.[2]

It was while the President's policy was still undecided, and while the Senate was inconclusively debating a resolution to arm American merchant ships, that the British Government made a carefully timed delivery to the Department of State (February 24, 1917) of a message which had come to the German Embassy in Washington more than a month previously over the Department of State's wires on January 17. It was a telegram from the German Minister of Foreign Affairs, Alfred Zim-

---

[1] See above, pp. 128-129.

[2] A filibuster by Senator Robert M. La Follette of Wisconsin, and a "little group of willful men," brought an adjournment of the Senate on March 4, 1917, without passage of a specific enabling statute; it was after this that the old law of 1797 was brought out.

mermann, to the Embassy in Washington, with instructions to be sent to the German Minister in Mexico. These instructions von Bernstorff had relayed promptly to Mexico City, on January 19, 1917. The telegraphic messages had been sent from the Foreign Office in Berlin in cypher through the hospitality of the American Embassy there and of the Department of State, after von Bernstorff had complained of the difficulty he had in communicating confidentially with his government on the peace overtures of President Wilson. The United States, whose hospitality was thus abused against itself, had required no key to the cypher, and had not attempted to read the letters entrusted to its courtesy.[1] By a double irony, the British secret service had intercepted the diplomatic communications between the American Embassy in Berlin and the United States Government in Washington, had extracted from it the German cypher messages, and with formidable resourcefulness had decyphered them. It then turned over to the United States the results of this particular espionage of American diplomatic communications, and the United States, in the circumstances, could do nothing but return thanks. The content of the telegrams was astounding. After informing the German Minister in Mexico that Germany would resume unrestricted warfare on February 1, it instructed him, *in case the United States should not remain neutral*, to propose to Mexico an alliance with the object of reconquering the "lost territory" in Texas, New Mexico, and Arizona, an alliance to which Mexico might invite immediate Japanese adherence. Once war existed between the United States and Germany, this was certainly not an abnormal measure to propose. One may even guess that Germany may have expected that the United States would decypher it and read it, and that its contents would give pause to a decision for war.

President Wilson gave the Zimmermann note to the press on March 1. It galvanized American opinion against Germany, and against the eleven filibustering senators who were striving to prevent the arming of American merchant ships. It was the unexpected Revolution in Russia on March 12, 1917, which crystallized the American decision for war. The welcome with which the United States first greeted the Revolution is witnessed by its prompt recognition (March 22, 1917) of the provisional government as the "Government of Russia"—a promptness which contrasts with the sixteen years of delay in recognizing the Soviet Government following the second revolution in November, 1917. If the Rus-

[1] Lansing, *War Memoirs, op. cit.*, p. 227.

sian Revolution had occurred three or even two months earlier, Germany, with the promise of victory and relief on the eastern front, would not have played the "last card" of unrestricted submarine warfare, the United States would not have entered the war, and Germany would have won,[1] or there would have been a compromise peace which would have kept Germany astride the war map. Coming just when it did, the Revolution was not only thus a decisive event in the history of the First World War, and, it was to prove, in the history of the twentieth century; it also had, in this its first phase, a decisive effect on American policy at a psychological moment, particularly on President Wilson, still struggling to keep his country out of actual war. "If our entering the war," he declared, "would hasten and fix the movements in Russia and Germany it would be a marked gain to the world and would tend to give additional justification for the whole struggle."[2] It made it seem truer that the Allies were fighting the battle of democracy against autocracy, as Secretary Lansing had reiterated to the President—faraway Japan counted little at that time of forced decision on European policy.

The President now concluded that armed neutrality would not be an adequate defense of the Freedom of the Seas against the unleashed submarine. Following an insistent public opinion, he went over to the cause itself of the Allies. He appeared before a special session of Congress, April 2, 1917, and recommended that a state of war, thrust on the United States by the acts of Germany, be formally recognized. Congress responded overwhelmingly; the resolution for war passed the House of Representatives by a vote of 373-50, the Senate by a vote of 82-6, April 6, 1917. A declaration followed belatedly against Austria-Hungary, December 7, 1917, delayed in the chance that that power might be moved to seek a general peace to preserve intact the territorial integrity of its empire. The United States did not declare war against the other two allies of Germany: with Turkey it severed diplomatic re-

---

[1] Churchill, *op. cit.*, III, pp. 212-215. "The beginning of 1917 was marked by three stupendous events: the German declaration of unlimited U-boat warfare, the intervention of the United States, and the Russian Revolution. Taken together these events constitute the second great climax of the war. The order in which they were placed was decisive. If the Russian Revolution had occurred in January instead of March, or if, alternatively, the Germans had waited to declare unlimited U-boat war until the summer, there would have been no unlimited U-boat war and consequently no intervention of the United States. If the Allies had been left to face the collapse of Russia without being sustained by the intervention of the United States, it seems certain that France could not have survived the year, and the war would have ended in a Peace by negotiation or, in other words, a German victory."

[2] David F. Houston, *Eight Years with Wilson's Cabinet, 1913-1920; with a Personal Estimate of the President* (2 vols., New York, 1926), I, p. 244.

lations, but with Bulgaria it remained quietly in formal diplomatic relations throughout the war.   Turkey and Bulgaria were more ·likely to
drift from their moorings in Central Europe in case of the worst weather;
Bulgaria, in fact, became the first to sue for peace.

Germany's resumption of unrestricted submarine warfare was what
forced the United States into the First World War.   The chemist in
his analysis adds to the test tube one reagent after another.   At last
there may be a precipitation.   This does not necessarily mean that it
is the final reagent alone which is the precipitant.   It means that, in
the order of additions, precipitation followed the last addition.   So it
may be with the historian's analysis of American neutrality.[1]   The
existing combination in 1917 contained the following ingredients: the
natural predisposition by cultural and political affinity of the American
people for the democracies of the British Empire, and of France, deep-
ened by Allied propaganda, much of it unscrupulous, some of it awfully
valid; the economic tie-up, fostered by private loans, between American
business and Allied war orders, which seized hold of American domestic
politics and led the Wilson Administration to ignore the compelling
diplomatic weapon of the embargo.   The submarine was the last reagent
necessary to precipitate war, although the reaction was not clear until
after the Russian Revolution.

In his war message President Wilson baptized American intervention
with the moral attributes of the Allied cause.   He epitomized it all, not
unjustly though history was to prove mistakenly, with the words: "The
world must be made safe for democracy"—by the crushing out of militarism and the creation of an international organization for the enforcement of world peace.   To the people it became a crusade.   It seemed a
war to end wars.   For this ideal many a gallant American was to lay
down his young life on European soil.

THE LUSITANIA

The commander of the German submarine did not know what ship it
was when he fired the torpedo.   Only as the vessel was sinking, with her
bow in the air, did he discern the name *Lusitania*.

The captain of the *Lusitania* was in possession of the general orders of
the British Admiralty, to commanders of British merchant vessels, to attempt
to ram submarines if they showed up off the bows "with obvious hostile
intent."   It has been argued, particularly by Germany, that this made it
impossible for the commanders of submarines to give warning safely, or to
hail for visit and search.   So it did; but we must remember that (before the

---

[1] I have borrowed the figure from Charles A. Beard.

Admiralty orders) Germany had announced her intention to proceed against belligerent merchant ships in the war zone without warning.

Germany also laid stress on a general warning, published over the name of the German Embassy, in New York newspapers, before the sailing of the *Lusitania*, warning American citizens not to take passage on belligerent merchant vessels bound for the war zone. The answer to this is that the German Embassy had no authority to communicate with American citizens through a newspaper advertisement, or in any other way than to the United States Government through the regular diplomatic channels. American citizens had a self-respecting and legal right to ignore statements made to them by the German Embassy through newspaper advertisements.

The existence of the 4,200 cases of cartridges and some fuses and shrapnel in the cargo of the *Lusitania* did not absolve the German authorities from the necessity of visit and search. Incidentally, these cartridges were not explosive *en masse*, and not so regarded as explosives by United States port laws for passenger ships. The ship was unarmed and carried no troops.

An extraordinary fact is that absolutely no convoy or protection was furnished for the *Lusitania* in the war zone by the British Admiralty, and that the captain ignored the general instructions of the Admiralty to proceed at full speed with a zigzag course on an irregular route when in the war zone. The captain exposed his ship on the regular track of shipping in the fullest possible way, even to the extent of slowing down. He did this despite receiving wireless messages apprising him of the activities of submarines in the vicinity.

Previous to the sinking of the *Lusitania* the Admiralty had on occasion convoyed merchant ships loaded with horses.

One might well wonder whether the British Government purposely exposed to attack the *Lusitania* and other British passenger vessels carrying American citizens, in order to lead the Germans on to a rash act which might bring the United States into the war. King George remarked to Colonel House, as the *Lusitania* was nearing her fate, "Suppose they should sink the *Lusitania* with American passengers on board." (*Intimate Papers, op. cit.*, II, p. 432.)

The same exposure, possibly deliberate, was true in the case of the unarmed cross-channel passenger steamer, *Sussex*, the torpedoing of which caused the German-American crisis of April, 1916. It was lumbering along, without escort, through a sea littered with the wreckage of recently torpedoed vessels.

The truth probably never will be known whether the British and French Governments deliberately exposed these ships for high diplomatic stakes.

Thomas A. Bailey discusses the facts and law concerning "The Sinking of the *Lusitania*," in *American Historical Review*, XLI (October, 1935), 26-54, although not with all the facts and suggestions in this note.

The First World War and the

Peace Settlement

THE United States in 1917 went over to the Allied cause unconditionally, wholeheartedly, overwhelmingly.

It is the unconditional feature of that decisive intervention which most concerns the historian of American diplomacy.

That the intervention was decisive we are told by British and French historians. They say that it marked the turning point of the war. They declare that, without this intervention, which followed the collapse of Russia, Germany would have won the war. We may believe this.[1]

This is not the place to say much about military participation in the last eighteen months of the First World War: the immediate joining of the American and British fleets; the bridling of the submarine with mine barrages and destroyer convoys; the industrial and financial mobilization of the nation; the conscription and training, behind the protection of secure sea power, of a civilian army of 4,000,000 men; the transport of 2,000,000 American troops to transfuse the bleeding man power of France and the British Empire; the collapse of the Central Powers in the autumn of 1918 before these freshened odds. It is rather the diplomatic history of the United States during this terrible war which concerns us here: (1) the relations with the nations associated in the war against Germany and Austria-Hungary, (2) the evolution of the American peace program, (3) the pre-Armistice negotiations, (4) the negotiation of peace at Paris, (5) the rejection by the United States Senate of the League of Nations and with it of the Treaty of Versailles, (6) the separate peace with the enemy, (7) the aftermath issues of neutral rights and the freedom of the seas.

The declarations of war against Germany and against Austria-Hungary did not in themselves signalize departure from the traditional policy of the

[1] See, for example, Churchill, *World Crisis, op. cit.*, III, pp. 212, 215 *et passim;* and Pierre Renouvin, *La Crise Européenne et la Grande Guerre (1904-1918)* (Paris, 1934), p. 420 *et passim.*

Fathers, from the Farewell Address and the Monroe Doctrine. The United States was careful to avoid any alliance with the partners in war. President Wilson studiously referred to them as "associates." He spoke of the "Allied and Associated Powers." Other associates rather than allies, like the United States, were, of course, those Latin-American nations which followed the call of the United States to declare war against Germany, namely: Brazil, Cuba, Costa Rica, Guatemala, Haiti, Honduras, Nicaragua, and Panama.[1] In the Far East, another associate, China, declared war in order to be able to defend her interests at the peace negotiations. Fighting by the side of the Allies, the United States studiously refrained from those infringements on neutral rights against which it had complained to Great Britain and to Germany. It is true that the United States helped to lay the barrage of mines across the northern entrance to the North Sea, thus aiding to shut German submarines out of the Atlantic, but we must remember that the caveat (rather than protest) filed against Great Britain on mined war zones in February, 1917, had acknowledged that this subject was "unsettled" in international law. The United States co-operated with the Allied blockade not by the use of naval force but rather by domestic embargoes, allocation of bunker fuel, and the wide extension of contraband, without distinction of conditional contraband. There were no naval captures of neutral ships and cargoes, no prize court decisions.[2]

The first question to come up between the Allies and the United States concerning the conduct of the war was the command of the American troops at the front. In their desperate need for man power to stem the final offensive of the Germans on the western front the British and French requested that American troops, as they arrived, be brigaded into the British armies. There was of course something reasonable to be said for this: time seemed of the essence in the general strategical situation, with Russia now out of the war and Germany preparing for a knockout offensive before an American army could appear in force; the British commanders had more experience; and the English language would make the command easily possible. Insuperable and highly proper reasons forbade the use of American troops to fill the British ranks. National pride alone made it impossible—there were the old

[1] Peru, Bolivia, Uruguay, Ecuador, and the Dominican Republic severed relations with Germany. The Latin-American nations which remained neutral were: Argentina, Chile, Colombia, Mexico, El Salvador, Venezuela, Paraguay.

[2] T. A. Bailey, *Policy of the United States toward the Neutrals, 1917-1918* (Johns Hopkins Press, 1942).

historical issues dating back to before impressment; further, to have accepted a British command would have destroyed the national identity of the American army and have greatly diminished American influence in the making of the final peace. So President Wilson insisted that, except for a few diversions in emergencies, the troops of the United States moved to the front as an army under the command of an American general, subject later, of course, like the British armies and those of the Allies, to the Generalissimo of the Allied and Associated forces, Marshal Foch. For this unity of command, indispensable to victory, the United States was an unswerving advocate.[1]

It would have been quite possible, and honorable, for the United States to have restricted itself to the maritime sphere, to defending the freedom of the seas, the violation of which had brought the Republic into the war. Toward the fighting on the continent of Europe it could have remained in only a state of war, like Brazil and Cuba, without sending an army to Europe or raising from its citizens huge loans for support of the Allies. At least this full endeavor could have been withheld until there was some sort of agreement upon the terms of a victorious peace which would be won now only by full American co-operation. That an explicit understanding of such a nature was not made a prerequisite by the Government of the United States showed diplomatic ineptitude. It meant that the United States gave without stint of its treasure and its manhood, of its power and its soul, with no guaranty that its ideals or its interests would be written into the peace of victory. That the Allies were prepared to expect some such demand as a reasonable condition of full American participation is indicated by the British mission led by Arthur Balfour which came to Washington in April, 1917, and the French mission which immediately followed. Balfour had full details about the secret treaties which the European Allies had made among themselves marking out the share which each was to have in the final victory.

These treaties were generally unknown in the United States when it entered the war, although American diplomatic advisers like Colonel House [2] knew the general nature of the contents of at least the European ones—they were published in the press in November—and had apprised the President; and Secretary of State Lansing knew at least of the

---

[1] The question of command is to be followed in *Intimate Papers, op. cit.;* T. C. Lonergan, *It Might Have Been Lost* (New York, 1929); General J. J. Pershing, *My Experiences in the World War* (2 vols., New York, 1931).

[2] *Intimate Papers, op. cit.,* I, p. 462; III, pp. 40-41.

Anglo-Japanese accord of 1915 with regard to the conquered German islands in the Pacific. These treaties,[1] which molded the final peace, were not so bad as some publicists have painted them. It is instructive to note that where they were followed there was no sore point left in the subsequent peace settlement.   Students of the war have excoriated the treaties as proof of the naked imperialistic designs of the Allies as contrasted with the hypocrisy of their professions of fighting for the defense of democracy and the rights of small nations.   That the treaties were tinctured with imperialism and selfishness is without question; but many commentators do not notice the obvious fact that these treaties were not the cause of the European War; they were negotiated *after* the war had already commenced. This holds true at least for the Allied powers which went to war in 1914. No spoils treaty antedated the war. In the cases of Italy and Rumania, the secret treaties by which they entered the conflict represented what the Allies had to promise to them in advance in order to bring them over.

There were five of these treaties or understandings, or groups of such, made to solidify the enthusiasm of the original Allies and to bring new ones into the circle.

(1) Russia secured her claims by a treaty with Great Britain and France made in March, 1915, at the beginning of the Allied attack on the Dardanelles. By this the two western Allies agreed that Russia might annex Constantinople and the Asiatic shore of the Bosporus and the Dardanelles, leaving free transit of the straits for the merchant ships of all nations. Russia on her part agreed to the separation of the Caliphate from Turkey and to sharing with France and Great Britain an influence over other portions of the Turkish Empire, reserving to England particular influence in the neighborhood of the Suez Canal and the Gulf of Persia—the British buffer of influence in Persia also was to be extended. These partitions of the Turkish Empire were marked out with more precision—conformable to the later mandates to France and Great Britain—in supplementary understandings (the Sykes-Picot agreement of May 16, 1916, and the agreement at St. Jean de Maurienne, April 17, 1917), reserving for Italy (in conformance with the Treaty of London) a share in the region of Adalia (which the entrance of Greece into the war later stopped her from taking, after the European peace). Thus did the Allies imperturbably dispose of the territory of Germany's Turkish ally, that vigorous "sick man of Europe" near whose bedside

[1] Seymour, *American Diplomacy during the World War, op. cit.,* p. 266.

the European powers for a century had been waiting either so anxiously or so eagerly.

(2) Italy's claim to expansion had been recognized in principle by the Treaty of London (April 26, 1915) which brought, or bought, that nation into the war. The Central Powers had been willing to promise a redemption of Italy's irredentist population at the end of the war, but not to deliver immediate occupation of the territory concerned. Ardent to weaken their enemy, the Allies promised the irredentist territory with strategical control of the Adriatic and of the Alpine passage into Austria, specifying a line which delivered over to Italy a Slavic and an Austrian *irredentum* at the head of the Adriatic and on its eastern shores.

Italy was also to have the strategic part of Albania, unchallenged government of the Dodecanese Islands in the Eastern Mediterranean, and a share in the partition of the Turkish Empire.

(3) Rumania was in a most favorable position for bargaining: the Central Powers offered her the irredentist province of Bessarabia (Russian); but the Entente Allies offered her the larger and more populous irredentist part of Hungarian Transylvania and even the Banat of Temesvár, where there was a numerous Serb population. After much wavering Rumania accepted the Allies' offer (Treaty of Bucharest, August 8, 1916), and entered on their side, only to be speedily crushed and occupied during the remainder of the war by German, Austro-Hungarian, and Bulgarian troops. Her separate treaty of peace in 1918 abrogated the obligations of the Allies.

(4) In the Far East, Japan and Great Britain by mutual understanding had divided up the conquered German islands in the Pacific: at the outset of the war British forces occupied those islands south of the Equator; Japan took over those north of that line. When it became apparent that the United States might enter the war Japan reached an understanding (February-March, 1917) with Great Britain, France, Italy, and Russia, sanctioning her claim to the transfer of all German rights in the Chinese province of Shantung, and, of course, to the islands north of the Equator.

(5) Finally there was the arrangement between France and Russia, also made (March 11, 1917) after the United States had broken relations with Germany, just on the eve of the first Russian Revolution. Each gave the other a free hand in arranging its frontier on the side of Germany—this meant at least Alsace-Lorraine for France and the Polish provinces for Russia.

Such were the famous secret agreements which Arthur Balfour presumably had in his portfolio, with their boundaries drawn on a large map, when he hurried to Washington in April, 1917, to secure full American participation in the war on the continent of Europe. To his surprise he found the United States enthusiastic for winning the war first and talking peace only afterward. Congress was appropriating (April 24, 1917) $7,000,000,000, of which $3,000,000,000 was to be loaned to Allied governments, the first great credit of a total which rapidly amounted to $7,077,144,750 before the armistice of November 11, 1918, and $2,170,200,000 more after it.

The President felt it would be a pity to let Balfour go home without a thorough discussion of the peace terms of the Allies. Colonel House thought it would be inadvisable at that time to have a general discussion with *all* the Allies: "If the Allies begin to discuss terms among themselves," he wrote to the President, "they will soon hate one another worse than they do Germany and a situation will arise similar to that in the Balkan States after the Turkish War. It seems to me that the only thing to be considered at present is how to beat Germany in the quickest way." Balfour easily concurred in House's sentiments. During the Balfour mission peace terms were nevertheless canvassed in long conferences. To Colonel House Balfour showed his map with the territorial lines of the secret treaties drawn on it. With the President and House, he went over the same ground. Russia had now collapsed, and the British spokesman did not defend her claims in Washington: Constantinople might be a free city, and Poland a resurrected state, though it would be a problem to find an outlet for that state to the sea. Rumania could have Bessarabia (Russian). As to the surviving Allies, the British Secretary insisted on keeping the bargains made with them.[1] There appears to have been no mention of the freedom of the seas.

Upon House's request, Balfour promised to furnish copies [2] of the secret treaties and agreements, but he returned to London without any new American demands. With the sequent French, Belgian, and Italian missions which had hurried to the United States, there was no discussion of peace terms, so far as we know.

President Wilson had agreed with his confidential adviser that it would not be well to disturb Allied unity before the enemy with any discussion of peace terms. He seems to have felt that his defense of

[1] House recorded the substance of these conferences, and it is printed in *Intimate Papers, op. cit.*, III, pp. 29-63.
[2] We do not know when these were delivered.

immutable principles, together with American military and financial power, would be so unchallengeable at the final peace conference that he could brush aside these secret agreements by the force of his prestige and that of his country. In this he was sadly mistaken. Having neglected the opportunity presented by the Balfour mission, at a time when it would have been a fatal mistake for the Allies to have cooled the military ardor of America, the President's crystallizing American peace terms began to conform more and more to the obligations to each other of the surviving Allies—objectives which themselves were of no mean service to the principle of nationality—and more and more he was forced to fall back on the unexceptionable principle of a League of Nations as the protected refuge for his peace policy and the sanctuary of his hopes for the future.

There was no longer any doubt that the United States would use all of its resources to help win the war. The Allies had found an ideal Associate, better than a real ally who would have extracted an equivalent for his sacrifices. A national conscription act passed Congress, May 18, 1917. A few weeks later the President promised Arthur Balfour a million and a half American troops on the western front by the end of 1918. The diplomats settled down now to the difficult task of gearing American resources to the military requirements of the Allies.[1] In August the President rejected as impossible the Pope's proposal to the belligerents for a peace without victory on the basis of mutual restoration, disarmament, organization for future arbitration, indemnity for civilian damages, general condonement, "community" of the seas, with a negotiated settlement of territorial questions like Alsace-Lorraine and the Trentino. These would have been ideal Wilsonian terms the previous January.

A peace of victory, would it be really possible? The military situation had steadily blackened. The near collapse of Italy after the Austrian victory of Caporetto, in the autumn of 1917, eased the Central Powers on that flank. American troops could not appear in force before the summer of 1918. The collapse of Russia was made complete and definitive by the Bolshevik Revolution of November, 1917. Straight-

[1] Seymour, *American Diplomacy during the World War, op. cit.,* pp. 212-252, is the only satisfactory account of the diplomatic labors of co-ordinating Allied requirements to American resources in shipping, food supply, credits, munitions, and questions of military and naval administration; and the creation of the inter-Allied Supreme War Council with which the United States cooperated without political commitment. Colonel House was the chief American spokesman in arranging these difficult but vital matters to a point where technical men could work out the details.

way the Russian revolutionists began the negotiation of a separate peace (signed at Brest Litovsk, March 3, 1918) which assured the Central Powers a free hand in regulating and expanding their eastern frontiers for future penetration beyond, and complete liberty to concentrate their whole war efforts on the western front of battle.[1]   The Bolsheviki in December, 1917, tore open the archives of the Czar and published to the world the secret treaties by which the Allies after the beginning of the war had pre-arranged a territorial settlement of Europe and the Near East.   It was an appeal to the laboring masses of the Allied countries to repudiate a war for what the revolutionists now branded as imperialistic ambitions hitherto masked by moral professions.   In France mutiny was brewing among the weary patriotic troops.   In Flanders the German high staff, nervous at popular restiveness, and disappointed by the Allies' checking of the submarine campaign, were preparing for a last mighty offensive to break through into France before their man power should give out in face of the American reinforcement.

It was in this black winter of the war that the Allies looked desperately for some moral impetus to their cause which would hold their peoples fighting together against complete military disaster.   It was then that President Wilson made his notable pronouncement to the Congress (January 8, 1918) of Fourteen Points for a peace acceptable to the United States.   The Fourteen Points were formulated by the President and Colonel House, after the latter had become convinced that the President must take a hand himself in a liberal crystallization of Allied war aims, if the Russians were to be kept in the war, and the morale shoved up of the Allied peoples.   House had studied carefully the previous expressions of the Allies' terms of peace, as they had been conveyed to him in his contact with Sir Edward Grey and Arthur Balfour, and as they had been proclaimed by Great Britain and France in January, 1917.   If we bear in mind the new Russian situation, the Fourteen Points did not conflict seriously with the secret treaties which Balfour had discussed in the White House.[2]   They proposed if possible to remake Europe along boundaries of nationality which perhaps would break up the Austro-Hungarian Empire and destroy the military strength of the Central Powers.   The American emphasis came in a demand

---

[1] H. W. V. Temperley, *A History of the Peace Conference of Paris* (6 vols., London, 1920-1921), I, pp. 1-14.

[2] This is seen by a comparison with the British Prime Minister's statement to the British Trades Unions Congress of Allied peace terms, January 5, 1918, the very day that the Wilson address was finally drafted.

for the freedom of the seas and insistence on a league of nations to organize peace after the war with a general guaranty thereafter of political independence and territorial integrity to great and small states alike. The authors of the Fourteen Points carefully phrased them so as to be useful under any of the three following conditions: (1) complete victory, (2) a stalemate war and a peace of compromise, (3) defeat. Witness the use of the words *must* and *should* which we have italicized:

The program of the world's peace, therefore, is our program, and that program, the only possible program, as we see it, is this:

1. Open convenants of peace, openly arrived at, after which there shall be no private international understandings of any kind, but diplomacy shall proceed always frankly and in the public view.

2. Absolute freedom of navigation upon the seas, outside territorial waters, alike in peace and in war, except as the seas may be closed in whole or in part by international action for the enforcement of international covenants.

3. The removal, so far as possible, of all economic barriers and the establishment of an equality of trade conditions among all the nations consenting to the peace and associating themselves for its maintenance.

4. Adequate guarantees given and taken that national armaments will be reduced to the lowest point consistent with domestic safety.

5. A free, open-minded, and absolutely impartial adjustment of all colonial claims, based upon a strict observance of the principle that in determining all such questions of sovereignty the interests of the populations concerned *must* have equal weight with the equitable claims of the government whose title is to be determined.

6. The evacuation of all Russian territory and such a settlement of all questions affecting Russia as will secure the best and freest co-operation of the other nations of the world in obtaining for her an unhampered and unembarrassed opportunity for the independent determination of her own political development and national policy and assure her of a sincere welcome into the society of free nations under institutions of her own choosing; and, more than a welcome, assistance also of every kind that she may need and may herself desire. The treatment accorded Russia by her sister nations in the months to come will be the acid test of their good will, of their comprehension of her needs as distinguished from their own interests, and of their intelligent and unselfish sympathy.

7. Belgium, the whole world will agree, *must* be evacuated and restored, without any attempt to limit the sovereignty which she enjoys in common with all other free nations. No other single act will serve as this will serve to restore confidence among the nations in the laws which they have themselves set and determined for the government of their relations with one another. Without this healing act the whole structure and validity of international law is forever impaired.

8. All French territory *should* be freed and the invaded portions restored, and the wrong done to France by Prussia in 1871 in the matter of Alsace-Lorraine, which has unsettled the peace of the world for nearly fifty years, *should* be righted, in order that peace may once more be made secure in the interest of all.

9. A readjustment of the frontiers of Italy *should* be effected along clearly recognizable lines of nationality.

10. The peoples of Austria-Hungary, whose place among the nations we wish to see safeguarded and assured, *should* be accorded the freest opportunity of autonomous development.

11. Rumania, Serbia, and Montenegro *should* be evacuated; occupied territories restored; Serbia accorded free and secure access to the sea; and the relations of the several Balkan states to one another determined by friendly counsel along historically established lines of allegiance and nationality; and international guarantees of the political and economic independence and territorial integrity of the several Balkan states *should* be entered into.

12. The Turkish portions of the present Ottoman Empire *should* be assured a secure sovereignty, but the other nationalities which are now under Turkish rule *should* be assured an undoubted security of life and an absolutely unmolested opportunity of autonomous development, and the Dardanelles *should* be permanently opened as a free passage to the ships and commerce of all nations under international guarantees.

13. An independent Polish state *should* be erected, which *should* include the territories inhabited by indisputably Polish populations, which *should* be assured a free and secure access to the sea, and whose political and economic independence and territorial integrity *should* be guaranteed by international covenant.

14. A general association of nations *must* be formed under specific covenants for the purpose of affording mutual guarantees of political independence and territorial integrity to great and small states alike.

The President and Colonel House studiously went over the whole document after they had first drafted it, qualifying it with their *musts* and *shoulds*.

The Fourteen Points, it proved, were to be interpreted under conditions of complete victory and solely by the Allied and Associated Powers, with the defeated enemy reaching desperately to the Wilsonian principles in the hope to save at least something. In these circumstances it was easy for the victors to interpret *should* to mean *must*.

The final German offensive in the west failed in July, 1918. The Turkish, Bulgarian, and Austrian allies began to crack all along their respective fronts and at home. With the victory now surely in sight, the Allies themselves were reeling with exhaustion. During 1918 there took place a series of long-distance exchanges of peace views in the shape of pronouncements from the rostrums of the different governments.[1] These varied in their force according to the military situation. At no time were the Allies driven to accepting a "peace by compromise and negotiation" which the Central Powers offered. Meanwhile President Wilson in public addresses had piled the Fourteen Points with further general principles of durable peace which included: the destruction or at least reduction of arbitrary power capable of upsetting the peace of the world, satisfaction of "well-defined national aspirations," prohibition of especial leagues or embargoes within the proposed League of Nations, no secret treaties, self-determination for peoples and territories whose sovereignty was in question, and, finally, "impartial justice." [2]

The end of the war suddenly appeared when Bulgaria signed an armistice of military surrender and occupation, September 29, 1918. Already Austria-Hungary (September 16, 1918) had proposed to the enemy a discussion of peace by all belligerents. Facing complete collapse, and in panic at the furious and general advance of the Allies and Associates all along the western front, General Ludendorff and the Field Marshal von Hindenburg, the German Chief of Staff, urgently advised the Government to sue for peace and to try to salvage something by an appeal to the Wilsonian principles. On October 6, Germany, and on October 7, Austria-Hungary, transmitted to the United States (instead of to the Allies) a request for an armistice. With victorious troops exultantly pushing through on all fronts the President made the most of his advantage, and kept control of the preliminary moves for peace. He used in a masterly way the strategy of delay. In a correspondence with Germany he insisted that he must know that he was treating with a government that really had the support of the people; to Austria he replied that the recent recognition of the belligerency of Czechoslovakia by the United States had modified Point X, which stressed "autonomy" for the peoples of Austria-Hungary: now it was the Czechoslovaks themselves, and also the Yugoslavs, who must themselves judge of their own rights and destiny.

Before the discussion with the United States could be completed the crumbling and vanishing Austro-Hungarian Empire signed (November 3, 1918) an armistice with the Italians, technically with the Allied and

---

[1] They are printed by the Carnegie Endowment for International Peace, Division of International Law. Pamphlet No. 11 (Washington, 1921).

[2] Since these points became a part of the discussions for an armistice, and were actually embodied in the German armistice, they should be added to the Fourteen Points. Note the more imperative tone, which we have stressed by italics, in the note at the end of the chapter.

Associated Powers. The Wilsonian principles, therefore, were not made a certain condition of peace in the Austro-Hungarian surrender. The historic but volatile empire had suddenly exploded before it could securely seize hold of them. Turkey had accepted a controlling British armistice, October 31, 1918, before its appeal to Wilsonianism could be heard and transmitted to the Allies.

A frantic constitutional reformation of the German Government did not prevent the proclamation of a socialist republic in Berlin, but it induced President Wilson at least to transmit to the triumphing Allies the German request for an armistice, making it first well understood to Germany that it must be an armistice of complete surrender. The Kaiser abdicated (November 9, 1918), fleeing ignominiously to Holland. The Central Powers, who had almost grasped the fringe of victory's robes in the spring of 1918, were now at the mercy of their enemies.

Germany had appealed to the United States for peace on the basis of President Wilson's pronouncements, particularly the Fourteen Points. The President had leisurely consented to transmit the appeal to the Allies. He had left it unreservedly to the commanding generals in the field, notably to Marshal Foch, the Generalissimo of the Allied and Associated armies, whether the military situation justified an armistice. Foch replied yes, if Germany agreed to an effectual disarmament he was ready to sign. In view of obstinate public ignorance it is necessary to emphasize what British and French historians and statesmen have repeatedly pointed out:[1] that President Wilson did not interfere with the command in the field and force them to agree to an armistice without further invasion and the complete pulverization of Germany. It was Marshal Foch who dictated the military terms of the armistice and was completely content with it, as were the other commanders, except Pershing. The French General said: "One makes war only to get results." In the military and naval surrender of Germany and her allies the results would be obtained, so far as they could be had by war.

It was for the Allies to decide among themselves what political conditions they would attach to the military surrender. Could they all agree to the Fourteen Points and later pronouncements of President Wilson as the fundamental basis of peace, to be interpreted to suit themselves in the condition of complete victory, then to be dictated to Ger-

[1] *The Memoirs of Marshal Foch* (translated by T. Bentley Mott, New York, 1931), p. 463; B. H. Liddell Hart, *The Real War, 1914-1918* (London, 1930), p. 409; Pierre Renouvin, *op. cit.*, p. 596.

many? Were there any other conditions to attach to the Fourteen Points before accepting a German surrender?

In the important pre-Armistice negotiations between the United States and the Allies, conducted by Colonel House as the personal representative of the President, Great Britain reserved her interpretation of Point 2, the freedom of the seas, the historic American principle. Prime Minister Lloyd George said he could not give up control of a means which had enabled the Allies to win the war, notably by transporting American troops to France. Premier Clemenceau of France agreed to this; and on his part insisted on specifying broadly for "reparation for damages." He insisted that there must be compensation by Germany, "for all damages done to the civilian population of the Allies and their property by the aggression of Germany by land, by sea and from the air." House, and Wilson behind him, contented themselves with a general understanding that Point 2 might be made the subject of future discussion with the Allies. With these two essential modifications, the significant emasculation of the freedom of the seas and the sweeping provision for reparation, the Fourteen Points and the subsequent pronouncements of the President became by the terms of the armistice of November 11, 1918, the agreed basis of the peace to be negotiated between the Allied and Associated Powers and Germany.

The negotiation of the armistice had taken place while the American congressional elections of 1918 were approaching. Republicans and Democrats during the war had put away their political opposition in common patriotic endeavor. It had been the Republican spokesmen who had been more aggressive in demands on Germany than the Administration, more forward for war. During the war they had at least equaled their old political adversaries in their demand for the utmost national exertions. Including the two former Presidents, Roosevelt and Taft, they had demanded, during the autumnal political campaign, the election in November, 1918, of a Republican Congress to push through the war and control a peace of unconditional surrender by the enemy. Roosevelt in particular contemned the Fourteen Points as "soft."

President Wilson feared that if the Republicans should secure control of Congress they would sweep away his program for peace. He was nervous about reports of large sums of money being spent by his political opponents to carry the elections, notably in Michigan. A friend asked him, in a long conversation in the White House (September 13, 1918), what he would do in case he should lose the elections. Would he resign the Presidency, following his well-known convictions about responsible government? It was recalled to him that he had planned to resign that high office in case Charles Evans Hughes, the Republican candidate for the Presidency, had been elected in November, 1916, thus allowing the President-elect to come into office immediately without waiting until March 4. "I cannot do it," Woodrow Wilson now said, "on account of the world-wide situation, in which American influence is very important and may be decisive. It happens to be a case where, even if defeated by the people, I shall have to try to obtain the objects for which we went to war." [1]

It was this fear which led the President into what has been generally regarded as a strategical misstep. But for this mistake he might have kept his position as the leader of a politically undivided nation. He could have appealed to the voters to return senators and representatives, of whatever party, who would support him in finishing the war and settling the peace. With the end of the war in sight, he issued a public appeal for the election of a Democratic majority in both houses of Congress in order that he might be wholly unhampered in the approaching negotiations. It is true that President McKinley issued a similar call, successfully, in 1898. But it was unnecessary for President Wilson and unwise. Some of his political advisers counseled against it. The appeal invoked a partisan issue where previously there had been little for the public to discern between the two parties united in war. The country was normally Republican—Wilson had come to power and stayed in power only because of the division of his Republican opponents; now, with the war over, they united to meet his challenge.

The elections resulted in a clear Republican majority for the new Senate (and House too) which would meet after March 4, 1919, to consider the treaties of peace. Former President Roosevelt, presuming to speak for a reunited and victorious Republican Party, declared to the world after the election: "Our allies and our enemies, and Mr. Wilson himself, should all understand that Mr. Wilson has no authority whatever to speak for the American people at this time. His leadership has just been emphatically repudiated by them. . . ."

The world cried for peace. The overturn of three great empires, Germany, Austria-Hungary, and Russia, and their satellites displayed throughout the eastern half of Europe a panorama of confusion, anarchy, and chaos. The question of the hour was how to shape the machinery

[1] Statement to the author by the friend in question, the late William E. Dodd, who recorded the conversation at the time.

of procedure directly, and efficaciously, to dictate peace quickly on the terms of the Allied and Associated Powers, terms couched as yet in the very general Wilsonian principles. France had suggested to the United States, in a memorandum to Washington of November 29, 1918, that the five great victors (the United States, Great Britain, France, Italy, Japan) should sweep the table clear of all previous special agreements arrived at by some of the Allies only, and straightway agree among themselves on the principal bases of peace. The small belligerents, the neutral states, and the new states in formation could be called in for consultation as their special interests were touched on one by one. In subsequent conferences, after a preliminary peace had been dictated, garnished with the invocation of moral principles, all the nations could meet in a congress to work out the permanent organization of world peace in a League of Nations. Colonel House and Secretary Lansing were inclined to favor some such procedure. President Wilson did not even answer the French proposal. He had his mind first on a League of Nations. He was determined that it should be interwoven with the peace treaties, and that he himself would take the American delegation to Paris to make sure that this was done; otherwise the peoples of the embattled nations might be overreached by the more sophisticated spokesmen of their governments. He did not realize that actually the peoples could be more uncompromising than their spokesmen.

If repudiated by the electorate of his own homeland, it was at the apogee of his prestige in the world that Woodrow Wilson surveyed the European shore from the bridge of the *George Washington*. He arrived in Europe as a true friend of mankind, closer to the principles of Christian charity and justice than any other statesman in history. The new great ideal seemed really possible. If only he could bring Europe to agree to a peace of justice resting on the foundations of a league of democratic nations which would execute and regulate the treaties of peace, he was convinced that the opposition of Congress at home would have to yield to the force of public opinion. By the gospel of his principles he would overbear the Republican politicians in the Senate, as abroad he expected to sweep aside whatever obstacles the Allies' secret treaties presented to the application of his Fourteen Points.

The American Peace Commission consisted of executive agents appointed without the advice and consent of the Senate, a custom which had been engrafted by practice to the American constitutional system by virtue of the President's control over diplomatic negotiations.[1] In the language of the treaties which he later signed, the President was "acting in his own name and by his own proper authority." Very unwisely he did not include in the Commission, according to traditional practice, representatives from both parties in that Senate which would be called upon to ratify his treaties. He was also criticized, even by his own Secretary of State,[2] for jeopardizing his dominant position in the world by descending into a conference with the foreign statesmen in Europe. One of the real advantages of the American diplomatic system has been the reserve power which the President, back home across the ocean, has had to stiffen the demands of his plenipotentiaries in the give and take of negotiation; and back of this, and despite the shocking abuse of it by party politics, lies the still greater reserve power of the Senate in the right to advise and consent, by a two-thirds majority, to the ratification of any treaty. These advantages the President, in his convictions, threw away by going to Paris at the head of a personal executive delegation. The other members were: Secretary of State Lansing; Colonel House; General Tasker H. Bliss; and Henry White, veteran career diplomatist of pale Republican allegiance, who had never made any public statement hostile to the President. White was the only Republican on the Commission, and through him Senator Lodge, leader of the Republican Senate and chairman of the Committee on Foreign Relations, unsuccessfully tried to speak to the Allies behind the back of the President.[3]

A shipload of officials of the State Department, intelligence officers, specialists, and secretaries accompanied the Commission. The "experts" had been recruited quietly from academic and other walks of life under the direction of Colonel House. Organized unostentatiously under the name of The Inquiry, after the immemorial habit of professors everywhere they had diligently assembled during the previous twelve months a mass of facts and information of a special nature for the advice of the diplomatists who were to discuss the intricate political, territorial, and economic questions of several continents. These specialists played an important part in drafting the nondebatable articles of the peace treaties and in fortifying the plenipotentiaries in the diplomatic disputations.

[1] Henry M. Wriston has traced with a wealth of detail the growth of this practice in his *Executive Agents in American Foreign Relations* (Johns Hopkins Press, 1929).

[2] Robert Lansing, *The Peace Negotiations, a Personal Narrative* (New York, 1921).

[3] Nevins, *Henry White, op. cit.,* p. 353.

At the Peace Conference at Paris, which opened January 12, 1919, met the plenipotentiaries of twenty-seven nations, enemies of Germany or of her allies, or nations, like five of the Latin-American states, who had severed relations with Germany. There had never been such a diplomatic gathering in history. Even the Congress of Vienna, once consecrated to the Principle of Legitimacy as the Paris Conference was now consecrated to the Principle of Nationality, could not approach its vast importance. It was the focus of seething national rivalries, resentments, despairs, ambitions, triumphs. President Wilson, it must be generally conceded, was the only statesman of the great powers who had no selfish national interest to serve, no particular necessitous war bargain to fulfill. Each of the other war-weary nations, except for those like the South American Republics which had been only nominally at war, had some special right or attachment to protect, some vital or profitable interest to secure. Among the actual fighting belligerents only Canada stood in the American relationship, but she had her responsibilities to the British Empire. How can we blame the plenipotentiaries for not having made a perfect peace? The marvel is that they agreed to any peace at all.

Able participants, conscious of the historic importance of the occasion, have pictured the highlights of the momentous gathering and its vivid personalities: Clemenceau, who presided, the dauntless Premier of France, acclaimed by his compatriots as the Father of Victory, seventy-eight years old, ancient, wrinkled, with his black skull cap, his gray-gloved and imperturbably folded hands, his fringe of white hair, a tiger statesman, frank exponent of the balance of power, fighting first and always to sustain his rescued France; Lloyd George, Prime Minister of Great Britain, crystal of perspicacity, indomitable dynamo of human energy, the parliamentary chiefs of the daughter Dominions arrayed at his side, a prime minister conspicuously serving the interests of the British Empire but a sincere striver for permanent reconciliation with the enemy—providing no fleet were left him; Orlando, the Italian Premier, virile, ardent, eloquent, little concerned with anything but the questions which affected Italy; Saionji, aged Elder Statesman of Japan, who as a lad had fought in feudal wars with bow and arrow—quiet, inscrutable, intervening only to protect Japan's winnings and to make sure her position as an equal among the Great Powers; finally, Woodrow Wilson, President of the United States of America now come to Europe, his eager academic countenance alive with success, the crusader for organized world peace.

It had been the President's first thought that all the Allied and Associated Nations, great and small, should meet together at the conference to interpret and apply the Fourteen Points. The small nations would welcome the League more unconditionally. For all the powers, big and little, to meet equally to dispose of issues, proved impossible. The Big Five (the United States, Great Britain, France, Italy, and Japan) therefore agreed that their chiefs of state and foreign ministers should meet in a Council of Ten, settle things, and prescribe articles to be ratified at the plenary sessions of the Conference. Smaller powers would be consulted as their interests were touched. In reality this Council of Ten was an *alter ego* of the Supreme Allied War Council which had developed in recent months to deal with inter-Allied war interests. The Council of Ten appointed representative commissions, fifty-two in number, to study and report on particular questions. The meetings of the Council of Ten, always attended by a numerous entourage of advisers, interpreters, and experts, proved too cumbersome, and too public, for frank and expeditious settlement of delicate subjects. Eventually a Council of Four: [1] Wilson, Lloyd George, Clemenceau, and Orlando, began to meet confidentially together with only one secretary—sometimes none—to keep their records. Here the main points of the peace were settled. These meetings were really continuing the method instituted at the time of the conferences on the impending armistice, when Clemenceau, Lloyd George, Orlando, and House had settled essential points before they were treated in the Supreme War Council. Orlando quit the Four, when later in disposing of Austria-Hungary they would not award Fiume to Italy, so the last weeks of the conference were under the diplomatic tribunal of the Triumvirate of the chiefs of state of the United States, Great Britain, and France. Thus it was the principal powers which arranged the peace, as France had proposed after the armistice; but it was only after Wilson had persuaded them to agree on the League; on the other hand there had been no sweeping aside of the secret treaties as France at first was willing to suggest.

The history of the Conference can be divided into three stages. The first extended from January 12 to February 14, 1919, on which date President Wilson left Paris for a visit to the United States to attend to his constitutional duties at the close of the Congress. During these weeks Wilson's insistence forged the first draft of the League of Nations, setting aside, until the great Convenant could be agreed upon, the final

[1] Japan did not choose to sit in on discussions of debatable Occidental political and territorial subjects.

decision of the crucial territorial and political questions that were being examined by the commissions. The second stage was the interval of the President's absence, a month, during most of which Lloyd George was in England to attend to pressing duties at home, and Clemenceau lay stricken by the attack of an anarchist. It had been agreed that during the President's absence discussion should proceed on the territorial and political questions. During this period much important work was done by the special commissions appointed to consider territorial, economic, and other technical questions. The third and final stage was from March 14, when the President returned to Paris, until the signature of the Treaty of Versailles. This was the period in which the Four, and then the Three, made the most important decisions on the great issues among the victorious Allies and Associates.[1]

When Wilson returned to Paris on March 14 these paramount questions, though clarified by discussion, still remained to be settled. In the intimate discussions which followed among the Four, with Japan included where she so desired, it boiled down to this, from the American point of view: President Wilson, in his endeavor to mold the peace settlement to the matrix of the principles of his pronouncements as interpreted by the American delegation under his leadership, found himself obliged to make compromises with the special demands of the great Allies and their commitments to each other. He reached this point not only through the necessity of bargaining with the Allies but also after the conclusions of his own advisers that his principles were inapplicable in their entirety.

Great Britain and the Dominions wished to keep the colonies they had conquered from Germany in Africa and on the Pacific. A Dominion spokesman, General Jan C. Smuts of South Africa, had proposed the system of mandates for the regions detached by the war from the Ottoman Empire, but he did not apply that also to Africa and the islands of the Pacific. Nobody on that side of the Atlantic thought of returning to Germany any of these conquests, despite Point 5, "a free, open-minded, and absolutely impartial adjustment of all colonial claims. . . ." This, in victory, was interpreted by all the victors to mean the claims only of the victors to the colonial spoil. To adjust the colonial question, Wilson acceded to the compromise suggestion of a graded mandate system for

[1] Robert C. Binkley has made a notable and critical analysis, from records then available, of the procedural history of the conference in relation to the great issues, in his "New Light on the Paris Peace Conference," *Political Science Quarterly*, XLVI (September, December, 1931), 335-361, 509-547.

all the conquered colonies, as well as for Asia Minor and Mesopotamia. The appointed mandatory under the direction of the League of Nations, in each instance, proved to be either the conqueror, or the beneficiary of a secret treaty.   Men have sneered at this as an hypocritical disguise of annexation; at least it was an appeal to an international control of backward peoples and colonial areas, stakes of imperialistic con- tention.   The efficacy of the system would depend on the strength of the League of Nations.

France required a demilitarized buffer Rhineland state to protect her from dreaded German attacks in the future; and she insisted on repay- ment of separation allowances and military pensions to civilian relatives and survivors of soldiers.   Here were the most difficult issues.   They were settled by France agreeing to content herself with Alsace-Lorraine and her old frontiers, back of a military occupation for fifteen years [1] of the left bank of the Rhine and its bridgeheads, and a demilitarized zone in Germany for a depth of fifty kilometers east of the Rhine; in return France was to possess the Saar Valley, with its rich coal mines, subject to a determining plebiscite in 1935 (as a result of which the district was finally returned to Germany).   Clemenceau, against the advice of Marshal Foch, agreed to this only when Lloyd George and Wilson signed a tripartite alliance pledging their countries to come to the aid of France if attacked in the future by Germany.   It was strictly and significantly stated that the alliance would not apply unless ratified by all three parties, according to their respective constitutional require- ments.   Great Britain and France ratified.   The United States Senate, as President Wilson probably knew it would and as Premier Clemenceau must have suspected it would, refused to consider the proposed pact, so radically contrary to George Washington's historic advice against "permanent alliances."   The President made no great battle for this treaty in the Senate.   It was a way the diplomatists had to get around a difficult corner.   The President and the Prime Minister readily agreed to Clemenceau's demand that the dubious allowances for military sep- aration and pensions be added to the German debt of reparations under category of "civilian damages" sanctioned by the Armistice.   Computa- tions of this kind could double the already astronomical character of calculating reparations debits—projecting their reckoning even unto the outer spaces of the ether drift beyond the great Magellanic Cloud.

[1] With provisions for evacuation of successive zones by five-year periods in case Ger- many fulfilled the treaty loyally.

In the case of Italy, the President assented to the strategical frontier of the Treaty of London, with some modifications, but not including the city of Fiume. The treaty of peace with Austria gave Italy possession of the Alpine passes into Austria, creating an Austria *irredenta* in the Tyrol of some 250,000 souls, in place of the old *Italia irredenta*. It remained to fix the boundary between Italy and the new state of Yugoslavia at the head of the Adriatic and along the Dalmatian littoral. President Wilson sought to apply Point 9 of the Fourteen Points to temper the extreme Italian claims, but it is uncertain whether Italy was explicitly bound by the Fourteen Points in the armistice with Austria-Hungary. Wilson, Lloyd George, and Clemenceau were willing to make generous strategic concessions to Italy beyond the line of the Treaty of London, but not to give to Italy the half-Slavic city of Fiume, necessary for a usable outlet for Yugoslavia to the sea, a city of mixed population with an entirely Slavic hinterland. The peace conference ended without this intricate question being settled.[1]

Japan insisted on two things: an explicit recognition in the Covenant of the League of Nations of the principle of equality of all races, and title to her conquests from Germany in the Chinese province of Shantung as well as control of the conquered former German islands north of the Equator. She was willing to accept a mandate for the islands, a mandate of the class which administered them as integral parts of the mandatory state, except for prohibiting fortifications; and she even made the promise ultimately to get out of Shantung in her own way, a promise subsequently fulfilled. Unfortunately the Council did not agree to the principle of racial equality. If also it had refused to transfer to Japan the German holdings in Shantung, Japan undoubtedly would have left the Conference and refused the treaty; with European powers still on the Mainland of Asia, she was determined not to have dictated to her, after 1895, another relinquishment of the fruits of victory. To secure Japanese assent to the treaty and hence to the League, President Wilson reluctantly accepted the Japanese position in Shantung, contrary as it was to the gospel of self-determination. China then refused to sign the Treaty of Versailles, but became a member of the League of

---

[1] In 1920, by the Treaty of Rapallo, Italy and Yugoslavia agreed on a frontier, and created a nominally independent city-state of Fiume with a finger of territory stretching along the Adriatic to Italy; and giving Italy possession of the strategic islands of the Dalmatian shore, where there were heavy, if spotty, Italian populations. By a treaty of 1924 between Italy and Yugoslavia after Mussolini's capture of the Italian state, Fiume was annexed by Italy. This final settlement left a rankling *Yugoslavia irredenta* of over half a million people.

Nations by ratifying the Treaty of St. Germain with Austria, which cost her none of her own territory, though it also violated in Central Europe the consecrated principles of self-determination and nationality.

All these major concessions in principle the President made in order to secure the consent of all the great victor powers to the League of Nations as an integral part of the treaty. He believed that the regrettable compromises in each case justified the great end in view.

The other provisions of the treaties with Germany, Austria, and Hungary involved no essential difficulty, although there was intense disputation in regard to the regulation of the status of the Saar Valley before the plebiscite postponed until 1935, and concerning the establishment of the Free City of Danzig at the mouth of the Polish corridor. They contained, among the countless routine articles: creation of the special commission to calculate and to charge up to Germany the total sum due for reparations, with no indemnity for war expenses by the Allies; the shaping of the nine new remnant and succession states in Central Europe—Austria, Hungary, Czechoslovakia, Yugoslavia, Poland, Lithuania, Latvia, Estonia, Finland; the Polish corridor; the marking off of patches of German peripheral territory for determination of sovereignty by plebiscites; the regulation of the Kiel Canal and the rivers within enemy territory; the effectual disarmament of Germany and her allies on land, on sea, and in the air "in order to render possible the initiation of a general limitation of the armaments of all nations"; and the one hundred and one incidental details of so vast a settlement of peace.[1] The Principal Allied and Associated Powers

[1] R. C. Binkley appraises the authorities for the peace conference in "Ten Years of Peace Conference History," *Journal of Modern History*, I (December, 1929), 607-629, and "New Light on the Paris Peace Conference," *Political Science Quarterly*, XLVI (1931), 335-361, 509-547, to which Paul Birdsall's article serves as a sequel: "The Second Decade of Peace Conference History," *Journal of Modern History*, XV (September, 1939), 362-378. The standard account is Temperley, *Peace Conference of Paris, op. cit.*, a co-operative work by specialists, British and American. Shorter and more general are: C. H. Haskins and Robert H. Lord, *Some Problems of the Peace Conference* (Harvard University Press, 1920) by two specialists from the American delegation; and Edward M. House and Charles Seymour, *What Really Happened at Paris; the Story of the Peace Conference, 1918-1919, by American Delegates* (New York, 1921), a series of chapters by members of and advisers to the American Peace Commission. Ray Stannard Baker's *Woodrow Wilson and World Settlement* (3 vols., New York, 1922) is informing but premature and one-sided, and his later biography of Wilson does not cover the peace conference. Harold Nicolson's *Peace Making, 1919* (New York, 1939) is a glancing literary essay of a disillusioned middle-aged man who participated in the conference in his youth. A better balanced account of the fate of Wilsonian principles at Paris is Paul Birdsall, *Versailles Twenty Years After* (New York, 1941). A most valuable source for American diplomacy at Paris is David Hunter Miller, *My Diary at the Conference of Paris* (20 vols., privately printed in 40 copies only, 1928). The official record of the

were easily agreed on the famous Article 231 and its sweeping provisions:

The Allied and Associated Governments affirm and Germany accepts the responsibility of Germany and her allies for causing all the loss and damage to which the Allied and Associated Governments and their nationals have been subjected as a consequence of the war imposed upon them by the aggression of Germany and her allies.

Strictly speaking, this article required Germany to accept responsibility for damages done by the war, rather than "war guilt"; but it has been denounced on many occasions as an unjust branding of that nation as solely responsible for the war itself.

Only the Russian enigma remained unsettled. At the signing of the peace treaties Allied and Associated forces still remained on Russian territory, in the bleak and distantly separated sectors of Archangel and Vladivostok, whither they had been sent during the war to stay the dizzy collapse of Russia's resistance to the Central Powers.[1]

As for Germany and Austria and Hungary, they were permitted to show cause why the dictated terms should be altered. In a few details only, like that of the boundary of Silesia, did the victors condescend to change the drafted treaty. Perforce they accepted, they the vanquished. Obscure German plenipotentiaries signed the Treaty of Versailles, June 28, 1919, in the Hall of Mirrors, in the historic palace

United States Government is *The Paris Peace Conference, 1919* (12 vols., Washington, G.P.O., 1942-1947), supplementary to the regular volume *Foreign Relations* for the year 1919.

[1] See below, p. 217, for Siberian expedition.

In May, 1917, the United States sent to Russia a special diplomatic mission under Elihu Root to institute ways and means of counteracting Germany's efforts to bring Russia to a separate peace. The net result of the Root mission was to open up for the provisional government credits to the extent ultimately of $325,500,000 for the purchase of military supplies in America, of which $187,729,750 had been advanced in cash before the withdrawal of credit after the Bolshevik *coup* of November 7, 1917.

Another commission of railroad experts was sent to Russia under the command of John F. Stevens, with the rank of minister, to facilitate the transport of war material, particularly across Siberia from Vladivostok.

Point 6 of President Wilson's Fourteen Points, it is remembered, demanded the evacuation of all Russian territory, and unembarrassed self-determination for the people of Russia. "The treatment accorded Russia by her sister nations in the months to come will be the acid test of their good will. . . ." Within a few months, however, the sister nations had intervened in Russia. At Paris in 1919 Clemenceau and Orlando successfully opposed the efforts of Wilson and Lloyd George to invite representatives of all the contending Russian parties to the Peace Conference. They finally agreed to sound out the Russian groups about sending delegates to a special conference with representatives of the Allies at Prinkipo Island, in the Sea of Marmara; but the failure of all the opposing factions to agree to send delegates resulted in the default of this proposed conference. The Bolsheviki on their part were willing to send representatives.

of Versailles, where in 1871 after the prostration of France the German princes in arms had proclaimed, amidst a mass of military glory, King William I of Prussia to be German Emperor.

In all this dictation of peace one great factor stands out. It was an imperfect but not a Carthaginian peace. If it did violence in certain regions to the Wilsonian principle of self-determination, it is also true that more millions of peoples enjoyed self-determination and national identity after the peace than before it. It did not undo the legitimate part of Bismarck's work, crowned in this same Hall of Mirrors forty-eight years before. It disarmed Germany. It took away her great navy. It dismantled her air force. It stripped her of her colonies. It levied an unfairly excessive amount of reparations, by including separation allowances and military pensions. It pared her of territory inhabited by conquered alien populations. But it did not destroy the Reich. It left a united nation. That vital fact is often ignored. The living core remained to rise again.

The Treaty of Versailles of the twenty-seven nations with Germany filled a stout volume, with smaller supplementary volumes for the Treaty of St. Germain with Austria (signed, September 10, 1919), and the Treaty of the Trianon with Hungary (signed, June 4, 1920).

There were two other treaties of peace, with Bulgaria (signed at Neuilly, November 27, 1919) and with Turkey (signed at Sèvres, August 10, 1920). The Bulgarian treaty, settling the present boundaries of the Balkan state, and fixing a staggering total of reparations for that small country, does not concern American diplomacy. The treaty with Turkey registered the dismemberment of the Ottoman Empire. This treaty did not stand. Before it could be executed a revolution of Turkish nationalists under the leadership of the redoubtable Mustafa Kemal, still master of that new republic, cast off the victor's bridle, drove out foreign forces from Anatolia, redeemed Constantinople, did away with extraterritoriality and the capitulations, fixed boundaries along the lines of nationality, and made no mention of indemnities or reparations. The United States at the same time (1923) signed a separate treaty with Turkey, of amity and commerce, also abolishing the capitulations, and re-establishing relations between the two republics, important to the United States because of the heavy interest of American philanthropic, religious, and educational endeavor there. This treaty failed to pass the Senate, because of opposition aroused against any treaty with the "red-handed" Kemal régime, which many expected to fall. But the Kemal Government proved permanent. A short, new treaty (signed,

1931, ratified, 1933) finally fixed relations of establishment and sojourn of nationals, on a most-favored-nation basis, between the two countries. With all nations except Russia normal diplomatic relations had been now established in Europe.

President Wilson and his plenipotentiaries signed the treaties of peace in 1919. How would the new Republican Senate in Washington look upon his diplomatic handiwork?

THE FOUR SUPPLEMENTARY POINTS OF PRESIDENT WILSON OF FEBRUARY 11, 1918; THE FOUR ADDITIONAL POINTS OF JULY 4, 1918; AND THE FIVE ADDITIONAL POINTS OF SEPTEMBER 27, 1918.[1]

(Address to Congress, February 11, 1918)

First, that each part of the final settlement *must* be based upon the essential justice of that particular case and upon such adjustments as are most likely to bring a peace that will be permanent;

Second, that peoples and provinces *are not* to be bartered about from sovereignty to sovereignty as if they were mere chattels and pawns in a game, even the great game, now forever discredited, of the balance of power; but that

Third, every territorial settlement involved in this war *must* be made in the interest and for the benefit of the populations concerned, and not as a part of any mere adjustment or compromise of claims amongst rival States; and

Fourth, that all well defined national aspirations *shall be* accorded the utmost satisfaction that can be accorded them without introducing new or perpetuating old elements of discord and antagonism that would be likely in time to break the peace of Europe and consequently of the world.

(Address at Mount Vernon, July 4, 1918)

I. The destruction of every arbitrary power anywhere that can separately, secretly, and of its single choice disturb the peace of the world; or, if it can not be presently destroyed, at the least its reduction to virtual impotence.

II. The settlement of every question, whether of territory, of sovereignty, of economic arrangement, or of political relationship, upon the basis of the free acceptance of that settlement by the people immediately concerned, and not upon the basis of the material interest or advantage of any other nation or people which may desire a different settlement for the sake of its own exterior influence or mastery.

III. The consent of all nations to be governed in their conduct towards each other by the same principles of honor and of respect for the common

[1] Italics inserted.

law of civilized society that govern the individual citizens of all modern States in their relations with one another; to the end that all promises and covenants may be sacredly observed, no private plots or conspiracies hatched, no selfish injuries wrought with impunity, and a mutual trust established upon the handsome foundation of a mutual respect for right.

IV. The establishment of an organization of peace which *shall make* it certain that the combined power of free nations will check every invasion of right and serve to make peace and justice the more secure by affording a definite tribunal of opinion to which all *must* submit and by which every international readjustment that can not be amicably agreed upon by the peoples directly concerned *shall* be sanctioned.

(Address at opening of Fourth Liberty Loan Campaign, September 27, 1918)

First, the impartial justice meted out *must* involve no discrimination between those to whom we wish to be just and those to whom we do not wish to be just. It *must be* a justice that plays no favorites and knows no standard but the equal rights of the several peoples concerned;

Second, no special or separate interest of any single nation or any group of nations *can be* made the basis of any part of the settlement which is not consistent with the common interest of all;

Third, there *can be no* leagues or alliances or special covenants and understandings within the general and common family of the League of Nations;

Fourth, and more specifically, there *can be no* special, selfish economic combinations within the League and no employment of any form of economic boycott or exclusion except as the power of economic penalty by exclusion from the markets of the world may be vested in the League of Nations itself as a means of discipline and control;

Fifth, all international agreements and treaties of every kind *must* be made known in their entirety to the rest of the world.

9

The Great Debate and the Separate Peace

WOODROW WILSON was the true founder of the League of Nations, but of course it was not his original idea. Philosophers and publicists had invoked for centuries the concept of a league or confederation of the nations for peace, but only in the twentieth century had statesmen begun to urge it as a practical measure. In the United States, former President Theodore Roosevelt had been a vigorous advocate since 1910, when he declared, in accepting the Nobel peace prize: "It would be a master stroke if those great Powers honestly bent on peace would form a League of Peace, not only to keep the peace among themselves, but to prevent, by force if necessary, its being broken by others." [1] He repeatedly urged, during the earlier years of the First World War, such a "solemn agreement in a great world league for the peace of righteousness," a "solemn covenant." The elder statesmen of both parties were for it: Roosevelt, Taft, Bryan, Elihu Root, Lodge, and finally Wilson, although Lodge was to desert the idea when Wilson later coupled it with a proposed peace without victory. None of these took exception to the proposal of a league of nations before 1917, and after then, among the prominent leaders, only Lodge. As the war continued, and American neutrality became more and more uncertain, enlightened public interest in a league of nations became more pronounced. The interest crystallized in the formation in June, 1915, of the nonpartisan civic League to Enforce Peace,[2] a propagandist organization for a league of peace at the

---

[1] Quoted by Denna F. Fleming, *The United States and the League of Nations, 1919-1920* (New York, 1932). This excellent historical tract is full of disconcerting *tu quoque* quotations for the later Republican opponents of the League, among whom Roosevelt cannot be classed. He died, January 6, 1919, before the first draft of the Covenant was formulated at the Paris Conference. We can only guess what his views would have been on the Covenant, remembering the intense partisan that he was, his intimate friendship with Lodge, and that he probably would have been the Republican nominee for the Presidency in 1920.

[2] Its statement of principles was summarized as follows:

(1) Submission of all justiciable questions to an international court of justice "both upon the merits and upon any issue as to its jurisdiction of the question."

[*Footnote continued on next page*]

end of the war, in which over a thousand distinguished citizens, including Senator Lodge, took part.

Only when the movement, like the demand for military preparedness, had gained a large volume of public support, and when it seemed that the United States might at any time become involved in the war, namely, after the *Sussex* exchange of notes with Germany, did the President publicly champion a league of nations, as he also advocated military and naval preparedness. His first utterance was to the League to Enforce Peace, in May, 1916, and, it so happened, speaking from the same platform with Lodge.

In England, and to a less degree in other countries, similar organizations and advocates urged such a league to accompany the peace settlement. Under the horror of war the idea was taking hold of a thoughtful mankind. Various plans for the constitution of a league of nations appeared during 1918 in Great Britain, France, and the United States. A committee of British specialists, acting under the chairmanship of the jurist, Lord Phillimore, drew up the first actual draft (March 20, 1918). It was mild and juridical. It called for only voluntary arbitration of international disputes and avoided political or territorial guaranties. It limited membership to selected Allied and Associated Powers and a few neutrals. A French official plan (June 8, 1918) provided for a similarly restricted membership, a tribunal of arbitration, an international political council which would have power if need be to carry out its decisions with economic, military, and naval force, and an international police force recruited pro rata from the members. This was characteristic of all French thought on a league: an international force to maintain the *status quo* established by the victor powers, which meant of course the protection of triumphant France against the future recovery of an aggressive or revengeful Germany.

The American plans came from Colonel House and President Wilson. House worked out a plan (July 16, 1918) in collaboration with David Hunter Miller, later one of the legal advisers to the American Peace Commission. It contained provision for guaranties of territorial in-

(2) Submission of all other questions to a council of conciliation for hearing, consideration, and recommendation.

(3) Agreement "to jointly use forthwith both their economic and military forces" to coerce any member committing acts of hostility against another before submitting to arbitration or conciliation.

(4) Periodic conferences to formulate and codify international law.

Except for the vital novelty of coercion this program was closely in line with the practice of American diplomacy hitherto. The exception, of course, was a tremendous one, contrary to the traditions of the Republic's policy since Washington and Monroe.

tegrity and political independence of members of the league, subject to changes pursuant to the principle of self-determination if approved by the delegates of two thirds of the members. The House plan also provided a secretariat and a permanent court, with compulsory arbitration. It provided for economic sanctions against outlaw states. President Wilson himself worked out a draft in the late summer of 1918 in which he borrowed the prominent features of the House draft, and added military and naval sanctions when necessary, with a provision (later Article XI of the League) expressing not only "concern" (as House's plan did) but providing for consultation and possible action in case of any threat to the peace of the world. Force against outlaw nations was characteristic of President Wilson's ideas of a league, as it had been of Theodore Roosevelt's. Yet his first draft for a league of nations called for "the reduction of national armaments to the lowest point consistent with *domestic* [1] safety."

General Smuts of South Africa drafted a plan (December 16, 1918), accompanied by a lengthy exposition, which urged, among many other things, the abolition of conscription, the nationalization of the munitions trade with international inspection, a council of the great powers, and a system of mandates for the separated portions of the Ottoman Empire (but not for the conquered German colonies in Africa and in the Pacific), and *ipso facto* war against covenant breakers.

At Paris President Wilson formulated two more drafts, in which he incorporated ideas from the Smuts plan and from a memorandum by Miller and by James Brown Scott, legal advisers to the American Commission. At the same time Lord Robert Cecil had drawn up a draft which became the official British suggestion. The last Wilson draft and the Cecil draft were referred to Miller and Sir Cecil Hurst, British legal adviser, and worked into a draft which President Wilson accepted and presented to the first meeting (February 3, 1919) of the special commission of the Peace Conference for the formulation of a league of nations. The commission deliberated almost continually for the next ten days and reported the first conference draft of the League of Nations, proposed to be incorporated as the first chapter of the treaty of peace with Germany. The plan naturally contained many features and much phraseology of the basic Miller-Hurst preliminary draft, to which the earlier British and American drafts had in turn made their contributions. The Conference published it to the world on February 14,

[1] Italics inserted.

when President Wilson left Paris for his necessary trip to the United States to be present at the ending of the Congress, and to introduce the proposed covenant to the people of the United States.[1]

Well-wishers to the Covenant criticized the President, and hostile partisans blamed him bitterly, for not having taken the document directly to the Senate, then in session, to ask for its advice. He could then have known in advance the indispensable amendments which would satisfy that body. Instead he discussed the document first in public addresses, and after this met informally the Committee on Foreign Relations of the Senate jointly with the Committee on Foreign Affairs of the House in an unsatisfactory dinner conference at the White House. This may have been another strategical mistake in handling the Senate; but if the other powers in Paris had realized that there were certain formulated amendments which the President must have in order to secure the consent of the Senate they could have held him up for further diplomatic equivalents at Paris. Nations do not concede favors gratuitously.

This proposal for the League, now formulated into actual articles and presented to the world, elicited a widespread sympathy and approval in both Europe and the United States. William Howard Taft, then the only living former President, hailed it as a partnership with the world not incompatible with the sovereignty of the United States "regulated by international law and morality and consistent with the same sovereignty as other countries." He pleaded publicly for the Senate's unanimous support of the document. Academic and religious leaders acclaimed it as a bright new dispensation for harassed mankind. Presently more cautious heads began to discern difficulties and to qualify their support. Even the proponents of the League feared it might be impossible to live up to such serious limitations on the sovereign rights of the United States. The partisan opposition, of course, stressed these vigorously, and brought up all other conceivable objections.

Cutting through a great medley of expression of opinion, both in the Senate and out of it, one may say that a responsible public demand

[1] Historians will always be grateful to David Hunter Miller, as they have been to James Madison for his notes on the Federal Convention at Philadelphia in 1787. Miller published the preliminary drafts of plans for a League of Nations, the minutes of the special commission on the League at the Paris Peace Conference, with ancillary documents, together with his own valuable commentary: *The Drafting of the League of Nations* (2 vols., New York, 1928). He had interpreted these data in a popular lecture in 1921, "The Making of the League," published in House and Seymour, *op. cit.*

In his history, *The Society of Nations, Its Origin and Constitutional Development* (Washington, Brookings Institution, 1932), Felix Morley traces its origin in great detail.

for a certain minimum of amendments to the proposed Covenant was apparent in the United States. In noting these objections to the text as it then stood, we give the gist of President Wilson's responses to them, either then or later.

First and foremost there was a demand for an explicit recognition of the Monroe Doctrine as a reserved policy for the United States quite beyond the touch of the League. Wilson declared that Article X had now made a world doctrine of the principles of Monroe. Article X was the one which guaranteed "the territorial integrity and political independence" of all members of the League. Then there was a demand for an explicit reservation that no sanctions could be shared by the United States in the enforcement of Article X or any other article of the League without an express vote of Congress. The President had declared that there was nothing in the document legally to oblige such sanctions, though he would not deny a moral obligation. There was much objection to Article X itself, particularly by Elihu Root, voiced later. To the President this was the "heart of the covenant." It was, as we have seen already, the keystone of the proposed pact of 1916 to Pan-Americanize the Monroe Doctrine. He had now given it a global concept. It was indeed his principal contribution to the great constitution. He would not change it.

With the tariff and Oriental immigration particularly in mind, cautious students insisted that all subjects of domestic legislation should be excluded from the League's purview. The President explained that the League could take cognizance of no dispute without unanimity of the Council powers (one of which would always be the United States), even though one or more of them be involved in the dispute and obliged to withdraw from sitting in judgment on its own case when later the Council by unanimous vote might take the dispute under examination. This was only an interpretation of what at best was not clearly defined in the Covenant; it would remain for future practice to confirm or reject it. There was a strong demand for an explicit statement about unanimity. There was also a desire for a provision for withdrawal from the League, although Wilson implied that such was not necessary if a power wanted to withdraw.

Friends to the League suggested amendments to cover these objections. One or more of these suggested amendments had the support of statesmen like Elihu Root and William Jennings Bryan, and of public leaders like A. Lawrence Lowell, president of Harvard University, and Charles Evans Hughes, and many other eminent citizens. Their supporters felt that such changes would secure the loyal membership of their country, that they were necessary to overcome the opposition of a strong partisan group of Republican senators. There were other men, particularly in the Senate, who were opposed to any League in any shape or form. They would vote for amendments when the time came, but frankly they would not, in the final decision, vote for the treaty even with their amendments. During the great debate in the Senate, these senators were known as the "Irreconcilables." The Irreconcilables joined with other Republican senators not opposed to a League in principle to demand that the whole idea be separated from the negotiations at Paris; that a peace be first made with the enemy, and the League taken up later. Under the leadership of Senator Lodge, whose precise attitude toward the League may never be known, thirty-nine Republican senators or senators-elect, declared, as Congress was closing, March 4, 1919, that it was the sense of the Senate that peace terms should first be negotiated with Germany, "and that the proposal for a League of Nations to insure the permanent peace of the world should be then taken up *for careful consideration.*" [1] This was not a resolution of the Senate, but it was a clear-cut ultimatum from more than one third of the membership of the next Senate in which a two-thirds majority would be necessary for the ratification of any treaty.

President Wilson met this challenge by declaring in a parting public address, in New York City, on the eve of his return to France, that the Covenant would be made a part of the treaty, "not only in it, but so many threads of the treaty tied to the covenant that you cannot dissect the covenant from the treaty without destroying the whole vital structure." Speaking from the same platform former President Taft declared that the Covenant ought to be a part of the treaty and urged the President to make it so.

It was evident that if the President did not at least secure some of the generally supported amendments that the otherwise sympathetic Republican senators would join with the Irreconcilables to defeat the whole thing.

After the President's departure Taft became alarmed at the rising tide of criticism and opposition and cabled to him in Paris that to carry the treaty and League in the Senate it would be advisable to secure reservations in regard to the Monroe Doctrine, domestic legislation, unanimity of Council voting, and withdrawal from the League.

[1] Italics inserted.

Taft cabled to Wilson (March 18, 1919):

If you bring back the treaty with the League of Nations in it make more specific reservation of the Monroe Doctrine, fix a term for the duration of the League, and the limit of armament, require expressly unanimity of action of Executive Council and body of Delegates, and add to Article XV a provision that where the Executive Council of the Body of Delegates finds the difference to grow out of an exclusively domestic policy, it shall recommend no settlement, the ground will be completely cut from under the opponents of the League in the Senate. Addition to Article XV will answer objections as to Japanese immigration, as well as tariffs under Article XXI. Reservation of the Monroe Doctrine might be as follows:

"Any American State or States may protect the integrity of American territory and the independence of the Government whose territory it is, whether a member of the League or not, and may, in the interests of American peace, object to and prevent the further transfer of American territory or sovereignty to any power outside the Western Hemisphere."

Monroe Doctrine reservation alone would probably carry the treaty, but others would make it certain.

A second telegram (April 13), from Taft and A. Lawrence Lowell, added:

Friends of the covenant are seriously alarmed over report that no amendment will be made more specifically safeguarding Monroe Doctrine. At full meeting of Executive Committee of League to Enforce Peace, with thirty members from eighteen States present, unanimous opinion that without such amendment Republican Senators will certainly defeat ratification of treaty, because public opinion will sustain them. With such amendment, treaty will be promptly ratified.[1]

Once a draft of the Covenant had been agreed upon it was not easy to secure amendments. Once the door to revision was opened other governments proposed amendments, too, or opposed them as their political exigencies dictated. French and British representatives in the commission on the league of nations opposed the President's desire for an amendment on the Monroe Doctrine. The British withdrew their objections after a private understanding that the President would agree to a future limitation of naval armaments.[2] Wilson then arranged a personal bargain with Clemenceau, regarding the disposition of the Saar Valley, in order to secure French approval in the commission for a curiously qualified exemption for the Monroe Doctrine, in the shape of

[1] Fleming, op. cit., pp. 183-187.
[2] Intimate Papers, op. cit., IV, pp. 416-417; Miller, Drafting of the Covenant, op. cit., I, pp. 338, 419-427.

a new article, XXI: "Nothing in this covenant shall be deemed to
affect the validity of international engagements, such as treaties of
arbitration, or regional understandings like the Monroe Doctrine, for
securing the maintenance of peace." This gave to the Monroe Doctrine a puzzling international recognition. What is a regional understanding (*entente régionale,* in the equally official French text) like the
Monroe Doctrine? This question is very difficult for even most learned
jurists to answer precisely. There was also another amendment in the
final text of the Covenant, as incorporated in the Treaty of Versailles,
permitting states to withdraw, after having fulfilled their obligations,
upon two years' notice. There were many small changes in the wording
and arrangement of the final Covenant.[1] At the final session of the
commission the Japanese delegates labored for an amendment, as important for them and, be it said, to the world, as the Monroe Doctrine was
for the United States: "the endorsement of the principle of equality of
nations and just treatment of their nationals." With his eyes downcast
on the table, Lord Robert Cecil, the British delegate, said that under
instructions from his government he refused the amendment.

At the close of the regular session of Congress, on March 4, 1919,
a Republican filibuster had defeated appropriation bills with the design
of forcing the President to call a special session of Congress before the
end of the fiscal year June 30, while the treaty was still in negotiation.[2]
The special session of the new Congress, with its Republican majority
in both houses, convened May 19, 1919. Senator Lodge now declared,
in June, that the amended Covenant would not do. His friend on the
Peace Commission, Henry White, had confidentially cabled him to send
over the texts of the amendments that in Lodge's opinion would satisfy
the Republican Senate. This the senator had refused to do. His refusal
of White's invitation to agree on amendments suggests that Senator
Lodge's real motive was to load the Covenant and the treaty with such
amendments as to make it unacceptable to the President and his supporters in the Senate.[3] He acknowledged that public opinion overwhelmingly favored the League. The man in the street did not know

---

[1] Miller gives complete minutes of the commission and its discussion of amendments.

[2] Fleming, *op. cit.,* p. 212.

[3] That is the testimony of his daughter, who was apparently unusually intimate with
his political activity; but his grandson states that he really wanted the League with
reservations. Fleming, *op. cit.,* p. 476. Lodge's own apologia, *The Senate and the
League of Nations* (New York, 1925), does not reveal whether he really wanted the
treaty and League even with his reservations.

what it was all about, he said, but "the preachers of sermons," and the university teachers, and generally the newspaper editors favored it as it stood.[1]

It was by way of delay, by interminable hearings, by slow formulation of amendments and reservations that the Committee on Foreign Relations, with a majority of its members hostile to the League, at least as it stood, proceeded to consider the treaty. In Paris, the President and his advisers had felt, that with the Monroe Doctrine amendment, the Republican opposition had no chance of defeating the League or the treaty—such a repudiation of the President before the world, followed by a separate peace with the enemy, seemed unthinkable. Senator Lodge once had said something like this to the Senate.

He had declared:

Suppose we reject the treaty; what follows? Let us look at it practically. We continue the state of war, and every sensible man in the country, every business interest, desires the re-establishment of peace in law as well as in fact. At the same time we repudiate the President and his action before the whole world, and the repudiation of the President in such a matter as this is, to my mind, the humiliation of the United States in the eyes of civilized mankind and brands us as a people incapable of great affairs or of taking rank where we belong, as one of the great world powers.[2]

But this declaration was in 1899 when he was advocating the ratification of a treaty negotiated by a Republican President, a treaty which acquired the Philippines and entangled the United States in the international politics of Asia where it had no vital interests. Now it was a Democratic President, whose success with the treaty and the League might make the Democratic Party, instead of the Republican Party, the normal party in power in the United States.

Woodrow Wilson, too, as a younger man had appreciated the force of this argument, when in his treatise on *Congressional Government*, he had pointed out that the President, with his control over negotiation,

---

[1] "I said to Senator Borah" (one of the Irreconcilables, a member of the Committee on Foreign Relations), "it seemed perfectly obvious to me that any attempt to defeat the treaty of Versailles by a straight vote in the Senate, if taken immediately, would be hopeless, even if it were desirable." Believing that "the interests and safety of the United States might be so protected by amendments or reservations that a large majority of Republicans could vote for it, I told him that in any event there was only one thing to do and that was to proceed in the discussion of the treaty by way of amendment and reservation." *Ibid.*, p. 147. It would have been very easy for the Senator mistakenly to have believed, in his remembrance of the conversation, that he had used the phrase "even if it were desirable."

[2] *Congressional Record*, January 24, 1899.

could so commit the country in the eyes of the world that it would be most difficult, if not impossible, for the Senate to use its constitutional power to repudiate him.

It became apparent after Wilson's return from Paris that with the strategy of delay the opposition was making considerable headway with public opinion. It had raised a fund for speakers and writers against the League, "the evil thing with a holy name." [1]

Contrary to custom, the hearings of the Committee on Foreign Relations were in public.[2] "Pitiless publicity" was turned against the President. There was appearing an increasing conviction that the Covenant had not been sufficiently amended. A natural reaction, "the slump in idealism," had set in, in the United States, and all over the world, weary as the peoples were of war and international politics. The President, resorting to his most effective political weapon, started on a speaking tour of the country, to rally public opinion to his support and to that of an unamended treaty. His plea was for the League of Nations as the hope of the world, against a separate treaty as a shameful desertion of the associates in war. In the midst of this tour the overworked statesman collapsed, September 26, 1919. He was never to recover his health. The cause had lost its most eloquent champion.

The Committee on Foreign Relations at last submitted its report to the Senate, September 10. It recommended forty-five amendments to the treaty, and four reservations. Most of these amendments [3] were to separate the United States from any responsibility in executing the political and economic provisions of the treaty in Europe. The reservations were to protect, in every conceivable way, American sovereignty from the League of Nations. A minority report, from six Democratic members of the Committee, recommended the ratification of the treaty as it was signed. The Senate proceeded first to vote on the proposed amendments and reservations. These it could accept or reject by majority vote, before the final vote on the treaty itself, which required a

[1] The principal contributors to the fund were Henry C. Frick and Andrew W. Mellon, industrialist millionaires of Pennsylvania. Mellon became the Secretary of the Treasury under subsequent Republican Administrations.

[2] The hearings were promptly published for public consumption, *Hearings before the Committee on Foreign Relations of the United States on the Treaty of Peace with Germany Signed at Versailles on June 28, 1919* (66th Congress, 1st Session, Senate Document, No. 106, Washington, G.P.O., 1919). This publication is a rich mine of source material.

[3] There were only two amendments recommended for the Covenant, both designed to insure equality of voting between the United States and the whole British Empire, regardless of Dominions.

two-thirds majority. By the time the treaty had advanced to a vote on advice and consent, fourteen reservations had been added, the so-called Lodge reservations:

(1) Reservation to the United States in case of its withdrawal from the League of sole judgment whether it had fulfilled its international obligations under the Covenant.

(2) Disavowal of any obligation to preserve the territorial integrity or political independence of any other country, or to interfere in controversies between nations, under Article X, or any other article of the entire treaty, or to employ the military or naval forces of the United States for any purpose except by act of Congress.

(3) No mandate to be accepted by the United States without vote of Congress.

(4) Exclusion of domestic questions from the consideration of the Council or of the Assembly of the League.

(5) Declaration that the Monroe Doctrine was "wholly outside the jurisdiction of the League of Nations" and entirely unaffected by any provision of the treaty.

(6) Withholding assent of the United States to the Shantung settlement, and reserving complete liberty of action.

(7) Reservation to Congress of the right to enact law for the appointment of representatives of the United States to the League.

(8) That the Reparations Commission should have no right to interfere with trade between the United States and Germany, without the approbation of Congress.

(9) Necessity of an act of Congress for appropriation of expenses of the United States in the League.

(10) Right to increase armaments of the United States, under any League plan of disarmament, in case the United States is threatened with invasion or engaged in war.

(11) Right to allow nationals of covenant-breaking states, residing in the United States, to continue their normal relations.

(12) Freedom to regulate private debts, property, rights and interests of citizens of the United States.

(13) Withholding assent to the section of the treaty setting up an international labor organization, until Congress should have voted approval.

(14) Protecting the United States against any unequal vote, in the League, of the entire British Empire, notwithstanding the votes of self-governing Dominions or Colonies.

As we look back on the Lodge reservations today, they do not appear to be so exorbitant as they did in 1919. President Wilson opposed them, and advised his senatorial supporters to oppose them; they would nullify the treaty, he said, not ratify it. The assertion failed to persuade his opponents.

The Senate voted three times on the Treaty of Versailles on November 19, 1919. Two votes were for the treaty with the Lodge reservations. The Democrats, loyal to Wilson's desires, joined the Irreconcilables to vote it down: first vote 39 for, 55 against; second vote 41 for, 51 against. Senator Gilbert M. Hitchcock, Democratic leader, asked for reconsideration of the defeated treaty with only five reservations attached: the right of Congress to authorize or forbid the use of American forces for League sanctions; the Monroe Doctrine; equality of voting power of the United States with the British Empire, including each Dominion; the right of withdrawal; exemption of domestic questions from the League's jurisdiction. The Senate rejected Hitchcock's plea: 41 for, 51 against. But it allowed itself to vote once more on the treaty, without reservations. Again the reservationists joined with the Irreconcilables: 38 for, 53 against.[1]

The rejection of the treaty provoked a widespread popular demand for still another vote. The Senate reconsidered and voted again, March 19, 1920. This time the President told his followers he would not object to mild interpretative reservations. But the Senate again attached the fourteen Lodge reservations, and added a fifteenth, expressing sympathy with Ireland's struggle for independence. For the last time the Senate voted down the treaty with the Lodge reservations: 49 votes for, 35 against. Some League defeatists voted for Ireland, confident the treaty would not get a two-thirds majority. In his successful attempt to get the League of Nations written into the treaty, Woodrow Wilson had made great concessions from his principles to the national interests of Great Britain, France, Italy, and Japan. Now he would not make necessary concessions to his political opponents at home. He rejected the sage counsel of his friend Colonel House to leave to the Senate, this second time, full responsibility on the treaty.[2] Now a shadow fell between the two men, darkening one of the strangest friendships in history.

There is good reason to believe, from the brief mission of Viscount Grey,[3] as Ambassador to the United States in the winter of 1919-1920,

---

[1] For best analysis of the Great Debate, see T. A. Bailey, *Woodrow Wilson and the Great Betrayal* (New York, 1945).

[2] "Practically every one who is in close touch with the situation admits that the Treaty cannot be ratified without substantial reservations. You must not be a party to those reservations. You stood for the Treaty as it was made in Paris, but if the Senate refuses to ratify without reservations, under the circumstances, I would let the Allies determine whether or not they will accept them. . . . If you take the stand indicated, it will aid rather than hinder those working for mild reservations. It will absolutely ensure the passage of the Treaty and probably in a form acceptable to both you and the Allies." Seymour, *Intimate Papers, op. cit.,* IV, pp. 510-511.

[3] As Sir Edward Grey he had been the former British Secretary for Foreign Affairs.

that the Allies would have accepted whatever reservations the Senate might have voted, as Colonel House had advised the President they would probably do. Ostensibly on account of his desperate illness, Wilson refused to receive the new British Ambassador who retired after a brief mission of three months.

It has been bitterly and rather generally remarked that if Woodrow Wilson had been a Republican President, presenting the same treaty to the same Senate, he would have secured its ratification according to his heart's desire. That is probably true. The vice of partisan politics explains the rejection.[1] Partisan politics, nevertheless, is a part of the American system of constitutional government, on which Woodrow Wilson was an authority. In this case the opposition stood on secure constitutional ground with an elected majority behind them. One must feel that the Democratic President would have had less trouble with the Senate if he had appointed the plenipotentiaries to the Paris Peace Conference with due deference to its new Republican leadership, and with the Senate's confirmation. As it was, he could have had the treaty ratified with the Lodge reservations, at the very worst.

Passionately interested students and commentators have debated the question: Who was responsible for the defeat of the treaty and the League in the United States? The answer is easy, very obvious: both Lodge and Wilson. In effect these personal enemies united, for opposite motives, to kill the treaty. Lodge was content. Wilson died broken and bitterly disappointed. It will be for the historian of the future to decide whether the succession of academic and political defeats which opened and closed the career of Woodrow Wilson transcend the political victories which fell to Henry Cabot Lodge.

There is one more chapter to the great debate. Before the last vote on the treaty, the President had announced that if it were rejected, he would take the issue to the people in a "great and solemn referendum," making it the outstanding issue between the two parties in the approaching national election of 1920. Success here was presumably his hope when he opposed uncompromisingly the Lodge reservations and rejected the advice of Colonel House.

In that election it did not prove to be a clear-cut issue for the voters. The Democratic platform came out for the League, "without reservations which would impair its essential integrity"; but did not oppose

---

[1] W. S. Holt, *Treaties Defeated by the Senate, op. cit.*, has the most acute analysis of the political struggle. See also Fleming, *op. cit.*, and H. B. Learned's chapter in the sixth volume of Temperley, *Paris Peace Conference, op. cit.*

the acceptance of any reservations making clearer or more specific the obligations of the United States to the League associates. The Republican Party stood "for agreement among the nations to preserve the peace of the world." It continued with ambiguous and latitudinarian phrases:

Such an international association must be based upon international justice, and must provide methods which shall maintain the rule of public right by the development of law and the decision of impartial courts, and which shall secure instant and general international conference whenever peace shall be threatened by political action, so that the nations pledged to do and insist upon what is just and fair may exercise their influence and power for the prevention of war.

The Republicans would not take a stand clearly against the League. The Democrats would not oppose reservations.

The Democratic candidate, Governor James M. Cox of Ohio, advocated the League and lost. The Republican candidate, Senator Warren G. Harding, who had voted for the League twice with the Lodge reservations, declared that he was for "an association of nations." He allowed his party followers to believe what they pleased from that. The Irreconcilables said this meant that he was against the League. Republicans who wanted the League asserted that "association" meant *the* League. Thirty-one eminent Republicans (including Elihu Root, Charles Evans Hughes, Herbert Hoover, A. Lawrence Lowell, Nicholas Murray Butler, John Grier Hibben, and presidents of several other leading universities) signed a statement assuring the American people that this meant the League. No one knows how many people thought they were voting for the League (with the reservations, of course) when they voted for the Republican ticket. Harding and Coolidge were elected by an overwhelming landslide.

The election was not a referendum, nor was it even solemn. On the League there was no clear issue. Nor was there much on any other subject. The Republican campaign leaders plastered the country with huge billboards, bearing flattering likenesses of the candidates framed in red, white, and blue, with the ridiculous and meaningless slogan: "Let us be done with wiggle and wobble." It is easy to see that the Republican platform wiggled and wobbled more than the Democratic statement on the League.

Inaugurated, President Harding declared that "the Administration which came into power in March, 1921, definitely and decisively put aside all thoughts of entering the League of Nations. It doesn't pro-

pose to enter now, by the side door, back door, or cellar door." [1]   Before
he made this announcement the most eminent two of his cabinet members, who had signed the assurance of the Thirty-One that "association"
meant really the League, had accepted office under his Administration.[2]

Congress interpreted the election to be a mandate from the people
against joining the League. If there be question what the people meant
in 1920, and certainly there must be question, there is no question what
they later felt. If there were a majority sentiment discernible for it,
the politicians would have been quick to put a League plank in a party
platform; but from 1920 to 1940 no political party in the United States
dared to come out for the League.

To many of us who lived through those war years and who ardently
hoped for a better world to follow the tragedy of the nations, it seemed
as though the partisans of 1919, on both sides, in the great debate on the
League of Nations, joined in folly to defeat the League, each group for
opposite reasons: the Irreconcilables because they wanted no League at
all; the Wilsonians because they would have no essential reservations.
It seemed, too, as though the election of 1920 was a joke on the people,
so far as any great and solemn referendum was concerned. It seemed
in short as though the United States foolishly threw away the victory
it had won at war.

The defeat of the Treaty of Versailles, both in the Senate and (so
the Republican Party immediately proceeded to construe it) in the
national election of 1920, meant a separate peace with the enemy. Hostilities had ceased to exist since the armistice of November 11, 1918,
and trade with Germany had already set in following the European
peace. In the United States the technical state of war terminated with
a resolution of Congress, July 2, 1921, which declared the war with
Germany to be at an end, reserving to the United States all rights which
would have accrued to it by benefit of the Treaty of Versailles, or by the
European treaties of peace with the remnants of the Austro-Hungarian
Empire. During the war the Government had sequestered German and
other enemy private property within the United States as pawn for
American claims against Germany and Austria-Hungary.[3] The resolution ending the war retained custody of this property pending separate
treaties by the United States which would satisfy claims over a wide

[1] Fleming, *op. cit.*, p. 472.

[2] Charles E. Hughes, Secretary of State, and Herbert Hoover, Secretary of Commerce.

[3] This was in violation of the treaty of 1828 with Prussia, reviving Article XXIII of
the treaty of 1799, but that treaty had long since been thrown overboard by German
naval practices.

field. The act of one belligerent, of course, cannot terminate a war unless the other parties to the war acquiesce. There was no question but what the former enemy acquiesced, but it remained to make treaties settling outstanding uncertainties. In a short treaty of August 25, 1921, Germany confirmed to the United States all the rights, privileges, indemnities, reparations, or other advantages which had been set forth in the resolution of Congress, including also "all the rights and advantages stipulated for the benefit of the United States" in the Treaty of Versailles. A similar treaty was signed (August 24, 1921) with Austria, in reference to the Treaty of St. Germain; and with Hungary (August 29, 1921), in regard to the Trianon Treaty.[1] Both were ratified promptly. The United States thus secured from the enemy all the advantages of the treaties made by the Allies and none of their obligations, and, let it be added, none of the hatreds left in their wake. A series of treaties established normal diplomatic relations and amity with the seven new European succession states, and with Turkey.[2]

It remained to settle the claims against Germany and Austria-Hungary arising out of protested acts during the period of neutrality, notably the submarine cases, and to wind up the war claims of nationals on both sides. This was done not by a treaty, but by executive agreements of extraordinary significance for the treaty-making power.

The Mixed Claims Commission the United States and Germany, set up by the agreement of August 10, 1922; and the Tripartite Mixed Claims Commission the United States, Austria, and Hungary, set up under the agreement of November 26, 1924; and the American arbiter provided by the War Claims Act of March 10, 1928, for the settlement of American, German, Austrian, and Hungarian claims; involved property on both sides of hundreds of millions of dollars, by far the greatest amount ever submitted to adjudication in the history of arbitration. The total of actual awards by the two commissions and the arbiter was more than ten times greater than the total awards of the tribunals set up under Jay's Treaty of 1794 with Great Britain, and under the Treaty of Washington of 1871 with Great Britain, including the Geneva Arbitration. The Commission with Germany consisted of one commissioner from each side and an umpire (whose decision was final) chosen by agreement of the two governments. It was at the suggestion of Germany that the umpire was appointed by the President of the United States. The Tripartite Com-

---

[1] C. C. Hyde in *American Secretaries of State, op. cit.,* X, pp. 225-230, 253-256, briefly describes the technical questions involved.

[2] For Turkey, see above, pp. 145-146.

mission was limited to one sole commissioner to be agreed upon by the three governments (he proved at first to be the same person [1]) who also acted as umpire of the Mixed Claims Commission the United States and Germany, and later as the American war claims arbiter.

In addition to the claims of American nationals against Germany, Austria, and Hungary that went before the respective arbitral commissions, there were large claims of German nationals and relatively much smaller claims of Austrian and of Hungarian nationals against the United States, that were adjudicated by the American arbiter. Most of these involved the seizure, after the outbreak of the war, of German merchant ships which had been interned in American harbors during the period of neutrality, and of patents and a radio station. The War Settlements Act of 1928, passed by the Congress of the United States, provided for the adjudication of these claims by an American arbiter appointed by the President, and for the payment of all awards by the arbiter for German, Austrian, and Hungarian claims; and by the Mixed Claims Commission for claims of nationals of the United States. This legislation proved acceptable to both the foreign and the American claimants.

A tabulation of the intricate work of these arbitral settlements—which occupied the greater part of two decades—and of the partial payment of the awards achieved before the collapse of German reparations in 1932, is given on the next page.

The settlement of War Claims Act of 1928 provided for the complicated pay-off of the awards to the claimants of all nations concerned in these arbitrations, by creating a pool or special German deposit fund in the Treasury of the United States, made up of: appropriations by the United States Government; 20 per cent of the proceeds of German enemy property sequestered during the war (after all properties under $10,000 had been unconditionally released) plus accumulated interest on the whole of it while in sequestration; and moneys received and to be received from Germany on account of reparations (after certain sums had been set aside on account of the satisfaction of occupation costs of the United States army in the Rhineland).[2]

Thus approximately $199,300,000—of which Congress appropriated ap-

---

[1] Edwin B. Parker, who died October 30, 1929, before he could complete the umpire's work of the Mixed Claims Commission the United States and Germany. He was succeeded by Roland Boyden, who died in 1931, and was in turn succeeded by Owen J. Roberts of the United States Supreme Court, who carried the work forward.

[2] See note at end of chapter.

TABULATION OF ADJUDICATION AND PARTIAL PAYMENT OF CLAIMS OF UNITED STATES, GERMANY, AUSTRIA, AND HUNGARY

	Principal	With interest [1] accumulated to January 1, 1928, in accordance with the Settlement of War Claims Act of 1928	With arrears of interest accumulated on unpaid principal to September 30, 1940	Amount paid or in process of payment by April 7, 1941
Awards of the Mixed Claims Commission, United States and Germany, to nationals of the United States and to the United States Government				
Total awarded to nationals of the United States:	$139,316,214.04	$201,507,975.18	$254,274,158.89	$161,608,544.66 [2]
Total awarded to the Government of the United States:	42,034,791.41	61,244,119.63	100,274,695.87	
Awards of the Tripartite Mixed Claims Commission, the United States, Austria, and Hungary:	*Principal and Interest to date of award:*			
Against Hungary	$172,619.70			Substantially paid } [3]
Against Austria	370,032.14			Substantially paid }
Awards of the American Arbitrator:	*Principal and Interest to December 31, 1928, in accordance with Settlement of War Claims Act of 1928*			
To German nationals:	$86,738,320.83		$116,301,476.57	$43,368,899.61
To Austrian nationals:	912,687.94			Substantially paid } [3]
To Hungarian nationals:	53,799.56			Substantially paid }

191

1 Interest allowed on awards for property damage during neutrality, from date of spoliation at 5 per cent. Interest allowed on awards for property damage during belligerency, from November 11, 1918, at 5 per cent. Interest allowed on death or personal injury awards from date of award, at 5 per cent.

2 This includes approximately $23,000,000 paid in January, 1941, on account of the sabotage awards entered October 30, 1939, plus approximately $2,222,000, being a 5-per-cent dividend on account of Class III awards in process of payment in April, 1941. Payment on account of the sabotage awards, which stated as of January 10, 1941, amounted to approximately $52,000,000, was delayed for over a year due to litigation instituted in the Federal Courts by certain holders of prior awards in an endeavor to have the sabotage awards set aside by the Courts. The decision of the Court of Appeals of the District of Columbia [114 Fed. (2d) 464] dismissing the bill of complaint was affirmed in a decision of the Supreme Court of the United States handed down January 6, 1941 (311 U. S. 470).

3 These payments had not been completed because of the failure of claimants to file applications required by law.

proximately $86,700,000—was made immediately available pursuant to the Settlement of War Claims Act for the satisfaction of these awards on both sides; the remaining unpaid part of awards was to be taken care of by the proceeds of German bonds deposited under a Debt Agreement that would replenish the pool in future years until all financial obligations were satisfied.

American claimants possessing awards for injury or loss of life, or for other claims under $100,000, were to be paid in full; those with awards over $100,000, and for other than death or personal injury, were to receive in cash preferential pro rata payments on account of their awards until such time as the total payments to American nationals equaled 80 per cent of the total awards to such nationals; the balance of these awards was to be paid in installments. German claimants with awards from the arbiter were to be paid 50 per cent in cash and 50 per cent in installments, and the 20 per cent of temporarily withheld alien property funds, plus the unallocated interest fund, was to be paid back eventually out of the pool. The comparatively small sums of the awards to American, Austrian, and Hungarian claimants by the Tripartite Commission and the American arbiter were to be paid in cash out of the Austrian and Hungarian special deposit accounts provided for in the act.

The United States Government under the Settlement of War Claims Act had to wait for the payment of its awards by the Mixed Claims Commission until all claims of American and German nationals were fully satisfied. No provision was made in the act for the satisfaction of the army of occupation costs of $247,865,645. This, however, was fully provided for in the Debt Funding Agreement of June 23, 1930. The treatment measured out to former enemy claimants and property holders was nearly as good as that secured by the victorious government for its own nationals. The whole settlement contrasts brightly with the loss of private property by German aliens in the European [1] Allied countries, where enemy property was sequestered and totally credited after the war to the huge reparations bill charged up to Germany; this amounted to confiscation in all but name.

Arrangements for the German reparation payments, part of which was to flow into the pool for the payment of awards on both sides, and part of which was set aside for the satisfaction of army occupation costs, were made under a series of three executive agreements with several powers concerned. The Wadsworth Agreement of May 25, 1923, regulated

---

[1] Japan returned all of the German enemy property seized within the territorial limits of the Japanese Islands.

the amounts and payments by installments for army occupation costs only. The other two agreements, the Paris Agreement of January 14, 1925, with the Allies, and the German-American Debt Agreement of June 23, 1930,[1] accommodated all German payments to the United States to the readjustments of the general reparation problem effected by the Allies through the Dawes Plan (1925) and by the Young Plan (1929) which was expected to supersede the Dawes Plan.

The collapse of German reparations payments in 1932 upset the remaining payments to German claimants; and to American claimants (for installments, on awards over $100,000, of the 20 per cent which remained to be paid to them). In 1932 Germany postponed indefinitely payment of the coupons on the occupation bonds, though some interest was paid (part of it in marks deposited or "blocked" in Germany) on account of the postponed coupons. Of the total occupation costs of $247,865,645 Germany had paid by 1932 $65,998,512.13. Germany also suspended payments on the second series of bonds for the obligations of the awards of the Mixed Claims Commission, according to an announcement of the President of the United States on March 2, 1935.[2] The payment of the remainder of the awards due the creditor claimants on both sides was thus indefinitely held up.[3] Having repudiated this obligation in 1932, Germany, under the Hitler régime, directed money (which otherwise might pay reparations, at least in part) to rearming on land, on sea, or in the air. There was no way for the victors of 1918 to stop this except to go to war again. This they were still unwilling to do.

[1] The effect of the last of these agreements was to spread German payments to the United States, separately on claims and on army occupation costs, over a long period of years. To cover these payments Germany deposited with the Secretary of the Treasury of the United States two series of noninterest-bearing bonds: one series totaling RM. 1,048,100,000 (approximately $250,000,000) to satisfy original army occupation costs by installments over a spread of thirty-six years; and another series of RM. 2,121,600,000 (approximately $505,000,000) to satisfy obligations on account of awards of the Mixed Claims Commission, payable by installments through the next fifty years, or as long as might be necessary short of fifty years to complete the awards. This was the stream expected to flow into the pool above referred to.

[2] For summary of the work of the Mixed Claims Commissions, see: *Report [1934] of Robert W. Bonynge, Agent of the United States before the Mixed Claims Commission, United States and Germany* (Washington, G.P.O., 1935); and *Report of Robert Bonynge, Agent of the United States before the Tripartite Claims Commission, United States, Austria, and Hungary* (Washington, G.P.O., 1930).

In this summary of claims and awards and payments, I am indebted to an unpublished memorandum of October 24, 1935, prepared by H. H. Martin, counsel to the United States agency before the Mixed Claims Commission of the United States and Germany.

[3] The comparatively equal amount due to claimants on each side (approximately $40,000,000 each) made possible the consideration of reciprocal assumption by the governments concerned, at least to that amount. This would have greatly simplified the final solution.

None of the treaties with the former enemy states, and none of the executive agreements, said anything about settling the principles of submarine warfare which caused all the trouble. Three later multilateral international conventions, to none of which Germany was an original signatory, defined the law of submarine warfare: the unratified treaty of 1922 among the United States, the British Empire, France, Italy, and Japan, signed during the Washington Conference; the treaty of 1930 among the United States, Great Britain, and Japan, signed at the London Conference for the limitation of naval armaments; and the Pan-American treaty of 1928.

The attempt to regulate submarine warfare in 1922, an attempt which failed because France did not ratify the treaty, stipulated:

The Signatory Powers recognize the practical impossibility of using submarines as commerce destroyers without violating, as they were violated in the recent war of 1914-1918, the requirements universally accepted by civilized nations for the protection of the lives of neutrals and noncombatants, and to the end that the prohibition of the use of submarines as commerce destroyers shall be universally accepted as a part of the law of nations they now accept that prohibition as henceforth binding as between themselves and they invite all other nations to adhere thereto.

This convention, if ratified, also would have outlawed the use of poison gas among the signatory powers.

The Pan-American Convention of Maritime Neutrality of 1928 laid down rules of visit and search for the purpose of identifying the real nationality, cargo, and destination of a ship, and added:

If the merchant ship does not heed the signal to stop, it may be pursued by the warship and stopped by force; outside of such a case the ship cannot be attacked unless, after being hailed, it fails to observe the instructions given it.

The ship shall not be rendered incapable of navigation before the crew and passengers have been placed in safety.

Belligerent submarines are subject to the foregoing rules. If the submarine cannot capture the ship while observing these rules, it shall not have the right to continue to attack or destroy the ship.

This convention by September, 1935, had been ratified by the United States and four small Caribbean states, protectorates of the United States, none of which has a navy, Dominican Republic, Haiti, Nicaragua, and Panama, and by the landlocked South American state of Bolivia.

Finally, the London Naval Treaty of 1930 among the United States, the

British Commonwealth of Nations, and Japan stipulated that the following are accepted as established rules of international law:

(1) In their action with regard to merchant ships, submarines must conform to the rules of International Law to which surface vessels are subject.

(2) In particular, except in the case of persistent refusal to stop on being duly summoned, or of active resistance to visit or search, a warship, whether surface vessel or submarine, may not sink or render incapable of navigation a merchant vessel without having first placed passengers, crew and ship's papers in a place of safety. For this purpose the ship's boats are not regarded as a place of safety unless the safety of the passengers and crew is assured, in the existing sea and weather conditions, by the proximity of land, or the presence of another vessel which is in a position to take them on board.

The United States, Great Britain, and Japan ratified the treaty. The London Naval Treaty expired by its own limitation on December 31, 1936. Before then, on November 6, 1936, the United States, Great Britain, France, Italy, and Japan signed a special protocol renewing indefinitely these articles for the regulation of submarine warfare. They invited other powers to adhere. Germany adhered, November 23, 1936, and Russia on February 19, 1937. Though codification of existing law is not necessary to make it law, nevertheless the formal acceptance of these principles by all of the great submarine powers confirms their binding character. It was on the basis of such principles of international law that the United States chose to defend its citizens, to the extent of going to war with Germany, even when those citizens were traveling under a foreign, even a belligerent flag. Their validity is not contested.

The controverted issues of neutrality between the United States and Great Britain were brought to an end without arbitration. The entrance of the United States into the war against Germany weakened the moral if not the technical force of the American neutral protests and caveats before 1917. In 1926 an examiner of the Department of State, acting in collaboration with a British opposite, eliminated all but 95 of 2,658 American neutral claims against Great Britain, and found that only 11 had conspicuous merit. "We are one of the principal naval forces of the world," he reported, "and should we become involved in another war it would be to our interest to have our naval forces free to operate in any way which would make them most effective against the enemy." [1]

Under this persuasion the United States then made with Great Britain

[1] *The Foreign Relations of the United States, 1926* (Washington, Government Printing Office, 1926), II, p. 287.

the notable War Claims Agreement of May 19, 1927. It agreed reciprocally not to claim any damages or demand arbitration of damages to its nationals growing out of the "war measures" of Great Britain. Each government retained its right to maintain in the future such position as it might deem appropriate with respect to the legality or illegality under international law of measures such as those giving rise to the claims which it had agreed in this instance not to present. The American claimants were left mostly to the judgment of the British prize courts to be held in England.

Thus did the historic question of neutral rights emerge uncertainly from the diplomatic aftermath of the war. We cannot dismiss the subject without referring to the crystallization of public opinion and legislation in the meditative years since then.

The United States as a champion of neutral rights found that the defense of those rights led not to neutrality but to war, when violation touched American lives rather than American property. Reflective opinion slowly began to ask whether legal neutral rights, the defense of which spells war rather than neutrality, were after all the best sort of rights. An inquiry by Congress in 1934 and 1935 into the munitions industry and traffic recalled the war profits of this enterprise in 1914-1917, and the economic tie-up between the United States and the Allies. Publicists [1] appealed to a public realization of the horrors of war by stressing this economic relationship with the Allies, without pausing to remember that this would not have brought war except for Germany's unrestricted submarine warfare. These reflections and the persisting uncertainty of the law of contraband and of blockade, and the status of armed merchant ships, gave rise to much searching of mind among students of international law and of American diplomacy.[2] Increasing precariousness of world peace in recent years suggested the recurrence of a neutrality which might mean another war for the United States, as in 1917. The threat to the general peace of Europe caused by the Italo-Ethiopian crisis precipitated the passage by Congress of the neutrality legislation of 1935, amended in 1936 and 1937. This legislation provided for the prohibition, in time of war between foreign states, or of foreign "civil strife," of the export from the United States of arms, ammunition, or implements of war, as defined by the President's proclamation, "to any port of such belligerent state, or to any neutral port for transshipment

---

[1] Grattan, *Why We Fought*, and Millis, *Road to War, op. cit.*

[2] Charles Warren published the most effective of these inquiries, "Troubles of a Neutral," *Foreign Affairs*, XII (April, 1934), 377-394.

to, or for the use of, a belligerent country," with an exception [1] in favor of an American republic at war with a non-American state. Loans or credits, or dealing in such, by an American national, with the same exception,[1] were also prohibited. This much was mandatory on the President, though it was left to him to define the existence of a war. The act of 1937 gave the President discretionary power (for two years) to forbid export on American ships to belligerent countries of articles or materials other than arms, ammunition, or implements of war, and to forbid the export of any American property in such articles or materials on foreign ships. The neutrality law provided for the control of the munitions industry in time of peace as well as in time of war. It required the licensing, with full publicity, of the exports of arms, ammunition, and implements of war, during times of peace. This was in response to a persuasion, which had taken such a hold on public opinion as to be of influence on Congress, that munitions makers were "merchants of death" and conspired wars for their own profit. The law specifically forbade any vessel, domestic or foreign, in time of war, to take out from American ports "men, or fuel, arms, ammunition, implements of war, or other supplies" to belligerent warships or tenders. It empowered the President to forbid to belligerent submarines or armed merchant ships the use of American neutral ports. It made it unlawful for American citizens to travel under a belligerent flag, except as prescribed by the President. It forbade the arming of American merchant ships trading to belligerent countries.

The neutrality legislation of 1935-1937 showed prevailing conviction not only of inadequacy of previous legislation in regard to neutral rights, but also of the unsatisfactory status of acknowledged neutral rights, subject to encroachment by belligerents' retaliations against each other. Incidentally it set up a neutral definition of contraband [2] and supported the doctrine of continuous voyage to ultimate destination, the British practice of the First World War. The most significant feature of the new legislation was expression of the policy that it was not worth while to go to war for rights which were undoubtedly legal in 1914-1917. It abandoned Wilson's policy of protecting neutral American citizens against violations of international law even when those violations were directed

[1] The law of May 1, 1937, states: "This Act shall not apply to an American republic or republics engaged in war against a non-American state or states, provided the American republic is not co-operating with a non-American state or states in such a war."

[2] Proclamations of September 25, 1935, and May 5, 1937, enumerated a list of arms, ammunition, and implements of warfare. It included among these: tanks, military armored vehicles and armored trains, vessels of war of all kinds, aircraft assembled or dismounted, and equipment for same, flame-throwers, and poison gas.

against a belligerent ship and flag, even a belligerent armed ship and flag. A most significant sequent announcement was the statement of President F. D. Roosevelt (October 5, 1935), when applying (October 5, 1935, to June 20, 1936) the law to the Italo-Ethiopian War, that "in the specific circumstances all transactions" of American citizens with belligerent countries would be at the risk of those citizens. Here was a formula for co-operating with the League of Nations' sanctions to the extent of not insisting upon neutral rights for the carriage of goods to belligerents when the League intervened. It meant that in the face of the League of Nations the United States was willing to abandon the traditional policy of the Freedom of the Seas. It was the existence of the League of Nations which had made possible such a radical change in neutral policy.

The cost, direct and indirect, of the First World War to the belligerents in lives and property will never be precisely measured. An estimate of the Carnegie Endowment for International Peace is 10,000,000 lives and 6,300,000 seriously wounded and approximately $200,000,000,000 of direct costs.[1] It cost the United States 223 neutral lives lost on the high seas, without mentioning those neutral passengers injured but not killed; 47,949 soldiers and 2,307 sailors killed in battle or died of wounds, and 83,390 severely wounded; and $35,000,000,000, without counting interest on moneys borrowed, which in the end would double the cost. To this direct cost must be added payments to veterans in the shape of "adjusted" compensation (bonus) by states and federal government, hospitalization, and other expenses, including those of administration, totaling by June 30, 1935, in the case of the federal government alone, $7,754,422,529.06.[2] Here was only a small part of this heavy continuing item. The economic dislocation wrought by the war exacerbated the inevitable Great Depression by wearing down the machines of national and international finance. The loss in men fortunately was small [3]

[1] The indirect cost of the First World War—loss of earning power, care of crippled, economic wastage, etc.—was estimated in 1919 at approximately $170,000,000,000. E. L. Bogart, *Direct and Indirect Costs of the Great World War* (New York, 1919), prepared for the Carnegie Endowment for International Peace; and J. M. Clark, *The Costs of the World War to the American People* (Yale University Press, 1931), also prepared for the same Endowment.

[2] Of this $1,043,846,740 was disbursed from insurance premiums, allotments, and vocational rehabilitation gift fund.

[3] Compare the annual loss, in 1934, of 36,000 men, women, and children killed by automobiles in the United States; and 954,000 injured, of which 105,000 were disabled (statistics from American Automobile Association). These deaths and mutilations are fully as horrible as those of war, many being burned to death *and much easier to prevent than war.*

for the United States; the loss in money certainly was great but not necessarily vitally grievous (unless combined with domestic folly). It was diplomatic ineptitude which caused the greatest losses, that ineptitude which neglected the embargo weapon, and which extended unstinted war effort *unconditionally* at the side of the Allies. The blunders of diplomacy were balanced, on the other hand, by the largest measure of idealism that a nation has ever brought into a world conflict, personified in Woodrow Wilson and his gallant, if imperfect, fight for the League of Nations. Unfortunately it did not make the world safe for democracy. The rise of the dictators completely upset the basis of Wilson's hope for world peace: a league of *democratic* nations.

What the United States really gained from the First World War was the overthrow for a generation of the military German Empire, which, victorious, would have been in a position for an inevitable Japanese alliance that would have caught the nations of the New World in the jaws of a crushing vise of Occidental and Oriental military and naval power. The price of temporary immunity, while high, was hardly excessive.

NOTE ON THE WAR CLAIMS ACT OF 1928

A more detailed analysis of the increments making up the special deposit fund of the War Claims Act of 1928 indicates:

(a) The unallocated interest fund (approximately $21,750,000), being the earnings and profits on German enemy property held by the Alien Property Custodian and accruing prior to March 4, 1923, the date of the passage of the Winslow Act (releasing amounts under $10,000).

(b) 20 per cent of the proceeds (approximately $32,950,000) of the liquidation of the German enemy property seized by the United States during the war and held by the Alien Property Custodian—the remaining 80 per cent (that is, 80 per cent of approximately $165,000,000) of the German enemy property was to be immediately returned to the former owners.

(c) The moneys received by the United States (approximately $32,200,-000) as its share under the Paris Agreement of January 14, 1925, of the annuities paid by Germany under the so-called Dawes Plan; in addition to these payments the United States likewise received under this Agreement the sum of approximately $39,200,000 on account of the costs of the army of occupation. These payments represented the percentages of German reparation payments which the Allies were willing to have diverted to the United States. There had already been received by the United States from Germany under the Wadsworth Agreement of May 25, 1923, the sum of approximately $14,700,000 on account of army occupation costs.

(d) Proceeds of German bonds (approximately $19,500,000) deposited under the Debt Funding Agreement of June 23, 1930; in addition there has been received by the United States under this same Debt Agreement the sum of approximately $12,000,000 on account of army occupation costs.

(e) The appropriation by the Congress (approximately $86,700,000) as provided for in the Settlement of War Claims Act to satisfy the awards of the arbiter for German ships, German patents used by the United States, and for the German radio station at Sayville, Long Island. Fifty per cent of this appropriation was to be paid immediately to German nationals. The remaining 50 per cent was to be used toward the satisfaction of awards of the Commission.

Among the former German ships that were paid for by the United States under the provisions of the Settlement of War Claims Act were seven, with a total gross tonnage of 62,888, that were sunk by German submarines during the war. These seven ships had a total valuation as found by the arbiter of $7,379,000, including interest to December 31, 1928. The former German owners of these vessels have consequently already been paid 50 per cent of this valuation. These seven vessels included the former Hamburg-American S.S. *Cincinnati* that became the U.S.S. *Covington,* and the former S.S. *President Lincoln* of the same line, that continued to be called the [U.S.S.] *President Lincoln.*

(f) In addition to these amounts there was also placed in the pool the amount of approximately $8,200,000, representing earnings and profits on investments of funds by the Secretary of the Treasury and interest on German bonds, payment of which was postponed in accordance with the provisions of the Debt Funding Agreement of June 23, 1930.

10

Oriental Immigration; The Problem

of the Pacific—1914-1921

THE principal focus of American diplomacy in the years immediately after the First World War and the separate peace settlement was the Far East. Across the Pacific a serious issue was rapidly developing with Japan. The gravest difficulties of Japanese-American affairs were involved in the relation of American policy in the Far East to Japanese ambitions on the continent of Asia, but the main issue was aggravated by the feeling that had arisen in Japan because of legislation in the United States concerning Oriental immigration and alien land ownership. Before passing presently to the larger aspects of the Problem of the Pacific, we should at this time review the question of Oriental immigration and attendant subjects.

Oriental immigration to the United States began with the American settlement of the Pacific Coast after the acquisition of California. The comparatively higher wages (low for California) proved a lure for Chinese workmen, generally imported by labor contractors. By 1852 there were 25,000 Chinese [1] there, mostly in California, approximately one tenth of the population at that time; by 1867, 50,000. The treaty negotiated by the plenipotentiary of China, Anson Burlingame, in 1868 at Washington was really a cheap-labor treaty signed readily by Secretary William H. Seward when labor was greatly in demand for completing the Central Pacific Railroad. It guaranteed to Chinese subjects "visiting or residing" in the United States, "the same privileges, immunities, and exemptions in respect to travel and residence as may there be enjoyed by the citizens or subjects of the most favored nation," except for the right of naturalization—from the first appearance of Oriental immigration the United States has refused to extend naturalization to Orientals. [2] It may have been a mistake in policy for the United States ever to have

[1] The Census of 1850 showed for California a total population of 92,597, of whom 660 were listed as foreign-born Chinese; the figures in 1860 were total 379,994, Chinese 34,935; in 1870, total 560,247, Chinese 49,277.

[2] States were not forbidden to do so until 1882.

introduced into treaty obligations any reference to the sovereign right of
regulation of a domestic subject like immigration, but in doing so in the
Chinese treaty it was simply following the practice of previous treaties
with the European nations. The influx of Chinese, so much desired at
first, soon created a serious racial, economic, and political problem.[1]
China yielded to American representations and signed the treaty of 1880,
which recognized the right of the United States to "regulate, limit or
suspend" but not to prohibit the immigration of Chinese laborers, and
guaranteed most-favored-nation treatment for Chinese already established in the United States—a contemporary treaty stringently prohibited
American citizens from engaging in the Chinese opium trade. Congress
in 1882 suspended immigration of Chinese laborers for ten years, and
later renewed the restriction. After over a decade of painful diplomatic negotiations and unedifying domestic legislation, a new immigration treaty was ratified with China in 1894 which prohibited for ten
years the entry of laborers. Teachers, students, merchants, travelers, and
officials were exempted. When this treaty expired in 1904 Congress
re-enacted all existing laws without term. After the annexation of
Hawaii and the Philippines the Chinese exclusion laws had been extended to those possessions, too. Following exclusion, the Chinese population within the United States has decreased to an insignificant number.[2]
Since 1943 China has been on a quota, allowing a nominal immigration
into the United States.[3]

The Japanese replaced the Chinese as a factor in the problem of
Oriental immigration at the turn of the century.[4] At the beginning the
Japanese Government followed the policy of discouraging undesired
labor emigration to the United States, though in later decades it actively
encouraged it to countries where Japanese laborers have been welcome,
like some countries of Latin America. The treaty of 1894 between Japan
and the United States allowed, reciprocally, free entry regardless of pur-

[1] "South China had a superabundant population; California was sparsely settled and
yielded large returns not merely in its mines but in its agriculture to the plodding, in-
defatigable labor of the Oriental. If natural laws were permitted, unchecked, to assert
themselves, it was only a question of time when the Chinese, with lower standards of
living and lower wage standards, would be able to displace the whites. The condition in
the southern states after the emancipation of the slaves was ever before the citizens of
California, so many of whom had come from the South." Tyler Dennett, *Americans in
Eastern Asia, op. cit.,* p. 539.

[2] 77,504 by the census of 1940, including 40,262 American citizens born of Chinese
parents. Chinese population was at its maximum in 1882, at 132,300.

[3] See below, p. 356.

[4] Raymond Leslie Buell has a convenient summary of *Japanese Immigration,* World
Peace Foundation Pamphlets, VII, Nos. 5-6 (Boston, 1924).

pose, but reserved for domestic control the regulation of immigrant laborers, as well as trade or public security. The Japanese Government fended off statutory exclusion by itself withholding passports, after August, 1900, to labor immigrants going to the mainland of the United States, but not to those destined for Hawaii.[1] Coolie immigrants fell off by 50 per cent thereafter, although the Japanese restriction was imperfectly administered. There were also vestibules of Japanese immigration via Hawaii (to which passports continued to be issued by Japan) and via Canada and via Mexico.

DISTRIBUTION OF ADULTS AND MINORS BY RACE IN HAWAII AFTER
CENSUS OF 1940

	Native-born		Foreign-born				
Racial origin	Adults	Minors	Natural-ized adults	Alien adults	Un-known	Minors	Total
Hawaiian	9,051	5,324	....	....	..	....	14,375
Part Hawaiian	17,405	32,503	14	10	..	3	49,935
Caucasian	61,235	34,605	5,013	2,757	4	177	103,791
Chinese	11,347	12,583	193	4,535	2	114	28,774
Filipino	36,318	16,251	....	....	..	....	52,569
Japanese	39,888	80,664	147	36,932	10	264	157,905
Korean	1,213	3,248	37	2,342	..	11	6,851
Puerto Rican	3,694	4,602	....	....	..	....	8,296
Negro and other	457	329	13	32	..	3	834
Total	180,608	190,109	5,417	46,608	16	572	423,330

In the Kingdom of Hawaii Oriental immigration, once actually contracted for by the Hawaiian Government, had taken root. There were 12,000 Japanese there in 1890 and 15,000 Chinese, out of a total population in the islands of 90,000, and Japan was insisting on the same rights of citizenship and officeholding for Japanese immigrants as for native-born Hawaiians. At the same time Japanese law rigorously maintained (until 1924) that an emigrant or even an emigrant's son could not divest himself of allegiance to the Emperor until he had done military service in Japan. A Japanese warship appeared at Honolulu to lend its presence to these demands, based on treaty. Until the annexation of the islands by the United States, Japan successfully opposed Hawaiian plans to exclude Oriental immigrants. Japan's very positive attitude in Hawaii, indeed, was one of the factors which hastened the Hawaiians

[1] This has been sometimes referred to as the First Gentlemen's Agreement.

toward American annexation in 1898. The immigration of Japanese into Hawaii continued after annexation so that by 1940 the population of Japanese extraction composed 37.3 per cent of the population.

Because every person born in Hawaii since annexation is a citizen of the United States, it was only a question of a relatively short time before American citizens of Japanese extraction would be a majority of the voting population.

Agitation against the admission of Japanese immigrants developed on the Pacific Coast; and in October, 1906, the San Francisco school board ordered that all Japanese school children [1] attend a school in which Oriental children were segregated. Japan, flushed with national pride after her recent great victory over Russia, quickly protested this act as a violation of most-favored-nation treatment to which her people in the United States enjoyed treaty guaranties. President Theodore Roosevelt recognized the justice of this protest. With difficulty he persuaded the school board to rescind its action on the understanding that he would somehow bring about a cessation of further Japanese immigration. The school board capitulated only when a hasty amendment to the immigration act of February 20, 1907, opened the way for this. It authorized the President to refuse entrance to the continental United States to immigrants with passports "to any other country than the United States." President Roosevelt promptly applied this to Japanese coming from Hawaii and Mexico, but not from Japan directly. This last was effected under an understanding—the so-called Gentlemen's Agreement of 1907—that Japan would not object to this restriction of Japanese coming to the mainland of the United States from adjacent countries or from Hawaii; and that Japan herself would not issue passports to laborers wishing to emigrate to the continental United States, excepting returning immigrants, and excepting also parents, wives, and children under twenty years of age of emigrants already established there. Though not by the terms of this unwritten understanding, Japan also in practice cut down passports to Hawaii.[2] In return the United States did not exclude Japanese immigrants. Exclusion was accomplished, in fact, by Japan. It was the year after the Gentlemen's Agreement, and in con-

[1] A few were very mature boys whose presence among young school children of both sexes created at least the apprehension of a social problem.

[2] See annual reports of the United States *Commission of Immigration,* 1909, 1910, in *Department of Commerce and Labor* reports for those years, 219 (for 1909) and 279 (for 1910).

sequence of it, that President Roosevelt, who felt that his sympathetic handling of the problem of Japanese immigration was regarded by Japan as due to fear on his part and that of his countrymen, sent the American battleship fleet on a cruise around the world,[1] really as a naval demonstration that the United States was not only willing to negotiate a settlement like that of 1907 but resolute and ready to defend a just position, if necessary, in the future. At Japanese invitation the fleet visited Yokohama and was most cordially entertained there. The cruise proved of great potency for peace, at least in the then immediate future.

After the Gentlemen's Agreement of 1907 had come into operation the United States ratified a treaty, in 1911, with Japan, which omitted the clause of the treaty of 1894, reserving the question of domestic legislation for the regulation of immigration; but the United States Senate, in the resolution of advice and consent to ratification, made the reservation that the treaty should not be deemed to repeal or affect any of the provisions of the immigration act of February 20, 1907.[2] This treaty granted, reciprocally, the free entry, residence, and privilege of owning or leasing houses, shops, and land *for the purpose of residence and trade,* but not regardless of purpose as had been provided by the treaty of 1894 (subject to the latter treaty's reservations concerning domestic legislation for the regulation of immigrant laborers).

The unwritten Gentlemen's Agreement solved fairly well the problem of Japanese immigration until 1924.

In the fifteen years during which the Agreement was in operation a total of 8,681 more Japanese arrived in the continental United States than departed; the net gain of Japanese residents in Hawaii was 7,415. The Japanese population in California nevertheless continued to increase more rapidly than the Occidental population because the birth rate of Japanese women, a relatively young group, was three times[3] that of Occidental women and because Japanese men brought in women as wives,

[1] See above, p. 24. Thomas A. Bailey has described the relation of the fleet's trip around the world to Japanese-American affairs in *Theodore Roosevelt and the Japanese-American Crises; an Account of the International Complications Arising from the Race Problem on the Pacific Coast* (Stanford University Press, 1934). For additional details and documents on the Gentlemen's Agreement, see Philip C. Jessup, *Elihu Root* (2 vols., New York, 1938).

[2] This act did not exclude Japanese coming directly to the mainland of the United States from Japan.

[3] It should be remembered that these Japanese women immigrants were then nearly all of childbearing age, as compared with average life groups of indigenous Occidental women.

selected by picture postcards and married by proxy in Japan.[1] This was eventually to lead to a renewal of demands on the Western Coast for exclusion by federal law.

The Gentlemen's Agreement did not solve the social and economic problem of Japanese already in the United States. The Japanese proved superior workers and savers. They quickly established a dominance in certain agricultural industries and localities. Of a different race, they found impediments as well as difficulties in assimilating themselves to American society,[2] and they tended (more than Occidental immigrants) to stick together and set up their own schools and churches. Meanwhile, even those born in the United States (and consequently American citizens) continued by Japanese law to owe allegiance to the Emperor until after they had done military service for him.

It was the economic and social aspects of Japanese immigration, rather than these legal anomalies, which provoked the legislation of western states that created another diplomatic issue. These laws, beginning with the California land law of 1913,[3] denied to alien residents ineligible for citizenship (i.e., Oriental aliens) the right to own, and even to lease, land directly or indirectly *for agricultural purposes,* though sometimes expressly observing all treaty rights (which included the right to own or lease land "incident to or necessary for trade").[4] These laws hit the Oriental agricultural landowner and leaseholders in California, Arizona, Arkansas, Delaware, Idaho, Kansas, Missouri, Montana, New Mexico, Texas, and Washington. Japan protested against such state laws, but ineffectually because technically they did not violate a treaty. This indirect discrimination by the states—which applied principally to Japanese aliens, and was so intended—coupled with the

---

[1] The growth of Japanese population in the continental United States by decennial censuses has been:

Year	Number	Native-born	Year	Number	Native-born
1870	55		1910	72,157	4,502
1880	148		1920	111,010	29,672
1890	2,039		1930	138,834	68,357
1900	24,326	269	1940	126,947	79,642

Compilation from Y. Ichihashi, *Japanese in the United States; a Critical Study of the Problems of the Japanese Immigrants and Their Children* (Stanford University Press, 1932), p. 64, plus census of 1930 and 1940.

[2] For a careful study of the social as well as economic position of Japanese immigrants, including the second generation, citizens of the United States, see *ibid.*

[3] Thomas A. Bailey, "California, Japan, and the Alien Land Legislation of 1913," *Pacific Historical Review,* I (1932), 36-59.

[4] California, Kansas, and Missouri have clauses protecting treaty rights of alien landholders.

naturalization laws of the United States which withheld citizenship from Orientals—rankled the spirit of a proud people; [1] but Japan herself had argued before the Hague Permanent Court of Arbitration (in the Japanese house tax case) that a sovereign power possesses the right to make all reservations concerning the land situated within its territory; and she herself then had laws which prohibited the owning or leasing of land by foreigners for agricultural purposes. As long as the principal problem of immigration was delicately handled by the Gentlemen's Agreement, and treaty rights were not overtly violated, these questions remained subordinated to the routine of diplomacy. Once the Gentlemen's Agreement of 1907 should be discontinued, Japan would fall back on her new treaty of 1911 to argue against discrimination in exclusion. [2]

During the century or more when the foundation of American foreign policy was being laid and the Republic was expanding westward through the continent, Europe's distresses were America's advantage. Similarly in the twentieth century the distresses of the Occident have made for the advantage of Japan in the pursuit of her vast objectives on the continent of Asia. The parallel would be more striking if Japan, like the United States, had started a career of expansion through an empty continent obstructed by no foreign barriers in force. Japan, however, had to confront and to saddle the teeming continent of Asia, to throw down old kingdoms, and to do this in a region where the imperialistic powers of Europe had ensconced themselves in possessions of territory, of military and naval posts, fortified also by diplomatic influence over China, in such a way as to be able to stop the advance of Japanese imperialism as long as their own continent of Europe remained quiet behind them. British opposition, for example, had prevented Japan from intervening in the Manchurian provinces of China as late as 1911, the year in which the Anglo-Japanese alliance was renewed for the last time. The American doctrine of the Open Door, to which had been added the principle of the administrative and territorial integrity of China, was also at least a principle, to which Japan herself had subscribed, which stood in the way of both Occidental and Oriental imperialism in China.

When the First World War convulsed Europe, there appeared the

[1] Iichiro Tokutomi, in *Japanese-American Relations* (New York, 1922, translated from the Japanese) presents, *suaviter in modo fortiter in re,* the Japanese case against exclusion laws.

[2] For the United States immigration act of 1924 in effect excluding Japanese laborers and thus terminating the Gentlemen's Agreement of 1907, see below, p. 237.

prospect of comparatively secure freedom for Japan to pursue her ambitions for the domination of China and of Eastern Asia and its littoral, the necessary step toward her goal of the greatest of world powers and the most powerful of imperial peoples. Thanks to the convulsed and confused condition of the Occident since 1914, particularly since 1917, Japan in three astonishing decades was able to take giant strides toward what her rulers beheld as her manifest destiny and her manifest opportunity.

When the war broke out in Europe the United States proposed to the belligerents that they limit the area of hostilities in the Far East, so as to preserve the *status quo*. Both Great Britain and Germany were anxious to do this, though Germany apparently had reservations as to what she might wish to do as to Russian forces there; but Japan delivered an ultimatum to Germany, requiring immediate surrender of her bases in that region and withdrawal from the East, and delivered it without fully consulting her ally. All circumstances considered, the British Government deemed it judicious to announce to the world that the two governments had agreed to take action against Germany in the Far East under their alliance of 1911, "keeping specially in view the independence and integrity of China as provided for in that agreement." Japan then signed the London pact of September 5, 1914, by which Great Britain, France, and Russia agreed to make peace only in common. By the Anglo-Japanese Alliance she had not, of course, been bound to such a general obligation.[1]

The first step for Japan was to capture the German naval base at Tsingtao, in Kiaochow Bay, together with the German concessions in Shantung which had been forced from China in 1899. The Japanese quickly blockaded the place from the sea, and marched an army of 20,000 from the northern shore of Shantung across that Chinese province—a distance as long as from New Haven to Cambridge—to invest it from land. This they did without the slightest regard for Chinese neutrality. Great Britain ignored this offense to Chinese sovereignty by her ally and even participated, without enthusiasm of the Japanese, in the naval and military operations, though not passing her

---

[1] A detailed survey of the diplomatic history of the Far East is contained in H. B. Morse and H. F. MacNair, *Far Eastern International Relations* (New York, 1931). A shorter account, more sympathetic to Japanese policy, is Payson J. Treat, *The Far East; A Political and Diplomatic History* (New York, 2d ed., 1935). See also the selected documents in *British Documents on the Origins of the War*, XI (London, 1926), Documents Nos. 499, 534, 549, 571, 641.

Map 4. Th

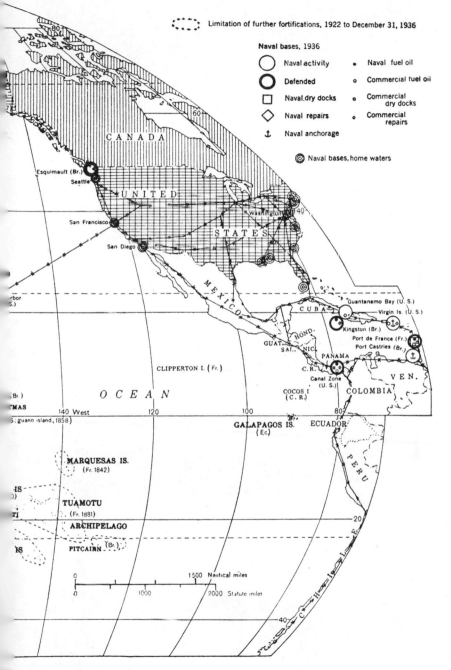

Limitation of further fortifications, 1922 to December 31, 1936

Naval bases, 1936

○	Naval activity	•	Naval fuel oil
◉	Defended	○	Commercial fuel oil
□	Naval dry docks	⊙	Commercial dry docks
◇	Naval repairs	⊙	Commercial repairs
⚓	Naval anchorage		

◎ Naval bases, home waters

CANADA

Esquimault (Br.)
Seattle

UNITED

San Francisco

Washington 140

San Diego

STATES

MEXICO

Guantanamo Bay (U. S.)
Virgin Is. (U. S.)
CUBA
Kingston (Br.)
Port de France (Fr.)
Port Castries (Br.)

rbor
S.)

GUAT.
SAL. NIC.
HOND.
PANAMA
C. R.
V E N.

CLIPPERTON I. (Fr.)

(Br.)
MAS

O C E A N

Canal Zone
(U. S.)
COCOS I
(C. R.)
COLOMBIA

140 West   120   100   80

S.: guano island, 1858)

GALAPAGOS IS.
(Ec.)
ECUADOR

MARQUESAS IS.
(Fr. 1842)

PERU

IS
)

TUAMOTU
(Fr. 1881)

TI

ARCHIPELAGO

20

IS

PITCAIRN (Br.)

| 0 | | 1500 Nautical miles |
| 0 | 1000 | 2000 Statute miles |

40

own troops outside the German leasehold.[1] Hopelessly overpowered, the German garrison surrendered (November 7, 1914).

While the operations against Tsingtao were under way, British naval contingents from Australia and New Zealand had made a sweep of the German colonial possessions in Micronesia and Polynesia from New Guinea to Samoa. In addition to German islands south of the Equator, an Australian contingent had proclaimed occupation (September 12, 1914) of the Solomon, Marshall, Caroline, and Mariana Islands which Germany had acquired from Spain in 1899. A few weeks later a Japanese squadron took possession of several of the islands in these groups; this notwithstanding the fact that the British announcement of Japanese operations under the Alliance had declared to the world that "it is understood that the action of Japan will not extend to the Pacific Ocean beyond the China Seas, except in so far as it may be necessary to protect Japanese shipping lines in the Pacific, nor beyond Asiatic waters westward of the China Seas, nor to any foreign territory except territory in German occupation on the continent of eastern Asia."[2] In a few weeks Japan had established by conquest her claim to the German concessions and leaseholds in China and to the German islands north of the Equator, a string of nesting places for submarines and roosting places for airplanes that would thrust future Japanese naval and aerial power far out eastward into the Pacific, across the communications between Hawaii and the Philippines. These had later powerful strategic value notwithstanding the fact that the condition of the later mandate of the League of Nations prohibited any fortification. It remained for Japan in the peace settlement to clinch her title to these advantages.

In the ultimatum to Germany, Japan had demanded unconditional withdrawal from the leased territory at Tsingtao "with a view to eventual restoration of the same to China." Japanese policy was eventually to return to China nominal possession of Shantung but before

---

[1] The Japanese did not even ask the consent of China to march across Shantung, and did it over Chinese protest. After the Japanese landing the Chinese proclaimed a war zone, to which the Japanese paid little attention. Japan let it be understood by China that she would be opposed to China's declaring war on Germany to get back Kiaochow for herself. See Morse and McNair, *op. cit.*, who differ widely from Treat, *op. cit.*

The case of Belgian neutrality is, of course, quite different from either that of China (or of Greece) and far more heinous: Belgian neutrality was guaranteed by solemn international covenant to which Germany, the ravishing power, was a party. Chinese neutrality had never been guaranteed, though the lack of guaranty gives no right to violate.

[2] *Foreign Relations, 1914, Supplement,* p. 171. Charles Roger Hicks has probed *Japan's Entry into the War, 1914* (University of Nevada Press, 1944).

then to have reduced all China itself to a Japanese sphere of influence as a first step to the establishment of a protectorate over the entire country. It is easy to let go an arm if one has a strangle hold on the whole body. This was revealed very suddenly to the world by Japan's presentation of an ultimatum (May 7, 1915) embodying drastic demands on China. As originally put forth they consisted of Twenty-One Demands, in five groups. Despite Japanese insistence on secrecy, the President of China, Yuan Shih-kai, dared to let them leak out. At first the Japanese Government denied them, then admitted part of them. In a note to the United States the text of the Twenty-One Demands was conveyed, with an explanation that some of them were not really demands—they were only requests. Nevertheless in the negotiations with China the Japanese representative insisted for a long time that a request was just as important as a demand. The demands were lengthy and detailed, every word of them packed with anesthesia for Chinese sovereignty. In their entirety they amounted to a protectorate over China.[1] That vast region, since 1910 an enfeebled republic, was, it seemed, about to become, very suddenly, Japan's India.

Actually the position of the United States caused Japan to hesitate with the result that her mastery of China was postponed for at least twenty years. This partial frustration by American diplomacy of Japan's principal national ambition was the cause of the chronic tension between the United States and Japan during those two decades, a tension which was to be strained further by American immigration policy, the alien land legislation of various states in the American Union, and the strategically vulnerable position of the Philippine Islands *vis-à-vis* Japan.

In appraising the effect, from this point on, of the United States on Japanese policy in Asia we must keep in mind the varying force of American diplomacy in 1915-1917, when the Republic was unprepared for war and under the governance of pacifist statesmen, and in 1917-1921, when it had effectively expanded its forces on land and sea to a position second to none.

When the Twenty-One Demands became known to the world in 1915 the United States was in no position to enforce singlehanded against Japan—even if it cared to do so, which it did not—its traditional policy of the Open Door, expanded in the Root-Takahira Agreement of 1908 to a formula for preserving the common interest of all powers in China

---

[1] Thomas Edward LaFargue, *China and the World War* (Stanford University Press, 1937).

by supporting by all *pacific* means at their disposal the independence and integrity of China as well as the principle of equal opportunity for commerce and industry of all nations in that Empire.

The Root-Takahira Agreement [1] of 1908, one recalls, had stipulated (among other things) that: "Should any event occur threatening the *status quo* as above described or the principle of equal opportunity as above defined, it remains for the two Governments to communicate with each other in order to arrive at an understanding as to what measures they may consider useful to take." It was on the basis of this article that Secretary Bryan directed a note (March 13, 1915) to the Japanese Ambassador in Washington, the content of which he also communicated by cable to China, while the Twenty-One Demands were under discussion between Japan and China. He stated that while the demands might be argued not to infringe on the territorial integrity of China (as Japan had pointed out when communicating to the United States on February 8 an abridged version of them) it was difficult to reconcile them with the maintenance of the unimpaired sovereignty of China "which Japan, together with the United States and the Great Powers of Europe, has reaffirmed from time to time during the past decade and a half in formal declarations, treaties and exchanges of diplomatic notes." The United States, therefore, "could not regard with indifference the assumption of political, military, or economic domination over China by a foreign Power." This note was tempered by a significant passage declaring that the activity of Americans in China had never been "political," and a frank recognition that in regard to Shantung, South Manchuria, and Eastern Inner Mongolia, "territorial contiguity creates special relations between Japan and these districts." The note closed with a very tactfully couched hope that Japan would find it consonant with her interests "to refrain from pressing upon China an acceptance of proposals which would, if accepted, exclude Americans from equal participation in the economic and industrial development of China and would limit the political independence of that country," and would thus create a situation which it was confidently believed that Japan did not desire.

During the discussions between Japan and China over the original Twenty-One Demands, they were considerably modified, coincidentally with friendly expostulations of the United States, and finally presented (May 7, 1915) as an ultimatum to China to be accepted within forty-eight hours. China accepted. Immediately the Chinese acceptance became known by telegraph in Washington, Secretary Bryan cabled (May

[1] See above, p. 25.

11, 1915, while the *Lusitania*[1] crisis was at its height) to Japan and China the following caveat:

In view of the circumstances of the negotiations which have taken place and which are now pending between the Government of Japan and the Government of China, and of the agreements which have been reached as a result thereof, the Government of the United States has the honor to notify the Imperial Japanese Government [Republic of China] that it cannot recognize any agreement or undertaking which has been entered into or which may be entered into between the Governments of Japan and China, impairing the treaty rights of the United States and its citizens in China, the political or territorial integrity of the Republic of China, or the international policy relative to China commonly known as the open door policy.[2]

Chinese acceptance of the Japanese demands was embodied in two treaties of May 25, 1915, and certain contemporary exchanges of notes. Group V of the Demands, the most serious of all for Chinese sovereignty, was "postponed for later negotiations."

It remained now for Japan to solidify diplomatically her position in China, as won by these Demands of 1915. The European War played admirably into her purposes. While Russia was so fully occupied with the other Allies against the Central Powers, Japan secured her acceptance of a treaty which openly pledged the two governments to unite their efforts for the maintenance of a "permanent peace in the Far East"— a phrase which decorates many an Asiatic agreement; and secretly the contracting parties agreed to "enter into open-hearted dealings" to "safeguard" China from the political domination of "any third power whatever, having hostile designs against Russia or Japan." Presumably these words meant the United States.[3] Thus was distressed Russia brought

---

[1] There was no relation between the sinking of the *Lusitania* and the delivery of the Japanese ultimatum (which had already arrived in Peking as early as May 6), although both occurred on the same day, May 7. Of course, the Japanese Government could not have been unaware of the possibility of difficulties between Germany and the United States over submarine warfare, particularly after Wilson's "strict accountability" note of February 10, 1915.

[2] For the notes, and the diplomatic correspondence of the Department of State, relating to the Twenty-One Demands, in so far as that correspondence has been published, see *Foreign Relations, 1915*, p. 146.

[3] Morse and McNair, *op. cit.*, p. 589, marshal the following reasons for believing that this "third power" could have been only the United States: (1) the well-known policy of the United States of the Open Door, and its attitude toward the Twenty-One Demands; (2) the United States was still a neutral in 1916; (3) it could not have been Germany because if Germany were defeated in the war there would be nothing to fear from her, while if she were victorious the Russo-Japanese alliance would be useless [and, we may add, the Anglo-Japanese alliance, too]; (4) there was no reason to keep secret a pact against Germany; (5) the Bolshevists published it from the Russian archives in 1918 under the title: "Secret Treaty between Russia and Japan, with reference to a possibility of their armed conflict together against America and Great Britain in the Far East before the summer of 1921."

in line with Japanese policy. The desperate situation of the other Allies following the resumption by Germany of unrestricted submarine warfare on February 1, 1917, next gave Japan her opportunity to secure pledges from them on the eve of the entry of the United States into the war. In return for the assistance of Japanese convoys in the Mediterranean—thus releasing Allied naval forces for work in critical fighting areas—Great Britain agreed (February 16, 1917) to support at the peace conference Japan's claims to Shantung and to retention of the German islands north of the Equator. France similarly agreed (March 1, 1917) to support Japan's claims, in return for Japan's obtaining from China a rupture of diplomatic relations with Germany (which among other advantages would make available for the Allies the German ships interned in Chinese ports). Russia (March 5, 1917) and later Italy also pledged themselves to support the Japanese claims at the end of the war.

The entrance of the United States into the war seemed an immediate advantage and possibly an ultimate disadvantage to Japan's policy of expansion in Eastern Asia. It meant that in the near future all American energies would be occupied by the war in Europe and on the Atlantic; it also meant the arming of the United States on land and sea to a formidable strength which might give renewed emphasis after the war to the traditional American policy for the integrity and independence of China. It was the objective of Japanese diplomacy therefore to commit the United States to the new program in China while it was still fully occupied in the war against Germany. This was the real object of the special mission to Washington of Viscount Ishii, announced in June, 1917, as a natural sequel to the other Allied missions which had visited the United States to arrange effective military and financial coöperation.

When the United States severed diplomatic relations with Germany, it had invited the neutral powers, including China, to do the same. The Chinese Parliament so declared, March 9, 1917. Then followed a confused domestic situation in that hapless republic, the seat of contest among President, Parliament, and Premier, and among the military provincial governors. Japanese policy encouraged this confusion by loans to the rival groups of shifting control, in return for economic concessions. It was the old story of *divide et impera*. Many Japanese leaders dreaded the economic, moral, and military energy of a united China independent of their control, and for that reason resisted the entrance of China into the war. Nevertheless the Chinese Government momentarily united sufficiently to declare war on Germany (August 14, 1917). Thus it insured itself a place at the peace conference where it could claim Shantung. Japan, on her part, now strove to bring under her management the military efforts of a divided China, meanwhile avoiding encouragement of Chinese unity. During the period of confusion between the rupture by China of diplomatic relations with Germany and her declaration of war, the United States invited (June 4, 1917) Great Britain, France, and Japan to co-operate for the restoration of Chinese national unity and internal peace as of first importance to itself and to the world, and to relegate the question of China and the World War to a second place. The failure of these powers to unite in any common policy here rendered useless this move for stiffening the integrity of China.

It was the effort of Viscount Ishii, appearing in Washington in the critical period of the First World War, to get from Lansing a recognition of Japan's "paramount interests" or at least "special influence" in China. Lansing on the other hand desired a reaffirmation of the Open Door and was willing to admit no closer "special relations" than Bryan had conceded two years previously. Ishii introduced the ominously suggestive statement, delicately but significantly put, that the German Government had three times sought to persuade Japan to withdraw from the Allies and to remain neutral, but that in every case his government had firmly rejected the suggestion.[1] The special Japanese envoy also mentioned a conversation which he had had in London in 1915 with Sir Edward Grey in which he had told the British Foreign Secretary that although Japan intended to restore Shantung to China at the end of the war, she was determined to keep the German islands north of the Equator; and that Grey "practically consented" to a division of the islands on the line of the Equator. Lansing would make no comment on such an agreement. Ishii did not mention the formal Anglo-Japanese agreement of February 16, 1917.

The result of this diplomatic logomachy was the cautiously phrased Lansing-Ishii Agreement[2] embodied in a public exchange of notes of November 2, 1917, by which the two cobelligerents in the war against Germany shelved their China issue with an ambiguous formula. Each

[1] Robert Lansing, *War Memoirs, op. cit.*, p. 293. K. Ishii, *Gaiko Yoroku* (Tokyo, 1930), published in an abridged English edition, William R. Langdon translator, under the title, *Diplomatic Commentaries* (Johns Hopkins Press, 1936).

[2] The negotiations are described by Julius W. Pratt, in *American Secretaries of State, op. cit.*, X, pp. 126-139, who had access to Lansing's papers which the former Secretary used in his *War Memoirs*.

party made nominal concessions to the other's position but sought cover for its own policy in studiously worded language. The agreement read:

The governments of the United States and Japan recognize that territorial propinquity creates special relations between countries, and, consequently, the government of the United States recognizes that Japan has special interests in China, particularly in the part to which her possessions are contiguous.

The territorial sovereignty of China, nevertheless, remains unimpaired, and the government of the United States has every confidence in the repeated assurances of the Imperial Japanese Government that while geographical position gives Japan such special interests they have no desire to discriminate against the trade of other nations or to disregard the commercial rights heretofore granted by China in treaties with other powers.

The governments of the United States and Japan deny that they have any purpose to infringe in any way the independence or territorial integrity of China, and they declare, furthermore, that they always adhere to the principle of the so-called "open door" or equal opportunity for commerce and industry in China.

Moreover, they mutually declare that they are opposed to the acquisition by any government of any special rights or privileges which would affect the independence or territorial integrity of China or that would deny to the subjects or citizens of any country the full enjoyment of equal opportunity in the commerce and industry of China.[1]

During the negotiations with Ishii, Secretary Lansing desired to include the following agreed statement: "They [the Governments of the United States and Japan] will not take advantage of the present conditions to seek special rights or privileges in China which would abridge the rights of the subjects or citizens of other friendly states." Ishii objected to putting this in the published exchange of notes. So a secret protocol, signed by Lansing and Ishii, accompanied the published exchange of notes that constituted the Lansing-Ishii Agreement. It stated: "It was, however, well understood that the principle enunciated in the clause *which was thus suppressed* was in perfect accord with the declared policy of the two Governments in regard to China." This secret ambiguity made the ambiguity of the public clauses of the Agreement doubly ambiguous. Though considered by the United States Government as an inseparable part of the Lansing-Ishii Agreement, it was not

[1] A convenient text of the note, with superficial information about the mission of Ishii, appears in Publication No. 15 of the Carnegie Endowment for International Peace, *The Imperial Japanese Mission, 1917* . . . (Washington, D. C., 1918). The publication significantly publishes together the texts of the Root-Takahira Agreement of 1908 and the new Lansing-Ishii Agreement of 1917.

published until long after the Lansing-Ishii Agreement had been superseded by the Nine-Power Treaty of Washington of 1922.[1]

Ishii was content with this agreement, which in Tokyo was regarded
as a diplomatic victory. He believed the time would come when Japan
could interpret it to her own satisfaction. Japan translated the document into Chinese in words that meant "paramount interests." Lansing
told the disheartened Chinese—and later the American Senate—that the
Agreement recognized only the "special interests" of an economic nature
created by geographical propinquity—"an axiom and nothing more."
He was convinced that it had resulted in commitments by Japan more
far-reaching and vital to the preservation of China's sovereignty than
the Root-Takahira Agreement of 1908, and that the "special interests"
which in return the United States had ratified were only the natural
economic interests of geographical propinquity, not political interests.
Ishii continued to believe and to declare in his country that it was essentially a political rather than an economic agreement which he had signed
with Lansing.[2]

Before the First World War ended, Japan, in co-operation with
her allies and associates, had made another significant intervention on
the continent of Asia—this time in Siberia, where Russian control collapsed after the Bolshevist Revolution. Japan was eager to make advantage of the confusion and take charge of that region. Great Britain
and France, anxious to marshal anti-Bolshevik forces against the Russian communists, in order to keep Russia in the war, urged the United
States to agree to a Japanese occupation of Siberia along the railroad
clear to the Urals. All major factions of the Russian people feared
Japanese intervention as a danger to their future sovereignty. The
United States persistently opposed such a step, even a joint occupation,
on the ground that it would antagonize Russia and throw her into the
arms of Germany; and stood obstinately in favor of letting the Russian
people work out their destiny unembarrassed. But after the German-
Russian peace of Brest Litovsk in the spring of 1918 the situation in
Siberia became so involved and volatile that Japanese intervention was
imminent. After this peace a legion of 50,000 Czechoslovaks, prisoners
of war organized by Russia to fight against the Central Powers, started
on a desperate anabasis across Siberia to Vladivostok. They were striving

---

[1] *Foreign Relations of the United States. The Lansing Papers, 1914-1920* (Department
of State Publication No. 1421, Washington, G.P.O., 1940), II, pp. 450-451. Italics inserted.
[2] Both diplomatists have left on record their recollections of these conversations and
negotiations, and their significance, records apparently based on contemporary diaries:
Lansing in his *War Memoirs, op. cit.*, and Ishii in his *Gaiko Yoroku, op. cit.*

to reach the western front in Europe, via America, to fight for the liberation of their newly revolted nation and homeland.   There was danger that these heroic troops might be cut off and destroyed by Bolshevist and other forces, and that the depot of munitions of the former Czarist Government at Vladivostok might become available to the Germans.   Japan was opposed to the re-establishment of any kind of stable Russian Government in Eastern Siberia, whether Czech, Bolshevist, or Cossack.   The looseness of the situation, and its danger to the Allied cause in Europe, presented an admirable opportunity for intervention, even with the applause of the European Allies.   A step in this direction was the Sino-Japanese military convention of May 16, 1918, which Japan secured from China in return for loans to the Anfu faction then in control of the Chinese Government at Peking.   This pact put China in Japanese lead-strings so far as military activity during the war was concerned; further, it provided for "joint" military operations in the Siberian provinces of Transbaikalia and the Amur "to assist Czechoslovak forces and to drive out German and Austrian forces and such as may be rendering assistance to them." [1]

The Japanese move led to a joint occupation by the Allies and the United States, in the summer of 1918, of the strategic port of Vladivostok and its hinterland.   To forestall an exclusive Japanese occupation and control of eastern Siberia, the Government of the United States proposed a Japanese-American expedition of a "few thousand men" to Vladivostok, to protect the rear of the eastward-moving Czechoslovak legion.   Japan (with the other powers) in agreeing to this reaffirmed her "avowed policy of respecting the territorial integrity of Russia and of abstaining from all interference in her internal politics."   She further declared that upon the realization of the objects above indicated (the relief of the Czechoslovak legion) she would immediately withdraw all Japanese troops from Russian territory. [2]   In the discussions accompanying the framing of these statements of intention, Viscount Ishii again suggested the words "special interests," this time to describe Japan's relationship to Siberia.   Acting Secretary of State F. L. Polk opposed the inclusion of any such declaration in the Japanese or American explanation of action and purpose.   The American expeditionary force was limited to 7,500 troops and less than a thousand additional civilian workers; and British, French, Italian, Rumanian, and Serbian con-

---

[1] Morse and McNair, *op. cit.*, pp. 649-668.

[2] Statement of the Japanese Ambassador to the Acting Secretary of State, August 2, 1918. *Foreign Relations, 1918, Supplement, Russia*, II, p. 325.

tingents were well below that limit; but Japan soon had 72,000 soldiers in Siberia.

In Siberia, more friction [1] than co-operation developed between the United States and Japan, for it was apparent that the American insistence on a joint, if any, intervention, had grouped Japan's opportunity. It was the object of American diplomacy to bring the joint intervention to steady the efforts of the Russians for self-government while protecting the ammunition stores at Vladivostok and the retreating Czechoslovaks, thus to remove the necessity for further intervention. It was the purpose of the Allies to bolster their position by building another front against Germany in the East. It was the aim of Japanese diplomacy to take advantage of this desire of the Allies for intervention, but to keep the Siberian situation confused in order to prolong intervention, by Japan alone when the other powers should step out. [2] One point at issue, outside of Siberia, was control of the Chinese Eastern Railway, running east and west across Manchuria to Vladivostok, a road formerly under Russian control. Japan was impelled by the joint intervention in Siberia to consent that it should be placed under the temporary control of an Inter-Allied Railway Commission. After the defeat of Germany, the foreign forces, with the exception of the Japanese, were withdrawn from Siberia by April, 1920. [3] But Japanese troops remained in Eastern Siberia. They were there when the Washington Conference assembled in November of 1921. Other Japanese forces were still in occupation of Shantung.

We recall, at the Peace Conference at Paris, President Wilson acquiesced to the agreements by which Japan had secured the support

---

[1] William S. Graves, *America's Siberian Adventure, 1918-1920* (New York, 1931).

[2] The Department of State has published a voluminous record of the diplomatic correspondence, and relevant documents, relating to the Siberian intervention, in *Foreign Relations, 1918, Russia* (3 vols., Washington, G.P.O., 1932). For Siberia, see Vol. II, pp. 1-467. It was the documents therein published which later induced Russia to waive all claims to damages on account of American participation in the Siberian intervention.

[3] The United States also participated with 4,500 troops in 1918-1919 in the joint intervention of Allied and Associated forces (British, 6,000, French, 1,500 men, with small contingents from other Allied nations) in the Murmansk region of northern Russia in Europe. At first with the co-operation of the Bolsheviki these troops occupied that region for the purpose of preventing that depot of ammunition and supplies from falling into the hands of Germany after the German-Russian peace of Brest Litovsk. The United States did not participate in the interventions of France and Great Britain in Russia from the Black Sea after the Armistice in Europe. For the Murmansk intervention, see *Foreign Relations of the United States, 1918, Russia* (Washington, G.P.O., 1932), II, pp. 468-577. Leonid I. Strakhovsky in a paper, "The Origins of American Intervention in North Russia, 1918," read at the American Historical Association at Chattanooga, Tennessee, December 27, 1935, showed the co-operation of Bolshevik authorities with this intervention, later protested by Russia. Russia nevertheless has not yet waived claims to damages for American participation.

of the European Allies to her conquest of the German concessions in Shantung and of the German islands in the Pacific north of the Equator. He had felt obliged to make this concession in order to secure Japan's signature to the treaty and to the League of Nations. In the discussions at Paris about the mandated islands the President had entered an oral reservation as to the status of the island of Yap, in the Carolines, nodal point for American cables running between the United States and the Far East. Japan after the peace settlement refused to recognize this reservation, and an issue arose between the two countries concerning the status of the tiny island, which aggravated the other complications of the Far East and the question of the Pacific.

At the Peace Conference, it is further recalled, neither Great Britain nor the United States, unfortunately, would recognize the demand of Japan for recognition in the League of Nations of the principle of racial equality. This was, and remained, a sore spot with the Japanese But Japan had emerged from the First World War in a triumphant position, with an equality in power and prestige, her feet well planted in new regions on the continent of Asia, in Shantung and in Siberia, grasping tenaciously a network of treaties thrown over China with the design of reducing that country to Japanese protection. She was also in occupation of the Russian half of the island of Sakhalin (northernmost island of the Japanese group) which Japan had seized as security for a satisfactory settlement for the slaughter by Bolshevik forces of the Japanese garrison of 640 men in a collision at Nikolaevsk across the strait in Siberia in March, 1920. Far out in the Pacific she had hold of the former German islands north of the Equator. It was the rapid rise of Japanese power in the First World War which brought to a head the vast diplomatic problem of the Pacific Ocean and the Far East.

11

The Washington and London Naval Treaties

THE First World War ended with the Allied and Associated Powers
of the Occident in a strong bond of friendship and military strength
despite their varying interests. After their defeat of Germany they were
in a position to look with less preoccupation upon the problems of the
Far East and the Pacific and their continuing interests there. It was
evident that a serious situation was shaping itself between the United
States and Japan, who now regarded her old friend as an inimical power
whose diplomacy had repeatedly stood in the way of her expansionist
ambitions, first and continually in China, and now in Siberia; and whose
laws as to citizenship and state landownership seemed incompatible
with the spirit of the Gentlemen's Agreement of 1907. The United
States in particular had emerged from the war in a position of great
military strength, in fact promising soon to be the greatest naval power
once the building of the program of 1916 should be completed. Great
Britain and Japan were anxious to see that naval power limited in line
with their own resources. If Japan were to gainsay the American policy
for the independence and integrity of China, and now for the same in
Siberia, naval force was imperative. The way the naval programs of
the three powers were then progressing, the most favorable relationship of Japanese naval power to that of the United States would seem
to be likely in the year 1923: after that Japan might steadily fall behind in the race for naval armament. The year 1923 loomed ahead as a
possible date for war.

The shadow of a coming Japanese-American crisis that might precipitate a war of the Pacific sobered the British Dominions, bordering on
that ocean, which also had their problems of excluding Oriental immigration. What would be the relation of the Dominions, particularly
Canada, to such a war, presuming the still unfettered scope of the Anglo-
Japanese Alliance? That alliance had been renewed for ten years in
1911, to continue after the decade subject to abrogation by either side at
one year's notice.

220

The alliance had stipulated that in case the interests of either party in the regions of the Far East should become endangered as a result of "an unprovoked or aggressive act wherever arising," [1] they should fight such a war together. When the treaty was renewed in 1911 it contained a clause to the effect that it should not apply to powers with which either party had a general treaty of arbitration. In 1911 President Taft had been engaged in negotiating a general arbitration treaty with Great Britain. The Senate did not ratify his treaty. Hence the United States was not immune from the touch of the Anglo-Japanese Alliance.[2] In case of a Japanese-American war Canada might be called upon to take sides against her southern neighbor and greatest friend, almost relative. This possibility was uppermost in the minds of Canadian leaders when they met with the other statesmen of the Empire in the Imperial Conference at London in the summer of 1921. In March, on the eve of that significant gathering, the Crown Prince of Japan, Hirohito—the present Emperor—made a visit of state on a Japanese battleship to the capital of the British Empire. It seemed, particularly to Canadian statesmen, backed emphatically by Canadian public opinion, that Britain must now choose between the United States and Japan.

The insistence of Canada, under her vigorous Prime Minister, Arthur Meighen, in guarding against any renewal of the Anglo-Japanese Alliance such as might involve her in a break either with the United States or with the new British Commonwealth of Nations, brought to focus

[1] Conceivably it might arise in the United States, over an incident of immigration or landownership, which might be made the pretext for a war of larger issues.

[2] In 1914 Great Britain seems to have made a secret statement to the Japanese Government that it would regard the Bryan conciliation treaty with the United States—the so-called "cooling-off" treaty—as an arbitration treaty in the sense of the Anglo-Japanese Alliance. The statement was not made public until 1921. Japan does not appear on her part ever to have accepted the interpretation.

Great Britain persuaded Japan to make a joint statement to the League of Nations, July 8, 1920, that the alliance, "though in harmony with the spirit of the Covenant," was not entirely consistent with its "letter," and that they recognized that, if renewed, it must be put in a form consistent with that Covenant. On July 13, 1921, six days before the ten-year term of the Alliance would have expired (though it continued unless denounced), the two allies notified the League of Nations that pending further action they were agreed that, "if any situation arises whilst the agreement [i.e., the Anglo-Japanese Alliance] remains in force in which the procedure described by the terms of the agreement is inconsistent with the procedure prescribed by the terms of the Covenant of the League, then the procedure prescribed by the said Covenant shall be adopted and shall prevail over that prescribed by the Agreement."

This did not remove the United States from the scope of the Alliance, because the United States had rejected the Covenant of the League of Nations. See Raymond L. Buell, *Washington Conference* (New York, 1922), pp. 113, 133. Note that the statement was made during the Imperial Conference of 1921 when Canada was protesting against any renewal of the Alliance.

the whole group of issues in regard to Anglo-American and Anglo-Japanese policy, the status of the Far East, the question of the Pacific, and postwar rivalry of naval armaments. The British Government was on the point of proposing to the interested powers a conference to settle these issues when it learned of the intention of the United States to do so and yielded the initiative to President Harding.

The President's call for a conference was based on the prime necessity of an understanding on naval armaments, but he proposed a discussion at the same time of Pacific and Far Eastern problems, a solution of which, he said, was of "unquestionable importance." He directed the invitations first to the Principal Allied and Associated Powers (except Russia, which had dropped out of the group after the Bolshevist Revolution) during the war against Germany and her Allies.[1] All accepted, Japan after some hesitation about the vague scope of the agenda. Later it was agreed to include in the Conference the Netherlands, which had large colonial holdings in the East Indies; Portugal, which possessed the settlement of Macao, near Canton; Belgium, which had an interest in Chinese railways and a concession at Tienstin; and China herself, the principal patient for the diplomatic doctors at Washington. Bolshevist Russia, the other patient, was in no condition to come to the clinic. For her only absent treatment could be indicated. Germany already had been operated on, and her convalescence was not disturbed. Austria-Hungary was deceased.

Back of the whole complex of issues, which were turning the face of the United States from the Atlantic to the Pacific, lay the fact that American diplomacy, though traditionally involved, was not vitally interested in the independence and integrity of China, to say nothing of Siberia. American leaders realized that their people would not then fight for these principles in Asia and that Congress could not be counted on for continuing big naval appropriations, notwithstanding rejection of the League of Nations Covenant. Under these circumstances Secretary Hughes was anxious for a diplomatic settlement. In the British Empire, in the United States, and in Japan the situation made for peace as well as for war.

President Harding's advisers profited by the recent experience of the Wilson Administration in dealing with the Senate. As in the case of the delegates to the Peace Conference at Paris, the American represen-

---

[1] Of these five powers, Great Britain, Japan, and France had territory in Eastern Asia. Italy and Belgium had small concessions in Tientsin, and Belgian capital was interested in some of the Chinese railways.

tatives were executive agents, with the rank of ambassador, except for the Secretary of State, who headed the delegation with his own title. Even though Congress was in session when the conference was called the President did not nominate the ambassadors to the Senate; [1] but he was careful to select his agents with regard to the Senate's power over treaties (he already had the advantage of a Republican Congress). In addition to Secretary of State Charles E. Hughes, there were Senator Henry Cabot Lodge, Republican leader in the Senate and Chairman of the Committee on Foreign Relations; Senator Oscar Underwood, ranking Democratic member of that committee; and former Secretary of State Elihu Root, an ex-senator.

Secretary Hughes opened the negotiations with the trump card of high naval strength, actual and potential, backed by undoubted support of the Republican Senate. Quite to the astonishment of the delegates, and perhaps with not perfect success, he played his trump at the first meeting. He proposed that "preparations for offensive war stop now." He then offered an itemized plan for the reduction of armaments according to an agreed ratio finally fixed at 5—5—3—1.7—1.7 (or 10—10—6—3.4—3.4),[2] corresponding generally to the existing ratio before the conference, which involved the sinking or scrapping of designated ships, built or building, of the three great naval powers, and a naval holiday in the construction of capital ships for ten years, with only limited replacements of superannuated ships thereafter until 1936. For Great Britain and Japan this program meant the scrapping mostly of old battleships and ships under construction, but including the monster Japanese battleship, *Mutsu,* already launched and over 90 per cent finished; for the United States it meant the scrapping of old battleships, of two new battleships already launched but not quite finished, plus seven battleships and six heavy cruisers on the ways. The delegates accepted in principle Hughes' startling proposal, and the several committees of experts proceeded to discuss it in detail as the Conference went into the consideration of the broad political subjects of the agenda. It was obvious that no naval agreement could be ratified at that time unless the political questions of the Far East and the Pacific also could be adjusted. The Hughes proposal emerged from the Conference fairly intact in treaty form, although modifications had to be made because of

[1] The Senate voiced no word of criticism at this procedure. "This appears to indicate that a tacit agreement has been reached to the effect that executive agents are not officers" [that is, in the sense of the Constitution, requiring nomination to the Senate and confirmation]. Wriston, *Executive Agents, op. cit.,* pp. 311-312.

[2] Great Britain, 5; the United States, 5; Japan, 3; France, 1.7; Italy, 1.7.

the refusal of Japan to scrap the *Mutsu;* but balanced by the acceptance of a proposal by Japan limiting fortification of certain of the islands of the Pacific, including the Philippines and Aleutian but not the Hawaiian Islands.

The following principal limitations of fortification were established by Chapter I, Article XIX, of the naval treaty:

The United States, the British Empire and Japan agree that the status quo at the time of the signing of the present Treaty, with regard to fortifications and naval bases, shall be maintained in their respective territories and possessions specified hereunder:

(1) The insular possessions which the United States now holds or may hereafter acquire in the Pacific Ocean, except (a) those adjacent to the coast of the United States, Alaska and the Panama Canal Zone, not including the Aleutian Islands, and (b) the Hawaiian Islands;

(2) Hongkong and the insular possessions which the British Empire now holds or may hereafter acquire in the Pacific Ocean, east of the meridian of 110° east longitude, except (a) those adjacent to the coast of Canada, (b) the Commonwealth of Australia and its Territories, and (c) New Zealand;

(3) The following insular territories and possessions of Japan in the Pacific Ocean, to wit: the Kurile Islands, the Bonin Islands, Amami-Oshima, the Loochoo Islands, Formosa and the Pescadores, and any insular territories or possessions in the Pacific Ocean which Japan may hereafter acquire.

The maintenance of the status quo under the foregoing provisions implies that no new fortifications or naval bases shall be established in the territories and possessions specified; that no measures shall be taken to increase the existing naval facilities for the repair and maintenance of naval forces, and that no increase shall be made in the coast defenses of the territories and possessions above specified. This restriction, however, does not preclude such repair and replacement of worn-out weapons and equipment as is customary in naval and military establishments in time of peace.

The treaty left the United States and Great Britain each 15 capital ships of 525,000 tons total; Japan 9 of 272,070 tons; and France and Italy free to build up to a maximum of 175,000 tons each. The United States and Great Britain might have each 135,000 tons additional of aircraft carriers; Japan, 81,000 tons; and France and Italy each 60,000 tons. Roughly this kept to the ratio of 5—5—3—1.7—1.7. The real effect of the naval agreement, including the ancillary part on fortified areas, was to make it impossible for any one of the three navies alone to fight an offensive war against one of the others in the Pacific. To forestall two of the navies suddenly leaguing against the third was the purpose of a new ten-year quadruple consultative pact for preserving the *status quo* of the Pacific which replaced the Anglo-Japanese Alliance. In case the rights of any party in the region of the Pacific Ocean were threatened by the aggressive action of any power, the four treaty powers (the United States, France, Great Britain, and Japan) agreed "to communicate with each other as to the most efficient measures to be taken, jointly or singly, to meet the exigencies of the particular situation." Thus Japan protected her own islands against any likely attack from Pacific waters, and established an irresistible dominance of her power in Eastern Asia. For a recognition of this position the other powers demanded, and received from Japan, certain pledges, which in form of a nine-power treaty were made binding on all, for the observance of the Open Door, the administrative and territorial integrity of China, and the abstention by all powers from seeking special privileges in China. Japan announced that she would now totally abandon Group V of the Demands of 1915, which she had hitherto reserved for future consideration. With the ratification by Japan and the United States of the Nine-Power Treaty for the conservation of the integrity of China, the public part of the Lansing-Ishii Agreement of 1917 was formally annulled by an exchange of notes, April 14, 1923.

The secret protocol[1] of the Lansing-Ishii Agreement had become the first part of paragraph 4 of Article I of the Nine-Power Treaty, by which the contracting powers other than China agreed "to refrain from taking advantage of conditions in China in order to seek special rights or privileges which would abridge the rights of subjects or citizens of friendly states, *and from countenancing action inimical to the security of those states.*" The last, italicized words were new, not in the secret protocol of 1917. Their significance has never been sufficiently noticed. What powers other than Japan could feel their *security* endangered by special foreign rights and privileges in China?

Japan during the Conference made a separate treaty with the United States recognizing American cable rights on Yap Island, and a separate treaty with China for the speedy return of Shantung (subject to the inviolability of private contracts, multifarious in number and character, procured during the Japanese occupation) and the purchase by China, in installments, of the former German railway there for *yen* 61,000,000. As to Siberia, Japan successfully protested against any disposition of that subject by the assembled powers, but on her own responsibility pledged herself to withdraw. The pledge was spread on the minutes

---

[1] See above, p. 215.

of the Conference. Japan evacuated Siberia in October, 1922. Not until 1925 did she restore the northern half of Sakhalin to Russian sovereignty, after securing exclusive concessions for the exploitation of oil and coal fields in that region, and further concessions for the lease of fisheries and the working of other national resources in Siberia.

The Washington treaties did not much undo the special privileges and concessions which had been forced from China by the imperialistic powers in the past: they were merely a general self-denial ordinance for the future. Nevertheless a series of formal resolutions opened the way, at least, for tariff autonomy for China, the removal of foreign post offices and radio stations, and the anticipation if not the consummation of the abolition of extraterritoriality.[1]

The Washington Conference amounted to a face-saving retreat of the United States from active diplomacy in the Far East under the cover of a multilateral international agreement for the observance of the traditional American policies for the Open Door and the administrative, political, and territorial integrity of China. In case of any future violation of these solemn pledges, which was not anticipated, redress of the wrong would as much concern, at least juridically, the nine powers parties to the treaties and resolutions in regard to China as it would the United States. After 1921 the United States was no longer sole proprietor of these policies, nor, because of the naval limitations, able to rely on anything stronger than peaceful means for co-operation.

The Washington naval treaty of 1922 limited only capital ships— over 10,000 tons displacement;[2] it said nothing about auxiliary craft: Class A cruisers (carrying 8″ guns), Class B cruisers (carrying 6″ guns), destroyers, submarines. For three years the United States did not lay down a keel of any kind, and for three years more a very small number of new ships were begun;[3] but in 1928, after the other powers, first of all Japan, had engaged in a formidable program of armaments in cruisers, destroyers, and submarines; six more Class A cruisers were laid down, and, in 1930, three more, in a belated effort to catch up with the new ri-

---

[1] W. W. Willoughby, who served as adviser to the Chinese Government before and during the Conference, has published expert analyses of China's problems in diplomacy in *Foreign Rights and Interests in China* (2 vols., Johns Hopkins Press, revised edition, 1927) and *China at the Conference, a Report* (Johns Hopkins Press, 1922).

[2] None could be built over 35,000.

[3] In 1925, 1 submarine.
   In 1926, 1 Class A cruiser and 6 river gunboats, and 2 submarines.
   In 1927, 1 Class A cruiser and 2 submarines.
   In 1928, 6 Class A cruisers.
   In 1929, none.

valry. During these years the United States had pressed for further limitations, in the auxiliary categories to which competition had transferred itself after 1922. It took the initiative for a preliminary conference under the auspices of the League of Nations at Geneva in 1927, which failed. Meanwhile all projects of the nations for a limitation of land armaments and armies also failed.[1]

The advent in the United States in 1929 of the Republican Hoover Administration, and in England of the new Labor Government, and a personal conference of the Prime Minister, Ramsay MacDonald, with President Hoover at Washington, and Rapidan, Virginia, laid the basis for another naval conference, of the five great naval powers, the United States, the British Commonwealth of Nations (as it had now come to be known), Japan, France, and Italy. The London Treaty of 1930 postponed until 1936 the replacements in capital ships allowable under the Washington Treaty after 1931, and extended limitations to the auxiliary ships (subject to certain allowable replacement), limitations which were to be worked up or down to by December 31, 1936, after which all surplus tonnage in the stipulated categories must be disposed of according to a fixed schedule. The new limitations were vigorously opposed by naval authorities in the United States, Great Britain, and Japan (France and Italy did not subscribe to the principal limitations, and finally did not ratify the treaty at all), which seems fairly good evidence that the treaty contained a reasonable compromise; but the three powers ratified the agreement, good until December 31, 1936, and providing for a third naval conference in December, 1935, one year before the expiration of the treaty.[2] On the following page is represented a tabulation of the fleets, ratios, and tonnage, with which the powers emerged from the London Treaty.[3] An "escalator clause" permitted any contracting party to step up out of the limitations in case a noncontracting party should modify seriously the existing situation of naval construction.[4] It proved to be of utmost importance when the time came, December 31, 1936, to begin disposing of the surplus tonnage, over and above the stipulations of the limited categories. By then the naval race had begun again, due to Japan's breakoff on the one hand, and the

---

[1] The United States with its small standing army of 165,000 could not be a great factor in these efforts.

[2] Benjamin H. Williams has published a very summary and wishful history of *The United States and Disarmament* (New York, 1931).

[3] For a more detailed statement, see "A Birdseye View of the Washington and London Naval Treaties," facing page 704 in *Diplomatic History, op. cit.* The treaty, an intricate document, must be carefully studied.

[4] Great Britain invoked it, May, 1936, and April, 1938.

NAVAL LIMITATION OF THE LONDON TREATY OF 1930 TO BE REACHED ON DECEMBER 31, 1936

Categories	United States		British Commonwealth of Nations		Japan	
	No. Ships	Total Tonnage	No. Ships	Total Tonnage	No. Ships	Total Tonnage
Capital Ships	15	464,300	15	474,750	9	272,070
Aircraft Carriers		135,000		135,000 (with 70,350 replacements)		81,000 (with 7,470 replacements)
Cruisers, Class A (8″ guns)	18	(No more than 10,000 tons each)	15	(No more than 10,000 tons each)	12	(No more than 10,000 tons each)
Cruisers, Class B (6″ guns)		143,500		192,200		100,450 (Replacement 1 ship in 1935)
Destroyers		150,000		150,000		105,500
Submarines		52,700		52,700		52,700 (with 31,200 anticipated replacement)

European situation on the other. The United States, therefore, did not scrap all its First World War decommissioned destroyers. Looking back on this situation after the critical days of 1940 we could be glad that these precious ships were not junked.

Notwithstanding the warnings of American naval experts that the London limitations were not safe for the secure defense of the United States and its territorial possessions, despite the ominous trend of international relations in Europe and in Asia since 1930, the United States (and to a small extent, Great Britain) underbuilt its navy beneath the treaty limits. Japan, on the other hand, built snugly up to the treaty line. Consequently in the last treaty year, the United States found itself particularly weak in underage warships, notably in cruisers, destroyers, and submarines. Japan surpassed the United States in effective Class B cruisers, destroyers,[1] and submarines; and crept perilously close in new tonnage of aircraft carriers and Class A cruisers.[2] With warships, as with automobiles, victory is likely to go to the new models. Under her right as a party to the Washington Treaty, Japan in December, 1934, gave formal notice of the cessation of any continuation of that agreement after its lifetime ending December 31, 1936,[3] when the London Treaty also expired. Great Britain, alarmed in 1936 by the Italo-Ethiopian War for the security of her Mediterranean route to India and for her African Empire, prepared for vigorous additions to her naval armament.

Under these unpromising conditions the treaty powers assembled for another naval conference in London in December, 1935, as provided by the terms of the London Treaty, only to prove themselves unable to agree on any effective limitations. The naval *status quo* of 1936, thanks to underbuilding by the United States during 1931-1936, was, as the reader will observe by the tables at the end of this chapter, much more favorable to Japan than was the *status quo* of 1931. These figures show that on July 1, 1935—the year in which the Washington period of naval truce came to an end—these were the *de facto* ratios of the five principal navies:

[1] This superiority in these categories of new tonnage was increased by the construction by Japan of an unknown number of small torpedo boats, under 600 tons. There were no treaty restrictions on this size of warship.

[2] For detailed tables of tonnage and ratios in 1922, 1930, and 1935, see note at end of this chapter.

[3] Without such notice registered by one of the parties the treaty by its terms would have continued for two additional years.

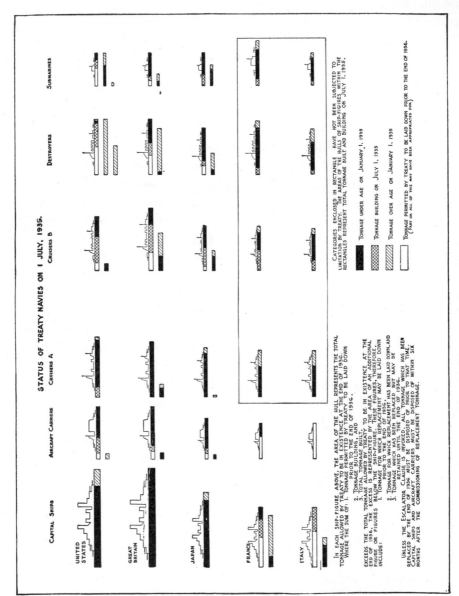

Pictorial Diagram of Treaty Navies, 1935

TOTAL TONNAGE OF UNDER-AGE SHIPS OF ALL CATEGORIES

United States	Great Britain	Japan	France	Italy
7.46	10	6.62	3.78	3.01

In underage tonnage in the categories of light cruisers, destroyers, and submarines, Japan by 1935 had already forged ahead of the United States under the treaty regime of 1922-1936. By secret encroachments on the treaty limits, revealed by the Second World War, she brought her actual fighting ratio even higher than the above *de facto* figures show.

The statesmen of the great powers left Washington in 1922 with the certainty that the tension had been relaxed and that a breathing spell was at hand, for at least fifteen years, for the development of peace and prosperity in the Pacific. Good will had taken the place of fear and suspicion. That happy atmosphere was suddenly vexed by the passage of the American immigration law of 1924, which superseded the Gentlemen's Agreement, under which the immigration of Japanese to the United States had been regulated since 1907 without discrimination directly or indirectly against the Japanese. Over the opposition of the President and of the Secretary of State, Congress declared that "aliens not eligible for citizenship," which by existing law meant all Orientals born outside of the United States, were excluded from admission into the United States and its territories, except for certain exempted classes of individuals. This really was intended for Japanese, since other Orientals, including Chinese, had been excluded by previous legislation. The exempted classes were: government officials, those coming to the United States as tourists, travelers, seamen, former residents returning from temporary absences, professors, ministers of religion, students, and those who entered solely to carry on trade in pursuance of existing treaty provisions. President Coolidge felt obliged to sign the act in order to have the advantages of the general regulation of immigration which it placed on the statute books, in the face of a menacing deluge of postwar European immigrants. To Japan it was a bitter blow: not the exclusion—Japan had accepted that in fact, and was willing to help block up any holes in the previous arrangements—but the essential discrimination. When the bill was being debated in Congress, and seemed likely to pass, the Japanese Ambassador, Mr. Hanihara, lodged with the Department of State a note of protest which stated that "grave consequences" were likely to ensue if it were enacted. There is reason to believe that this note was prepared in collaboration between the Japanese Embassy and the Department of State for the purpose of staying the hand of Congress. When Secretary of State Hughes transmitted a copy of it to Congress it was taken as a threat of war. Probably there was enough sentiment in the Senate to have carried Japanese exclusion by a narrow margin anyway, but Hanihara's veiled threat turned the vote in Congress into a veritable landslide for exclusion.[1]

Toward the end of this volume we shall return to Japan's program in Asia, her conquest of China in defiance of the principles so solemnly agreed to in the Nine-Power Treaty, the patient caveats and protests of the United States, and Japan's treacherous attack on the Hawaiian Islands and the Philippines in the momentous war that began on Sunday morning, December 7, 1941.

[1] Rodman W. Paul wrote an undergraduate essay on *The Abrogation of the Gentlemen's Agreement* (Harvard Phi Beta Kappa Prize Essay for 1936, Cambridge, 1936) worthy of a doctoral dissertation.

12

The United States and Europe during the

Interbella Period

In a previous chapter we have described the peace settlement of 1919-1921 and the liquidation of those questions of neutral rights that were such an intricate legacy of the First World War. The first fifteen years of diplomatic relations between the United States and Europe in the interval beween the two World Wars concerned largely certain other issues arising from the aftermath of the first war and its train of revolution: reparations, intergovernmental war debts, the organization of peace, recognition of Soviet Russia, disarmament. Historians hardly realized that as soon as they had placed these issues in their proper perspective they would have to deal with another world war.

The policy which the United States pursued toward Europe after the separate peace with Germany, Austria, and Hungary, following the rejection of the League of Nations, may be compared to that of Great Britain after the Napoleonic wars and the peace settlement of 1815. Great Britain refused to make of the Quadruple Alliance, in which the great powers had united to overthrow Napoleon, a pedestal for the Holy Alliance, which was to mold Europe in the principles of absolute monarchy invoked at Vienna under the mantle of Legitimacy. Unchallenged in her absolute control of the sea, and thus safe behind the English Channel, she preferred to stand aloof from the issues of continental politics as long as no one upset the balance of power. Similarly a century later the United States, safe behind the Atlantic, rejected Woodrow Wilson's ideal of internationalism and stepped back from Europe to its own continent after the defeat of Germany. It refused any direct participation in the succeeding conferences,[1] after Versailles, that met to execute and adjust the peace settlement of 1919 which straitjacketed Europe again, this time under the principle of Nationality. It refused membership in the League of Nations, which Wilson had founded to enforce the peace henceforth all over the globe by guaranteeing the

[1] London, San Remo, Hythe, Lympne, and Spa, in 1920; Cannes, London, and Genoa, in 1922; London, 1924; Locarno, 1925; Genoa, 1926.

existing political independence and territorial integrity of its members. Its Senate even rejected membership in the Court of International Justice, the judicial organ of the League, set up by separate statute so that a nation might belong to it without necessarily being a member of the League. Only in numerous humanitarian, cultural, economic, and technical international conferences held under the aegis of the League did the United States take a full part; and in membership in the separately organized International Labor Office, for the co-ordination, by separate sovereign legislation, of national labor legislation throughout the world.[1]

For more than a decade after 1921, this policy of "isolation" encountered a steady, vigorous, and highly articulate opposition on the part of the intellectuals, speaking through the pulpit, the public forum, the textbooks, and the universities; but following the appearance of the European dictatorships, and the clanging appeals to force for the rearrangement of political and economic frontiers in Europe, Asia, and Africa, it became obvious that Woodrow Wilson's conception of a league of *democratic* nations to enforce world peace was only delicately viable under new stresses.

Default by the European Allies [2] of their so-called "war debts" to the United States, and the tangled question of reparations, rooted in the Versailles Treaty, had been at least a minor factor in this revulsion of opinion in the United States from the League of Nations. Before we turn to the American peace policy, as manifested in the network of treaties for voluntary arbitration and conciliation, and the pledges against war as an instrument of national policy, and against intervention in the foreign or domestic affairs of any foreign state, it is necessary to set forth these sore and chafing issues of "war debts" and reparations, legally separate yet actually joined, theoretically unconnected yet really related.

Entering the First World War, the United States opened its credit unstintedly to the Associated Governments, at the moment when they were hardest pressed for money, even as it raised its armies and finally hurled them against the enemy on the continent of Europe. The Allies were desperate to borrow, in the hour of their darkest need; and the United States, intent on winning the war, was eager to lend to sustain the fighting strength of its Associates while American man power was being

---

[1] Denys P. Myers has traced the history of these multifarious activities in the *Handbook of the League of Nations* (World Peace Foundation, Boston, 1935).

[2] In using the word *Allies,* reference is made to the European Entente Allies allied among themselves. They were Associates of China, the United States, and the belligerents of the New World.

drilled to take its place in battle at the European front. The United States lent without stint and later it fought without condition. Before the armistice of November 11, 1918, it had loaned to the Allies a total of $7,077,114,750.00 in cash, nine tenths of which was spent in the United States for supplies useful in prosecuting the war, not only munitions but also many kinds of materials for war-busy populations.

These sums thus loaned before the armistice, and hence during the hostilities of the war, may properly be called *war debts*. There was some difference of opinion expressed in the debates in Congress as to whether they might in the end be treated as subsidies or loans; but there was no misunderstanding concerning the terms on which they were furnished to the Allied Governments. They were loaned on promises to pay, backed by the national faith of the borrowing governments, the terms of repayment to be agreed upon later, interest at 5 per cent to be charged meanwhile. The United States Government in turn secured the money by its own credit from its own citizens by the sale of bonds, the "liberty bonds," on which the Government promised to pay back principal and interest, usually 4¼ per cent, in dollars of the weight and fineness of gold which existed at the time of issue of the loan, and according to a schedule stipulated in the bonds. So if the Allies should not pay their debts, for these moneys borrowed in the hour of direst distress to help them save their very lives, then the burden of their indebtedness, principal and interest, would rest upon the people of the United States, on the lenders instead of the borrowers. That burden did so rest, as a matter of fact, upon the American people immediately after the war, when interest payments were suspended,[1] at least until the day should arrive for the funding of the payment of these sums.

After the armistice of November 11, 1918, the United States loaned in addition to the sums above mentioned, the sum of $2,533,288,825.45 cash, and $740,075,499.25 war supplies and relief supplies—total $3,273,364,324.70. This was not used for fighting, but for relief of civilian populations, rehabilitation of credit of the Allied nations, big and little, old and new, and sustenance of the new remnant and succession states of Europe while they were staggering to their feet amid the ruins from which they rose: Poland, Czechoslovakia, Rumania, Serbia, Estonia, Lithuania, Latvia, Finland, even Austria and Hungary.[2] These were really *peace debts,* incurred after Germany and her allies had surren-

---

[1] Interest payments in most cases were kept up by the debtors during the war, for the compelling reason that they might not be able to borrow more if they did not pay interest on the previous loans.

[2] As noted in the tabulation below, this included a loan of $10,000,000 to Cuba, $431,849.14 to Nicaragua, and $26,000 to Liberia.

dered, some of them borrowed by the former enemy. The United States Government, however, made no distinction between these war debts established before the armistice and the peace debts created after November 11, 1918. Nor was any such distinction ever made in the later funding of the debts (except in the case of Belgium) nor during the few years in which the debtor nations paid on their debts according to the agreed schedule.

The following statement [1] shows the total principal of these original debts to the United States, $10,350,479,074.70.

PRINCIPAL OF FOREIGN INDEBTEDNESS TO THE UNITED STATES, BY COUNTRIES, DIVIDED INTO PRE-ARMISTICE AND POST-ARMISTICE LOANS

| | Pre-Armistice | Post-Armistice | | |
Country	Cash Loans	Cash Loans	War Supplies and Relief Supplies	Total Indebtedness
Armenia			$ 11,959,917.49	$ 11,959,917.49
Austria			24,055,708.92	24,055,708.92
Belgium	$ 171,780,000	$ 177,434,467.89	29,872,732.54	379,087,200.43
Cuba	10,000,000			10,000,000.00
Czechoslovakia		61,974,041.10	29,905,629.93	91,879,671.03
Estonia			13,999,145.60	13,999,145.60
Finland			8,281,926.17	8,281,926.17
France	1,970,000,000	1,027,477,800.00	407,341,145.01	3,404,818,945.01
Great Britain	3,696,000,000	581,000,000.00		4,277,000,000.00
Greece		27,167,000.00		27,167,000.00
Hungary			1,685,835.61	1,685,835.61
Italy	1,031,000,000	617,034,050.90		1,648,034,050.90
Latvia			5,132,287.14	5,132,287.14
Liberia		26,000.00		26,000.00
Lithuania			4,981,628.03	4,981,628.03
Nicaragua			431,849.14	431,849.14
Poland			159,666,972.39	159,666,972.39
Rumania		25,000,000.00	12,911,152.92	37,911,152.92
Russia	187,729,750		4,871,547.37	192,601,297.37
Yugoslavia	10,605,000	16,175,465.56	24,978,020.99	51,758,486.55
	$7,077,114,750	$2,533,288,825.45	$740,075,499.25	$10,350,479,074.70

In addition to these loans of the United States Government, the people of the United States contributed, through the Red Cross and other agencies, over a billion dollars for the relief of war-stricken populations between 1914 and 1921.[2]

[1] From mimeographed "Memorandum Covering the Indebtedness of Foreign Governments to the United States and Showing the Total Amounts Paid by Germany under the Dawes and Young Plans," Treasury Department, Office of Commissioner of Accounts and Deposits, revised March 1, 1935 (Washington, D. C.), p. 16.

[2] See statement of Senator S. P. Spencer, Congressional Record, March 4, 1921. Through the Red Cross was contributed $978,512,225; by Congressional appropriations for European relief, $100,000,000. Spencer's report estimates $490,000,000 (one half the Red Cross total) contributed through other channels.

In the Peace Conference at Paris the French and British spokesmen desired to make some all-round agreement for the settlement of inter-Allied indebtedness in relation to the reparations which were to be demanded from Germany on account of her damages to civilian populations on land, at sea, and from the air, as interpreted by the victorious Allies. In 1923 Great Britain was a creditor for $10,447,761,000 lent to Allied nations outside the Empire ($4,321,976,000 of it to Russia), and a debtor for $6,489,492,000 of which $4,277,000,000 was to the United States. Assuming that revolutionary Russia would never pay the Czar's war debts, Great Britain would come out more than even in any general cancellation. She was therefore not unwilling, in fact she was ready to agree to collect no more than she had to pay. France was a creditor for $3,463,744,000 ($1,165,720,000 of this to Russia) and a debtor for $7,020,616,000 ($3,404,818,945 to the United States); Italy was a creditor for $389,988,000 and a debtor for $4,747,527,000 ($1,648,034,050 to the United States); these two nations were naturally eager for a general cancellation.[1] If each power could have canceled off its debits against its credits, and made the payment of any surplus debits left over dependent and contingent upon its receipts from German reparations—leaving the immediate cash to be raised from a bonded loan from America secured by anticipated proceeds of German reparations—the burden of the war debts could then be paid partly by the people of the defeated nation, Germany, and partly by the people of the United States. Then if unforeseen contingencies should in future interrupt the flow of reparations from Germany, it need disturb only the holders of the German reparation bonds which, it was often thought, could be sold to people in the United States. The ally which failed to collect its German reparations would stop contingent payment on its own war debts.

The United States had loaned vast sums, and borrowed none. Therefore proposals of this nature would have made the payment of the uncanceled portion of the debts of its Associates depend upon the collection of German reparations, a problem of European political complexities and entanglements. Incidentally such an arrangement would have made the United States interested in the inter-Allied machinery for the enforcement and collection of reparations against Germany, just as the creditors of the thirteen original states once were made interested, by Alexander Hamilton's fiscal device of federal assumption of state debts,

[1] H. E. Fisk, *The Inter-Ally Debts; an Analysis of War and Post-war Public Finance, 1914-1923* (New York, 1924), pp. 348-349; and Treasury "Memorandum Covering the Indebtedness," *op. cit.*

in the success of the new federal government of the United States after 1789. Woodrow Wilson and his colleagues successfully resisted all suggestions of melting together at Paris the debts to the United States and the reparations to be extracted from Germany.[1]

The peace-makers at Paris could not agree on any sum of total reparations to be required of Germany, so vast were the damages alleged to civilians from Germany and her allies, so astronomical were the implications of the interpretation [2] placed by the victorious powers on civilian damages to include war pensions and separation allowances. Article 231 of the treaty of Versailles stated:

The Allied and Associated Governments affirm and Germany accepts the responsibility of Germany and her allies for causing all the loss and damage to which the Allied and Associated Governments and their nationals have been subjected as a consequence of the war imposed upon them by the aggression of Germany and her allies.

This responsibility for civilian damages (as so interpreted by the victors) to Allied and Associated nationals was limited to the period of the belligerency of nations in the war. Such guaranteed little to the United States, whose claims for damages, as is recalled, were mostly for outrages against American neutral lives and property in violation of international law, before the period of American belligerency.[3] The treaty required 20,000,000,000 gold marks to be paid by Germany on account during the two years while reparations were being figured up, together with a schedule of payments in kind. The final calculation was referred to a special Reparations Commission, created by the treaty, to report before May 1, 1921, the total demanded from Germany, to arrange a schedule of payments, and to supervise its execution. The Commission was also empowered by the treaties with Austria and Hungary to fix and supervise the payments of reparations due from them. The Commission duly announced the colossal sum of 132,000,000,000 gold marks, or approximately 33,000,000,000 gold dollars in the currency of that time. As if in its inner wisdom the Reparations Commission doubted the

---

[1] They presented to the French and Italian commissioners the following statement from the Treasury of the United States, March 8, 1919: "The Treasury . . . will not assent to any discussion at the Peace Conference or elsewhere of any plan or arrangement for the release, consolidation, or reapportionment of the obligations of foreign governments held by the United States." Thomas W. Lamont, in House and Seymour, *What Really Happened at Paris, op. cit.,* p. 289.

[2] See above, p. 167.

[3] After the separate peace with Germany these claims for spoliations on neutrals were adjudicated by the Mixed Claims Commission United States and Germany. See above, p. 189.

capacity of Germany to pay the 132,000,000,000 gold marks even over a long time, it divided the sum into three categories; established the order of priority of each; and ordained a schedule of payment for each, in the form of three classes of bonds, with dated coupons for interest and amortization. Germany was called upon first to assume the service by payments partly in cash and partly in kind, of the Class A bonds totaling 12,000,000,000 gold marks and the Class B bonds, totaling 38,000,-000,000 gold marks bearing 6-per-cent coupons, representing 5-per-cent interest and 1-per-cent amortization. The Class C bonds, 82,000,000,000 gold marks, held in abeyance without interest, were never actually issued.

Needless to remind the reader, Germany never paid any more than a few years' installments toward serving the Class A and B obligations. While doing this, and making huge payments in kind, she depleted her currency and went through a catastrophic cycle of inflation. When she failed to pay more, France occupied (1923) the Ruhr Basin, Germany's principal industrial region, a coercive step allowed by the treaty; and Great Britain deducted 26 per cent from the payments by her nationals for current imports from Germany, applying the proceeds to reparations account. These coercive measures proved ineffective as a means of adequate collection, though not as a means of coercion. The only way to try to collect all was to use further force, and this was too costly, even if force could overcome passive resistance. Germany on her part was still helpless after military defeat and inflation. Alarmed by the occupation, she was willing to agree to a new compromise schedule. At the indirect suggestion of the Secretary of State of the United States, Charles E. Hughes, the Reparations Commission invited American financial experts, General Charles G. Dawes, and Owen D. Young, to head successive international commissions to devise a receivership for a bankrupt, helpless, and, it must also be said, unwilling, conquered debtor nation. First by the Dawes Plan (in operation, 1924 to 1929), and then by the Young Plan (which dated from 1929) successively lighter schedules of payments were prescribed and accepted.

The Young Plan (agreed upon December 22, 1928) stepped German reparations down to an annual burden that was possible for the Third Reich to bear. It laid down a new schedule of a "final and definitive settlement" based on a revised total liability over fifty-nine years. During this period Germany was to make unconditional payments of 612,000,000 gold marks per year (approximately $153,000,000 pre-devalued gold dollars). Conditional payments (contingent on German prosperity) might rise above the unconditional annuities to a total of

RM.1,641,600,000 ($410,000,000) per annum to RM.2,352,700,000 ($588,-175,000) in 1965, and descending to less than a billion marks ($250,000,-000) for the last three years of the long term. The unconditional annuities represented an amount almost precisely equal to what the Allies had agreed, meanwhile, to remit per annum to pay their funded debts to the United States. A part of the unconditional annuities was pledged for another immediate "mobilization loan" of a $200,000,000 bond issue to commute into ready cash for the creditors that much of Germany's revised obligations. In return for a German pledge to pay these new annuities all established controls and coercions were abandoned by the Allies. Contemporaneously they agreed to evacuate all occupied zones of German territory (held since the armistice) by 1930.

Defeated Germany no longer had any great domestic war debt (it had been withered up by the catastrophe of inflation and deflation), and her small army and navy were strictly limited by the Treaty of Versailles. The reparations debt was now no more of a burden to Germany than were their war debts to the victorious powers (where the burden of war debts in many cases had also been alleviated by inflation and devaluation) ; but the Allies had to spend huge sums on armies and navies necessary, in the background, to hold Germany down to these terms of defeat. And Germany under Adolf Hitler was able *within five years*, 1934-1939, to spend upwards of 90,000,000,000 reichmarks [1] (re-established German currency) at first secretly then openly on rearmament for the purpose of tearing up the treaty obligations of Versailles and conquering the victors of 1918! This sum should be compared to the original total reparations bill to be paid over a stretch of sixty years. The additional military expenses spent by Germany after the beginning of the Second World War quickly equaled and surpassed the *total* original reparations bill of 132,000,000,000 gold marks (of which 82,000,000,000 was never bonded).

While the Allies were saddling on Germany the terms of reparations the United States was patiently awaiting a settlement of the debts due to it, interest on which had been suspended by the debtors at the end of the war. An act of Congress (February 9, 1922) had created a World War Debts Funding Commission, appointed by the President, by and with the advice and consent of the Senate, with the Secretary of the Treasury as chairman. The law authorized the Commission to fund anew the debts into bonds bearing 4.25-per-cent interest, to be

[1] See Hitler's Reichstag speech of September 1, 1939, in collection of Adolf Hitler's speeches in English translation, entitled *My New Order* (New York, 1941), p. 689.

completely paid off, principal and interest, by 1947. This corresponded generally to the obligations of the United States for the payment of its own bonds from which had come the money that was loaned to the Associates in war and in peace. The funding agreements, made by the Commission with the different debtor nations between 1923 and 1930, were much more lenient than these terms allowable by the statute, because of radical cuts in interest and lengthening of terms of payment; but Congress by separate acts ratified each revision. The tabulation [1] on the following page shows the terms on which the total debts were funded, without distinction between war debts and peace debts, and excluding the unfunded debts of Armenia, Nicaragua, and Russia.

Calculating on the basis of an original obligation to pay 5-per-cent interest, these funding agreements represented a cancellation of approximately 51.3 per cent of the *then value* of the total indebtedness, ranging from a minimum of 30.1 per cent cancellation allowed to Great Britain to 80.2 per cent cancellation allowed to Italy. On a 4.25-per-cent interest basis (corresponding to domestic liberty-loan rates) this cancellation would be 43.1 per cent of the whole, ranging from 19.7 per cent of the British to 75.4 per cent of the Italian.

Though the sums were large, some thought impossible, the terms were generous. The Allies pledged their faith and started to pay to the United States. Meanwhile they made among themselves other funding agreements for the settlement of inter-Allied war indebtedness.[2] There was no legal connection between the inflow of German reparations and the service on inter-Allied war debts with the obligated remittances to the United States; but actually the Allies intended to pay no more to their creditors, including the United States, than they collected in the end from German reparations. Great Britain, for example, in the average of years would take in from her debtors slightly more than she paid out to the United States; and debtors to Great Britain, like France, relied on Germany. So, in reality, the payment of war debts was made to rest upon the payment by Germany of reparations. And, in reality again, Germany's payments rested on her capacity to borrow from private foreign capital, over a third of it American.

The United States, which had refused to allow war debts to be coupled with reparations, was not unwilling to couple them with disarmament.

[1] From Treasury "Memorandum Covering Indebtedness of Foreign Governments," *op. cit.*, p. 22.

[2] In dealing with this tremendous and intricate subject the author has relied heavily on Harold G. Moulton and Leo Pasvolsky, *War Debts and World Prosperity,* published by the Brookings Institution (New York, 1932).

STATEMENT SHOWING PRINCIPAL AND INTEREST COMPUTED AT THE RATES SPECIFIED IN DEBT AGREEMENTS ON INDEBTEDNESS OF FOREIGN GOVERNMENTS TO THE UNITED STATES AT TIME OF FUNDING, CREDIT ALLOWANCES, THE CASH PAYMENTS ON EXECUTION OF AGREEMENTS, AND THE TOTAL DEBT AS FUNDED.

Country	Indebtedness at Time of Funding			Credit Allowances and Cash Payments on Execution of Agreements		Funded Debt
	Principal	Interest	Total	Applied on Principal	Applied on Interest	
Austria	$ 24,055,708.92	$ 559,176.08	$ 24,614,885.00	......	......	$ 24,614,885
Belgium	377,029,570.06	40,767,664.60	417,797,234.66	......	$ 17,234.66	417,780,000
Czechoslovakia	91,879,671.03	25,978,742.91	117,858,413.94	......	2,858,413.94 [1]	115,000,000
Estonia	13,999,145.60	1,765,219.73	15,764,365.33	$1,932,923.45 [2]	1,441.88	13,830,000
Finland	8,281,926.17	727,389.10	9,009,315.27	......	9,315.27	9,000,000
France	3,340,516,043.72	684,870,643.17	4,025,386,686.89	386,686.89		4,025,000,000
Great Britain	4,074,818,358.44	529,309,727.30	4,604,128,085.74		4,128,085.74	4,600,000,000
Greece	27,167,000.00 [3]	3,127,922.67	30,294,922.67	2,922.67	......	30,292,000
Hungary	1,685,835.61	253,917.43	1,939,753.04	......	753.04	1,939,000
Italy	1,647,869,197.96	394,330,268.38	2,042,199,466.34	199,466.34	......	2,042,000,000
Latvia	5,132,287.14	647,275.62	5,779,562.76	......	4,562.76	5,775,000
Lithuania	4,981,628.03	1,049,918.94	6,031,546.97	......	1,546.97	6,030,000
Poland	159,666,972.39	18,898,053.60	178,565,025.99	......	5,025.99	178,560,000
Rumania	36,116,972.44	8,477,479.10	44,594,451.54	4,451.54	......	44,590,000
Yugoslavia	51,037,886.39	11,819,226.00	62,857,112.39	7,112.39	......	62,850,000
	$9,864,238,203.90	$1,722,582,624.63	$11,586,820,828.53	$2,533,563.28	$7,026,380.25	$11,577,260,885
Cash received upon execution of agreements	600,639.83	4,167,966.31	4,768,606.14			
Credit allowances	1,932,923.45 [2]	2,858,413.94 [1]	4,791,337.39			
	$2,533,563.28	$7,026,380.25	$9,559,943.53			
Amount funded	$9,861,704,640.62	$1,715,556,244.38	$11,577,260,885.00			

242

[1] Amount of interest written off in compromise settlement with Czechoslovakia.
[2] Allowance for total loss of cargo of S. S. *John Russ* sunk by a mine in Baltic Sea.
[3] Includes 4-per-cent twenty-year loan of $12,167,000 authorized by Act of February 14, 1929.

In discussions of possible further cancellation—that is, of *transfer* of the burden from European taxpayers to American taxpayers—it was always observable that the European debtors, who asserted that the burden was becoming impossible to bear, were expending vast sums on increased armaments, greater than before the war; France was even loaning money to Poland and Czechoslovakia for new armaments in defense against a possible German eruption. It was just as illogical to couple further cancellation with disarmament as with reparations; but President Hoover intimated that the United States might be willing to make additional concessions in exchange for real relief everywhere, by international agreements, from the staggering and mounting burden of increased armament cost. No disarmament, beyond the naval agreements of 1921 and 1930, proved possible in a European world ruled by fear. This was particularly galling to disarmed Germany. The victors of 1918, never really trusting her, feared she would be able some day to tear up the Treaty of Versailles, which had suggested that German disarmament was the first step of general disarmament.

Contemporary with the funding of the Allied debts and the inauguration of the Dawes Plan, a flood of foreign money, mostly American, poured into Germany and Europe, in the form of bonded loans to municipalities and corporations. It was these funds, filtering through the German state, which really paid such reparations as were remitted.

As long as private loans [1] continued, they freshened the bloodstream of German national economy sufficiently to support the payments under the Young Plan. But in 1931, in the second year of the Great Depression, private investors became nervous and ceased to loan to Germany. In the summer of that year a political factor of international character helped precipitate a financial panic in Austria and Germany: French credit to Austrian banks was withdrawn following the attempt to set up a German-Austrian customs union as a step toward a political union (*Anschluss*). This caused the failure of the leading Austrian commercial bank, the *Creditanstalt*, which already was in a straitened condition. In turn this threatened the leading German private banks and insurance companies, and started a renewed flight of capital from Germany. The German budget became unbalanced. American private credits to Germany, held by banks in the United States, were endangered. If the impending collapse could not be prevented, the second bankruptcy of

[1] Much of the borrowed money was used for permanent, private or public, improvements, which must remain in Germany, embedded in steel and concrete, no matter what the fate of the loans.

Germany threatened widespread bank failures in foreign countries, particularly in the United States. To fend this off, President Hoover, June 20, 1931, proposed [1] to the foreign governments a one year's standstill agreement on the payment of all intergovernmental debts, the year's arrears to be postponed and spread over the next ten years.

The passing months brought no certainty that payments would be resumed all around when the year's moratorium should expire. With difficulty the principal central banks (including the Federal Reserve Bank of New York) sustained the German financial institutions against collapse by short-time loans totaling $100,000,000. In September, 1931, the increasing intricacy of the financial situation forced Great Britain off the gold standard, and with it those dependencies and European countries which in times past had linked their currencies, by exchange, with that of England. Meanwhile the debtor governments, eager to rid themselves of the burden of indebtedness, anxiously considered what should be done at the end of the year's standstill. Could a belated all-round cancellation of war debts and reparations clean up the whole mess?

This general cleanup would be at the expense of the United States. The European Allies easily agreed that the service charges on their "war debts" to America were so heavy as not to be possible to pay out of their own resources in gold or cash without stripping the currency reserves of the debtor governments and bringing on economic chaos, damaging to creditor and debtor alike. The annual payments could be remitted only in bills of exchange; bills of exchange could be purchased only from firms having money due them for goods sold to American customers —that is, payment of "war debts" depended upon the United States being willing to accept an increasing volume of imports from the debtor countries. Economists in the debtor states argued that the American tariff walls kept out the foreign goods and thus made impossible payment of such huge debts. American economists overwhelmingly agreed with this: that a creditor country, as the United States was believed to be since the war, could not successfully remain a high tariff country. It is nevertheless instructive to note that in 1934 and 1935 Great Britain, France, and Belgium exported to the United States, without stripping their currency cover or seriously injuring it, several times more gold

---

[1] The President had to make this proposal contingent upon approval of Congress. He hurriedly sounded out a sufficient number of members to pledge approval once Congress should assemble in December. The "Hoover Moratorium" was promptly approved by Congress, when it convened.

(privately owned) than was necessary to pay public debt installments for those years.[1] This gold was seeking refuge in the United States. In the case of Italy, organized for war, all private export of gold was prohibited, but the phenomenon shows that the debtors could have paid during those years, if they preferred to, without upsetting their currency.[2]

For the debtor countries any program of general cancellation of war debts and reparations, at the end of the "Hoover year" of relief, depended on what the United States would do.

The European governments promptly took the initiative. In a conference meeting at Lausanne (June-July, 1932) they wrote off, contingently, 90 per cent of German reparations due under the Young Plan, lumping them into one easily supportable principal bonded 5-per-cent debt of RM.3,000,000,000 ($750,000,000) to be redeemed by a 1-per-cent per annum sinking fund. In addition Germany would pay off by regular schedule the loans received in the Dawes Plan and Young Plan, totaling $400,000,000. The Lausanne Agreement, which thus canceled nine tenths of Germany's surviving obligations for reparations, and reduced her payments on that account to only $43,000,000 a year (plus the service on the Dawes Plan and Young Plan loans), was not to go into effect until ratified by Belgium, France, Great Britain, Italy, and Japan, as well as Germany. The creditor powers signed among themselves a memorandum embodying a "gentlemen's agreement" that they, on their part, would not ratify until a "satisfactory settlement is obtained between them and

---

[1] The following shows the amount due by the principal debtor countries in the years of default 1934 and 1935, and the amount of gold exported by those countries in those years to the United States:

		Defaulted Installment of "War Debt" Due to U. S.	Private Gold Export to U. S.
Great Britain	1934	$182,780,000	$510,161,190
	1935	181,660,000	316,092,897
France	1934	75,000,000	290,530,897
	1935	80,000,000	934,301,508
Italy	1934	15,075,500	898,783
	1935	15,459,750	4,310
Belgium	1934	6,150,000	12,968,055
	1935	6,650,000	3,257

In the cases of Great Britain, France, and Belgium these huge exports of gold were made without any great fluctuation of exchange, and with no damage to currency cover. The transfer was not for the purpose, principally, of settling commercial accounts. It was capital seeking a safe refuge. If to seek refuge this transfer could be made without injuring currency cover, the question arises, could not the debt installments have been safely made?

[2] The governments could have purchased enough of this exportable gold from their nationals for shipment on their own government accounts.

their own creditors." In case of no ratification, the *legal* status of the reparations question would continue to be the same as before the Hoover year, namely, the Young Plan.

The Hoover year expired as the United States was in the midst of a national electoral campaign. Neither party dared to pledge itself to scale down war debts proportionately to the proposed Lausanne schedule. There was widespread feeling among voters of both parties that the debtors had pervertedly spent money on armaments which might have been paid on account of the "war debts" already eased by the generous funding agreements. No proposals of further concessions were tolerated unless the European powers were willing to pare down their armament burdens. In Europe such disarmament was impossible because of the rise of the dictators in Italy and Germany, leaders who preferred war to peace, because war might undo the restrictions on expansion imposed by the Treaty of Versailles. The Hoover Administration went out and the Roosevelt Administration came in without any essential change in the corrosive questions of war debts, reparations, and increasing armaments.

Before giving up office, the Hoover Administration did agree to send representatives to a general economic conference to be held at London in the spring of 1933 to consider some international agreement on these vital economic problems: (1) monetary and credit policy; (2) prices; (3) resumption of the movement of capital; (4) restrictions on international trade; (5) tariff and trade policy; (6) organization of production and trade. Debts were not included in the agenda, but credits were, which might mean the same thing. Following the example of the British Prime Minister, Ramsay MacDonald, the French and Italian Governments sent distinguished statesmen to Washington, to try to reach some agreement with the incoming Roosevelt Administration for a workable program (presumably on international debts) at the approaching conference, which public opinion hailed as one of the most significant of contemporary history. Little seems to have been accomplished in these preliminary conversations. President-elect Roosevelt and his advisers were preoccupied with the rapidly approaching débâcle of American credit which had made its ominous appearance in December, 1932, and January, 1933, as the incoming Administration came closer to power. The ensuing conference at London was a fiasco. Before it met, the United States had gone off the gold standard, deliberately, as a means of raising prices at home, and meeting foreign competition abroad. The new President suddenly refused, in a telegram to the American delegation, to agree to any program of stabilization which would "peg" the dollar in international exchange. Aside from agreement on a program of silver purchasing, the delegates left London with no real accomplishment.

Germany never paid any more reparations after the Hoover year (though she kept up, in case of certain favored nationals,[1] the service on the Dawes Plan and Young Plan loans). Most of the debtor governments then stopped payment on their installments to the United States, and to each other. Great Britain, Italy, Latvia, Lithuania, and Yugoslavia made "token payments" toward interest, throughout 1933, hoping that some general scaledown, proportionate to the reparations scaledown, might be possible with the new Roosevelt Administration. Then they stopped. Only Finland adhered to her bonded word, in full and without question.

It was bitterly disIllusioning for American bondholders and taxpayers to read the net results of:

REPARATION PAYMENTS AND DEBT PAYMENTS COMPARED IN RELATION TO FOREIGN LOANS TO GERMANY (AT TIME OF STOPPAGE OF PAYMENTS IN 1931)

Total private capital borrowed by Germany [2]
In U.S.A. (estimated) $2,475,000,000
In other countries (estimated) 3,809,000,000

Total $6,284,000,000

Total cash reparations paid by Germany... $4,470,000,000.00
Total war debts paid by Allies to U.S.A.... 2,606,340,987.52

This meant that:

(1) Germany really paid her cash reparations out of long-term loans from the gullible victors and had $1,814,000,000 left over, which she devoted to rearmament for another war.

(2) The Allies paid to the United States on account of war debts an amount approximately equal to the American share (39.37 per cent) of the private capital thus loaned to Germany and its nationals.[3]

[1] In 1934 the German consulate at New York announced willingness of Germany to pay Dawes Plan currency loan coupons, 50 per cent in foreign exchange, and 50 per cent in German marks blocked against export from Germany; and to pay to nationals of certain countries only (Great Britain, France, Switzerland, Holland, Belgium, Sweden and Italy), who held Young Plan bonds, their coupons in foreign exchange. American holders, however, had to take 5/6 in blocked Reichsmarks. *Foreign Bondholders Protective Councils, Inc., Annual Report for 1934* (New York), pp. 90-92.

[2] Estimates summarized from the Wiggin-Layton figures of the Report of the Committee appointed upon the recommendation of the London Conference, 1931. See Royal Institute of International Affairs Information Department, *Memorandum on Foreign Short-term Loans in Germany, 1919-1932* (London, 1933), p. 49. This statement includes also the long-term loans.

I have converted dollars into marks at four marks to the dollar.

[3] Of the total of American private loans to Germany, a major portion was repatriated by German purchase of low-priced defaulted bonds, but more precise statistics for this have not been available.

As the years passed, defaulted reparations and war debts receded farther and farther into history. Every party to them but the United States wanted to forget about them, because every one but the United States was a debtor. A disgusted Congress in 1934 passed the Johnson Act forbidding the making of loans within the jurisdiction of the United States to any foreign government which had defaulted on its debts to the United States. But during the Second World War, Congress passed legislation (March 11, 1941) permitting the President to lend, lease, *or otherwise dispose of* property of the United States to nations defending themselves against aggression and thereby helping to defend the United States. The neutrality laws of 1935-1939 prohibited making loans to belligerent governments but were amended, February 21, 1942, so as not to apply when the United States is at war, with the Johnson Act left standing. Under this Lend-Lease Act of 1941 over $50,000,000,000—five times the war loans of 1917-1919—were extended to allies all over the world with little expectation of repayment. This is a good example of how politics controls economics in diplomacy, rather than economics controlling politics—as is sometimes maintained.

Only eleven years before the nations became engulfed in the Second World War, they had made a solemn agreement, entered into upon the initiative of the United States and France, known as the Pact of Paris, or the Briand-Kellogg Pact, after the two ministers of foreign affairs who drafted it:

Article I. The High Contracting Parties solemnly declare in the names of their respective peoples that they condemn recourse to war for the solution of international controversies, and renounce it as an instrument of national policy in their relations with one another.
Article II. The High Contracting Parties agree that the settlement or solution of all disputes or conflicts of whatever nature or of whatever origin they may be, which may arise among them, shall never be sought except by pacific means.

The treaty is perpetual. The preamble expresses enigmatically the conviction that a resort to war *denies to a Power the benefits furnished by the treaty.* Did these words mean that neutrality could no longer exist when a power resorted to war as an instrument of national policy? That where in violation of the treaty it waged aggressive war it subjected itself to all the sanctions which the use of force could impose? The Nuremberg trials of 1946-1947 and the trials of the major Japanese war criminals of 1946-1948 were to answer these questions with an awful affirmative.[1]

This agreement arose from an informal suggestion made by the French Minister of Foreign Affairs, Aristide Briand, in 1927, that the United States and France, who were then facing a renewal of a general treaty of arbitration which was due to expire in 1928, should pledge themselves in a treaty of perpetual friendship never to go to war with each other under any circumstances. Though possibly not intentionally so, this was tantamount to an agreement that either party, France or the United States, would remain neutral in case the other were involved in war with a third party. This, one recalls, was a feature of many an alliance, for example the Anglo-Japanese alliance of 1902. Secretary Kellogg eluded the implications of this proposal by consenting to agree to such a treaty if it were general in its membership. Consequently the two governments formulated the above articles and the United States, by pre-concerted arrangement with France, invited fourteen other nations to sign jointly: Great Britain, and the several self-governing Dominions, Belgium, Czechoslovakia, France, Germany, Italy, Japan, and Poland. After considerable interchange of observations, all fifteen nations signed the above-quoted Pact of Paris (August 27, 1928). The other nations [2] of the world, invited by the United States to join the Pact, speedily adhered. Sixty-three nations are now members. Only seven [3] nations have failed to adhere.

The United States Senate, in ratifying the treaty, this time attached no reservation, after Secretary Kellogg had included in the diplomatic record a statement explaining that the pact did not preclude a war of self-defense, and after the Committee of Foreign Relations had reported that "the United States regards the Monroe Doctrine as a part of its national security and self-defense." The other powers accepted the pledge only after Secretary Kellogg had made assurances, in the record of the negotiations leading to the pact, that each power was the sole judge of what constituted self-defense, and that the proposed treaty could not be construed to impair existing treaty obligations, like the European

---

[1] See below, Chapter 21.

[2] France it was who conveyed the invitation to Russia, with which nation the United States was not then in diplomatic relations.

[3] On May 15, 1949, those nations which had not adhered were: the Argentine Republic, Bolivia, El Salvador, Israel, Lebanon, Syria, and Yemen. New states arising out of the British Commonwealth and Empire are presumed to have inherited the obligations of the Pact of Paris.

Locarno treaties and the League of Nations (which might require war as an instrument of international policy). The French Government, for example, which had stood out for limiting its anti-war agreement to a pledge not to fight a war of "aggression," was not willing to accept the formula of the multilateral treaty until it was clear that it alone could construe its own necessities of self-defense. It was professedly as an act of self-defense that Japan had since sent large armies into China, and had detached great areas of her territory, and that Italy had conquered Ethiopia. In neither case had a formal war been declared. Such a *declared* war would be illegal!

The British reservation to the Kellogg Pact was very far-reaching:

. . . there are certain regions of the world [unspecified] the welfare and integrity of which constitute a special and vital interest for our peace and safety. His Majesty's Government have been at pains to make it clear in the past that interference with these regions cannot be suffered. Their protection against attack is to the British Empire a measure of self-defense. It must be clearly understood that His Majesty's Government in Great Britain accept the new treaty upon the distinct understanding that it does not prejudice their freedom of action in this respect.

The Russian Government, of the Union of Soviet Socialist Republics, in accepting the pact, lamented that it did not unequivocally forbid any kind of aggression or armed conflict short of war, or provide for disarmament, and noted with emphasis the sweeping nature of the British reservations, which it refused to accept as binding upon itself inasmuch as they had not been communicated officially to Russia.

Following the adoption of the Pact of Paris,[1] the United States, under the direction of Secretary Kellogg, negotiated with most of the non-American[2] nations a new series of bilateral treaties. They adjusted the old Root arbitration treaties to the new resources of arbitration and con-

[1] Several American commentators have written on the Kellogg Pact. Professor James T. Shotwell, who stimulated public opinion following Mr. Briand's original suggestion by presenting academic propositions for an anti-war treaty, describes the negotiations, and as an advocate of peace analyzes the document in his *War As An Instrument of National Policy and Its Renunciation in the Pact of Paris* (New York, 1929). Hunter Miller interprets juridically this unique treaty in *The Peace Pact of Paris; a Study of the Briand-Kellogg Treaty* (New York, 1928), with a documentary appendix. See also Denys P. Myers, *Origin and Conclusion of the Paris Pact; the Renunciation of War as an Instrument of National Policy* (World Peace Foundation Pamphlets, XII, No. 2, Boston, 1929).

[2] In the case of the nations of the New World the Root-Bryan conciliation treaties have given way to a multilateral inter-American conciliation treaty (on a Bryan chassis), the so-called Gondra Convention; and the Root arbitration treaties to a multilateral inter-American treaty of arbitration (on a Kellogg chassis). See Chapter 14 below.

ciliation presented by the League of Nations, to which the non-American partners to the treaties were now pledged. The Root treaties had been for short periods of time, generally five years, requiring repeated renewals to keep them alive. The formula adopted in the new Kellogg arbitration treaties called for the arbitration by the Hague Permanent Court of Arbitration, or *any other competent tribunal,* of all justiciable disputes which could not be settled by diplomacy or by the Bryan devices of conciliation through inquiry.[1] The Root treaties, it is recalled, had excluded from the purview of arbitration all disputes involving national honor, independence, or vital interests; and the Senate had reserved its right to pass upon the *compromis* which in each case would define the subject and scope of a particular arbitration. In ratifying the Kellogg treaties, the Senate made similar reservations to pass upon the *compromis.* The twenty-eight [2] new Kellogg treaties excluded from the scope of arbitration any dispute which:

(a) is within the domestic jurisdiction of either of the high contracting parties,

(b) involves the interest of third parties,

(c) depends upon or involves the maintenance of the traditional attitude of the United States concerning American questions, commonly described as the Monroe Doctrine,

(d) depends upon or involves the observance of the obligations of [the other non-American treaty party] in accordance with the Covenant of the League of Nations.

Significant abstentions from Kellogg arbitration treaties with the United States were Great Britain, Japan, Russia, and Spain.

Contemporaneously with the new arbitration treaties, Secretary Kellogg set on foot negotiations for treaties of conciliation on the Bryan model with non-American states which had not yet entered into such with the United States. There were in January, 1942, thirty-five of these Bryan "cooling-off" treaties in effect. The most notable exception was Japan, which had neither conciliation nor arbitration treaty with the United States. Both, however, had pledged themselves to the Pact of Paris.

The provision in the new Kellogg treaties, for arbitration before *any other competent tribunal,* doubtless envisaged the accession of the United

---

[1] The Bryan conciliation treaties depended on parties to a dispute cooling off through a stipulated period of investigation and report by a commission of inquiry.

[2] The United States on May 15, 1949, was a party to Kellogg bilateral arbitration treaties with the following twenty-eight countries: Albania, Belgium, Bulgaria, China, Czechoslovakia, Denmark, Egypt, Estonia, Ethiopia, Finland, France, Germany, Greece, Hungary, Iceland, Italy, Latvia, Liberia, Lithuania, Luxemburg, Netherlands, Norway, Poland, Portugal, Rumania, Sweden, Switzerland, and Yugoslavia.

States to the protocol embodying a statute for the establishment of a Court of International Justice, which had been set up under the patronage of the League of Nations, as anticipated in the League of Nations Covenant. Though technically this Court, established in 1921, was an organ of the League of Nations, non-League members could join it without being parties to the League, or might without being statutory members of the Court avail themselves of its judicial facilities. The purpose of this court, the so-called World Court, was to decide on the basis of law rather than arbitration cases brought before it, and to give advisory decisions when requested by the League of Nations. In part, therefore, the Court fitted in with the traditional American aspirations for a truly international court of justice to make international law a regnant concept in the voluntary settlement of disputes and to build up by a series of judicial rather than arbitral decisions an expanding body of law.

The distinguished American jurist and elder statesman, Elihu Root, was one of the principal formulators of the original statute. Another most eminent American international lawyer and *genro,* John Bassett Moore, was selected at the outset (1922-1928) as judge of the Court, and, after his resignation, the former Secretaries of State, Charles E. Hughes (1928-1930) and Frank B. Kellogg [1] (1930-1935) served in the Court. American Presidents since 1923 without exception recommended to the Senate the adoption, with reservations, of the protocol which would make the United States a supporting member, but the Senate steadily refused to accept the Court until after the Second World War and the ratification of the covenant of a new league of nations: the Charter of the United Nations.[2]

We have already observed in a former chapter how normal relations were restored by the United States after the First World War with all but one great nation, Russia, and its 168,000,000 people in Europe and Asia. Following the failure of the Peace Conference at Paris in 1919 to devise any solution of the problem of Soviet Russia, the United States during sixteen years refused to extend recognition to that republic. The fundamental reason for this was the irreconcilability of the revolutionary communistic theory and practice of government with the theory and practice of American democracy and capitalism. The Soviet Government strengthened this determination of the United States Government by its

---

[1] In 1936 Professor Manley O. Hudson, of the Harvard Law School, an unquenchable protagonist of American entry into the League of Nations as well as the Court of International Justice, was chosen judge.

[2] See below, Chapter 21.

refusal to sanction the loans and contracts made by previous Russian governments with the United States and its nationals, and by its refusal to extend to American citizens in Russia the type of protection customarily extended to aliens in the other countries of Europe. Further, the ardor of revolutionary propaganda, not technically from the Soviet Government in Moscow, but from its international image, the *Third Internationale,* or international communistic revolutionary society, militated against American recognition. So long as a foreign community permitted its nationals to propagate seditious activities within the United States and to seek to overthrow by revolution the existing government and Constitution of the United States, it was not difficult to understand why that government should shrink so inveterately from extending its own recognition to the source of the subversive activities. The passage of time, however, tended to smooth down the hitherto insuperable asperities and difficulties and incompatibilities between the two peoples. One by one the great powers of Europe had recognized Russia; and in 1934 Russia took its place in the League of Nations. Even without recognition a very considerable volume of trade, more indeed than existed after recognition, sprang up between the two republics. Their citizens visited each other even without directly visaed passports. The more radical features of Russian government gave way to a slightly less rigorous state communism. To keep in friendly relations with the states of the capitalistic world, the Russians temporarily abated their revolutionary ambitions and made agreements not to excite propaganda in foreign states. Above all, the increasing tension of Far Eastern politics, where the interests of Russia and the United States supported each other more than they did Japanese policy, impelled the two nations, so different in their constitutional structure and social organization, to close up the gap of diplomatic irreconcilability.

The opportunity for attempting normal relations with Russia came in the autumn of 1933, when President Franklin D. Roosevelt, unembarrassed by recent party commitments on Russian policy, invited the President of the All Union Central Executive Committee to send a representative to the United States to discuss ways and means of effecting a re-establishment of regular relations between the two peoples. The Soviet Government immediately sent to Washington its Minister for Foreign Affairs, Maxim Litvinoff. On November 16, 1933, regular relations were resumed, after a lapse of sixteen years, on conditions which were laid down in a series of notes exchanged between President Roosevelt and Litvinoff:

1. Direct assurances by the Russian Government scrupulously to respect a policy of noninterference with life and affairs within the jurisdiction of the United States.

2. Pledge by the Russian Government to refrain from, and to restrain all persons and organizations directly or indirectly under its control—or receiving money from it (without indicating by name the *Third Internationale*)—from agitation or propaganda within the United States or its territories, or from violation of the territorial integrity of the United States or its possessions.

3. Pledge by the Russian Government not to permit formation or residence within Russian jurisdiction of any organization or group revolutionary to the United States, or to lend its support to such.

4. Reasonable expectations (but not guaranties) given by the Russian Government to the United States to secure freedom of conscience and religious liberty for American citizens residing temporarily or permanently within Russian jurisdiction.[1]

5. Promise of a consular convention to be negotiated with most-favored-nation provisions, including right of fair trial for American citizens accused of crimes in Russia.

6. Existing claims between the two countries to be adjusted by negotiations to be undertaken after resumption of regular relations, the Russian Government waiving all claims on account of United States intervention in eastern Siberia (but not in northern Russia) ;[2] the Russian Government meanwhile to respect the previous and future acts of the United States and its courts regulating the property of the Russian Government or its nationals.

The complicated negotiations for an adjustment of the outstanding claims of both governments, including war debts of the former Czarist government and the provisional revolutionary government of 1917, have not yet been settled, although ambassadors were duly exchanged in 1934. With the re-establishment of formal diplomatic relations with Russia the circle of normal contacts of American diplomacy, interrupted by the First World War, was complete at last even though the promises of Soviet Russia in the Roosevelt-Litvinoff agreement proved to be no settlement of the questions broached in it.

[1] This may be said to have adjusted an issue with the Czarist Government, arising over exclusion of Jews who were naturalized American citizens, which caused American abrogation, in 1913, according to form, of the Russian-American treaty of commerce of 1832.

[2] See above, pp. 170, 218, n. 3.

13

Economics and Diplomacy: The New

Reciprocity

THE United States in 1860 was already over the threshold of the persistently expanding Industrial Revolution which since then has so profoundly modified American life, running successively and quickly from steam and rail to electricity, the internal combustion engine, concrete highway, automotive transportation, general instantaneous communication, automatic machinery, and great technology. President Lincoln freed the black human slaves, and the American people acquired new mechanical slaves on farm and in factory, speechless, nerveless slaves who could work day and night, with the power of thousands of horses, expanding and transforming production, competing for the markets of the world with other oily slaves of steel and copper toiling for corporate masters in the industrial countries across both oceans.

The Civil War marked a turning point in American economic history, as well as in the political evolution of the United States. The demands of the armies furnished quick and powerful impetus to manufacturing. Wartime tariff primarily for revenue gave way after the return of peace to protective tariffs quietly legislated into being amid the noisy domestic politics of the Reconstruction Era,[1] to become a protean part of the American national system. For a generation after the war agriculture, grazing, and mining, thanks to the expanding frontier and the settlement of the Far West, held their predominant place in the face of the new industrial forces for which they created a growing home market. By 1900 manufactured products [2] constituted, nevertheless, 35.38 per cent of the total exports of merchandise from the United States, as compared with 15.32 per cent in 1860. During the next decade the character of exports showed a radical change. The frontier had disappeared by 1890, although it took a few years for the effect of this to be felt clearly in foreign trade. The West was filling up. Population was rapidly agglom-

[1] H. K. Beale, *The Critical Year; a Study of Andrew Johnson and Reconstruction* (New York, 1930), dissects the motives of business protection in the politics of the reconstruction era.

[2] Not counting manufactured foodstuffs, which were 23.32 per cent.

255

erating in new cities and towns west and east. The continuing Industrial Revolution entered a phase of scientific intensification. The United States became in our times primarily an industrial nation. By 1913, before the First World War, manufactured articles [1] accounted for approximately one half the total exports of the United States. The war slowed up this tendency to proportionate increase of manufactured exports, because of the great demands for raw materials, particularly foodstuffs. After the war the exports of finished manufactures surpassed those of the extractive industries. As manufactured goods assumed increased weight in exports, the total of imports showed a heavier share of raw materials and lighter receipts of foreign manufactures,[2] at least until the Great Depression. As the shift took place in imports toward raw materials, non-European countries slowly began to contribute a larger share of the total imports. For a long while it was protectionist policy to raise the tariff on manufactures and to keep raw materials on the free list—this increased the imports from the countries of simple economy notably in the New World, Asia, and Africa. There was, it seemed, a healthy equilibrium for a complex economy in the United States. Foreign capital poured into the Republic. The United States remained a debtor nation (we speak of course of private debts), serving its debts with an excess of exports over imports, with a surplus left over debt charges to pay for foreign freightage, tourist expenditures abroad, immigrant remittances, and foreign insurance premiums.

These new conditions of a complex national economy [3] cannot be ignored by any historian of American diplomacy. In previous chapters we have noted some of their effects. At first they served the apostles of sea power to stimulate by false reasoning an imperialistic expansion in the Far East. Later they united with the politics of American neutrality to cause the Wilson Administration to keep its hands off the irresistible weapon of the embargo. Today they meet in an even greater world crisis of economy and thought which remains to be solved. With these reflections in mind we may observe the historical development of American policy to secure freedom of commerce and navigation from national discriminations.

[1] Not including manufactured foodstuffs.

[2] G. G. Huebner, "The Foreign Trade of the United States Since 1789," in *History of Domestic and Foreign Commerce of the United States* (2 vols., Carnegie Institution of Washington, 1915), II, p. 69 (citing the *U. S. Bureau of Statistics*); and John H. Frederick, *The Development of American Commerce* (New York, 1932).

[3] John Donaldson has presented a lucid analysis of the evolving character of American national economy, in its reference to foreign policy, in "Fundamentals of the Foreign Economic Processes and Policy of the United States," in *Weltwirtschaftliches Archiv*, XXX (Juli, 1929), 4-77.

Until the close of the nineteenth century American commerce continued to flow pretty much in the old channels of trade, with increases most marked in commerce to the prosperous industrial nations of the world. Canada became an increasingly important factor in American foreign commerce, as it filled up with an English-speaking population. The doubling of the volume of trade with British North America in the period 1865-1900 counterbalanced a depression in the commerce with other portions of the New World, notably Central America and the West Indies. It was not until the twentieth century that the channels of foreign commerce began to change notably.

In the first half of the national period of American history it had been one of the main objects of foreign policy to clear away the barriers of European colonial monopolies, particularly in the New World, which restricted the entrance of American ships and goods. This was accomplished by the beginning of the period under review in this chapter. With a growing export of manufactures searching for markets abroad the resources of American diplomacy turned next to the objective of securing, wherever possible, at least equal or even special advantages for American trade and incorporating them in treaties. The United States generally adhered throughout the century to the *conditional* type of most-favored-nation clause [1] in its treaties of commerce, in order to protect itself against general and unrequited diffusion to most-favored nations of particular trade privileges bargained for corresponding equivalents. This ran counter to the desire of most of the great trading nations of Europe, who preferred the unconditional interpretation of a most-favored-nation clause. It was to the advantage, so the opinion ran, of the greater trading nations to keep down the general level of tariffs throughout the world. They preferred therefore the unconditional most-favored-nation formula, by which a tariff concession or privilege of nation A to nation B, must also be extended to nations X, Y and Z if the latter had unconditional most-favored-nation articles in their treaties with A; that is, it must be extended no matter what unique equivalents B had paid to A for the privilege.[2]

Commercial bargains by give-and-take, written into reciprocity treaties, became the objective of the Department of State in its negotiations for

[1] Exceptions were Switzerland (1850), Orange Free State (1871), Serbia (1881). Only one of these nations, Switzerland, ever protested tariff rates on the basis of the clause, and the United States recognized the validity of the protest, but presently (with due notice) abrogated the treaty.

[2] Benjamin H. Williams has analyzed, with a historical background, the various factors and implications of the most-favored-nation formula, and its relation to commercial reciprocity, in his *Economic Foreign Policy of the United States* (New York, 1929).

treaties with foreign nations. Such treaties would purchase, on each side, particular privileges in return for particular concessions, and would be protected by a *conditional* most-favored-nation article against possible extension automatically to conventional most-favored nations. Such was the objective of the Department of State, it is true, but the objective met two obstacles: many greater trading nations, for reasons explained, were unwilling during the nineteenth century to negotiate reciprocity treaties except when coupled with an unconditional most-favored-nation article; and the Senate, imbued with the philosophy of protection, would not ratify reciprocity treaties which lowered the tariff through the treaty-making power, even when tariff acts authorized the President to make such changes (subject, of course, to ratification in regular treaty form). The net result was only two reciprocity treaties—following the termination of the Marcy-Elgin Canadian reciprocity treaty of 1854-1866—with Hawaii (1875) and with Cuba (1902). In each of these cases there was an obvious political and strategical interest which made the Senate willing to accept them.

It should be remembered that during the half-century after the Civil War the Government of the United States was under the control of political parties which either espoused outright the political economy of protection, as did the Republican Party, or secretly accepted it, publicly preaching against protection but actually tolerating it when in power, as did the Democratic Party. That this assisted the one-sided industrial development of the United States at the expense of agriculture, few thoughtful historians today would deny. When we speak, then, of domestic tariffs, we do not mean protective taxes on imports that were based on any scientific calculation. There was little thought to approach the question from a balance sheet of commercial needs adapted to the best economy of the nation and people as a whole. Tariff schedules contained largely what representatives of powerful industrial interests, to which both parties responded, persuaded Congress was necessary for the prosperity of, first, those industries, and next, the people dependent upon them.[1] The negotiation of a treaty of commercial reciprocity was less susceptible to lobbying, but after signature it must secure an approval of two thirds of the Senate.

It was the agrarian nations, relatively untouched by industrial revolution or the political economy of protection, like Canada and the republics

---

[1] There is a stimulative rush of thought, not without historical *ex-parte* argument, on this in Charles A. Beard's two notable books, *The Idea of National Interest* (New York, 1934) and *The Open Door at Home* (New York, 1934).

of Latin America, which seemed most inviting for reciprocity treaties. But Canada competed, more than the tropical or subtropical countries, with the raw materials of the United States, lumber, fish, and agriculture. Hence it could not be such good bargaining ground as the Latin-American nations. Great Britain made repeated proposals for a renewal of commercial reciprocity with Canada: in 1869, 1874, 1888, 1889. They all failed. A system of imperial preferences inaugurated in 1897 tended to improve the Canadian market for British manufactures. Meanwhile Canada herself entered the infant industry stage, and the new native manufactures blunted her desire for reciprocity with a competitor so close at hand.

The Latin-American countries offered the greatest hopes for reciprocity without any essential undermining of the American protective system. The United States, under proper treaty arrangements, could admit most of their raw materials, some of them exotic, cheaply or altogether freely, and with advantage to its own economy; they in turn could profitably lower their tariffs to American manufactures. Widespread reciprocity with the nations of Latin America meant, indeed, the capture, in the face of European competition, of those growing markets for the increasing manufactures of the United States. It was one of the factors which led to the Pan-American movement—conceived by Secretary of State James G. Blaine as a device for getting himself out of some embarrassing diplomatic predicaments relative to Peru and Chile.

But the Arthur Administration abruptly displaced Blaine at President Garfield's death, and turned its attention from the channels of Pan-American trade negotiations to individual treaties of commercial reciprocity. A treaty was quickly negotiated in Washington (January, 1883) with Mexico. It granted free entry for twenty-eight products of Mexico, including tobacco and sugar, at a sacrifice of less than $90,000 annual duty hitherto collected. Mexico in turn agreed to let in duty-free seventy-three American articles, many of them manufactured, upon which previously a high tariff had been collected. It was a most advantageous treaty for the United States; but protectionist influences in the Senate delayed action on it for a year. Finally advice and consent to ratification were made dependent upon the passage by Congress of legislation to allow to Mexico the lowered tariffs fixed by the treaty. Under these conditions the President withheld final ratification. Similar reciprocity treaties signed with the Dominican Republic, and with Spain for her West India Islands (Cuba, Puerto Rico) encountered much delay in the Senate. When these treaties appeared likely to be consummated the British Government saw disaster for its sugar planters in the West Indies if they should not secure at least similar tariff reductions in the markets of the United States. With some alacrity it opened reciprocity negotiations for the trade of those islands, to which the Arthur Government eagerly responded; but failure of the United States to agree to an unconditional most-favored-nation article (to which Great Britain then stood committed in her treaties with other nations) resulted in the collapse of these discussions.[1] When President Cleveland came into office he withdrew from the Senate the pending treaties with Spain and the Dominican Republic.[2] The Democratic Party, which now took over the government for the first time since 1861, professed belief in a general lower tariff by legislation, rather than by treaties; and Cleveland made unsuccessful efforts to accomplish this in Congress.

Reciprocity reappeared as an objective of American diplomacy when the Republicans came back under the Harrison Administration in 1889, with Blaine again Secretary of State. It offered a means of consoling that element of opinion which could not brook immitigable high protection. Blaine was now able to go ahead with his ambitious project of a Pan-American Congress, for the promotion of peace by arbitration and the removal of barriers to inter-American trade, a project which President Arthur, under the influence of partisan politics,[3] had quashed after President Garfield's death and Blaine's resignation. In fact, invitations to an inter-American conference at Washington had already been sent out by Bayard, Cleveland's Secretary of State, in response to an act of Congress (1888) for inviting a conference of the Latin-American governments with that of the United States in Washington for settling a plan of arbitration and for considering questions relating to the improvement of business intercourse, communications, and commercial relations. It

[1] By an executive agreement of January 2, 1884, between Spain and the United States (negotiated pursuant to the old law which authorized the President to add or remove extra duties) in reference to nations discriminating against the United States, the United States removed a previously imposed extra duty of 10 per cent on products and articles coming in from Cuba and Puerto Rico. In return Spain removed all discriminating duties on American ships and products in Cuba and Puerto Rico.

[2] George Frederick Howe, *Chester A. Arthur, a Quarter-Century of Machine Politics* (New York, 1934), pp. 267-271.

[3] Blaine was the most dynamic personality in the Republican Party and a continual possibility for Presidential nomination (he became the defeated candidate of the party in 1884). He was also the leader of a faction which in Garfield's Administration, and previously, had opposed the Republican machine in Arthur's state of New York, a machine to which Arthur owed his nomination for the Vice-Presidency in 1880, and hence his position as President. It is easy therefore to understand why Arthur did not follow along with Blaine, who was his principal rival for the nomination for President in 1884.

was fitting that Blaine should preside over this conference when it assembled at Washington in October, 1889. It is noteworthy that a powerful motive for the conference was the expansion of the commerce of
the United States.[1] The very first activity on the program was a grand
official excursion by the delegates throughout the industrial United States
with inspection of factories.[2] The main purpose Blaine veiled in ora-
torical expressions of friendship, arbitration and peace, and the promotion of the general welfare of the American nations of the New World.[3]
Then the delegation of the United States brought forth the proposal for
a Pan-American customs union—commercial reciprocity approaching free
trade on a vast scale. It would have given the United States preference
over European nations in the markets of Latin America, in return for free
imports of articles many of which were already on the free list of the
United States. The project failed before the opposition of the Latin-
American delegates. Spurred on by European diplomacy, they were unwilling to damage their established trade with Europe for the advantage
of American manufacturers, and some of them feared the political effects
of a customs union.[4] The Conference shelved the proposed customs union
with a resolution declaring in favor of bilateral reciprocity treaties. The
achievements of the first Inter-American Conference were most meager,
but they led to the establishment of a permanent secretariat at Washington, which developed into the Pan-American Union, housed (after 1910)
in a beautiful building the gift of Andrew Carnegie, one of the delegates of the United States to that Pan-American Conference. Out of

[1] The agenda included in the act of Congress was: first, measures to preserve and
promote the prosperity of American states; second, an American customs union; third,
transportation and communication; fourth, uniform custom and port regulations; fifth,
uniform weights and measures and uniform laws of copyrights and patents and extradi-
tion of criminals; sixth, adoption of a common silver coin; seventh, a plan for the
arbitration of all disputes; eighth, any other subjects relating to the welfare of the
several states that might be represented.

[2] Described, with illustrations, by C. A. O'Rourke, *Congreso Internacional Americano*
(New York, 1890).

[3] Alice Felt Tyler, *The Foreign Policy of James G. Blaine* (University of Minnesota
Press, 1927), p. 177. Joseph B. Lockey has a good summary of the significance of the
First Inter-American Conference in his sketch of Blaine in *American Secretaries of State*,
VIII, pp. 164-181.

[4] "It is easy to foresee the squirmings of Europe," remarked Mr. Peña, an Argentine
delegate, "when she should feel the effects of a continental blockade, maintained, it is
true, not by warships but by belligerent tariffs. It would not be countries bound
together by political bonds that would enter into compacts inspired by a national sentiment. It would be the war of one continent against another, eighteen sovereignties
allied to exclude from the life of commerce that same Europe which extends to us her
hand, sends us her strong arms, and complements our economic existence, after having
apportioned us her civilization and her culture, her sciences and her arts, industries and
customs that have completed our sociologic evolutions." Williams, *op. cit.*, quoting
proceedings of *International American Conference* (Washington, G.P.O., 1890), I, p. 124.

this grew the notable Pan-American movement and the present Organization of American States, described in the next chapter.[1]

In his striving toward freer trade with the American nations Blaine was
impressed with the fact that the United States in 1889 imported from
the Latin-American republics $142,000,000 worth of goods in excess of
exports; that 87 per cent of commodities imported from these countries
came in free of duty, compared with only 10 per cent of products of the
United States entering free. Having failed to adjust this unbalance by
the Pan-American Conference, the Secretary next tried to do so through
a series of reciprocity treaties. To give him advantage in negotiation
he urged Congress, then debating the McKinley tariff bill, not to take off
the duties on sugar and coffee. The McKinley Act as passed placed
sugar, tea, coffee, hides, and molasses on the free list but authorized the
President to impose duties on the "tropical list" when, in his opinion, a
nation failed to extend similar tariff favors to the United States, or
treated its products in a "reciprocally unequal or unreasonable manner."
It was therefore by a series of executive agreements, made under threat
of the penalties of the McKinley Act of 1890, that Blaine secured tariff
concessions from ten countries: Austria-Hungary; Brazil; Dominican
Republic; Spain for Cuba and Puerto Rico; Salvador; the German Empire; Great Britain for Barbados, Trinidad, Leeward Islands, Windward
Islands, and British Guiana; Nicaragua; Honduras; and Guatemala.
Each of these countries granted lower tariffs on imports from the United
States in order to avoid the penalty duties otherwise to be encountered
on tea, coffee, hides, sugar, and molasses. Most of these agreements resulted in increased trade during their brief lifetimes, and suggest the
manifold advantages that might have been general in a Pan-American
customs union. The Democratic tariff act of 1894, however, placed a
duty on sugar and other commodities, free in 1890, and thus put an end
to these agreements which depended on legislative provisions rather than
treaty guarantees, legislative provisions that were subject to political
caprice or party overturns.

The Republican Dingley Tariff Act of 1897 renewed provisions for tariff
bargaining similar to those of the McKinley Act of 1890, with a "tropical
list" of somewhat different variety (not including sugar). It led to only

---

[1] The governments represented at the Conference did not act to give effect to this
resolution or to the plan of arbitration which was recommended; but they adopted
a resolution expressing the principle of illegality of conquest, in defiance of arbitration,
similar to that later invoked by the world in refusing to recognize conquests or
mutilations of territorial sovereignty in violation of the Pact of Paris (notably in Manchuria and South America).

one Latin-American agreement, with Brazil (1904-1922). There was another bargain list (the "argol list" [1]) designed for European countries. Using this leverage, a series of executive agreements (the "argol agreements") were negotiated with France, Germany, Spain, Portugal, and Bulgaria, and to a minor degree with Italy, Great Britain, and the Netherlands. These were terminated by the new Payne-Aldrich Tariff Act of 1909. The Dingley Act also authorized the President—as if, forsooth, such authorization were necessary—to negotiate treaties of commercial reciprocity, limited in time, in which the tariff rates of the United States might be reduced not over 20 per cent, with transfer of dutiable articles to the free list when they were not produced in the United States—all such treaties to be ratified by the Senate (as the Constitution required anyway). Several reciprocity treaties were signed between 1890 and 1899. Under "McKinleyism" reciprocity went hand in hand with a high protective tariff.[2] The Government of the United States, in fixing reciprocal tariff concessions, never proposed to lower duties on any major category of manufactured products. When the treaties came to the Senate it was evident that there was no willingness to lower the tariff—even in bargains—for *any* articles which could reasonably be produced in the United States. The Senate refused to ratify the treaties.[3] Reciprocity as a general policy was abandoned in 1903, not to be taken up again (except for Canada) until 1933.[4] For expansion of commerce the country turned confidently to the new colonial markets created by the Cuban protectorate (with its singular reciprocity treaty of 1902), and by the acquisition of the Philippines, Puerto Rico, and Hawaii. The two latter were incorporated into the United States and

[1] The list ran "argols, or crude tartar, or wine lees, crude; brandies," etc., etc.—hence the name "argol agreements."

[2] The standard work by J. Laurence Laughlin and H. Parker Willis, *Reciprocity* (New York, 1903) constitutes an argument for reciprocity with *unconditional* most-favored-nation policy.

[3] These unratified treaties (the so-called "Kasson treaties") were: Great Britain for Newfoundland (1890); Great Britain for Barbados, British Guiana, Turks and Caicos Islands, Jamaica and Bermuda (1899); Denmark for the Danish West Indies (1899); Dominican Republic (1899); Nicaragua (1899); Ecuador (1899); the Argentine (1899); France (1899). United States Tariff Commission, *Summary of the Report on Reciprocity and Commercial Treaties* (Washington, G.P.O., 1919).

[4] President Wilson made no use of the supererogatory provision of the Underwood tariff act of 1913 (on the whole lowering tariff schedules) enabling him to negotiate trade agreements subject to final approval by Congress.

Percy W. Bidwell has an unusually helpful review of *Tariff Policy of the United States; a Study of Recent Experience*, in his Report to the Second International Studies Conference on the State and Economic Life, London, May 29 to June 2, 1933, prepared for the American committee appointed by the Council on Foreign Relations (New York, 1933).

assimilated into its tariff structure. With the Philippines a system of preferential tariffs was built up—in general larger than those within the British Empire—to fasten the islands economically to the United States.

An exception to the new apathy toward reciprocity was Canada, next to Great Britain the biggest single foreign customer of the United States. The Payne-Aldrich Tariff of 1909, which repealed the bargaining features of the Dingley Act of 1897, introduced a two-column schedule of tariff rates—minimum rates for imports from countries which did not discriminate against imports from the United States, and maximum rates, 25 per cent higher, for all others. Since Canada had applied similar maximum rates against the United States, the new penalties of the Payne-Aldrich Act logically envisaged that Dominion. To avoid this and the disruption of trade which was likely to follow, President Taft negotiated an agreement with Canada arranging for reciprocal reductions on tariffs to be accomplished by legislation in each country. It provided for a free admission of nearly all the important products of Canada in return for lowered rates on American manufactures.

The appropriate law passed the American Congress; but political considerations, which had undoubtedly helped to pass the bill in Congress, wrought its defeat in the Canadian Parliament. In the midst of the debate in Congress, Champ Clark, Speaker of the House of Representatives, had declared: "I am for it [the bill] because I hope to see the day when the American flag will float over every square foot of British North American possessions clear to the North Pole." This indiscreet utterance provided ammunition for the Canadian nationalists and protectionists.[1] The issue of reciprocity became in the parliamentary elections an issue of annexation. The Liberal Government of Sir Wilfrid Laurier suffered defeat, and with it, for twenty-five years, Canadian-American reciprocity. The penalties of maximum rates of the Payne-Aldrich Tariff (and of later American tariffs) were never applied to Canada, nor indeed to any other country. Meanwhile foreign tariff systems developed the technique of restriction by ingeniously devised quotas of imports, administrative restrictions, exchange controls, and special bilateral agreements from the benefit of which the United States was excluded. They generally avoided specific discrimination in name but accomplished it in fact.

We have noted that before the First World War the industrialization

---

[1] W. G. Swartz analyzed the opposition to reciprocity of various economic groups in both countries, in "The proposed Canadian-American Reciprocity of 1911," *Journal of Economic and Business History*, III (1930-1931), 118-147.

of the United States had proceeded to the point where one half the total exports consisted of manufactured articles. That great war opened a phenomenal demand for manufactures at the very moment when American industrial production seemed, at least for the moment, to have geared up beyond the markets in reach. The demand for munitions alone produced an unheard-of commerce, the effects of which on the diplomacy of neutrality we have been obliged to analyze in a previous chapter. The demand spread to ordinary manufactures. Europe was no longer able to supply its overseas markets—or even its own home markets—and the United States quickly and easily supplanted its competitors in the New World, and even elsewhere. Before the war (for the year 1913) the United States supplied 25.03 per cent of the imports of the Latin-American states and took 30.78 per cent of their exports. At the close of the war (for the year 1919) it supplied 48.79 per cent and took 44.49 per cent,[1] American credit, too, largely displaced—to its misfortune—European credit and European banks in South America.

The demand for American goods and credit, although dislocated temporarily by the advent of peace, continued after the war for a decade in industrial products, but not in foodstuffs, which went back to pre-war levels, throwing agriculture into a prolonged distress. The war-torn European countries needed replacements of peacetime goods, and they were able to pay for these with loans tapped by their governments and corporations from surplus American industrial profits, through the sale of bond issues underwritten by American banks. In South America, which needed no war replacement of goods, governments found it was possible to borrow, without much examination of their credit, for ambitious projects of public works for which politicians are always so delighted to make contracts and disbursements. Agents of American banks, eager to collect commissions for these loans, urged them on the financially irresponsible republics. In the United States the banks easily resold the bonds to American investors, without being further responsible to them.

The phenomenal demand for American produce during and after the war seemed to extinguish altogether any lingering ideas of reciprocity agreements and treaties. With the world crying for American goods (and paying for them with American credits thrust on foreign governments and corporations) there seemed no need for reciprocity to sustain American commerce. The State Department became concerned

[1] *Latin American Foreign Trade in 1914, 1920, 1933.* Foreign Trade Series, Pan American Union.

with two major problems of foreign trade and investment: (a) to prevent the United States from being excluded or discriminated against in competitive regions of the world like the concessions and spheres in China, and the Class A and Class B mandates set up by the Treaty of Versailles;[1] and (b) to prevent discrimination in tariffs within national territories. To solve the last problem the Government resorted in 1923 to a fundamental change of policy in its formula of commercial treaties. In the new treaties made in 1923 and thereafter, the Government of the United States, whether in Republican or Democratic administrations (Secretary Hughes in the Harding Republican Administration was, however, responsible for the change in policy) inserted the *unconditional* most-favored-nation formula, in sharp contrast to the traditional *conditional* formula. Thus it adopted the policy and practice of the European nations before the war, the theory being that, by a network of *unconditional* most-favored-nation articles in treaties of commerce, discriminations would be done away with and the tariff walls lowered to a level consistent with the fundamental protectionist desires of each sovereign nation applied to commodities rather than to the source of origin. But after the First World War, European practice reversed itself in large measure. By quotas and bargain tariffs the nations embarked upon a new mercantilism[2] which aimed at autarchy, or building up, by national planning, among other things, as great as possible economic and military self-sufficiency, against war, or against the economic strife of peace, or even against the possibility of economic sanctions by the League of Nations. Consequently the reform in American commercial policy, so desired by some specialists[3] at the turn of the new century, and even after the First World War, came too late. To the extent[4] that

[1] Secretary Bainbridge Colby, in the Wilson Administration, and Secretary Hughes in the Harding Administration, were successful in securing equal treatment in these mandates (not administered as an integral part of the mandatory like Class C) on the ground that the United States as one of the principal Allied and Associated Powers had helped win the war and make the mandates possible.

[2] Ferdinand Fried [Friedrich Zimmermann] noted this most impressively in his two works *Autarkie* (Jena, 1932) and *Die Zukunft des Aussenhandels durch inners Marktordnung zur Aussenhandels Freiheit* (Jena, 1934).

[3] Laughlin and Willis, *op. cit.*

[4] These treaties, with year of possible termination, were with: Austria (at one year's notice), Germany (terminated 1935), China (no date of termination), Estonia (1936), Honduras (1938), Hungary (1936), Latvia (1938), Morocco (at one year's notice), Muscat and Zanzibar (no date), Norway (one year's notice), Poland (six months' notice), Danzig (six months' notice), El Salvador (1940), Siam (one year's notice), Turkey (one year's notice), Yugoslavia (one year's notice).

In addition, there were unconditional most-favored-nation provisions in executive agreements which could be terminated at short notice (ranging from 15 days to 6 weeks), or by conflicting legislation: with Albania, Belgo-Luxemburg economic union, Bulgaria, Chile,

it negotiated unconditional most-favored-nation treaties of commerce, the United States, best endowed in resources for a strife of autarchy, sacrificed one of its best bargaining assets for the negotiation of reciprocity treaties or agreement in the future. As we shall presently see, in a time of paralyzed international trade, the Republic was again to turn to reciprocity.

The United States had changed from the position of biggest debtor nation before the war supposedly to that of biggest creditor nation. But what were the credits, and what were they worth? First, there were the moneys loaned to the military Associates before the armistice for war purposes, and after the armistice for reconstruction, relief, and the maintenance of credit. The money was borrowed from American taxpayers who took United States government bonds, which were to be paid with interest in gold dollars of the same weight and fineness of gold as loaned. We recall how the debts were leisurely funded, at great concessions, according to the "capacity to pay" of each of the debtor Associates, transferring a large part of the interest burden to the American people; and how, after a few years, in 1932, the Associates suspended payment altogether, leaving the whole burden of their debts on the shoulders of the same American people. And we remember how the United States in 1934, after the debtors ceased payment, itself repudiated approximately 40 per cent of its own bonds and outstanding interest by devaluing the dollar notwithstanding the covenant of the bond. Such was the value of one class of these foreign credits, that owed to the United States Government by the countries where the American crusaders in arms had been so fervently and anxiously welcomed in 1917 and 1918.

The United States rapidly slid back toward its old position of a debtor nation. One reason for this was that some debtor nations were able to suspend payment of interest on their official dollar debts, and at the same time find money to buy back large quantities of bonds thus debased in value of principal. Others were able to provide huge sums for increased armaments amidst the hot rivalry of European nationalism. Finally European investors, frightened at the explosive nature of the politics of the Old World, sent their savings to the United States for the purchase of securities, apparently believing that an American promise to pay was (despite devaluation of the dollar in 1934) better than a European promise to pay. These investments, at long or short terms—mostly short terms—were owed to the foreign investors, and were subject to

Czechoslovakia, Dominican Republic, Egypt, Finland, Greece, Guatemala, Haiti, Iran (Persia), Lithuania, Nicaragua, Rumania, Saudi-Arabia, Spain, Sweden.

withdrawal according to their terms, or to liquidation and quick removal, whilst most of the credits of the United States and its citizens abroad, when solvent at all, were long-term investments. Under such conditions the foreign creditor could remove his money from the United States on much shorter notice than the United States creditor could remove his money, if at all, from abroad. Until the breakdown of American neutrality in 1941 the United States made no move to impound or sequester this rich horde of foreign private wealth within its gates as security for payment of defaulted foreign public debts. In 1940 and 1941, for obvious war reasons, it "froze" the property and funds of nationals and governments of some European and Asiatic countries; and after the outbreak of war sequestered enemy alien property.

The lesson of all this was that hard-pressed nations like individuals will pay for armaments to continue their security and what they conceive to be their vital national interests, even at the abandonment of debts for moneys which helped save their lives in crises happily passed. The credits of some of the Latin-American governments proved to be equally untrustworthy, after the general financial collapse of 1929. All except Argentina suspended payment on their dollar bonds, and even there full service on foreign loans contracted by some of the provinces was suspended. In Europe, even before the war of 1939, other government debtors, notably Germany, defaulted on their dollar [1] bonds (also Bulgaria, Greece, Hungary, Rumania, Russia, Yugoslavia, Czechoslovakia [provinces]).

Under the illusion of payments through first portions of the proceeds of loans flowing back to the United States, American industry—but not agriculture—had continued at its high level of production and export until the collapse of foreign credit in 1929-1932 and the precipitation of the Great Depression in the United States, with all its sociological and political consequences both in the Old World and the New.

The colossal defaults of government and private debtors brought about a collapse of the creditor position of the United States from nearly nineteen billions in 1929 to only half a billion in 1940,[2] while the huge defaulted private loans to Germany assisted in the recovery of her aggressive military might. By the outbreak of the Second World War the United States had practically ceased to be a creditor nation. In the new conflict it poured forth of its remaining wealth to the United

[1] For German defaults on foreign obligations in other currencies, see Chapter 12 above.

[2] For tabulations establishing the debtor-creditor balance of American economy with the outside world, see *A Diplomatic History*, 2d ed. (1942), pp. 752-753.

Nations in amounts many times the loans of the First World War, this time as contributions for the cause of freedom and liberation without thought of repayment except in terms of victory and principles of universal justice: the net total of "lend-lease" aid sent abroad 1941-1946 was $42,872,787,000,[1] a sum larger than the total national debt of the United States at the close of the First World War. The total lend-lease aid was $50,243,996,158.79; but against this was balanced generous estimates of $7,819,322,790.89 "reverse lend-lease," received by the United States from the aided nations.[2]

These enormous grants helped to place the United States after the Second World War more deeply than ever in the status of a debtor nation in the balance of international debits and credits. Even after these national war credits of the United States Government were written off in lend-lease settlements with some of the Allies after the war, or ignored by others like the USSR, the debtor-creditor position of American economy was as follows in 1946:

American-owned assets in foreign countries....$20,900,000,000
Foreign-owned assets in the United States (in-
      cluding gold reserves of $14,681,000,000)....$28,681,000,000 [3]

Taking into consideration the foreign assets and liabilities of the United States and its citizens in 1947 and the balance of international credits and debts, it can be said that the Republic ended up the Second World War as a *debtor nation* to the outside world of $7,781,000,000 and loaded with a national domestic debt of $252,000,000,000 as of 1949.

Demoralization of world commerce by the Great Depression, and cuts in American exports due to restrictive import systems of competing industrial, and even competing agricultural, nations wrought a reversion in American commercial policy, back to reciprocity. Amid the unprecedented depression in American agriculture which set in after 1921 and became worse after 1929, and the later crippling volume of industrial unemployment, the Democratic Administration of President Franklin D. Roosevelt frankly abandoned traditional tenets of Jeffersonian democracy, states' rights, and tariff for revenue only. In both

[1] *Documents of American Foreign Relations*, VIII, pp. 126-158; *Twenty-Third Report to Congress on Lend-Lease Operations, for the Period Ending September 30, 1946* (Department of State Publication No. 2707), p. 27.

[2] Edward R. Stettinius, Jr. described the stream of *Lend-Lease, Weapon for Victory* (New York, 1944). See tabulation at end of this chapter.

[3] *Foreign Assets and Liabilities of the United States and Its Balance of International Transactions* (80th Cong., 1st Sess., Sen. Finance Committee print, Washington, 1948).

of these directions the new Administration out-Hamiltoned Alexander Hamilton himself. It passed no lower tariff law. To placate low-tariff constituents, the new government embarked, as had the Republicans in the regime of McKinleyism, upon a program of three-year [1] reciprocity agreements for mutual lowering of tariffs (within a range of 50 per cent, increased another 50 per cent by the extension act of 1945) [2] on agreed articles, but with this far-reaching feature: the act of Congress of June 12, 1934 (successively extended to 1952) put into the new law the policy of extending gratuitously to all nations—unless, perhaps, they discriminated against the United States [3]—every advantage purchased by any [4] particular reciprocal trade bargain. The President was not obliged to except—and as a matter of fact excepted only Germany, and temporarily Australia—even the discriminatory nations from the benefit of the lowered tariff which thus spread out generally to all nations (whether or no they had made reciprocal argreements with the United States or even whether or no they had general commercial treaty commitments of either conditional or unconditional most-favored-nation nature with the United States) from the individual "reciprocity" arrangements.[5]

[1] Continuing thereafter as terminable at six months' notice.

[2] The extension act of 1948, passed by the Republican Congress, removed the Tariff Commission from the interdepartmental organization set up to advise and assist the President in formulating trade agreements and required the Commission to hold independent hearings and report to the President: (1) the point beyond which tariff concession could not be made without imperiling domestic industries; (2) what, if any, additional duties or import restrictions were required to prevent such injury. The Democratic Congress repealed these safeguards in the extension act of 1949.

[3] " . . . the President may suspend the application [of the new duties from a reciprocity agreement] to articles the growth, produce, or manufacture of any country because of its discriminatory treatment of American commerce or because of other acts or policies which in his opinion tend to defeat the purposes set forth in this section."

These very wide powers to the President enable him to except any recalcitrant nation from the advantages of the new duties; to date (1950) they have not been utilized in time of peace except in regard to Germany, and very briefly as to Australia.

The President also had power under the tariff act of 1930 (continued in this respect from the act of 1922) to levy retaliatory increases up to 50 per cent or new tariffs, against states discriminating against American commerce; and even to prohibit imports, in case discrimination continued. This was also applied to Germany (after June 4, 1936).

[4] Unique preferential tariff treatment was specifically reserved for Cuba.

[5] In negotiations under this act there was an effort to mitigate the descending bargaining power of American diplomacy, signalized by general extension of concessions in each successive agreement, by limiting the agreement to key products which more or less singularly dominated the trade of the two parties concerned; thus, coffee with Brazil, pulp with Canada, guava jelly with Honduras, etc.; but this device weakened as soon as negotiations were completed with a great industrial country. There was also in some of the agreements, i.e., that of Belgium, the ingenious clause which provided that if imports of specified commodities increased unduly from third countries, the general extension by the United States of the concessions would be withdrawn.

In addition to the new policy of general extension of reciprocity bargain concessions there was another striking difference between the reciprocity policy of McKinleyism and the new reciprocity policy sponsored by Secretary of State Cordell Hull. The reciprocity arrangements made in a halfhearted manner in the 1890's had required ratification by the Senate, if they were in the form of treaties, approval by Congress if they were in the form of executive agreements for mutually lowered rates. The reciprocity agreements to be worked out under the act of Congress of 1934 were ratified in advance by Congress, and were independent of competition with any national tariff law.

The advantages of the Hull policy of trade agreements were that it made possible the lowering of tariff with less pressure from a lobby of special interests, and according to the requirements of the national economy as measured by the Department of State and other official agencies. Of course, only a start had been made in measuring and planning for the national economy as a whole and adjusting tariff and trade agreements to it, when the Second World War occurred and deranged all international trade. The Hull policy thus marched in the direction of freer trade while the Democratic Party amidst a sea of unemployment did not dare to lower the tariff by domestic legislation. Opponents of the policy—that is, opponents for other than political reasons—argued plausibly that because the world was moving in the direction of higher tariffs and multiple special restrictions through the ingenious devices of the new mercantilism, it was hopeless to advance far with reciprocity agreements when they were accompanied by a gratuitous generalization of the advantages thus traded for; for one reason the shrewdest bargainer would hold out to the last before negotiating, until he garnered the greatest possible volume of concessions without having to bargain for such favors by the granting of particular concessions to the United States. And the major industrial nations were reluctant to make reciprocity agreements which undid the protection, or endangered the self-sufficiency, enjoyed by their own industry or agriculture. Critics also pointed out that the United States, being best endowed with natural resources and well advanced in technical industry, had a natural advantage in economic bargaining which in the age of the new mercantilism took up an increasing proportion of the activities of diplomacy. They contended that it was folly, like disarmament by example, to weaken this advantage by the generalization, gratuitously, of reciprocal concessions. They asserted that the increasing tendency toward state control of foreign trade, where the state rather than the individual merchant, firm, or even trust buys and sells its commodities on the basis of a planned economy, had radically altered the old liberalistic tendency toward free trade. It had also contracted the flow of international trade and finance. Because of the derangement of normal trade by the Second World War, its antecedents and aftermath, it is difficult to determine how much, if any, the reciprocal trade agreements have improved the foreign commerce of the United States. For several years immediately after the Second World War the labor costs of American manufacturing had mounted to such a level, and the demand for foreign products was so avid that wherever available they could have come in over almost any tariff wall.

Secretary Hull's reciprocal trade agreement program was only one feature of his determined attack on the new mercantilism, and all of its discriminations. In this larger sense we may refer to the Hull policy as the New Reciprocity. When the United States became a full belligerent in the Second World War the New Reciprocity was one of the first peace aims to crystallize as a cornerstone of American foreign economic policy. It became a condition of all the lend-lease agreements that were signed with the various co-belligerents following the Declaration of United Nations, that in the final settlement of accounts the respective signatories, together with all like-minded nations, would strive "in the light of governing economic conditions" for the elimination of all forms of discrimination in international commerce, and for the reduction of tariffs and other trade barriers.[1] That is, the recipients

[1] The standard formula was taken from Article VII of the Mutual Aid Agreement between the United States and Great Britain of February 23, 1942, as follows:

"In the final determination of the benefits to be provided to the United States of America by the Government of the United Kingdom in return for aid furnished under the [Lend-Lease] Act of Congress of March 11, 1941, the terms and conditions thereof shall be such as not to burden commerce between the two countries, but to promote mutually advantageous economic relations between them and the betterment of world-wide relations. To that end, they shall include provision for agreed action by the United States of America and the United Kingdom, open to participation by all other countries of like mind, directed to the expansion, by appropriate international and domestic measures, of production, employment, and the exchange and consumption of goods, which are the material foundations of the liberty and welfare of all peoples; to the elimination of all forms of discriminatory treatment in international commerce, and to the reduction of tariffs and other trade barriers; and, in general, to the attainment of all the economic objectives set forth in the Joint Declaration made on August 12, 1941, by the President of the United States of America and the Prime Minister of the United Kingdom.

"At an early convenient date, conversations shall be begun between the two Governments with a view to determining, in the light of governing economic conditions, the best means of attaining the above-stated objectives by their own agreed action and of seeking the agreed action of the other like-minded Governments." Department of State *Bulletin*, VI, No. 140 (February 28, 1942), p. 192.

of lend-lease agreed to pay the United States not in money or kind, but in principles of the New Reciprocity.[1]

The lend-lease settlements undoubtedly contributed to increasing the number of nations with which the United States had negotiated reciprocal trade agreements from twenty-three in 1942, to a total of forty-one as of December 1, 1949, including all the major countries excepting Germany, Japan, Spain, and the Soviet Union and its satellites (but not Czechoslovakia, which was party to a reciprocal trade agreement with the United States). The phrase "governing economic conditions" introduced a wide area of bargaining reservation on the part of those countries who resorted to state control of trading to repair their war-ravaged economies following the Second World War. This bargaining took place both in bilateral reciprocal trade agreements with the United States and in drafting the charter of an International Trade Organization which the United States proposed to the Economic and Social Council of the United Nations Organization.

President Truman considered the New Reciprocity to be "an integral part of our foreign policy," one of the three main objectives: "peace, freedom, and world trade."[2] It remained for his Administration to make it an international policy and objective.

Preliminary conversations with the Governments of the United Kingdom and Canada during the negotiation of a 50-year, 2-per-cent rehabilitation loan of $3,750,000,000 to Great Britain secured the limited cooperation of these two countries for such a world policy. The Economic and Social Council then invited nineteen countries,[3] including Soviet Russia, estimated to share among them two thirds of the world's trade, to take part in a Preparatory Committee meeting at Geneva, in April, 1947, to draw up the charter of an International Trade Organization, on the basis of a draft proposed by the United States. All except Russia accepted. The Preparatory Committee elaborated a new draft to be submitted to a plenary International Conference on Trade and Em-

[1] Notwithstanding her solemn agreements with the United States against discrimination, made in return for cancellation of lend-lease, the Anglo-American loan of 1947, and other huge rescue grants for British economy and defense, Great Britain, over the initial protest but later reluctant acquiescence of the United States, entered into a special bilateral trade treaty with Argentina, 1949, discriminating in favor of Britain's commerce and diverting much American trade from the Argentine.

[2] See statement of President Harry S. Truman, February 25, 1947, in Department of State *Bulletin*, XVI, No. 401 (March 9, 1947), p. 438; and his speech at Baylor University, Waco, Texas, March 6, 1947, in *ibid.*, XVI, No. 402 (March 16, 1947), p. 481.

[3] Australia, Belgium, Brazil, Canada, Chile, China, Cuba, Czechoslovakia, France, India, Lebanon, Luxemburg, the Netherlands, New Zealand, Norway, South Africa, the United Kingdom, the USSR, and the USA.

ployment [1] at Havana (December, 1947-March, 1948). While at Geneva the delegates also drew up a General Agreement on Tariffs and Trade, signed originally by twenty-three nations, as a sort of provisional code of fair competition in foreign trade practices,[2] as well as numerous bilateral trade agreements among themselves agreeing to tariff concessions covering nearly half the world's national imports.

At Annecy, France, in 1949, ten more countries [3] applied for accession to the General Agreement of Geneva and negotiated bilaterally new tariff schedules with twenty-one of the twenty-three original contracting parties, including the United States which generalized its own Annecy concessions into one schedule applying to all countries. Each country's accession and reciprocally lowered tariff rates are to become binding when two thirds of the parties have signed at Lake Success, N. Y., in respect to that party, the Annecy Protocol. Accession was to become effective from January 1 to May 30, 1950. The twenty-three original parties contracting at Geneva, plus the ten new ones acceding at Annecy, carried on among them four fifths of all world trade.[4] Meanwhile the Truman Administration announced that it would participate in negotiations with additional countries wishing to accede to the Geneva Agreement. The Annecy Agreement and the new tariff concessions to be expected would bring the United States tariff wall, already reduced approximately one half, still lower.

The Havana Conference of delegates from fifty-four countries [5] signed (March 24, 1948) a much modified Charter for an International Trade Organization. In its final form the Charter differed considerably from the original proposals of the United States for consideration by the peoples of the world. It represented a compromise between statism and non-discrimination, between the New Mercantilism and the New Reciprocity. It was a statement of guiding principles with wide reservations, more

[1] In addition to the eighteen states members of the Preparatory Committee, the following states signed: Burma, Ceylon, Pakistan, Southern Rhodesia, Syria. *U.S. and World Affairs, 1947-48,* pp. 244-246.

[2] All the signatories to the final Act of Geneva which contained the General Agreement on Tariffs and Trade gave the Agreement provisional application subject to denunciation on short notice.

[3] The ten additional countries were: Denmark, Dominican Republic, Finland, Greece, Haiti, Italy, Liberia, Nicaragua, Sweden, and Uruguay. The United States had entered previously into bilateral agreements with Finland (1936), Haiti (1935), Nicaragua (1936), Sweden (1935), and Uruguay (1942).

[4] *General Agreement on Tariffs and Trade: the Annecy Protocol of Terms of Accession and the Annecy Schedules of Tariff Concessions* (State Department Publication 3664, Commercial Policy Series 121, Washington, October, 1949).

[5] The USSR abstained from attending. Argentina and Poland did not sign.

than of compulsory obligations. Through the long, complicated, and difficult Charter runs the theme of the New Reciprocity, American plan.

Any advantage, favor, privilege, or immunity, granted by any Member to any product shall be accorded immediately and unconditionally to the like product originating or destined for all other Member countries.

Reservations, exceptions, and qualifying language to the numerous articles of the Charter attached at Havana greatly weighed down and hampered this fundamental principle of American foreign policy. For example, exceptions had to be made for important *existing* preferential systems, like the preferences within the British Empire and Common-wealth of Nations, and those (always cited by persons who argue for such preferences) between the United States and Cuba. Other exceptions gave leeway for quantitative restrictions to remedy current shortages of goods, and special situations. During difficulties in making balance of payments, some discriminatory quantitative restrictions could be per-mitted. But at least the Members agreed *not to increase* any existing preferences, and not to create any new preferential arrangements without permission of the Organization by majority vote of Members present in Conference—one half the membership necessary for a binding quorum. The Members undertook at least to "negotiate" with each other for sub-stantial reduction of the general level of tariffs; in principle they aban-doned the quota system as a protective device; they agreed to work for simplification and easing of customs formalities, and for bridling of pri-vate cartel activities. And they engaged to settle their economic disputes by peaceful means either within the machinery of the Organization or by the International Court of Justice.

The ITO was a bark designed by Mr. Hull's architects of economic amelioration and hopefully launched at Lake Geneva with a pretty name and fair sails, which descending to the open oceans of international trade got heavy-bottomed with barnacles of preferential nationalistic reser-vations picked up in Cuban waters. So encrusted, it was capable of slow progress even though most urgent winds might blow. And it could not even set forth from the port of Havana on its world voyage until a majority of the Charter parties signatory to the ship's articles had deposited "instruments of acceptance" with the Secretary General of the United Nations. Many of the signatories did not trust their future too confidently to this ship; otherwise they would not have built into it so many escape hatches. The period for ratification ended (September 30, 1949) without any of the signatories—not even its principal sponsor,

the United States—having accepted it.[1]   Meanwhile Washington itself
had taken steps in the direction of statism.   The United States Senate
ratified (June 13, 1949) a multilateral treaty (USSR and satellites not
parties thereto) fixing export quotas and prices of wheat for the next
four years; and agreeing in the Anglo-Canadian-American financial
conversations of September, 1949, to further discriminations by Great
Britain, with the help even of the Marshall plan, against the United
States, in order to bolster British economy and power to face the impending world crisis.   Nevertheless, thoughtful Americans wished well to the
ITO.   It was freighted with hopes for a better world.

During the war (Bretton Woods [N. H.] Conference, July 1-22, 1944)
American policy had sponsored and underwritten the establishment of an
International Monetary Fund of $8,046,500,000 (American quota, $2,-
750,000,000) to facilitate the expansion and balanced growth of inter-
national trade, and to promote exchange stability; and an International
Bank for Reconstruction and Development, authorized capitalization
$10,000,000,000 (American share, $3,175,000,000).   The International
Monetary Fund and the International Bank proved to be more than
many of the subscribers could afford unless with loans from the United
States.   Nevertheless, the two institutions were set up to care for an
economically creaking world.[2]   A measure of the International Monetary
Fund, during the momentous Anglo-Canadian-American financial discussions in Washington in September, 1949, was its recommendation to

---

[1] If a majority of the Charter signatories should not have accepted within one year
after signature (March 24, 1948) then it was to enter into force sixty days after
twenty Charter signatories should have accepted. If the Charter should not thus have
entered into force by September 30, 1949, then the Secretary General of the United
Nations was empowered to invite those Governments which had deposited "instruments
of acceptance" to enter into a consultation to determine whether and on what conditions they desired to bring the Charter into force.

The most thoughtful analysis (and sympathetic appraisal) of the ITO Charter and
the general agreements on tariff and trade is by William Adams Brown, Jr., *The United
States and the Restoration of World Trade* (Brookings Institution, Washington, 1950).

[2] The ratifying members of the United Nations Monetary and Financial Conference
(Bretton Woods) were the following signatories: Australia, Belgium, Bolivia, Brazil,
Canada, Chile, China, Colombia, Costa Rica, Cuba, Czechoslovakia, Dominican Republic,
Ecuador, Egypt, El Salvador, Ethiopia, France, Greece, Guatemala, Honduras, Iceland,
India, Iran, Iraq, Luxemburg, Mexico, Netherlands, Nicaragua, Norway, Panama, Para-
guay, Peru, Philippine Commonwealth, Poland, Union of South Africa, United Kingdom,
USA, Uruguay, Venezuela, and Yugoslavia. Haiti, Liberia, New Zealand, and the
USSR attended but did not sign. *United Nations Monetary and Financial Conference,
Bretton Woods, New Hampshire, July 1 to July 22, 1944. Final Act and Related Docu-
ments* (Department of State Publication 2187, Washington, G.P.O., 1944), pp. 25-27.
Haiti and Liberia have since applied for admission to the Bank and Fund Agreements.
By January 1, 1950, the following states not signatories had been admitted: Austria,
Denmark, Finland, Italy, Lebanon, Thailand, and Turkey.

countries whose exchange was strained for dollars that they devalue their currencies accordingly. The dramatic devaluation of the British pound and the currencies of the "sterling block" followed almost immediately, accompanied by far-reaching economic indulgences of the United States to Britain and Canada.

Neither the Fund, nor the Bank, nor the New Reciprocity magnified into the International Trade Organization, nor all the king's horses and all the king's men, proved sufficient to bring Europe together again, quick enough. Amid the stresses and strains, political and ideological as well as economic, that followed in wake of the Second World War, including the abstinence of Soviet Russia and its satellites, too little time has passed to measure the healing efficacy of these international institutions.[1] One thing seemed certain: their success in mending the economic disruption of the world depended upon the success of the United Nations; and the success of the United Nations depended upon the attitude of the Soviet Union. So far the USSR had refused to help man the economic machinery of the United Nations. As a powerful and permanent member of the Security Council it had braked and blocked the peace machinery too.

To hasten the recovery of Europe against the rising tide of communist revolution spearheaded by the USSR, the United States in 1947 took the astonishing step of initiating and underwriting to the amount of $20,000,000,000 a five-year European Recovery Program. Open to all the states of Europe, it was designed to bring their economies to a level of well-being 25 per cent above pre-war conditions. The USSR refused to participate in this unprecedented enterprise or to allow its satellite states to do so. It set up a plan of its own for them. The Soviet Union's attitude signalized a heading conflict between free economies and controlled economies, between free peoples and controlled peoples, in short between freedom and power in the world, a crisis in thought and action with which we close our final chapters.

[1] The USSR participated in the Bretton Woods Conference, but has had nothing to do since then either with the Fund or the Bank.

LEND-LEASE AND REVERSE LEND-LEASE

1941-1947 (June 30)

Recipient	Lend-Lease	Reverse Lend-Lease to U. S. A.
American republics:		
Bolivia	$ 5,523,113.77	
Brazil	372,018,982.63	
Chile	21,603,647.88	
Colombia	8,264,954.63	
Costa Rica	156,330.15	
Cuba	6,550,610.38	
Dominican Republic	1,617,315.60	
Ecuador	7,794,178.09	
El Salvador	878,275.90	
Guatemala	2,598,045.84	
Haiti	1,423,658.75	
Honduras	368,364.24	
Mexico	39,238,971.45	
Nicaragua	887,199.28	
Panama	667.33	
Paraguay	1,956,128.55	
Peru	18,925,731.36	
Uruguay	7,129,488.01	
Venezuela	4,523,680.08	
Total—American republics	$ 501,459,343.92	
Other governments:		
Belgium	$ 159,464,430.26	$ 191,215,983.35
British Empire	31,384,810,121.25	6,752,073,165.40
China	1,626,998,524.86	3,672,000.00
Czechoslovakia	641,839.17	
Egypt	2,319,691.15	
Ethiopia	5,251,480.09	
France and possessions	3,223,891,229.32	867,781,244.70
Greece	81,521,726.17	
Iceland	4,371,496.03	
Iran	5,303,624.18	
Iraq	891,469.57	
Liberia	11,554,901.20	
Netherlands and possessions	251,137,540.95	2,367,699.64
Norway	47,000,522.22	
Poland	12,475,376.00	
USSR	10,982,088,888.95	2,212,697.81
Saudi Arabia	18,984,227.45	
Turkey	42,876,877.88	
Yugoslavia	32,192,067.91	
Total—other governments	$47,893,776,034.61	
Total—charged to foreign governments	$48,395,235,378.53	

1941-1947 (June 30)

Recipient	Lend-Lease	Reverse Lend-Lease to U. S. A.
Not distributed by foreign governments:		
Transfers to Federal agencies......... $	725,589,141.95	
Losses on inventories and facilities.....	31,072,272.57	
Production facilities.................	720,641,686.66	
Miscellaneous charges...............	332,200,098.31	
Administrative expenses.............	39,257,580.77	
Total—not distributed by foreign governments................... $	1,848,760,780.26	
Grand total......................	$50,243,996,158.79	$7,819,322,790.90

Total Lend-Lease................ $50,243,996,158 79
Total Reverse Lend-Lease........   7,819,322,790.90

Net Lend-Lease................. $42,424,673,367 89 [a]

[a] *Twenty-fifth Report by the President to Congress on Lend-Lease Operations. Lend-Lease Fiscal Operations March 11, 1941, through June 30, 1947.*

14

The United States and Latin America

THERE have been a few small wars between the nations of the New World in the twentieth century, but compared to the Old World of Europe, Asia, and Africa, their general lot has been one of relative peace and serenity in international affairs. This is because the European political system has been fenced away (except in the case of Canada) by the American Revolution, by the successful revolutions from Spanish sovereignty of the Latin-American nations, by the defensive exertions of the South American states themselves unaided, and, more recently, by the Monroe Doctrine.

The Monroe Doctrine did not in itself at first "save" Latin America from the re-imposition of Spanish authority at the hands of the Holy Alliance. Nevertheless the United States speedily grew up to the stature of defending the Monroe Doctrine. Its attitude toward French or Spanish aggressions in Mexico, the Dominican Republic, and Peru, and British boundary policy in Venezuela; and Great Britain, Germany, and Italy later in Venezuela; gave pause to adventures of those monarchies across the Atlantic. One has only to compare the maps of Asia and Africa, recording as they do the advances of European and Japanese imperialism, with the map of South America and the persistence there of sovereign independence.[1]

In this chapter we shall treat of South America, as distinct from the Caribbean fringe, the Isthmus, and Central America, that nearer field of the Panama Policy of the United States, where a mild imperialism—now fully liquidated—was built up in an area from which European intervention had been held aside by the Monroe Doctrine. Before the days of aerial navigation the nations of Hispanic America, south of the Caribbean fringe, were quite as distant from the United States as from Europe. Indeed, from the geophysical point of view, Asia and Africa are more closely connected to Europe than is South America to North America. The United States had less contact with these South American

[1] See Map 5, between pp. 280 and 281.

Map 5. The New World with the Monr

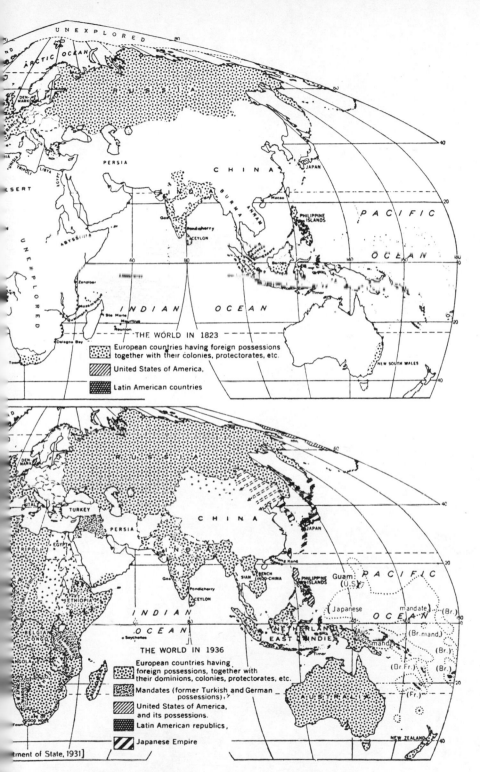

THE WORLD IN 1823

European countries having foreign possessions
together with their colonies, protectorates, etc.

United States of America,

Latin American countries

THE WORLD IN 1936

European countries having
foreign possessions, together with
their dominions, colonies, protectorates, etc.

Mandates (former Turkish and German
possessions),

United States of America,
and its possessions.

Latin American republics,

Japanese Empire

[ment of State, 1931]

nd the Old World without It 1823-1936

states, before the First World War, than with Europe. During the nineteenth century the noteworthy features of the history of the diplomacy of the United States with South America were: the extension of good offices on several occasions to end strife between South American nations; Blaine's attempt to freshen commerce by a system of reciprocity to be erected through the First Inter-American Conference, at Washington in 1889, and the resulting feeble beginnings of the Pan-American movement;[1] the *Baltimore* affair with Chile in 1891; and the sympathetic reaction of the United States in 1893 to the republican government in Brazil when it was threatened by a naval insurrection intent on restoring the old empire.

It has been a consistent policy of the United States to encourage peace in South America through the extension of good offices and proposals of mediation. One motive for this has been to enhance its good will at the expense of Europe; but the policy has by no means necessarily opposed similar good offices and mediations by European nations; the Monroe Doctrine has never been invoked to exclude peace at European hands from the American continents. It was under American[2] good offices, for example, that Spain's war with the Pacific coast republics of South America (1864-1871)—Ecuador, Peru, Bolivia, and Chile—came to a legal end long after actual hostilities had ceased. It was the United States which, after much discouraging diplomacy, eventually helped to end the Tacna-Arica controversy, which alienated Chile and Peru from the end of the War of the Pacific (1879-1883) until the Treaty of Santiago (1929).[3] President Hayes served as arbitrator of a disputed boundary between the Argentine Republic and Paraguay, by a treaty between those two countries in 1876. His decision in favor of Paraguay was accepted by the disputants. President Cleveland, in 1895, acted successfully as arbitrator for the settlement of another boundary dispute in the same general region, that between Brazil and Argentina, the Misiones arbitration. The American Minister to Argentina, W. I. Buchanan, served as umpire in a mixed Chilean-Argentine boundary commission, successfully bringing to a settlement a standing dispute over their long mountainous boundary line. These are examples of many good offices for the peaceful settlement of Latin America's vexing boundary disputes.

[1] Above, p. 261.

[2] For my justification for the use of this adjective for the United States, see above, p. 32.

[3] An adequate monograph is W. J. Dennis' *Tacna and Arica; an Account of the Chile-Peru Boundary Dispute and of the Arbitrations by the United States* (Yale University Press, 1931).

Map 6. Latin America, 1940

The nearest the United States ever came to any actual conflict with a South American nation was with Chile. A revolution in that distant republic against the praetorian practices of President Balmaceda broke out in 1891. The American Minister, Patrick Egan, of Irish birth, appeared to the Congressionalists to sympathize overmuch with the *Balmacedistas,* disfavored by British interests in Chile. The revolutionists sent a ship to San Diego, California, to buy a cargo of rifles and other military supplies. It was doubtful whether this was in violation of American domestic neutrality laws, but the vessel, the *Itata,* was detained on suspicions at that port and a United States marshal placed on board. The captain put out to sea notwithstanding, temporarily shanghaied the marshal, took on the military cargo at Catalina Island, and steamed away for Chile, followed by two American warships. At the port of Iquique, held by the Congressionalists, the revolutionary authorities complied with the request of the American naval officer for the surrender of the ship and cargo to be sent back to the United States for trial—where eventually it was acquitted of any violation of the neutrality laws. The Congressionalists nevertheless triumphed, with arms imported successfully from Germany.

Egan gave customary asylum in his legation to fleeing *Balmacedistas.* This, and the sentiments previously attributed to him, created bitter popular feeling against the United States. In such an atmosphere a mob of Chileans in the port of Valparaiso attacked (October 15, 1891) a party of 116 sailors on shore leave from the U.S.S. *Baltimore,* killed two, and seriously wounded several others. The new government made no efforts either to protect the visitors or to punish the assailants. It offered no apology or explanation; rather the contrary. Despite a wave of indignation in the United States, Secretary Blaine did not allow the Harrison Administration to be precipitated into a rupture. The *Baltimore* was called home, and an unhurried investigation of the incident took place. Then after due consideration Blaine despatched an ultimatum to Chile, demanding, under the alternative of a rupture of diplomatic relations, a suitable apology for the attack on sailors of the United States wearing the American uniform, and adequate reparation. At the same time President Harrison laid the whole matter significantly before Congress for ultimate decision. In Chile the personnel of the new government had meanwhile changed. A sincere expression of regret was promptly forthcoming, and the United States accepted a sum of $75,000 by way of reparation for the families of the victims. Since then relations between Chile and the United States have been of the most friendly nature.[1]

The United States was the first (outside of Latin America) to recognize the new republican government in Brazil, when that empire was overthrown by the bloodless revolution of 1889. A counterrevolution followed in 1893 by the monarchists, who secured control of the Brazilian navy. President Cleveland declined to recognize the belligerency of the

[1] H. C. Evans, *Chile and Its Relations with the United States* (Duke University Press, 1927) and W. R. Sherman, *The Diplomatic and Commercial Relations of the United States and Chile, 1820-1914* (Boston, 1926).

monarchists. An American squadron hastened to Rio de Janeiro, where warships from the European powers also appeared. At the cannon's mouth, the American admiral refused to permit the anti-republican warships to enforce a blockade on American vessels carrying alleged contraband into Rio. The insurrection had the sympathy of the European monarchical powers, which, particularly Germany, hoped for its success. There was a considerable concentration (300,000) of sturdy German immigrants in southern Brazil, for whom Pan-German enthusiasts had higher hopes than really could be justified because of the rapid Brazilianization of the majority of these people. The Kaiser secretly applauded the monarchical strivings. There was even a chance that Prince August von Coburg, a nephew of the late Dom Pedro, might be the new monarch: "Then we shall be the big people there," declared Wilhelm II. Germany was also jealous of the good will which the United States had created for itself in Brazil by its open sympathies for the republican government, and feared the intrusion and future competition of American trade there, as elsewhere in South America, under the impetus of a Pan-American movement for which the Brazilian republicans had shown enthusiasm (Brazilian-American reciprocity agreement, 1891-1894).

The attitude of the United States gave the European monarchical powers pause in their desire to recognize the belligerency of the monarchists. England refused to antagonize the United States by such a step. Count Caprivi, Bismarck's successor, considered that the Brazilian revolutionists were of more promise to Germany than the established republican government, because of their opposition to Pan Americanism and because of possible favors to be expected to German colonization, but he opposed any singlehanded recognition of their belligerency and the consequent legality of their blockade, because of its injury to German trade, including the munitions trade.[1] The successful suppression of the monarchists by the established republican authorities meant the triumph in Brazil of this form of government. The policy of the United States at that decisive hour of trial was an earnest to Brazil of the real feelings of the American people and laid the foundations for a persistent cordiality between the two republics ever since.[2]

The United States bought from the group of South American countries far more than it sold to them, though there have been notable exceptions in the case of individual countries, like Argentina; Europe sold more

[1] Alfred Vagts, *Weltpolitik, op. cit.,* II, pp. 1673-1700, has a full analysis of German policy.

[2] Lawrence F. Hill, *Diplomatic Relations between the United States and Brazil* (Duke University Press, 1932), is the best account.

than it bought. It was Secretary Blaine's effort to make use of an inter-American Conference (that of 1889) for the purpose of furthering reciprocal trade arrangements between the increasingly industrial United States and the agrarian republics of South America which would overcome this unprofitable disparity. We have seen that he failed; [1] but the Pan-American movement which followed "Blaine's Conference" has always had a reciprocity tinge,[2] and if only for this reason has been opposed by European diplomacy, particularly German.[3] European industrial nations feared that political amenities of the United States with South America would eat into the commercial predominance which they enjoyed down to the outbreak of the First World War, and which they endeavored to retrieve in the interlude of peace after 1919. They welcomed the appearance of countermovements, so far of no treaty or even diplomatic structure, like Pan Hispanism and Pan Iberianism, by which South American Yankeephobes tried to rally public sentiment about a common Latin culture, and with it to keep trade in European channels, and even to hope for political followings.[4]

The second inter-American Conference, at Mexico in 1901-1902, did not take place until after the Cuban-Spanish-American War, which had made some of the Latin-American nations suspicious of the platonic intentions of the United States. The Conference accomplished very little, except to put in motion a train of such conferences which have assembled more or less regularly (except for the interruption of the two World Wars) ever since. At first fruitful only of feeble accomplishments, the Pan-American movement, as represented by these conferences, has come in our own times to be an impressive vehicle for the organization of peace in the New World, with most elaborate machinery. Particularly with ultra-Caribbean nations of South America are the diplomatic relations of the United States now contained in the formula of Pan Americanism.

What is Pan Americanism? Is it a policy or is it a tendency? It is both. It may be described as a tendency, more or less pronounced, of the republics of the New World to associate together in a neighborly way for mutual understanding of common aspirations and interests and

[1] Above, p. 261.

[2] A European conception of this appears in Jens Jessen, "Die ökonomische Grundlage der panamerikanischen Idee," *Schmollers Jahrbuch*, LII, No. 5 (1928), 79-111.

[3] Vagts, *Weltpolitik, op. cit.*, I, pp. 72-75; II, pp. 1637-1814.

[4] For example, the *Ibero-Amerikanisches Institut* had its headquarters in Germany. An expression of this German patronage appeared in the Argentine historian, Ernesto Quesada's *Die Wirtschaftsbeziehungen zwichen Latein-Amerika und den Vereinigten Staaten* (Leipzig, 1931). Santiago Magariño presented the case for Pan Hispanism in his *Panhispanismo, su trascendencia histórica, política y social; obra premiada en el concurso hispano antillano de 1925* (Barcelona, 1926).

their realization. The greatest of these common aspirations is peace. It is a policy of the United States to encourage this tendency in order to cause the American nations not to look to Europe or to depend on Europe for leadership, because (as past and present history suggests) Europe might possibly exploit such tutelage for the selfish interests of particular European powers. This in turn might lead to the exercise of political influence or even sovereignty of a non-American power in the American world, which would be possibly a menace to the common American republican form of government and perhaps a threat to independence itself. Rather let the American republics look to themselves and their common counsel for such leadership. In this sense Pan Americanism may be considered as a complement to the Monroe Doctrine.

It has been called a "twin policy" to the Monroe Doctrine.[1] At first, 1888-1936, it was a movement, sponsored by the United States, toward *moral union* of the American republics under the protection of the Monroe Doctrine. Later, 1936-1950, it developed into a political regional arrangement of the republics of the New World in formal alliance—all for one and one for all—to protect the peace and security of the Western Hemisphere against attack or menace of aggression, from without or within.

Before the First World War the accomplishments of the Pan-American movement were meager. The intervention of the United States to clinch the secession of Panama, and the installation of the protectorates in the Caribbean and Central America, had provoked a vigorous skepticism of the good faith of the "Colossus of the North," a skepticism which overweighed the protection from European imperialism which had been secured by the Monroe Doctrine. The inarticulation of cultural backgrounds between the United States and Latin America made it difficult for the people of the southern republics to think and feel like their "Anglo-Saxon" neighbors north of the Rio Grande. This cultural incompatibility lent itself to a literary Yankeephobia among South American publicists [2] which frequently displayed (at least so it appeared to the North American mind) more emotion than common sense. North American imperialism in the Caribbean gave fuel for the flames of these burn-

---

[1] G. H. Blakeslee, *The Recent Foreign Policy of the United States; Problems in American Cooperation with Other Powers* (New York, 1925), p. 129.

[2] J. Fred Rippy has an analysis of South American opinion in his introduction to the English edition of Ugarte, *The Destiny of a Continent* (New York, 1925); and a further survey in his "Literary Yankeephobia in Hispanic America," *Jour. of International Relations*, XII (Jan., 1922), 350-371, 524-538. One of the best analyses of opinion at a later time is C. H. Haring, *South America Looks at the United States* (New York, 1928).

ing critics; and there was generally little consideration of the strategic necessities which had thrust up the Panama Policy of the United States in the Caribbean and in Central America. Successive inter-American conferences that followed Mexico City before 1914 (Rio de Janeiro, 1906, and Buenos Aires, 1910) really accomplished very little of vital importance. Their principal achievement was the abatement, by treaties, of trade nuisances: they provided for the international regulation of such common conveniences as bills of lading, trade-marks, copyrights, patents, publicity of customs dues, sanitary precautions, etc. Ancillary to these diplomatic conferences were held special Pan-American conferences of professional, scientific, and humanitarian representatives of the different American republics, meetings initiated by the diplomatic conferences themselves or organized by the Pan American Union from its headquarters in Washington: conferences of bankers, journalists, railroads, motor roads, advocates of the advancement of women's rights, educators, historians, geographers, and so on. These conferences did much to bridge the cultural gap and to tone down discordances among the leaders of thought.

For several reasons it was difficult to achieve multilateral political conventions. The South American states suspected that the United States would like to impose a political tutelage over them even while it would prevent non-American powers from doing so. They suspected the Monroe Doctrine of such import, and desired to pan-Americanize it. They resented the shadow of the Washington Monument falling across, so to speak, the Pan American Union in the capital of the United States. This shadow appeared in the persistent presiding over the Union by a citizen of the United States, either as chairman of the group of diplomatic representatives from the several American republics accredited to Washington, which chair according to the rules of the Union until 1923 was held *ex officio* by the Secretary of State of the United States; or as Director General of the Pan American Union, which office was held until 1947 by a citizen of the United States. Until 1923 only a recognized diplomatic representative at Washington could sit in the Pan American Union; hence the rupture of diplomatic relations, for whatever reason, with the United States, would deprive a republic of its seat.[1] In short, there lingered a general distrust which it has been a task of the Pan-

---

[1] The Sixth (Havana) Inter-American Conference adopted a convention controlling the organization of the Pan American Union, already reformed at Santiago de Chile in 1923. This adjusted these questions with this treaty article: "The government of the Pan American Union shall be vested in a Governing Board composed of the representatives

American policy of the United States to overcome. Nascent nationalism in South America itself, and racial differences in the midst of a common Hispanic heritage, also prevented Pan-American political agreements, like treaties for the limitation of armaments and the lowering of tariff walls. Nevertheless the Pan-American nations did agree, before the First World War, to the convention establishing the Hague Court of Arbitration which had been set up in 1899 by a conference in which they did not sit; to the Root arbitration treaties with the United States, and in many instances also to Bryan conciliation treaties.

It was one of the principal objects of Woodrow Wilson's foreign policy to wipe out this distrust and to reach a common understanding about the Monroe Doctrine as an instrument of protection, this with acceptance of the accomplished fact of a benevolent North American imperialism in the Caribbean and in Central America as evidenced by the protectorates in Cuba, Panama, the Dominican Republic, Nicaragua, and Haiti. In a notable speech at Mobile, Alabama, in the first year of his administration (October 27, 1913) on the eve of the opening of the Panama Canal, he took occasion to say that "the United States will never again seek one additional foot of territory by conquest." This assurance, the treaty of reparation negotiated with Colombia (not ratified however till 1921), and Wilson's sympathetic policy toward Mexico did much to win the confidence of the sister republics all over the southern continent and Central America. Particularly ingratiating, as evidence of the sincerity of Wilson's remarks, was his ready acceptance of the mediation of the joint ABC and other republics of South and Central America for the solution of Mexican peace.

Wilson's adviser, Colonel E. M. House, urged that this good will be capitalized, during the First World War, in the cementing of an inter-American pact which in effect would pan-Americanize the Monroe Doctrine by a common guaranty of the existing political independence and territorial integrity of every republic of the New World. In November, 1915, House and Wilson formulated the following articles:

that the American governments may appoint. The appointment may [not must] devolve upon the diplomatic representatives of the respective countries in Washington."

"The Board shall elect its Chairman and Vice-Chairman annually."

This convention does not go into effect until ratified by *all* the member states of the Union. The United States has ratified; but to January 1, 1949, ratifications were missing from: Argentina, Colombia, El Salvador, Honduras, Paraguay. The Charter of the Organization of American States, signed at the Ninth International Conference of American States, March 30-May 2, 1948, may be said to have superseded previous attempts to formulate the organization in treaty form. It required ratification by only two thirds of the signatories, and went immediately into provisional effect by resolution. See below, pp. 309-312.

Article I. That the high contracting parties to this solemn covenant and agreement hereby join one another in a common and mutual guaranty of territorial integrity and of political independence under republican forms of government.

Article II. To give definitive application to the guaranty set forth in Article I, the high contracting parties severally covenant to endeavor forthwith to reach a settlement of all disputes as to boundaries or territory now pending between them by amicable agreement or by means of international arbitration.[1]

When he broached the subject of such a broad pact, President Wilson encountered hesitations from Peru and Chile, arising out of the then unsettled Tacna-Arica dispute. Peru would not enter into any guaranty of the territorial status quo, so grievous to her; and Chile was not willing to assume a general obligation to submit boundary disputes to arbitration. Before negotiations for the consummation of such a Pan-American treaty could be pursued further, the rupture of diplomatic relations with Germany and the entrance of the United States into the First World War drew the President's attention from this pact and engrossed his energies with even larger affairs. It is emphatically noteworthy that during the period of belligerency of the United States the sympathy of the Latin-American republics, with the possible exception of Argentina, was with the great republic of the north. We recall that eight of the Latin-American republics declared war against Germany, at the invitation of the United States, and that five others broke off diplomatic relations.[2] In the Peace Conference at Paris Woodrow Wilson wrote into the Covenant of the League of Nations the principles of his proposed Pan-American pact, notably Article X, to him the most vital article in the Covenant. He believed that by this article he was globalizing the Monroe Doctrine, whereas previously he would have merely pan-Americanized it. At the instance of those who feared the defeat of the treaty without an article reserving the Monroe Doctrine specifically from the purview of the League, he secured the adoption of the equivocal Article XXI for that purpose.[3]

Republican administrations following Wilson did much toward pruning off the "Roosevelt Corollary" of the Monroe Doctrine, which an

[1] Seymour, *Intimate Papers, op. cit.*, I, pp. 207-234.
[2] Above, p. 149.
[3] Above, p. 181.
Article XXI of the Covenant: "Nothing in this Covenant shall be deemed to affect the validity of international engagements, such as treaties of arbitration or regional understandings like the Monroe Doctrine, for securing the maintenance of peace."

earlier Republican President had invoked to justify intervention by the United States in the Dominican Republic in 1905. The United States ratified in 1924 the so-called Gondra Convention, signed at the Fifth Inter-American Conference at Santiago in 1923, which has replaced, by a multilateral treaty among the Pan-American states, the series of Bryan conciliation treaties, previously in effect bilaterally in each case with the United States. The Pan-American nations, including of course the United States, at the Havana Inter-American Conference of 1928 adopted a resolution outlawing aggression as an international crime against the human species (without defining aggression), and another for the obligatory arbitration of all justiciable disputes, the minimum exceptions to justiciable questions to be worked out by a special conference on arbitration and conciliation appointed to meet at Washington the following year. The delegates at Havana signed a number of treaties, since ratified in less or greater degree, of a distinct political nature: they concerned the status of aliens,[1] asylum, civil strife,[1] aviation,[1] consular rights,[1] maritime neutrality,[1] alteration of the Pan American Union,[1] private international law, and rules governing treaties. Both at Santiago in 1923 and at Havana in 1928 the majority of the Latin-American countries displayed an antagonistic feeling toward the United States—because of American interventions then established in the Caribbean and Central America—a feeling which restricted the possibilities of still wider accomplishment. Notwithstanding the fact that the intervention of the United States then underway in Nicaragua, and the presence of American marines still in Haiti, served to prolong hesitations among the Latin-American delegations, the Havana Inter-American Conference of 1928 gave real impetus to the Pan-American movement, a headway which has since continued unchecked as it became increasingly evident that American policy toward intervention was undergoing a change.

At Havana, in a speech outside the Conference to the American Chamber of Commerce in that city, one of the delegates of the United States, former Secretary of State Charles E. Hughes, declared that the "pillars of Pan Americanism" were independence, and political stability to secure independence, together with good will and co-operation. He said that the interventions of the United States then in evidence were only for the purpose of ensuring stability as a means of securing independence. "We have no desire to stay. We entered to meet an imperative but temporary

[1] Since ratified by the United States.

emergency, and we shall retire as soon as possible." This may be considered as the last statement of the policy of intervention for prevention of political or economic disorder, the policy of the "Roosevelt Corollary" of the Monroe Doctrine.

As if to clarify the relation of the Panama Policy to the Monroe Doctrine, the Department of State prepared, after the Havana Conference, the "Clark Memorandum on the Monroe Doctrine," dated December 17, 1928, and later made public in 1930 under the imprimatur of the Department and over the name and title of the Undersecretary of State. Its principal purpose appears to have been to repudiate, by historical exegesis, the "Roosevelt Corollary" as an unwarranted interpretation of the Monroe Doctrine. Public addresses of Secretary of State Henry L. Stimson (February 6, 1931), and of the new Undersecretary of State, W. R. Castle (July 4, 1931), corroborated this irenic interpretation. Said Mr. Stimson: "The Monroe Doctrine was a declaration of the United States versus Europe—not of the United States versus Latin America." Mr. Castle declared that the Monroe Doctrine "confers no superior position on the United States," and said that it had been wrongly credited with giving the United States a right to interfere in the internal affairs of other nations. The next step of assurance to the nations of the New World that the United States was not going to interpret the Monroe Doctrine in an imperialistic way was signature of the two treaties worked out by the special Washington conference of 1929, the General Convention of Inter-American Conciliation, and the General Treaty of Inter-American Arbitration. The new conciliation convention empowered the commission of inquiry, provided by the Gondra Convention of 1923, to investigate into and report upon disputes not settled by diplomacy or arbitration, with function also of proposing modes of conciliating (as well as reporting). The arbitration convention of 1929 condemned war as an instrument of national policy and adopted obligatory arbitration as the means for the settlement of international differences of a juridical character between or among the contracting parties, when it has proven impossible to adjust them by diplomacy, viz.:

There shall be considered as included among the questions of juridical character:
(a) The interpretation of a treaty;
(b) Any question of international law;
(c) The existence of any fact which, if established, would constitute a breach of an international obligation;

(d) The nature and extent of the reparation to be made for the breach of an international obligation.[1]

There are excepted from the stipulations of this treaty the following controversies:

(a) Those which are within the domestic jurisdiction of any of the Parties to the dispute and are not controlled by international law; and

(b) Those which affect the interest or refer to the action of a State not a Party to this treaty.

Both treaties remain in force indefinitely, but may be denounced by any party on one year's previous notice.

In signing the arbitration treaty the delegates of several states (Venezuela, Chile, Bolivia, Honduras, Guatemala, Ecuador, Colombia, El Salvador) made a reservation (among others) that the obligation to arbitrate should not involve old disputes, and in some cases treaties, antedating the arbitration treaty. The Senate of the United States in advising and consenting to ratification attached the usual reservation stating that the special agreement (compromis) for any particular arbitration must be the subject of a special treaty negotiated by the President and ratified by the Senate; and that the general treaty should not be applicable to past or pending controversies or treaties. To date eighteen nations [2] (including the United States) have ratified the conciliation convention, and sixteen nations [3] (including the United States) the treaty of arbitration.

President Franklin D. Roosevelt, upon taking office in 1933, hit upon the happy phrase "the good neighbor" to characterize his foreign policy. In regard to Pan America, he continued, under the benevolent impulse of Secretary of State Cordell Hull, the trend which had been pursued by his Republican predecessors: to bring American policy back toward the pristine dicta of the Monroe Doctrine: for non-American nations, hands off the New World; for the United States also, hands off Latin America—accepting, of course, the accomplished fact of the Canal treaties. In the new order of naval security that followed the victory of the First World War, it seemed no longer necessary to pursue a policy which might provoke a challenge by a non-American power to the Monroe Doctrine. That

[1] This definition of justiciable questions is that of Article 36 of the Statute of the Permanent Court of International Justice.

[2] The conciliation convention had been ratified (on January 1, 1949) by: Brazil, Colombia, Cuba, Chile, Ecuador, El Salvador, United States, Guatemala, Haiti, Honduras, Mexico, Nicaragua, Panama, Paraguay, Peru, Dominican Republic, Uruguay, Venezuela; all except Argentina, Bolivia, and Costa Rica.

[3] The arbitration treaty had been ratified (on January 1, 1949) by: Brazil, Cuba, Chile, Colombia, Ecuador, El Salvador, United States, Guatemala, Haiti, Honduras, Mexico, Nicaragua, Panama, Peru, Dominican Republic, Venezuela; all except Argentina, Bolivia, Costa Rica, Paraguay, and Uruguay.

Doctrine alone, without any corollary of vicarious responsibility, seemed sufficient to protect the independence of the republics of the New World and the naval communications of the United States via the Isthmus of Central America. No more interventions would be necessary, unless for the immediate protection of the legitimate rights of American citizens generally recognizable and acceptable under international law and international conventions. This banned future political interventions. Accompanying this was a process of liquidation of the Caribbean protectorates, the result of past interventions.

The Good Neighbor Policy, at first greeted as a mere phrase, bore rich and friendly fruit at the Seventh Inter-American Conference at Montevideo in 1933. The old feelings of suspicion and resentment vanished before the proven sincerity of the Good Neighbor of the North. The delegates there assembled proceeded to the signature of a number of treaties which marked great advance in Pan Americanism, particularly in regard to the organization of peace, in the preservation of which the nations of the New World had a common vital interest. They adopted no less than 114 resolves and recommendations for the furtherance of worthy projects of inter-American life, enterprises of social, economic, and cultural value, which vastly extended the ancillary functions already increasingly developed through Pan-American channels. Since many of these projects required negotiation of treaties and conventions, and subsequent ratification, or at least a community of uniform national legislation, this part of the work of the Conference was a program and a tribute rather than an accomplishment. One of these resolves, for the removal of trade barriers, including high tariff walls, was very significant. It was the treaties which were most important. In addition to treaties defining the nationality of women, the requirements for naturalization in general, political asylum, the teaching of history [1]—treaties which have a long road to ratification by sufficient countries to make them important—the Conference adopted an additional protocol to the general convention of inter-American conciliation [2] and a convention henceforth to define the rights and duties of states, which had been drawn up by a special commission of American jurists appointed after the Sixth (Havana) Inter-American Conference of 1928. It was the last-

[1] "To revise the text books adopted for instruction in their respective countries, with the object of eliminating from them whatever might tend to arouse in the immature mind of youth aversion to any American country," and to found an "Institute for the Teaching of History" at Buenos Aires.

[2] In this the parties to the Gondra Convention of 1923 agreed to negotiate among themselves bilateral conventions setting up as between themselves particular commissions of investigation and conciliation.

named convention that was of fundamental importance as a capstone of
the new Pan-American policy of the United States and of the Pan-
American structure of peace. Ratified by the United States (June 29,
1934), it contained among other articles:

Article 2. The federal state shall constitute a sole person in the eyes of
international law.

Article 8. No state has the right to intervene in the internal or external
affairs of another.

Article 9. The jurisdiction of states within the limits of national territory
applies to all the inhabitants.

Nationals and foreigners are under the same protection of the laws and
the national authorities and the foreigners may not claim rights other or
more extensive than those of the nationals.

Article 10. The primary interest of states is the conservation of peace.
Differences of any nature which arise between them should be settled by
recognized pacific methods.

Article 11. The contracting states definitely establish as the rule of their
conduct the precise obligation not to recognize territorial acquisitions or
special advantages which have been obtained by force, whether this consists
in the employment of arms, in threatening diplomatic representations, or in
any other effective coercive measure. The territory of a state is inviolable
and may not be the object of military occupation nor of other measures of
force imposed by another state directly or indirectly or for any motive whatever even temporarily.

The first of these quoted articles, Article 2, settles a long-standing
question: whether a federal government is responsible for the acts of its
states or provinces.

Article 8 was the most significant of all. It was a self-denial of the
right of intervention in the internal or external affairs of any other state.
It would make impossible political interventions. It was a disclaimer
for the future, in the case of the United States, of such interventions as
Cuba, Panama, the Dominican Republic, Nicaragua, Haiti, in so far as
those interventions involved more than the protection of the rights of
American citizens under international law and treaties. It was therefore
a repudiation of the "Roosevelt Corollary." In signing this treaty Secretary Hull appended a lengthy reservation, repeated by the Senate in
ratifying, by which the United States, in cases of difference of opinion or
of interpretation as to its provisions, declared that it would follow "the
law of nations as generally recognized and understood."

Article 11 resembles the "Stimson Doctrine" already adopted as a resolution of the League of Nations,[1] which doctrine is really of inter-American origin conceived in essence in 1889. It had been reaffirmed, a few months after the "Stimson Doctrine," by an important Pan-American Declaration of August 3, 1932: the nineteen neutral American republics declared to Bolivia and Paraguay, engaged in the Chaco War, that they would "not recognize any territorial arrangement of this controversy which has not been obtained by peaceful means nor the validity of territorial acquisitions which may be obtained through occupation or conquest by force of arms." Article 11 of the Rights and Duties of States was designed to implement by moral and juridical force not only this Declaration but also the outlawry of wars of aggression (undefined) by the Sixth (Havana) International Conference of American States, and the renunciation of war as an instrument of national policy by the Pact of Paris and by the Inter-American Arbitration Treaty (Washington, 1929).

At Montevideo the delegates resolved to call upon their respective governments for the speedy ratification by all of them of the multilateral peace treaties which remained unratified by many of the signatories. The United States had accepted the inter-American convention for conciliation promptly in 1929, and in 1935 it ratified the inter-American convention for arbitration. It also signed and ratified (July 6, 1934) the Saavedra-Lamas Anti-War Pact, of Argentine initiative, originally signed October 10, 1933, by the Argentine Republic, Brazil, Chile, Mexico, Paraguay, and Uruguay. The pact condemned wars of aggression and territorial acquisitions secured by armed conquest, and declared that the signatories would recognize no territorial arrangement not obtained through pacific means, nor the validity of an occupation brought about by armed force.[2] It pledged neutrals to undertake in common "the political, juridical or economic means authorized by international law"— including the machinery of commissions of conciliation but not diplomatic or armed intervention—to restore peace between parties violating the pact. It prohibited intervention. In ratifying it, the United States reserved all rights under international law and existing treaties.

Before these treaties had been ratified by all principal American republics other than the United States, a Special Inter-American Conference for the Maintenance of Peace assembled in December, 1936, at Buenos Aires, at the initiative of President Franklin D. Roosevelt, to

[1] Below, p. 343.
[2] This treaty was open to any nation which wished to adhere.

add further blocks to the Pan-American peace structure. It adopted an Additional Protocol Relative to Nonintervention which removed any reservations about rights of intervention even under international law, by stating: "The High Contracting Parties declare inadmissible the intervention of *any one* [1] of them, directly or indirectly, and for whatever reason, in the internal or external affairs of any other of the Parties." Any question concerning the interpretation of the Additional Protocol, not settled by diplomacy, was to be submitted to conciliation, arbitration, or judicial settlement.

A Convention for the Maintenance, Preservation, and Re-Establishment of Peace provided for consultation of the parties "for the purpose of finding and adopting methods of peaceful co-operation," when peace among the American republics is threatened, "or in the event of an international war outside America which might menace the peace of the American Republics,"—with the possibility of co-operation "in some action tending to preserve the peace of the American Continent." There was at least the conception here of pan-Americanizing the Monroe Doctrine. A Treaty on the Prevention of Controversies provided for a series of bilateral mixed commissions, between the various pairs of American republics, to devise ways and means of eliminating the causes of future difficulties or controversies. An Inter-American Treaty on Good Offices and Mediation provided rules for mediation between disputants by some eminent citizen of a third American republic. A Convention to Coordinate, Extend, and Assure the Fulfillment of Existing Treaties between the American States pledged the signatories "to take counsel together, with full recognition of their juridical equality, as sovereign and independent states, and of their general right to individual action, when an emergency arises which affects their common interest in the maintenance of peace." In case, despite all the peace machinery, a war should break out between or among American republics, the nonbelligerent parties pledged themselves "through consultation, immediately [to] endeavor to adopt in their character as neutrals a common and solidary attitude, in order to discourage or prevent the spread or prolongation of hostilities" —including such means as restrictions or prohibitions on the sale and shipment of arms, munitions and implements of war, loans or other financial help to the states in conflict,[2] "in accordance with the municipal

---

[1] Italics inserted.

[2] Before the assembly of this special Inter-American Peace Conference, the United States Congress had made a significant amendment to the neutrality act of August 31, 1935, which was later extended by acts of February 29, 1936, and May 1, 1937: it excepted from embargo of arms, ammunition, and loans to belligerents, those American re-

legislation of the High Contracting Parties"—but nothing in the treaty was to affect the rights and duties of parties members at the same time of the League of Nations.[1]

In addition to the treaties for the maintenance of peace, the nations signed at Buenos Aires a Convention for the Promotion of Cultural Relations, proposed by the United States. It provided for the exchange of professors and students. This is a perfection of the traditional striving of the Pan-American movement to bridge the gap between differing cultures as a help to political solidarity.

The United States ratified these treaties and the Additional Protocol without reservation, June 29, 1937.

One of the sixty-four declarations, resolutions, tributes, recommendations, and pious wishes signed at Buenos Aires was a Declaration (No. XXVII) of Principles of Inter-American Solidarity and Cooperation, to stand in the face of future wars in the Old World. Because these principles were to become the basis of collaboration in critical years to follow, we beg the reader's leave to quote the entire document as an approved definition of Pan Americanism and of continental solidarity. Note particularly the paragraph which we have italicized.

The Governments of the American Republics, having considered:
That they have a common likeness in their democratic form of government and their common ideals of peace and justice, manifested in the several Treaties and Conventions which they have signed for the purpose of constituting a purely American system tending towards the preservation of peace, the proscription of war, the harmonious development of their commerce and of their cultural aspirations in the various fields of political, economic, social, scientific, and artistic activities;

That the existence of continental interest obliges them to maintain solidarity of principles as the basis of the life of the relations of each to every other American nation;

That Pan Americanism, as a principle of American International Law, by which is understood a moral union of all of the American Republics in defence of their common interest based upon the most perfect equality and reciprocal respect for their rights of autonomy, independence and free development, requires the proclamation of principles of American International Law; and

That it is necessary to consecrate the principle of American solidarity in all non-continental conflicts, especially since those limited to the American

publics which might be at war with a non-American power, the United States being neutral. This was a sign to the world that the United States might not be as coldly neutral in such an instance as it could be toward other wars.

[1] Space is lacking to detail the other conventions and resolutions adopted at the Buenos Aires Conference.

Continent should find a peaceful solution by the means established by the Treaties and Conventions now in force or in the instruments hereafter to be executed,

The Inter-American Conference for the Maintenance of Peace

DECLARES:

1. That the American Nations, true to their republican institutions, proclaim their absolute juridical liberty, their unqualified respect for their respective sovereignties and the existence of a common democracy throughout America;

2. That every act susceptible of disturbing the peace of America affects each and every one of them, and justifies the initiation of the procedure of consultation provided for in the Convention for the Maintenance, Preservation and Reestablishment of Peace, signed at this Conference; and

3. That the following principles are accepted by the American community of Nations:

(a) Proscription of territorial conquest and that, in consequence, no acquisition made through violence shall be recognized;

(b) Intervention by one State in the internal or external affairs of another State is condemned;

(c) Forcible collection of pecuniary debts is illegal; and

(d) Any difference or dispute between the American nations, whatever its nature or origin, shall be settled by the methods of conciliation, or unrestricted arbitration, or through operation of international justice.

To be sure, this was not a treaty, but the United States, along with all the other American republics, subscribed to it in good faith as an agreed declaration of principles.

The Pan-American policy of the United States was thus brought into line with the real tendencies of Pan Americanism. It is indeed exemplary and ideal. It may not be easy to live up to in a crisis. In pledging itself against resort to war as an instrument of national policy, and against intervention in the internal or external affairs of any other state, the United States was uninfluenced by the existence of $1,188,665,400 of South American dollar bonds defaulted as to interest, out of a total of $1,564,116,860 borrowed in the United States.[1] Huge expropriations of property owned by nationals of the United States, in Mexico,[2] and in Bolivia,[3] and confiscatory taxes on property in Ecuador under the Enriquez de facto government following acceptance in Washington of the Doctrine of Nonintervention, presented denials of justice which

---

[1] See tabulations printed at end of this chapter.

One may wonder whether the debtor countries have been uninfluenced in debt policy by the self-denial ordinances to which the United States has subscribed.

[2] See above, p. 95.

[3] In 1937 a de facto government in Bolivia outrageously confiscated, on the flimsiest pretexts, property belonging to a Bolivian subsidiary owned by the Standard Oil Com-

taxed the Good Neighbor's rights and patience, but these questions have now been adjusted.

Pan Americanism in no way impeded the membership of American republics in the League of Nations and their full co-operation with it. Nor did the Pan American peace structure, or the policy of the United States under it, brace itself against peace efforts in South America by the League of Nations, or by non-American powers. After some hesitation, the United States ungrudgingly welcomed the settlement by the League of Nations of the distressing Leticia dispute between Peru and Colombia; and the League efforts to stop the Chaco War between Bolivia and Paraguay. It co-operated with the League's embargo on arms and ammunition to the Chaco belligerents by the passage of an act of Congress (May 28, 1934) empowering the President to prohibit the sale of arms and munitions to those countries. This the President promptly did.[1] Nor has the United States stood in the way of arbitrations between an American republic and a non-American state; for example, the award in 1932 by the King of Italy to France, of Clipperton Island, about 1,300 miles west of the Panama Canal, in dispute between Mexico and that European power—not wholly dissimilar in principle to the arbitration between Venezuela and Great Britain in 1896 of their boundary.

As the European situation "deteriorated"—to use a gloomily current word of the diplomats in London and Washington—the tendency of the American republics to be firm in their solidarity became more and more pronounced, with one possible exception: Argentina. Militarization of the Rhineland by Germany in March, 1936, which gave the Nazi power the lead in Europe, had introduced a note of anxiety in Pan-American relations as early as the Buenos Aires Conference. We have mentioned how the signatories to the Convention for the Maintenance of Peace agreed to consult in the event of the peace of the American republics being menaced from either inside or outside the New World. We have just quoted the Buenos Aires Declaration of December 21, 1936, of Prin-

---

pany of New Jersey and then packed the courts, and stirred up public opinion so as to deny justice to the claimants in the tribunals of the country.

In 1942 the company accepted from the Bolivian Government $1,500,000 for property valued by the claimants at $17,000,000. The petroleum formerly exploited by the company was later diverted to Argentina by means of a state-owned Argentine company.

[1] Congress, however, would not go so far as to empower the President to embargo only one belligerent, Paraguay, as the League recommended, a step resented by Latin-American nations generally. Elton Atwater has published an authoritative history of *American Regulation of Arms Export* (Carnegie Endowment for International Peace, Washington, 1941). See pp. 193-203 for the Chaco Embargo.

ciples of Inter-American Solidarity and Cooperation *vis-à-vis* all non-continental conflicts. The forcible annexation of Austria by Germany in March, 1937, was a signal to the world of the growing might of Nazi Germany; Hitler's triumph at Munich made that unquestionable. With increasing alarm the American republics looked across the Atlantic. When the Eighth Inter-American Conference of States met at Lima in December, 1938, war in Europe seemed inevitable before the passing of another twelve months, providing Great Britain and France dared to resist the next German *Machtfrage*.

The Eighth Pan-American Conference met at Lima in December, 1938, three months after Munich, with the nations of the New World deter-mined by a solidary neutral front to keep out of the approaching con-flagration. The Lima Conference was more noteworthy for statements than for treaties. There were 112 resolutions, declarations, recommen-dations, tributes, etc.—a whole bookful of whereases and desires, but not a single treaty or convention requiring further ratification at home. Number 110 was a Declaration of American Principles, eight in number, introduced by Secretary of State Cordell Hull of the United States: (1) the doctrine of absolute nonintervention, (2) peaceful settlement of all international differences, (3) proscription of the use of force, (4) rule of international law, (5) respect for treaties, (6) peaceful collaboration and intellectual interchange, (7) economic reconstruction for international welfare, and (8) international co-operation. Henceforth these were to be guiding principles of the foreign policy not only of the United States but also of all the republics of the Western Hemisphere.

The Declaration of Lima, No. 109, was more than an enumeration of idealistic principles of inter-American relations. Not itself a treaty, it presumed to "improve" the process of consultation set up in the Buenos Aires treaties of 1936. Technically it was no more binding in force than any of the 111 other declarations, but in weight of content it had more force. It reaffirmed and elaborated the Declaration of the Principles of Inter-American Solidarity of Buenos Aires of 1936, quoted above. At Lima the twenty-one republics declared that, always acting independently in their individual capacities, they would consult in meetings of their Foreign Ministers, at the initiative of any one republic, for defense of their "peace, security, or territorial integrity."

This resolution gave further support to the program of solidarity which the United States had been advocating ever since Buenos Aires: con-sultation among the assembled Foreign Ministers whenever their com-mon interests should require it. At Buenos Aires in 1936 the United

States proposed, but Argentina had succeeded in defeating, a treaty that would have set up a Permanent Inter-American Consultative Committee of Foreign Ministers, to meet and consult "whenever emergencies arise which affect their common interests." Now a step toward this was taken by the Declaration of Lima, a resolution which was called on to do the work of a treaty. It is not likely that the Declaration of Lima would have been ratified by all the states, particularly Argentina, had it been signed as a treaty. As a declaration no state has objected to it.

From Lima on, Pan-American diplomacy, after the fashion of United States diplomacy, began more and more to resort to resolutions and declarations which are at most multilateral executive agreements, but do not require ratification by the constitutional processes that characterize the treaty-making power in most of the republics: ratification by one or more branches of the legislative body. The growth, strength, prestige, and binding force of executive agreements present an interesting study not only of constitutional history in individual states like the United States but also of inter-American relations; in fact, a multilateral executive agreement was the basis of the 1942 alliance of the United Nations in the Second World War. No sooner did consultations of Foreign Ministers begin to take place, under the provisions of the Buenos Aires treaties and the Declaration of Lima, than documents emanating from them commenced to refer to the "agreements" of Buenos Aires *and* Lima. Such official language helped exalt the power of a declaration to that of an agreement. These declarations or multilateral executive agreements have been taken over without demur by governments succeeding those which made them. Thus doth current custom speedily snatch away from senates their ancient treaty-making powers. We shall see that these consultations of Foreign Ministers soon came to have the importance, and indeed the character, features, procedure, and dignity, of full International Conferences of American States, like the periodic Pan-American Conferences (I through IX) with which we have become familiar for the years 1889-1948.[1]

The First Meeting of the Foreign Ministers was at Panama, September 23 to October 3, 1939, called for by that republic immediately after the outbreak of war in Europe. At the same time occurred in

---

[1] The Carnegie Endowment of International Peace has published all the treaties, conventions, resolutions, declarations, and other expressions of Inter-American Conferences and Meetings since the first Pan-American Conference of 1889-1890 down to and including the Havana Consultation of 1940: *The International Conferences of American States, 1889-1921* (Washington, 1931), and *Ibid., First Supplement, 1933-1940* (Washington, 1940). The latter volume also contains an enumeration of special technical con-

Washington a special session of the Congress of the United States summoned by President Franklin D. Roosevelt to revise the neutrality legislation of the United States so as to remove the embargo on the shipment to belligerents, in ships not flying the flag of the United States, of arms, ammunition, and implements of warfare. The purpose of this law, of course, was to permit France and Great Britain, who controlled the seas, to get arms to defend themselves in their struggle for existence against the might of German aggression. It was the first deviation in a series of acts, to be reviewed in later chapters, that brought collapse of the neutrality of the United States by the end of 1941 under pressure of German conquests in Europe and Japanese conquests in Asia.

By impressive coincidence this First Meeting at Panama took place simultaneously with the special session of Congress that revised the neutrality laws of the United States by the Neutrality Act of 1939. The purpose of the meeting on the Isthmus was to shape the neutrality policy of the American republics in a common front, with a "unanimous intention not to become involved in the European conflict." The effort of the United States was to mold that neutrality as much as possible after the policy of the United States: increasing benevolence toward Great Britain and France. The result was the Act of Panama. It was in effect a multilateral executive agreement, consisting of resolutions, declarations, and recommendations, but using very binding language, and frequently employing the imperative auxiliary *shall*, and the not uncertain word *will*.

If an inter-American declaration can modify an inter-American treaty, then the Act of Panama released the five states (United States,[1] Bolivia, Haiti, Nicaragua, and the Dominican Republic) which had ratified the Maritime Neutrality Convention signed at Havana in 1928, from the obligation to treat armed merchant ships as ships of war, and the implied obligation to allow to submarines the same rights of hospitality in neutral waters as enjoyed by surface warships. This made it possible for all the American republics to open their ports to armed merchant ships and close them to submarines, an obvious advantage to Great Britain and France over the situation which had prevailed at the outbreak of the war. President Roosevelt promptly put this into effect for the United States (November 4, 1939).

A Declaration of Panama, already almost forgotten, proclaimed as a

ferences, with synopses of their proceedings, and bibliography, and a list, with synopses, of permanent inter-American commissions and other bodies.

[1] The United States was not bound by the article on armed merchant ships, because it had attached a reservation to that when ratifying the treaty in 1932.

"measure of continental self-protection" a neutrality belt for several hundred miles out to sea from the shores of the neutral American republics and forbade any hostile act therein by any non-American belligerent nation. But the belligerents paid no more attention to the neutrality belt than the tides of the sea did to the commands of King Canute not to rise on his shores. This so-called Declaration of Panama remains only an interesting specimen in the historical museum of neutrality, armed or unarmed. More important still was another declaration of continental solidarity, and a joint suggestion for a second meeting of Foreign Ministers at Havana, October 1, 1940, or earlier, and the creation—by resolutions—for the duration of the war of an Inter-American Neutrality Committee of seven experts in international law, and an Inter-American Financial and Economic Advisory Committee.

The outstanding achievement of the Panama Meeting was a Resolution on the Transfer of Sovereignty of Geographic Regions of the Americas Held by Non-American States. We have seen that at Buenos Aires the American republics in effect had pan-Americanized one part of the Monroe Doctrine by the arrangements for consultation for common defense in case the peace of the Americas should be threatened from either inside *or outside* the New World. The resolution on the transfer of sovereignty pan-Americanized the remainder of the Doctrine, namely the Non-Transfer Principle, a principle older than the Monroe Doctrine, and generally regarded as an integral part of it since 1870.[1] Said this Declaration of Panama: "In case any geographic region of America subject to the jurisdiction of a non-American state should be obliged to change its sovereignty and there should result therefrom a danger to the security of the American continent, a consultative meeting such as the one now being held will be convoked with the urgency that the case may require."[2] This is a hemispheric landmark in the history of the Monroe Doctrine and of the foreign policy of the United States. Congress reaffirmed the principle, in a joint resolution of June 18, 1940, when the German occupation of Denmark, Norway, the Low Countries, and France made the danger seem very real:

(1) That the United States would not recognize any transfer, and would not acquiesce in any attempt to transfer, any geographic region of this

[1] Dexter Perkins, *The Monroe Doctrine, 1867-1907* (Johns Hopkins Press, 1937), pp. 1-64.

[2] At the instance of Argentina, who claimed the Falkland Islands, occupied by Great Britain since 1832, an article was added: "It is understood that this resolution shall not apply to a change of status resulting from the settlement of questions now pending between non-American states and states of the Continent."

hemisphere from one non-American power to another non-American power; and

(2) That if such transfer or attempt to transfer should appear likely, the United States shall in addition to other measures, immediately consult with the other American republics to determine upon the steps which should be taken to safeguard their common interests.

The German conquests of European colonial powers with holdings in the New World hastened the assembly of the Second Meeting of Foreign Ministers that had been scheduled for October, 1940. It met at Havana in July. Again the American republics confirmed the "non-transfer" principle of the Monroe Doctrine. In the first place they signed a resolution which declared that whoever committed an act of aggression against one of them committed an act of aggression against all of them, in which case they would consult again at the request of any one party to negotiate measures of common defense. In the second place, they signed a declaration, the Act of Havana, which declared that if necessary they would step in and take over any colonial possession of a non-American power in the New World which might be threatened by a non-American power. They also signed a convention settling details.

The Act of Havana provided for an emergency committee, composed of one representative of each American republic, to administer the territories thus taken over, for the twofold purpose of contributing to the security and defense of the Continent, and to the economic, political, and social progress of such regions, until the reasons requiring the provisional administration should cease to exist. Then the territories should be either organized as autonomous states under the principle of self-determination, or restored to their previous status, "whichever of these alternatives should appear to be the more practicable and just." The convention was to go into effect as soon as ratified by two thirds of the signatories, that is, fourteen states. Fourteen states ratified by January 8, 1942.[1] The Act further stated that in case of urgent emergency, any one or more of the signatories might act first and consult later,

[1] The first fourteen states to ratify were, in this order: United States, Dominican Republic, Costa Rica, Brazil, Peru, Panama, El Salvador, Haiti, Guatemala, Argentina, Venezuela, Colombia, Ecuador, Honduras. The Havana Convention was one of seven Pan-American treaties and conventions, out of ninety, which Argentina had ratified to January 1, 1949. Like the Non-Transfer Declaration, of Panama, it contained a paragraph excluding application to territories or possessions which are subject of dispute or claims between European powers and one or more of the Republics of the Americas. In ratifying the treaty Argentina attached a reservation stating its understanding that the Malvinas (Falkland) Islands were a part of Argentine territory "as was stated at the Panama meeting . . . and also with reference to other southern Argentine regions." Perhaps it is not too cynical to suppose that Argentina ratified the treaty with this

either before or after the treaty went into effect. This last provision was really a Pan-American mandate to the United States by itself alone to enforce the Non-Transfer Principle if urgently necessary. It was a striking act of confidence in the Good Neighbor Policy of the United States and in the Monroe Doctrine, pruned since 1930 of the Corollary of Theodore Roosevelt.

The climax of the Pan-American movement, and with it the great test of the reformed Latin-American policy of the United States, came with Japan's attack without warning upon the Hawaiian Islands and the Philippines, December 7, 1941, and the subsequent declarations of war on the United States by Japan, Germany, Italy, et alii. Immediately the United States, and several of the other American republics, called for a consultation of the Foreign Ministers, which took place at Rio de Janeiro, January 15-28, 1942, to determine what should be done now that an act of aggression had been committed against all the republics by an attack on one of them.

Before the Foreign Ministers assembled in the capital of Brazil for their third consultation, Cuba, Haiti, the Dominican Republic, Panama, Costa Rica, Nicaragua, Honduras, El Salvador, and Guatemala had already declared war on Japan, Germany, and Italy. Mexico, Colombia, and Venezuela had severed diplomatic relations with those three powers. As a result of the consultation five Latin-American republics—Brazil, Ecuador, Paraguay, Peru, Uruguay—broke off diplomatic relations with the Axis powers. In June, 1942, Mexico declared war. Only two Latin-American countries, Argentina and Chile, resisted the general desire, and even those two states [1] joined in a general resolution of the Foreign Ministers "recommending" the break by all, and signed the other significant resolutions and recommendations for the co-operation of all the republics in measures for common defense. These called for severance of economic and financial as well as diplomatic relations with the enemies of the United States; general economic mobilization for war and post-war purposes, including establishment of an international stabilization fund for currencies; hemispheric purging of Axis spies, saboteurs and

reservation, fancying that it gave some sort of Pan-American support to her century-old claim against Great Britain.

The six other Pan-American treaties ratified by Argentina are: the Argentine Anti-War Pact of 1933 (not at first a Pan-American treaty), two postal conventions, two sanitary conventions and a naturalization treaty. See the semiannual tabulations by the Pan-American Union of the *Status of Treaties and Conventions Signed at the International Conferences of American States and Other Pan-American Conferences.*

[1] They refused to recognize the American republics at war as belligerents.

fifth-columnists, and co-ordination of censorship; and unification of defense measures to be pointed up in a projected meeting immediately at
Washington of military and naval technicians representing the twenty-
one republics.[1] Straightway the United States concluded a series of
bilateral lend-lease agreements with the American republics, those who
had declared war and those who had broken off relations, opening to
them such supplies as could be afforded, and delivered, from the Arsenal
of Democracy. In short, the Rio Meeting made plans for a nonshooting
war against the Axis powers by the Latin-American states, belligerent
or nonbelligerent, with the United States in effect the dynamic co-
ordinator and economic and military supporter of all. Final success of
the Good Neighbor Policy, in principle as well as in practice, was testified by a Rio resolution extolling it as a "norm of American international
law."

Facing the heaviest threats of all their independent history, the American republics and their peoples huddled together instinctively under
the military wings of the Good Neighbor of the North. They made
exclusively available to the United Nations vitally important war
materials. They afforded to the United States highly important and useful temporary [2] naval and air bases for controlling strategic coastal
waters. This made possible a "corridor of victory" for the flight across
the South Atlantic of American men and arms to the African, European,
and Asiatic fronts. In return the fighting Republic made available to
the Latin-American belligerents and allies (all except recalcitrant Argentina) a golden flood of $500,000,000 ($10,000,000 of which was
distributed *after hostilities were over*) in lend-lease for military equipment and economic support of the war,[3] not to mention gigantic purchases
($2,500,000,000) of raw materials for war purposes, and $431,116,968
(net) loans by the United States Government, 1940-1947, after defaults
by Latin-American governments (excepting Argentina) on external
dollar bonds had dried up their private credit abroad.[4] In addition the

[1] The first meeting of the Inter-American Defense Board convened in Washington,
March 30, 1942.
[2] All bases were returned to their respective sovereigns after the war. In the case
of Ecuador the United States tried to purchase continuing rights to bases in the
Galapagos Islands. Failing to do so, it returned both the Galapagos base and the
Salinas base on the mainland under arrangements permitting United States troops to
remain there for the purpose of training Ecuadoreans in the use of the installations.
[3] See tabulations in *Twenty-Fifth Report to Congress on Lend-Lease Operations*
(Department of State Publication 3064, Washington, 1948).
[4] See Charts of Status of External Dollar Bonds of Latin-American Governments,
and of United States Government Credits to Latin-American Governments, at end of
this chapter.

United States Government contributed as actual gifts a total of nearly $80,000,000 to all and sundry republics of Latin America.[1]

Before the war ended all of the nations of the New World (including even unfriendly Argentina at the last moment) declared war on the enemies of the United States.[2] Brazil, in addition to extensive naval patrols, sent a division of troops to the Mediterranean; they engaged in heroic combat on the Italian front, and captured an entire German division. Before the Pacific war was over Mexico sent an air squadron to the Far East. Mexican and Cuban navies helped to clear the Gulf of Mexico of German submarines.

Argentina, ruled by a military dictatorship aping those of Europe, held aloof until the fag end of the war, hoping for and expecting a victory of the Axis powers. Only when the jig was manifestly up for Hitler's Germany did the Argentine Government scramble to get in on good neighborhood in the Western Hemisphere, begrudging even then the military and moral ascendancy of the United States, a nation "alien" to Latin-American culture and politics. The Argentine Government safely if unheroically declared war on Germany and Japan (March 27, 1945). Even then her Government furnished aid and comfort to the enemy.[3] Argentina was allowed to sign (April 4, 1945) the Act of Chapultepec, already signed by the other American republics in Mexico City, March 3, 1945, a declaration (not a treaty needing ratification)[4] for temporary alliance during the remaining days of the war.

At San Francisco, on June 26, 1945, all the American republics became charter members of the United Nations Organization.

It remained to forge inter-American solidarity of war into a pact for future defense of the Western Hemisphere: one for all and all for one. Acting under Article 51 of the United Nations Charter,[5] nineteen of the

[1] Foreign Assets and Liabilities of the United States, Committee Print for Committee on Finance, House of Representatives, 80th Cong., 1st Sess. (Washington, 1948), p. 36.

[2] The Memoirs of Cordell Hull (2 vols., New York, 1948), II, pp. 1377-1409, describe American diplomacy with Argentina, "The Bad Neighbor."

[3] As established in the United States "bluebook" issued on the eve of the Argentine national election in February, 1946: Consultation among the American Republics with Respect to the Argentine Situation (Department of State Publication No. 2473, Washington, 1946).

[4] Argentina had not ratified any of the inter-American treaties for inter-American peace and solidarity, except the Saavedra-Lamas Anti-War Pact of 1933.

[5] "Nothing in the present Charter shall impair the inherent right of individual or collective self-defense if an armed attack occurs against a Member of the United Nations, until the Security Council has taken the measures necessary to maintain international peace and security. . . ."

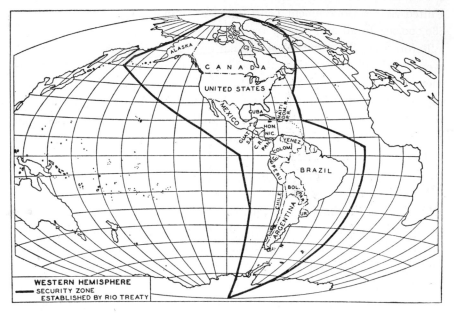

Map 7.   Regional Security Zone of Western Hemisphere as Defined by Treaty of
Rio de Janeiro, 1947 [1]

American republics (all except Nicaragua [2] and Ecuador) met in a
special Inter-American Conference for the Maintenance of Continental
Peace and Security, and concluded an Inter-American Treaty of Reciprocal Assistance—the Pact of Rio—signed at the Brazilian capital
September 2, 1947 (effective December 3, 1948, following required
ratification by two thirds of the signatories).   The essential articles of
this epoch-making alliance are the first and second:

1. The High Contracting Parties agree that an armed attack by any state
against an American State shall be construed as an armed attack against all
the American States, and consequently, each one of the said Contracting
Parties undertakes to assist in meeting the attack in the exercise of the inherent right of individual or collective self-defense recognized by Article 51
of the Charter of the United Nations.

2. On the request of the State or States directly attacked and until the
decision of the Organ of Consultation of the Inter-American System, each
one of the Contracting Parties may determine the immediate measures which
it may individually adopt in fulfilment of the obligation contained in the
preceding paragraph and in accordance with the principle of continental

[1] Reproduced from *Major Problems of United States Foreign Policy, 1949-1950*, p. 263,
with permission of Brookings Institution.
[2] Nicaragua later signed and ratified the treaty.

solidarity. The Organ of Consultation [1] shall meet without delay for the purpose of examining those measures and agreeing upon the measures of a collective character that should be adopted.

Thus the treaty left it to each of the signatories to determine what measures it would adopt pending decision as to future joint measures by a two-thirds majority of the Members of the Pact. No more could one state, like Argentina, paralyze joint and solid action by holding out against the wishes of the majority.

How about another equally great danger not constituting immediate armed attack by another state: such as a communist revolution, like those which had occurred in Greece and China after the Second World War, inspired and abetted by an outside power? In that case the parties agree to meet immediately in special consultation and decide what to do.

The Pact of Rio of 1947 became a prototype for the North Atlantic Alliance of 1949.[2]

The most recent efforts in inter-American organization for peace and solidarity in the World of Columbus that this volume can record, were the treaties signed at the Ninth International Conference of American States at Bogotá in 1948 under tragic circumstances (an attempted revolution in the capital of Colombia that caused considerable loss of life and great damage to the city).

First was a Charter for the Organization of American States, placing Pan Americanism at last on a treaty basis, within the framework of the United Nations.[3] Under the Charter the old Pan American Union at Washington is the central and permanent organ and general secretariat of the Organization. Its governing Council consists of a representative from each one of the member republics, who does not need to be the diplomatic representative of that government to the United States. The Director of the Union [4] becomes Secretary General of the Organization, elected by the Council for a ten-year term, not re-eligible or to be succeeded by a person of the same nationality. The Charter specifies the nature and purposes of the Inter-American Organization; its

[1] I.e., a special meeting of the Foreign Ministers of the American Republics, to be called by the Pan American Union at the request of any one of the American Republics.

[2] See below, p. 455.

[3] M. Margaret Ball in a scholarly dissertation analyzed *The Problem of Inter-American Organization* as it had developed up to 1944 (Stanford University Press, 1944). Manuel S. Canyes has described the relationship of the Charter of the Organization of American States to that of the United Nations (Pan American Union, Washington, 1949).

[4] Mr. Alberto Lleras of Colombia was elected March 11, 1947, by the Governing Council of the Union, for a term of ten years, to succeed Dr. Leo S. Rowe, deceased.

ORGANIZATION OF AMERICAN STATES

The International Organization of the 21 American Republics established by the Charter
signed at the Ninth International Conference of American States , Bogotá, Colombia,1948.

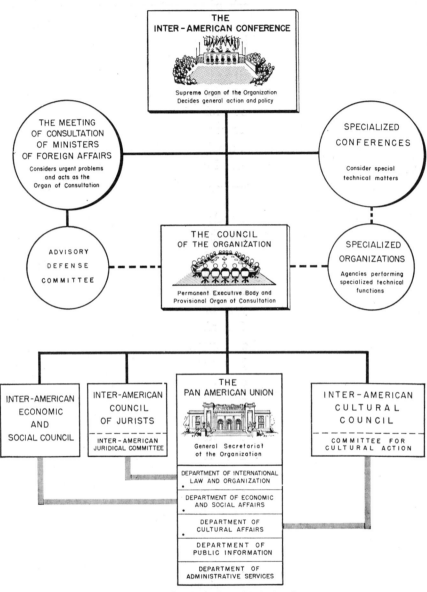

Courtesy of Mr. Alberto Lleras, Secretary General

principles; the fundamental rights and duties of states; the duty of pacific settlement of international disputes; inter-American solidarity and collective security; economic, social, and cultural standards; elaborates on the organs and departments of the Organization and the Pan American Union (see accompanying chart); and provides rules for quinquennial meetings of the Inter-American Conferences as the "supreme organ" of the Organization. Article XL of the resolution known as the Final Act of Bogotá provided that, pending ratification of the Charter by two thirds of the signatories, the old organs of the Union of American Republics (popularly known as the Pan American Union) should immediately adopt the nomenclature and provisions of the Charter, and that the new organs of the Charter should be established on a provisional basis. All this promptly took place in Washington.

Keystone of the Charter was Chapter V on Collective Security, with its two articles 24 and 25, extending the pledges of the Pact of Rio de Janeiro of 1947 to cover not only "armed attack" but also "every act of aggression" or "any other fact or situation that might endanger the peace of America." [1] Incorporated in the treaty was Article 15 denying the right of intervention not only to any *one* State, as previously denied in 1933 and 1936, but to any *group* of States for any reason whatever.[2] But Article 19 still allowed group intervention to maintain measures of peace and security in accordance with existing treaties.[3]

A second treaty brought together into one code all the complicated peace machinery of former inter-American treaties of arbitration, conciliation, and judicial settlement of international disputes.

[1] Article 24: "Every act of aggression by a State against the territorial integrity or the inviolability of the territory or against the sovereignty or political independence of an American State shall be considered an act of aggression against the other American States."

Article 25: "If the inviolability or the integrity of the territory or the sovereignty or political independence of any American State should be affected by an armed attack or by an act of aggression that is not an armed attack, or by an extra-continental conflict, or by a conflict between two or more American States, or by any other fact or situation that might endanger the peace of America, the American States, in furtherance of the principles of continental solidarity or collective self-defense, shall apply the measures and procedures established in the special treaties on the subject."

[2] Article 15: "No State or group of States has the right to intervene, directly or indirectly, for any reason whatever, in the internal or external affairs of any other State. The foregoing principle prohibits not only armed force but also any other form of interference or attempted threat against the personality of the State or against its political, economic and cultural elements."

[3] Article 19: "Measures adopted for the maintenance of peace and security in accordance with existing treaties do not constitute a violation of the principles set forth in articles 15 and 17."

Article 17 stipulates that the territory of a State is "inviolable."

A third lengthy treaty stipulated, within the framework of the United Nations Charter, principles of economic co-operation for the well-being of all the American republics.

There were also two conventions on the rights of women, political and civil.[1]

These treaties, epoch-making for the inter-American regional movement, adjusted to the United Nations, await (1950) ratification by two thirds of the signatories, to enter into effect.

Nothing was more hopeful, in disheartening post-Potsdam years of disillusion and world crisis, than the peaceful structure of inter-American organization and solidarity based on equal sovereignty, juridical equality, nonintervention, territorial inviolability, co-operation for the general welfare, peaceful settlement of inter-American disputes, and consultation for common defense on the agreed premise that an attack on one is an attack on all.

[1] The United States did not sign the last-named convention on civil rights for women, that subject not being constitutionally a power of the Federal Government.

Country	National Governments		States, Provinces, Depts.		Municipalities		Government Guaranteed Corporate Issues [2]		Totals		
	Outstanding	In Default as to Interest	Outstanding	In Default as to Interest	Outstanding	In Default as to Interest	Outstanding	In Default as to Interest	Outstanding	In Default as to Interest [5]	Default as to Sinking Fund Only
Argentina	250,904,500	....	87,424,900	81,725,900	22,960,000	10,329,500	....	....	361,289,400	92,055,400	4,222,500
Bolivia	59,422,000	59,422,000	....	....	....	....	....	....	59,422,000	59,422,000	....
Brazil	144,672,500 [3]	144,672,500	142,558,800	119,296,800	66,944,000	66,944,000	....	....	354,175,300	330,913,300	23,262,000
Chile	175,404,000	175,404,000	....	....	20,459,500	20,459,500	68,745,000	68,745,000	264,608,500	264,608,500	....
Colombia	51,223,500	51,223,500	59,989,500	59,989,500	22,145,900	22,145,900	10,296,500	10,296,500	143,655,400	143,655,400	....
Costa Rica	8,781,000 [3]	8,781,000	....	....	....	....	....	....	8,781,000	8,781,000	....
Cuba	91,878,100	40,000,000	....	....	....	....	....	....	91,878,100	40,000,000	51,878,100
Dominican Republic	16,292,000	....	....	....	....	....	....	....	16,292,000	....	16,292,500 [4]
El Salvador	12,619,300	12,619,300	....	....	....	....	....	....	12,619,300	12,619,300	....
Guatemala	2,214,000	2,214,000	....	....	....	....	....	....	2,214,000	2,214,000	....
Haiti	10,511,360	....	....	....	....	....	....	....	10,511,360	....	....
Mexico	62,037,500	62,037,500	3,252,000	3,252,000	....	....	....	....	65,289,500	65,289,500	....
Panama	15,214,000	11,356,000	....	....	416,000	....	3,097,500	3,097,500	18,727,500	14,453,500	416,000
Peru	87,210,000	87,210,000	1,189,000	1,189,000	2,887,000	2,887,000	....	....	91,286,000	91,286,000	....
Uruguay	52,947,500	52,947,500	....	....	10,420,000	10,420,000	....	....	63,367,500	63,367,500	....
TOTAL	$1,041,331,260	707,887,300	294,414,200	265,453,200	146,232,400	133,185,900	82,139,000	82,139,000	1,564,116,860	1,188,665,400	96,071,100

[1] "Latin-American Dollar Debts," *Commercial Pan America*, No. 37 (Pan-American Union, January, 1935).
[2] Includes only direct guarantees.
[3] Exclusive of bonds issued to fund interest.
[4] The Dominican Republic has made a proposal to bondholders concerning readjustment of the sinking fund which has been approved by the Foreign Bondholders Protective Council, Inc.
[5] Includes defaults in interest and in interest and sinking fund.

STATUS OF SERVICE (INTEREST, SINKING FUND, AND PRINCIPAL) ON LATIN-AMERICAN DOLLAR BONDS (PUBLICLY OFFERED) ISSUED OR GUARANTEED BY GOVERNMENTS OR POLITICAL SUBDIVISIONS THEREOF, AS OF DECEMBER 31, 1949.

Country	Issued	Outstanding	Receiving Full Service Int. and S.F.	Adjusted Service Available	In Default as to Int. and S.F.	In Default as to Principal	Maturities Extended
Argentina............	Retired	....	....	....	....	....	....
Bolivia.............	68,400,000	59,422,000	....	....	59,422,000	23,368,000 b	....
Brazil..............	391,013,145	162,252,455	....	162,252,455	....	3,457,800 b	28,667,550
Chile...............	296,592,000	119,547,000	....	119,547,000	....	645,000 b	11,958,000 c
Colombia............	169,289,960	78,480,400 a	....	78,480,400	....	14,292,800 b	14,457,300 c
Costa Rica...........	11,853,668	8,103,951	....	....	8,103,951	1,589,000	....
Cuba................	93,506,100	74,219,700	5,443,900	68,468,800	307,000 d	307,000 d	39,910,000 c
Dominican Republic...	Retired	....	....	....	....	....	....
Ecuador.............	14,437,800	12,262,700	....	....	12,262,700	12,262,700	....
El Salvador..........	18,515,400	7,463,800	....	7,463,800	....	241,500 b	1,262,000
Guatemala...........	1,749,000	478,000	478,000	....	....	....	....
Haiti...............	Retired	....	....	....	....	....	....
Mexico..............	381,782,429 e	240,199,716 e	....	24,358,746	215,840,970	60,188,609	....
Panama..............	16,941,600	15,099,350	3,789,850	11,309,500	....	....	....
Peru................	95,079,600	71,428,100	....	68,541,100	2,887,000	386,500 b	640,500
Uruguay.............	67,757,000	44,480,300	....	44,480,300	....	242,000 b	4,847,500
TOTAL...............	1,626,917,702	893,437,472	9,711,750	584,902,101	298,823,621	116,980,909	101,742,850

This table includes outstanding funding bonds, but excludes outstanding convertible scrip.

a Includes $3,456,000 principal amount, equivalent to 75 per cent (less unconverted scrip) of the old nonguaranteed corporate bank bonds of Colombia which have been exchanged for a National issue in accordance with the June 25, 1942, debt plan, without adjustment for retirements.

b In these countries debt plans are currently in effect, and bonds in default as to principal may have their maturities extended, if assented to the plans.

c In these cases it has not been possible, from the data available, to exclude those new bonds which were issued in exchange for formerly matured bonds in default as to principal, and which have been retired in accordance with the terms of the exchange plan, since they have been included along with a number of other issues exchanged for a single new issue of bonds; hence the acceptances to a particular debt plan without adjustments for retirements have been used.

d The Exchange Agent reports that $217,000 of these bonds have been exchanged (in Havana, Cuba) since the close of the debt plan of 1937 on June 30, 1941; these bonds are shown as uncanceled and outstanding on the records of the New York Fiscal Agent.

e Includes railways expropriated in 1937.

Source: Foreign Bondholders Protective Council, Inc. Report 1946 through 1949.

314

LATIN-AMERICAN REPUBLICS, JULY 1, 1940, THROUGH JUNE 30, 1947

(EIB = Export-Import Bank. RFC = Reconstruction Finance Corporation. ODS = Office Defense Supplies. State = Department of State. Treas. = Treasury Department.)

	Commitments				Utilizations			Collections		Outstanding
	Gross	Cancellations and expirations	Net	Unutilized	Total	Direct	By export banks	Principal	Interest and commissions	
American Republics	1,085,411,260	409,222,418	676,188,842	245,071,874	431,116,968	247,234,08-	183,882,881	183,039,948	27,186,149	248,077,020
EIB	1,082,100,160	408,758,735	673,341,425	245,071,874	428,269,551	244,386,670	183,882,881	181,387,605	27,168,722	246,881,946
ODS	924,627	463,683	460,944		460,944	460,944		377,242	17,427	83,702
USCC	2,138,441		2,138,441		2,138,441	2,138,441		1,071,134		1,067,307
State	248,032		248,032		248,032	248,032		203,967		44,065
Argentina (EIB)	93,690,000	93,090,000	600,000	210,000	390,000	390,000		390,000	28,376	
Bolivia	23,080,643	48,250	23,032,393	9,935,000	13,097,393	13,097,393		3,499,577	201,116	9,597,816
EIB	20,678,004	48,250	20,629,754	9,935,000	10,694,754	10,694,754		2,129,754	201,116	8,565,000
ODS	300,000		300,000		300,000	300,000		300,000		
USCC	2,102,639		2,102,639		2,102,639	2,102,639		1,069,823		1,032,816
Brazil	270,463,827	86,663,717	183,800,110	47,615,705	136,184,405	70,767,328	65,417,077	46,516,503	7,484,890	89,667,902
EIB	270,433,215	86,663,717	183,769,498	47,615,705	136,153,793	70,736,716	65,417,077	46,516,503	7,484,890	89,637,290
USCC	30,612		30,612		30,612	30,612				30,612
Chile (EIB)	89,756,008	6,991,378	82,764,630	47,538,294	35,226,336	7,525,228	27,701,108	17,061,865	2,021,825	18,164,471
Colombia (EIB)	50,243,456	907,154	49,336,302	14,864,714	34,471,588	10,947,974	23,523,614	15,459,320	2,462,611	19,012,268
Costa Rica (EIB)	8,723,000	1,463,393	7,259,607		7,259,607	7,035,878	223,729	456,632	1,178,482	6,802,975
Cuba (EIB)	90,366,535	26,888,062	63,478,473	7,310,000	56,168,473	30,130,973	26,037,500	43,947,348	1,044,467	12,221,125
Dominican Republic (EIB)	3,300,000	16,068	3,283,932		3,283,932	3,000,000	283,932	1,653,879	447,013	1,630,053
Ecuador	18,194,817	559,513	17,635,304	10,230,000	7,405,304	7,405,304		1,011,645	776,348	6,393,659
EIB	17,565,000	95,830	17,469,170	10,230,000	7,239,170	7,239,170		933,092	742,921	6,306,078
ODS	624,627	463,683	160,944		160,944	160,944		77,242	17,427	83,702
USCC	5,190		5,190		5,190	5,190		1,311		3,879
Haiti (EIB)	13,350,000	2,670,000	10,680,000		10,680,000	10,680,000		3,440,000	1,985,050	7,240,000
Honduras (EIB)	2,700,000	1,700,000	1,000,000		1,000,000	1,000,000	1,000,000	422,750	50,320	577,250
Mexico	154,287,315	5,993,309	148,294,006	79,701,623	68,592,383	48,714,046	19,878,337	14,392,105	2,468,919	54,200,278
EIB	154,069,446	5,993,309	148,076,137	79,701,623	68,374,514	48,496,177	19,878,337	14,205,117	2,468,919	54,169,397
State	217,869		217,869		217,869	217,869		186,988		30,881
Nicaragua (EIB)	5,235,000	585,000	4,650,000		4,650,000	4,000,000	650,000	2,360,500	701,857	2,289,500
Panama (EIB)	4,500,000	2,012,296	2,487,704		2,487,704	2,287,704	200,000	2,487,704	207,791	
Paraguay (EIB)	7,800,000	1,600,000	6,200,000		6,200,000	6,000,000	200,000	1,298,550	926,380	4,901,450
Peru (EIB)	37,450,000	37,000,000	450,000	73,494	376,506	376,506		28,238	7,231	348,268
Salvador (EIB)	1,726,000	250,000	1,476,000		1,476,000	1,476,000		218,628	167,285	1,257,372
Uruguay	43,615,163	29,211,125	14,404,038	2,593,044	11,810,994	11,810,994		227,726	702,258	11,583,268
EIB	43,585,000	29,211,125	14,373,875	2,593,044	11,780,831	11,780,831		210,747	702,258	11,570,084
State	30,163		30,163		30,163	30,163		16,979		13,184
Venezuela (EIB)	42,551,000	36,806,922	5,744,078		5,744,078	3,045,900	2,698,178	3,715,578	581,236	2,028,500
Unclassified (EIB)	124,378,496	74,766,231	49,612,265	25,000,000	24,612,265	20,044,815	4,567,450	24,451,400	3,757,794	160,865

From *Foreign Assets and Liabilities of the United States and Its Balance of International Transactions, A Report to the Senate Committee on Finance by the National Advisory Council on International Monetary and Financial Problems*, December 18, 1947. Printed for use of the Senate Committee (Washington, G.P.O., 1948), p. 20.
(Corrected to $1,000,000 for obvious misprint in case of Honduras, column 7, to make column balance.)

15

Canada, the Coupling Pin of
Anglo-American Relations

STRICTLY speaking, the Dominion of Canada is not a republic like the other American nations. It is a democratic kingdom which has the same king, today George VI, as Great Britain, Australia, New Zealand, and South Africa, and is an independent member of the British Commonwealth of Nations. But by history, culture, religion, economy, and general ways of life, it has been more closely associated with the United States than with any other foreign nation. So unrestricted and so natural have been the freedom of movement and interplay of populations,[1] that Canadians and Americans do not think of themselves as foreign to each other; rather in their neighborliness and consanguinity they consider themselves independent of each other.

The United States has always scrupulously respected Canada's independence. At various periods in North American history, always coinciding with economic depressions, there has developed a strong—but progressively weaker—minority in Canada which has desired annexation or at least commercial union with the United States. And before the First World War there was always an influential minority in the United States —surviving apostles of Manifest Destiny—who had been prophets and advocates of the peaceful and mutually voluntary union of the two countries. In this minority were included such men as William Henry Seward, Charles Sumner, Hamilton Fish, Ulysses S. Grant, Henry Cabot Lodge, Theodore Roosevelt. Even so, it is doubtful whether at any time an appeal by Canada for annexation would have been accepted by a majority of the United States Congress. Certainly not before the Civil War, because the Southern states feared being overwhelmed by antislavery territory; they wanted Cuba instead, where, reciprocally, they were opposed by the Northern states who feared the growing power of slavery. Remember that in 1866 when the United States had a million

[1] See the late Marcus Lee Hansen's *The Mingling of the Canadian and American Peoples* (Canadian-American Series, Carnegie Endowment for International Peace, Yale University Press, 1940).

veteran bayonets and a first-class navy, no step toward Canada was made; on the contrary, the army and navy were demobilized.

President Grant and Secretary Fish hoped that Canada, deprived of reciprocity after 1866, would seek and secure independence, and afterward seek and secure annexation. British statesmanship by the North American Act of 1867, creating the self-governing Dominion within the then British Empire, contented Canada just as British statesmanship in 1774, by the Quebec Act, had kept Canada out of the American Revolution. Recurring periods of prosperity lifted Canada's economic head above water handsomely, assisted from time to time by imperial commercial preferences.[1] As time went on, both nations became addicted to high protective tariffs. the United States under the long reign of the Republican Party; Canada under the continuing control of the Liberal Party. By 1910 high tariffs and other forces of domestic discontent in both countries threatened the parties in power. President Taft turned to Canadian reciprocity—in the form of an executive agreement to be made good by agreed legislation in both countries—as a means of offsetting tariff reform sentiment in the United States and propitiating the press (by duty-free newsprint paper) in favor of himself and his party. Prime Minister Sir Wilfrid Laurier accepted it as a means of restoring personal and party prestige by getting free entry into the United States for Canada's chief exports. Imprudent political bombast in both countries camouflaged reciprocity with the issue, the bogey, of annexation: reciprocity would be a step toward ultimate organic union. The issue ruined both the Republicans in the United States and the Liberals in Canada. After 1911 Canada became a confirmed protectionist nation.[2]

So strong have been the forces of tariff protection in the United States and the jealousy of sections, that it is extremely doubtful whether any enthusiastic minority, even since the Civil War, could have got a treaty of annexation through the Senate, had Great Britain been willing to negotiate one; or a joint resolution through Congress, if the Canadian Parliament had voted annexation on its part. Since the First World War annexation has had no political following in Canada. The Canadians do not want it. Neither do their neighbors to the south.

Canada established a legation at Washington in 1927, setting up direct

---

[1] Donald Frederick Warner, "The Movement for the Annexation of Canada to the United States, 1849-1893" (unprinted doctoral dissertation, 1940, Yale University Library).

[2] L. Ethan Ellis, *Reciprocity, 1911: a Study in Canadian-American Relations* (Canadian-American Series, Carnegie Endowment for International Peace, Yale University Press, 1939).

diplomatic relations independent of Great Britain.[1]   As such she continued the historic role which she had played as a part of the British
Empire.   As a member of the British Commonwealth of Nations (confirmed by the Statute of Westminster, 1931) she has continued her work
for peace between the United States and Great Britain, as illustrated by
the last hundred years of Anglo-American relations.

During the nineteenth century the British navy was the greatest power
in international politics, in both the Old World and the New.   It not
only carried an army of invasion to Washington and New Orleans in
1814; it also stood in the way of any conceivable intervention of Europe
to restore Spain's sovereignty over her revolted colonies in 1823.   But it
was not principally the British navy that preserved the independence
and territorial integrity of the Latin-American states in that really happy
century of British maritime power.   Remember the interventions in
Argentina and Uruguay, and in Central America; remember also that the
British navy helped at least to escort Napoleon III's army to Mexico,
and did nothing to stop French intervention in that republic or Spanish
intervention in Santo Domingo, in 1861-1865.   If any nations, other than
the Latin-American states themselves, can be credited with preserving
the republican liberties of the New World, certainly in North America
since 1823, and later in South America too, they are the United States and
Canada: the United States because of the Monroe Doctrine and in our
times the Good Neighbor Policy; Canada because she has always been in
effect a hostage for the benevolent conduct of the British navy toward
the United States and the Monroe Doctrine.

At no time during the nineteenth century could the United States have
withstood a challenge of the British navy on the seas; but at no time
since, say 1850, certainly since 1866, could Great Britain have defended
Canada against an overland movement by the United States on the long
exposed flank of her Empire.   Great Britain was cautious about forcing
mediation during the Civil War of 1861-1865, because of the military
strength of the United States and the consequent danger to Canada in
case of war.   War between the United States and Great Britain at any
time since 1866 not only would have been genuinely "unthinkable," but
also would have meant the loss of Canada to the Empire, either by conquest or by secession.   Canada's successful pressure on British foreign

---

[1] Other former parts of the British Empire to set up independent legations or
embassies at Washington were: Irish Free State, 1924; Union of South Africa, 1929;
Australia, 1940; New Zealand, 1943; India, 1946; Pakistan, 1947; Burma, 1947;
Ceylon, 1948.

policy on the eve of the Washington Conference to abandon the Anglo-Japanese Alliance, to choose the United States instead of Japan as a friend, shows how she read her own vital interests in that crisis.[1]

Canada has always been instinctively conscious of this position of hostage for the good conduct of Great Britain toward the United States. She has been aware of her terrible alternatives in case of any Anglo-American conflict. If only for this reason—among many other pleasanter ones—she has become the natural link of friendship, geographically, politically, economically, and culturally, between the two great English-speaking powers.[2] No nation has ever had a more pacific, a more praise-worthy, or a more easily successful role. Let it be understood in speaking of the historic role of Canada as the linchpin, or coupling pin, of Anglo-American amity, that the Great Dominion under the control of any other imperialistic power of the Old World, say Germany or Russia, would have been not a shield of peace but rather a base for the invasion of the Continental Republic.

The Monroe Doctrine has always applied to Canada in spirit if not in word. Even in word it has covered Canada through the Non-Transfer principle. From the very nature of North American security Canada as a part of the British Empire, or later as a member of the British Commonwealth of Nations, could be fairly certain that she would have the ultimate military protection of the United States in any war which she entered, as soon as that war came to threaten her own homeland. Such a threat would be a menace to the security of the United States, too. Thus Canada and, through Canada, Great Britain ineluctably have had a certain control over the foreign policy of the United States. And because the security of the Latin-American republics rests in the last analysis on the United States, Canada and her relative nations have an ultimate influence on the destiny of the whole New World, as illustrated by the World Wars of the twentieth century. So does the Dominion of Canada bind together the international politics of Europe and the Western World.

From this analysis it seems that Canada is as important to the diplomacy of the United States as all the Latin-American republics put together. The reader of this history may realize that Canadian-American

---

[1] See above, p. 221.

Professor J. Bartlett Brebner has explained the problem of "Canada, the Anglo-Japanese Alliance, and the Washington Conference," in *Political Science Quarterly,* L (March, 1935), 45-58.

[2] F. H. Soward, J. F. Parkinson, N. A. M. Mackensie, and T. W. L. MacDermot have analysed the position of *Canada in World Affairs, the Pre-War Years* (Canadian Institute of International Affairs, Toronto, 1941).

relations take up almost as much space in the diplomatic history of the United States as do contacts with all the countries of Latin America,[1] despite the greater variety of the latter and the more complicated nature of their problems. If Canada, because of her relationship both to Great Britain and to the United States, has such an influence on the destiny of the New World, why then has she not been a member of the Pan American Union?

During the First World War, in 1916, it had been the idea of Colonel House to commit the British Empire, on behalf of Canada, to the Pan-American Pact which President Wilson and he were then preparing. He suggested as much indirectly to the British Government, through Sir Edward Grey, then recently resigned from the Foreign Office and serving as a member of Parliament. "This, I told him, was one way [for Great Britain] to bring about a sympathetic alliance not only with the United States but with the entire Western Hemisphere. In my opinion it was an opportunity not to be disregarded, and its tendency would be to bring together an influence which could control the peace of the world." [2]

Grey thought it should be done, and agreed to try to arrange an interpellation in the House of Commons on the subject. But the Government demurred on the ground that "it would be somewhat hasty to have the question asked in the House of Commons, and an answer given just now, about the Pan-American Pact." Bonar Law, Secretary of State for the Colonies, cabled the Canadian Prime Minister and promised that "the matter will be brought out at the time considered most opportune." The intervention of the United States in the First World War, and President Wilson's taking over into the Covenant of the League of Nations his principles for the proposed Pan-American Pact, caused this suggestion to be lost from sight. Canada has evidenced relatively little interest in the Pan-American system, preferring to attach all her aspirations for peace to the League of Nations and the British Commonwealth of Nations,[3] and, more latterly, to the United Nations and the North Atlantic regional arrangement.

Canada's isolation from the Pan-American movement has suited perfectly the Latin-American policy of the United States. As long as the slender umbilical cord still remained which binds Canada to a non-Ameri-

[1] Cf. Chapters 13 and 15, versus 3, 4, 5, 13, and 14.
[2] Intimate Papers, op. cit., I, pp. 228-230.
[3] John P. Humphrey in a useful study of The Inter-American System, a Canadian View (Canadian Institute of International Affairs, Toronto, 1942), concluded that Canada should co-operate fully and wholeheartedly in an organized international American community.

can political group through the person of the British Crown, the Department of State resisted any movement to bring Canada into the purely American family, as some Latin-American spokesmen have thought of doing possibly as a fancied make-weight against the United States in inter-American councils. Such opposition has now ceased. Membership in the Organization of American Nations awaits Canada's convenience.

A word must now be said about purely Canadian-American diplomatic relations. They have been comparatively tranquil, like the relations of the Scandinavian nations. The heavy investment of United States capital in Canada—approximately $5,150,000,000 [1] as of January 1, 1948, more than in any other foreign land (and safer)—has created no political problems, has led to no cry of "economic imperialism." As already intimated, the highly important questions of boundaries, fisheries, commerce, and navigation would greatly occupy the reader of any full diplomatic history of either country. The principal problem of the twentieth century has been regulation of the waterways along the common frontier. It affords a distinctly Canadian-American contribution to the system of collective security in the New World.

The regulation of Canadian-American international waterways through commissions goes back to the period of British administration of Canadian foreign affairs, which continued until 1927. Joint commissions have been a favorite Anglo-American device for the settlement of Canadian-American questions. Several such commissions in the past had determined the arbitration of disputes over boundaries and fisheries. The Treaty of Washington of 1871, which involved many Canadian questions, was worked out by a joint commission of Canadians, Americans, and Englishmen. In 1899 another joint commission, of ten members, similar to the one of 1871, met at Washington and at Quebec to draw up a treaty for the adjustment of the Alaska boundary controversy and for the settlement of all outstanding questions, among them the regulation of waterways. Disagreement on the boundary question terminated the labors of this commission, without any disposition of the other questions. Following the settlement of the Alaska boundary question by the joint commission created in 1903, the remaining significant diplomatic issues between the United States and Canada were the North Atlantic fisheries controversy, the dispute over title to little islands in Passamaquoddy Bay, and the various questions constantly arising in regard to the common waterways along the northern frontier. The important fisheries dispute was referred to the arbitration of the Hague Court by a treaty of 1909, and a special boundary commission was established in

[1] Information from Division of Commercial Policy, Department of State (1949).

1910 which settled the question of the disputed islands. Contemporaneously with the disposal of these issues, Great Britain and the United
States agreed to a convention, in 1909, providing for the regulation of
boundary waters and setting up permanent machinery for the settlement
of future controversies.[1] Since there is no special treaty for conciliation,
or for arbitration, between Canada and the United States, this convention takes the place, in respect to Canada, of the bilateral and multilateral treaties which the United States has with most other nations.

The convention provides for the free and equal navigation, by nationals
of both parties, of the boundary waters, and also of the American Lake
Michigan, and sets up an International Joint Commission of six members
to regulate obstructions or diversions to the flow and level of boundary
waters, with particular regulations for the flow of water in the Niagara
River (much used for hydroelectric power), and in the St. Marys River
(much used for navigation between the Upper Lakes) and the Milk River
(used for irrigation in Montana, Saskatchewan, and Alberta). For these
purposes the Commission has administrative, investigative, and judicial
powers, deciding by a majority vote, or referring the question back to the
governments in case of a deadlock. In addition, the Commission has certain conciliatory and arbitral functions. Any other questions or matters
of difference (other than the regulation of waterways) arising between
them involving the rights, obligations, or interests of either in relation to
the other or to the inhabitants of the other *along the common frontier,*
shall be referred to the Commission for examination, and possible recommendation whenever either party so requests, the report and recommendation not to have the character of an arbitral award. Further, any questions or matters of difference involving the rights, obligations, or interests
of either party in relation to each other or to their respective inhabitants
may be referred with the consent of both parties (by and with the advice
and consent of the United States Senate, and His Majesty's Governor
General in Council) to the Commission *for decision* by a majority vote;
in case of a deadlock, to an umpire chosen according to the relevant rules
of the Hague Convention establishing the Permanent Court of Arbitration.

It was to this Commission that both governments referred in 1920 the

---

[1] The preamble states the desire of the parties "to prevent disputes regarding the use
of boundary waters and to settle all questions which are now pending between the
United States and the Dominion of Canada involving the rights, obligations, or interests
of either in relation to the other or to the inhabitants of the other, along their common
frontier, and to make provision for the adjustment and settlement of all such questions
as may hereafter arise."

study of an international improvement of the St. Lawrence waterway between Montreal and Lakes Ontario and Erie, so as to make ocean-going navigation possible to the Upper Lakes, and to divide the immense hydroelectric power resources of the St. Lawrence River. The report of the Commission prepared the way for the negotiation of the St. Lawrence deep-waterway treaty between Canada and the United States (signed July 18, 1932). This treaty provided for co-operation by the United States and Canada to complete by a uniform plan, each country working within its own jurisdiction but under the general direction of a special joint commission, a twenty-seven-foot channel in the St. Lawrence River and around the rapids, and improvements in the channels of the Upper Lakes; and a provision for the construction of hydroelectric plants, with equal division of the flow of water for power development. The total estimated cost, past and future, was $543,429,500. The expense was to be equally shared, with the stipulation that each country would receive credit for the cost of past works which entered into the project. This made the new costs to the United States $257,992,000 and to Canada only $38,071,500—Canada having just completed at immense cost the Welland Canal, between Lakes Ontario and Erie, as well as other important works which were to be a part of the general waterway.

This treaty also attempted to settle a dormant issue between Canada and the United States concerning the diversion of waters from Lake Michigan, which is not a "boundary water" within the meaning of the treaty of 1909, and which had therefore remained under exclusive American jurisdiction, except for the treaty servitude of 1909 which allows free navigation there to Canadian shipping. Lake Michigan is, of course, nevertheless a part of the Great Lakes system. The city of Chicago in 1900 tapped the waters of the Lake to flush out its sewage into the Illinois River and down the Mississippi. The increasing use of the waters, which eventually worked up toward 8,500 cubic feet a second, threatened to lower seriously the general lake level and the power flow of the Niagara River. Alarmed, several of the lake states and Mississippi River states [1] sued the Chicago Sanitary District in a case appealed to the Supreme Court of the United States, to prevent the diversion. The Court in 1930 decreed that Chicago must taper down the taking of water to 1,500 cubic feet a second by 1938. This was a purely domestic affair. But in 1926 the British Ambassador at Washington had complained that excessive

---

[1] Wisconsin, Ohio, Pennsylvania, Missouri, New York, Michigan, Kentucky, Tennessee, Louisiana, Arkansas. See note by J. W. Garner in *American Journal of International Law*, XXII (1928), 837-840.

diversion from Lake Michigan was a violation of Article III of the waterways treaty of 1909. This treaty, we have just noted, prohibited diversion from "boundary waters" without authorization of the International
Joint Commission. The lake states had really been pleading Canada's
cause, in fact but not in law; and the Supreme Court's decree mitigated
the grievance of Canada without recognizing it. The treaty signed in
1932, however, specifically agreed in Article VIII to limit diversion of
water from "the Great Lakes system," by December 31, 1938, to the
quantity permitted by the Supreme Court's decree of April 21, 1930. In
case the Government of the United States should propose an emergency
diversion, and the Government of Canada should take exception, the
issue might be submitted to an arbitral tribunal empowered to determine
any just and equitable diversion during an emergency. No other diversion from "the Great Lakes system" than that just provided was to be
authorized except by the International Joint Commission.[1] The treaty
of 1932 would thus create, for better or worse, an additional servitude
on the sovereignty of the United States over Lake Michigan, and thereby
would place the Chicago drainage issue definitely in the international
field.

The idea of a new servitude, of definitely merging Lake Michigan, a
recognized American lake, into the treaty formula of "the Great Lakes
system," created understandable if not justifiable opposition to the ratification. There was further objection to the much greater *new* American
expenditure. Strong sectional opposition also manifested itself both in
Canada and in the United States. Impartial economic analysis of the
advantages and disadvantages to the United States of the navigation and
power features of the project, as presented by the Brookings Institution
in 1929,[2] was also adverse in its conclusions. The treaty came first to a
decision on ratification in the Republic, where it was defeated in the
Senate (March 14, 1934) by a vote of 46 for and 42 against, the negative
votes coming particularly from New England, New York, the South,
and the Mississippi navigation states.

What could not be arranged by treaty President Roosevelt tried, like
President Tyler in the case of Texas and President McKinley in the
case of Hawaii, to carry by a majority vote of Congress. An executive
agreement between "The President of the United States and His Majesty
the King of Great Britain, Ireland and the British Dominions beyond the

---

[1] *Great Lakes-St. Lawrence Deep Waterway Treaty* (Department of State Publication
347, Washington, 1932). See also *Canadian Annual Review, 1932-1933.*

[2] H. G. Moulton, Charles S. Morgan, and Adah L. Lee, *The St. Lawrence Navigation
and Power Project* (Brookings Institution, Washington, 1929).

seas, Emperor of India, in respect of Canada," signed at Ottawa, March 19, 1941, created a Great Lakes-St. Lawrence Basin Commission, of five members from each country, to carry the great project through to completion. Nothing in the Agreement "shall confer upon either of them proprietary rights, or legislative, administrative, or other jurisdiction in the territory of the other, and the works constructed under the provisions of this Agreement shall constitute a part of the territory in which they are situated." This keeps Lake Michigan inviolate; and the Agreement extends, indefinitely, reciprocal navigation rights in Lake Michigan and in the St. Lawrence River which otherwise might be terminated by due notice under existing treaties. The Agreement has not yet been approved by the Congress of the United States and the Parliament of Canada.[1]

The International Joint Commission became a prototype for other Canadian-American commissions in a modern network of agencies for peaceful settlement and regulation of common concerns: the Wild-Life Services (1916); the International Halibut Commission (1924) for conservation of fisheries on the Pacific Coast; the Salmon Commission (1930); not to mention yet the later Permanent Joint Defense Board, and other wartime and later agencies.

To come back to the older International Joint Commission: it has, in addition to its powers for the regulation and investigation of the use of boundary waterways, contingent functions of conciliation and of arbitration. The conciliatory function may be invoked by only one party to suggest a settlement. The arbitral function may be invoked by both parties jointly to decide a dispute. To date it is only the administrative, investigative, and judicial powers of the Commission for the regulation of the boundary waterways which have been put to service—most effectively in numerous cases. But the machinery of conciliation and arbitration stands steadily available, whenever called for, just as does the apparatus of the multilateral treaties for peace provided for among the United States and the Pan-American nations. The Canadian-American International Joint Commission is thus a worthy adjunct to the system of collective security in the New World, a system which rests on the out-

---

[1] The President supported himself by opinions from the Solicitor of the Department of State, and the Attorney General of the United States, that an agreement of this kind, subject to ratification by a majority vote of both Houses of Congress, would be constitutional.

For text of the Agreement, and the legal opinions, see S. Shepard Jones and Denys P. Myers, *Documents on American Foreign Relations, 1938-39 to 1940-41* (3 vols., World Peace Foundation, Boston, 1939-41), III, pp. 187-199.

A vast amount of data is included in the publication compiled for the Department of Commerce by N. R. Danielian, director of the St. Lawrence Survey, in a report on *The St. Lawrence Survey* (7 vols., Washington, G.P.O., 1941-1942).

lawry of war and the pledge, without compulsion, to peaceful means for the settlement of international disputes. Further than this, both the United States and Canada have ratified the optional clause of the International Court of Justice, judicial organ of the United Nations, obligating each party to submit definitively all "legal" questions to the judgment of that court. For the perfection of peace and justice between them the United States and Canada still await a keystone treaty agreeing to submit *all* disputes to a standing tribunal of the best judicial talent in both countries,[1] to guarantee the heritage of freedom of both peoples.[2]

The First World War did very little to cement Canadian-American solidarity; on the contrary, it rather loosened traditional bonds. American neutrality, 1914-1917, tended to antagonize the Canadian people against their neighbors to the south, notwithstanding an inveterate admiration by people in the United States for the gallant qualities of Canadians and for their highly successful democracy. Somehow the Canadians were convinced that it was the United States's war as much as Canada's. They resented the slowness, so it seemed to them, with which the Republic turned to the Allied cause. After American intervention it was galling to some to think that the war would have been lost except for the belated, as they thought, entry of the United States. Later, others were convinced that the United States had deserted a noble cause in failing to accept the League of Nations, thus, in their opinion, crippling it from the start, though in 1936 Canada and the other Dominions themselves proved reluctant to support Britain in stopping remilitarization of the Rhineland, which placed Germany in a position to begin her program of conquest. Canadians further felt that the United States was immoral in expecting the "war debts" of the European Allies to be paid even according to capacity to pay; but Canada held none of their paper. This bitter distaste,[3] which was so difficult for Americans to realize, and which was not reciprocated by them, persisted to some degree after the common victory of 1919. Added to it was a curious but understandable culture complex. As a highly intelligent people, surpassed by no nation anywhere, Canadians resented the greater force of American culture coming from mere power of territory, natural resources, and infinitely greater population. They fancied that the United

---

[1] P. E. Corbett has published a critical study of methods and results in *The Settlement of Canadian-American Disputes* (Canadian-American Series, Carnegie Endowment for International Peace, Yale University Press, 1937).

[2] James T. Shotwell has described *The Heritage of Freedom,* in the Marfleet Lectures at the University of Toronto in 1932 (New York, 1934).

[3] Hugh L. Keenleyside discusses it temperately in his *Canada and the United States* (New York, 1929).

States did not pay enough attention to them, and even complained that Canadian events did not take up more space in metropolitan American newspapers!

In such murky atmosphere economic grievances quickly took root on both sides of the boundary and spread themselves like bad weeds. New tariffs of the United States in 1922 and 1930 were followed by the Canadian high tariffs of 1927 and 1930. The American tariffs restricted the market for Canadian products—hard wheat, lumber, cattle, dairy products, maple sugar—in the United States. The Canadian tariffs cut down, or at least heavily taxed, the importation of American manufactured products. By the Ottawa intra-imperial treaties of 1932 Canada took her place in a system of reciprocal preferences within the British Empire, and continued a tariff schedule of three rates: most-favored rates to the imperially preferred Dominions of the Ottawa intercommonwealth agreements of 1932; next-favored rates to those nations which had treaties of commerce with Canada; highest rates of all on goods coming from nations which had no treaties of commerce—that was, principally the United States. A tariff war sharpened psychological differences between two friendly nations while the non-American world teetered on the edge of the abyss. This was more than intellectual leaders and good folk on both sides of the weed-grown frontier could tolerate.

How a group of anxious scholars in the United States and Canada set about pulling these bad weeds and cultivating the traditional affinity on the eve of world crisis is one of the most inspiring examples of intellectual and moral co-operation in the history of American diplomacy. With the support of the Carnegie Endowment for International Peace, a series of biennial conferences (1935, 1937, 1939, 1941) on Canadian-American Affairs, meeting alternately at St. Lawrence University, Canton, New York, and Queen's University, Kingston, Ontario, brought together statesmen, scholars, philanthropists, diplomatists, and journalists of both nations to hammer out common problems on the anvil of determined friendship, with such utter frankness as is possible only between Canadians and Americans who, let it be repeated, regard themselves as independent of each other rather than foreign to each other. These extra-official conferences, and the continuing studies that they helped put in motion,[1] restored the old tone of fellowship, and made themselves felt in official policy.

[1] The proceedings of the four *Conferences on Canadian-American Affairs* have been printed by the Carnegie Endowment for International Peace (New York, 1936, 1938, 1939, 1940), edited by Professors Walter W. McLaren, Albert B. Corey, and Reginald G. Trotter.

One of the most notable products of this Canadian-American intellectual collaboration was a comprehensive historical study, in twenty-five volumes, on all phases, economic, cultural, social, and diplomatic, of *The Relations of Canada and the United States*. This unusually successful series was unprecedented in the field of internationl intellectual cooperation and was to be of continuing influence for peace with freedom. Capstone of the series was a volume focused on *The North Atlantic Triangle, The Inter-Play of Canada, The United States and Great Britain*.[1]

First fruit of the new feeling was the reciprocal trade agreement of January 1, 1936. Though this did not altogether overcome the imperial preferences of the Ottawa agreements, it nevertheless lowered tariffs radically on both sides. Impelled by the circumstances of the Second World War, Great Britain and Canada made simultaneous but separate reciprocal trade agreements with the United States, December 20, 1940. Most detailed and sweeping in their nature, they had the effect of doing away with the discriminations which either Canada or Great Britain hitherto had practiced against the United States, on the one hand, and of lowering United States tariffs drastically to both nations, daughter and mother. Undoubtedly there was a political motive as well as an economic impulse in the negotiation of these salutary trade agreements, the motive of Anglo-American solidarity. Once more Canada fulfilled her role of political accouplement between Great Britain and the United States.

Conclusion of the first trade agreement, in 1936, made it easier for President Franklin D. Roosevelt to put the coupling pin in place on the occasion of a visit (certainly not casual) to Queen's University, Kingston, Ontario, one of the homes of the Canadian-American Conferences to which we have referred. "The Dominion of Canada," he said apparently gratuitously, "is part of the sisterhood of the British Empire. I give to you assurances that the people of the United States will not stand idly by if domination of Canadian soil is threatened by any other Empire."[2] The Canadian Prime Minister, William Lyon Mackenzie King, acknowledged this assurance with appropriate expressions, but made no pledges on his part.[3]

---

[1] By the general editor, Professor J. Bartlett Brebner of Colombia University. The twenty-five volumes were published, 1940-1945, by the Yale University Press, the Ryerson Press of Toronto, and the Oxford University Press, for the Carnegie Endowment for International Peace. A list of titles and authors may be found on the inside rear flap of the folder to Brebner's capstone volume.

[2] Department of State *Press Releases*, XIX, No. 464 (August 20, 1938).

[3] F. R. Scott, *Canada and the United States* (World Peace Foundation, Boston, 1941), p. 53.

Canadian foreign policy before the war aimed at: (1) preserving Canadian neutrality in case of war between the United States and Japan,[1] (2) appeasement, if possible, of the European situation—this spirit disappeared after Munich, (3) reliance on the British navy and the Monroe Doctrine to protect the Canadian homeland in any event, (4) in the last analysis, to support Great Britain if she found herself at war in the Old World, mobilizing Canada's whole resources after the event. In line with this policy, Mr. King could do no more than say thank-you to Mr. Roosevelt in 1938, before Munich.

The outbreak of the Second World War put Canadian policy into motion. The fall of Denmark and Norway, the Low Countries and France in the spring of 1940, and the terrible danger to England threw Canada and the United States closer together.[2] In a meeting at Ogdensburg, New York, on August 17, 1940, during maneuvers of the United States Army, to which President Roosevelt invited Prime Minister King, the two executives announced an agreement—an executive agreement, not a treaty—to set up a Permanent Joint Board of Defense "to consider in the broad sense the defense of the northern half of the Western Hemisphere." The Agreement by Great Britain, September 2, 1940, to cede to the United States a naval and air base in Newfoundland punctuated Canadian-American collaboration for joint defense in a dramatic manner.[3]

After Ogdensburg, Canadian-American relations drew even more tightly together as German conquests in Europe became rapidly more threatening to both countries. The President and the Canadian Prime Minister in a meeting at the former's home on the Hudson laid down general principles for mobilizing the resources of the North American continent for the defense of Great Britain, in line with the "lend-lease" act of Congress of March 11, 1941. In the Hyde Park Declaration (April 20, 1941) they announced that the two governments would gear their production programs to fit each other, and that the United States would pay

---

[1] C. P. Stacey, "A Canadian View" of Defense and External Obligations, at *Conference on Canadian American Affairs,* St. Lawrence University, Canton, N. Y., June 19-22, 1939, pp. 190-193 (Carnegie Endowment for International Peace, New York, 1939), 182-197.

[2] We are, of course, alluding to events narrated more in detail in Chapter 18 below.

[3] A tripartite protocol signed by the United States, Canada, and Great Britain, March 27, 1941, on the occasion of the signing on the same date of the final lease agreement for United States bases in Newfoundland (see below, p. 383) "recognized that the defense of Newfoundland was an integral part of the Canadian scheme of defense and as such a matter of special concern to the Canadian Government." Nothing in this agreement was to affect arrangements already taken by the Joint Board of Defense, United States and Canada, relative to the defense of Newfoundland. In the future the Newfoundland Government was to participate in all consultations.

Canada $200,000,000 to $300,000,000 during the next twelve months for certain supplies, complementary to the American defense program, but a "small fraction of it." This payment would assist Canada in meeting part of her defense purchases in the United States. Further, the United States would furnish to Great Britain, under the lend-lease program, certain parts to be made up in Canada into finished products to go forward directly to Great Britain.[1] Thus the vast reservoirs of American cash and supplies were opened up to Canada for help to Great Britain in her hour of greatest peril—in order to keep that peril away from North American shores, if possible.

If United States help to Canada and Great Britain should lead to war with Germany, as it speedily did, in undeclared form, and that should bring Japan into war against the United States, according to the terms of the Triple Alliance of Germany, Italy, and Japan, of September 27, 1940, what would be the position of Canada toward Japan? That was the principal question of Canadian-American relations as a real shooting war began between American and German naval forces on the Atlantic.[2]

Japan answered the question. After her staggering surprise attack on Pearl Harbor, December 7, 1941, she declared war on the United States *and* Great Britain. Canada, perforce, and the other Dominions, declared war in turn on Japan. Promptly the United States and Canada announced a joint declaration, by their War Production Committees, of a policy of all-out war production and the removal of any and all barriers (legislative, administrative, tariff, customs, "or restriction of any character") standing in the way of total war effort.[3] Canada signed the Declaration of the United Nations in Washington, January 2, 1942. Both nations and the British Commonwealth, and their Allies, joined their destinies in the greatest and most fateful war of history. Throughout the great conflict the bars of nationality were let down, so to speak, for cooperation in a common military effort, without impairment of the sovereignty or national integrity of either nation.

At the close of the Second World War both the United States and Canada committed themselves unreservedly to the Charter and program of the United Nations. But the increasing insecurity of North America in the new unbalance of power, and the failure so far of the Security

---

[1] S. Shepard Jones and Denys P. Myers, *Documents on American Foreign Relations, 1938-39 to 1940-41, op. cit.,* III, pp. 161-169.

[2] For discussion of this vital question, see *Conference on Canadian-American Affairs, Queen's University, Kingston, Ontario, June 23-26, 1941* (New York, 1941), pp. 241-242.

[3] Department of State *Bulletin,* V, No. 131 (December 27, 1941), 578-579. R. Warren James has published a study of the United States and Canada in the field of *Wartime Economic Cooperation* (Canadian Institute of International Affairs, Toronto, 1949).

Council to reconcile the great crisis of thought and action between the East and the West, kept the two independent countries ever more closely together, within the integrity of each people's sovereignty, notwithstanding complicated and vexing minor problems of imperial preference treaties, aerial navigation, and numerous other technical puzzles. In 1947 the two Governments announced their decision to continue indefinitely the Permanent Board of Joint Defense, first established in 1940 as a war measure. This common defense planning depended on no treaty, no executive agreement, no contractual obligation.[1] It rested on the anxiety of each party for the maintenance of its own security and freedom in an uncertain and dangerous world.

More than ever each people realizes that its independence and liberty depend on the independence and liberty of the other. In the North Atlantic Security Pact of 1949 Canada became in very firmest fit the coupling pin of Anglo-American solidarity for the defense of the freedom of both the Old World and the New.

[1] Department of State *Bulletin*, XVI, No. 339 (February 23, 1947), 361.

16

The United States and the Far East between
Two World Wars

THE Washington treaties of 1922 left Japan in a position of paramount military and naval power in the Far East, but they pledged the powers, including Japan, against *further* imperialism in China, to the maintenance of the Open Door and the political independence and territorial integrity of China, and to the continuance of the *status quo* in the region of the Pacific Ocean. These traditional American—and British—policies were thus written into multilateral pacts. Nobody could foresee the Great Depression and the rise of the European dictators, phenomena which would present tempting advantages and opportunities for Japanese power at the expense of the plighted word of her rulers. For nearly a decade Japan pursued loyally the policy of the Washington treaties. These years witnessed the crystallization and spread of a new Chinese national movement of profound significance to Japan's ambitions for the future of Asia.

The Chinese Nationalist movement took new shape at Canton in 1923 under the leadership of Dr. Sun Yat-sen, who turned for material support to the Russian Bolshevists. An understanding between Sun and the Soviet Commissioner, Joffe, agreed that the Soviet system could not actually be introduced into China because conditions were lacking for the successful establishment of communism or sovietism. In 1924 a diplomatic agreement and sequent treaty were reached between China and Russia, by which China recognized the Soviet Government. Russia abandoned all the special treaty rights and concessions procured from China under the Czarist régime, including extraterritoriality. This meant another step [1] in freeing China of the burden of "unequal treaties." The Sino-Soviet treaty regulated the Chinese Eastern Railway, hitherto a joint Sino-Russian enterprise, financed by Russia, by making it a purely commercial affair controlling its own business operations, with all other matters affecting the national and local governments of China

---

[1] The "unequal treaties" with Germany and Austria-Hungary had been thrown off in the peace settlement of 1919.

to be administered by Chinese authorities. This divested the railroad of the political attributes originally granted to the Czarist Government, including the right to guard it with armed guards.[1] Russian assistance in the form of military training, supplies, and funds now streamed into South China to support the campaign for national unity and control by the Kuomintang (Nationalist Party) of all China, this as a first step to the economic, social, and moral regeneration and national galvanization of that chaotic republic under modern, and eventually Soviet, ideas.

Notwithstanding the terms of the working agreement between Russian communism and Chinese nationalism, the destitute condition of the Chinese people presented a favorable medium for the cultivation of communist principles; behind the Kuomintang armies developed a wave of social and labor unrest, strikes and industrial violence particularly against foreign-owned factories. In 1927, however, after evidence was received that the Soviet mentors were plotting the overthrow of the Kuomintang in order to establish a thoroughly communist government, the Nationalists expelled the Bolshevik comrades and took reprisals on their native followers. Rapidly breasting the tide and confusion of Chinese political life, the Nationalist armies pressed northward until by 1928 they had established an enthusiastic but loose authority over all of China south of the Great Wall, with a new capital at Nanking. North of the Great Wall, the Manchurian provinces had lain under the control of war lord Chang Tso-lin, hitherto politically backed by Japan, but increasingly sympathetic to the Nationalists. Murderously the Japanese got rid of him in 1928 by blowing up his railway coach in a trackage area under their military guard. Next step in the Nationalist program of unification was control over the Manchurian provinces of China, long a theater of international rivalry, particularly between Russia and Japan.[2] Japan viewed with disfavor this territorial extension of authority by the Chinese Nationalist Government and made overt but unsuccessful efforts to prevent it.

The advance of the Nationalist movement was accompanied by some revival of animosity against the imperialist powers, a limited reincarnation of the Boxer revolt animated by more modernistic sentiment. It was convenient for the leaders to attribute the troubles of China not to their essential internal causes but to the unequal treaties, and to sustain enthusiasm by exciting their followers to a frenzy of criticism and un-

[1] R. T. Pollard, *China's Foreign Relations, 1917-1931* (New York, 1933), pp. 160-204.
[2] This account of the Chinese Nationalist Revolution is of course vastly simplified, based on the summaries in Morse and McNair, *Far Eastern International Relations, op. cit.*, and George N. Steiger, *History of the Far East* (New York, 1936).

rest against the foreigners and their concessions. Meanwhile the events of the First World War had weakened the white man's prestige, so powerful in China before 1914. Clashes with foreigners (at Shanghai, May 30, 1925, and also at Canton, June, 1925; Wanhsien incident on the upper Yangtze River, September, 1926) culminated in the premeditated and organized attack on foreign nationals in Nanking (March 24, 1927), resulting in the deaths of three British, one American, one French, and one Italian national, the assault on many others without distinction as to sex or nationality, and the violation of the American, British, and Japanese consulates. Only the laying down of a barrage of shells from British and American destroyers in the river made possible the evacuation of foreigners without more general slaughter. The affair at Nanking led to a demand, presented in identic notes (April 11, 1927) by the American, British, French, Italian, and Japanese Governments for punishment of the commanders of troops responsible for the outrage, complete reparation, and apology in writing by the commander in chief of the Nationalist armies, including an express written undertaking to refrain from all forms of violence and agitation against foreign lives and property. Contingents of foreign forces from the protesting powers arrived, including a regiment of American marines, and hastened to Shanghai for the protection of the foreign settlement and the refugees clustered there. Of the total of 40,000 troops, there were about 11,000 British. Meanwhile there was almost a complete evacuation of foreign nationals from the interior of the Yangtze Valley and South China.

The Nationalist Government, then under the control of radicals at Hankow, undertook to reply to the powers individually, and at first offered no adequate satisfaction. Great Britain, France, and Italy wished that the aggrieved powers jointly adopt measures to enforce compliance with their demands. Japan, before the fall of Baron Shidehara, was willing to follow. The United States refused to go that far, or to join in an ultimatum. After the establishment of the government at Nanking, the leadership of the Nationalists fell into more conservative hands, and the powers were able to make a friendly settlement without the use of force, involving mutual apologies, reparations, and guaranties by the Nationalist Government.[1] In this incident, as traditionally, the United States took a stand which bolstered the integrity of China.

Unlike the Boxer agitation, the Nationalist movement was not stimu-

---

[1] R. T. Pollard, *op. cit.*, pp. 293-307. The terms of settlement in 1928 may be found in G. H. Blakeslee's *The Pacific Area; an International Survey* (World Peace Foundation Pamphlets, XII, No. 3, Boston, 1929), pp. 155-159.

lated by threatened encroachments of the powers. It was directed against the accumulation of privileges forced from China in the past. It came to a head after the Washington Conference when the powers under American impulsion were pledged to a policy of patience and sympathy with China. In November, 1927, the commander of the Nationalist forces, General Chiang Kai-shek, announced: "We will execute no treaties such as were signed by former governments, nor will we at any time recognize any treaties or agreements which were made with other nations by any government in China previous to that of the Nationalist forces." These bold words went further than actual accomplishment, but the Kuomintang did secure the abolition of the old tariff treaties, and a diminution of concessions (notably the British relinquishment of concessions at Hankow, Kiukiang, Chinkiang, Amoy, and the restoration of Weihaiwei). It did not succeed in throwing off the trammels of extraterritoriality. A powerful instrument in its program of liberation was the device of boycotts. These menaced the security of foreign trade, first British, later Japanese. During these boycotts American trade prospered at the expense of the boycotted nations.

Particularly to Japan did the Nationalist movement assume an alarming aspect. Japanese leaders feared that the moral and political regeneration of China would block any plans of Japan for eventual control of that vast country. The increasing population of Japan (at the rate of 1,000,000 a year) depended for its support on the industrialization of the islands. This required expanding markets, of which China was the nearest and greatest. Few things could be a more painful blow to Japan in time of peace than a successful Chinese boycott of her exports. To all China also, particularly to the provinces of Manchuria, Japan looked for a continuing supply of raw materials to sustain her own island people, and for a possible (but not proven) outlet for her pressure of population.[1] Should the Nationalists establish themselves strongly, and extend their authority over Manchuria, Japan's career of future expansion on the continent of Asia might be permanently blocked.

Whether to continue the policy of conciliation with China became the paramount question of Japanese politics. Baron Shidehara, Japanese Minister of Foreign Affairs, 1924-1927, endeavored against increasing opposition to pursue conciliation and friendly co-operation based upon the Washington treaties. Those treaties, it is recalled, had not con-

[1] Tatsuji Takeuchi has the best presentation available in English of the Japanese point of view in Chapter XXVI of his *War and Diplomacy in the Japanese Empire* (New York, 1935).

tested Japan's treaty rights in Manchuria. It was Shidehara's belief that this policy would win China's confidence and the confidence of the world in Japan's motives toward China, and that a policy of moderation generally in foreign affairs would increase the markets for Japan's expanding industries on which her growing population depended so imperiously. Under his guidance, for example, Japan did not participate in the protective barrage laid down by British and American naval forces at Nanking in 1927, despite the fact that the Japanese consulate was fired on, and several Japanese subjects wounded; and it was the British rather than the Japanese who bore the brunt of that incident before the Chinese boycotts. While Shidehara's policy reigned there was no special feeling against Japan, and Japanese commerce flourished.

The Nanking incident fired Japanese public opinion against Shidehara's friendly policy. His government was immediately overthrown in April, 1927, by Baron General Tanaka, personification of a more "positive" policy, spokesman at that time of the army which was constantly pressing against the more liberal and conciliatory elements. The displaced moderates were allied with "big business" in Japan and wanted peace. The army in turn appealed strongly to the small landowners and peasants, an agrarian class increasingly ground down by the rapid industrialization and urbanization of Japan. This class furnished many of the officers. Supporting the army, and firing public sentiment by appeals to a fanatical patriotism, stood various fraternal chauvinistic societies devotedly militaristic in nature and closely akin to fascist thought and action.

The Tanaka Government came into power in Japan as the Kuomintang forces were pushing north from the Yangtze Valley toward Peking. Japan landed troops in Shantung, in 1927, and again in 1929, to keep the civil war out of that province and to protect her interests there, as well as to deflect and embarrass the northward movement of the Nationalists. These interventions, though withdrawn, brought on costly and persisting boycotts on Japanese imports. In May, 1928, the Japanese Government declared to the rival Chinese groups in Nanking and Peking that it would not tolerate the extension of the war into Manchuria and Mongolia; that if the disturbances should spread Japan would "be constrained to take appropriate and effective steps for the maintenance of peace and order in Manchuria." In December of that year Chang Hsueh-liang, war lord of Manchuria, son of Chang Tso-lin, acknowledged allegiance to the Nanking Government. The following spring (1929) Chinese forces in Manchuria seized the Chinese Eastern Railway, hitherto under joint Chinese-Russian management, and arrested the Russian officials and employees of the road. Diplomatic relations broke off. Border clashes began. War appeared imminent, although both China and Russia had just become parties to the Pact of Paris of 1928 for the renunciation of war. It became evident, however, that China could not withstand Russia in any conflict in Manchuria. The American Secretary of State, Henry L. Stimson, and Aristide Briand, French Minister of Foreign Affairs, representing the two governments originally sponsors of the Pact of Paris, reminded the two disputants of their obligations under it. China, realizing her weak military position, hastened to accept a peaceful settlement based on the restoration of the *status quo ante*. Russia took occasion to snub the United States for venturing to apply to the Soviet Government with advice and counsel, when by its own choice it had no official relations with it; but the Soviets accepted a peaceful solution which was really a check to China.

Japan applauded the invocation of the Pact of Paris to keep the peace between Russia and China in Manchuria. China's action toward Russia was an earnest of what might confront Japan's treaty position in those provinces, were the Chinese successful. On the other hand, Soviet successes might strengthen Russia's position in an area which Japan coveted for herself. The Nationalists were as desirous of redeeming South Manchuria, where existed the Kwantung (southern tip of the Liaotung peninsula) leased area and the Japanese railway and ancillary concessions,[1] as they were to restore their sovereignty over North Manchuria *vis-à-vis* Russia. As the Nationalists spread their authority into Manchuria they began to contest the broad interpretations attached by Japan to her special treaty rights in that region: particularly the right to station a limited number of guards along the South Manchuria Railway; the administrative powers which that state railway enjoyed over areas which had passed under its proprietorship or lease; the police powers and juris-

---

[1] See above, pp. 22 ff. These treaty rights were based upon the transfer from Russia to Japan by the Peace of Portsmouth (1905) of all Russian rights south of Changchun, which was in turn ratified by the Sino-Japanese Treaty of Peking (1905), and extended by the Sino-Japanese treaties of 1915, following the presentation of the Twenty-One Demands. Extensive areas tributary to the South Manchuria Railway had been acquired before and after 1915, when such leases were regularized and placed under the semipolitical jurisdiction of the railroad, which was in itself an instrument of the Japanese Government. C. Walter Young's elaborate studies of *Japan's Special Position in Manchuria; The International Legal Status of the Kwantung Leased Territory;* and *Japanese Jurisdiction in the South Manchuria Railway Areas* (all three published by the Johns Hopkins Press, 1931) are conveniently digested by T. A. Bisson's analysis of "Basic Treaty Issues in Manchuria Between China and Japan," in *Foreign Policy Reports,* VII, No. 21 (December 23, 1931).

dictional powers which Japan assumed in these "railway areas" outside the Kwantung leasehold; and the expanding consular police which Japan set up in Manchuria, even in regions distant from the railway areas. Similar powers to these in North Manchuria the Soviet Government had already relinquished in 1924. The Chinese endeavored to undermine the power of the Japanese South Manchuria Railway by setting up a system of competing parallel roads, financed through foreign loans, which would drain away Manchurian commerce, at fares payable in cheap currency, to a new Chinese port (Hulutao) at the head of the Gulf of Pechili. On other feeder roads, previously constructed by Japanese capital, they defaulted in their loans. They also interposed difficulties in the way of leasing lands by Japanese subjects, who by the treaties of 1915 were enabled to make such leases.

If Japan were to have Manchuria some day for her own, as the proponents of the "positive" policy so ardently advocated,[1] or if she were to continue to control its destiny (as nearly all Japanese leaders desired), she must act before either Russia or China became too strong there. The situation was exacerbated by the occurrence of provocative affairs of the sort which lead up to conflict. One incident which incensed the Japanese military was the arrest and execution, in the interior of China, of a Japanese officer, one Major Nakamura, who was making a military reconnaissance there in civilian attire. Bitter anti-Chinese riots then followed in Japanese Korea, which in turn intensified anti-Japanese boycotts in China. Baron Shidehara, who had been called back to the

---

[1] Japanese policy after 1931 in Manchuria, Mongolia, and other adjacent provinces of China exhibited a striking similarity to the policy and action advocated in alleged official documents given to the world through Chinese channels after the outbreak of hostilities. One of these was a confidential memorial of July 25, 1927, to the Throne attributed to Baron Tanaka. It advocated the economic and political penetration and conquest of Manchuria and Mongolia, particularly through the construction and control of strategic railways, as a means of ensuring Japan an abundant supply of natural resources and an outlet for population, and as a first step for the control of all China. The Honjo Memorial, alleged to have been directed by the commander of Japanese forces in Manchuria to the Minister of War, General Minami, projected plans beyond this: it outlined an eventual conquest of the Philippines, Malaya, Australia, and a subjugation of Western Europe and Africa "until we would share equally with the United States the good things of this world." The Japanese Government has declared these documents to be forgeries by a venal subject, and has been able to point out obvious impossibilities in some of their details; but the array of carefully organized information (particularly in the so-called Tanaka Memorial) is astonishing; and the sequence of actual events in Manchuria, examined in the light of that memorial, is startling. For discussion of authenticity, see debate between Japanese and Chinese delegates before the League of Nations in *Official Journal* of League of Nations, XIII (July-December, 1932), pp. 1882, 1893, 1895, 1898, 1902. In 1950 one is surprised at the reluctance of the world to have believed in the authenticity of these programs.

Ministry of Foreign Affairs in 1929,[1] found himself overwhelmed by mounting demands for a stronger policy toward China.

In Japan the army, like the navy, was responsible only to the Emperor directly, not to the government which rested on a parliamentary support. Demands for a "positive policy" meant a challenge to the League of Nations, to the Nine-Power Treaty of Washington of 1922, and to the Pact of Paris of 1928, and ultimately to the accompanying naval treaties of 1922 and 1930, all of which Japan had accepted freely. For such a challenge the world situation of international politics was propitious. In Europe the peace edifice of Versailles was beginning to show signs of cracks, and the international economic structure was collapsing. The Hoover standstill agreement for a year's moratorium on intergovernmental debts had just been proclaimed. Great Britain had gone off the gold standard, and the United States was pressed. The Great Depression gripped and paralyzed the nations of the Western world. In the ensuing intervention which was precipitated by the Japanese army command in South Manchuria and which led to the establishment of the unrecognized puppet state of Manchukuo, the world came to realize what the reader must constantly bear in mind: that it was the army and navy authorities, not the Cabinet, which directed and controlled Japanese military policy; that the Foreign Office proposed, professed, and pretended, *vis-à-vis* the world, but the army command really defined, determined, and disposed for the destiny of Japan's continental policy in Asia, leaving it to the Foreign Office to smooth over things as best it could with the foreign treaty powers. The military were confident that a patriotic and warlike people would sustain them. They scorned the façade of treaties for the Open Door, the political independence, and territorial integrity of China. They contemned the naval limitations of Washington and London. Theirs was the power. To them appeared the opportunity: the distresses of the Occident were obviously the advantage of Japan. They continued to be so, even more, perhaps, than Japanese radical militarists could have foreseen in 1931.

The military command in the Kwantung leased area took matters into its own hands on the night of September 18-19, 1931. Following a minor explosion on the railway, the Japanese army occupied "with swiftness and precision" [2]—as if it had been prepared and waiting for such

[1] He remained in that office in the ensuing Hamaguchi and Wakatsuki Cabinets until December 13, 1931.

[2] The phrase is from the *Report of the Commission of Enquiry* of the League of Nations (Lytton Report) which analyzes the evidence.

an event—the principal cities in Southern Manchuria (excepting, for the time being, Chinchow and Harbin), and took over the public services. Notwithstanding professions of the Foreign Office to the United States that there was no intention to occupy Chinchow, they followed (after the fall of the moderate *Minseito* Party, including Baron Shidehara) with further operations so that by the end of 1932 all of Manchuria was under their control. The Chinese troops withdrew with little fighting. In February, 1932, under Japanese tutelage the "independent" state of Manchukuo declared itself under the regency of "Mr. Henry Pu-Yi"— former Manchu boy-emperor of China, who had been living under Japanese patronage since leaving Peking in 1924. With the "new state" of Manchukuo, Japan negotiated a treaty, September 15, 1932. It confirmed and guaranteed all rights and interests possessed by Japan or her subjects within the territory of Manchukuo by virtue of Sino-Japanese treaties, agreements or other arrangements, or of Sino-Japanese contracts, *private as well as public.* "Japan and Manchukuo, recognizing that any threat to the territory or to the peace and order of either of the High Contracting Parties constitutes at the same time a threat to the safety and existence of the other, agree to co-operate in the maintenance of their national security; it being understood that such Japanese forces as may be necessary for this purpose shall be stationed in Manchukuo."

Manchukuo was to remain under *de facto* Japanese control until September, 1945. The Japanese crowned Henry Pu-Yi as Emperor Kang Te, March 1, 1934. Japanese troops meanwhile had pushed the boundaries of the new puppet state west and south to the Great Wall, including within it the additional Chinese province of Jehol, and leaving open the frontiers into Mongolia for further expansion. China, unable to secure help from the outside world, was forced to acquiesce, by the military truce of Tangku (May 31, 1933), signed in the outskirts of Tientsin. The Chinese Nationalist Government agreed to evacuate a demilitarized zone south of the Great Wall. Only when the Japanese authorities were sure that the Chinese were completely withdrawn were they to remove their forces out of the zone. The terms of the truce left Japan free to do as it pleased north of the Great Wall. This armistice—for technically it was only such—amounted to a *de facto* acceptance of the supremacy of Japan in Manchukuo. As if there were other, unpublished terms, the Chinese began immediately the suppression of anti-Japanese propaganda and boycotts. Any tendency to their renewal met a threat of the occupation of Peiping and the immediate detachment of more provinces.

This "positive" action of Japan in Manchuria was a clean-cut violation of the Covenant of the League of Nations, of the Nine-Power Treaty, and of the Pact of Paris. It took place over the impotent protests of China and the Western world, of the League of Nations, and the United States. We must now turn back to the reaction brought about by this challenge to the machinery of peace to which the nations of the world had pledged themselves since 1919 under the New Dispensation, and to the relation of the United States thereto.

China immediately appealed Japanese aggression in Manchuria to the Council of the League of Nations under Article XI of the Covenant (which declares "any war or threat of war" a "matter of concern"). The Council asked the two disputants not to aggravate the situation while peaceful measures were being sought. Secretary of State Stimson (September 22, 1931) told the Japanese Ambassador in Washington that the United States was profoundly concerned on account of the Nine-Power Treaty and Pact of Paris. Trusting that the civilian element in the Japanese Government represented by the Foreign Office could restrain the aggressive military leaders from making way with Manchuria, Stimson at first inclined to encourage China and Japan to settle the controversy directly.[1] This only emboldened Japan. The Council (i.e., including China and Japan) passed a resolution (September 30, 1931), requesting both China and Japan to do all in their power to hasten the restoration of normal relations, but Japan blocked the unanimity of another resolution (October 24, 1931) which called for the withdrawal of her troops.[2] Meanwhile the Council, as if anxious to take advantage of an opportunity to bring the United States into close co-operation with the League in a crisis, invited (over the protests of Japan) the United States to sit in on the case. Secretary Stimson immediately appointed Prentiss Gilbert, consul of the United States at Geneva, to be present at public sessions of the Council, but instructed him not to participate in discussions except when the subject of the Pact of Paris had been raised by someone else; then he could take a part in helping to mobilize world opinion against war. To this degree only did American participa-

[1] Sara S. Smith has analyzed *The Manchurian Crisis, 1931-1932* as *A Tragedy in International Relations* (Columbia University Press, 1948). Apparently she completed her study before the publication by the Department of State of voluminous official documents in *Foreign Relations of the United States, 1931* (Washington, G.P.O., 1946), Vol. III, and *ibid., 1932*, Vols. III and IV (1948). Richard W. Van Alstyne in *Far Eastern Quarterly*, VIII (1949), 222-225, feels that the materials in the *1931* Vol. III support Miss Smith's thesis that the incompetence of the American foreign service at this juncture, together with Stimson's confusion of policy, encouraged Japan's contumacy.

[2] The resolution of September 30 was unanimous, including Japan and China. The resolution of October 24 was voted over the dissent of Japan.

tion extend in the functioning of the League on the Manchurian question; the Government of the United States was careful not to appoint any delegate to any of the committees of the League which dealt with the Sino-Japanese disputes. Nevertheless, in supplementary diplomatic conversations the United States made plain its willingness to "reinforce" any action by the Council and to co-operate with the Council Powers in their effort to find a formula for peace which could be resolved by the Council. This formula, to which the representatives of both Japan and China agreed, was adopted by the Council in a resolution of December 10, 1931, providing for the appointment of a neutral commission of investigation to study the dispute on the spot and to report back to the Council. The members of this commission, which included an American army officer, Major General Frank McCoy, with an Englishman, Lord Lytton, as chairman, did not represent any particular government: they were employed by the Council only.

President Hoover was resolved not to let the League leave the abandoned Chinese "baby" on America's doorstep. He would not have the United States join in any sanctions against Japan, lest they lead to war. Nor, for that matter, was the League ready to resort to such. Secretary Stimson wanted to keep Japan guessing about the attitude of the United States, fearful of sanctions.[1] But Japan would not be bluffed. Her forces moved all the way into Manchuria.

Dismayed by the power of the Japanese military, Secretary Stimson proceeded to draw up a caveat, like that of Secretary Bryan in 1915,[2] notifying both China and Japan that the United States did not intend to recognize any treaties, understandings, or situations which Japan and China might enter into impairing the treaty rights of the United States or their citizens in China or impairing the sovereignty, independence or territorial or administrative integrity of China, or affecting the Open Door policy, or which might be arrived at by steps contrary to the Kellogg-Briand Pact of Paris. He called in the British and French Ambassadors separately and read each a draft of his proposed note. He suggested that Great Britain—and France—might take similar steps. Such parallel statements[3] he thought might tide over a bad situation until a future

---

[1] *Foreign Relations of the United States, 1931*, Vol. III, and *ibid., 1932*, Vol. IV. Ernest Ralph Perkins has used these documents in his careful analysis of "The Non-application of Sanctions against Japan, 1931-1932," in *Essays in History and International Relations in Honor of George Hubbard Blakeslee* (Clark University Publication, 1949), pp. 215-233.

[2] Above, p. 212.

[3] Memorandum by the Secretary of State, January 5, 1932. *Foreign Relations, 1932*, III, pp. 3-4.

occasion could redeem it. Without waiting for the reply of either Great
Britain or France, Stimson independently dispatched his note to Japan
and China, the "Stimson Doctrine." After observing that with the recent
operations about Chinchow the last remaining administrative authority
of the government of the Chinese Republic in South Manchuria as it
existed prior to September 18, 1931, had been destroyed, the note went
on to state (January 7, 1932):

> The American Government continues confident that the work of the
> neutral commission recently authorized by the Council of the League of
> Nations will facilitate an ultimate solution of the difficulties now existing
> between China and Japan. But in view of the present situation and of its
> own rights and obligations therein, the American Government deems it to
> be its duty to notify both the Imperial Japanese Government and the Govern-
> ment of the Chinese Republic that it cannot admit the legality of any situa-
> tion *de facto* nor does it intend to recognize any treaty or agreement entered
> into between those governments, or agents thereof, which may impair the
> treaty rights of the United States or its citizens in China, including those
> which relate to the sovereignty, the independence, or the territorial and ad-
> ministrative integrity of the Republic of China, or to the international policy
> relative to China, commonly known as the open-door policy; and that it
> does not intend to recognize any situation, treaty, or agreement which may
> be brought about by means contrary to the covenants and obligations of
> the Pact of Paris of August 27, 1928, to which treaty both China and Japan,
> as well as the United States, are parties.

To this note the Japanese Government replied (January 12, 1932)
intimating that a new state would be set up in Manchuria by the Chinese
people there who were "not destitute of the power for self-determination."

Neither Great Britain nor France was willing to take any such parallel
step. From the British—not to mention the French Government—the
United States met a pointed rebuff, communicated to the world at large
in the form of a press communiqué: in view of former statements by
Japanese representatives that Japan would adhere to the Open Door
policy and would welcome participation and co-operation in Japanese enterprise, the British Government did not consider it necessary to address any formal note to Japan on the lines of the American note, but
had requested the Japanese Ambassador to obtain confirmation of these
early assurances from his Government.[1]

While the Lytton Commission was proceeding to the scene of the
trouble in the Far East, Japan, undismayed, proceeded with her "positive
policy" and set up the "independent" state of Manchukuo. To stamp

[1] Henry L. Stimson, *The Far Eastern Crisis* (New York, 1936), pp. 98-104.

out the disastrous boycott to which the Nationalists had resorted as a defensive measure, Japanese military and naval forces attacked and occupied Shanghai, after severe and prolonged fighting (January 28-March 3, 1932) followed, with great loss of life [1] and destruction of property.

The attack on Shanghai, and the refusal of Great Britain to co-operate with the United States, led to a significant restatement of the Stimson Doctrine by the Secretary of State of the United States, and it impelled China to appeal her dispute with Japan from the Council to the Assembly of the League, according to the provisions of Article XV. The restatement of Mr. Stimson's doctrine was contained in a public letter addressed to Senator William E. Borah, chairman of the Senate Committee on Foreign Relations, February 24, 1932. He stated that the treaties of Washington were all dependent on each other, and intimated that a party to the Nine-Power Treaty could not ignore its obligations under that treaty and continue to enjoy the advantages of the others.

The appeal to the Assembly mobilized the judgment of the small states of the League. In the Council the great powers had been less eager to pronounce against Japan. In the Assembly they could not withstand the moral pressure of the small powers, who for their own future safety were anxious to secure small or weak states from the aggression of great powers. The result was a resolution of the Assembly (March 11, 1932) by the unanimous vote of 45 delegates (China and Japan abstaining) which:

1. Proclaimed the binding nature of the Covenant and of the Pact of Paris.
2. Declared: "that it is incumbent upon the members of the League of Nations not to recognize any situation, treaty, or arrangement which may be brought about by means contrary to the Covenant of the League of Nations or to the Pact of Paris."

This resolution meant the implementing of the League of Nations and the Pact of Paris with the peaceful weapon of nonrecognition. It was equivalent to a statement that if the Lytton Commission should find Japan in the wrong, or that if Japan should not accept the recommendation of the League made after the report was rendered, then the League members would not recognize Manchukuo, for to do so would stamp Japan's conquest with the seal of international validity. The League resolution was not as sweeping as the Stimson Doctrine which had preceded it. That Doctrine rested on agreement and treaties between

[1] The Lytton Report cites estimates by the Chinese as 24,000 officers, men, and civilians, and $1,500,000,000 Mex.

Japan and the United States as well as on the multilateral treaties of Washington and the Pact of Paris. It implemented the League of Nations only indirectly.

The Lytton Commission finished its labors in September, 1932. The League published its report on October 2. An expert, conscientious, and unbiased inquiry, it is the most authoritative history and analysis which exists of the whole issue between Japan and China to that time. Briefly summarized, its conclusions were:

(1) In regard to the original attack on South Manchuria the night of September 18-19, 1931: "The military operations of the Japanese troops . . . cannot be regarded as measures of legitimate self-defence."

(2) "The present regime [Manchukuo] cannot be considered to have been called into existence by a genuine and spontaneous independence movement," and the Japanese were in actual control.

(3) The maintenance of the present regime in Manchuria would be unsatisfactory, and not "compatible with the fundamental principle of existing international obligations, nor with the good understanding between the two countries upon which peace in the Far East depends."

(4) A mere restoration of the *status quo* would be no solution.

(5) A recommendation for the creation of an autonomous Manchuria within the Chinese Republic; a recognition of the rights and interests of Japan in a new Sino-Japanese treaty which would restate those rights and interests; negotiation of a new Sino-Japanese commercial treaty; and, finally, temporary international co-operation in the internal reconstruction of China, as suggested by the late Dr. Sun Yat-sen.

After a committee of nineteen of the Assembly had endeavored to persuade Japan to accept a settlement along these lines (for which China was willing), the League unanimously [1] voted a resolution, framed by the committee:

1. That any plan of agreement should observe the principles of the League Covenant, the Pact of Paris, and the Nine-Power Treaty of Washington.

2. It should observe the provisions of the Assembly's resolution of March 11, 1932, especially those concerning a scrupulous regard for treaties and the mutual obligations of the League Members to respect and preserve their territorial integrity and political independence against external aggression, and the submission of disputes arising among them to methods of peaceful settlement.

3. It should conform to the principles and conditions laid down in the Lytton Report.

[1] China voted for the adoption of the report, Japan against it, and Siam abstained from voting. The President of the Assembly of the League of Nations announced that under Article XV of the Covenant the votes of the parties to a dispute did not count in reckoning unanimity.

After the Japanese attack on Shanghai, in the British sphere of the Yangtse Valley, Great Britain was more anxious than she had been when Manchuria alone was the prey of Japan. In the Assembly she supported the above resolution.

Following the adoption of the resolution Mr. Matsuoka, the Japanese delegate, and his staff walked out of the Assembly. Soon thereafter his Government gave the required notice (March 27, 1933) for withdrawal from the League, which became effective March 27, 1935. Japan quitted that League of Nations which her greatest diplomatist, Viscount Ishii, had so recently extolled in his *Diplomatic Commentaries* as "a house of correction for disturbers of world peace."

The League sat in legal judgment only. It resorted to no sanctions against contumacious Japan. It did not do so, because the great powers who were members were not willing to make the necessary sacrifices of trade and treasure, perhaps of men, in a region of the world where their interests seemed not sufficiently vital.[1] This was also true in two great tests of the League after Manchukuo: the Italo-Ethiopian War in 1935-1936, and the German garrisoning of the demilitarized Rhineland in 1936.

Except for nonrecognition [2] the League did nothing about the violation of the Covenant, the Nine-Power Treaty and the Pact of Paris. Except for the pronouncement of the "Stimson Doctrine" the United States also did nothing. That doctrine had been a signal to the League that the United States was on the same track.

Secretary Stimson in the restatement of the "Stimson Doctrine" in the letter to Senator Borah, noted above, made the point that the treaty structure of Washington must stand or fall as a whole. Japan had taken a passage from that book of treaties to create a doctrine to her particular advantage, while ignoring the obligations which she took upon herself so solemnly, along with other powers, when ratifying those treaties. The secret protocol to the Lansing-Ishii Agreement of 1917 had stated that the two governments would not "take advantage of the present [i.e., First World War] conditions in China in order to seek spe-

---

[1] See some very perspicuous comments in the late Frank H. Simonds' *American Foreign Policy in the Post-War Years* (Johns Hopkins Press, 1935).

[2] El Salvador and Germany (after she quitted the League) were the only states before 1936 to recognize Manchukuo *de jure*. Soviet Russia was not a member at the time of its judgment on the Sino-Japanese crisis and hence was not a party to the nonrecognition resolution. In 1935 Russia sold the Chinese Eastern Railway to Manchukuo, for *yen* 140,000,000, one third in cash, two thirds in goods, the payments guaranteed by Japan. China filed a protest. This agreement between Russia and Manchukuo might be argued to constitute at least a *de facto* recognition.

cial rights or privileges which would abridge the rights of citizens or subjects of friendly states." Paragraph 4 of Article I of the Nine-Power Treaty of 1922 had stipulated that the contracting parties would "refrain from taking advantage of conditions in order to seek special rights or privileges in China which would abridge the rights of the subjects or citizens of other friendly states, *and from countenancing action inimical to the security of such States.*" [1] The Nine-Power Treaty thus took over, multilaterally, and continued beyond the period of the First World War, the obligation previously but secretly agreed upon by the United States and Japan to be in perfect accord with the *declared* policy of the two governments in regard to China. In thus embodying in the Nine-Power Treaty of 1922 the formula of the secret Lansing-Ishii protocol of 1917, the diplomatists at Washington had added the words just italicized.

Japan ignored those portions of the Nine-Power Treaty which had been inconvenient to her, but clung to the italicized phraseology of the article here quoted in an effort to construct for the Far East a new and exclusive policy. During the London Naval Conference in 1930 reference was made in Japan to the role of that Empire as "guardian of peace in the Pacific." Before Japan quitted the League, the Japanese delegation at Geneva stated to the Assembly (February 21, 1933): "Japan is responsible for the maintenance of peace and order in the Far East." Shortly afterward (February 25, 1933) her representative at the League of Nations announced "the insistence of Japan not to allow any party to intervene in the Manchurian problem." Successive Japanese spokesmen repeated this statement of policy and expanded it to include the rest of China,[2] then Eastern Asia, next "Greater Eastern Asia," finally "Japan's Co-Prosperity Area," whatever those descriptions might comprise.

[1] Italics inserted. Notice that in the Nine-Power Treaty the word "present" is omitted, but the word "friendly" retained. Presumably the retention of "friendly" at that time excluded Russia.

[2] One of the most conspicuous utterances of this nature was by Mr. Eijii Amau, referred to by the newspapers as the "spokesman of the Foreign Office" at Tokyo, in 1934. Although the Amau pronouncement was not a state paper, its validity was confirmed by a statement attributed to the Japanese Ambassador in Washington, Mr. Saito, in the New York *Times* (April 24, 1934) and by a statement by Foreign Minister Hirota to the United States Embassy, reported in the *Times* (April 26, 1934). Said Amau in a long statement: "We oppose any attempt on the part of China to avail herself of the influence of any other country in order to resist Japan. . . . The supplying to China of war planes, the building of airdromes in China and the detailing of military instructors and advisers to China, or the contracting of a loan to provide funds for political uses would obviously tend to alienate the friendly relations between Japan and China and other countries and to disturb the peace and order of Eastern Asia. Japan will oppose such projects."

Under this concept Japan even objected to a League of Nations technical mission for reconstruction and internal improvements in China, including roads, waterways, education, rural credit, hygiene, and flood control.

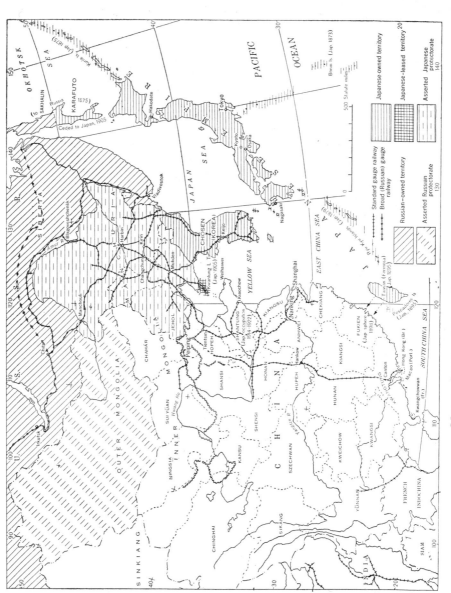

Map 8. Japan and Russia in Eastern Asia, 1936

This expression of a policy of hegemony over "Greater Eastern Asia" was frequently referred to by Japanese spokesmen as the Asiatic or Japanese Monroe Doctrine.[1] It was similar to the Monroe Doctrine to the extent that Japan insisted that no outside power should take action in China inimical to the security of Japan. It was scandalous to compare it otherwise to the Monroe Doctrine. Japanese publicists cited the interventions under the Panama Policy of the United States to justify intervention in Manchuria. But these American interventions were not used to exploit the land and resources of the temporary protectorates that were established under them; and, as the reader of the preceding chapters of this volume is well aware, the protectorates had been liquidated, and the United States had ratified a treaty never to intervene in the external or internal affairs of Latin-American republics, directly or indirectly, or for whatever reason.

The best comparison of the so-called Japanese Monroe Doctrine with the real Monroe Doctrine of the United States would be the treatment accorded by Japan and the United States respectively to Manchuria and Mexico. Even if the interventions of the United States in Cuba, in Panama, the Dominican Republic, Nicaragua, and Haiti were cited—as they have been—as precedents for Japan's interventions in China, one must note this most significant fact: these interventions were not in violation of solemnly ratified multilateral treaties. It may be contended, and the present author agrees, that the Panama intervention was unjust—reparation was later paid for the wrong—and that it violated at least the spirit of the treaty of 1846 with New Granada; but it did not take control of the land and people of the Republic of Panama, the independence of which moreover was promptly recognized by the nations of the world.

An essential thing in all these comparisons of Japanese interventions with previous interventions of the United States, Great Britain, France, and other great powers was the New Dispensation: the solemn treaties of the League of Nations, the Washington treaties, the Pact of Paris, the instruments by which the statesmen of the world, including Japan's statesmen, sought to establish a reign of international peace after the First World War. If Japan had withdrawn her armed forces from China and had agreed with the recognized states of Asia as the United States had agreed with Latin America, that no one state has a right to intervene in the internal or external affairs of another state; if she had

[1] George H. Blakeslee has described the development of "The Japanese Monroe Doctrine," in *Foreign Affairs*, XI (1932-1933), 670-681.

observed the obligations of the Washington treaties as well as enjoyed their advantages; if she had accepted the recommendations of the League of Nations on the Manchurian and Shanghai and other issues with China, then the world might well have applauded the Japanese claim to an Asiatic Monroe Doctrine.

For the New Dispensation Japan had only hatred and contempt. Further, she interpreted the Philippine independence act of March 3, 1934,[1] and the efforts of the United States to bring about limitation of naval armament, not as evidence of good will and peaceful ideals, but rather as an indication of softness. The distresses of the Occident, signalized by the continuing Great Depression and the rise of Italian and German power in Europe, encouraged Japanese militarists to go ahead rapidly with the conquest of China while the Western powers were unable to stop them. Japan next attacked Peiping [2] (July 7, 1937) and extended the Second Sino-Japanese War for the thorough conquest of that vast country. She had now entered with spectacular earnestness a further phase of the designs expressed by Lord Hotta to the Shogun back in 1858: "to command universal vassalage" and "hegemony over all nations."

Such an empire, erected on the ruins of ancient China, accompanied by a German empire built on the ruins of a conquered Europe, presaged an unbalance of power in the Old World which ought to be the nightmare of every anxious American student of international affairs. It brought back the danger that had been removed for a generation by American intervention in the First World War. It cast power politics in the shape of a future totalitarian vise pressing out the life of the republican New World. It foreshadowed the possibility of a two-ocean war to be fought with a one-ocean navy. It signalized the close of that foolproof period of American diplomatic history when the distresses of the Old World had been uniformly the advantages of the New World. It meant the end of the long period of isolation and peace in which the

---

[1] This law provided that the Philippine Islands, after a period of ten years as an autonomous commonwealth under the protection of the United States, should become an absolutely independent republic. At the end of the ten-year period, which began with the inauguration in 1936 of the new commonwealth of the Philippines, all American military forces were to be withdrawn from the islands, and the two governments jointly were to decide whether, and on what terms, the United States should maintain a naval base in the islands. This act seemed to indicate a withdrawal for good and all by the United States from the Philippines at the end of the prescribed decade. Notwithstanding Japan's temporary conquest of the Philippines in 1942, Philippine independence went into effect as scheduled, July 4, 1946, following the defeat and surrender of Japan.

[2] Historical usage sanctions the name Peking for the capital of China before 1928, when the Nationalists shifted it to Nanking and renamed the former capital Peiping. In 1949 the Communists established Peking, with the old spelling, as their capital.

Continental Republic had been created in the empty spaces of North America, working out its Manifest Destiny between wide ocean barriers.

In the face of such doubly ominous portents President Roosevelt tried to thwart German aggression in Europe and Japanese aggression in Asia by throwing the weight of American neutrality in favor of the victims of aggression, and at the same time keeping the United States out of war in either Asia or Europe. To do this, first in the case of Japan, later in the case of Germany, he had to get around some of the apparent obstacles of the neutrality resolution of April 30, 1937, designed, so to speak, to keep the United States out of the First World War rather than the Second World War. We recall that the law stipulated a mandatory embargo on the export of arms, ammunition, and implements of warfare, and credits, from the neutral United States to belligerent countries, but left it to the discretion of the President to "find" or not to "find" a war in existence which required the application of this domestic law.

President Roosevelt hesitated to proclaim neutrality, in this phase of the Second Sino-Japanese War.[1] Under the domestic law of May 1, 1937, this would have instantly embargoed the export of arms, ammunition, and implements of war to both China and Japan, and would have given the President discretionary power to prohibit the export to *both* belligerents of other articles [2] *in American ships,* but not in foreign ships. Japan had ships. China had no ships. So Japan would continue in any event to import from the neutral United States other war material than arms, ammunition, and implements of war, that is, gasoline, oil, and scrap iron, to feed her war machines in China.

Such a neutrality, flowing from the mandatory provision of the law of May 1, 1937, was distasteful to the President because it would operate more favorably to Japan, considered to be the aggressor, than to China, esteemed to be the victim. He preferred that circumstances might not oblige him to "find" a war in existence. As the Sino-Japanese War developed, Japan proved equally unwilling to be involved in further "international difficulties" as long as the Western powers were not fully occupied by distresses in the Occident. She was not prepared to assert belligerent rights against neutral shipping on the high seas. Thereupon

[1] The First Sino-Japanese War was in 1895. The Second Sino-Japanese War may be said to have begun in 1931 with the conquest of Manchuria, and to have been in existence, with short truces, to 1945.

[2] This provision of the Act covering the export in American ships of articles other than arms, ammunition, and implements of warfare was on the statutes only between May 1, 1937, and May 1, 1939.

the Government began to license the export, in privately owned ships of the United States, of arms to Hong Kong to be transshipped to China. It also furnished credit to the Chinese Government for the stabilization of exchange and the purchase of supplies, as did European governments.[1] By "moral embargoes" it endeavored to persuade American exporters not to export arms, ammunition, or implements of warfare to nations (like Japan) which bombed civilian populations in open cities.

President Roosevelt now took another look across the Pacific Ocean. He could not, for the life of the United States, see a war anywhere. Hostilities, battles, marches, and countermarches of invading armies, the bombing of civilian populations, the sack of great cities, indescribable human suffering and death, all this he could see clearly, but no war that required the proclamation of neutrality according to the Act of April 30, 1937.[2]

It is not a duty of neutrality to keep the weight of power even between two belligerents locked in mortal combat, and accordingly to regulate the flow of supplies so as to make up for the deficiencies of the one

---

[1] At first, beginning July, 1937, the $2,000,000,000 "gold profit" stabilization fund created as a result of the gold devaluation act of 1934, was used to stabilize the Chinese currency, to buy and sell dollars and *yuan*. On December 13, 1938, the Export-Import Bank, a government corporation, extended a commercial credit of $25,000,000, and on March 7, 1940, a second credit of $20,000,000, to the Universal Trading Company of New York, guaranteed in both instances by the Central Bank of China, for the purchase of agricultural, industrial and manufactured articles (including motor trucks).

These loans were paralleled by loans for the purchase of supplies, from the British, French, Russian, Czechoslovakian, and Belgian Governments. In the case of the French Government the loans were also for construction of the railway between Szechuan and Yunnan. See *Documents on American Foreign Relations, op. cit.,* III (1940-1941), pp. 245-246.

[2] "We have not put into effect the neutrality proclamation," he explained in a then off-the-record special press conference with members of the American Society of Newspaper Editors, April 21, 1938, "for the very simple reason that if we could find a way of not doing it, we would be more neutral than if we did.

"Now, if we declared neutrality, what would happen? Japan could not buy any munitions from us, but they are not buying them anyway. China is buying munitions from us via England, via Singapore, via Hong Kong—not direct—through English purchases and, undoubtedly, American munitions are going into China today. But, on the other hand, Japan has complete, free access to all of our raw material markets because they dominate the ocean. They are buying their copper, their oil, their cotton—they are buying all kinds of things, scrap metal by the shiploads, which is going into munitions, and they would be able, under the Neutrality Act, to continue to buy oil and copper and scrap metal.

"Therefore, by virtue of this excuse [of the Japanese] that they are not at war—it is only an excuse—we are maintaining, in fact, a neutral position."

"We are achieving that, despite the neutrality?" asked one of his listeners.

"Despite the neutrality law," continued the President, "and that is the trouble with a neutrality law that attempts to tie the hands of an administration for future events and circumstances that no human being can possibly guess." *Public Papers and Addresses of Franklin D. Roosevelt,* 1937 volume: *The Constitution Prevails* (New York, 1941), p. 287.

which is weaker in sea power, or armament, or money, or man power. But it may be imperative as a matter of policy to sacrifice a juridical neutrality to help one of the belligerents sustain itself against an aggressor lest the triumph of the aggressor build up an irresistible power to be turned against the whilom neutral. President Roosevelt's use of his discretion, under the letter of the neutrality law of April 30, 1937, was a diplomatic, not a juridical decision, a grave diplomatic step, let it be said, which was supported by the nation. The House of Representatives made no move to question, much less to challenge, the President.

Soon after the Second Sino-Japanese War broke out, Secretary of State Hull made a broad pronouncement (July 16, 1937) of general foreign policy invoking the principles of the Good Neighbor Policy, which the Secretary now applied to the Far East.

"We avoid entering into alliances or entangling commitments," he said, "but we believe in co-operative effort by peaceful and practicable means in support of the principles hereinbefore stated." [1]

Secretary Hull did not stress or mention the integrity of China. He did express willingness, as he had offered since 1934, to modify treaties, when need arose for it, "by orderly processes carried out in a spirit of mutual helpfulness and accommodation." He left the door open for peaceful negotiations to settle the China question, either by another conference, or by negotiation between the United States and Japan.

Once more China appealed to the League of Nations (September 12, 1937), and once more the United States accepted the League's invitation to sit in on its consideration of the conflict without voting. A committee of the League reported Japan guilty of violating the Pact of Paris and the Nine-Power Treaty, and called upon the signatories of the latter treaty, including Japan, to meet in conference to seek some method of ending the Sino-Japanese conflict by agreement.[2] The same day (October 5, 1937) President Roosevelt in a sensational public address at Chicago appealed to the "peace-loving nations" to make a concerted effort "in opposition to those violations of treaties and those ignorings of human instincts which today are creating a state of international anarchy and

---

[1] In a supplemental statement on August 23, 1937, Mr. Hull explained that the principles expressed on July 16 applied in the Pacific area as elsewhere. "It embraces the principles embodied in many treaties, including the Washington Conference treaties and the Kellogg-Briand Pact of Paris. . . . This Government is endeavoring to see kept alive, strengthened, and revitalized, in reference to the Pacific area and to the world these fundamental principles." Department of State *Press Releases*, XVII, No. 407 (July 17, 1937) and XVII, No. 413 (August 28, 1937). See also F. D. Roosevelt, *Public Addresses and Papers*, 1940 volume, pp. 589, 590.

[2] A. W. Griswold, *Far Eastern Policy of the United States* (New York, 1938), pp. 456-460.

instability from which there is no escape through mere isolation or neutrality." War, he said, should be quarantined like an epidemic disease. The next day Secretary Hull declared that Japan's action in China was inconsistent with the Nine-Power Treaty and the Kellogg-Briand Pact of Paris, and that the Government of the United States was in general accord with the conclusion of the Assembly of the League of Nations on these points.

Given the dangerous international situation in Europe, none of the great European powers parties to the broken Nine-Power Treaty dared to call a conference to mend it. They prevailed on little Belgium to extend the invitation. If any government expected the United States to take the lead at Brussels in quarantine measures against Japan, it was disappointed. The President himself explained that the delegation of the United States went to Brussels without any commitments to any other governments. In the conference Japan declared she would tolerate no outside interference in the settlement of her dispute with China. Italy, who had left the League after its rebuke to her on Ethiopia, could be counted on to block unanimity of resolve on any action that might be proposed against Japan. The meeting adjourned without accomplishing anything more than an empty reaffirmation of the principles of the demolished Nine-Power Treaty.

After the failure of the Brussels Conference the United States began to evacuate its nationals and its forces [1] from Chinese territory, in order to avoid incidents that might lead to war. Japanese militarists took this as a sign of weakness. Some irresponsible officers bombed from the air and destroyed the U. S. gunboat *Panay* (December 12, 1937) in the Yangtze River. The United States was quick to protest and demand reparations. Japan even more quickly apologized in advance, and paid the reparations demanded without question: $2,214,007.36.[2] She did not want war with the United States while Europe was still at peace.

The United States continued to keep a list of Japanese violations of the treaty rights of American citizens, their persons and property, and to file protests and caveats against a future reckoning. Japan on her part continued her conquests deep in China. Wherever she went she

---

[1] Since the Boxer Protocol of 1901 the United States and other powers had maintained small detachments of marines to guard the legations, as long as they existed at Peking, and since 1927 they had contributed small forces to defend the international settlement at Shanghai. The United States also had maintained, in company with Great Britain and France, nine small gunboats to patrol Chinese rivers against depredations to American citizens and commerce. In 1937 there were 528 marines at Peiping (Peking), 814 infantry at Tientsin, 2,555 marines at Shanghai. Griswold, *op. cit.*, p. 462.

[2] No punitive reparations were assessed.

slammed shut, in the face of the Washington treaties of 1922 and all other treaties, the old Open Door, and locked it tight with all sorts of devices: discriminatory tariffs, taxes and railroad rates, exchange controls, import and export controls, restrictions on shipping and port facilities, monopolies, and other contrivances in violations of treaties.[1] As to the integrity of China, her armies tore it to pieces.

Japanese-American relations by now were raising greater questions than the Open Door or the treaty rights of American citizens in China. They were testing right and wrong, according to the respective lights of the two governments, in what was coming slowly to be interpreted as a challenge of power to the principles of liberty everywhere.[2]

The diplomatic capitulation of Great Britain and France to Germany at Munich in September, 1938, and the certainty that they would be involved indefinitely and deeply in European dangers, encouraged Japan in her Asiatic policy and sharpened her effrontery toward those powers in the Far East, although for the time being she dealt more cautiously with the United States and its nationals as long as that Pacific power was not definitely involved in Europe. While the United States protested to Japan against indiscriminate slaughter of civilian populations by the bombing of undefended cities in violation of Hague Conventions, Japan was making in the United States huge purchases of oil and gasoline with which to lubricate and fuel her growing fleets of warships and planes, and of scrap iron with which to perfect her armaments against any or all comers. Public opinion in the United States, incensed at Japanese bombings of civilians and conscience-stricken at the provenance of Japan's supplies, increasingly demanded an embargo on exports of war materials to Japan. Such an embargo, at least in time of peace (i.e., no recognized war between China and Japan, as testified

---

[1] William C. Johnstone has listed and analyzed these treaty violations in his study of *The United States and Japan's New Order* (American Council of the Institute of Pacific Relations, New York, 1941).

[2] So wrote Secretary Hull, in a public letter to Vice President Garner, January 10, 1938: "The interest and concern of the United States in the Far Eastern situation, in the European situation, and in situations on this continent, are not measured by the number of American concerns residing in a particular country at a particular moment nor by the amount of investment of American citizens there, nor by the volume of trade. There is a broader and more fundamental interest—which is that orderly processes in international relations must be maintained. Referring expressly to the Far East, an area which contains approximately half the population of the world, the United States is deeply interested in supporting *by peaceful means* influences contributory to preservation and encouragement of orderly processes. This interest far transcends in importance the value of American trade with China or American interests in China, it transcends even the question of safeguarding the immediate welfare of American citizens in China." Department of State *Press Releases*, XVIII, No. 433 (January 15, 1938). Italics inserted.

COMPARATIVE NAVAL STRENGTH OF THE SEVEN PRINCIPAL POWERS IN JULY, 1939

TYPE	TOTAL BUILT		UNDER AGE		OVER AGE		BUILDING AND APPROPRIATED FOR	
	NUMBER	TONS	NUMBER	TONS	NUMBER	TONS	NUMBER	TONS
UNITED STATES								
CAPITAL SHIPS	15	464,300	14	438,200	1	26,100	8	300,000
AIRCRAFT CARRIERS	5	120,100	5	120,100	0	0	2	34,500
CRUISERS A	17	161,200	17	161,200	0	0	1	10,000
CRUISERS B	17	137,775	17	137,775	0	0	8	60,000
DESTROYERS	221	273,490	54	84,190	167	189,300	43	68,380
SUBMARINES	89	83,175	22	34,435	67	48,740	25	35,250
BRITISH EMPIRE								
CAPITAL SHIPS	18	495,500	18	495,500	0	0	9	335,000
AIRCRAFT CARRIERS	9	148,600	7	127,700	2	20,900	7	138,000
CRUISERS A	15	145,620	15	145,620	0	0	0	0
CRUISERS B	47	294,635	24	185,945	23	108,690	25	146,500
DESTROYERS	178	233,359	107	154,114	71	79,245	37	37,350
SUBMARINES	55	56,919	45	52,469	10	4,450	18	15,690
JAPAN *								
CAPITAL SHIPS	11	308,480	10	301,400	1	7,080	3	121,000
AIRCRAFT CARRIERS	11	146,520	11	146,520	0	0	2	25,000
CRUISERS A	17	153,050	12	107,800	5	45,250	0	0
CRUISERS B	23	132,635	15	97,555	8	35,080	5	44,000
DESTROYERS	111	141,748	75	106,798	36	34,950	9	14,900
SUBMARINES	59	76,863	40	59,261	19	17,602	3	6,000
FRANCE								
CAPITAL SHIPS	7	163,945	7	163,945	0	0	4	140,000
AIRCRAFT CARRIERS	2	32,146	2	32,146	0	0	2	36,000
CRUISERS A	7	70,000	7	70,000	0	0	0	0
CRUISERS B	11	79,725	11	79,725	0	0	3	24,000
DESTROYERS	71	121,201	70	120,286	1	915	30	46,776
SUBMARINES	75	72,709	75	72,709	0	0	27	24,252
ITALY								
CAPITAL SHIPS	10	108,730	9	99,498	1	9,232	4	140,000
AIRCRAFT CARRIERS	0	0	0	0	0	0	0	0
CRUISERS A	7	70,000	7	70,000	0	0	0	0
CRUISERS B	14	80,918	12	74,488	2	6,430	14	56,344
DESTROYERS	130	133,163	100	111,936	30	21,227	12	15,200
SUBMARINES	105	79,704	98	77,248	7	2,456	28	30,986
GERMANY								
CAPITAL SHIPS	7	108,080	5	82,000	2	26,000	4	150,000
AIRCRAFT CARRIERS	0	0	0	0	0	0	2	38,500
CRUISERS A	2	20,000	2	20,000	0	0	3	30,000
CRUISERS B	6	35,600	6	35,600	0	0	4	28,000
DESTROYERS	44	51,081	32	42,844	12	8,237	10	18,110
SUBMARINES	50	19,709	50	19,709	0	0	21	11,573
RUSSIA **								
CAPITAL SHIPS	3	69,878	3	69,878	0	0	3	105,000
AIRCRAFT CARRIERS	1	9,000	1	9,000	0	0	2	24,000
CRUISERS A	3	24,030	3	24,030	0	0	5	40,000
CRUISERS B	5	28,994	3	17,034	2	11,960	0	0
DESTROYERS	37	40,907	23	25,024	14	15,883	10	26,295
SUBMARINES	122	64,265	114	59,897	8	4,368	19	12,158

* Best obtainable data due to the fact that the Japanese Government did not release figures. Japanese tonnage was probably greater than indicated above, and particularly so in the categories of aircraft carriers, cruisers, destroyers, and submarines.

** Best obtainable data due to the fact that the Soviet Government did not release figures. Soviet tonnage was probably greater than indicated above, and particularly so in the categories of destroyers and submarines.

SOURCE: Compiled from figures furnished by United States Navy Department to House of Representatives indicating comparative naval strength of the seven principal powers as of 2 July, 1939. To be found in Congressional Record, 76th Congress, 2nd Session, Volume 85, Part I, pages 1065-66.

Compiled by Anthony C. J. Davidonis

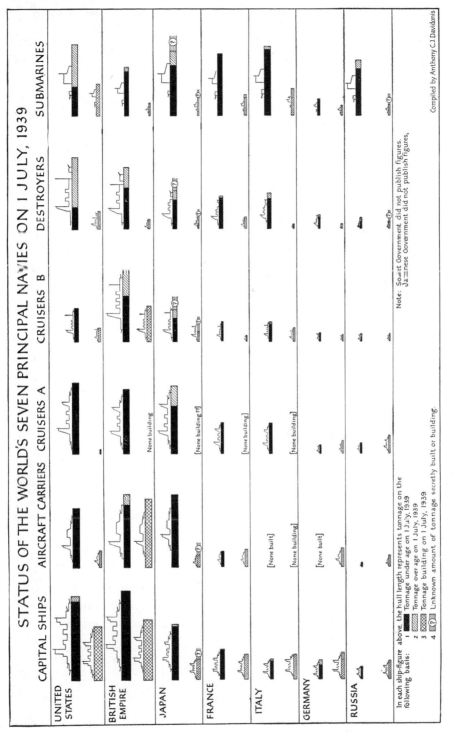

STATUS OF THE WORLD'S SEVEN PRINCIPAL NAVIES ON 1 JULY, 1939

CAPITAL SHIPS   AIRCRAFT CARRIERS   CRUISERS A   CRUISERS B   DESTROYERS   SUBMARINES

UNITED STATES

BRITISH EMPIRE

JAPAN

FRANCE

ITALY

GERMANY

RUSSIA

In each ship-figure above, the hull length represents tonnage on the following basis:

1   Tonnage under age on 1 July, 1939
2   Tonnage over age on 1 July, 1939
3   Tonnage building on 1 July, 1939
4   Unknown amount of tonnage secretly built or building.

Note: Soviet Government did not publish figures.
        Japanese Government did not publish figures,

Compiled by Anthony C.J Davidonis

357

by the inanimity of the neutrality laws), would have been unquestionably in violation of the treaty of commerce of 1911. If the United States was standing for the sanctity of treaties all over the world, it could not very consistently violate this one by imposing an embargo, not to mention political reasons for hesitating to discriminate against Japanese commerce. Widespread demand for abrogation of the treaty, with the stipulated six months' notice according to its terms, brought up proposed resolutions in Congress urging such a step on the executive. Before a resolution could be passed, Secretary Hull announced, as an executive act, that the requisite notice had been given, July 26, 1939. The treaty accordingly expired January 26, 1940, four months after the beginning of the European war. It left the way open for commercial discriminations and embargoes against Japan.[1]

In the next two chapters of this volume, we shall see how the unbalance of power in Europe and Asia and its mounting danger to the New World merged to break down the neutrality of the United States for the third time in its history. During that great conflict China was to rise suddenly to unheard-of prestige. As ally of the United States she succeeded in abolishing American extraterritorial rights by the treaty of January 11, 1943, thus accompanying the termination of the unequal treaties by the last of the other powers. The United States further recognized the new position of China by repealing the Chinese exclusion acts, admitting Chinese citizens to an immigration quota, and making Chinese aliens resident in the United States eligible at last for citizenship.[2] Entering the United Nations as a charter member, China became one of the five permanent members of the all-powerful Security Council along with the United States, Great Britain, France, and the Soviet Union. It seemed that a new day of equality and prosperity had come for that great nation, most populous state on the globe, vast seat of the world's oldest civilization. In the penultimate chapters of this book we shall have to read the sad climax for China of the Second World War: the Yalta agreement, the entrance of Russia into the war, the surprising surrender of Japan, which caught the Chinese off guard, so to speak; the Communist Civil War; and defeat in victory for the Nationalist Government.

[1] For pre-Pearl Harbor studies of Japanese-American relations and Far Eastern issues see: Harold S. Quigley and George H. Blakeslee, *The Far East, an International Survey* (World Peace Foundation, 1938); T. A. Bisson, *American Policy in the Far East, 1931-1940* (Institute of Pacific Relations, New York, 1940); W. W. Willoughby, *Japan's Case Examined* (Johns Hopkins Press, 1940). M. Royama, *Foreign Policy of Japan, 1914-1939* (Japanese Council, Institute of Pacific Relations, Tokyo, 1941).

[2] For the treaty and the act of December 17, 1943, repealing the exclusion acts, see *Documents on American Foreign Relations, 1944, 1945*, V, pp. 485-500, VI, pp. 607-619.

17

Isolation and Neutrality—1937-1939

WHAT caused the second war in Europe, twenty-five years after the beginning of the First World War, was the recrudescence of German military power and will to conquest under a new Napoleonic genius, Adolf Hitler. Taking advantage of the apathy and division of the nations that had checked and beaten Germany in the First World War, he fired the German people with a religiously fanatical nationalism determined to avenge the defeat of 1918 and to conquer Europe: today Europe, to-morrow the entire world. He molded them into a totalitarian folk under his own dictatorship, resting on revolutionary repudiations of popular sovereignty and democracy, a military technocracy called National Socialism. Before Great Britain and France [1] could fully awake to the swift and deadly facts of German power, Hitler had rearmed and fortified the Rhineland, had united Austria with Germany by force, and had built up a mighty mechanized army and overwhelming armadas of the air.

By threatening the Allies with war in the summer of 1938, Hitler achieved the greatest success possible in diplomacy: he won the fruits of a war without fighting one. He made the Allied leaders come to Munich and sign a peace with him and his new fascist ally, Premier Mussolini of Italy, a peace which at one stroke shattered the Treaty of Versailles in Europe and broke up the alliances of France that had protected the small countries in the central and eastern parts of that continent against another eruption of German power. Helpless at Munich, Britain and France tried to divert the German lightnings away from their own dooryards by opening a field for German conquest in middle Europe and in Russia: in Russia, the actual ally of France, excluded at Munich!

Vainly Prime Minister Chamberlain and Premier Daladier hoped against hope that Munich would bring peace in their time in the west.

---

[1] Arnold Wolfers has analyzed conflicting strategies of peace since Versailles in *Britain and France between Two Wars* (Yale Institute of International Studies, 1940).

Foolishly they put faith in Hitler's pledge that he would never change another frontier in Europe. But the thunderbolts had been forged, and now they could be hurled in any direction from the mountaintop of Berchtesgaden. Too late the men of Munich woke up to this when they saw Czechoslovakia, sacrificed in 1938 by cession of her northern "Sudeten" provinces, next trampled under the treads of German tanks in the spring of 1939 and annihilated, her vast stocks of armaments added to the conqueror's arsenals for use against the next victim. The League of Nations, which had guaranteed the political independence and territorial integrity of each convenanting party, was not even consulted in this dismemberment and extinction of a signatory state.

Belatedly Great Britain and France prepared for the war that was certain soon to come when Hitler's avalanche of armaments should move against another nation. Not to resist the next time would mean definitive surrender to a power that could not afterward be checked. It would mean the death of the British and French Empires and the democracies on which they rested at home, the end of the small nations of the continent, the unification of Europe by that conquest which successive captains of war had tried and failed to accomplish during the last three hundred years, and its enfeoffment to German Nazism.

As soon as the crops had been harvested, Hitler struck again, on September 1, 1939, this time at Poland, immediately after signing a dramatic nonaggression pact with Russia, the outcast of Munich, the only one of the former Allies of 1938 who had been willing to fight for Czechoslovakia, the former ally whom Great Britain had wooed again in vain. In desperation Great Britain and France declared war on Germany, September 3, rather than by neutrality to contribute to their own certain destruction. By fighting there was some chance to save themselves; by not fighting, none. From a bedeviled continent the holocaust flamed up, to light the whole world in its lurid glare.

Unlike the days of 1914, when the American public, and even the United States Government, was taken by surprise by the sudden outbreak of war in Europe, the advent of war in 1939 was not unexpected either by the people or by the Government. They were watching for it. They had been dreading it for years.

The Roosevelt Administration came into power almost simultaneously with the accession of Hitler to the Chancellorship of Germany. Although at first absorbed with the economic debacle at home, the new President continued the efforts of the Hoover Administration to further international agreements for disarmament in order to promote peace. As early as May 27, 1933, the United States delegate to the disarmament conference at Geneva declared that his Government was willing "to consult the other States" in case of a threat to peace, with a view to averting conflict.

"Further than that," he declared, "in the event that the States, in conference, determine that a State has been guilty of a breach of the peace in violation of its international obligations and take measures against the violator, then, *if we concur in the judgment rendered* as to the responsible and guilty party, we will refrain from any action tending to defeat such collective effort which these States may thus make to restore peace." [1]

President Roosevelt made it plain at the time of the Ethiopian crisis of 1935, and again on the occasion of Japan's next attack on China in 1937, that the United States did concur in the judgment made by the League and would respect any sanctions that it might take to block aggression. In May, 1936, he appealed to all the chiefs of state the world over to enter into nonaggression pacts. He declared publicly at Chicago, October 5, 1937, after mentioning the Kellogg-Briand Pact of Paris, the Covenant of the League of Nations, the Nine-Power Treaty, and the new Pan-American treaties outlawing aggression and intervention in the New World, that aggressor states ought in effect to be quarantined. [2]

All these speeches, and numerous other expressions, indicated a disposition to co-operate for the maintenance of international peace, in order, as the President put it, to keep the United States out of war and to cut the expense of armament. They indicated also anxiety as to whether the United States could avoid involvement in any war that did come in Europe. No such anxiety existed in the Government of the United States in the years before the First World War. The new concern was reflected in the rising appropriations for army and navy bills.

Whatever the anxiety of the Government may have been as to the ultimate effect of another European war, there was no question of its policy of keeping out of war in the Old World, whether in Europe or Asia. That policy had been fixed in the neutrality legislation of 1935-1937, written on the statutes and signed by the President, in a wave of disillusionment arising from a review of the last war, and of fear that

[1] Statement of Norman Davis to the General Commission of the Disarmament Conference, May 22, 1933. Italics inserted. Department of State *Press Releases* (May 27, 1933).

[2] *Public Papers and Addresses of Franklin D. Roosevelt, op. cit.,* 1937 volume, pp. 406-411.

the United States might be "dragged" into another one like it. The President favored the new neutrality laws in principle, but felt that they were too rigid, that situations might arise in which the wholly inflexible embargo might have exactly the opposite effect from that intended.[1] The people did not realize that the next war might not be like the last one. They were largely isolationist.

When during the European war crisis of September, 1938, all the peace machinery of the times seemed to have failed, President Roosevelt at the eleventh hour appealed to Great Britain, Germany, France, and Czechoslovakia, and to Hitler and Mussolini personally, to save the peace of Europe. This was more than Woodrow Wilson had done in 1914. Until archives are opened up years hence, it is not possible to say, probably it will never be possible to say, precisely what influence, if any, the President's appeal had in bringing about the Munich Conference. The motive of the Government was to insure the safety of the United States by preserving the peace of Europe. Every man and woman in the United States, it was explained officially, shared in the universal feeling of relief that war had been averted.[2] Roosevelt's reaction to the crisis of September, 1938, as contrasted with Wilson's passivity in July, 1914, is a gauge of the extent to which a quarter century of contemporary history had tightened up the relationships of the Old World and the New, for good or ill, in our age of Great Technology.

After Czechoslovakia had ceased to exist, if such a euphemism is permissible, President Roosevelt in the spring of 1939 addressed identic notes to Chancellor Hitler and Premier Mussolini stating that the possibility of a new war was of definite concern to the people of the United States, for whom he spoke, "as it must be also to the peoples of the other nations of the entire Western Hemisphere."[3] "All of them know," he continued, "that any major war, *even if it were confined to other continents,* must bear heavily on them during its continuance and for many generations to come." Speaking for the United States as one of the

[1] Note by President Roosevelt, *Public Papers and Addresses, op. cit.,* 1939 volume, p. 523.

[2] Message to Czechoslovakia, Germany, Great Britain, and France, September 26, 1938. To Chancellor Adolf Hitler, September 27, 1938. *Ibid.,* pp. 531-538. Department of State *Press Releases,* XIX, Nos. 470, 471 (October 1, October 8, 1938) for the correspondence. Undersecretary of State Sumner Welles summarizes the correspondence with Mussolini, which is not printed in the President's *Papers and Addresses.* The last two sentences of the above text are taken almost *verbatim* from Mr. Welles's radio address of October 3, 1938, explaining the crisis.

[3] "You will note that I did not assume to speak for them," he explained to the Press Conference of April 15, 1939, in a running exegesis of the note, which went out on April 14. *Ibid.,* pp. 208-217. I have inserted italics in quoted passages.

nations of the Western Hemisphere "not involved in the *immediate* controversies which have arisen in Europe," he challenged the dictators to make good their professions of peace by asking them outright if they were willing to give assurances that their armed forces would not attack or invade the territory or possessions of the following independent nations: Finland, Estonia, Latvia, Lithuania, Sweden, Norway, Denmark, the Netherlands, Belgium, Great Britain and Ireland, France, Portugal, Spain, Switzerland, Lichtenstein, Luxemburg, Poland, Hungary, Rumania, Yugoslavia, Russia, Bulgaria, Greece, Turkey, Iraq, the Arabias, Syria, Palestine, Egypt, and Iran.

In case Germany and Italy would engage in "reciprocal assurances" with the enumerated governments, Roosevelt offered to participate, in the resulting peaceful surroundings, in a general international discussion for the limitation of armaments and the elimination of international trade barriers—in other words a great international conference with guns "parked" outside.

The dictators did not deign to answer this plain proposal, except by tirades from their own rostra. It was evident they intended to make war.

In case of another European war and consequent proclamation of the neutrality of the United States under the Act of April 30, 1937, a mandatory embargo would immediately go into effect on the shipment of arms, ammunition, and implements of warfare,[1] directly or indirectly from the United States to any of the belligerent powers. Included in such category, by official listing under the act, were airplanes and their component parts. Similarly the granting of credits to belligerent governments, other than for ordinary current transactions, would be blocked by domestic law. The neutrality law also prohibited citizens of the United States from traveling on belligerent merchant ships; and it prohibited the arming of neutral United States merchant ships. From the then current disillusionist historiography of American intervention in the First World War, the nation had drawn the conclusion that it had been impolitic to insist on traditional and indubitable neutral rights. To do so again might get the country into another war.

Thus had been forsworn in a trice, as it were, the American birthright of Freedom of the Seas, written into the early treaty structure of the United States, and subsequently into international law, doctrines which

[1] The Act of 1937 had contained a two-year section authorizing the President, at his discretion, to embargo the export overseas in American ships of other articles than arms, ammunition, and implements of warfare; and to forbid the export of any *American-owned* property in such articles or materials on foreign ships; but this section of the act expired on May 1, 1939. See above, pp. 196-197.

the great Republic of the West had championed in two previous major
wars. This was not only a discouragement to the small nations of the
world who hoped to be neutrals and to have neutral rights in the next war.
It was also an ominous portent for Great Britain and France. It would
make it impossible for those powers to draw upon the neutral United
States as a storehouse for munitions as they had done in the First World
War. We have seen that without that neutral reservoir, and sea power
to protect transatlantic imports, the Allies could not have armed themselves adequately in 1914-1917 to resist their enemies. The neutrality
laws of 1935 and 1937 closed this neutral storehouse to the powers that
controlled the seas. The mandatory embargo on munitions, announced
to the world by the United States for application automatically to the
next war, was in effect an assurance to Germany that if her ruler attacked
a European State, and thus provoked a general war, his enemies, Great
Britain and France, could not rely on these vital succors from the United
States as they had done in the last war. Given the greater preparation
of Germany, the neutrality of the United States under the new *domestic*
legislation of 1937 would insure the defeat of the Allies, laggard as they
had been in preparing themselves for a new attack by Germany. The
existence of this legislation was thus a powerful advantage to Adolf
Hitler. At the same time it was perfectly obvious that in another war,
as in the last war, the United States had nothing to fear or to lose from
a victory of the Allies, but much to fear and to lose from a German
victory.

President Roosevelt saw this. Vainly he strove, in the summer of
1939, following an unprecedented visit of the British monarchs to Washington and Hyde Park, to get the neutrality statute amended before war
should break out in Europe. To alter it radically *after* the outbreak of
war, by a change that would operate in favor of one belligerent side,
would be unneutral. The President did not ask for the repeal of the
entire law, including embargo on credits, prohibition to American citizens
to travel on belligerent ships, and prohibition of the arming of American
merchant ships. It was only the mandatory, inflexible embargo that
he urged Congressional leaders to repeal, retaining the other features
calculated to keep the United States out of war. To go "back to international law" on the export of munitions, he felt, would be to benefit
the friends of the United States rather than to help those powers who
were not its friends.

There is as yet no evidence to show that the President insisted upon a
diplomatic equivalent from Great Britain and France—such as cession

of island bases or continental territory vital to the defense of the United States and the New World—before he urged Congress to repeal the embargo. He advocated it gratuitously, in the interests of the United States. So vital was the interest of the Allies in a repeal of the embargo that undoubtedly they would have given much to obtain it, if they had to.

An amendment to the Neutrality Act repealing the embargo passed the House of Representatives in the summer of 1939, but stuck in the Senate. Despite the warnings of Secretary of State Hull that war was imminent, the disillusionists were able to block the amendment. Senator Borah of Idaho, distinguished isolationist and former leader of the Irreconcilables of 1919, assured his colleagues that he had his own sources of information which made it clear that there would be no war. The Senate listened to him rather than to the Secretary of State or to the President. Congress adjourned without the amendment having passed. In a certain sense that body had "bet" that war would not break out in Europe before Congress reconvened in January, 1940.[1]

President Roosevelt promptly (September 5, 1939) proclaimed the neutrality of the United States, putting into effect recognized obligations under international law, and other obligations under the domestic neutrality laws including the embargo on arms, ammunition, and implements of warfare. "The laws and treaties of the United States," he declared in the preamble of the proclamation, *"without interfering with the free expression of opinion and sympathy,*[2] nevertheless impose upon all persons who may be within their territory and jurisdiction the duty of an impartial neutrality during the existence of the contest."

In a separate radio address to the people the President said: "This Nation will remain a neutral nation, but I cannot ask that every American remain neutral in thought as well. . . . I hope the United States will keep out of this war. I believe that it will. And I give you assurances that every effort of your Government will be directed toward that end. As long as it remains within my power, there will be no blackout of peace in the United States."[3]

The overwhelming majority of the American people, 99 and 44/100

[1] "The action of the majority of the members of Congress in refusing to amend the 'neutrality' legislation and thus permit this country to throw its influence in favor of peace constituted, in a sense, a 'bet' by them that there would be no war until after Congress reconvened in January, 1940." Note by President Roosevelt, *Public Papers and Addresses, op. cit.,* 1939 volume, p. 524.

[2] Italics inserted.

[3] *The Neutrality of the United States, Laws, Proclamations, Orders, Regulations, and Inter-American Declarations Applicable during the Present War in Europe.* Documents covering the period September 3-December 14, 1939. (World Peace Foundation, Boston, 1939.)

per cent of them, favored neutrality. Even if they had wanted to go to war, the nation was hopelessly unprepared. The army, antiquated in matériel by the standards of 1939, was smaller than that of third-rate European powers. Despite renewed naval building at exorbitant cost, the aim of naval construction had been "a treaty navy by 1942." This meant that by 1942, six years after the expiration of the Washington and London naval treaties, the United States might catch up to the limits allowed by those long-dead treaties! During the interval the rival powers had built far beyond those now ancient treaty ratios.

About 90 per cent of the American people passionately wanted the Allies to defeat Germany. They had desired Great Britain and France to take steps to stop Hitler and Mussolini in Europe, just as the British and French people had wanted the United States to take steps to stop Japan in Asia! Peace was the American passion, nevertheless. The people said and sang God Bless America and pasted those words on their windshields and were glad they were not like other less-favored lands and peoples. They took comfort in the wise neutrality legislation, so they conceived it, that would keep their peaceful nation from being dragged or "colonel-housed" into a repetition of the events of 1914-1917.

So convinced was public opinion that the United States would and could keep out of the new war by applying the putative lessons of the last war that the President would have risked impeachment had he failed to "find" a war in existence in Europe which required the proclamation of neutrality.[1] Nor was the argument brought forth that already had been suggested by theorists, and which was to gather influence as the war developed: that a State which violated the Kellogg-Briand Pact of Paris, as Germany had in 1939, had deprived herself of any right to

---

[1] "When the war actually broke out, I was bound by the terms of the 'Neutrality' Act [of 1937] to impose an embargo upon the shipment of arms and munitions." Note by President Roosevelt in his *Public Papers and Addresses, op. cit.,* 1939 volume, p. 524. Compare his attitude toward the Sino-Japanese War, or toward the first Russo-Finnish War that began in 1939, in which the neutrality laws were not invoked. Loans were made through the Export-Import Bank to help Finland, a victim of aggression, as they were being made to help China, a victim of aggression; and "moral embargoes" were resorted to to dissuade American exporters from selling to governments which were bombing civilian populations (i.e., Russia and Japan), war materials other than arms, ammunition, and implements of warfare (i.e., airplanes, aviation gasoline, molybdenum, aluminum, etc.). Public opinion was overwhelmingly indignant at this unprovoked Russian attack on Finland, despite a previous treaty of nonaggression of 1932; and Finland had a warm place in American sympathies if only because of its unique record of paying to the United States Government its schedule of war debts.

On the other hand, when Germany, Italy, and other allies, including Finland, declared war on Russia in June, 1941, President Roosevelt did not proclaim the neutrality of the United States. *Documents on American Foreign Relations, op. cit.,* II (1939-1940), pp. 381-392, 725-727; III (1940-1941), pp. 769-772.

the obligations of neutrals—that there could no longer be any real neutrality.[1] To insure neutrality the President proclaimed (September 8, 1939) a limited national emergency to exist—to the extent necessary for the proper observance, safeguarding, and enforcement of the neutrality of the United States and the strengthening of national defense within the limits of peacetime authorizations.[2]

The uncomfortable truth kept staring people and President in the face: neutrality, with its embargo, would help Hitler defeat Great Britain and France because they could not buy munitions in the United States as they did in the First World War. Accordingly Roosevelt summoned a special session of Congress to repeal the embargo and prohibit American ships from entering such war zones as the Chief Executive should map out. At the same time, the Government of Panama called for a significant Meeting of Foreign Ministers of the American Republics to take place at the capital of that isthmian state. It was a striking coincidence that the meeting at Panama occurred simultaneously with the special session of the 76th Congress of the United States.[3]

The "Neutrality Act of 1939" became law on November 4 of that year, after six weeks of thorough debate within Congress and without. It had the approval of the public notwithstanding the warning of international lawyers that to change the domestic rules of neutrality *during the course of a war,* so as to benefit one side—in this instance the naval powers—was a departure from neutrality,[4] even though it was a "return to international law." The title of the Act showed that it had a wider purpose than strict juridical neutrality. It was a "Joint Resolution to Preserve the Neutrality and the Peace of the United States *and to Secure the Safety of Its Citizens and Their Interests."* [5] Thus did Government essay to combine neutrality and peace with safety and interest while German and Russian armies overran Poland and the modern Alexander planned his next strokes against the Western Powers, enemy and neutral alike.

The Neutrality Act of 1939 repealed the embargo on arms, ammunition, and implements of war. Such foreign nationals as could cross the

[1] Former Secretary of State Stimson argued so, most plausibly, in 1935. *Proceedings of the American Society of International Law,* 29th Annual Meeting, Washington, D. C., April 25-27, 1935 (Washington, 1935), p. 127.
[2] The legal character of such an emergency is difficult to appraise.
[3] See above, p. 302.
[4] *Research in International Law under the Auspices of the Harvard Law School,* published as a Supplementary Section to the *American Journal of International Law,* Vol. XXXIII (1939), 316-317.
[5] Italics inserted.

seas, belligerent and neutrals, could come, buy for cash, and take away anything they wanted; hence this feature of the Act was dubbed the "cash-and-carry" section.[1] American ships were forbidden to carry arms, or to take goods or passengers to any state named in the President's proclamation, or to enter such combat zones as he should mark out. Otherwise the principal features of the old legislation were retained. By abandoning the traditional freedom of the seas for American citizens, ships, and cargoes, the United States strove to avoid that choice of neutral policy which had led Woodrow Wilson step by step along the road to war in 1914-1917. At the same time it opened to the maritime Allies, Great Britain and France, *after the war began,* the resources of its private industry for their armament, an arsenal that had been closed to them at the beginning of the war. In this respect American neutral policy turned back, while the war was in progress, to where it was before 1935—to the advantage of the democratic sea powers of Europe so far as control of exports was concerned.[2] But it did not go back to the Freedom of the Seas.

Immediately after the passage of the Neutrality Act of 1939 the President lifted the embargo and proclaimed "combat zones," shown on the accompanying map,[3] into which American ships were forbidden to take cargoes or passengers. These zones were arranged to administer the law in such a way as to make impossible under any pretext such

---

[1] A limited "cash-and-carry" feature had existed by the Act of May 1, 1937. This act gave a two-year discretionary power to the President to forbid the export *in American ships* of articles other than arms, ammunitions, and implements of warfare, further to prohibit the export of such articles in foreign ships unless all title to the articles had passed from American owners previous to their being carried away from American jurisdiction. Present usage of the phrase "cash-and-carry" applies to the later Neutrality Act of 1939 rather than to the temporary provisions of the act of 1937, which had expired on May 1, 1939.

[2] In requesting a repeal of the embargo features of the neutrality laws of 1935-1937, President Roosevelt thus explained the way in which they had reversed the traditional neutral position of the United States: "The enactment of the embargo provisions did more than reverse our traditional policy [of neutrality under international law]. It had the effect of putting land powers on the same footing as naval powers, so far as sea-borne commerce was concerned. A land power which threatened war could thus feel assured in advance than any prospective sea-power antagonist would be weakened through denial of its ancient right to buy anything anywhere. This, four years ago, gave a definite advantage to one belligerent as against another, not through his own strength or geographical position, but through an affirmative act of ours. . . . The step I recommend is to put this country back on the solid footing of real and traditional neutrality." *Public Papers and Addresses, op. cit.,* 1939 volume, pp. 512-525. This includes the President's own notes of explanation of his address of September 21, 1939, to the Congress.

[3] Map 9, pp. 370-371.

torpedoing incidents as had challenged the American concept of the Freedom of the Seas in 1914-1917.

Zone 1, including the waters around the British Islands, the entire European coast, neutral and belligerent from Bergen to the Spanish border, was absolutely closed to American ships, by sea or air. Goods could not leave the United States even in foreign ships for ports in that area unless title to the articles had first passed out of American ownership.

Zone 2 contained the Atlantic coasts of Canada (except for ports on the east coast of the Bay of Fundy), Newfoundland and Labrador, and belligerent coasts of Morocco, Gibraltar, and British and French territory in the Mediterranean. To these belligerent coasts the same restrictions applied as of Zone 1, but did not apply to neutral territory within Zone 2.

All other waters and coasts were included in Zone 3. To these ports, whether belligerent or neutral, American ships and trade might operate without restriction, except for the absolute embargo on the export of arms, ammunition, and implements of warfare to belligerents. By proclamations of April 11, 1940 (after the invasion of Denmark and Norway), the President expanded Zone 1 to include the entire Scandinavian and Kola peninsulas and the White Sea, the entire Mediterranean, and the entrance to the Red Sea.[1]

Following up the resolutions of the Foreign Ministers of the American States at Panama (September 23-October 3, 1939) as well as the new Neutrality Act, the President also forbade the entrance of belligerent submarines (both commercial and ships of war) into the territorial waters of the United States, while allowing armed belligerent merchant vessels the use of such waters.[2] The consultation of Panama [3] was an inter-American supplement to the President's neutrality policy: a neutrality calculated to favor the Allies as much as possible.

[1] The Red Sea prohibition was removed April 11, 1941.

[2] Despite much discussion by publicists after the First World War, and a tendency to assimilate armed merchant ships to the status of warships (see *Research in International Law* under the auspices of the Faculty of the Harvard Law School, *Supplement Section to American Journal of International Law*, XXIII [1939], 222-231), the United States had never committed itself to that position as regards merchant ships armed for defensive purposes. The neutrality laws of 1935 and 1937 and 1939 prohibited American citizens from traveling on belligerent armed ships except under such condition as the President might allow (i.e., to get them home after the outbreak of war), and gave the President discretionary power to exclude belligerent armed merchant ships, or belligerent submarines, or both, from American territorial waters. The Neutrality Law of 1939 forbade the arming of United States merchant ships; but this prohibition applied to time of peace and neutrality; it was repealed, November 17, 1941. When war began the United States as a belligerent armed its merchant ships as fast as it could.

[3] See above, p. 302.

Map 9. War Zones under Neutrality Act of 1939

ZONE 1—Combat Areas Proclaimed by the President (Indicated by crosshatching)

(a) It is unlawful for any citizen of the United States or American watercraft or aircraft to go into or through this area except under rules and regulations as may be prescribed. (Sec. 3.)

(b) Goods, except copyrighted articles or materials, must not leave the United States bound for a belligerent country in Zone 1, even on a foreign vessel, unless all right, title, and interest has been transferred to a foreign government, agent, or person, and a declaration under oath to that effect filed with the collector of the port of export. (Sec. 2(a).)

ZONE 2—Restrictions in this area relate solely to belligerent countries and their possessions, which are indicated by feathered shading

(a) It is unlawful for American vessels to carry any passengers or any articles or materials to belligerent ports in this zone. It is lawful for American vessels to travel in this zone provided they go to neutral ports and provided their voyage does not penetrate Zone 1.

(b) It is unlawful for American vessels to carry any passengers or any articles or materials to ports in Canada east of 66° west longitude. (Sec. 2(g).)

(c) It is lawful to extend credit on all goods for shipment to neutral countries in Zone 2.

ZONE 3—Covers rest of the world

(a) It is lawful to extend credit on goods other than arms, ammunition, and implements of war, shipped to Canada (except that portion of Canada in Zone 2) by inland waterway, railroad, or other vehicle, or aircraft, provided the goods are not purchased by a belligerent Government, its political subdivisions, or their agents, or a belligerent Government monopoly or its agents, and it is not necessary to pass all right, title, and interest in the goods. (Sec. 2(f).)

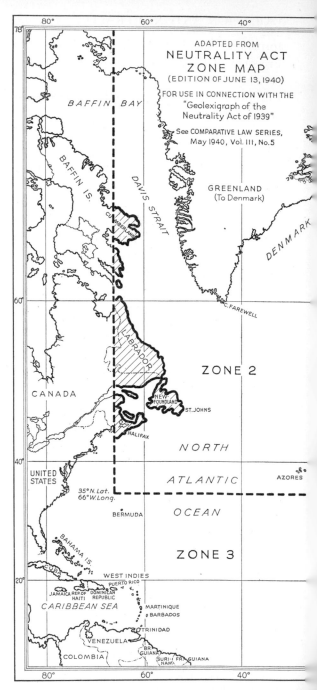

ADAPTED FROM
NEUTRALITY ACT
ZONE MAP
(EDITION OF JUNE 13, 1940)

FOR USE IN CONNECTION WITH THE
"Geolexigraph of the
Neutrality Act of 1939"

See COMPARATIVE LAW SERIES,
May 1940, Vol. III, No.5

GREENLAND
(To Denmark)

DENMARK

BAFFIN BAY

BAFFIN IS.

DAVIS STRAIT

CUMBERLAND

C. FAREWELL

LABRADOR

CANADA

NEW FOUNDLAND

ST. JOHNS

HALIFAX

ZONE 2

NORTH

UNITED STATES

35° N. Lat.
66° W. Long.

ATLANTIC

AZORES

BERMUDA

OCEAN

BAHAMA IS.

ZONE 3

CUBA

WEST INDIES
PUERTO RICO
JAMAICA REP.OF DOMINICAN
HAITI REPUBLIC

CARIBBEAN SEA

MARTINIQUE
BARBADOS

TRINIDAD

VENEZUELA

COLOMBIA

BR. GUIANA
SURI-FR. GUIANA
NAM.

(b) American vessels and citizens may carry on commerce and trade in any part of the world not included in Zones 1 and 2 without passing title to the goods, except goods considered arms, ammunition, or implements of war destined for a belligerent country.

370

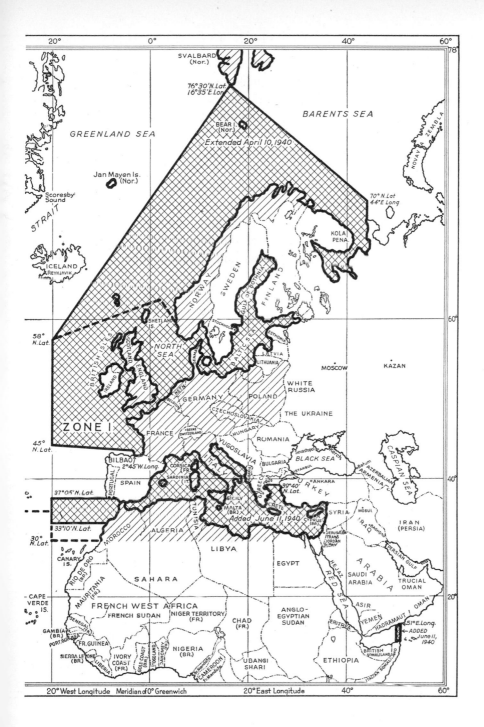

The Neutrality Act of 1939 and its sequels demonstrate that it was not possible, in this war, to reconcile peace and neutrality with safety and interest, even by forswearing the American birthright of the Freedom of the Seas. The new law was also a signal to Great Britain and France that the United States was on their side as much as a neutral could be, that they need not fear any very strenuous protests to their own belligerent practices.

Before we observe the successive developments that followed this first deviation until the ultimate collapse of neutrality, after Hitler had overrun the scrupulously neutral kingdoms of Europe, let us turn to the development, in the initial years of the Second World War, of the opposing belligerent maritime systems and to the position of the neutral United States between them.

18

The Collapse of Neutrality

THE victory of the United States and the Allies in the First World War had greatly strengthened the validity of the naval measures which Great Britain had taken in 1914-1917 *vis-à-vis* the neutral United States, and which she was prepared to put into effect again in 1939. After entering the war in 1917 the United States had proclaimed a sweepingly expansive definition of contraband, had thrown aside all distinction between absolute and conditional contraband, and had applied the doctrine of continuous voyage and ultimate destination to all contraband.[1] In consequence, Great Britain in 1939 did not proclaim "measures of blockade" such as she had instituted against Germany by way of retaliation on March 1, 1915. Instead she proclaimed, at the outset of the war, a "contraband control" which served the same purpose, was easier to maintain, more effective, and less subject to objections on the ground of imperfect blockade.

All neutral ships bound for Europe were "invited" to call at designated ports (Weymouth, Ramsgate, Kirkwall, Gibraltar, and Haifa) for examination and clearance to a neutral destination. Or, on leaving their home port, they could, if they were that obliging, obtain from British consuls certificates of innocent character, called "navicerts."[2] This was a British practice initiated in 1916 at the suggestion of the neutral United States Government.[3] If a neutral ship ignored this control she was brought by force into a British port, under the doctrine of continuous voyage and ultimate destination applied to an all-inclusive definition of

[1] Instructions for the Navy of the United States Governing Maritime Warfare, June 30, 1917, Savage, *Policy of the United States toward Maritime Commerce in War, op. cit.,* II, pp. 615-638. Note paragraphs 23, 24, 69, 70, 71. The Secretary of the Navy to the Secretary of State, June 18, 1918, *ibid.,* II, p. 779.

[2] *Commerce Clearing House War Law Service,* Nos. 40,620, 65,501, 65,502, 65,556, 66,005, and 66,015, cited by C. H. McLaughlin in his pioneer scholarly review of "Neutral Rights under International Law in the European War, 1939-1941," *Minnesota Law Review,* XXVI (1941-1942), 1-49, 177-222.

[3] H. Ritchie has described the origin and development of *The "Navicert" System during the [First] World War* (Carnegie Endowment for International Peace, 1938).

contraband. There she was searched and handed over to the prize courts if alleged to be carrying contraband. While the neutral ship was in a British control port, whether voluntarily or by compulsion, the neutral mail bags were examined for contraband (including money and securities) and the letters censored.

The next step was to stop German exports. In retaliation against alleged German violations of international law—torpedoing or aerial bombing of merchant ships without warning and indiscriminate sowing of mines on the high seas—Great Britain by an Order in Council of November 27, 1939, proclaimed the "detention" of all goods of German origin, even if neutral property.[1] This was contrary to the ancient doctrine of free ships free goods, universally accepted in international law since the Declaration of Paris of 1856, to be excused if at all only under the principle of retaliation.

Thus by her contraband control Great Britain stopped all goods destined for Germany; by her retaliation she stopped all goods being exported across the seas from Germany. Further, she prohibited her own subjects from any relations with a published blacklist of neutral firms suspected of trading with the enemy.[2] To enforce these regulations the British Government established a Ministry of Economic Warfare, significant appellation.

France followed very closely the practice of her ally and tutor in these naval measures.[3]

The United States could not very well protest the British definition of contraband as it did in the previous war, because in 1939 the British employed almost word for word the same definition that the United States had used as a belligerent in 1917![4] So did Germany. The category of contraband simply evaporated, for all practical purposes, by being expanded to include anything useful to the enemy. With it, and with the neutrality acts of 1935-1939, disappeared almost the last vestiges of the traditional Freedom of the Seas, so dear to American diplomacy during the first century and a half of the independence of the United States. Nor could the United States any more protest the British blacklists, because it had used them itself in 1917-1918. The Secretary of State did protest against the detention of goods of German origin, against

---

[1] McLaughlin, *op. cit.*, p. 47.

[2] September 13, 1939. Halsbury's *Statutes of England*, XXXII, 1095.

[3] All the belligerents in their first contraband lists observed a theoretical distinction between absolute and conditional contraband.

[4] Department of State *Bulletin*, I, No. 12 (September 16, 1939), 250, cf. Savage, *op. cit.*, II, pp. 615-638.

diversion of American ships into the war zones for examination at British control ports, and against search and censorship of neutral mail bags on board American ships in British ports.[1]

The strongest of these protests was against the last-mentioned grievance: diversion for search. Since the Neutrality Act of 1939 had forbidden American ships to visit European belligerent ports at all, and the President's accompanying proclamation of war zones had blocked off entry also to Scandinavian neutral ports below Bergen, all American ships by necessity were carrying cargo only between neutral ports. "Such cargo," said the Secretary of State, "is entitled to the presumption of innocent character, in the absence of substantial evidence justifying a suspicion to the contrary." The State Department argued that, because United States ships en route to neutral ports had voluntarily co-operated with British control by "putting aside certain of their rights under international law," they should be entitled to "a corresponding degree of accommodation and flexibility" so as not to give occasion for forcible diversion of American vessels to British control ports which the law of the United States forbade them to enter. It thus admitted by implication the propriety of diversion to control ports, particularly if there were reasonable grounds to suspect the ships of carrying contraband ultimately destined to the enemy.

Pending further examination and action, said the protest of December 14, 1939, the United States reserved for itself and its nationals all its and their rights in the matter and expected that compensation for losses and injuries resulting from the infraction of such rights would be made as a matter of course.

This perfunctory caveat left the door open for further argument throughout the war and possible adjudication after the war. At most the argument was directed against details that had been moot in the last war. For the implacable essentials of British practice the Governments of George VI and his ally had abundant United States precedent—that is, for their interpretation of contraband and the doctrine of continuous voyage to ultimate enemy destination. The State Department's notes encouraged rebuttal. As to mails, was it not worse, the British promptly asked, what Germany was now doing: not even examining ships to see whether they were neutral or belligerent, but sinking them mail and all by torpedo or bombs from the air?[2] To this question, and to other

[1] In notes of December 8, 1939 (re detention of goods of German origin); and December 14, 1939, and January 20, 1941 (re diversion); and December 27, 1939 (re mails), *Documents on American Foreign Relations, op. cit.*, II (1939-1940), pp. 705-719.
[2] Department of State *Bulletin*, II, No. 31 (January 27, 1940), 91-93.

British replies, the United States made no rejoinder. Soon it was co-operating with the British in these very practices, while still a nominal neutral.

We recall that after the First World War multilateral treaties, like the Inter-American Convention of Maritime Neutrality of 1928 and the London Naval Treaty of 1930, had applied to submarines the rules of surface warships: the necessity of visit and search, and provision for the safety of passengers and crew and ship's papers before destroying a merchant ship.[1] Only in case of persistent refusal to stop or of active resistance to visit or search could a warship, whether surface vessel or submarine, sink the ship or render it incapable of navigation without first having observed these precautions. Of her own free will Germany accepted these rules in 1937 by adhering to a special protocol of November 6, 1936, that had continued them after the expiration of the London treaty.

Did this mean that an armed merchantman—which could, if it chose, sink a submarine that stopped to visit and search—had all the treaty privileges of a merchant ship? International law had not settled that vitally important point. Only one multilateral treaty, the Inter-American Convention of Maritime Neutrality of 1928, just mentioned, had declared armed merchant ships to be ships of war, and this article had not been ratified by any naval power.[2]

The United States had avoided such a commitment, anticipating a day when it might want to arm its own merchant ships in defense against enemy submarines that would not obey international law. But by the Neutrality Act of 1939 it had forbidden the arming of its neutral merchant ships, so that it could never be alleged, as a pretext for submarine attack, that the belligerent warship could not in its own safety take the risk of visit and search of an American ship. Since no American ship was allowed to enter the war zones proclaimed by the President and all American merchant ships on the high seas were conspicuously marked

---

[1] Of course, a prize cannot be taken legally unless there is evidence of enemy owner-ship or of a neutral carrying contraband or of violating contraband. Even then the captor must take the ship into his prize court for judgment, unless imperious circumstances pre-vent; in that case he may destroy the prize, after making proper provisions for the safety of passengers and crew, keeping the ship's papers as evidence.

[2] Only Bolivia, Ecuador, Haiti, Nicaragua, Panama, and the Dominican Republic had ratified the Convention without reservation of this article on armed merchant ships. The United States ratified the Convention with a reservation of the article. It is recalled (p. 302 above) that the Declaration of Panama of October 3, 1939, nullified this obliga-tion on the part of these Caribbean States that had ratified.

and lighted, there could be no reasonable pretext for mistaking them for armed enemy merchant ships.

Great Britain never renounced the ancient custom of arming merchant ships for defensive purposes. During the last war, after Germany had declared her submarine blockade of the British Islands—for which Woodrow Wilson chose to hold her to strict accountability as regarded American nationals or ships—the British Admiralty had instructed captains of merchant ships to ram or fire upon submarines if they showed "hostile intent." After the German announcement of February 4, 1915, no British sea captain could see an enemy submarine, certainly not one in the "blockade" zone which did not manifest hostile intent. Immediately upon the outbreak of the war in 1939 the unarmed British ship *Athenia*, en route from Scotland to Canada with about 1,400 passengers of whom approximately one half were Americans, was sunk September 3, 1939, by an exterior explosion, in the presence, it was alleged, of a German submarine. Twenty-eight American citizens lost their lives. The German Government denied responsibility and asserted that a British submarine had sunk the ship in order to accuse Germany of the crime and get the United States into the war. The naval records of Hitler's Government later captured by the American Army prove that this was a deliberate lie, but in 1939 the momentum of "neo-neutrality" was still so powerful that President Roosevelt's Government did not consider the evidence of torpedoing conclusive enough to warrant a protest to Germany! Actually it was in principle a repetition of the *Lusitania* affair, if possible even more heinous because in studious violation of solemn treaty pledges by the Third Reich not to torpedo passenger ships without summons, visit, and search.

The British Government took speedy action for protection of its ships and subjects against dreaded torpedoing without warning. Winston Churchill, First Lord of the Admiralty at the outbreak of war in 1939, as he had been at the beginning of the previous conflict, stated in the House of Commons, September 26, 1939, that the whole British merchant marine would be armed defensively against attack by submarines and aircraft. Britain, with her experience of the last war, and the *Athenia* tragedy recently to remind her of it, would not trust German promises not to attack without visit and search.

During the first two months of the war, as long as it was possible that United States neutral ships might be in British or French waters or near them, Germany professed to follow the rules of surface warfare (unless an exception be recorded for the *Athenia* tragedy)—that is, her submarine commanders tried to let crews and passengers get into lifeboats before sinking ships; in some cases commanders actually towed the boats toward safety.[1]   During the few weeks of war before the passage of the Neutrality Act of November 4, 1939, German submarines observed the law toward American ships going to the British Islands; [2] the Neutrality Law of 1937 prohibited these neutral vessels from carrying arms, ammunition, and implements of warfare.   But after the Neutrality Act of 1939 became law, German submarines and aviators began to sink without warning any ship, neutral or belligerent, that was proceeding to or from the British Islands, or believed to be submitting to British contraband control, or accepting enemy convoy.   Germany justified this practice on grounds of retaliation.   She proclaimed a "blockade" of the British Islands, similar to that of 1915.[3]   "Any neutral ship which in the future enters those waters is likely to be destroyed." [4]

Again, as in the other historical struggles between the Leviathan of the Seas and the Colossus of the Land (1793-1802; 1803-1815; 1914-1918), each mighty belligerent had reached for his most deadly weapon of war in a bitter struggle for life or death, with only incidental concern for the technicalities of international law.   Great Britain resorted to her maritime measures to cut off German contact with overseas neutrals by her contraband control and retaliatory detention of neutral goods of German origin; Germany reverted to her use of unrestricted submarine warfare, the employment of mines of all sorts, and started bombing merchant ships from the air.

British measures had the weight of Anglo-American precedent back of them; German submarine action was in violation of a treaty—that is, if defensively armed merchant ships were not to be regarded as warships; even then Germany did not stop to see whether a ship was armed or not, or neutral or not.   Since the last war devices had been perfected by which a submarine did not have to stick its periscope above the water to "see" its prey and aim its torpedo; now it could aim accurately and destroy from beneath the surface, guided by "hearing" apparatus.   By

[1] This was not, of course, a perfect compliance with the treaty.

[2] On September 11, 1939, a German submarine detained the S.S. *Wacosta*, American flag, bound from New York to Glasgow with general cargo and a few passengers, for three hours of searching, and allowed it to proceed. Department of State *Bulletin*, I, No. 12 (September 16, 1939), 249.

[3] See Map 3, B, p. 133.

[4] New York *Times*, August 18, 1940, for text, p. 25.

the use of mines, greatly perfected since the last conflict, Germany also took an alarming toll of belligerent and even more of neutral merchant ships in the waters around the British Islands.[1] This led to protests by the Scandinavian neutrals, but not by the United States. It had been too deeply involved in mine laying during the previous war to justify a protest. Besides that, the Neutrality Act of 1939 prohibited American merchant ships from entering the war zones.

Unlike the period of American neutrality in 1914-1917, no serious controversies arose with either belligerent side during the latest war until after American neutrality had collapsed for other reasons than violations of neutral rights. The weight of Anglo-American precedent was too greatly in favor of British maritime practice by 1939 to justify a very effective protest to Great Britain, not to mention the strength of public opinion and sympathy in favor of the cause of Great Britain and France. So far as Germany was concerned, the Neutrality Act of 1939, forswearing for expediency's sake the Freedom of the Seas, kept American neutral ships out of harm's way.

The overrunning by German armies of neutral Denmark, Norway, the Netherlands, and Belgium, and the fall of belligerent France, all in the spring and summer of 1940, put a different aspect on the war for the United States. Adhering to the doctrine of nonrecognition of the fruits of aggression, the Washington Government refused to recognize any change of sovereignty in those conquered kingdoms and continued diplomatic relations with their exiled governments, as with Poland's.

The conquest of England itself seemed alarmingly close in June, 1940, when Italy characteristically entered the war at what appeared the last hour of the enemy's resistance. Germany's military successes now threatened to destroy the balance of power in Europe and the supremacy of British sea power, behind which the United States, because of its peculiar position in reference to Canada, had rested in such security for a century. Then Hitler might either possess himself of the British navy, or, in possession of the combined shipbuilding resources of all Europe outside of Russia, be speedily in the way of building the instruments of invasion of the New World before the United States could brace itself adequately to meet the shock in the Atlantic while required to maintain at the same time a defensive fleet in the Pacific.

It was at this hour of history that the United States, in desperate disregard of neutral obligations, reached hastily into its own national

[1] McLaughlin, *op. cit.*, p. 7, note 20.

arsenals and sent arms to Englishmen—and Canadians—with which to defend themselves. Already it had been doing so furtively by rigging the neutrality laws so as to permit the export of airplanes to Canada and Great Britain while making it impossible to Germany. Beginning in the summer of 1940 a series of further steps led during the course of the next twelve months to the collapse of American neutrality and to undeclared naval hostilities with Germany: (1) Facilitation of purchase of military aircraft by Great Britain and France by giving increasing priorities to them over military orders from the United States Government with American manufacturers. (2) Gradual dropping of the encumbrances of neutrality on the export of military aircraft under their own locomotion, driven by belligerent pilots within the United States or by American pilots over belligerent territory. Great armadas of flying ships of war built in the United States sped on their way across the Atlantic ultimately destined to bomb military objectives in Germany. (3) Rushing from United States Government arsenals in the summer of 1940, through the intermediary of private corporations, of large supplies of rifles, machine guns, anti-aircraft guns, trench mortars, field pieces, and other military equipment to England's new levies of men in her hour of vital need. (4) The executive agreement of September 6, 1940, with Great Britain, trading fifty United States destroyers of First World War age for American naval bases in British islands of the Western Atlantic and Caribbean and in British Guiana. (5) Sale of 229 old First World War tanks to Canada in September, 1940. (6) The sale by the United States Maritime Commission of old First World War merchant ships to Great Britain in December, 1940. (7) President Roosevelt's speech of December 29, 1940, declaring that the United States would be the "arsenal of democracy" for the defense of Great Britain and her allies against Germany and her allies. (8) Successive statements by the Secretary of State and the President that it was the policy of the United States to aid any victim of aggression who would defend itself against the aggressor. (9) Passage of the Lend-Lease Act of March 11, 1941. (10) Seizure of merchant ships belonging to Germany, her allies, and captive countries, and their transfer to Great Britain, during March-July, 1941. (11) Measures for the defense of Greenland, April 7, 1941, taken under the Act of Havana.[1] (12) Proclamation by the President of an unlimited national emergency (May 27, 1941) because of the plain objectives of the Axis belligerents to overthrow exist-

[1] See above, p. 304.

ing democratic order throughout the world and to establish a world-wide domination of peoples and economies through the destruction of all resistance on land and sea and in the air.[1] (13) Establishment of direct relations with the independent Government of Iceland, April, 1941, and military occupation of Iceland at first jointly with British and Canadian troops, July, 1941. (14) Announcement, July 7, 1941, that the sea lanes to Iceland would be kept open by the American navy to prevent threats to Greenland and the northern part of the American Continent, and to protect the flow of munitions to Great Britain. (15) Construction, under outright ownership [2] of the British Government, of armament factories in the United States. (16) Blacklisting throughout the other American republics of persons and firms deemed to be acting for the benefit of Germany or Italy, and forbidding exports from the United States to them, in the interests of national defense. (17) Building, as if by anticipation, of a naval base in Northern Ireland, under nominal British auspices.

Most spectacular and far-reaching of these deviations from neutrality for the purpose of securing the defense of the United States [3] were: (18) the destroyer-naval base deal with Great Britain; and (19) the Lend-Lease Act, the former effected by an executive agreement before the Presidential election of 1940, the latter enacted by Congress after the re-election of President Roosevelt for a third term.

Faced with imminent invasion of her unfortified island in the late summer of 1940, Great Britain needed more naval defense than ever before in her history, not only to defend the Channel, but also to protect the Atlantic transit for the armaments that were being sent from United States arsenals and factories. On the other hand, the downfall of England would have given Germany and Italy control of the Atlantic and would have opened up the New World to invasion by the Axis powers (as Germany and her allies had come to be designated). Against such a menace the United States realized the vital need of naval bases in the British islands of the Western Atlantic and the Caribbean Sea

[1] In response to a Senate Resolution requesting definition of the executive powers under such an emergency, the Attorney General declined to give an opinion, but transmitted a list of relevant statutes. *Documents on American Foreign Relations, op. cit.,* III (1940-1941), pp. 754-755.

[2] The British Government refused to pay local taxes on such properties in Connecticut on the ground that the property of a foreign sovereign was not subject to taxation, in international law.

[3] "We have made no pretense about our self-interest in this aid. Great Britain understands it—and so does Nazi Germany." Address by President F. D. Roosevelt, May 27, 1941. *Ibid.,* p. 49.

for the protection of the continental homeland, even as the Hawaiian
Islands served that purpose in the Pacific. American diplomacy, in the
midst of an opportunity in the first part of 1939, had been negligent on
that score. The Government must now act quickly or it might be too
late. There was grave doubt whether the President had constitutional
power [1] by executive agreement to trade away any or all of the navy
for naval bases in foreign territory; in fact, Congress had just passed a
law preventing him from giving or trading certain new naval units to
Great Britain. To negotiate a treaty with Great Britain and get it
through the Senate was practically impossible, so confused was the state
of public opinion. Even if ratified, a treaty would take so much debate
and time that it might be too late. The danger of inaction or delay
was much greater than the danger from doubt of executive powers.

In this predicament the President turned to the Attorney General for
assurance that he had the powers to make such a deal by executive
agreement. To these demands for advice Attorney General Robert H.
Jackson responded with what might be called at any rate resourcefulness
and ingenuity: it was he who called upon a comma to save a kingdom.[2]
The resulting executive agreement was another devastating encroachment upon the treaty-making power of the Senate.

A mere exchange of notes, September 2, 1940, between Secretary of
State Hull and the British Ambassador, "consummated an arrangement"
far more important than most of the seven or eight hundred treaties
that the Senate has ever ratified. In exchange for the immediate transfer
of fifty destroyers, the British Government agreed to lease to the United
States for ninety-nine years naval bases, with all rights for their operation
and protection, in the Bahama Islands, Jamaica, Santa Lucia, Trinidad,
Antigua, and British Guiana. These were only agreements to lease;
the leases themselves with their conditions, still had to be negotiated in
more time; [3] but the destroyers were handed over immediately. In addition, the British Government agreed to secure for the United States,

---

[1] "The Congress shall have Power to dispose of and make all needful Rules and Regulations respecting the Territory or other Property belonging to the United States; and
nothing in this Constitution shall be so construed as to Prejudice any Claims of the
United States, or any particular State." Article IV, Section 3, Paragraph 2, of the
Constitution of the United States.

[2] The opinion of the Attorney General of August 27, 1941, is conveniently printed, along
with other documents pertaining to the Agreement in *Documents on American Foreign
Relations, op. cit.,* III (1940-1941), pp. 207-228. For critical analysis of the legal merit of
the Attorney General's opinion, see Quincy Wright (*pro*) and Edwin M. Borchard (*con*)
in *American Journal of International Law,* XXXIV (October, 1940), 680-697.

[3] The supplementary lease agreements were signed March 27, 1941.

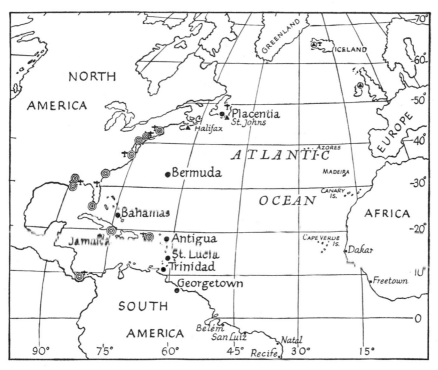

Map 10. New Bases Acquired from Great Britain, 1940

◎ Old bases, home waters.   ✝ New air bases, home coasts.

▲ British bases.   Ⓐ British-American bases later established, 1941.

● The new bases, 1940.   (See Map 4 for old bases.)

freely and without consideration, similar leases for naval bases in Bermuda and Newfoundland.[1]

How could the Government be sure that this fleet of destroyers, built by the United States and hitherto a part of its own navy, would not be used against itself in case Germany conquered England? It could not be sure that this would not happen, though the purpose of the transfer was to prevent the defeat of England; but before he signed the bargain Secretary Hull secured a statement from the British Ambassador that it was "the settled policy of His Majesty's Government" never to sur-

[1] See Map 10. Rather than make a formal contract in an exchange of letters, by which Great Britain would pay for the destroyers such undefined concessions as might be required in the judgment of the United States, in the islands and places mentioned for American naval bases, Prime Minister Churchill would have preferred to make outright gifts of well-defined facilities, Great Britain the final judge of what she gave. Winston Churchill, *The Second World War*, Vol. II, *Their Finest Hour* (Boston, 1949), pp. 399-416.

render or to sink the British fleet in the event of the waters around the British Islands becoming untenable. Having made the deal by executive agreement, President Roosevelt tersely and triumphantly informed Congress about it: "the most important action in the reinforcement of our national defense that has taken place since the Louisiana Purchase."

The Senate did not demur. The House did not object. The people approved the deal. In the Presidential election campaign of 1940 Wendell L. Willkie, Republican candidate, made no issue on this point of executive procedure. Both candidates favored "all-out" aid to Great Britain "short of war." Both advocated a conscription law (passed September 16, 1940) and full preparedness. Both party platforms pledged against entry into foreign wars, or sending American forces to fight in foreign lands outside America—unless attacked, said the Democratic platform. Both Roosevelt and Willkie pledged against leading the United States into a foreign war, against sending American forces overseas under any circumstances.[1] The conscription law had prohibited the use of the new army outside the Western Hemisphere. The principal issue of the election of 1940 was not peace or war: it was whether Wendell Willkie would make a more capable and more reliable President than Franklin Delano Roosevelt in the critical times immediately ahead.

A strong minority of anti-interventionists, under the national leadership of Charles A. Lindbergh, the eminent aviator and conqueror of the Atlantic, still favored strict neutrality in the European war. Only by arming to the teeth and conserving military strength at home, argued Lindbergh, could the United States be safe from Europe's wars. He was against extending aid to England. He lamented not so much the fact that Hitler was conquering Europe as that the Occidental nations were bleeding each other to death for the advantage of Japan and Russia. The election of 1940 was a measure of persistence in the United States of this isolationist sentiment that had been so strong in 1939.

Following the election of 1940 Prime Minister Churchill addressed a long, confidential letter, made public first in 1949, and already famous, setting forth in forceful detail Great Britain's needs for survival, in terms of implements of war and munitions, airplanes, cargo ships and warships and convoys—he did not then think it was the kind of war in which Great Britain would be able to match the great armies of Germany in

---

[1] Charles A. Beard, *American Foreign Policy in the Making, 1932-1940; a Study in Responsibilities* (Yale University Press, 1946).

Secretary Hull was much more cautious in his campaign speeches on behalf of the Administration. He made no promises of this kind.

any field where their main power could be brought to bear.[1] Roosevelt responded with his renowned speech of December 30, 1940, calling for "all-out aid" to Great Britain and her allies, the captive kingdoms of Europe, by the United States as an "arsenal of democracy." At his impulse the Lend-Lease bill HR 1776 was immediately introduced into Congress. In the interests of national defense it overrode many of the prohibitions of the Neutrality Act of 1939 and of other statutes, and it disregarded the obligations of neutrality under international law. Subject to the necessary appropriations by Congress (which were promptly forthcoming), this unprecedented law gave the President full powers at his discretion, and under his direction, and on terms to be arranged by him, to put the material resources of the Government (but not yet the nation's ships or man power) at the disposal of countries whose defense he believed vital to the defense of the United States. Never in history had a President, even in times of war, received such a grant of power as this.[2] It was a measure of the alarm that the people felt in the midst of

---

[1] Churchill to Roosevelt, 10 Downing St., Whitehall, December 8, 1940. *Their Finest Hour, op. cit.,* pp. 558-569.

[2] These were the powers which it gave to the President:

(1) To manufacture in arsenals, factories and shipyards under their jurisdiction, or otherwise procure, to the extent to which funds are made available therefore, or contracts are authorized from time to time by the Congress, or both, any defense article for the government of any country whose defense the President deems vital to the defense of the United States.

(2) To sell, transfer title to, exchange, lease, lend or otherwise dispose of to any such government any defense article, as described by the act, but only after consultation with the Chief of Staff of the Army or the Chief of Naval Operations of the Navy, or both.

(3) To test, inspect, prove, repair, outfit, recondition, or otherwise to place in good working order, any defense article for any such government, under appropriations or contracts authorized by Congress, or to procure any or all such services by private contract.

(4) To communicate to any such government any defense information, pertaining to any defense article furnished to such government under paragraph (2) of this subsection.

(5) To release for export any defense article disposed of in any way under this subsection to any such government.

The act further enabled the President to arrange terms, conditions, and benefits, direct or indirect, to be rendered by governments receiving such aid. Under this power the colossal aid to Great Britain was soon written off as subsidies, by an executive agreement of February 25, 1942, after certain understandings had been reached by the two Governments as to the nature of the principles that should govern the future peace.

The act further stipulated that nothing in its provisions should be construed to authorize or permit convoying of vessels by the naval forces of the United States. This was more of a gesture than a prohibition, because the Executive had the power of convoy, as Commander in Chief.

More authoritative was another stipulation that nothing in the act should authorize or permit the entry of an American vessel into a combat area in violation of the Neutrality Act of 1939; but even here the President had the power to make or unmake the combat zones.

their confusion at what might happen to them if Germany should defeat Great Britain before the United States had armed itself adequately.

It would have been folly to make of the nation this arsenal of democracy only to have the armaments sunk before they reached the hands of a fighting friend. The occupation of Iceland was a step to strengthen the shipping lanes of the North Atlantic against rupture by German naval and aerial forces. Iceland had proclaimed its complete independence from the Crown of Denmark following the German occupation of that little neutral kingdom. But under British occupation Iceland was belligerent territory like Denmark under German occupation. Germany (March 25, 1941) expanded her retaliatory "blockade" of the British Islands to include Iceland, even as far as Greenland's icy waters,[1] and began to torpedo neutral ships going to Iceland as well as to the British Islands.

President Roosevelt had not included Iceland within the Class I combat zone proclaimed by him under the Neutrality Act of 1939, the zone into which American ships were forbidden to take passengers and cargo of any kind. That strategic island lay within Zone 2 where American ships could go to neutral countries with cargo and passengers, but not with arms, ammunition, and implements of warfare.[2] Once American troops were in Iceland a service of supply ships was necessary. This led to the convoy of American ships, then of other neutral ships, finally of belligerent British ships along the way. Convoys led to naval engagements between American destroyers and German submarines.[3] An undeclared shooting war began on the North Atlantic in the summer of 1941.

Before these engagements occurred a German submarine had sunk, May 21, 1941, an unarmed American merchant ship, the *Robin Moor*, New York to Capetown with a mixed cargo not containing arms, ammunition, or implements of warfare prohibited to American ships by the Neutrality Act. The attack took place in the middle of the South Atlantic, far outside any war zone proclaimed by belligerent or neutral. There was no visit or search, although crew and passengers, including

[1] See Map 11.
[2] See Map 9.
[3] There were preliminary engagements as early as May, without casualties. On September 4, 1941, the United States Government announced that the destroyer U.S.S. *Greer* (which had been tracking a German submarine while a British plane dropped depth charges) had been attacked by torpedoes which missed their mark. On the night of October 16-17, 1941, a submarine attacked the destroyer U.S.S. *Kearny* while engaged in convoy work to Iceland, with the resulting loss of eleven men of the destroyer's crew. On October 31 the destroyer U.S.S. *Reuben James*, also engaged in convoy duty, was torpedoed off Iceland with a loss of ninety-six men and officers.

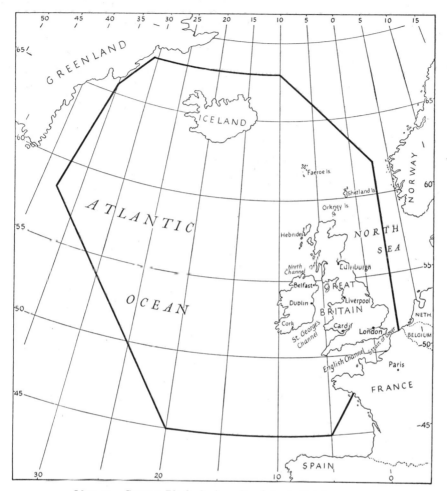

Map 11. German Blockade Area Proclaimed March 25, 1941

women and children, were allowed to take to open lifeboats. After many days of suffering they were saved, fortunately and fortuitously, by friendly vessels. This incident was a flagrant violation of treaty obligation. The United States demanded full reparation. Germany did not reply but did the same thing over again.[1] By this time [2] the neutrality of the United States already had collapsed from other reasons.

[1] The *Lehigh*, cargo ship under the American flag, sunk in the South Atlantic, just south of the Equator, off the African coast, October 19, 1941.

[2] After the passage of the Lend-Lease Act the President revoked (April 11, 1941) the combat zone of his proclamation of June 11, 1940, barring off the Red Sea, in order to allow American-flag ships to deliver lend-lease material to British armies in Egypt. In this maritime backdoorway one of them, the U.S.S. *Steelseafarer* was sunk by an aerial bomb, September 5, 1941.

Armed with the Lend-Lease Act, President Roosevelt had it within his power to reach an understanding with Great Britain on the principles of a future peace settlement before he opened wide the sluiceways of American supplies.   Meanwhile most momentous problems had arisen calling for joint attention and anxiety of the United States and Britain: the islands of the Eastern Atlantic, and the menace of Japan in the Western Pacific: if Germany occupied Spain as a causeway to North Africa, someone would have to occupy the Spanish Canaries and Cape Verdes and the Portuguese Azores lest they fall into the hands of Hitler and become submarine bases to cut Britain's remaining route around Africa to Egypt and also menace the security of the Western Hemisphere. Japan's advance from China into French Indo-China threatened Singapore and menaced the Philippines: should the United States and Great Britain serve joint notice on Japan to stop?

In the summer of 1941 President Roosevelt had a meeting off the coast of Newfoundland with Prime Minister Winston Churchill, who was dreaming and working for the day when the United States might come into the war at Britain's side.[1]   The two statesmen, after visiting back and forth to their respective flagships in Argentia Bay, announced eight principles of policy on which they based the hopes, the desires, the beliefs, the endeavors, and the promises of the Governments of the United States and Great Britain for a better future for the world: the Atlantic Charter, August 14, 1941.

As in the case of the Fourteen Points of President Wilson of 1918, the historian may well underline the carefully chosen verbs and their auxiliaries.

First, their countries seek no aggrandizement, territorial or other;

Second, they *desire* to see no territorial changes that do not accord with the freely expressed wishes of the peoples concerned;

Third, they respect the right of all peoples to choose the form of government under which they will live; and they *wish* to see sovereign rights and self-government restored to those who have been forcibly deprived of them;

Fourth, they *will endeavor*, with *due respect for their existing obligations,* to further the enjoyment by all States, great or small, victor or vanquished, of access, on equal terms, to the trade and to the raw materials of the world which are needed for their economic prosperity;

Fifth, they *desire* to bring about the fullest collaboration between all

[1] "That ['the United States unitedly and wholeheartedly in the war with us'] is what I have dreamed of and worked for, and now it is come to pass." Speech of Prime Minister Winston Churchill to the House of Commons announcing the fall of Singapore, February 15, 1942.

nations in the economic field with the object of securing, for all, improved labor standards, economic advancement, and social security;

Sixth, after the final destruction of the Nazi tyranny, they *hope* to see established a peace which will afford to all nations the means of dwelling in safety within their own boundaries, and which will afford assurance that all the men in all the lands may live out their lives in freedom from fear and want;

Seventh, such a peace *should* enable all men to traverse the high seas and oceans without hindrance;

Eighth, they *believe* that all of the nations of the world, for realistic as well as spiritual reasons, must come to the abandonment of the use of force. Since no future peace can be maintained if land, sea, or air armaments continue to be employed by nations which threaten, or may threaten, aggression outside of their frontiers, they *believe*, pending the establishment of a wider and permanent system of general security, that the disarmament of such nations is essential. They will likewise aid and encourage all other practicable measures which will lighten for peace-loving peoples the crushing burden of armaments.[1]

The use of the word *charter* implied a treaty or an agreement of the most solemn kind. The Atlantic Charter was not a treaty, not a signed document, not even a state paper. It was only a press release,[2] carefully phrased by the two statesmen. It was nonetheless a most solemn and significant understanding, later incorporated in the signed Declaration of United Nations—testament of the grand alliance against the Axis powers—and in subsequent bilateral agreements on Lend-Lease for the winning of the war.

Hitler's decision not to invade Spain relieved Roosevelt and Churchill of the necessity of announcing any agreement they may have reached at that time regarding the Spanish and Portuguese islands of the Eastern Atlantic. As we shall see in the next chapter, they agreed at the Argentia

---

[1] Department of State *Bulletin*, V, No. 112 (August 16, 1941), 125. Italics inserted.

[2] See statement of President Roosevelt in press conference of December 18, 1944. New York *Times*, December 19, 1944. There is a growing literature on the Atlantic Conference: Forrest E. Davis and Ernest K. Lindley, *How the War Came* (New York, 1942), pp. 250-285; Sumner Welles, *Where Are We Heading* (New York, 1946), pp. 6-18; Elliott Roosevelt, *As He Saw It* (New York, 1946), Ch. II; Robert E. Sherwood, *Roosevelt and Hopkins* (New York, 1948), pp. 349-365; *Memoirs of Cordell Hull, op. cit.*, II, pp. 974-976, 1012-1027; see also Sumner Welles's "Memoranda" on Atlantic Conferences in *Pearl Harbor Attack*, joint Congressional Committee hearings, Part 14, pp. 1268-1299, exhibits 22B, 22C, 22D (Committee Print, Washington, G.P.O., 1946). Derogatory are: George Morgenstern, *Pearl Harbor, the Story of the Secret War* (New York, 1947), pp. 117-126; John T. Flynn, *The Roosevelt Myth* (New York, 1948), pp. 299-303, 332-338, 385-386; Charles A. Beard, *President Roosevelt and the Coming of the War* (New Haven, 1948), pp. 118-133.

Students of the subject look forward to the third volume of Winston Churchill's matchless memoirs, *The Grand Alliance* (Boston, 1950).

Conference on a war warning to be sent to Japan, but Secretary of State Cordell Hull turned it into an olive branch.

Neutrality collapsed altogether in the Atlantic during the autumn months. On November 17, 1941, Congress, at the behest of the Administration, repealed the most essential features of the Neutrality Act of 1939: it permitted American merchant ships to carry goods of any kind, including arms, ammunition, and implements of warfare, to belligerent ports; and it removed the prohibition to arm American merchant ships. After consultation with the exiled Dutch Government, United States forces occupied Surinam (Dutch Guiana), on November 24, 1941, the Brazilian Government being also invited to assist in the defense of that colony.

The United States and Germany by then had drifted into an undeclared state of hostilities as yet confined to naval action.[1] An interesting feature of this conflict, to the historian of American diplomacy, is that it came to pass despite the neutrality legislation of 1935-1937. The disillusionists had told their fellow-countrymen that they had been unnecessarily "dragged" into the First World War. Congress had taken these seers and prophets at their word. It had passed neutrality laws that repudiated completely Woodrow Wilson's choice of neutral policy of 1914-1917. A pacifist people, anxious to keep out of the next war, applied to its foreign policy the lessons of the last war, without success. The United States did not get into war again with Germany and her allies in 1941 because of torts against American citizens traveling on belligerent ships; they were prohibited from embarking on them. The munitions makers did not involve the country in the European conflict; their business was strictly licensed. Loans to belligerent governments were not a cause; they were prohibited by law. American merchant ships had been forbidden to go into danger zones. They were not allowed to arm themselves lest they get into trouble with belligerents outside the war zones. Propagandists had been registered. One by one the disillusionists had picked out and quarantined the causes of the last war, only to find themselves lost in academic and legal theory as the modern conquerors sprang upon their victims.

Despite and notwithstanding the neutrality acts, the United States drifted into war with Germany at the end of 1941 because it was scared

---

[1] Diplomatic representatives still remained in the respective capitals. The United States expelled German and Italian consular agents, and "froze" the assets of the European nations in the United States, in June, 1941. Reciprocal measures followed immediately in Germany and Italy. Russian assets in the United States were frozen at the same time but released after the German attack on Russia.

for its own national safety. It resorted to unneutral action to prevent the defeat of Great Britain whilst it armed itself to meet the mounting danger. The people of the New World had seen the scrupulous neutrals of Europe go down one by one under the heel of the conqueror: Denmark, Norway, the Netherlands, Belgium, Luxemburg, Albania, Yugoslavia, and Greece. Then they had seen Hitler attack Russia in unblushing violation of the treaty of nonaggression that he had concluded with that power on August 23, 1939, a week before he began the war. The United States feared that if Great Britain fell its turn would come next. In this desperate fear for its own safety it had come to throw its lot in gradually with the British Empire, including Canada.

But how about the Pacific War, the Japanese blow that brought the United States formally into the Second World War? This was caused by a collision of Japan's conquest in Asia with the Far Eastern policy of the United States, to which subject we must now turn again.

19

Pearl Harbor and the United Nations

IN PREVIOUS chapters we have seen how skillfully Japan's diplomacy since 1902 had taken advantage of the divisions and conflicts of the Western powers in order to advance her interests and conquests in Asia. To the Japanese the revolution of the European situation after Munich and the ensuing war came as a divine wind richly laden with further opportunities for lavish successes. At last Japan was in a position to cut off the supplies which China had been importing from the United States and Europe to sustain her defense against the neighboring island empire.

Desperately resisting Japan's invasion, China had been equipping her armies largely with articles imported from overseas through the adjacent colonies of British Hong Kong and French Indo-China, and by way of British Burma over the new Burma motor road. Other succors came overland from Soviet Russia. Japan now laid plans to stop these. Immediately after Munich, Japanese forces occupied South China, including Canton and the coast behind British Kowloon; this cut off supplies coming in by way of Hong Kong. Other actions followed at the expense of the European powers, as fast as opportunities presented themselves. Thus when Hitler took over the remainder of Czechoslovakia in 1939, Japan promptly occupied the large Chinese island of Hainan, controlling the Gulf of Tonkin; next she took possession of the strategic Spratly Islands in the midst of the South China Sea, equidistant from the Philippines, Indo-China, Siam, Borneo, Java, and Singapore. Again as German armies were turning the Maginot Line in June, 1940, Japan made a treaty of amity and guaranty of territorial integrity with Thailand (Siam), providing for the exchange of information and mutual consultation on matters of common interest. After the actual fall of France, Japan occupied northern French Indo-China (September, 1940), thus stopping up that source. These conquests enabled Japan to shut off supplies coming to China through the Pacific littoral. The next step was to cut off the Burma Road.

Following the passage of the Lend-Lease Act in the United States,

Japan stirred up hostilities between Thailand and remaining French forces in Indo-China in order to fashion an opportunity for a mediation which gave her a further hold on Thailand (March, 1941) from which she might reach into Burma. After Hitler's surprise attack on Russia, Japanese forces proceeded to occupy southern Indo-China (July, 1941). With naval bases and air bases in this French territory, Japan was in a position to outflank Singapore from the land, as well as to move on Burma. In building their base at Singapore, British policy had never counted on Japanese power rushing into a vacuum in French Indo-China and flowing down the narrow Malay peninsula to attack that key to the Empire in Asia, Malaysia, and Australasia. Singapore's costly fixed defenses all pointed out to sea!

In Europe the fall of the Low Countries and of France and the peril of England not only had provided Japan with an opportunity to prepare a blow against Singapore that might break up the British Empire as well as end the China War; it had also opened a menace. A German triumph in Europe might lead Hitler into Iran and India, to repossession of the former German islands of the Pacific, abandoned at Versailles, even to China where German generals were training Chinese armies; more than that, to sovereignty over the Dutch East Indies, richest tropical archipelago in the world, with their vast stores of petroleum and rubber. Therefore Japanese policy had to guard against substituting a German for a British Empire in the Far East. Accordingly Japan struck a bargain with Germany and her satellite Italy: an alliance (September 27, 1940) to confirm a German "new order" in Europe—that is, a German conquest of that continent, in return for a Japanese "new order" in the Far East, which meant a Japanese conquest of the Far East and the expulsion of Occidental power from the protean area of "Greater East Asia." The alliance further stipulated that in case either of the three contracting parties were attacked by a power (other than Russia) not at present involved in the European war or the Sino-Japanese conflict, the other parties would come to its assistance.[1]

---

[1] The Triple Alliance of Germany, Italy, and Japan, signed on September 27, 1940, stipulated:

"Article 1. Japan recognizes and respects the leadership of Germany and Italy in the establishment of a new order in Europe.

"Article 2. Germany and Italy recognize and respect the leadership of Japan in the establishment of a new order in Greater East Asia.

"Article 3. Germany, Italy and Japan agree to cooperate in their efforts on aforesaid lines. They further undertake to assist one another with all political, economic and military means if one of the three Contracting Powers is attacked by a Power at present not involved in the European War or in the Chinese-Japanese conflict.

"Article 4. With the view to implementing the present pact, joint technical commis-

In preparing herself for this division of the Old World into a New German Order and a New Japanese Order, of totalitarian empires, Japan could not ignore the position of Russia, her only really dangerous neighbor, the sharp edge of whose armament she had tested out recently in informal but bloody battles on the Manchurian border, a power which was well armed and in a position to strike with deadly effect by sea and air from Vladivostok. Russia needed to cover her Siberian front against the menace of a German attack in Europe; Japan needed to protect herself against conflict with Russia while she planned her war in the Pacific. Like Germany under Hitler, and unlike the United States, neither Japan nor Russia chose to involve herself in a war on two fronts at the same time. So they signed a five-year pact of nonaggression and neutrality, at Moscow, April 13, 1941, resembling the first Anglo-Japanese alliance of 1902.[1] It protected Japan from attack in the north while she herself prepared to attack the Western powers in the south; but the articles as published did not forbid Russian aid to China. When Germany attacked Russia in June, 1941, another source of succor dried up for China—the overland source.

The Triple Alliance was directed against the United States, now committed to all-out aid to Great Britain "short of war" with Germany, and still sponsor of the Open Door and the integrity of China. It left it to the two greatest potential enemies of the United States to choose the moment when together they and their satellites would regard American aid to Britain or China to have crossed beyond the boundary short of war. Meanwhile Japan prepared for that day by the purchase of vast stores of gasoline, fuel oil, and scrap iron. Avidly she bought these and other war materials in the United States as long as that Government hesitated to restrict exports, particularly petroleum products, for fear

sions, to be appointed by the respective Governments of Germany, Italy and Japan, will meet without delay.

"Article 5. Germany, Italy and Japan affirm that the above agreement affects in no way the political status existing at present between each of the three Contracting Parties and Soviet Russia.

"Article 6. The present pact shall become valid immediately upon signature and shall remain in force ten years from the date on which it becomes effective." *Documents on American Foreign Relations, op. cit.*, III (1940-1941), pp. 304-305.

[1] "Article I. Both Contracting Parties undertake to maintain peaceful and friendly relations between them and mutually respect the territorial integrity and inviolability of the other Contracting Party.

"Article II. Should one of the Contracting Parties become the object of hostilities on the part of one or several third Powers, the other Contracting Party will observe neutrality throughout the duration of the conflict." *Ibid.*, p. 291.

such an embargo might impel Japan to seize the latter in the Dutch East Indies.[1]

Before the conclusion of the Triple Alliance the United States had been, generally speaking, in process of retirement from the Far East. It had pledged the independence of the Philippine Islands for 1946. It had responded only with protests and caveats to Japan's progressive violations of the Nine-Power Treaty and the Open Door. Repeatedly the Secretary of State had expressed the readiness of the United States to adjust Japanese-American relations, even existing treaties, by peaceful diplomacy; this had signified a willingness to reappraise and repair the Far Eastern situation in a diplomatic settlement with Japan. The White House at one time even went so far in the critical summer of 1940, when it seemed that England might go under, as to throw out indirectly a suggestion that there might be distinct and separate Monroe Doctrines for Europe, Asia, and for the American World.[2] But a general Japanese-American diplomatic settlement became extremely difficult when, by signing the Triple Alliance, Japan stepped from the backyard of American diplomacy to take a place in the frontyard too. By this act she projected herself into the affairs of the Atlantic, where American policy had pitched its all on an effort to hold England's head above water while preparing the defense of the United States and the Western Hemisphere amidst a world revolution of power. Japan's action after the fall of the Netherlands and France made it evident that compliance in her grand design of conquest would further weaken the British Empire at a time when the United States was taking all measures to sustain that Empire against Germany. It would completely unbalance both Europe and Asia against the United States. From then on American policy toward Japan stiffened uncompromisingly.

As Japan advanced through Indo-China toward Singapore and Burma,

---

[1] Statement of President Roosevelt, New York *Times*, July 25, 1941.

[2] Statement of Stephen A. Early, Secretary to the President, attributed to the President, printed in the New York *Times*, July 7, 1940, p. 1. The statement was actually made from Hyde Park. It was immediately welcomed by German and Japanese spokesmen and opposed by Generalissimo Chiang Kai-shek. Secretary Hull in a press statement on July 6 (New York *Times*, July 7) declared that the Monroe Doctrine contained "not the slightest vestige of any implication, much less assumption of hegemony on the part of the United States. It has never resembled, and does not today resemble, policies which appear to be arising in other geographical areas of the world, which are alleged to be similar to the Monroe Doctrine, but which, instead of resting on the sole policies of self-defense and of respect for existing sovereignties, as does the Monroe Doctrine, would in reality seem to be only the pretext for the carrying of conquest by the sword. . . ."

Mr. Early modified his statement (July 7) more in the direction of Secretary Hull's exegesis. See Arthur Krock in New York *Times*, July 9, 1940, p. 20.

and thus threatened increasingly the Dutch East Indies and the Philippines, the Secretary of State and the President uttered expressions and warnings against these aggressive steps and sought in various ways to counter them. More loans [1] were issued to China. When Great Britain, to appease Japan, closed the Burma Road for three months during the rainy season of 1940, the United States frowned on the closure.[2] In the following months American exports of war materials, including aviation gasoline, scrap iron, and ultimately petroleum, were embargoed or licensed, not against Japan specifically, but in the interest of national defense.[3] In July, 1941, Japanese credits in the United States were blocked, and reciprocally American credits in Japan. In August, 1941, an American lend-lease mission was sent to China, and supplies of all kinds began to go forward to that country by way of Rangoon and the Burma Road, under the Lend-Lease Act.[4] Finally, when Japanese aviators from Thailand and Indo-China began to bomb the Burma Road, the United States furnished China with military planes and allowed trained aviators to resign their commissions in order to take service under China to give air protection to that lifeline of military and other supplies.

The United States and Japan were on the verge of open war from the summer of 1941, as were the United States and Germany. Curiously enough, the American public did not appear greatly alarmed over what had been a matter of deepest concern to students of American diplomatic history: the possibility of a two-ocean war with a one-ocean navy to fight it with. Instead of scanning the two oceans of world politics with national binocular vision, the people looked out from their Continental Republic under the impairment of a peculiar political strabismus. They beheld now with one eye the Atlantic scene while blind to the Pacific, and now again they viewed the panorama of conflict across the Pacific while the Atlantic war picture remained occluded. In the proprietary polls which purported to sample if not to guide the trend of public opin-

---

[1] March 7, 1940, the Export-Import Bank authorized a loan of $20,000,000, to be repaid in tin, on September 25, 1940, a loan of $25,000,000 guaranteed by the Bank of China; and in addition a $30,000,000 purchase of tungsten by the Metals Reserve Corporation, a subsidiary of the United States Reconstruction Finance Corporation. A further loan of $60,000,000 was announced November 30, 1940, in connection with a plan of the Metals Reserve Company to purchase a stock of wolframite, antimony, and tin from the National Resources Commission of China. *Public Papers and Addresses of Franklin D. Roosevelt, op. cit.,* 1940 volume, p. 595.

[2] See statement made by Secretary Hull to the press, July 16, 1940. *Documents on American Foreign Relations, op. cit.,* III (1940-1941), p. 269.

[3] For a list of the restrictions to June 5, 1941, see *ibid.,* pp. 473-495.

[4] Department of State *Bulletin,* V, No. 114 (August 30, 1941), 166; V, No. 122 (October 25, 1942), 313.

ion on vital political issues, professional pollsters never put the question: "Are you in favor of going to war with Japan, Germany, and Italy at one and the same time if necessary to prevent the defeat of England?"

Any war was certain to be a double war, a two-ocean war. If there had remained any doubt of what Japan would do in case the United States went to war with Germany, there was the Triple Alliance of September 27, 1940, to make the answer unmistakable. Yet the question which these ministers of public opinion asked was: "Are you in favor of going to war against Germany if necessary to prevent the defeat of England?" Increasingly the citizens were reported to answer yes, their gaze fixed primarily across the Atlantic.

Throughout the year 1941 Secretary of State Cordell Hull strove to work out with Japan some broad-gauged program of peace for the entire Pacific area, including the Far East, a settlement to be based really on recently established principles of inter-American diplomacy. Secretary Hull's "exploratory conversations" with the new Japanese Ambassador, Admiral Nomura, later joined by a second plenipotentiary, a Mr. Kurusu, remind one of the Lansing-Ishii conversations of 1917, but with this difference: during the First World War, Japan had threatened to switch to the enemy Germany if the United States would not, like the other powers, recognize her "special interests" in China; during the Second World War, Japan was already allied with Germany (not to mention Italy) and implicitly threatened war with the United States if her paramount interest, military, economic, and political, in China and "Greater East Asia" were not recognized. If she could get this by diplomacy, if she could win the fruits of war without going to war, she was willing to interpret *defensively* [1] her obligations to Germany—and Italy—in the Tripartite Pact: i.e., not to consider hostilities between the United States and Germany in the Atlantic as an "attack" which would bring Japan into war against the United States in the Pacific. To Japan time was of the essence. She must win a diplomatic triumph over the United States before Germany invoked the *casus foederis* of the Tripartite Pact. In case the negotiations should prove unsuccessful, Japan was preparing with all her might and main for a Pacific war, to be opened by a carefully drilled surprise attack on Pearl Harbor.

At the Atlantic Conference, in August, 1941, Roosevelt and Churchill had drafted identical warnings for their two Governments to deliver to Japan: (1) that "any further encroachment by Japan in the Southwestern Pacific would produce a situation in which the United States Government

[1] See Article 2 of the Pact, above, p. 393, n. 1.

[His Majesty's Government] would be compelled to take counter measures even though these might lead to war between the United States [Great Britain] and Japan"; and (2) "If any third power becomes the object of aggression by Japan in consequence of such counter measures or of their support of them, the President would have the intention to seek authority from Congress to give aid to such Power [His Majesty's Government would give all possible aid to such Power]." [1] This would have been practically a war ultimatum. Secretary Hull, engaged in conversation with Japan, succeeded in toning down the reference to contingent conflict and holding forth in its place an olive branch.[2]

Prince Konoye, Premier of Japan—he whose Government had used a lead pencil to answer Secretary Hull's patient expostulations against Japanese advances into French Indo-China—suggested a Pacific Conference (at Honolulu, or elsewhere) between Roosevelt and him, like the Atlantic Conference between Roosevelt and Churchill. Ambassador Grew, hoping to avoid a double war, urged such a conference, and Roosevelt toyed with the idea, but he was unwilling to go unless terms of a peaceful settlement could be agreed on in advance without selling China down the river. Japan's insistence on keeping troops in China and her military occupation of all of Indo-China (July 21, 1941) in the midst of these parleys made a meeting impossible.

Historians [3] will linger for centuries over the character and details of the Hull-Nomura negotiations of 1941. We can only summarize the position of each party.

The Japanese demands for a general peaceful settlement were included

---

[1] *Roosevelt and Hopkins, op. cit.*, p. 354.

[2] *Memoirs of Cordell Hull, op. cit.*, II, pp. 1018-1020.

[3] Already a massive literature has been built up. Forrest Davis and Ernest K. Lindley were favored with a limited inside official knowledge to write their book on *How War Came* (New York, 1942). Ambassador Joseph C. Grew's account of his *Ten Years in Japan* (New York, 1944) rests on his contemporary diaries and official correspondence. Two publications present the official documents on the American side: *Peace and War: United States Foreign Policy, 1931-1941* (Department of State Publication No. 1983, Washington, G.P.O., 1943); *Foreign Relations of the United States: Japan, 1931-1941* (Department of State Publication Nos. 2008 and 2016, 2 vols., Washington, G.P.O., 1943). Of the successive reports of investigations into the Pearl Harbor disaster, the most complete is *Pearl Harbor Attack*: hearings before the Joint Committee, 79th Cong., 1st Sess. (39 vols., Washington, G.P.O., 1946). The Majority and Minority Committee Reports are in Sen. Doc. 244, 79th Cong., 2d Sess. (Washington, G.P.O., 1946). Two disillusionist studies are: George Morgenstern, *Pearl Harbor, The Story of the Secret War* (New York, 1947), and C. A. Beard, *President Roosevelt and the Coming of the War, 1941; A Study in Appearances and Realities* (New Haven, 1948). A later corrective is Basil Rauch's study of *Roosevelt from Munich to Pearl Harbor* (New York, 1950). See also H. L. Stimson and McGeorge Bundy, *On Active Service in Peace and War* (New York, 1947), and, most important, *The Memoirs of Cordell Hull, op. cit.*, II, pp. 982-1083.

in a memorandum handed to the Secretary of State on November 20, 1941:

(1) The Governments of Japan and the United States undertake not to dispatch armed forces into any of the regions, excepting French Indo-China, in the Southeastern Asia and the Southern Pacific area.

(2) Both Governments shall cooperate with the view to securing the acquisition in the Netherlands East Indies of those goods and commodities of which the two countries are in need.

(3) Both Governments mutually undertake to restore commercial relations to those prevailing prior to the freezing of assets. The Government of the United States shall supply Japan the required quantity of oil.

(4) The Government of the United States undertakes not to resort to measures and actions prejudicial to the endeavors for the restoration of general peace between Japan and China.

(5) The Japanese Government undertakes to withdraw troops now stationed in French Indo-China upon either the restoration of peace between Japan and China or the establishment of an equitable peace in the Pacific Area; and it is prepared to remove the Japanese troops in the southern part of French Indo-China to the northern part upon the conclusion of the present agreement.

These demands show the vast gulf, as wide as the Pacific Ocean, that separated the principles of the good neighbors of the American world, and the rule of force in the Far East. Japanese forces presented a definite challenge to those principles for the governance of Asia.

There was no ultimatum attached to the Japanese demands. The Japanese representatives at Washington, the Ambassador, Admiral Nomura, and the Special Plenipotentiary, Mr. Kurusu, recently arrived as an Envoy Extraordinary, professed to be willing to explore further the possibilities of an agreement, at least for a couple of weeks more. Already Japanese naval forces, with air complements, had left their home bases for the neighborhood of the Hawaiian Islands, timed to strike without warning on Sunday morning, December 7, before negotiations were broken off.

The United States replied to Japan's demands with a tentative Outline of Proposed Basis for Agreement, dated November 26, 1941. After repeating the general American principles of territorial integrity, nonintervention, equality, and conciliation, Secretary Hull proposed that the two nations govern themselves in their *economic* relations with each other and with other nations and peoples by the following principles:

(1) The principle of nondiscrimination in international commercial relations.

(2) The principle of international economic co-operation and abolition of extreme nationalism as expressed in excessive trade restrictions.

(3) The principle of nondiscriminatory access by all nations to raw material supplies.

(4) The principle of full protection of the interests of consuming countries and populations as regards the operation of international commodity agreements.

(5) The principle of establishment of such institutions and arrangements of international finance as may lend aid to the essential enterprises and the continuous development of all countries and may permit payments through processes of trade consonant with the welfare of all countries.

As specific steps to be taken by the Governments of the United States and Japan to carry out these principles in a broad settlement of existing issues, the United States outline further proposed:

1. The Government of the United States and the Government of Japan will endeavor to conclude a multilateral nonaggression pact among the British Empire, China, Japan, the Netherlands, the Soviet Union, Thailand, and the United States.

2. Both Governments will endeavor to conclude among the American, British, Chinese, Japanese, the Netherland, and Thai Governments an agreement whereunder each of the Governments would pledge itself to respect the territorial integrity of French Indo-China and, in the event that there should develop a threat to the territorial integrity of Indo-China, to enter into immediate consultation with a view to taking such measures as may be deemed necessary and advisable to meet the threat in question. Such agreement would provide also that each of the Governments party to the agreement would not seek or accept preferential treatment in its trade or economic relations with Indo-China and would use its influence to obtain for each of the signatories equality of treatment in trade and commerce with French Indo-China.

3. The Government of Japan will withdraw all military, naval, air, and police forces from China and from Indo-China.

4. The Government of the United States and the Government of Japan will not support—militarily, politically, economically—any government or regime in China other than the National Government of the Republic of China with capital temporarily at Chungking.

5. Both Governments will give up all extraterritorial rights in China, including rights and interests in and with regard to international settlements and concessions, and rights under the Boxer Protocol of 1901.

Both Governments will endeavor to obtain the agreement of the British and other Governments to give up extraterritorial rights in China, including rights in international settlements and in concessions and under the Boxer Protocol of 1901.

6. The Government of the United States and the Government of Japan will enter into negotiations for the conclusion between the United States

and Japan of a trade agreement, based upon reciprocal most-favored-nation treatment and reduction of trade barriers by both countries, including an undertaking by the United States to bind raw silk on the free list.

7. The Government of the United States and the Government of Japan will, respectively, remove the freezing restrictions on Japanese funds in the United States and on American funds in Japan.

8. Both Governments will agree upon a plan for the stabilization of the dollar-yen rate, with the allocation of funds adequate for this purpose, half to be supplied by Japan and half by the United States.

9. Both Governments will agree that no agreement which either has concluded with any third power or powers shall be interpreted by it in such a way as to conflict with the fundamental purpose of this agreement, the establishment and preservation of peace throughout the Pacific area.

10. Both Governments will use their influence to cause other governments to adhere to and to give practical application to the basic political and economic principles set forth in this agreement.

A week passed without any response from Japan, ten days, eleven, twelve. Then on Saturday, December 6, President Roosevelt made a fervent personal appeal to the Emperor of Japan to give thought in this definite emergency to ways of dispelling the "dark clouds." "None of the peoples of whom I have spoken [inhabitants of Indo-China, Philippines, East Indies, Malaya, Thailand]," the President cabled, "can sit either indefinitely or permanently on a keg of dynamite."

Before the Emperor could respond, the Japanese Government's reply to the United States, timed to be delivered after war had commenced without declaration,[1] was handed in at Washington. After lengthy recrimination, it declared that in view of the attitude of the American Government, Japan could not but consider that it was impossible to reach an agreement through further negotiations.

Already Japan had struck her first blows at Pearl Harbor, Manila, and Hong Kong. Characteristically the American Government had shown the resourcefulness to "crack" the Japanese secret code and read the diplomatic and military correspondence of the Japanese Government on the eve of Pearl Harbor. Characteristically it neglected to make full and vigilant use of that valuable intelligence in order to ward off a wellnigh fatal surprise blow. By this one stroke Japan caught a careless democratic nation inexcusably off guard on a sleepy Sunday morning.

---

[1] "The Contracting Powers recognize that hostilities between them must not commence without a previous and unequivocal warning, which shall take the form either of a declaration of war, giving reasons, or of an ultimatum with a conditional declaration of war." Article I of Hague Convention III, of 1907, Relative to the Commencement of Hostilities. The United States, Great Britain, Germany, Italy, and Japan were all parties to this Convention in 1941.

At the start Japan crippled the American navy and air force in the Hawaiian Islands and turned to the conquest of the Philippines, the Dutch Indies, Malaya, and Burma as the first phase of the war. It was the greatest defeat and humiliation in American history.

In a trice, by December 11, 1941, the United States, Great Britain, and her Dominions were formally at war with Japan, Germany, and Italy. The satellites of the Triple Alliance, Hungary, Rumania, and Bulgaria, declared war on the United States December 13; another one, Thailand, on January 25, 1942. The United States returned the compliment, June 4, 1942, to Hungary, Bulgaria, and Rumania.

In previous years the United States had been unwilling to stand fast at all costs for the Open Door and the integrity of China. For the security of the Philippine Islands it had made repeated concessions on its Far Eastern policy to Japan since the Russo-Japanese War (1905, 1908, 1915, 1917). From 1931 to 1941, during the various phases of the Second Sino-Japanese War, the United States had not been willing, for the sake of the Open Door and the integrity of China, to risk a war with Japan, even when Japan had no allies. Why then in 1941, after Japan had secured the most powerful allies possible for her to get in a war with the United States, and in addition had neutralized Russia, did the United States for the first time take an unflinching stand not only for the Open Door and the integrity of China, but also for the integrity of French Indo-China, British Malaya, and the Dutch East Indies, actually urging the evacuation of Japanese forces from China, where they had been during ten years of conquest, and from French Indo-China?

The answer to this staggering question is that the German conquests in Europe and the Japanese conquests in Asia, and the Triple Alliance between the conquerors forbidding the United States to come into the war to save England or China from defeat, had so completely upset the balance of power in the Old World [1] and with it the whole basis of American foreign policy—Europe's distresses America's advantage—that if the United States was to defend itself and its principles, and the whole global cause of freedom, against the merging torrents of conquest it must do so *while still there was time, while there were left alive effective allies to fight with,* Great Britain, China, and Russia. Otherwise it would surely have to face alone in the New World and in its own homeland the victorious conquerors of the Old World. On the eve of Pearl Harbor,

---

[1] Nicholas J. Spykman has given us a perspicuous analysis of the United States and the balance of power in *America's Strategy in World Politics* (Yale Institute of International Studies, 1942).

Roosevelt had prepared a war message to Congress in response to Japan's moves against British Malaya and the Dutch East Indies.[1] The perfidious Japanese blow, before a declaration of war, in violation of Hague Convention III of 1907, made this unnecessary.

Within seven hours after the faithless Japanese attack on Pearl Harbor naval orders went out from Washington: "Execute unrestricted air and submarine warfare against Japan," in violation of the London Naval Treaty of 1930.[2] During the war against Japan, 1941-1945, American submarines sank 1,750 Japanese merchant ships and took the lives of 105,000 Japanese civilians.[3] Thus did the United States forswear and throw overboard its ancient birthright, the Freedom of the Seas, for which it went to war with Germany in 1917 and collected adjudicated indemnities, after the victory, for torts against its own citizens by illegal German submarine warfare, 1914-1918.[4]

Pearl Harbor ended in one hour all previous debate in the United States on "measures short of war," or on the wisdom of intervention or nonintervention. At the cost of a terrible defeat and national humiliation it welded the United States into an immediate union with the other nations, conquered and still unconquered, who were fighting for their existence as free men against the power and skill of the conquerors in Europe and Asia. During a dramatic visit to Washington of Winston

[1] George Morgenstern, *Pearl Harbor, op. cit.*, pp. 296, 403.
American, British, and Canadian military staff conversations in Washington in January-March, and American, British, and Dutch conversations in Singapore in April, 1941, had envisaged the possibility of such a message in case Japanese forces should cross designated lines of defense (Japan crossed them December 5, 1941), but this was not a "secret alliance," or any "alliance" at all, as Morgenstern avers. These staff conversations did not constitute a treaty. They were not even an executive agreement, unless by some secret understanding with Prime Minister Churchill not yet revealed. They could not bind Congress. They were more like the Anglo-French staff conversations which planned defensive measures to meet any German invasion of Belgium in 1914.
Admiral Stark and General Marshall rejected the ABD staff plan of Singapore. "Nevertheless, on November 5, 1941, the United States chiefs-of-staff passed on to President Roosevelt the exact recommendations made by the Singapore Conference as to the three contingencies any one of which should be met by an American declaration of war on Japan." Samuel Eliot Morison, *The Rising Sun in the Pacific* (Boston, 1948), pp. 55-56.
[2] For text, see above, p. 195.
[3] Navy Department News Release, February 2, 1946. See also New York *Times*, February 3, 1946.
[4] In answer to formal interrogations by former Gross Admiral Doenitz, at the request of the International Military Tribunal at Nuremberg, Germany, where Doenitz was tried as a war criminal, Fleet Admiral Chester W. Nimitz, Chief of Naval Operations, U.S.N., testified as follows: "The unrestricted submarine and air warfare ordered by the Chief of Naval Operations on 7 December 1941 was justified by Japanese attacks on that date on U.S. bases, and on both armed and unarmed ships and nationals, without warning or declaration of war." Navy Department Press Release, May 24, 1946.

Churchill, President and Prime Minister announced the terms of an alliance of the two English-speaking powers and all who cared to join it. This international agreement, the most important and far-reaching since the treaty of peace and independence of 1783, was not a treaty made by and with the advice and consent of the Senate. It was another executive agreement, signed by the executive authorities of twenty-six governments, in the form of a joint declaration, January 1, 1942, for the overthrow of Hitlerism and its allied forces and for ultimate peace on the basis of the Atlantic Charter. Mexico and the newly established Philippine Republic later signed this joint agreement in an impressive ceremony at Washington on June 14, 1942.

DECLARATION BY UNITED NATIONS

A Joint Declaration by The United States of America, The United Kingdom of Great Britain and Northern Ireland, The Union of Soviet Socialist Republics, China, Australia, Belgium, Canada, Costa Rica, Cuba, Czechoslovakia, Dominican Republic, El Salvador, Greece, Guatemala, Haiti, Honduras, India, Luxembourg, Netherlands, New Zealand, Nicaragua, Norway, Panama, Poland, South Africa, Yugoslavia.

The Governments signatory hereto,

Having subscribed to a common program of purposes and principles embodied in the Joint Declaration of the President of the United States of America and the Prime Minister of the United Kingdom of Great Britain and Northern Ireland dated August 14, 1941, known as the Atlantic Charter,

Being convinced that complete victory over their enemies is essential to defend life, liberty, independence and religious freedom, and to preserve human rights and justice in their own lands as well as in other lands, and that they are now engaged in a common struggle against savage and brutal forces seeking to subjugate the world, *Declare:*

(1) Each Government pledges itself to employ its full resources, military or economic, against those members of the Tripartite Pact and its adherents with which such government is at war.

(2) Each Government pledges itself to cooperate with the Governments signatory hereto and not to make a separate armistice or peace with the enemies.

The foregoing declaration may be adhered to by other nations which are, or which may be, rendering material assistance and contributions in the struggle for victory over Hitlerism.[1]

[1] Department of State *Bulletin*, VI, No. 132 (January 3, 1942), pp. 3-4.

American Diplomacy during the

Second World War

The principal concern of the United States in the diplomacy of the Second World War was, of course, the winning of the war as soon as possible. All diplomatic goals were sighted to that surviving purpose: to sustain and fortify the tottering British Empire, to keep alive the defeated French nation, almost inanimate under Hitler's heel but still alive and stirring in North Africa; to arm and accouter the swarming Russian legions; and to prevent the remaining neutrals, Spain, Portugal, Sweden, Switzerland, and Turkey, from falling prey to the enemy: in short to win the war in Europe, then with Russia's hoped-for aid to knock out Japan in Asia: first VE-Day, then VJ-Day.

Thanks to the Good Neighbor Policy, the republics of the Western Hemisphere, all except Argentina, had already lined up on the side of the United States and the United Nations.[1]

In Europe, amidst the uncertainty and anxiety following the military collapse of France and the Franco-German armistice of June 22, 1940, the United States remained in formal diplomatic relations with the Vichy Government, despite the rupture between Great Britain and France. As President George Washington had refused to break with the French Revolutionary Government of the First Republic after the overthrow of the monarchy of Louis XVI, so President Roosevelt kept up a formal contact with the "neutral" National Revolutionary Government of Marshal Pétain long after the downfall of the Third Republic, even until after American entrance into the European war.

The reason for this connection with an unrespected regime was not so much perfect propriety under international law as convenience for American purposes: (1) to prevent, if possible, the French fleet (demobilized by the Franco-German armistice) from being turned over to the Germans to be used against Great Britain—and the United States; (2) to try to prevent Vichy from yielding to Germany or Italy any bases in French Africa or French colonies in the New World;[2] (3) generally

1 See above, pp. 305-306.
2 In October, 1940, Admiral Greenslade, U.S.N., entered into a separate under-

to stiffen Marshal Pétain's Government against co-operation and col-laboration with Germany and Italy beyond the terms of the armistice. During 1940-1942 the United States, still unprepared for war on a suf-ficient scale, could exert little military pressure on the situation, but its diplomatic influence was by no means negligible: for France to lose the historical friendship and potential support of the United States might extinguish her last hope of resurrection from German conquest. The American Ambassador to Vichy, Admiral William D. Leahy—succeeding William C. Bullitt—was at least a bare rock to cling to after the Nazi tide swirled over France.

Aside from the French Navy, which the Pétain Government pledged itself to scuttle rather than make over to the Germans, North Africa was the vital concern of the United States. It was a springboard for an Axis invasion of the New World, not to mention advanced Atlantic sub-marine bases for Germany. By the same token it was a coveted military platform on which the United States might some day stage a Mediter-ranean invasion of Italy and the German fortress of Europe.

The first American implement for the security of French North Africa was the Murphy-Weygand agreement of February 26, 1941, made in the name of the President by Robert D. Murphy, counselor of the United States Embassy in France, with the French commander in North Africa, and countenanced by Vichy. Under its terms the United States agreed to provide a small revictualing of Morocco and Algeria to be controlled and administered by an increased number of American vice consuls. The real function of these numerous officials was to maintain contact with General Weygand, encourage resistance to German intrusion, and furnish intelligence in preparation for a military occupation not to be resisted, perhaps even to be assisted, by the French North African army.

Germany checkmated the American design for French North Africa by bringing about the removal of General Weygand, but (thanks to Hitler's war and disaster in Russia) was not able to invade the southern continent before the United States and Great Britain landed massive forces in Morocco and Algeria, November 8, 1942. This led to German occupa-

standing with the French High Commissioner at Martinique, Admiral Robert, em-bodying guarantees immobilizing French war vessels in American waters and holding at the island heavy shipments of gold en route to France from the United States—also allowing an American observer and naval and air patrol to enforce the understanding. Secretary of State Cordell Hull to Senator James M. Mead, June 2, 1941. *Documents on American Foreign Relations, op. cit.,* III (1940-1941), pp. 95-96. The agreement did not survive the rupture of relations between the United States and Vichy in November, 1942, after which the United States Navy had to take the problem into its own hands. *Ibid.,* V (1942-1943), pp. 470-473. *Memoirs of Cordell Hull, op. cit.,* II, pp. 1160, 1223.

tion of all of metropolitan France and to a final rupture of the Allies with Pétain and the other men of Vichy, including the precious German tool, Pierre Laval—all of them by then discredited in their own country. Henceforth the French people put their faith in "underground" resistance inspired and led by General Charles de Gaulle in exile, supported by Allied military efforts. Pending the liberation of France and the establishment of a provisional government by the choice of free Frenchmen, the United States tried to sustain and unite the dissident overseas groups into one French Committee of National Liberation recognized by the Allies as administering such territories of France as acknowledged its authority.[1] At best our Vichy policy was an opportunist gamble with fate to cover the successful landing of an American army in North Africa and the turn of the tide of war.[2]

Allied operations in North Africa, prelude to a strike at *Festung Europa* from the Mediterranean, depended to a considerable degree on the attitude of Falangist Spain. There the dictator General Francisco Franco owed the success of his revolt against the established republican government, in the Spanish Civil War of 1936-1939, to the intervention of Fascist Italy and Nazi Germany, unsuccessfully opposed by the intervention of Soviet Russia—rehearsal for larger wars soon to come. But he could also burn a candle of thanks to the unprecedented attitude of the United States along with fellow democracies, Great Britain and France. By applying the new neutrality legislation to civil as well as international wars, the United States had reversed the old rule of the law of nations which permitted established governments to buy munitions

---

[1] Statement of President Roosevelt, August 26, 1943. *Documents on American Foreign Relations,* VI (1943-1944), p. 666.

[2] William L. Langer has written a scholarly history of *Our Vichy Gamble* (New York, 1947) with the aid of documents furnished uniquely to him by President Roosevelt and the Department of State. See also Hull, *Memoirs, op. cit.,* I, pp. 844-855, II, pp. 948-967, 1127-1165. Langer judges the North African phase of our Vichy diplomacy to have been an "unqualified success" (p. 388), but admits that it was not the deciding factor either in preventing parts of the French Empire, or the French fleet at Toulon (scuttled, November 27, 1942), from falling into the hands of the enemy. He considers its principal significance was that of providing military intelligence and contacts with French officers to lay the groundwork for the Allied invasion. But General Eisenhower found our intelligence none too good upon launching the campaign in North Africa. Louis Gottschalk, reviewing Langer's book and thesis at length, contends from the evidence therein presented that "Our Vichy Gamble" was really "Our Vichy Fumble," in *Journal of Modern History,* XX (No. 1, March, 1948), 47-57. He alludes to the considerable body of literature already building up on this question. See also Eugene Rostow, "Wartime Policies toward Vichy and Franco," *World Politics,* I (No. 3, April, 1949), 389-394. For the naval and military history of the landings see: Samuel Eliot Morison, *History of United States Naval Operations,* Vol. II: *Operations in North African Waters* (Boston, 1947), and Dwight D. Eisenhower, *Crusade in Europe* (New York, 1948). See also Winston Churchill's *The Grand Alliance, op. cit.*

of war from the citizens of a neutral nation.[1] Now in 1940 after the fall of France, Franco's heavy-caliber shore batteries commanded the Straits of Gibraltar and the Rock itself. Across the Straits there were 150,000 Spanish troops in the Rif, resting on the immediate left flank of the American invasion route. The Canary and Cape Verde Islands could make an ideal base for the German *Luftwaffe* and U-boats. And the Spanish peninsula could become an easy causeway for German armored might rolling down from France to Algeciras to be ferried across to Africa under the protection of Spanish guns.

At the outbreak of the war in Europe, General Franco had proclaimed a strict neutrality. When Germany conquered France and Mussolini's Italy entered the war like a jackal, the Spanish Caudillo changed suddenly from neutrality to "nonbelligerency" in order to be more benevolent to his fellow-dictator friends against his old enemy Soviet Russia. He had to face the German Führer in a personal meeting at Hendaye on the French frontier, October 23, 1940. Exhausted by the recent civil war at home, which had bled Spain a million lives, Franco seems not to have wanted another war, unless it were short and sure, without peril, bringing great rewards. But Hitler's astonishing victories might make it unsafe to stay out. In a spirit of appeasement rather than determined bellicosity, Franco offered a pact with the devil. He proposed to come in on Hitler's side, and had already named his price: Gibraltar, traditional Spanish gauge of war with England; French Morocco; the province of Oran in Algeria; plus additions to the colony of Rio de Oro on the west coast of Africa south of Morocco; also Spain to be supplied with food and armament.[2] When Hitler refused to meet these terms unequivocally and continued his efforts to reduce England first, Franco was relieved;[3] doubly so when, failing to conquer England,

[1] Compare the situation in 1948 when the United States Government having repealed the neutrality legislation of 1935-1937, furnished the Chinese Government with economic aid, military supplies, and equipment for defense of "individual liberty, free institutions, and genuine independence" during the communist revolt and civil war. See Foreign Assistance Act of 1949, Title IV, approved April 3, 1948. For economic and military aid rendered under this act, see New York *Times*, October 12, 14, November 13, December 16, 19, 1948.

[2] Langer, *Vichy Gamble, op. cit.,* pp. 90-100.

[3] So opines Professor Carlton J. H. Hayes, Ambassador of the United States to Spain, 1942-1945, in his *Wartime Mission in Spain* (New York, 1945), pp. 64-66. Franco's Foreign Minister, the Falangist commander, Serrano Suñer, was more eager for an alliance on Hitler's terms than Franco. Langer, *op. cit.,* p. 91. Franco dropped Serrano Suñer in September, 1942. Herbert Feis's account of *The Spanish Story* (New York, 1948), pp. 93-111, affirms that a secret Spanish protocol with the Axis was actually signed, November 11, 1940, and endorsed by Franco, stipulating in principle that Spain would enter the war, but not saying when, and vague as to particulars. When later Hitler pressed Franco to set a date, the Caudillo managed to put him off

Hitler madly attacked Russia in June, 1941. All Spain breathed easier as the storm veered from the direction of the Iberian Peninsula to those roomy Scythian steppes that had lured the French Napoleon to his fate over a century before.

After Hitler's and Mussolini's declarations of war on Russia and six months later on the United States, Franco explained that Spain's "non-belligerency" applied only to the war between Hitler and Franco's old enemy Soviet Russia; in the war between the Western Allies and the Axis Powers he professed still to be neutral. It was the task of American Ambassadors at Madrid, successively Alexander C. Weddell and Professor Carlton J. H. Hayes, to keep uncertain Spain really neutral. In the dark days of 1940-1942, when American forces were still insufficient for a two-ocean war, about all that these diplomats had to rely on was poise and propaganda, manipulation of overseas exports, particularly petroleum, to the Peninsula, and costly "preclusive" buying of war materials—like tungsten ore (wolfram)—to prevent their going to Germany. Spain's real attitude finally became clear when her shore batteries remained silent as the Allies marshaled their planes and ships under range at Gibraltar and in the Bay of Algeciras.[1]

As the tide of war turned against Italy and Germany, Franco, despite continuing diplomatic problems, became more and more friendly, finally benevolently neutral to the Allies. At American behest the Spanish Government drastically reduced the shipment of vital products to Germany. Spain became not a causeway for German invasion but a vestibule for the escape of thousands of Allied airmen and able-bodied refugees out of France for service in the armies fighting Hitler and Mussolini in Africa and Italy. It was also an American listening post for German military movements in France before the Normandy invasion. The signed photo-

with one reason or another. Captured German archives have not yet revealed the full text.

[1] Winston Churchill acknowledged in a speech to the House of Commons, May 24, 1944, that Spain on this occasion had made full amends for her former unfriendly attitude: "We had sometimes 600 airplanes crowded on this [Gibraltar] airfield in full range and full view of Spanish batteries . . . apart from the aircraft, enormous numbers of ships were anchored far outside of the neutral waters inside the Bay of Algeciras, always under the command of Spanish shore guns. We would have suffered the greatest inconvenience if we had been ordered to move those ships. Indeed, I do not know how the vast convoys would have been marshalled and assembled." *Parliamentary Debates, House of Commons*, Vol. 400, p. 700.

At the time of the landings in North Africa, President Roosevelt conveyed written assurances to the Chiefs of State of Portugal (November 8, 1942) and Spain (November 13, 1942) of complete respect for the continental or island possessions of each power. In turn Franco's Ambassador in Washington assured the United States of continued maintenance of Spain's "absolute neutrality." *Documents on American Foreign Relations, op. cit.*, V (1942-1943), pp. 592-594.

graphs of Mussolini and Hitler disappeared from the walls of General Franco's reception room; only the Pope's autographed portrait remained.[1]

Portugal, though at first anticipating German victory, did not desert her ancient British ally, but for a long time she stayed neutral. After the entrance of the United States into the war, and on British nomination, she allowed the establishment of an American air base in the Azores Islands.[2]

In the Eastern Mediterranean and the Near East, Turkey was a strategic complement to Spain and Portugal in the West. Likewise the neutrality of Turkey depended not so much on the diplomacy of the Allies as it did upon the strategical decisions of Adolf Hitler and his consequent fatal invasion of Russia. As the war turned against Mussolini and Hitler, Turkey too became more and more benevolently neutral toward the United Nations, and finally embargoed the export of much-needed chrome ore to the Axis and its satellites. As Hitler's edifice of power and hate began to crumble into rubble around the bunkers of Berlin, Turkey technically declared war on Germany and Japan (February 23, 1945) and entered the company of the United Nations.

Switzerland and Sweden remained neutral to the end of the war, thanks to their own location and convenient resources, so open to Germany; but even there the United Nations were able to prevail on those governments, as the twilight of the war descended on the false gods of Fascism and Nazism, to embargo war materials, like ball bearings, for Germany, and to close their frontiers, like the other neutrals Spain and Portugal, to escaping war criminals.

The Second World War was a war of dramatic personal conferences between Chiefs of State almost as much as it was a war of colossal battles on land, on sea, and in the air. The Allied leaders winged their way over the oceans to cement unity face to face in quick decisions on problems of high strategy. We recall that, during the First World War, Woodrow Wilson had stayed at home until the final peace conference at Paris, but had used a representative without office, Colonel Edward M. House, for the purpose of personal collaboration with the Associated war chiefs. President Franklin D. Roosevelt found his *alter ego* in Harry L. Hopkins, a New York social-service worker who had risen rapidly to high rank in the administration and familiar councils of the New Deal and had served for a while as Secretary of Commerce. For three and a half years he lived

[1] Hayes, *Wartime Mission, op. cit.*, p. 242.
[2] Still allowed and maintained for other purposes (1950).

in the Lincoln Study in the White House. It was Hopkins, acting without portfolio, who made the first personal contacts for Roosevelt with Churchill in London and Stalin in Moscow, preparing the way for the President's later conferences on both sides of the Atlantic.

Harry Hopkins all but set aside the higher responsibilities of the Secretary of State, and President Roosevelt as Commander in Chief of the armed forces all but usurped the treaty-making power of the Senate. A liaison officer had to be appointed to serve between the White House and the Department of State! In personal conferences Roosevelt made international agreements on subjects of the greatest possible significance, reserving for treaties only the new league of nations and the final peace settlement.[1] The Argentia (Atlantic Charter) and Arcadia [2] (United Nations Declaration) conferences of Roosevelt and Churchill were the first of eight meetings of the two statesmen for the conduct of the war and the promise of the peace, climaxed by their conferences with Stalin at Teheran and Yalta.

Hopkins's earlier confabulations had secured British agreement to General Marshall's plan for an Anglo-American second front to take shape on the Channel coast of France (after the collapse of the first second front during Soviet Russia's nonaggression agreement of 1939 with Hitler) to relieve German pressure on Russia in the year 1942, later to be extended into the heart of Germany by more extensive operations during 1943. President Roosevelt authorized V. M. Molotov, on the occasion of that Russian envoy's secret visit to Washington during the last days of May, 1942, to tell Joseph Stalin to expect a second front that very year. To suffering Soviet Russia, ravaged by Hitler's legions so deep within her frontiers, this was the most important factor in Allied diplomacy, and it meant to the Russians one thing: a second front *in France.*

A second front in France in 1942 was too big a promise to make and keep in the military situation that followed. Germany and Japan spoiled the plans. They seemed to be winning the war on every side. Military disasters in all theaters led to conferences between Roosevelt and Churchill at Hyde Park and Washington (June, 1942) that shifted the

[1] Robert E. Sherwood has written from forty boxes of Hopkins's personal papers an intimate history of *Roosevelt and Hopkins* (New York, 1948), which is as important to the historian of American diplomacy during the Second World War as is Charles Seymour's *Intimate Papers of Colonel House* for the First World War. Sherwood writes history like a playwright, selecting and excluding his materials to throw his characters into dramatic highlights, and exhibiting high disdain for precise documentation.

For Charles E. Bohlen, whom Hopkins persuaded Roosevelt to appoint to a post in the White House where he could act as liaison with the Department of State, see Sherwood, pp. 774-775.

[2] See above, pp. 388, 403.

projected invasion from the English Channel to North Africa. The Prime Minister undertook the difficult duty of explaining the decision personally to Stalin in Moscow (August, 1942). The mistrustful Russian leader acceded to the change only because he could not help it.

As the enemies' lightnings quivered and flashed through black clouds on every horizon, neither England, nor Russia, nor the United States faltered, nor did their war leaders. At length for stout hearts the tide of war turned. The first, isolated naval and air Battle of Midway put Japanese strategy on the defensive in the Pacific and made it safer for the United States to devote its principal war effort to the European arena. In November, 1942, came by a narrow margin the next victories: at El Alamein before the gates of Egypt; at Stalingrad on the Volga; in the waters of the distant Solomon Islands; and with the successful landings of American and British armies in Morocco and Algeria. Thenceforth the Allies could look forward not to defeat and slavery but to victory and freedom. The later great personal conferences took place in a spirit of increasing confidence.

At Casablanca (January, 1943) Roosevelt and Churchill met behind the new front in North Africa and made their military decisions for carrying the war into Sicily and Italy. It was at Casablanca that the President, in a joint press conference with the Prime Minister, announced to the world that the Allies would fight on implacably until the "unconditional surrender" of their enemies.[1] This time there would be no Fourteen Points. At Quebec in August, 1943, the two statesmen prepared for the surrender of Italy [2] and for a second front at last in France.

Secretary of State Cordell Hull, for once allowed to participate in an international war conference in Europe, conveyed such plans and as-

[1] Roosevelt later explained that the phrase "popped into his mind" from thoughts about General Grant and Lee during the American Civil War, but Sherwood, *op. cit.*, pp. 695-697, shows that the President used the phrase deliberately, reading from prepared notes. And Churchill, backed by the British Cabinet, had already agreed with the President on unconditional surrender—at least for Germany. See parliamentary exchange between Foreign Secretary Ernest Bevin and former Prime Minister Winston Churchill, November 17, 1949, printed in New York *Times,* November 18, 1949.

[2] Strictly speaking, the surrender of Italy, although it followed the formula of unconditional surrender in regard to full powers over the internal, financial, economic, and military life of Italy, left the Italian royal house (soon deposed by internal protest) in authority. Later, the provisional Italian government declared war on Germany, October 13, 1943, and on Japan, February 27, 1945.

For terms of Armistice between General Eisenhower, "acting by authority of the United States and Great Britain and in the interest of the United Nations" and Marshal Pietro Badoglio, "Head of the Italian Government," see Department of State *Bulletin,* XIII, No. 333 (November 11, 1945), 748-760. Howard McGaw Smith has written a history of "The Armistice of Cassibile," in *Military Affairs,* XII (No. 1, Spring, 1948), 12-36.

surances to Marshal Stalin in Moscow at the first meeting of foreign ministers and chiefs of staff of the Big Three (October, 1943). The Russian leader reciprocated by stating gratuitously and unequivocally, for delivery to President Roosevelt, that as soon as the Allies had succeeded in vanquishing Germany the Soviet Union would then join them in defeating Japan. The representatives of the three Allied Governments then proclaimed a solemn warning to all Nazis guilty of war atrocities that they would be brought back to the scene of their abominations to be charged and punished according to the laws of the countries that had suffered them. They set up an European Advisory Commission in London to examine European questions as they should arise and make joint recommendations to the three Governments—this Commission later was given the task of preparing the conditions to be imposed on Germany and Austria after the surrender, as well as delimitation of the zones of Allied occupation.[1] They also declared for a democratic regime in Italy and for the independence of Austria after the war. Most important of all for prevailing opinion in America was a Four-Power Declaration, sponsored by the American Secretary of State, pledging the United States, China,[2] Great Britain, and Russia to take the necessary steps for the establishment of a general international organization to insure world peace. What the Secretary of State then had in mind was inter-American principles of international co-operation applied on a world scale;[3] the structure of the new United Nations organization had not been drafted; but Hull wanted to get it going even during the war, lest postwar debate frustrate its inception.

The Four-Power Declaration of Moscow had the effect of joining a movement in both political parties in the United States for a new league of nations, only they would not call it that. It led to the passage by the Senate of the Connally Resolution, presented by the Committee on Foreign Relations, Tom Connally of Texas chairman, by a vote of 85 yeas, 5 nays (six Senators not voting). This epoch-making resolution, foreshadowing a diplomatic revolution in the history of the United States, looked to the consummation of a treaty "under constitutional process" with free and sovereign nations for the "establishment and maintenance

---

[1] Hajo Holborn has described the work of this Commission and other diplomatic antecedents of *American Military Government* (Washington, 1947).

[2] The Chinese Ambassador was empowered to sign the Declaration originally, thus making it a four-power document and considerably enhancing the prestige of China then in the eighth year of resistance to the invasion of Japan.

[3] *Memoirs of Cordell Hull, op. cit.*, II, pp. 1274-1318, notably p. 1281, p. 1298 and p. 1309. *Documents on American Foreign Relations, op. cit.*, VI (1943-1944), pp. 225-232.

of international authority with power to prevent aggression and to preserve the peace of the world."

Thus did the Senate of the United States, which had four times refused the Treaty of Versailles, and which had joined with the House
of Representatives in the passage of the neutrality legislation of 1935-
1937, repudiating American intervention in the First World War, come
back at last to Woodrow Wilson—Congress had already repealed the
neutrality laws. At last, for the first time since 1920 an American
political party, both American political parties, advocated the entry of
the United States into an international organization for the maintenance
of world peace. In the party conventions of 1944 the only debate was
how to enforce the peace to come, whether the police force was to be
an international army, or navy, or air force.

It was Roosevelt's ardent wish to meet Stalin face to face and convince him of the good faith and comradeship of the United States and
Great Britain with Russia for the winning of the war and a future
reign of peace. He had a "hunch" that he could treat him trustingly and
not suspiciously.[1] But repeated postponements of the second front had
chilled the Soviet Marshal. Only after the new assurances at Moscow did
Stalin give Secretary Hull to understand that he would meet with the
other two Chiefs of State if the place could be no farther away from the
pressing Russian front than Teheran. (Roosevelt had suggested Basra
on the Euphrates River, in Iraq.) Promptly the President and Prime
Minister decided to pack their bags and fly [2] to the distant Iranian capital.
But no place in the world was distant any more. At Oran, Tunis, Malta,
Egypt, even in the Persian rendezvous of fabulous Teheran, the President signed or vetoed bills of Congress and returned them within the
ten days prescribed by the Constitution.

In Cairo, en route to Teheran, Roosevelt and Churchill and their
military and political advisers (including always the faithful Harry
Hopkins) held a prearranged conference with Chiang Kai-shek, Generalissimo of the embattled Chinese Republic, now desperately at bay
against the Japanese invaders. Since Russia was not yet a party to
the war with Japan, no Soviet representative participated. At the Con-

[1] According to an undated conversation with William C. Bullitt, recounted by the
latter in his article on "How We Won the War and Lost the Peace," *Life* Magazine
for August 30 and September 6, 1948, Vol. XXV, Nos. 9 and 10.

[2] Roosevelt and Hopkins went as far as Oran on the new U.S.S. *Iowa*. They flew
from there via Tunis to Cairo, and from Cairo to Teheran and back. From Cairo
they returned by air to Tunis, where the President apprised General Eisenhower of his
appointment to command the whole Allied second front; then to Malta and Sicily,
and back from Malta by battleship to the United States.

ference of Cairo (November 22-26, 1943) the Sphinx and the Pyramids, not to mention the chic costumes of the Wellesley College alumna, Mrs. Chiang Kai-shek, illustrious spouse and interpreter to the Generalissimo, lent romantic color to the grim realities of war.[1] After the several military missions agreed upon future operations against Japan, Roosevelt, Churchill, and Chiang Kai-shek made a joint statement of purpose: to strip Japan of all the islands in the Pacific which she had seized or occupied since the beginning of the First World War in 1914 (this, of course, included the islands under mandate to the League of Nations), and to restore all the territory stolen from China, such as Manchuria, Formosa, and the Pescadores Islands. They further declared: "The aforesaid three great powers, mindful of the enslavement of the people of Korea, are determined that in due course Korea shall become free and independent."

Explaining Cairo in a radio address on December 24, 1943, President Roosevelt further said that the three Chiefs of State had "discussed" simple and fundamental long-range principles that recognized "the right of millions of people in the Far East to build up their own forms of self-Government without molestation." Generalissimo Chiang in a message to the Chinese people referred to "absolute assurances" received at Cairo that all the oppressed and maltreated Asiatic peoples both in the Pacific and the Asiatic mainland might look forward with hope for liberation.[2] Prime Minister Churchill did not elaborate.

These statements were calculated to offset deceptive Japanese propaganda addressed with much effect to the subordinated peoples of Asia: that Japan was the real sponsor of freedom in the Far East. Roosevelt was constantly stressing the example of the United States in the Philippines as a model for all the great powers of the West. And China, enjoying for the time being her novel classification as a great power, relished also the temporary role of liberator. The statements seemed to imply a willingness on the part of the white man to ease himself as soon as he could after the war of the burden of a century of imperialism. But only one white man joined in this promise at Cairo. Nevertheless, the action of Great Britain since Cairo speaks louder than the proverbial silence of the Sphinx of Ghizeh.

From Cairo, Roosevelt and Churchill flew on to meet at Teheran the other great partner in the European war. In order to win the war the Big Three had to agree among themselves. At the Persian capital (No-

[1] *Roosevelt and Hopkins, op. cit.,* p. 771.

[2] For the public statements on the Cairo Conference, see *Documents on American Foreign Relations,* VI (1943-1944), pp. 232-234.

vember 28-December 1, 1943) the Big Three laid their plans for war and peace on this planet while about them hovered the envious ghost of Alexander the Great.

Stalin's most anxious question was about the second front. The two Western statesmen described their concerted plans in detail, not only for the second front in Europe, but also their recent conference with Chiang Kai-shek and their plans for concerted campaigns in Asia. Stalin repeated the assurance he had given to Hull in Moscow: that, when the Allies had defeated Germany, Russia would begin a second front of her own against Japan in Manchuria. This looked like a promise of one Russian Eastern second front against Japan on the Pacific in return for one Western second front against Germany on the Atlantic.

"Who will command OVERLORD?" the Russian Marshal asked, referring to the code name for the second front already in preparation. "Until that is done, OVERLORD cannot be said to be really in progress." [1] Stalin did not insist then and there on a specific answer to that vital question. Roosevelt appointed the commander before he got home.

The declaration of the Three Powers at Teheran (December 1, 1943) was brief: they had concerted plans for the destruction of German forces; as to the future "enduring peace" they said: "We shall seek the co-operation and active participation of all nations, large and small, whose peoples are in heart and mind dedicated, as are our own peoples, to the elimination of tyranny and slavery, oppression and intolerance. We welcome them, as they may choose to come, into a *world family of democratic nations.*" [2] Nobody paused to define democracy—the Americans and British did not think it necessary to make clear the obvious. Was it not implicit in the Atlantic Charter?

There was also a declaration of the same date respecting Iran (Persia), to which the Big Three had referred in the earlier declaration as "our ally." [3] They expressed a common "desire" to maintain the "inde-

---

[1] *Roosevelt and Hopkins, op. cit.,* pp. 787-788.

[2] Italics inserted.

A few days before at a Thanksgiving Day dinner of the British and American delegations at Cairo President Roosevelt had alluded to the family tradition in the American Thanksgiving, and said that this year America and Great Britain formed one family, which was more united than ever before. Roosevelt had opened the formal meetings of the Conference of Teheran by saying that he was glad to welcome the Russians as new members of "the family circle."

"If there was any supreme moment in Roosevelt's career," remarks the playwright Sherwood, "I believe that it will be fixed at this moment, at the end of the Teheran Conference. It certainly represents the peak for Harry Hopkins." *Ibid.,* pp. 775, 778, 799.

[3] Iran declared war on January 16, 1943, against Germany, Italy, and Japan.

pendence, sovereignty, and territorial integrity of Iran." "They count upon the participation of Iran together with all other peace-loving nations in the establishment of international peace, security and prosperity after the war in accordance with the principles of the Atlantic Charter, *to which all four governments have continued to subscribe.*" [1]

Such were the public "declarations" of Teheran. They were not treaties or even formal executive agreements but they had the import of treaties. Behind the scenes much more went on. The Three talked about getting the Turks into the war, but Stalin was unenthusiastic. Churchill mentioned possibilities of an Allied military diversion from the Adriatic via the Balkans into the Danube basin. Neither Roosevelt nor Stalin responded to that.[2] Churchill told Stalin he would welcome a warm-water port for Russia and the sight of her merchant marine and navy on every sea; Roosevelt proposed some kind of an international trusteeship that would ensure free passage to and from the Baltic Sea. The President also thought that Dairen, in Manchuria, might be made a free port under international guaranty, to which Russia might have access; he thought China would not object to the proposal.[3] Of course the Russian Marshal had no objections to such thoughts; in his turn he suggested that the islands in the vicinity of Japan would have to be used —he did not yet say by whom—to contain Japan against future aggression. And Roosevelt ventilated his ideas about a future United Nations organization for peace: an Assembly, an Executive Committee, and Four Policemen.

[1] Italics inserted.

[2] "I never at any time heard Mr. Churchill urge or suggest complete abandonment of the Overlord plan. His conviction, so far as I could interpret it, was that at some time in the indefinite future the Allies would have to cross the Channel. But he seemed to believe that our attack should be pushed elsewhere until the day came when the enemy would be forced to withdraw most of his troops from northwest Europe, at which time the Allies could go in easily and safely." Eisenhower, *Crusade in Europe, op. cit.,* p. 198.

It is fortunate for England, as well as for the entire Allied cause that Churchill's urgings did not succeed in diverting American military strategy from piercing directly to the heart of Germany from a second front in France based on England. Without stopping to discuss the difficulties of mountainous terrain in Yugoslavia (Tyrol, Styria, Carniola, Bosnia) so far from a major Allied base, it seems certain that Hitler would have pulverized England as a base and pounded it into surrender with V-2 projectiles if the American and British armies had not captured his launching platforms in the Low Countries barely in the nick of time. See *General Marshall's Report* (Washington, 1945).

See also Hajo Holborn, "The Collapse of the European Political System, 1914-45." *World Politics,* I (No. 4, July, 1949), 442-466.

[3] "It is my understanding," states Sherwood, who had access to the record of Teheran in the Hopkins Papers, "that Roosevelt was not merely guessing at this—that he had, in fact, discussed this very point with Chiang Kai-shek at Cairo a few days previously." *Roosevelt and Hopkins, op. cit.,* p. 792.

"Would this Executive Committee have the right to make decisions which would be binding on all the nations?" asked Stalin, anticipating his attitude toward a new league of nations.

They deliberated on the possible dismemberment of Germany. Stalin remarked that Poland's western boundary should be the Oder; he was less clear about the eastern boundary—he and Churchill had a conference separately on that question.

On the way back from Teheran, Roosevelt, Churchill, Harry Hopkins, and Anthony Eden met with the President and Foreign Minister of the Turkish Republic at Cairo (December 4-6, 1943),[1] but despite "useful" and "fruitful" discussions the Turkish officials would not commit themselves to entering the war while there was still danger of the destruction of Constantinople. The Second Cairo Conference was more important for further military deliberations between the leaders and staffs of the United States and Great Britain, preparing for the Normandy invasion, than it was for the talks with the Turks;[2] shortly afterward President Roosevelt announced the appointment of General Eisenhower to command OVERLORD.[3]

Roosevelt and Churchill did not meet again until after the second front had been mounted successfully and France liberated. This interval was the period of greatest strain between the two Atlantic Allies. Finally in a second Quebec Conference (August 11-24, 1944) President and Prime Minister and numerous military, naval, financial, and diplomatic staffs— Harry Hopkins instead of the Secretary of State—reached decisions with regard to the completion of the war in Europe and the "destruction of the barbarians in the Pacific," the United States to bear the principal burden of the last-named assignment.[4]

---

[1] *Documents on American Foreign Relations, op. cit.,* VI (1943-1944), pp. 237-238.

[2] *Roosevelt and Hopkins, op. cit.,* pp. 798-804.

[3] Decided on, December 7, 1943. *Crusade in Europe, op. cit.,* p. 208.

[4] Joint Statement of the President and Prime Minister, September 16, 1944. *Documents on American Foreign Relations, op. cit.,* VII (1944-1945), p. 347. At this conference Secretary of the Treasury Morgenthau, invading the province of the Secretary of State, Cordell Hull, who did not attend, secured adoption of his plan for dismantling Germany to an agrarian economy as a means of ensuring the future peace of Europe. The Secretary of State, Cordell Hull, and the Secretary of War, Henry L. Stimson, were unalterably opposed to the plan, but Roosevelt OK'd it and Churchill acquiesced, apparently in return for a promise by Morgenthau of a huge postwar subsidy to Great Britain: $3,500,000,000 cash, and $3,000,000,000 more later. Roosevelt later acknowledged that he had initialed this proposal without thinking enough about it, and soon dropped it: "I dislike making detailed plans for a country which we do not occupy." Memorandum of Roosevelt to Hull, October 20, 1944. Five years later Churchill said in Parliament (July 21, 1949): "I did not agree with it [the Morgenthau Plan], and I am sorry I put my initials to it." New York *Times,* July 22, 1949. See also *Memoirs*

The most vexing Anglo-American problem resolved at Quebec was the respective zones of occupation for American and British armies after the surrender of Germany. This had to be settled before the two governments could finally agree with Russia about the eastern Soviet zone. Roosevelt wanted the northwestern zone of Germany nearest to the sea. Churchill was happy to see American armies involved as deeply and constructively as possible in the heart of the continent for the protection of England and the salvation of Europe.[1] He naturally preferred that British armies should occupy the regions nearest to England as a buffer between Russia and the North Sea, and where Britain could do a thorough job of demolishing all naval works and destroying or at least controlling industrial war potential. The President finally gave in to Churchill and agreed that Britain should have the northwestern area, including the Ruhr Valley, the seacoasts, and the Kiel Canal; the United States would have all of southern Germany, including Bavaria, with Bremen in the north as an American port of entry enclaved in the British zone.[2] In southern Germany the American occupation forces would find themselves between the Soviet and the French Zones, at the end of a long corridor, through British-held territory, from the sea. If a liberated France should go communist it would be an untenable military position.

Stalin did not attend this conference if only because Russia was not yet an enemy of Japan.[3] As a matter of fact, he was not anxious for a conference anyway. The second front in the West was an accomplished fact and success. Everything was now going Russia's way. Therefore why limit one's freedom of action for revolutionary reshaping of a

of Cordell Hull, op. cit., II, pp. 1602-1622; *Roosevelt and Hopkins, op. cit.,* 817-819; Henry L. Stimson and McGeorge Bundy, *On Active Service in Peace and War, op. cit.,* pp. 568-583.

[1] "The United States has entered deeply and constructively into the life and salvation of Europe. We all three set our hands to far-reaching engagements, at once practical and solemn." Speech of Winston Churchill in House of Commons, Feb. 27, 1945. New York *Times,* February 28, 1945, pp. 14-15. Announcement of the zones was not made until June 5, 1945. Department of State *Bulletin,* XII, No. 311 (June 10, 1945), 1052, and even then the boundaries were not described. They were later indicated on a map in *ibid.,* XIII (No. 321, August 19, 1945), 275.

[2] Hull, *Memoirs, op. cit.,* II, pp. 1609-1616. According to Hull, "the United States Chiefs of Staff, however, proposed that the British and American spheres be exactly reversed" from what Churchill (and the Combined Chiefs of Staff) had proposed. Whatever the United States Chiefs of Staff had proposed, the Secretary of War Henry L. Stimson certainly opposed American instead of British occupation of the northwestern zone. "He [Roosevelt] is hell-bent to occupy the northern portion. We all think that this is a mistake—that it will only get us into headlong collision with the British." *On Active Service, op. cit.,* pp. 568-569.

[3] To protect its eastern flank against the possibility of a war with Germany, the USSR had signed (April 13, 1941) a five-year nonaggression pact with Japan; this was not due to terminate until April 13, 1946, and even then it would continue unless specifically denounced by either party on one year's notice.

Map 12. Zones of Military Occupation in Europe, Beginning 1945

NOTE: The Ruhr area has no accepted geographical definition but is generally taken to include the industrial cities of Duisburg, Essen, Bochun, Dortmund, Wuppertal and Düsseldorf.   A French proposal for an international economic regime for the Ruhr included a precise geographical description of the area involved (text in New York *Times*, February 5, 1947).   The Saar territory shown on the map covers the area which was under the League of Nations from 1920 to 1935, to which France added, in July, 1946, the Rhineland districts of Saarburg and Wadern, thus extending it as far as the Luxemburg border.   (Reproduced by permission of Council on Foreign Relations from their book, *The United States in World Affairs, 1945-1947*, by John C. Campbell, New York, 1947, p. 168.)

ruined continent?   There was, however, one answer to give pause to Stalin: the Western Allies were reaching the peak of their military power in Europe. It might be best for the time being to play along with them until the United States should retire back across the ocean after the defeat of Germany.

A formidable group of questions now faced the Big Three. Although there seemed to be firm assurances, since Moscow and Teheran, that Russia would join the United States and Great Britain in the war against Japan as soon as Germany surrendered in Europe, there was not any agreement on what to do with Germany after the war. What would be the boundaries of the fourth Reich? Or should the Reich continue to exist at all as a state? Ought France, now liberated and functioning under the provisional government of General Charles de Gaulle, be admitted to a share of the occupation and control of defeated Germany? Stalin objected to French participation; Churchill desired it in order to bolster the West. And how should the victors deal with the other liberated countries, notably those in Eastern and Central Europe into which Russian influence and armed forces were now pouring?

Czechoslovakia had already made her own fateful choice. Deserted at Munich in 1938, and most likely to be occupied by Russian troops upon the defeat of Germany, she had been first to link her destiny to Moscow, hoping and trusting to keep her freedom. President Beneš in exile had signed in Moscow an alliance offensive and defensive with Russia (December 12, 1943) against the day of liberation from Hitler's power. In Poland and Yugoslavia, Soviet Russia refused to extend a helping hand to the old-line nationalist patriots under General Bor and General Mikhailovich, and insisted that the Western Allies ignore them in favor of the revolutionary partisans. Stalin was determined to make these Slavic border countries Russian satellites under communistic governments subject to leaders of his own appointment already schooled in Moscow. There was still no agreement among the Three on the future frontiers of Poland, through which invading armies had advanced for the conquest of Russia ever since the time of Napoleon Bonaparte. The United States had taken the position that the fixing of frontiers (there were thirty of them unsettled in Europe alone) [1] must await the final peace settlement, and that it would not guarantee any frontier except collectively as a member of the world peace organization agreed to in principle at Moscow in October, 1943, and already being formulated at Washington under the fatherly countenance of Cordell Hull (Dumbarton

---

[1] *Memoirs of Cordell Hull, op. cit.,* II, p. 1438.

Oaks Conference, August 21-October 7, 1944). Finally, how would the big powers (the United States, Great Britain, Russia, China; perhaps France) vote on decisive matters in the Security Council of the new league of nations? Would they have to be unanimous? Would each therefore have in effect an absolute check on the others, a *liberum veto*?

With all these issues brooding under the spreading Soviet wing, Prime Minister Churchill wanted another conference of the Big Three to settle the future of Europe before things got out of hand for England. But Roosevelt held off until after the national election, scheduled over a century before to take place the first Tuesday after the first Monday of November, 1944. Churchill could not wait. He and his Foreign Minister Anthony Eden flew to Moscow and made an agreement with Stalin (Anglo-Russian Conference of October 9-18, 1944) on the future boundaries of Poland (in the east approximately the Curzon Line recommended by British diplomacy in 1919; in the west the line of the River Oder, deep in the heart of Prussia) and on spheres of influence in the Balkans (predominantly for Russia in Rumania, Bulgaria, and Hungary; for Great Britain in Greece; jointly for both in Yugoslavia).[1] Roosevelt let it be known that he would not be bound by anything decided by Russia and Great Britain in the Moscow Conference.[2] As the aurora of victory began to light up the horizon of Europe, the Allies seemed to be drifting apart.

It was in this uncertain dawn that Roosevelt and Hopkins and top American military advisers, and the new[3] Secretary of State, Edward R. Stettinius, Jr., and James F. Byrnes, Director of the Office of War Mobilization and Reconversion, chief "trouble-shooter" for the Administration, set forth for the Russian Crimea immediately after the President's fourth inauguration. They were on their way to the Crimean —Yalta—Conference, most famous in the annals of American secret diplomacy. For during the Second World War the United States, through the power of the Commander in Chief of the armed forces of the nation to make "military" agreements, had become engaged for better or worse

---

[1] The Anglo-Soviet communiqué of October 21, 1944, describes the discussion only in veiled terms. *Documents on American Foreign Relations, op. cit.,* VII (1944-1945), p. 347. *Memoirs of Cordell Hull, op. cit.,* II, p. 1485. The documentation is not fully available for these temporary arrangements. Vernon Van Dyke summarizes the evidence in his memorandum on "American Support of Free Institutions in Eastern Europe." *Yale Institute of International Studies,* No. 28 (August 10, 1948).

[2] *Roosevelt and Hopkins, op. cit.,* p. 834.

[3] Cordell Hull, who had held that office with great distinction since March 4, 1933, longer than any other Secretary of State in American history, resigned in a collapse of health on November 30, 1944.

in the practice of secret diplomacy,[1] hitherto a relatively unknown phenomenon in American history.

The Yalta Conference (February 4-11, 1945) was one of the most dramatic personal parleys in modern history, rivaling in that respect the memorable meeting of Napoleon and Alexander I on a raft in the middle of the Niemen River.   There, amidst the soft airs of the ravaged Crimea, on the seats of the mighty in the old Livadia palace of the Czars, sat in joyful situation Joseph Stalin, the man of steel, dictator of the Russian proletariat, father of a new Pan-Slavism, implacable *Realpolitiker* of the Revolution, sponsor of a future WUSSR.   On the other end of the row of three sat Winston Churchill, dauntless leader of large enterprises, greatest statesman of English history, somber man of blood and tears and toil and sweat, and now of smiling victory, striving for a peace that would make the world safe for a disintegrating British Empire.   Between them sat the amiable Roosevelt, civilian Commander in Chief[2] of the armies and navies and airfleets of the United States, new dealer of good will and promises to the common man and voter, would-be good neighbor to all the world, preacher of the four freedoms to all the men in all the lands.   Graven on his anxious visage were the fatal ravages of illness and fatigue.   The last task of his life was to wean Stalin away from the inexorable revolutionary goal of a World Union of Soviet Socialist Republics into a peaceful World Family of Democratic Nations.

The joint public announcement of the results of the Yalta Conference masked the secret agreements of the three Chiefs of State.   They told the world that they had agreed on the timing, scope, and co-ordination of military plans for the defeat and unconditional surrender of Germany and enforcement by military occupation by the United States, Great Britain, Russia, and France, in separate zones, with a joint Allied Control Commission of their respective commanders in that field.   They declared that they would root out all vestiges of Nazism in order to give hope for a future decent life for Germans and a place for them in the comity of nations.   They made known that they would call a conference of the

---

[1] By this is meant not secret and confidential discussions or negotiations, but secret international agreements not even known to the Senate, or the House of Representatives. The American delegation, listed in the joint Report on the Crimean Conference, included no member of either house of Congress.

[2] "Following Pearl Harbor, he preferred to be called Commander in Chief rather than President.   He relished the title.   He may have felt that this all-important position was now more essential than that of President.

"At a Cabinet dinner, probably in 1942, where I was to propose the toast, the President asked me, before I rose to speak:

"'Please try to address me as Commander in Chief, not as President.'" *Memoirs of Cordell Hull, op. cit.,* II, p. 1111.

signatories of the United Nations Declaration to meet at San Francisco April 25, 1945, to agree upon a world peace organization on the basis of the proposals of Dumbarton Oaks. They revealed that they had reached an agreement, to be announced in due course, on the voting formula of the big powers within the Security Council of such an organization. They broadcast their resolution to endow the liberated nations of Europe with provisional governments representative of all the democratic elements in the population pledged to free elections of *de jure* governments responsible to the will of the people. They did not define democracy, any more than they had done at Teheran, but they reaffirmed their faith in the principles of the Atlantic Charter.

They conceded that a new situation had been created in Poland, as a result of her complete liberation by the Red Army, that called for the establishment of a more broadly based provisional government, to include democratic leaders from Poland itself and from Poles abroad; this government would be pledged to hold free and unfettered elections as soon as possible on the basis of universal suffrage and secret ballot to be participated in by all democratic and anti-Nazi parties. They recognized that the eastern boundary of Poland "should" follow the Curzon Line, with minor deviations in favor of Poland, and that Poland "must" receive substantial accessions of territory in the north and west—as compensation for her losses in the east. They agreed to the establishment of a new government in Yugoslavia under Marshal Tito—the Soviet protégé—but with a broader basis including former members of parliament who had not compromised themselves by collaboration with the enemy. They provided for periodic meetings of the foreign secretaries of their respective governments, by rotation in the three capitals, to follow after the United Nations Conference on World Organization.

The most important products of Yalta were the three secret supplementary agreements, not included in the public declaration of February 11, 1945, but of the same date: (1) an agreement on the repatriation of citizens of the USA and the USSR, and on prisoners of war and civilians liberated by American and Soviet forces respectively; (2) on the voting formula for the Big Four in the Security Council kept secret only until cleared with France and China;[1] and (3) conditions agreed upon for the entrance of Russia into the war with Japan "in two or three months after Germany has surrendered."

[1] Secretary Stettinius made a public announcement of the Yalta voting formula during the Chapultepec Conference at Mexico City, March 5, 1945.

The latter agreement pledged the United States and Great Britain "unquestionably" to fulfill for Russia, after Japan's defeat: (1) the *status quo* of outer-Mongolia—named as The Mongolian Peoples' Republic—which had severed itself from China and accepted Russian protection; (2) restoration to Russia of her former status in Manchuria before the Russo-Japanese War of 1904-1905, with specific safeguarding of the "pre-eminent interests" [1] of Soviet Russia in the internationalized free port of Dairen, in a naval base (by lease) at Port Arthur, and in joint Sino-Russian control and operation of the Chinese-Eastern and South Manchurian Railroads; (3) the Kurile Islands and the southern half of the island of Sakhalin to be handed over to the USSR. [2]

The pledges at Yalta to Stalin, which the Russian leader was careful to have written down explicitly over the signatures of the Big Three, ran directly counter to the promises which Roosevelt and Churchill had made to Chiang Kai-shek in the Cairo Declaration. They placed the President under the "unquestionable" requirement of obtaining from the Generalissimo his consent,[3] a most mortifying function for the United States. Further, by failing to stipulate the Open Door for the USA along with the "pre-eminent interests" of the USSR in Manchuria, Roosevelt overlooked a fundamental of American foreign policy in the very region that originally called forth that doctrine and led to its pronouncement for all of China in 1899.[4]

Roosevelt signed the last, secret pact of Yalta—relating to Russia's entry into the war with Japan—while personally closeted with Stalin and Churchill. It was this agreement which provoked the most severe animadversions among the President's countrymen when the text became

---

[1] Compare this phrase with the words "paramount interests" which Viscount Ishii attempted unsuccessfully to substitute for "special interests" in the Lansing-Ishii Agreement of 1917. See above, pp. 215-216.

[2] For the text of the Yalta Three-Power Declaration of February 12, 1945, and the supplementary agreements signed on February 11, and official explanations by President Roosevelt and Secretary of State Stettinius, see *Documents on American Foreign Relations, op. cit.,* VII (1944-1945), pp. 360-364, VIII (1945-1946), pp. 919-924.

According to Sherwood, Stalin asked Roosevelt whether any foreign troops would be stationed in Korea, and Roosevelt replied in the negative, whereupon Stalin expressed his approval. *Roosevelt and Hopkins, op. cit.,* p. 868.

[3] This was given in the Sino-Soviet Treaty of Friendship and Alliance, signed at Moscow, August 14, 1945, the very day of Japan's capitulation, formally attested in the instrument of surrender, September 2, 1945. The text of the Alliance is in *Documents on American Foreign Relations, op. cit.,* VIII (1945-1946), pp. 826-829.

[4] Russia had never unequivocally accepted the Open Door and was not a party to the Nine-Power Treaty of 1922. See above, p. 222. In conversations in Moscow in May, 1945 (after Yalta), Stalin remarked to Harry Hopkins that he agreed with America's Open Door policy. *Roosevelt and Hopkins, op. cit.,* p. 903.

known.[1] Roosevelt had led the United States into a double war in order
to preserve a global balance of power. At Yalta, on the eve of certain
victory, he made concessions to Stalin at the expense of China which unhinged the balance of power in both Asia and Europe. Yet it is difficult
to see how, short of turning on the ally Russia in actual war, either the
United States or Great Britain could have prevented in fact the flow of
Russian power into the vacuums east and west that were being created
by the defeat of Germany and Japan. To be sure, in return for these concessions Roosevelt received pledges from Stalin in other arrangements at
Yalta to support democratic principles in the liberated states of Eastern
Europe and elsewhere—just as Chamberlain received guaranties from
Hitler at Munich not to advance any farther in Europe after taking part
of Czechoslovakia. Placing this promise of Stalin's on record for these
principles was a most important factor in the great issues that were to
follow. Nevertheless, in its aftermath of deception, Yalta was in a
sense equivalent to another Munich.

President Roosevelt's top military advisers, present at Yalta, must
bear with him the heavy responsibility. They thought it greatly necessary to induce Russia to enter the Japanese war in order to save a million
American casualties and another year of war in a direct assault on the
islands of Japan then being planned.[2] But former Secretary of State

[1] James F. Byrnes, who was present at Yalta and took stenographic notes of the
deliberations did not know of this secret agreement when he became Secretary of
State on July 3, 1945. He first learned of it from Russia, and then he went to the
White House to find out, as he tells it, how many IOU's were outstanding against
the United States. Admiral Leahy got the text of the agreement out of a safe in the
Map Room of the White House, and Byrnes took it to the Department of State. *Speaking Frankly* (New York, 1947), p. 43. Edward R. Stettinius, Jr., Hull's successor as
Secretary of State, was present at the Crimea Conference and knew about the signed
agreement on the Far East. Harry Hopkins had told him about it before the
Conference convened, and President Roosevelt and Ambassador (to Russia) W. Averell
Harriman discussed the subject with him during the Conference. The State Department,
however, did not handle this matter, despite Harriman's participation. Harriman at
that time was more than an ambassador: he was the co-ordinator of all civilian
and military activities. I am indebted for this information to the late Mr. Stettinius and
to Professor Walter Johnson, his historical collaborator. Mr. Stettinius's account of
Roosevelt and the Russians: the Yalta Conference was published posthumously (New
York, 1949).

[2] Rear Admiral Ellis M. Zacharias has explained "The Inside Story of Yalta," in
United Nations World (January, 1949), pp. 12-16, in terms of poor intelligence furnished to Roosevelt by the Combined Chiefs of Staff grossly exaggerating Japan's army
strength at 5,000,000 effectives instead of 2,000,000 men of all kinds. As late as July,
1945, scarcely a month before VJ-Day, Secretary of War Stimson believed that the
United States would need 5,000,000 men to defeat Japan in her own islands. *On Active
Service, op. cit.*, pp. 618-619. This was after the Japanese navy had been all but destroyed and the main Japanese archipelago cut off from the island conquest and connections endangered even with the continent of Asia!

Hull has indicated that Stalin had already pledged the USSR to come into that war as soon as Germany was defeated and has suggested that it was scarcely necessary to tender equivalents to perform what he had already agreed to do.[1]   It is too early, and we have too inadequate a record, to pass secure judgment on Roosevelt's diplomacy at Yalta.   Perhaps the best explanation is that the President, realizing there could be no future world peace without Russian-American co-operation and reciprocal good will, went more than half way to get it.   That the effort failed because of Soviet Russia's subsequent violations of the agreement does not disprove that it was a persevering attempt to convince Marshal Stalin of the sincerity of American intentions.[2]

Roosevelt and Hopkins, and the whole American delegation, left Yalta in a mood of supreme exultation.   They felt that they could live with the Russians and get along with them in as far a future as any one of them could imagine.[3]   The President persisted against mounting mistrust in his sanguine expectations of Russian good will, until the day of his death, April 12, 1945.   Only an hour before he collapsed from a sudden cerebral hemorrhage, Roosevelt dictated this last message, to Winston Churchill:

I would minimize the general Soviet problem as much as possible because these problems, in one form or other, seem to arise every day and most of them straighten out as in the case of the Berne meeting.

We must be firm, however, and our course thus far is correct.[4]

ROOSEVELT'S INTERVIEWS WITH EMPEROR HAILE SELASSIE, KING FAROUK, AND KING IBN SAUD, 1945

On the way home from Yalta the President stopped at Suez to meet personally the Emperor Haile Selassie of Ethiopia, King Farouk of Egypt, and King Ibn Saud of Saudi Arabia.

[1] *Memoirs of Cordell Hull, op. cit.*, II, p. 1310.   Hopkins, Roosevelt's principal confidant, admits that, at Teheran, Stalin had made a first commitment in so far as Soviet participation in the war against Japan was concerned, but says it "needed to be clarified as to precise dates and the extent of Soviet participation." *Roosevelt and Hopkins, op. cit.*, p. 842.   But the Yalta secret protocol clarified neither the one nor the other, except in the loose phrase "two or three months."

[2] Rudolph A. Winnacker asks the question: "Yalta—Another Munich?" in the *Virginia Quarterly Review*, XXIV (No. 4, Autumn, 1948), 520-537.

[3] *Roosevelt and Hopkins, op. cit.*, pp. 870-873.

[4] Byrnes, *Speaking Frankly, op. cit.*, pp. 56-59.   Reference to the Berne meeting is to a contretemps between Roosevelt and Stalin arising from the latter's unjustified accusations that the Allies had parleyed with German officers for a surrender of German forces in Italy without participation of Soviet representatives.

In the ceremonial exchange of gifts that accompanied the interview with Ibn Saud on board the U.S.S. *Quincy* the King presented Roosevelt with a freshly slaughtered sheep, and the President gave his own wheel chair—plus a United States naval plane—to the King. He asked Ibn Saud, as a spokesman for the Arab world, to agree to admit more Jews into Palestine, but ended up by promising himself to take no step in Palestine without full consultation of both Arabs and Jews. "I will take no action in my capacity as Chief of the Executive branch of the Government," he further declared, "which might prove hostile to the Arab people." [1] Thus did the United States make dubious entry into the Palestine question. [2]

[1] New York *Times*, March 14, October 19, 1945.

[2] The scope of this history does not include the issues raised before the United Nations Organization, such as Palestine, Greece, Iran, Indonesia, etc.

World Family of Democratic Nations
Versus
World Union of Soviet Socialist Republics

THE immediate purpose of the United Nations, in their diplomacy as in their military effort, great or small or merely nominal, had been to win the global war by complete defeat of Germany and Japan, not to mention Italy and the lesser captives of the Axis powers. After that, to win the peace. Here the policies of the greater powers diverged radically into two postwar worlds.

There was the One World [1] of general Western preference and renewed American fancy. It rested on the political thought of Burke and Bagehot and Woodrow Wilson. It was what Franklin D. Roosevelt thought of as a World Family of Democratic Nations. It envisaged collective security for individual liberty and political democracy, functioning nationally and constitutionally under a new league of nations, backed this time by an international force of righteousness.

On the other hand there was the Revolutionary World of Marx and Lenin and Joseph Stalin. It was based on totalitarian power, to be seized and wielded in the name of the proletariat. It sacrificed the freedom of the individual to the omnipotence of the state. The Marxian World, under its mighty Russian dictatorship, avowed an irreconcilable conflict between capitalism and communism. The First and the Second World Wars were classic convulsions, already marked down in the primer of revolution, to be encountered along the rapidly shortening way to the collapse of capitalism. The Strange Alliance [2] with the Western democracies against the Axis powers was a profitable episode in

---

[1] The phrase captivated public opinion following the publication of the quick brochure *One World* (New York, 1943) by Wendell Willkie, Roosevelt's Republican contender in 1940, who in 1942 made a flying trip around the world in the interests of Allied unity.

[2] General John R. Deane, head of the United States Military Mission in Moscow, 1943-1945, told the history of American efforts at wartime co-operation with Moscow in *The Strange Alliance* (New York, 1947).

more ways than one. To Soviet statesmen winning the peace did not
mean collective security for peace-loving political democracies under
a new league of nations. Russia had just been expelled summarily
from the old League for the attack on Finland in 1939. To the leaders
of the USSR victory meant not only defense of Holy Russia in a great
patriotic war. It also warranted the prestige and power of the Soviet
Union all over the globe. It presented a world-shaking opportunity to
expand out of the Asiatic Heartland into the places of Germany and
Japan west and east in the World Island of Eurasia, massive pedestal for
world power in the complete sense of the word. The ultimate end would
justify any means. The end in view was a revolutionary World Union
of Soviet Socialist Republics. That was the one world of Lenin and
Stalin.

It was otherwise among the Western democracies, particularly in
America. To them victory meant world peace. Amidst the heartily un-
wanted anxieties, agonies, and responsibilities which a new World War
had thrust upon them, thoughtful Americans began to talk remorsefully
of the "lost peace"—meaning that of 1919! Actually no peace had been
lost *then*. The United States and its Associates had emerged from the
First World War altogether victorious. They had dictated a peace—a
very fair peace, all things considered—to their own liking. That peace
was lost in Europe in 1936, not in Washington in 1919. Great Britain
and France, jealous of each other,[1] had allowed Adolf Hitler to re-arm
Germany and tear up the Treaty of Versailles while Uncle Sam, entranced
by a disillusionist historiography, had buried his addled head and strong
shoulders in the drifting sands of pacifism and neutrality legislation.
Good folk suddenly found themselves believing fondly that if only the
great Republic of the West and its vanished army had been all along a
member of the League of Nations the world would not have got so
speedily unhinged.

In the black spring of 1942 old college grads, veterans of the First
World War, came back to their twenty-fifth reunions to do honor to their
alma maters. Their own sons had just gone forth to the wars to fight
over again on a large scale what they battled for in their own youth.
Military boots had worn bare the campus greens. Motors and propel-

---

[1]Arnold Wolfers, *Britain and France between Two Wars; Conflicting Strategies of
Peace since Versailles* (New York, 1940); Harold Butler, *The Lost Peace, a Personal
Impression* (New York, 1942); Leopold Schwartzschild, *The World in Trance* (London,
1942).

lers and anti-aircraft parts crowded the classrooms. The blackboards were covered with military logistics. "It must not happen again!" declaimed the men of 1917, Commencement orators of 1942. So said the teachers and the preachers everywhere. So felt the man in the street.[1] The politicians echoed the universal thought. They called for a new league of nations as Professor Wilson had called for one when President, got it, and lost it.

As the war progressed, a new school of historiography, students of the "lost peace," who had written their books in recent anxious years, held forth their warnings on President Wilson's mistakes with the Senate.[2] But the historians of Woodrow Wilson's supposedly lost peace were no more successful in teaching President Franklin D. Roosevelt how not to lose the next peace than their predecessors, the historians of Wilsonian neutrality, had been in teaching him how not to become involved in the Second World War. They and the American people about them, engrossed in their war against the two colossi of Europe and Asia, had too little comprehension of the changing balance of power and the consequently shifting strategy of American defense and diplomacy. They did not realize how quickly the totalitarian power of Soviet Russia would fill the vacuums left by the collapse of Germany and Japan, how mightily it would congeal there, what new dangers it would produce.

New historical prophets made the American people League-of-Nations-conscious again, if they had not made them conscious of the possibilities of new problems of power. Complete defeat of the enemies and collective security under the United Nations in a charter to be forged while the Allied arms still smoked hot on land, at sea, and in the air, became the most cherished goal of the United States and that of the Western Allies. They expected Russia after the war to sit down like a good neighbor to the bourgeois board of peace in a brave new world at ease from totalitarian dictators.

The United Nations Conference on International Organization, scheduled at Yalta, took place on time at San Francisco, April 25-June

---

[1] Thomas A. Bailey would fain educate *The Man in the Street* (New York, 1948) to cope responsibly with major problems of foreign policy and diplomacy. As a step toward this competence the Man might well read Professor Bailey's many books on the subject, including *A Diplomatic History of the American People* (New York, 1946).

[2] Paul Birdsall, *Versailles Twenty Years After* (New York, 1941). Thomas A. Bailey, *Woodrow Wilson and the Lost Peace* (New York, 1944), and *Woodrow Wilson and the Great Betrayal* (New York, 1945). Sumner Welles, *The Time for Decision* (New York, 1944). H. C. F. Bell, *Woodrow Wilson and the People* (New York, 1945).

26, 1945, called to order by Franklin D. Roosevelt's successor, President Harry S. Truman. Already a rift had appeared between the East and the West, over the democratization of Poland, over the amount of reparation in kind to be extracted from surrendered Germany and shared by the victors, and over the apparent lack of interest and enthusiasm manifested by Soviet Russia for the San Francisco Conference.[1]

The other United Nations met at San Francisco in a general fervor of conviction. Nowhere was this evangelism at higher pitch than in the United States. The Government fanned the fervor and galvanized it. From all over the land it brought teachers and civic leaders to the Golden Gate of World Peace as consultants or secretaries or assistants or advisers. They returned home as apostles to gather up and focus public opinion on the Senate of the United States. Foreign negotiators at San Francisco— notably the Soviet delegates—capitalized upon this popular insistence for the new league, as they had done at Paris in 1919, in Woodrow Wilson's time.

Most of the constructive work for the new league of nations had been done already by professional diplomatists and specialists at Dumbarton Oaks, and at Yalta the Big Three had compromised the vital controversial questions hitherto raised by Russia: (1) representation in the Assembly, (2) voting procedure in the Security Council. Stalin at first had talked about one membership in the Assembly for each one of the sixteen Soviet Republics, but he came down to three at Yalta, one for the USSR and one each for two of the components, Byelorussia, and the Ukraine. To match Stalin, Roosevelt had in mind before he went to Yalta to ask for one membership and vote for each one of the forty-eight states of the United States. Actually at Yalta he agreed to three for Russia, but wanted a certain "insurance" understanding, to which Stalin assented: in case the Senate objected (the President doubtless remembered the Great Debate of 1919-1920) to the three votes of Russia, the United States could have at least three votes too,[2] if desired, in the Assembly.

The Charter of United Nations, completed at San Francisco, June 26, 1945, attempted to remedy the defects of the Covenant of the League of

---

[1] In contrast to the other nations big and little, the Soviet Government did not attach enough vital importance to the conference to think it worth while to send its Minister of Foreign Affairs, Molotov, to San Francisco. Only after much urging by the United States and other powers did Stalin finally send Molotov, who was there for the opening of the Conference and during the first two weeks. Anthony Eden, the British Foreign Minister, left on May 13, four days after Molotov. New York *Times.*

[2] *Roosevelt and Hopkins, op. cit.,* pp. 854-857, 876-877.

Nations. As originally framed at Dumbarton Oaks, the Charter had
endowed the Security Council (composed permanently of the United
States, the United Kingdom of Great Britain and Northern Ireland, the
Union of Soviet Socialist Republics, France, and China, plus six small
powers elected in rotation by the General Assembly from the other members) with control over any question affecting the peace of the world. On
all but procedural matters a decision of the Council required seven votes,
including *unanimity of the five permanent members*. This gave a veto
to each one of the Big Five.

At first Stalin had insisted, at Yalta, that this veto power apply even
to admission of any question for consideration by the Council, but had
finally conceded that unanimity of the Big Five need not be required
merely to discuss a question, and that disputant parties could not vote
in judgment on themselves in the Council. The President and the
British Minister esteemed this Russian concession to be a great victory
for peace; in turn they agreed that for any *action* by the Security Council
there must be unanimity among the five major powers.[1] It meant, in
brief, that there could be no enforcement of world peace except the Big
Five agree.[2] This merely enacted a fact of life. The United States
clung to the veto power on enforcement action if only to protect the
Monroe Doctrine and matters of domestic jurisdiction from outside intervention. As revolution has spread since then in the world the veto
power has become more and more of a comfort against the possibility of
members of the Security Council, even permanent members, going communist.

The most important addition to the Charter at San Francisco came
by way of the Chapultepec meeting of the American republics,[3] voicing
a desire for more immediate security, individually or collectively, for the
states of the New World. With the support of the United States the
small nations succeeded in inserting Article 51, which declared that nothing in the Charter should impair the inherent right of individual or collective self-defense, if an armed attack should occur against a member of
the United Nations, until the Security Council should have taken
measures necessary to maintain international peace and security.[4] This

---

[1] *Roosevelt and Hopkins, op. cit.*, pp. 854-855.
[2] See William T. R. Fox, "The United States and the Other Great Powers," in
A Foreign Policy for the United States (University of Chicago Press, 1947), p. 316.
[3] See above, p. 307.
[4] It meant that the Security Council could take no action against an American
republic until the United States, sponsor of the Monroe Doctrine and party to the
Inter-American Doctrine of Nonintervention, agreed to it as a permanent member of

made possible the regional inter-American defensive pact of Rio de Janeiro of 1947 [1] ; but it could apply, of course, to any region of the world, like the Middle East, the Balkans, Eastern Europe, or the North Atlantic countries. Article 51 of the Charter made the United States the watchdog within the Security Council for the liberties of the American republics, because the Council could take no action, like intervention in the Western Hemisphere, without consent of the United States. *Per contra,* the USSR built up regional pacts among its satellite states.[2]

Another feature added at San Francisco was a broader forum function for ventilation in the Assembly of problems which the Security Council might not be considering at the moment or, conceivably, might not even be willing to consider. But when all was said and done, whether at Dumbarton Oaks, or at Yalta, or at San Francisco, the future peace of the world depended on co-operation and agreement among the superpowers, particularly between the USA, exponent of the Four Freedoms in a World Family of Democratic Nations, and the USSR, dictator for the proletariat in a World Union of Soviet Socialist Republics.

"It must not happen again!" The Charter of United Nations, in treaty form, and the Court of International Justice, as a statute annexed thereto, went through the Senate of the United States with flying colors in less than a month, to be ratified overwhelmingly by a final vote of 89-2 (July 28, 1945), with not a single reservation. It was not necessary for President Truman to make use of the card which Stalin had let Roosevelt have at Yalta to keep up his sleeve in Washington: three votes for the USA in the Assembly.[3] The Senate advised and consented without demur to a new league of nations which might, through the Security Council (subject to the veto of the American representative) place armed forces of the United States (as part of an United Nations police force) in action to preserve the peace anywhere in the world without a vote of the United States Congress.

The Senate further agreed (August 14, 1946) under an option of the statute, to submit in advance as compulsory *ipso facto,* and without

the Council. See the analysis of W. T. R. Fox, who participated in the Conference, of "The Super-Powers at San Francisco," *Review of Politics,* VIII (No. 1, January, 1946), 115-127.

[1] See above, p. 308.

[2] See below, p. 444.

[3] Whether President Truman knew of this reservation at the time of the Senate deliberations is not yet clear.

further special agreement (*compromis*) any purely "legal" [1] dispute with any nation which similarly registered in advance its agreement to accept the same obligation. This was the greatest step ahead ever made by the United States in the history of judicial settlement of international disputes. [2]

The United States had pinned its hopes to the banner of the United Nations. [3] "We have solemnly dedicated ourselves and all our will to the success of the United Nations Organization," President Truman declared to the Congress, January 14, 1946.

Impelled by a vast surge of public opinion, the United States, repudiator of Woodrow Wilson's League of Nations, had led the movement for a new league and set its seal to the Charter before the global war was finished. Already Hitler and his archprophet Goebbels had committed suicide in the bunkers of Berlin, and Germany had surrendered unconditionally, May 5, 1945. Another personal conference of Chiefs of State was necessary to sit on the ruins of the Reich and fix in detail the terms of occupation and reparation, and to arrange for the expected European peace conference.

No man has ever been called more suddenly, and with less preparation, than Harry S. Truman to the exalted duty of Commander in Chief of the armed forces of a great power—at the moment perhaps the greatest military power in all history—who, with his military and political advisers, represented the United States at the Conference of Berlin (July 17-August 2, 1945). Clement Attlee, the new British Prime Minister who had succeeded Winston Churchill as a result of a staggering British election held in the middle of the Conference, had far more experience

---

[1] The language of the Senate Resolution of August 14, 1946, included a reservation declaring that the obligation did not apply to:

  a. Disputes entrusted to other tribunals by treaties already existing or by treaties which might be concluded in the future.

  b. Disputes with regard to matters "essentially within the jurisdiction of the United States of America as determined by the United States of America."

  c. Disputes arising under a multilateral treaty, unless (1) all parties to the treaty affected by the decision are also parties to the case before the Court, or (2) the United States of America agrees to the jurisdiction.

  Documents on American Foreign Relations, op. cit., VIII (1945-1946), p. 516.

[2] The following countries have also accepted (1949) the compulsory jurisdiction of the International Court of Justice: Australia, Belgium, Bolivia, Brazil, Canada, China, Colombia, Denmark, Dominican Republic, El Salvador, France, Guatemala, Haiti, Honduras, India, Iran, Luxemburg, Mexico, Netherlands, New Zealand, Nicaragua, Norway, Pakistan, Panama, Paraguay, Philippines, Sweden, Switzerland, Thailand, Turkey, Union of South Africa, United Kingdom, Uruguay.

[3] Radio Address of Secretary of State James F. Byrnes to the Overseas Press Club, February 28, 1946. Department of State *Bulletin*, XIV, No. 349 (March 10, 1946), 355.

in politics [1] than the Vice President who succeeded Franklin D. Roosevelt. Truman followed the advice of his new Secretary of State, James F. Byrnes, and of his admirals and generals.

At Berlin it was not a question so much of what was done as of what was left undone or referred to subordinate commissions or councils. The zones of occupation had already been laid down by the European Advisory Commission [2] and agreed to by the three Governments, and the victors were seated there in all their might. At Potsdam the Big Three (though personally no longer the Big Three of Teheran and Yalta) dismissed the European Advisory Commission and set up a Council of Foreign Ministers to prepare, for submission to the United Nations, treaty drafts of peace with Italy, Rumania, Bulgaria, Austria, Hungary, and Finland. They looked forward to the ultimate admission of those states into the United Nations. The Council of Foreign Ministers also received the task of preparing terms of peace to be accepted by Germany when a German government adequate for that purpose should be established—nobody could say when that would be. The Big Three meanwhile agreed that supreme authority in Germany would be exercised by each occupational commander (American, Russian, British, French) within his respective zone, and by a Control Council of all four commanders in matters affecting Germany as a whole—the Control Council set up zones for each of the four powers respectively in the jointly occupied city of Berlin, embedded deeply within the Russian zone. The three Chiefs of State came together on principles to govern the treatment of Germany in the initial period of control: the rooting out of all traces of Nazi power and authority in German life and complete disarmament and demilitarization of Germany, to prepare for the eventual reconstruction of the Reich on a "democratic basis"—again no definition of democracy, but was it not in the Atlantic Charter? They agreed to share equally—among the Three—what was left of the German navy and ocean-going merchant marine. They provided that during the occupation period Germany should be treated as a single economic unit, and primary emphasis given to the development of agriculture and peaceful domestic industries. They left German frontiers to be fixed in the future peace treaty; but pending final delimitation of Poland's western frontier in the peace settlement they agreed on a line running from the Baltic Sea immediately west of Swinemünde and thence up the Oder River to the confluence of the

---

[1] Winston Churchill had brought him along to Berlin to be familiar with the proceedings, just in case!

[2] Announced June 5, 1945. See above, Map 12.

western Neisse and to the Czechoslovak frontier—Stalin's maximum desire for Poland. They left the city of Königsberg and a large part of East Prussia meanwhile under Soviet control.

At the Yalta Conference the Big Three had laid down as a "basis of discussion" reparations of $20,000,000,000 "in kind" (including German labor to restore damage), 50 per cent to go to Russia. Much discussion had taken place since then, including the deliberations of a reparations commission, but no further agreement had been reached; for one thing the Russians, under the guise of war "booty" rather than accounted reparations, were stripping Germany, Austria, and Hungary of movable property (including American-owned property previously confiscated by the Nazi forces). At Berlin it finally was stipulated that the reparation claims of the United States and the United Kingdom and other Western countries should be met from the Western zones, plus appropriate German external assets; reparations and assets for Russia (and for Poland) should come from the Eastern zone, plus 10 per cent for Russia of the usable and complete capital equipment available for the purpose in the Western zone, furthermore another 15 per cent in exchange for an equivalent value of commodities more plentiful in the Russian zone. Austria would not be required to pay reparations.[1]

Looking out from the rubble of Berlin over a ravished Europe, Truman, Churchill, and Stalin reaffirmed their determination to bring to "sure and swift" justice the major war criminals whose crimes had no particular geographical localization—this was already being arranged in discussions by American, British, French, and Russian representatives in London.[2]

[1] Control machinery and zones of control for Austria, similar to those in Germany, were later agreed to by the Governments of the United States, the United Kingdom, Soviet Russia, and the provisional government and released to the press by the Department of State, August 8, 1945. Department of State *Bulletin*, XIII, No. 320 (Aug. 12, 1945), pp. 221-22.

[2] The agreement setting up the International Military Tribunal at Nuremberg for the trial of major German war criminals was signed at London, August 8, 1945. For text see Department of State *Bulletin*, VI, No. 320 (August 12, 1945), pp. 222-28. The Nuremberg trials lasted from October 14, 1945 to October 1, 1946. The surviving major German war criminals who were convicted and received the death sentence, and were hanged on October 15, 1947, were: Von Ribbentrop, Keitel, Kaltenbrunner, Rosenberg, Frank, Frick, Streicher, Sauckel, Jodl, Seyss-Inquart. Göring succeeded in committing suicide the night before. Martin Bormann, never apprehended, was condemned to death *in absentia*. Those who received less than the death sentence were: Hess, Funk, Raeder, life imprisonment; von Schirach, Speer, twenty years imprisonment; von Neurath, fifteen years; Dönitz, ten years. Acquitted were: Schacht, von Papen, and Fritzsche.

For the voluminous record of the trials, see *Trial of the Major War Criminals Before the International Military Tribunal*, Nuremberg, October, 1945-October, 1946 (pub-

Berlin was the last of the spectacular conferences of the Chiefs of State of the United States, Great Britain, and Soviet Russia,[1] and the final chapter of Allied unity.

President Truman hopefully reported to his fellow-Americans that the three great powers were now more closely bound than ever before in their determination to achieve a just and lasting peace. But the American delegation left Berlin far less sanguine than the group which came back with such exaltation from Yalta. Stalin and Molotov and Vishinsky had revealed a disturbing disposition to lay down the law as much as to co-operate—an ominous portent for the future. In the later words of James F. Byrnes, Potsdam was a success that failed.[2]

During the Conference, President Truman and Prime Minister Attlee, with the concurrence of Generalissimo Chiang Kai-shek, proclaimed the

lished at Nuremberg, Germany, 42 vols., 1946-1949). The documents in the exhibit are of greatest historical importance. The American case of prosecution is published in *Nazi Conspiracy and Aggression* (8 vols., Washington, G.P.O., 1946).

UNITED STATES WAR CRIMES PROGRAM FOR ALL THEATERS, AS OF OCTOBER 1, 1949

	Germany			Japan				
	Nurem-berg*	Dachau†	IMTFE‡	Yoko-hama	China	Manila	Italy	Navy
No. of cases......	12	491	1	317	11	97	9	25
No. of defendants tried..........	177	1,682	25	993	75	215	14	116
No. of defendants convicted......	142	1,416	25	850	67	195	11	108
No. of defendants acquitted......	35	266	0	143	8	20	3	8
No. of defendants on trial or awaiting sentence....	0	0	0	2§	0	0	0	2
No. of death sentences adjudged	24	428	7	124	10	92	5	28
No. of confirmed death sentences executed.......	7	259	7	43	6	52	5	11

* Does not include trial of Göring, *et al.*, which was concluded on October 1, 1946.
† Includes cases tried in Austria.
‡ IMTFE = International Military Tribunal for the Far East.
§ During October these two remaining cases were tried, the defendants found guilty, and sentenced to a term of years.
Sentences other than capital punishment were imprisonment for various periods of years. One death sentence commuted.

[1] Report on the Tripartite Conference at Berlin, released to the press by the White House, August 2, 1945. Department of State *Bulletin*, XIII, No. 319 (August 5, 1945), 153-61. See also *Documents on American Foreign Relations, op. cit.*, VII (1944-1945), pp. 924-938. This, and the comments in Secretary Byrnes's *Speaking Frankly* and Edward R. Stettinius, Jr.'s *Roosevelt and the Russians* are all we know at the present writing (1949) of the proceedings of the Conference.
[2] *Speaking Frankly, op. cit.*, pp. 67-87.

Potsdam Declaration (July 26, 1945) of acceptable terms for Japanese surrender, thus altering, for the now impotent Pacific Colossus, the formula of unconditional surrender:

Elimination for all time of Japanese militarism and the authority and influence of those who had deceived the Japanese people into embarking on world conquest.

Allied military occupation of Japan.

The terms of the Cairo Declaration to be carried out and Japanese sovereignty to be limited to the islands of Honshu, Hokkaido, Kyushu, Shikoku, and such minor islands as might be determined by the victors.

Japanese military forces after being completely disarmed to be permitted to return to their homes with the opportunity to lead peaceful and productive lives.

No intention to enslave or destroy the Japanese as a nation, but stern justice to be meted out to war criminals.[1]

The Japanese Government to remove all obstacles to the revival and strengthening of democratic tendencies among the Japanese people. Freedom of speech, of religion, and of thought, as well as respect for the fundamental human rights, to be established.

Japan to be restricted to an economy of peace.

"The occupying forces of the Allies shall be withdrawn from Japan as soon as these objectives have been accomplished and there has been established in accordance with the freely established will of the Japanese people a peacefully inclined and responsible government."

Russia, not having yet entered the war, was not a party to the Declaration. At Potsdam, Generalissimo Stalin had told President Truman about peace feelers he had received from Japan, and Truman had revealed to Stalin the perfection of the atomic bomb (first secretly demonstrated at Alamogordo, New Mexico, July 16, 1945). The Russian leader did not seem too much impressed at that time.[2] The conventional American bombings of Tokyo and Yokohama had been already impressive enough.

The USSR had given on April 6, 1945, the required one year notice for the termination of the Russo-Japanese nonaggression pact of 1941,[3]

---

[1] The major war criminals were tried before a military international tribunal, sitting two and a half years from May 3, 1946, to November 12, 1948. The following were found guilty, sentenced to death, and executed by hanging on December 23, 1948: Hideki Tojo, Prime Minister at the time of the Pearl Harbor attack, and the following other high officials: Koki Hirota, General Kenji Dohihara, General Iwane Matsui, General Akira Muto, Seishiro Itagaki, General Heitaro Kimura. Sixteen others received life imprisonment, one twenty years, and one seven years.

For summary of trials and judgments by United States military courts of all Japanese war criminals, see above, pp. 437-438, n. 2.

[2] Byrnes, *Speaking Frankly, op. cit.,* p. 263.

[3] See above, p. 394.

explaining that circumstances had changed because of Japan having gone to war against the United States and Great Britain, allies of the Soviet Union. But the pact had still nearly a year to run. To make the Allies complicitous to the abrupt break-off of the treaty Stalin suggested that the USSR be requested by the Allies in the name of the United Nations to join them in the war against Japan in order to maintain world peace and security. President Truman made the request as suggested.[1]

While Japan was delaying and pondering surrender, the two atomic bombs were dropped successively over Hiroshima (August 6, 1945) and Nagasaki (August 8, 1945). Russia hastened to declare war on Japan (August 9, 1945). This happened to be three months to a day after the surrender of Germany, according to Stalin's promise at Yalta.[2]

Within a week the Red armies engulfed Manchuria. They were already there when Russia concluded (August 14, 1945) the Sino-Soviet treaty of alliance, draped with the Soviet servitudes coming from Yalta.[3] Russia in the nick of time barely managed to get in on the war and its booty. Another week and it might have been too late, at least with any Allied agreement.

Faced with utter destruction, Japan already had opened up negotiations with the Allies via neutral Switzerland. She accepted the Potsdam Declaration (August 14, 1945), but without prejudice to the prerogative of the Emperor as sovereign ruler. In answer the Allies (the USA, Great Britain, the USSR, and China) by implication allowed the Emperor to stay on his throne, but required him to authorize and ensure surrender terms necessary to carry out the provisions of the Potsdam Declaration.[4]

Such were the commanding terms of the definitive instrument of Japanese surrender, signed on the USS *Missouri* in Tokyo Bay at 0908 o'clock on September 2, 1945, almost a century after the Japanese soldier had shoved Commodore Biddle on the occasion of the first, friendly visit of the American Navy to Japan in 1846.[5]

Soviet Russia's acceptance of the surrender terms along with the other Allies then made the USSR, of course, a party to the stipulations of the governing Potsdam Declaration.

The Second World War had ended, so far as actual fighting was con-

---

[1] Byrnes, *Speaking Frankly, op. cit.,* pp. 208-209.

[2] See above, p. 424.

[3] See above, p. 425.

[4] For Potsdam Declaration, and documents relating to the Japanese surrender, see *Documents on American Foreign Relations,* VIII (1945-1946), pp. 105-111.

[5] For this incident, see *Diplomatic History, op. cit.,* p. 354.

cerned. Military movements connected with the occupation of Italy, Germany, Austria, and Japan, including Korea, prolonged a technical state of hostilities until December 31, 1946.[1] The vacuum of power left in Korea by Japan's surrender attracted the occupation of American and Russian armies if only to keep order in that liberated country. Pending re-establishment of Korea as an independent state with a democratic government, the United States and Russia partitioned the country into two zones of occupation, divided by the parallel of 38° N.L., under the authority of a Soviet-American Commission.[2] Soviet troops withdrew from North Korea in October, 1948, after setting up and arming a communist "People's Republic" there with the aim of extending it by revolutionary force into all Korea. United States troops evacuated South Korea in June, 1949, after the Assembly of the United Nations had sponsored a Korean republic under fair and free elections. Evacuating American troops left armament and military advisers to protect the new republic. Korea remained a potential battlefield for the first military engagements of the "Cold War" that followed the Second World War.

Russia proceeded to take over the Kurile Islands and Southern Sakhalin, promised to her at Yalta. The United States occupied all the other Japanese islands in the Pacific. The Security Council of the United Nations by an unanimous vote (April 2, 1947) approved a trusteeship for the former German islands north of the Equator, later under mandate to Japan by the League of Nations, now placed under the full strategic authority and control of the United States.[3] The other Japanese islands (like Okinawa, Iwo Jima, etc.) occupied by the United States still (1950) await disposition by the eventual Treaty of Peace.

A final peace settlement would not be possible without the sincere desire and collaboration of the remaining superpowers, particularly the USA and the USSR. The Council of Foreign Ministers wrangled over the provisions of the minor peace treaties until December, 1946, with the Soviet representative trying to secure heavy reparations from Italy (to be pumped out of that prostrate state as expected American relief money poured in), to get the port of Trieste for Yugoslavia, to obtain for Russia

[1] President Truman formally proclaimed "the cessation of hostilities of World War II" as of twelve o'clock noon, December 31, 1946. *Documents on American Foreign Relations, op. cit.,* VIII, 112.

[2] *Ibid.,* 834-842.

[3] Department of State *Bulletin,* XVI, No. 409 (May 4, 1947), 783-792.

Russia voted in favor of this trusteeship, possibly as a result of an understanding reached at Yalta in exchange for the Kuriles; but, if so, the text of such an agreement has never been revealed.

a trusteeship over Italian colonies in North Africa, and to keep the Western Allies from any free navigation of the Danube River. The five peace treaties finally concluded with Bulgaria, Finland, Hungary, Italy, and Rumania, made relatively small territorial changes in the map of Europe, already vastly altered *de facto* by Russian absorption of the Baltic states, the coast of East Prussia, eastern Poland, northern Bucovina, and Bessarabia.[1] The former satellites of Germany were laid under heavy indemnities to Russia,[2] Yugoslavia, and Greece, with token indemnities to Albania and Ethiopia. Trieste became a provisional Free Territory under the guaranty of the United Nations, occupied by American, British, and Yugoslav troops until a neutral (i.e., not Yugoslav or Italian or Trentino) governor, to be appointed by the Security Council, should decide upon their withdrawal.[3] The Italian treaty left the disposition of Italian colonies in Africa to the Council of Foreign Ministers the more to dispute about, with the provision that if it was not settled by September 1, 1948, it should be determined by the General Assembly of the United Nations. (On November 22, 1949, the Assembly voted to establish Libya as an independent state not later than January 1, 1952;

[1] For map and tabulation of territorial changes in eastern Europe, and Finland, see *The United States in World Affairs, 1945-1947* (Council on Foreign Relations, 1947), 445-53.

[2] The five minor peace treaties levied the following indemnities by way of reparations:

Against Finland:
  $300,000,000 to USSR

Against Hungary:
  $200,000,000 to USSR (lowered to $100,000,000 in 1948)
      70,000,000 to Czechoslovakia
      30,000,000 to Yugoslavia

Against Rumania:
  $300,000,000 to USSR (lowered to $150,000,000 in 1948)

Against Bulgaria:
  $25,000,000 to Yugoslavia (canceled in 1947)
      45,000,000 to Greece (Bulgaria refused to pay because she would not recognize
                    the Greek Government!)

Against Italy:
  $125,000,000 to Yugoslavia
    125,000,000 to Greece
    100,000,000 to USSR
      25,000,000 to Ethiopia
        5,000,000 to Albania
  _____
  $380,000,000 (total)

The above noted reductions by Russia are largely nominal because the countries had already been stripped in kind under the sense of "war booty." They however had a certain propaganda value. The other cancellations are parts of the political treaties between the new communist states of the Balkans.

[3] The Security Council, not being able to agree on the setting up of the Free Territory, a *status quo* of military occupation has continued in Trieste (1950).

to give independence to Somaliland after ten years under Italian trusteeship; and deferred the disposition of Eritrea pending further study.) It
was agreed to call a conference of the Big Four plus the riparian states
to regulate freedom of navigation on the Danube River. (It assembled
at Belgrade in the summer of 1948, where seven of the eleven states signed
a convention excluding nonriparian states from the International Danubian Commission, which was equivalent to excluding them from navigation.) [1]

The minor treaties disarmed the Balkan states and Italy and thus
left Yugoslavia a heavily preponderant military power in southeastern
Europe. They were far from satisfactory to the United States, but the
Senate ratified them and the President proclaimed them,[2] obstinately
hoping thereby to introduce some element of stability into European affairs and to make way for peace treaties with Austria and Germany.

What appealed most to the people and Government of the United
States was the article common to all the minor treaties by which the
former enemy state solemnly guaranteed to "take all measures necessary
to secure to all persons under [its] jurisdiction, without distinction as to
race, language, or religion, the enjoyment of human rights and of the
fundamental freedoms, including freedom of expression, of press and of
publication, of religious worship, of political opinion and of public
meeting."

Trustful Americans hoped that the minor peace treaties would be the
forerunner of a general peace, first in Europe and then in the Far East,
protected and administered by a World Family of Democratic Nations.
This hope crumbled slowly in the following months and years. Soviet
Russia carried forward her revolutionary program, first in contiguous
states, next in remoter regions, finally through fifth columns of com-

[1] This shut-out of the nonriparian states was a victory for Vishinsky, leader of the
Russian delegation. Since the USSR controlled state navigation corporations of the
Danubian states, the practical result of such a convention was Russian control of the
Danube. It was a humiliating blow to an age-long fundamental of American foreign
policy, the freedom of navigation of international waterways, as guaranteed on the
Danube River by pre-war treaty rights. The United States, the United Kingdom,
France, and the provisional government of Austria registered a formal protest at the
majority decision of the conference and refused to accept it. See United States Department of State, *Documents and State Papers*, Vol. I (Nos. 8 and 9, Nov. and Dec.,
1948), 487-514; II (No. 4, July, 1948), 250-275, for treaties and conventions relating
to navigation on the Danube River.

[2] The United States was the only one of Russia's allies which did not declare war
on Finland after that nation became involved in war as a concomitant of Hitler's
invasion of the USSR in 1941. Therefore the United States was not a party to the
Finnish peace treaty of 1946.

munists all over the world. Russian power flowed irresistibly into the vacuums left by the collapse of German and Japanese authority in Europe and Asia. The USSR clenched its hold on the territorial occupations in Eastern Europe. Then it intervened with the force of revolution, syphoned out of Soviet military might, to overturn the principles of real democracy and free and unfettered elections agreed to at Teheran and Yalta. One by one it installed communist governments in the satellite states to the west and southwest and imposed upon them a structure of alliances and political and economic control in the form of "co-operation" and "collaboration" for cultural and economic purposes: with Czechoslovakia, Rumania, Yugoslavia, Hungary, Albania, Poland, Bulgaria.[1] In Eastern Europe the *Comintern* (Communist International, politely suspended during the Strange Alliance) reappeared in the shape of the *Cominform* to implement these Soviet alliances. It invoked the solidarity of the several states in their forthcoming struggle against "Anglo-American imperialism."[2] In Northern Europe, Finland, and behind Finland, the Scandinavian countries, Sweden, Norway, and Denmark, trembled before the aggressive advances of the Revolutionary Colossus.

To the Far East, Soviet expansion thrust rapidly into the great continent of Asia. A mutual-assistance treaty (February 27, 1946)[3] brought the "Mongolian People's Republic" into the Russian power system; communistic revolutionary governments were installed in Manchuria, Inner Mongolia, Northern Korea, and for all practical purposes in

[1] It was not the formal content of these treaties that caused concern so much as it was increasing Russian control over the satellite states, despite the word-service of the treaties to the principle of nonintervention and to the peace organization of the United Nations. The general pattern of the articles as published provides for friendship, co-operation and mutual aid in cultural and economic matters, and mutual military assistance in case of aggression from Germany or other powers allying themselves directly or in any other way whatever. Each party agrees not to join any alliance or coalition erected against the other, and not to intervene in the internal affairs of the other party, and both invoke the international peace system of the United Nations charter. Texts of the treaties in "The Soviet Alliance System, 1942-1945," and "New Links in the Soviet System of Alliances, 1948-49," may be found in United States Department of State, *Documents and State Papers,* No. 4, July, 1945, 219-250, and Nos. 12 and 13, March and April, 1949, 681-685. I am indebted to Dr. Andrew Gyorgy of Yale University for the opportunity to read in manuscript the relevant pages of his *Governments of Danubian Europe* (New York, 1949) in which he describes the network of bilateral treaties between the non-Russian states of Eastern Europe and the Balkans. The USSR and the remaining satellites denounced and abrogated unilaterally the Yugoslav treaty, September-October, 1949.

[2] Resolution of the *Cominform* on World Affairs, October 5, 1947, originally published in *For a Lasting Peace, For a People's Democracy,* Vol. I, No. 1. (Belgrade, November 10, 1947).

[3] This supplemented an earlier treaty of March 12, 1936, which became the prototype of similar pacts between the USSR and the Baltic States before the latter were occupied and annexed.

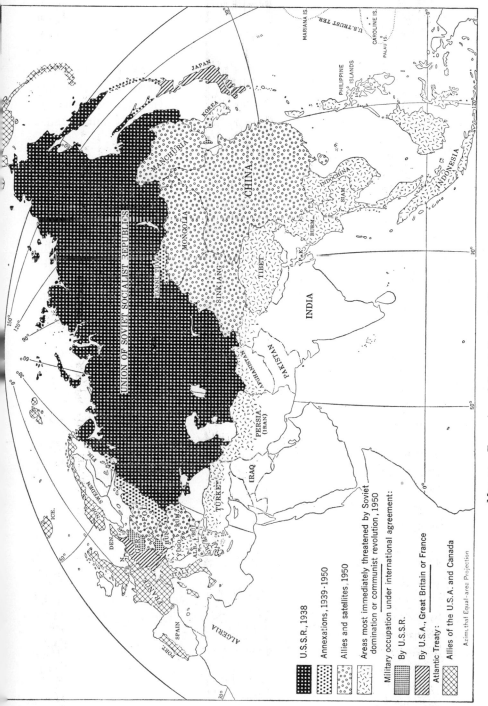

Map 13. Expansion of Soviet Power in Eurasia, 1939-1950

Legend:

U.S.S.R., 1938

Annexations, 1939-1950

Allies and satellites, 1950

Areas most immediately threatened by Soviet domination or communist revolution, 1950

Military occupation under international agreement:

By U.S.S.R.

By U.S.A., Great Britain or France

Atlantic Treaty:

Allies of the U.S.A. and Canada

Azimuthal Equal-area Projection

Sinkiang. The tiny territory of Tannu Tuva, on the border between Outer Mongolia and Russia—tiny by Asiatic standards, but with a thinly populated area as large as Great Britain—went through the whole cycle of Red imperialism: from Chinese province to autonomy, from autonomy to Soviet protectorate, from a "people's republic" to an actual province of the Soviet Union.[1] Beyond these former buffers of inner Asia lay the vast prize of China itself and the restive peoples to the south—India, Malaya, and the East Indies.

Thus the Iron Curtain closed down between the West and one Soviet satellite after another in Europe and Asia. Next might come Greece, where a communist revolt had been smoldering since the end of the war; then Turkey, and Iran; and still further to the south lay Africa, as tempting for the future as were China and the Indies to the east. Africa could be what it threatened to be if controlled by Nazi Germany, a springboard for a jump of power to South America. The Revolution, to use the words of its guides and fellow travelers, was "on the march" from the Heartland toward the Rimlands of the World Island. Beyond the Rimlands of the Old World, communist fifth columns, with leaders of revolution schooled in Moscow, mapped out the political terrain in every country everywhere. The United States, with its wide liberties and meager policing, afforded unparalleled facilities.

Meanwhile the Western Allies were demobilizing and putting their faith in the United Nations Organization, with its permanent headquarters established in New York as if to flatter the United States and hold it to the purpose of collective security. The United Nations proved to be but an international debating society like the first League of Nations, only more vituperative. Competent observers had generally agreed that it would need force to make it work, and the Charter had provided for national constituencies of armed forces, with a staff committee to put into effect the decisions of the Security Council. But the big powers had not shown the slightest indication of being able to agree on such a force, and even if they had done so each one held an absolute veto on its use. More and more the Security Council became merely a sounding board for Russia's aggressive diplomacy and the Western democracies' coalescing resistance. The issues of a troubled world produced a series of spectacular deadlocks in the Council while the various peace organs of the Organization proceeded to form their special councils and commissions: the professional Secretariat; the

---

[1] David J. Dallin has portrayed the expansion of *Soviet Russia in the Far East* (Yale University Press, 1948).

ORGANS OF THE UNITED NATIONS

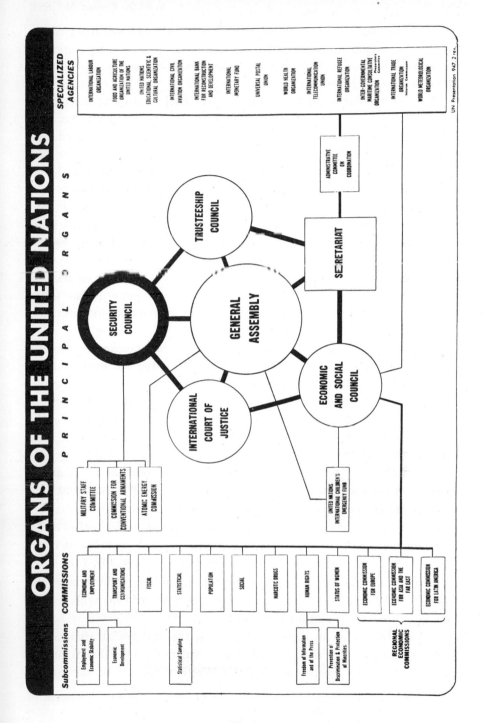

447

Trusteeship Council; the Economic and Social Council, with its twelve permanent commissions; and the thirteen specialized agencies appending to the Secretariat, including the Educational, Scientific and Cultural Organization (UNESCO).

Most spectacular of all the deadlocks was that relating to the control of atomic weapons and energy. The USA presented to the Security Council a proposal for the outlawry of the atomic bomb and placing the manufacture of atomic energy under international control *and inspection*. The USSR proposed to outlaw and destroy the bombs first and create an international control next but not to submit to any international inspection.[1] It proposed an all-round reduction of armaments by one third, well knowing that such a program would leave unchanged the relative strength of the rival powers. The aggressive antagonism of the USSR within the United Nations made it terrifyingly clear to the Western world that despite the five little peace treaties no real peace existed, that a far greater totalitarian power [2] had taken the place of Germany, Italy, and Japan to menace national independence and democratic liberty and the rights of man.

The agreements of Teheran, Yalta, and Berlin had invoked democratic principles as the basis of the coming peace. To the Soviet authorities democracy meant communism enforced only in the name of the people, without their free consent, by a dictatorship, with ruthless suppression of the freedom of speaking, meeting, publishing and voting. To the Western countries democracy meant the rights of man won from divine-right monarchy through centuries of constitutional struggle. It rested on universal suffrage freely expressed by secret ballot. It meant freedom of the common man, worker or drone, to speak, meet, print, and vote on perfect equality with the uncommon man, everybody equal before the law, as interpreted by independent courts of justice, enforced by a government of the people's own free choice. Such a government could regulate the people's economy as the voters desired, whether by capitalism and free enterprise or by socialistic or communistic collectivism—the fundamental principle of this democracy was a government truly of the people by the people and for the people.

Soviet intervention in the satellite states, the new Soviet alliances in Eastern Europe, and the increasing preponderance of Russian armed force, and gradual realization by the Western nations of the Soviet

[1] *The International Control of Atomic Energy; Growth of a Policy* (Department of State Publication No. 2702, Washington, G.P.O., 1947 [?]).

[2] Edmund J. Walsh, *Total Power* (New York, 1948).

program for world revolution,[1] frightened the democracies fringing on the Atlantic.   Their heritage of freedom, so recently and so valiantly preserved, with Russia's aid, against the fascist conquest, seemed doomed to another even more formidable trial from their Ally of yesteryear.

The new fear focused first and foremost on the German Question.   It became all too obvious that the Soviet Union intended to make Germany and its decisive war potential another satellite of Soviet power, a dominating thrust of the Revolution into Western Europe—to set up a communist Reich as an unchallengeable menace to Western democracy.   Secretary of State James F. Byrnes tried to neutralize that danger by proposing a four-power treaty (United States, France, Great Britain, Russia) designed to hold Germany to military impotence for twenty-five, even forty years, and thus make possible Allied evacuation and a German peace treaty safe to all.[2]   But Russia would have none of it.

The next reaction, this time from the war-weary and semisocialist democracies of Western Europe, was the Anglo-French alliance, the Treaty of Dunkirk (March 4, 1947), a regional security pact within the framework of the United Nations Charter, Article 51.   Waiting for the other powers to make such a treaty as proposed by Secretary Byrnes, they joined in a military alliance of mutual defense in the event of any threat to the security of either "arising from the adoption by Germany of a policy of aggression, *or from action by Germany designed to facilitate such a policy*." [3]   The words italicized could, of course, envisage the action of a communist Germany set up by Russia, just as the Soviet alliances with the border satellite states looked toward action by states allied directly with Germany "or in any other way."

Germany and Austria were all that stood between the Western democracies and the colossus of the Soviet Revolution.   Germany and the democracies of Western Europe were all that stood between the USA and the USSR to the east of the New World, even as Japan and China were all that stood across the Pacific between the two superpowers.

Closely following the Treaty of Dunkirk, President Truman declared to a joint session of Congress (March 12, 1947) that it was the policy of the United States "to support free peoples who are resisting attempted subjugation by armed minorities or by outside countries."

[1] Synthesized from Stalin's writings and speeches in a remarkable anonymous essay "Stalin on Revolution," by "Historicus," in *Foreign Affairs*, XXVII (January, 1949), 175-214, which was widely reprinted in digested form in the United States.

[2] For draft of treaty proposed, April 29, 1946, to the Council of Foreign Ministers, by Secretary Byrnes, and subsequent Stuttgart Speech, September 6, 1946, see *Documents on American Foreign Relations, op. cit.,* VIII (1945-1946), pp. 205-211.

[3] Text in New York *Times*, March 5, 1947.

Specifically he asked for appropriations of $400,000,000 (enacted July 30, 1947) to provide economic assistance to Greece, struggling against a communist revolt sustained from the north, and to fortify Turkey to hold the line of the Near East against the threatened advance of Soviet power. The action of the United States Government ("Truman Doctrine") in furnishing loans, military and naval equipment, not to mention military and naval staff personnel, to the Government of Greece, and also to the Government of China, when they were engaged in domestic strife against communistic revolts, was without doubt an intervention in these civil wars, like similar action already taken, less openly, by the USSR and satellites to foment and sustain the revolts.[1] The pattern of American resistance to the Soviet menace was beginning to resemble that of President Roosevelt's build-up of defense against Nazi Germany in 1939-1941, with public opinion, lulled by the earnest vision of collective security, following reluctantly but determined. It was what the journalists called a "cold war." [2]

The next step of the United States to stiffen overseas democracies against the Soviet menace was the European Recovery Program. Originally proposed by Secretary of State George C. Marshall (June 5, 1947), it offered a $20,000,000,000 five-year program to the co-operation of all the nations of Europe (except Falangist Spain) to transfuse their war-famished continent with American (i.e., United States Government) capital, livestock, new machinery, and raw material, calculated to raise the national economies to 25 per cent above the pre-war level and make them impervious to communistic revolution. It was a gigantic continuation and expansion of lend-lease in time of peace, including even tobacco and cigarettes, supported by the American taxpayer. The Soviet Government refused to participate or allow its satellites to do so, but the program went into effect with sixteen other nations (Act of June 28, 1948). The huge purchases from outside the United States necessary to carry out this unprecedented departure spilled out largesses into Canada and Latin America and splashed all over the world outside and even inside the Soviet area. Congress added to the European Recovery appropriation $400,000,000 for aid to China—too late to prevent the collapse of Chiang

---

[1] Technically there was no violation of neutrality. The belligerency of the communist insurrection had not been recognized. The provisions of the joint resolutions of Congress of January 8, 1937, and May 1, 1937, enabling the President to proclaim an embargo on arms, ammunition, and implements of war to a state wherein civil strife existed, when necessary to promote the security or protect the lives or commerce of citizens of the United States, were repealed by Section 19 of the Neutrality Act of 1939.

[2] Walter Lippmann, *The Cold War* (New York, 1947).

Kai-shek's Nationalist Government before the onslaughts of the communist revolution encouraged and guided from Russia.

The rather belated Soviet reply (January 25, 1949) to the European Recovery Program was the formation among the western satellites (exclusive of seceded Yugoslavia) of an opposing Council for Economic Mutual Assistance, open like the ERP to the other countries of Europe.

The European Recovery Program,[1] or the "Marshall Plan," as this American succor was popularly called, stiffened Italy and France successfully to resist revolutions at least for the time being. It encouraged Great Britain, France, the Netherlands, Belgium, and Luxemburg—all alarmed at the communist *coup d'état* in Czechoslovakia (February 20-25, 1948)—to expand the Dunkirk idea into the Western Union, a military regional defensive alliance based on Article 51 of the United Nations Charter against an "armed attack" on any one of them "in Europe."[2]

Soviet Russia's reply to the Pact of Brussels (March 17, 1948) setting up the new regional alliance was to walk out (June 16, 1948) of the joint Allied Control Council or *Kommandatura* of Berlin and, in violation of previous occupation agreements,[3] to blockade (June 23, 1948) passage of Allied personnel and matériel through the general Soviet zone of occupation into the American, British, and French zones of the enclaved city. It was a measure designed to maneuver the Western Allies out of the German capital and make of it a metropolitan magnet in the communist field of all Germany, under Soviet control and manipulation. Faced by this blow, the American and British forces resorted to a costly air lift of foodstuff and fuel from their Western zones into their respective areas of Berlin, barely enough to keep the people there from starving or freezing during the blockade. Efforts to adjust the ugly impasse by a Conference of Foreign Ambassadors at Moscow collapsed in the summer of 1948.[4] Further attempts to conciliate the controversy in the United Nations Security Council also failed. But a vital minimum of truce was reached by the Council of Foreign Ministers when the Soviet Government lifted the blockade of Berlin, May 12, 1949, restored the joint *Kommandatura,* and revived hopes for an Austrian treaty. After this the United States and Great Britain eased off the air lift.

[1] *The European Recovery Program.* Sen. Doc. 111, 80th Cong., 1st Sess. (Washington, G.P.O., 1947).

[2] Text in New York *Times,* March 18, 1948.

[3] For a list of Soviet violations of treaty and other agreements, see Department of State *Bulletin,* XVIII, No. 466 (June 6, 1948), 738-744.

[4] *The Berlin Crisis. A Report on the Moscow Discussions, 1948.* (Department of State Publication 3298, September, 1948). See also Walter Bedell Smith, *My Three Years in Moscow* (Philadelphia, 1950).

Meanwhile Soviet forces had set up a German communist administration and militia in their Eastern Zone of occupation, while the United States, Great Britain, and France recruited democratic German officials to administer their respective zones. Then the Allies set up in all the Western Zones of occupation a single German Federal Republic (September, 1949) on a democratic basis, hoping that a government of the German people by the German people and for the German people, with individual freedom and human rights anchored in a republican constitution, would some day prevail all over the prostrate Reich, out of the hands of Russia. In turn the USSR set up a communist state (October, 1949)—a "German Democratic Republic"—in their Eastern Zone, on the model of similar communist governments installed after revolution in Poland, Czechoslovakia, Hungary, Rumania, Bulgaria, Albania, and Yugoslavia, hoping that it would some day extend over all of Germany, out of control of the Allies. Germany and its future war potential remained the biggest battlefield of the "cold war."

Unexpectedly fortunate for the American policy of containment all round the circle [1] of Soviet aggression, revolutionary expansion, and Red imperialism, was the defection (June 28, 1948) of Marshal Tito, Moscow-schooled communistic dictator of Yugoslavia, from the *Cominform*, and his denunciation of the Soviet-Yugoslav Alliance of June 8, 1946. It was the initial crack in the Soviet system of alliances against the Western democracies. It held out encouragement to suppressed nationalist majorities in the other satellite states. It withdrew twenty ready military divisions from the Soviet bloc of power. It eased the Trieste Question and the Italian Question, if not the Greek Question (still sustained from Bulgaria and Albania). It gave pause to any plans that the USSR might have had for a hot war in the summer of 1948. It gave time for the further coagulation of Western resistance. But the communist military triumph in 1949 in the Chinese Civil War that had continued after the fall of Japan overbalanced the relief brought by Yugoslavia's secession from Moscow. And Soviet achievement of their first atomic explosion (announced by President Truman, September 23, 1949) weakened the American policy of containment in Europe as well as in Asia.

The communist victory in China, and affiliation in their new revolutionary constitution [2] (October, 1949) with the foreign policy of the USSR, unhinged American policy in the Far East. The United States had risked

[1] The articulator of this policy was "X" in his essay "Sources of Soviet Conduct," *Foreign Affairs*, XXV (No. 4, July, 1947), 566-582. "X" is widely believed to be George Kennan of the Department of State; and the assertion has never been denied.

[2] The USSR recognized the new communist government of China, October 1, 1949.

and won a double war in 1941-1945 in order to prevent China and the British Commonwealth of Nations from conquest in the East by Japan, while America for its own security was trying to hold Britain up in the West as a buffer against Germany. After the Second World War the British Empire was disintegrating in the East, and the component Commonwealths were threatened by a bloc of Russian power, actual and potential, following the communist conquest of China, larger than ever Japan had been able to mass on the continent of Asia. These revolutionary developments negated the American victory over Japan, one half the victory of the double war. In the other half of the globe Russia was counteracting the victory in Europe. Reappraising its China policy,[1] the Department of State decided not to interfere further in the Chinese Civil War, hoping that China under Mao Tse-tung, sworn enemy of the United States, would "go Tito" like Yugoslavia, once the Chinese people realized how Soviet imperialism was depriving China of her fairest provinces in the north and west. Accordingly the American delegate to the United Nations, Dr. Philip C. Jessup, sought to pledge the powerless Assembly to the traditional American principles of self-determination for China and the political, territorial and administrative integrity of that nation.[2]

The patient, if irresolute, American position conceivably may have been of some moral advantage and unacknowledged help to the Chinese Communists in the diplomatic negotiations then under way between Mao and Stalin in Moscow, in enabling the Chinese leader to resist to some extent Red imperialist pressure. The resulting thirty-year Sino-Soviet Alliance, announced February 15, 1950, was directed against a recrudescence of Japanese aggression, "or any other state which directly or indirectly would unite with Japan in acts of aggression." The published articles followed the pattern of Soviet pacts with the satellite states of Eastern and Central Europe. Supplementary agreements, only partially revealed, defined Sino-Russian relationships in Manchuria and Sinkiang, without leaving any real assurance that Soviet Russia would give up her dominating influence in those outlying parts of China.[3] Whatever contemned

---

[1] *United States Relations with China, with Special Reference to the Period 1944-1949,* based on the files of the Department of State (Department of State Publication 3573, Far Eastern Series 30, released August 1949) presents official documents apparently intended to demonstrate that "nothing this country did or could have done within the limits of its capabilities could have changed that result [the communist triumph in China]; nothing that was left undone by this country has contributed to it."

[2] Statement of Dr. Philip C. Jessup, United States Ambassador at Large, to the Political and Security Committee of the United Nations General Assembly at Lake Success, N. Y., November 28, 1949.

[3] One of these agreements was said to have promised a loan of $300,000,000 to China. Another was reported to have promised sole control to China of the Changchung Rail-

comfort the Chinese may have taken from the irenic attitude of the
United States did not prevent that vast Asiatic country from becoming a
great and dangerous satellite of Soviet Russia in the Far East. The
world outside the Iron Curtain suspected the existence of secret protocols
which would give to the USSR naval and air bases on the Chinese coast,
together with Russian bases in Eastern Siberia, the Kuriles, and Sakhalin
Island. These would seed the whole Pacific Ocean with Russian submarines. They would also bring Japan, and her former island possessions
transferred to American trusteeship in 1946, under range of an arc of
Soviet Power from Kamchatka in the north to Hainan Island. If so,
they threatened speedily to neutralize the whole power position of the
United States in the Far East so recently secured by the victory over
Japan in 1945.

It was under circumstances of the increasingly bitter "cold war," and
at the outset of the Presidential campaign of 1948 in the United States,
that the Senate passed (June 11, 1948) the bipartisan Vandenberg Resolution, outstanding signal of the reorientation of American foreign policy
to a system of defensive alliances within the United Nations. It pledged
the United States to associate itself by constitutional process—that is,
by treaty requiring the advice and consent of the Senate—with "regional
and other collective arrangements"—the Senate still eschewed the
traditionally forbidding word *alliance*—for individual or collective
self-defense in case of an "armed attack" threatening the national
security. This took the "cold war" out of the Truman-Dewey Presidential
campaign of 1948, except for the exhortations of Henry Wallace,
candidate of the Progressive Party, who, reflecting the Soviet line of
propaganda, vigorously but ineffectually attacked in Europe as well as
in the United States the current foreign policy of his own country.
Backed by the Vandenberg Resolution, Secretary of State George C.
Marshall began the negotiation of a treaty to expand the Western Union
into a defensive military alliance along the lines of the Rio Pact of 1947,
based on Article 51 of the United Nations Charter.[1] The collapse of
General Marshall's health left the completion of the task to his successor,
Secretary of State Dean Acheson. President Truman greeted the plenipotentiaries when they assembled at Washington (April 4, 1949) to sign

---

way and the ports of Dairen and Port Arthur as soon as a Japanese peace treaty should
be made, but the specific text of these agreements was not made public. See *New
York Times* of February 15, 1950.

[1] The Department of State prepared a background statement on *Collective Security in
the North Atlantic Area* (Foreign Affairs Outlines, *Building the Peace*, Spring, 1949),
Department of State Publication 3377.

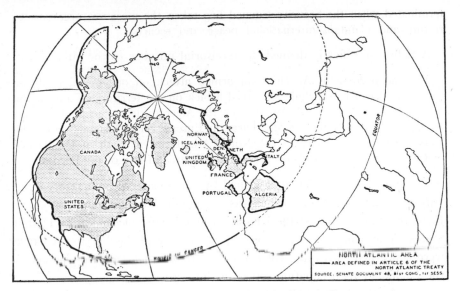

Map 14. North Atlantic Area as Defined in Atlantic Treaty, 1949 [1]

the North Atlantic Treaty, following two World Wars of aggression. "Our peoples, to whom our Governments are responsible," he told the diplomatists, "are determined that *these things shall not happen again.*" [2]

The President sent the Treaty to the Senate on April 12, 1949. It provided (Article 1) that the signatories, Belgium, Canada, Denmark, France, Iceland, Italy, Luxemburg, Netherlands, Norway, Portugal, the United Kingdom, the United States, would consult together whenever the territorial integrity, political independence, or security of any one of them were threatened; this was hardly more than they would do anyway. Key to the new ten-year alliance, completing a revolution in American foreign policy, was Article 5:

The Parties agree that an armed attack against one or more of them in Europe or North America shall be considered an attack against them all; and consequently they agree that, if such an attack occurs, each of them, in exercise of the right of individual or collective self-defense recognized by Article 51 of the Charter of the United Nations, will assist the Party or Parties so attacked by taking forthwith, individually and in concert with the other Parties, *such action as it deems necessary,*[2] including the use of armed force, to restore and maintain the security of the North Atlantic area.

Any such armed attack and all measures taken as a result thereof shall immediately be reported to the Security Council. Such measures shall be

[1] Reproduced from *Major Problems of United States Foreign Policy, 1949-1950*, p. 270, with permission of Brookings Institution.
[2] Italics inserted.

terminated when the Security Council has taken the measures necessary to restore and maintain international peace and security.

Article 6 specifically defined the territorial purview of the alliance:

For the purpose of Article 5 an armed attack on one or more of the Parties is deemed to include an armed attack on the territory of any of the Parties in Europe or North America, on the Algerian departments of France, on the occupation forces of any Party in Europe, on the islands under the jurisdiction of any Party in the North Atlantic area north of the Tropic of Cancer or on the vessels or aircraft in this area of any of the Parties.

The North Atlantic Treaty, ratified by the Senate without reservation, July 21, 1949 (by a vote of 82 yeas, 13 nays), left uncovered the Near East, the Far East, and the islands of the Pacific Ocean. The United States alone would have to cope—so far as any pledges of the Alliance were concerned—with an attack on its territory, such as the islands of the Pacific, or its occupation forces in those areas.

Even in the North Atlantic area the pledges of the Allies were not absolute and automatic: each Party pledged itself only to *such action as it deemed necessary*. If and when the attack should come, how much action would each of the twelve allies "deem necessary"?

One of the reasons for the qualified nature of the pledge was the inability of the executive branch of the Government of the United States to bind Congress to vote to take any action, including the use of armed force, in advance of any situation. Despite the inroads of executive agreements by-passing the Senate, that body's advice and consent was still considered necessary for a treaty of alliance, and the Senate would not have advised and consented to a treaty that ignored the power of Congress to appropriate moneys and to declare war. The qualifications introduced into the treaty in deference to the Congress of the United States also served as "outs" for each of the other eleven Parties.

The North Atlantic Treaty was thus an uncertain alliance, which circumstance might further debilitate—*or further strengthen*. Congress implemented it (September, 1949) with an appropriation of $1,314,010,000 for military assistance to the Atlantic Allies; to Greece and Turkey; to Iran, "right flank" of the Atlantic defense line; to China (within the President's discretion); to Korea, the only remaining continental citadel of the rear guard in Asia; and to the island outposts of the Philippine Republic. The aid proved to be too little and too late to prevent the Red onslaught in Asia—Europe too remained unsafe in 1950.

Such was the posture of American foreign affairs as the first half of our century drew to a disheartening close. The United States and its Allies had fought the Second World War to a brilliant military triumph. Five years later it looked like defeat in victory. The Republic of the West had spent 352,799 lives in the war. It had 668,653 wounded service [1] men and dependents to care for, and hundreds of thousands more invalided, not to mention pensions and allowances for millions of others, totaling, for veterans of all wars of the United States $6,495,232,236 in the year 1949 alone.[2] In the Second World War it had spent a third of a trillion dollars ($330,000,000,000) in military efforts and lend-lease. As in the case of all previous wars, pension costs in future years will multiply

---

[1] However tragic for individuals and families, the comparatively small loss of life and other military casualties to the United States in the two World Wars were by no means serious to the nation. Compare the equally sanguinary casualties from automobile accidents within the United States during the years of the Second World War, men, women, and children killed, crippled, or maimed, a toll of death and injury which the public bears without revolt—and speeds on:

Year	Deaths	Nonfatal Injuries
1941	39,969	1,400,000
1942	28,309	1,000,000
1943	23,823	800,000
1944	24,282	850,000
1945	28,076	1,000,000
	144,459	5,055,000

Accident Facts (published by the National Safety Council, 20 North Wacker Drive, Chicago, 1948).

[2] An Associated Press despatch from Washington, February 15, 1949, doubtless a news release from the Veterans Administration, presented the following historical summary of pensions and other compensations to veterans of the armed forces of the United States in previous wars:

Veterans, their dependents or heirs from World War II back to the Mexican War received a total of $6,495,232,236 in various benefits during the fiscal year ending June 30, 1948.

This amount is roughly one billion less than the all-time high of the previous fiscal year.

Compensation or pension benefits for 2,918,325 veterans totaled $1,827,641,507. The rest went for subsistence, tuition, unemployment allowances, and insurance payments.

The lingering cost of wars is shown by the following breakdown of compensation and pension payments:

Mexican War—$22,440 to the heirs of 36 veterans.

Indian Wars—$757,444 to 710 living veterans; $1,135,869 to heirs and dependents of 2,090 dead veterans.

Civil War—$94,491 to 49 living; $8,924,774 to 16,323 dead.

Spanish-American War—$126,906,930 to 106,698 living; $38,190,878 to 776,336 dead.

World War I—$317,396,870 to 449,609 living; $154,444,088 to 252,626 dead.

World War II—$974,139,086 to 1,714,535 living; $1,759,121,779 to 241,362 dead.

Regular Establishment—$23,378,857 to 43,438 living; $6,226,601 to 13,513 dead.

Congress may have raised pension costs further by the time the reader peruses this astonishing note!

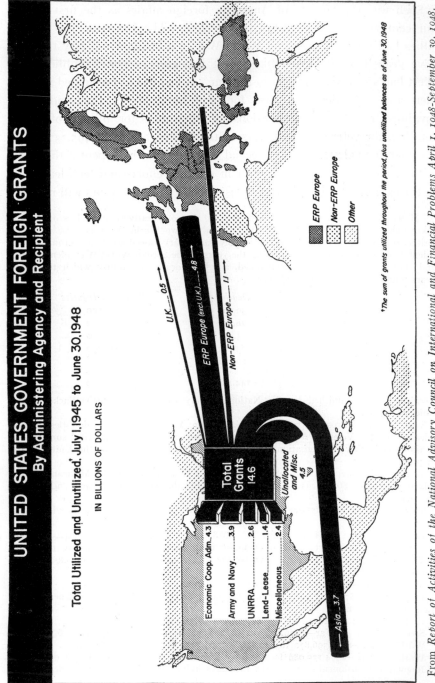

UNITED STATES GOVERNMENT FOREIGN GRANTS

By Administering Agency and Recipient

Total Utilized and Unutilized, July 1, 1945 to June 30, 1948

IN BILLIONS OF DOLLARS

Economic Coop. Adm. _ 4.3
Army and Navy _ 3.9
UNRRA _ 2.6
Lend-Lease _ 1.4
Miscellaneous _ 2.4

Total Grants 14.6

Unallocated and Misc. 4.5

U.K. _ 0.5
ERP Europe (excl. U.K.) _ 4.8
Non-ERP Europe _ 1.1
Asia _ 3.7

ERP Europe
Non-ERP Europe
Other

*The sum of grants utilized throughout the period, plus unutilized balances as of June 30, 1948

From *Report of Activities of the National Advisory Council on International and Financial Problems April 1, 1948–September 30, 1948.*

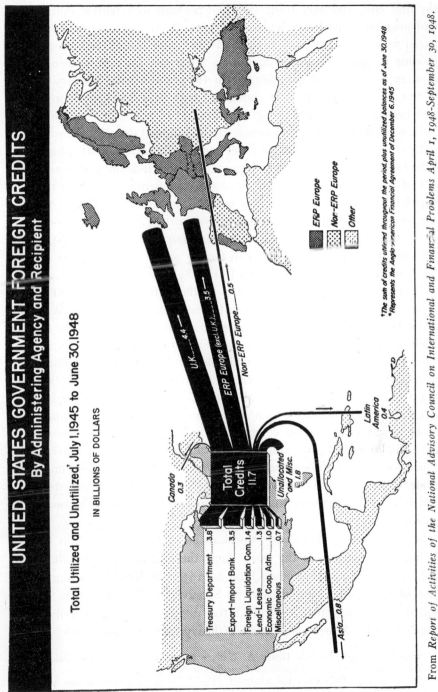

UNITED STATES GOVERNMENT FOREIGN CREDITS
By Administering Agency and Recipient

Total Utilized and Unutilized, July 1,1945 to June 30,1948

IN BILLIONS OF DOLLARS

Treasury Department......3.8
Export-Import Bank.......3.5
Foreign Liquidation Com..1.4
Lend-Lease...............1.3
Economic Coop. Adm.......1.0
Miscellaneous............0.7

Total Credits 11.7

Canada 0.3

U.K.——4.4
ERP Europe (excl. U.K.)——3.5
Non-ERP Europe——0.5

Unallocated and Misc. 1.8

Latin America 0.4

Asia——0.8

ERP Europe
Non-ERP Europe
Other

*The sum of credits utilized throughout the period, plus unutilized balances as of June 30,1948
†Represents the Anglo-American Financial Agreement of December 6,1945

From *Report of Activities of the National Advisory Council on International and Financial Problems April 1, 1948–September 30, 1948.*

the first cost, and may bring the total perhaps to a trillion dollars. It had acquired a national debt of $258,286,383,109 (1947 peak) as compared with $48,961,443,536 in 1941. It had come to military conscription in time of peace. It was maintaining an armed force of 1,991,096 men in 1949 as contrasted with 683,591 in 1939, and a total military budget of $11,745,000,000 in 1949 as contrasted with $1,068,854,207 in 1939. It had become really a debtor in the disguise of a creditor nation in the balance of international payments. It had dipped deep into its depleted natural resources. In postwar relief and rehabilitation of friend and foe, it had spent a larger amount of treasure than any indemnity ever squeezed out of a defeated people by a victorious conqueror—and the stream of hopeful tribute continued to flow out and out from the victor: $5,809,-990,000 for the European Recovery Program for the fiscal year July 1, 1949, to June 30, 1950, and $1,314,010,000 more for military assistance to the Atlantic Treaty Allies; and to Greece and Turkey and the others: total in grants and credits since VJ Day, $43,000,000,000.

To give still more generous gush to the outflow President Truman, apparently taking his cue from an earlier suggestion of Henry A. Wallace,[1] proposed as Point Four of his inaugural address of January 20, 1949, a "bold new program" for making the benefits of American scientific advances and industrial progress available for the growth of undeveloped areas of the world.[2] The Foreign Economic Assistance Act ($3,120,-555,000 authorized for the fiscal year 1950-1951) included an item of $35,000,000 as a starter for Point Four: to organize and sustain a program of technical assistance in co-operation with the United Nations, with individual governments, and with private organizations. Later steps, which would have to be provided for by subsequent legislation, might include United States Government guaranties for American private loans and foreign governments wishing to co-operate and otherwise unable to borrow money.

In the midst of these vast American expenditures to sustain the remaining free nations of the world came the first military assault of the Cold War. At 4 A.M. Sunday, June 25, 1950, the Kremlin, acting in the face of the United Nations and its Supervisory Commission in Korea, pulled the strings that controlled the puppet "People's Republic" of North Korea. A formidable force of heavy tanks Russian models rolled

---

[1] Address of Vice President Henry A. Wallace to the Free World Association, New York City, May 8, 1942. *International Conciliation,* No. 381 (June, 1942), 369-376.

[2] The Brookings Institution has analysed "The Problem of United States Assistance to Underdeveloped Areas," as one of the *Major Problems of American Foreign Policy, 1949-1950* (Washington, 1949), pp. 295-350.

down over the free Republic of South Korea, followed by at least a hundred thousand well-prepared ground troops well-armed from Russian arsenals. If the United Nations did nothing about this naked aggression, it was the end of collective security; other assaults, successive challenges, could be expected to follow in numerous exposed places all around the Eurasian perimeter of the USSR and its satellites.

That same Sunday afternoon (Western time) the Secretary General of the United Nations, Trygve Lie, called an emergency meeting of the Security Council at Lake Success, New York. The representative of the USSR had absented himself from meetings of this vital organ ever since January 13, 1950, because of the Council's refusal to unseat the delegate of Nationalist China after the triumph of the communist revolution. By a vote of 9 to 1, Russia absent and Yugoslavia abstaining, the Security Council adopted, with revisions, a resolution presented by the United States. It declared that a breach of the peace had occurred, requested the North Korean authorities to withdraw north of the 38th parallel, and asked Member States to carry out the resolution and not to assist the North Korean forces.

In conformance with this resolution President Harry S. Truman, Commander in Chief of the armed forces of the United States, immediately ordered American air and sea units to give cover to the defending South Korean troops. He further directed the United States Navy to forestall any communist attack on the island of Formosa, last refuge of Generalissimo Chiang Kai-shek, and called upon the Nationalist Government there to cease all air and sea operations against the Chinese mainland. In response to an appeal from the United Nations Supervisory Commission in Korea, the Security Council adopted, on June 27, by a vote of 7 for and 1 (Yugoslavia) against, with the USSR still absent and India and Egypt not participating,[1] a resolution presented by the United States delegate Warren R. Austen. It recommended that Member States "furnish such assistance to the Republic of Korea as may be necessary to repel the armed attack and to restore international peace and security in the area." The Council on July 7 adopted a further resolution recommending that all military forces and other assistance be made available to a unified command under the United States and the flag of the United Nations. In Washington the Council of the Organization of American

---

[1] The delegates of India and Egypt did not participate because they had not yet received instructions. At a later meeting of the Security Council (June 30) the representative of India reported that his government "accepted" the resolution of June 27, and the representative of Egypt declared that he would have abstained in the voting had he then received his instructions.

States lent its moral support and prestige to these measures of collective security. It declared, June 28, that all its members were also members of the United Nations and therefore obligated by the terms of the decisions of its "competent organs," and expressed "firm adherence" to those decisions—it also reaffirmed the pledges of continental solidarity which unite all the American States.

Approval of the resolutions of the United Nations flowed in from the freedom-loving nations with promises at least of token forces (the United Kingdom, Australia, New Zealand, the Netherlands, Siam, Turkey, and distant Bolivia among the first; then Canada, Costa Rica, France, Belgium, Denmark, Greece, and the Union of South Africa), while the Soviet Satellites from their several capitals screamed against the action.[1] In Moscow, André Gromyko, Deputy Minister of Foreign Affairs of the USSR, charged that the Council's Resolution was "illegal" because it had only six votes,[2] the seventh necessary vote being that of "the Kuomintang representive" who, he asserted, had no right to represent China, and "illegal" because the Charter required the concurring votes of all five permanent members—the USSR and communist China being absent. Acceptance of this argument would have meant that any Council power—in this case the USSR—could inspire and prepare an aggression and then block all defense by absenting itself from the Council. As for the question of China's proper representation, that was for the Council itself to decide.

The fact was that the USSR had tried to paralyze collective security by absenting itself from the Security Council, and the United Nations had gone ahead and acted without Russia! The World Family of Democratic Nations had taken a definite stand, within the United Nations, against the aggression of the USSR behind its satellites. Realizing this, the Soviet representative, Y. A. Malik, came back into the Security Council, August 1, to accuse the United States of aggression and to try to paralyze further action unless the Council should first unseat the delegate of Nationalist China. This the Council refused to do; the United States delegate, Warren R. Austen, demanded a restoration of South Korea first. Malik's effort seemed calculated to bring Communist China into the war against the United States and the United Nations.

Under the banner of the United Nations and the flag of the United States, General Douglas MacArthur in supreme command, three divisions

---

[1] *Korean Crisis* (Dept. State Pub. 3922, July, 1950).

[2] Actually India's approval on June 30 made seven votes, even if one should not count the vote of Nationalist China.

of green American troops landed in South Korea during July in a desperate attempt to stem the invasion and hold a beachhead until effective force could be brought up. Congress backed the President's international "police action" with prompt appropriations to sustain the Korean War and to increase the armed forces for any other contingency that might follow.

Convinced that "it must not happen again," the American people and their Government had led the way into a new league of nations, putting their large-hearted faith in the trust that their Allies would co-operate for peace as they had worked for war. Disconsolately they faced the fact that the peace was all but lost, that the freedom-loving nations were outbalanced by the power of the USSR.

The revolutionary USSR would not clasp the proffered hand of friendship. It stood firmly based in the Heartland of Eurasia, one mighty foot by 1950 planted on the Asiatic Rimland of the World Island, the other poised to tread Atlantic shore.

> WHO RULES EAST EUROPE COMMANDS THE HEARTLAND:
> WHO RULES THE HEARTLAND COMMANDS THE WORLD-ISLAND:
> WHO RULES THE WORLD-ISLAND RULES THE WORLD.[1]

Within the United Nations Organization a new opposition of alliances and counteralliances had arisen. The best that men could hope for seemed a long armed peace. Only a political miracle could resolve truly and peaceably the issue between a World Family of Democratic Nations and a World Union of Soviet Socialist Republics. America had never faced so great a challenge to her heritage of freedom. America had arisen before triumphantly to meet great challenges at home and abroad—when there had been time to rise. Would there be time, once more?

[1] H. J. Mackinder, *Democratic Ideals and Reality: A Study in the Politics of Reconstruction* (New York, 1919, 1942).

NORTH ATLANTIC TREATY

Preamble

The Parties to this Treaty reaffirm their faith in the purposes and principles of the Charter of the United Nations and their desire to live in peace with all peoples and all governments.

They are determined to safeguard the freedom, common heritage and civilization of their peoples, founded on the principles of democracy, individual liberty and the rule of law.

They seek to promote stability and well-being in the North Atlantic area.

They are resolved to unite their efforts for collective defense and for the preservation of peace and security.

They therefore agree to this North Atlantic Treaty:

Article 1

The Parties undertake, as set forth in the Charter of the United Nations, to settle any international disputes in which they may be involved by peaceful means in such a manner that international peace and security, and justice, are not endangered, and to refrain in their international relations from the threat or use of force in any manner inconsistent with the purposes of the United Nations.

Article 2

The Parties will contribute toward the further development of peaceful and friendly international relations by strengthening their free institutions, by bringing about a better understanding of the principles upon which these institutions are founded, and by promoting conditions of stability and well-being. They will seek to eliminate conflict in their international economic policies and will encourage economic collaboration between any or all of them.

Article 3

In order more effectively to achieve the objectives of this Treaty, the Parties, separately and jointly, by means of continuous and effective self-help and mutual aid, will maintain and develop their individual and collective capacity to resist armed attack.

Article 4

The Parties will consult together whenever, in the opinion of any of them, the territorial integrity, political independence or security of any of the Parties is threatened.

Article 5

The Parties agree than an armed attack against one or more of them in Europe or North America shall be considered an attack against them all; and consequently they agree that, if such an armed attack occurs, each of them, in exercise of the right of individual or collective self-defense recognized by Article 51 of the Charter of the United Nations, will assist the Party or Parties so attacked by taking forthwith, individually and in concert with the other Parties, such action as it deems necessary, including the use of armed force, to restore and maintain the security of the North Atlantic area.

Any such armed attack and all measures taken as a result thereof shall immediately be reported to the Security Council. Such measures shall be terminated when the Security Council has taken the measures necessary to restore and maintain international peace and security.

Article 6

For the purpose of Article 5 an armed attack on one or more of the Parties is deemed to include an armed attack on the territory of any of the Parties in Europe or North America, on the Algerian departments of France, on the occupation forces of any Party in Europe, on the islands under the jurisdiction of any Party in the North Atlantic area north of the Tropic of Cancer or on the vessels or aircraft in this area of any of the Parties.

Article 7

This Treaty does not affect, and shall not be interpreted as affecting, in any way the rights and obligations under the Charter of the Parties which are members of the United Nations, or the primary responsibility of the Security Council for the maintenance of international peace and security.

Article 8

Each Party declares that none of the international engagements now in force between it and any other of the Parties or any third state is in conflict with the provisions of this Treaty, and undertakes not to enter into any international engagement in conflict with this Treaty.

Article 9

The Parties hereby establish a council, on which each of them shall be represented, to consider matters concerning the implementation of this Treaty. The council shall be so organized as to be able to meet promptly at any time. The council shall set up such subsidiary bodies as may be necessary; in particular it shall establish immediately a defense committee which shall recommend measures for the implementation of Articles 3 and 5.

Article 10

The Parties may, by unanimous agreement, invite any other European state in a position to further the principles of this Treaty and to contribute to the security of the North Atlantic area to accede to this Treaty. Any state so invited may become a party to the Treaty by depositing its instrument of accession with the Government of the United States of America. The Government of the United States of America will inform each of the Parties of the deposit of each such instrument of accession.

Article 11

This Treaty shall be ratified and its provisions carried out by the Parties in accordance with their respective constitutional processes. The instruments of ratification shall be deposited as soon as possible with the Government of the United States of America, which will notify all the other signatories of each deposit. The Treaty shall enter into force between the states which have ratified it as soon as the ratifications of the majority of the signatories, including the ratifications of Belgium, Canada, France, Luxembourg, the Netherlands, the United Kingdom and the United States, have been deposited and shall come into effect with respect to other states on the date of the deposit of their ratifications.

Article 12

After the Treaty has been in force for ten years, or at any time thereafter, the Parties shall, if any of them so requests, consult together for the purpose of reviewing the Treaty, having regard for the factors then affecting peace and security in the North Atlantic area, including the development of universal as well as regional arrangements under the Charter of the United Nations for the maintenance of international peace and security.

Article 13

After the Treaty has been in force for twenty years, any Party may cease to be a party one year after its notice of denunciation has been given to the Government of the United States of America, which will inform the Governments of the other Parties of the deposit of each notice of denunciation.

Article 14

This Treaty, of which the English and French texts are equally authentic, shall be deposited in the archives of the Government of the United States of America. Duly certified copies thereof will be transmitted by that Government to the Governments of the other signatories.

In witness whereof, the undersigned plenipotentiaries have signed this Treaty.

Done at Washington, the fourth day of April, 1949.[1]

AMERICAN FOREIGN POLICY AS OFFICIALLY DEFINED IN 1945 [2]

The foreign policy of the United States is based firmly on fundamental principles of righteousness and justice. In carrying out those principles we shall firmly adhere to what we believe to be right; and we shall not give our approval to any compromise with evil.

But we know that we cannot attain perfection in this world overnight.

[1] For original twelve signatories, see above, p. 454.
[2] Address of President Harry S. Truman, Navy Day, October 27, 1945, at New York City. Department of State *Bulletin*, XIII, No. 331 (October 28, 1945), 654-655.

We shall not let our search for perfection obstruct our steady progress toward international cooperation. We must be prepared to fulfil our responsibilities as best we can, within the framework of our fundamental principles, even though we recognize that we have to operate in an imperfect world.

Let me restate the fundamentals of that foreign policy of the United States:

1. We seek no territorial expansion or selfish advantage. We have no plans for aggression against any other state, large or small. We have no objective which need clash with the peaceful aims of any other nation.

2. We believe in the eventual return of sovereign rights and self-government to all peoples who have been deprived of them by force.

3. We shall approve no territorial changes in any friendly part of the world unless they accord with the freely expressed wishes of the people concerned.

4. We believe that all peoples who are prepared for self-government should be permitted to choose their own form of government by their own freely expressed choice, without interference from any foreign source. That is true in Europe, in Asia, in Africa, as well as in the Western Hemisphere.

5. By the combined and cooperative action of our war Allies, we shall help the defeated enemy states establish peaceful, democratic governments of their own free choice. And we shall try to attain a world in which Nazism, Fascism, and military aggression cannot exist.

6. We shall refuse to recognize any government imposed upon any nation by the force of any foreign power. In some cases it may be impossible to prevent forceful imposition of such a government. But the United States will not recognize any such government.

7. We believe that all nations should have the freedom of the seas and equal rights to the navigation of boundary rivers and waterways and of rivers and waterways which pass through more than one country.

8. We believe that all states which are accepted in the society of nations should have access on equal terms to the trade and the raw materials of the world.

9. We believe that the sovereign states of the Western Hemisphere, without interference from outside the Western Hemisphere, must work together as good neighbors in the solution of their common problems.

10. We believe that full economic collaboration between all nations, great and small, is essential to the improvement of living conditions all over the world, and to the establishment of freedom from fear and freedom from want.

11. We shall continue to strive to promote freedom of expression and freedom of religion throughout the peace-loving areas of the world.

12. We are convinced that the preservation of peace between nations requires a United Nations Organization composed of all the peace-loving nations of the world who are willing jointly to use force if necessary to insure peace.

That is the foreign policy which guides the United States now. That is the foreign policy with which it confidently faces the future.

It may not be put into effect tomorrow or the next day. But none the less, it is our policy; and we shall seek to achieve it. It may take a long time, but it is worth waiting for, and it is worth striving to attain.

INDEX

(Including authors cited in footnotes)